D0908753

FRONTIERS OF LEADERSHIP

B

Frontiers of Leadership
An Essential Reader

EDITED BY
MICHEL SYRETT AND CLARE HOGG

BLACKWELL
Oxford UK & Cambridge USA

658.409
F935

Copyright © Basil Blackwell Ltd 1992;

Every effort has been made to trace all the copyright holders but if any have been inadvertently overlooked the publishers will be pleased to make the necessary arrangement at the first opportunity.

First published 1992

Blackwell Publishers
108 Cowley Road, Oxford, OX4 1JF, UK

3 Cambridge Center
Cambridge, Massachusetts 02142, USA

All rights reserved. Except for the quotation of short passages for the purposes of criticism and review, no part of this publication may be reproduced, stored in a retrieval system, or transmitted, in any form or by any means, electronic, mechanical, photocopying, recording or otherwise, without the prior permission of the publisher.

Except in the United States of America, this book is sold subject to the condition that it shall not, by way of trade or otherwise, be lent, re-sold, hired out, or otherwise circulated without the publisher's prior consent in any form of binding or cover other than that in which it is published and without a similar condition including this condition being imposed on the subsequent purchaser.

A CIP catalogue record for this book is available
from the British Library.

Library of Congress Cataloging in Publication Data
Frontiers of leadership: an essential reader/edited by Michel
Syrett and Clare Hogg.
p.   cm.
Includes bibliographical references and index.
ISBN 0–631–16865–6 (acid-free paper) – ISBN
0–631–18387–6 (pbk.: acid-free paper)
1. Leadership. 2. Management. I. Syrett, Michel. II. Hogg,
Clare.
HD57.7.F76   1992
658.4'092 – dc20   91–30908   CIP

Typeset in 10 on 12pt Ehrhardt
by Hope Services (Abingdon) Ltd.
Printed in Great Britain by T.J. Press Ltd.,
Padstow, Cornwall

This book is printed on acid-free paper

Contents

UNIVERSITY LIBRARIES
CARNEGIE-MELLON UNIVERSITY
PITTSBURGH, PENNSYLVANIA 15213

The Contributors

The Editors

Michel Syrett is the editor or author of eight books on management subjects. He is co-director, with Clare Hogg, of The Directors' Forum, a management development centre specializing in seminars and briefings for boardroom executives.

Clare Hogg is an established consultant and journalist. She is a regular contributor to *The Times*, founder of *Multinational Employer*, and was editor of the acknowledged personnel management series, *Factsheets*. She runs her own company, DCR Enterprises, and is a co-director, with Michel Syrett, of The Directors' Forum.

Other Contributors (Alphabetical)

John Adair is author of *Training for Leadership, Action-Centred Leadership* and *Effective Leadership*. More than one million managers throughout the world have been through the Action-Centred Leadership course that he pioneered, and Britain's three armed services base their leadership training on his approach. In 1978 he was appointed as the world's first Professor of Leadership Studies at the University of Surrey, where he is still a visiting professor.

F. G. Bailey is Professor of Anthropology at the University of California, San Diego. His publications include *Humbuggery and Manipulation* and *The Prevalence of Deceit*.

Kate Ballen began her career by becoming US Editor for the Oxford Literary Review. She is a winner of the National Press Award and currently writes for *Fortune* magazine.

Bernard M. Bass is Distinguished Professor of Management, and Director, Center for Leadership Studies, at the State University of New York, Binghampton. He has published twenty-one books, over three hundred articles and monographs on leadership and organizational behaviour and is currently involved in transformational leadership research and training in Europe and the USA.

After two years working at the *Economist* as a researcher, **Clare Bebbington** joined EuroBusiness as Assistant Editor, where she was responsible for Eastern Europe. She now works for BP Exploration as a writer.

Meredith Belbin is the author of the well-known *Management Teams: Why they Succeed or Fail*, and Director of Belbin Associates Ltd, Chairman of Cambridge Product Innovation Ltd, Chairman of Group Personnel, and visiting Fellow of Henley

Management College. His approach to team building has influenced management thinking in developed countries around the world.

Peter Benton has had a varied career in several countries including the Chairmanship of a group of engineering companies, and management consulting with McKinsey, A. D. Little, and Nolan Norton. He has been Managing Director and Deputy Chairman of British Telecom, and Director General of the British Institute of Management. He is the author of *Riding the Whirlwind* (Blackwell Publishers).

Jan Carlzon is President and Chief Executive Officer of the Scandinavian Airlines Group. At the time he joined the airline, it had been in the red for two years to the tune of £30 million, following an unbroken string of 17 years of profitability. He positioned SAS as 'The Businessman's Airline' and replaced former production orientation with a strong sense of customer orientation. Within a year, SAS had more than recouped its losses with a profit of some £60m and has gone from strength to strength ever since.

Simon Caulkin is a business journalist and writer. He edited *Management Today* from 1983 to 1986. He is the author of *The New Manufacturing: Minimal IT for Maximum Profit* and has contributed articles to a number of British, European and American publications.

Sir Geoffrey Chandler CBE spent 22 years with Shell, serving both in the UK and overseas. He was Director General of the National Economic Development Office 1978–83 and Director of Industry Year 1986. He is currently Industry advisor to the Royal Society for the encouragement of Arts, Manufactures and Commerce and Chair of the National Council for Voluntary Organizations.

David C. Charlton founded Celmi, an educational residential resource in Snowdonia. From 1976 until 1980 he developed his knowledge of management behaviour, working with the Mars Corporation, ICI and other business organizations. In 1980 he established Celmi Experience Ltd as a management development resource with a focus on experiential heuristic learning.

Jay A. Conger is an Associate Professor of Organization Behaviour at the Faculty of Management, McGill University. He is the author of over fifty articles, papers, and book chapters on the subjects of leadership, empowerment, and the management of change. His most recent books are *Charismatic Leadership* and *The Charismatic Leaders*.

Cary L. Cooper is Professor of Organizational Psychology and Deputy Chairman of the Manchester School of Management at the University of Manchester Institute of Science and Technology. He is author of over fifty books, mainly on the subject of stress at work, has written over two hundred articles for academic journals, and is a frequent contributor to newspapers including the *Guardian*, the *Daily Telegraph*, *The Times* and the *International Herald Tribune*. He is the co-author of *High Fliers* (Blackwell Publishers).

Charles J. Cox has been a lecturer in organizational psychology at the Manchester School of Management at the University of Manchester Institute of Science and Technology since 1966. His main teaching area is management and organizational development which links with his research interests in the development and evaluation of management training techniques. He is the author of four books, co-author of *High Fliers* (Blackwell Publishers), and has written numerous published academic papers.

Geoff Deehan joined BBC Radio in 1974, producing many documentaries on just about every aspect of science and medicine. He moved to BBC Television in 1981 and worked as a producer on 'Medical Express', 'QED', and 'A Guide to Armageddon', which won the BAFTA prize. He returned to BBC Radio and became editor of all science programming. In 1989 he joined Channel Four Television as science consultant, with, in particular, editorial responsibility for 'Equinox'.

John Delaney is Associate Professor of Management and Organizations at The University of Iowa. In 'Society, Law and Business', a course that is required for all Iowa MBA students, he uses real world examples to help students assess the ethical issues that arise in business.

Norman F. Dixon is an Emeritus Professor in Psychology at University College, London, and a Fellow of the British Psychological Society. After ten years in the British Army, he became a psychologist, in 1974 being awarded the University of London Carpenter Medal 'for work of exceptional distinction in Experimental Psychology'. He is author of several books, the latest of which was *Our Own Worst Enemy*.

Peter Drucker was for more than twenty years Professor of Management at the Graduate Business School of New York University. Since 1971 he has been Clark Professor of Social Science at Claremont Graduate School in California. In addition he is renowned for his management books, and also his prophetic books analysing politics, economics and society. He is one of the most renowned management writers of the post-war period.

John D. Elliott was Chairman and Chief Executive of Elders IXL between 1985 and 1990. He is now Chairman of Harlins Holdings Ltd, a major shareholder in the Fosters Brewing Group.

Peter Evans, is a broadcaster, writer and producer with extensive experience of scientific and behavioural subjects. He is the author of twelve books on scientific, medical and psychological topics. He is presenter of 'Science Now' on BBC Radio Four.

Frank Field is Labour Member of Parliament for Birkenhead. From 1969 until 1979 he was Director of the Child Poverty Action Group. From 1974 until 1980 he was director of the Low Pay Unit.

Jaclyn Fierman joined the staff of *Fortune* magazine in 1982 as a Reporter/Researcher. In 1987 she was promoted to Associate Editor. Prior to this she was associate Editor for *World Business Weekly*, a reporter for the Commodity News Service and a writer for Tree Communications.

Bob Garratt is an independent strategy consultant based in London and Hong Kong. His work involves the simultaneous development of directors and their organization through action learning processes. He is Chairman of the Association for Management Education and Development and on the Professional Development Committee of the Institute of Directors. His latest book is *Creating a Learning Organisation: A Guide to Leadership, Learning and Development*.

Peter A. D. Giblin is Chairman and Chief Executive of Axiom Advisors Limited, a management consultancy specializing in executive search and management evaluation. Previously Senior Vice-President International of Russell Reynolds, Managing Director-Administration of Samuel Montagu and President and Chief Executive of Carré, Orban & Partners. He is a member of the New York Bar.

Clive Goodworth was for twenty years a Royal Air Force officer. In 1970, after two years as a training adviser, he worked as a senior personnel executive with an international oil company. In 1975 he went into teaching as Senior Lecturer in Management and Professional Studies at the Huntingdonshire College. Eight years ago he became a freelance management author, trainer and consultant – and has written eleven books and many articles on management topics.

Jan Grant, a psychologist, lectures in community and behavioural studies and is the course co-ordinator for graduate programmes in Counselling and Applied Womens' Studies at the Western Australian College of Advanced Education. She works also as a consultant in organization development.

Lynda Gratton is Assistant Professor in Organizational Behaviour at London Business School. An authority on selecting, assessing and developing senior managers, she lectures and writes widely on succession strategies and assessment technology. She is author of *Heirs Apparent: Succession Strategies for the 90s*.

Valerie Hammond is director of the Ashridge Management Research Group, whose current research interests include management for the future, developing effective leaders, cultural and organizational change, and issues relating to women in management.

Charles Hampden-Turner is Visiting Professor at Roffey Park Management College. He is the author of *Corporate Culture: Vicious and Virtuous Circles* and *Charting the Corporate Mind* (Blackwell Publishers), and, together with Fons Trompenaars is writing *The Seven Cultures of Capitalism*, and co-teaching cross-cultural management at the Erasmus University in Rotterdam.

Charles Handy is Britain's leading business commentator. He is the author of *The Future of Work* (Blackwell Publishers), and visiting professor at the London Business School. His most recent books are *The Age of Unreason* concerning the changing work patterns in tomorrow's world and *Waiting for the Mountain to Move*, a collection of his Radio 4 'Thoughts for Today'.

Sir John Harvey-Jones is one of Britain's best-known and most admired businessmen. His television series, 'Troubleshooter', with its clear-sighted look at ailing British companies, became a national talking point, and as Chairman of ICI he topped the *Sunday Times* poll of captains of industry five years running. He is now Chairman of the *Economist*, Deputy Chairman of Guinness Peat Aviation and Deputy Chairman of Grand Metropolitan.

Wendy Hirsh joined the Institute of Manpower Studies in 1979, advising public and private sector organizations on manpower planning, recruitment, personal information systems and career management. She has developed successful Institute training programmes and lectures widely at universities, conferences and management training establishments.

Sir Antony Jay has been a freelance writer and producer since 1964, and was Chairman of Video Arts from 1972 until 1989. He is co-writer of the BBC Television series, 'Yes, Minister' and 'Yes, Prime Minister'. He is author of several books.

Andrew Kakabadse is Professor of Management Development and Head of the Human Resources Team at Cranfield School of Management. He has recently completed a major world study of Chief Executives. He has published thirteen books and over sixty articles, including best sellers such as *Politics of Management*, *Working in Organisations* and *The Wealth Creators*. He holds positions on the boards of a number of companies. He is Editor of the *Journal of Managerial Psychology* and Associate Editor of the *Leadership and Organisation Development Journal*.

Rosabeth Moss Kanter is the Class of 1960 Professor at the Harvard Business School, and Editor of the *Harvard Business Review*. She is author of ten books, the best known of which are *When Giants Learn to Dance*, and *The Change Masters*. Dr Kanter is the recipient of many national honours, including the Guggenheim Fellowship, thirteen honorary doctoral degrees, and five 'Woman of the Year' awards from national organizations. In 1990 she was named one of the '50 Most Powerful Women in America' by *Ladies Home Journal*.

John Keegan is Defence Editor of the *Daily Telegraph*. Formerly he was senior lecturer in Military History AMA Sandhurst from 1960 until 1986. He is a Fellow of the Royal Historical Society and Fellow of the Royal Society of Literature. His latest book, *The Mask of Command* is a companion volume to his classic study of the individual soldier, *The Face of Battle*. He was appointed OBE in the Gulf War Honours List.

Manfred F. R. Kets de Vries holds the Raoul de Vitry d'Avaucourt Chair of Human Resource Management at the European Institute of Business Administration (INSEAD), France. He is a practising psychoanalyst. He has held professorships at McGill University, the Ecole des Hautes Etudes Commerciales, Montreal and the Harvard Business School. Kets de Vries' books and papers have been translated into ten languages. He has been a regular consultant on organizational design and strategic human resource management to US, Canadian and European companies.

Christopher Knowlton joined the staff of *Fortune* magazine in 1985 as a reporter/researcher and in 1988 was promoted to Associate Editor. He is author of *The Real World*.

John P. Kotter is Konosuke Matsushita Professor of Leadership at the Harvard Business School. He is the author of nine books, the latest of which are *The Leadership Factor* and *A Force for Change: How Leadership Differs from Management*. He is the winner of the Johnson, Smith and Knisely Award for New Perspectives in Business Leadership.

Kenneth Labich joined the staff of *Fortune* magazine in 1983 as an Associate Editor.

Michael M. Lombardo is Director, Leadership Development Research group at the Centre for Creative Leadership in Greensboro, North Carolina. He is lead author of *Looking Glass: An Organisational Simulation* and is the author of numerous articles and technical reports. He is the recipient of the Johnson, Smith and Knisely Executive Leadership Award (as an author of *The Lessons of Experience*) and of the American Society for training and Development Award for Excellence in Executive Development Research.

Christopher Lorenz is Management Editor of the *Financial Times*, specializing in strategy and organization and product design, development and technology. He is the author of several books including *The Design Dimension* (Blackwell Publishers), and is a board/council member of The Strategic Management Society; the editorial board of the *Long Range Planning Journal*; the UK Design Council; and the advisory committee of the London Business School Centre for Design Management. He lectures and teaches widely within companies and business schools and for conference organizations.

Clare Lorenz writes and researches on ethical issues in business and architecture. She is Education Director of the Mensa Foundation for Gifted Children, and is engaged in research on the ability of business to meet young people's aspirations for their working lives.

Morgan W. McCall Jr is Professor of Clinical Management and Organization in the School of Business Administration and a Senior Research Scientist with the Centre for Effective Organizations at the University of Southern California. He is a regular contributor to research and writing about executive leadership and author of several books.

Roz Morris is a writer and broadcaster on women's career issues. She writes for a number of national newspapers and magazines including the *Guardian* and *Options*. She is a working mother with three children, working from her office at her home in North London and is Executive Secretary of Network, the top businesswomen's organization.

Virginia O'Leary is Professor and Chair of the Department of Psychology at Indiana State University. She has held visiting positions at The George Washington University, Boston University, and Radcliffe College. She is on the Board of the American Psychological Society. She is author of many books, and twice won the Association of Women in Psychology's Distinguished Publication Award.

Tom Peters is the co-author of *In Search of Excellence* (with Robert H. Waterman Jr) and *A Passion for Excellence* (with Nancy Austin). He is founder of the Tom Peters Group in Palo Alto, California.

Ann Reilly Dowd is an Associate Editor of *Fortune* magazine. Since joining the magazine in 1983 she has been based in Washington DC, covering politics and economic policy, including the 1988 Presidential election.

Tudor Rickards is a lecturer at Manchester Business School and Visiting Professor at the State University of New York, working mainly on creativity and innovation. Originally he worked with the Unilever Group specializing in new product management. As director of a consulting firm he works with corporations such as IBM, ICI, British Airways and Ciba Geigy. He writes and lectures widely on creativity.

Wess Roberts served in the US Army, and for many years was Vice President, Human Resources at American Express. A Professor of psychology, he has published numerous professional papers on leadership.

Philip Sadler was Principal of Ashridge Management College from 1969 until 1987, and from 1988 until 1990 Chief Executive of the Ashridge Trust. Prior to 1969 he was involved in research and consultancy in the field of organizatonal behaviour. He has published many articles and a number of books including *Managerial Leadership in Post-Industrial Society* and *Designing Organisations*.

Marsha Sinetar is an exponent of the practical value of self-actualization. She is the author of several books dealing with gifted, creative leadership, the latest of which, *Developing a Twenty-first Century Mind*, suggests a breakthrough method of creative problem-solving.

Donna Sockell is Director of Credit Programs and Professor of Management and Labor Relations at Rutgers, the State University of New Jersey. In addition to her research on ethics in the work place, she has designed and taught ethics programmes for several corporations and commodities exchanges. She is also gathering additional information on how firms' ethical practices affect employees.

Robert H. Waterman Jr is a partner in the consulting firm Waterman and Miller, and an author of business management books. Among his published works are two New York Times best sellers: *In Search of Excellence*, a book that sold more than five million copies, and *The Renewal Factor*.

Craig M. Watson was, at the time of writing, financial director of business projects for the international division of Merck & Co. Inc. He later became Division Vice President Finance for The Pepsi Cola Co. He is now Director of Investment Analysis and Financial Planning for FMC Corporation in Chicago.

The Cult of Leadership
by Bertie Ramsbottom

Since first from earth's primeval slough
Societies emerged somehow
And, retrogressing now and then,
Produced the dominance of Men,
It has been commonly agreed
There must be people who can lead.

The prince, the father or the priest
Met some criteria, at least,
For making in the infant state
Their leadership legitimate,
Though often, too, the biggest stick
Determined who might make the pick.

And then to leadership's chagrin
Democracy came creeping in,
With radical ideas which said
The followers should choose instead;
Or, at least, should have a voice
To influence their masters' choice.

Except, that is, strange to relate,
Within the corporate estate,
Where leaders, we are told, instead
Leap fully-clothed from Zeus's head
Protected, unlike other things,
By some divine right of the kings.

Suggestions that the lesser fry
Have any right to choose defy
The consecrated rights of bosses,
Whether making gains or losses,
To answer only for their sin
To priests who put the money in.

xviii

And those who hew the wood and hump it
Are firmly told that they can lump it –
A system known to learned sages
To mark the neolithic ages,
But now unknown to observation
Outside the business corporation.

So leadership, as a result,
Is consecrated as a cult,
Endowed with charismatic powers
Light-years from the likes of ours;
Particularly useful while
The new machismo is in style.

So might it not be best to say
That leaders, too, have feet of clay,
And any claim to lead is hollow
Unless the troops consent to follow?
If not, I think the special pleaders
Should find another word than 'leaders'!

From Bertie Ramsbottom's, *The Bottom Line*, Century Hutchinson Ltd., 1985. (Bertie Ramsbottom is the creation of Ralph Windle, originally of the *Financial Times*, by permission of Bertie Ramifications Ltd.

Introduction

Leaders must be seen to be up front, up to date, up to their jobs and up early in the morning.

Lord Sieff
Former Chairman
Marks and Spencer

Leadership is learned although I cannot explain entirely how it is learned. The ability to lead and inspire others is far more instinctual than premeditated and it is acquired somehow through the experiences of everyday life, and the ultimate nature and quality of that leadership comes out of the innate character and personality of the leader himself.

Harold Green
Former Chief Executive
International Telephone & Telegraph Company

Throughout history, the quality of leaders and leadership has been of prime importance: progress has depended on it, so has the defence of achievements already made. Effective leadership in business is no less important than in the guidance of states, the direction of wars, and the development of local communities; and in business, as in military, political, and social affairs, the need for leadership increases in times of turbulence, crisis and of course, change.

The recent interest in business leadership, which we have tried to reflect in this book, arose from the feeling that many companies in the 1980s were overmanaged and underled at a time of commercial instability, new technology, and the growing interdependence of national economies worldwide. Management developers, charged with the job of creating better leaders, were forced to ask first what exactly it is that makes leaders effective. As they (and we) discovered, this is not an easy task. 'Leadership is an endless subject and endlessly interesting because you can never get your conceptual arms fully around it', says Warren Bennis, acknowledged expert on the subject. 'I always feel rather like a lepidopterist chasing a butterfly.'

The deliberations of many of the practitioners, academics, and consultants who have contributed to this book revolve around one principal issue: Do all leaders possess common qualities, regardless of their sex and race, the time in which they live and the context of their work? And are these qualities inalienable or capable of being developed in others?

Sifting through the mass of material on the subject, a number of characteristics seemed to be common to a Nelson, a Socrates, and a Richard Branson. A capacity for hard work, an ability to inspire respect (largely by example), a caring attitude, good judgement, and highly developed communication skills are just a few. These and others are explored in greater depth in the early chapters.

Yet we were also struck by Christopher Lorenz's claim that few modern business leaders and politicians last in their role for more than a decade. The personal qualities of effective leadership may be common to all ages; the style of individual leaders, it seems, reflects the immediate needs of their contemporary society.

Our own experience confirms this. In the period it took to compile this book, the demands made on business leaders changed. When it was commissioned in 1988, Western economies were only just beginning to feel the effects of the October crash of the previous year. The prospect of a single European market seized the imagination. Entrepreneurial leaders like Jan Carlzon, Lee Iacocca, Akio Morita, and Anita Roddick were folk heroes. The founding of young companies like Virgin, Amstrad, and the Body Shop, and turnaround of corporate giants like SAS and ICI was the stuff of bestsellers, marketed prominently on the shelves of high street stores and airport bookshops.

When the manuscript was delivered to the publishers, the economies of Britain and the United States were in recession. Germany was in political turmoil following an over-hasty union and the collapse of industry in East Germany. A report by Britain's City University was predicting that up to half the factories and business units in Europe were under threat from cross-boundary competition. The EC was proving more of a struggle to get off the ground than many had expected. Even the Japanese economy was being affected by a particularly severe global credit squeeze.

Many of the companies that had been held up as exemplars of corporate efficiency and success in the 1980s were in liquidation, performing badly or the subject of takeover bids. SAS was struggling against bigger rivals and ICI was about to fall victim to a well-publicized acquisition scare by Lord Hanson.

Poor performance in a number of public companies was prompting large institutional investors on both sides of the Atlantic to question whether management was being granted too great a licence by their boards – leading to calls for a majority of independent directors on the board and greater curbs on senior managers' ability to determine their own pay, protect themselves by anti-takeover measures, and grant themselves generous pay-offs. A rash of mergers and acquisitions had given way to more sophisticated business alliances and joint ventures.

The most recent contributions to the book reflect this change. They describe a world of complex interlocking relationships where business success cannot be achieved purely through acquisition and brute force. Common purpose and performance between a company and its subcontractors, suppliers, and distributors are essential to ensure focus, cost flexibility, and speed of response. Strategic alliances in different parts of the world blur the distinction between competitors and partners. The interests of shareholders have to be reconciled with those of employees, the environment, local communities, governments and other 'stakeholders' in the business.

Business leaders, as a consequence, need to 'feel comfortable with ambiguity and chaos' (Warren Bennis). They need to be 'multifaceted and ambidextrous', able to work across functions, industries and local cultures, and compete in a way that enhances rather than undercuts co-operation (Rosabeth Moss Kanter). They have to manage the grey areas that exist both inside and outside the firm (Peter Williamson). Humility and high ethical standards are necessary to inspire trust in sensitive alliances and a willingness to learn from new situations.

It all seems a far cry from the certainty and stock solutions that featured so prominently in the coffee-table books on business that crammed the shelves of the aspiring young managers three or four years ago. Yet they are common features of self-effacing or less predatory heroes of the companies that see through bear markets like Peter Holmes of Shell, Yutuka Kume of Nissan, and Glaxo's Sir Paul Girolami, a CEO who scorns takeovers as 'buying your way to the top'.

Where does this all leave the people responsible for developing the next generation of business leaders? Although most senior personnel practitioners and academics agree with Jay Conger's argument that, in general, leaders are bred not born (see chapter 14), they still face the problem that the factors that most determine leadership potential occur early in life and have as much to do with upbringing, education, and personal life experiences as they do with the quality of company training.

Succession planning is still founded on the early identification of potential in young managers and a long-term programme of personal development, based on job rotation across business functions, peer and collegiate feedback, business school education, and (increasingly) individual coaching and counselling.

A number of social and economic factors threaten this approach. Diversification and globalization are making it harder to design programmes which embrace all business functions. Multinational corporations now incorporate a variety of businesses at different stages of development, requiring different and often contrasting management skills. Leaders of large corporations no longer need to know one business market and national culture well to make strategic trade-offs. Their careers need to encompass more experiences than it is arguably possible to achieve in twenty years of early in-company development.

Secondly, a growing number of young managers are no longer willing to make the sacrifices in their personal lives which are necessary in a conventional fast-track career. While academics may be divided on the exact contribution a female influence may bring to leadership (see chapter 12), there is a general consensus that too few women reach the boardroom; and that one reason is that growing numbers of female middle managers – even those who have benefited from company maternity leave in their early careers – are simply not prepared to destroy their family lives as the price for breaking through the glass ceiling barring them from senior executive positions. Research by Robert Goffee from the London Business School also shows that many talented MBA-educated managers of both sexes aspire to broader life-goals than slogging their way up the corporate ladder, and are prepared to sacrifice promotion for a richer, more holistic lifestyle.

Finally, even the best MBA education and fast-track development are not sufficient on their own to equip senior executives throughout their careers. The task management developers face is no longer merely getting these people into place – it is also keeping them sufficiently well educated to remain abreast of what is happening in the world once they are there.

Business school academics have learned to their cost (and the considerable diminishment of their egos) that world-class leaders do not respond to traditional learning methods. Programmes for chief executives require tuition that responds to their individual needs and tutors that act as 'facilitators of learning', creating comfortable but challenging environments in which groups of peers are enabled to draw on each other's experiences in discussions disciplined by academic rigour. Few consultants and academics have the ability, and can inspire sufficient credibility among participants, to achieve this task effectively.

And leaders themselves need the humility to accept the need for this kind of continuous learning. Among the many characteristics of modern business leadership, this is perhaps the most important. As Warren Bennis recently concluded: 'My heroes are the people who are continuous learners, who have their eyebrows always raised in curiosity and who can say to themselves "The more vulnerable I am to my people, the more I can influence them".'

Michel Syrett
Clare Hogg
1991

Part I
Definitions

Chapter 1
Leadership and Management:
Is There a Difference?

Introduction

Any book on a specialized subject should start by defining the topic. Leadership has emerged as one of the most important business requirements at a time of permanent discontinuity. Yet any attempt at a definition presupposes that leadership is different from management and that good leaders have skills and personal qualities that distinguish them from good managers. Is this in fact true?

Yes, according to all three contributors in this chapter. Leadership skills have become important because the more fragmented and diversified an organization becomes, the more leaders it requires; and the faster moving an organization's markets or commercial environment, the more it needs 'changing' rather than 'running'.

Therein lies the fundamental difference between the tasks of leaders and managers. Managers do things right, leaders do the right thing. Managers accept the *status quo*, leaders challenge it. Leaders create and articulate vision, managers ensure it is put into practice.

In the opening article, Britain's leading business commentator, Charles Handy, points out that new concepts of leadership have gone hand in hand with new concepts of the organization. Businesses, according to Handy, are human organisms to be influenced, motivated and 'led' rather than precision pieces of engineering to be serviced, oiled and 'managed'.

Vision – the thing that most sets aside leaders from managers – has to be built around a number of principles. It must be different. It must have an element of surprise. It has to be understandable. And it requires the trust and support of others to ensure it is realized. Thus the business leader requires not just an original mind but the communication skills to get others to 'buy into' his aims.

But if the roles of leader and manager are separate and distinct, does this mean that different people are required for them? John Kotter argues that although individuals with mutually exclusive skills as managers or leaders should be recognized and valued equally lower down in the organization, top executives should be groomed to provide both. His views are supported by Craig Watson in an article written in 1983. Watson concludes that outstanding companies are not distinguished by the leaders who head them or by the managers who run them, but by the manner in which leadership and management are harmonized by a common culture.

The efforts currently being made by companies to improve the number and calibre of their leaders should not be interpreted as a sign that they no longer need good managers. Organizations need both. And while most commentators are united in their belief that businesses are, for the most part, overmanaged and underled, the article from *The Economist* points out the problems equally faced by companies that are overled and undermanaged. The importance of charismatic leaders who can influence collective organizational behaviour stems from US and UK attitudes to business. German and Japanese styles of management place an equal, and perhaps unfashionable, emphasis on the need for planning and co-ordination.

1
The Language of Leadership

Charles Handy

Leadership is back in fashion. No longer does the word carry its overtones of militarism and macho heroics. Gone are the days when it conjured up images of an officer class, of glory linked to privilege. Today leadership is the stuff of best-selling tracts on business, the theme of ambitious researchers and of up-market training conferences. How has this come about? Is it a passing fashion or should we take it seriously? What does it take to be a leader? Can one learn it, or develop it, or recognize it only when it's there?

The leadership industry is, I suggest, a symptom of a deeper and more far-reaching change in our thinking about organizations. We have exchanged the language of engineering for the language of political theory, and the study of organizations will never be quite the same again. It used to be that organizations were thought of as pieces of engineering, flawed pieces maybe but capable in theory of perfectibility, of precision, of full efficiency. They were things to be 'designed', 'planned' and 'managed' – full of 'human resources', 'feedback loops' and 'control systems'. The very word 'management', with its origins in the running of the household or, some say, of the army mule trains, implies control backed by authority (which is perhaps why it is a word much disliked in all the professional and voluntary bodies that value autonomy).

The new language of organizations is different. The talk today is of networks and alliances, of 'adhocracy' and federalism, of shared values, cultures and consensus. The key words are options not plans, the possible rather than the perfect, involvement instead of compliance. These are the words of political systems not of engineering, they are the language of leadership not of management.

Originally a paper presented to the Irish Management Institute, 34th National Management Conference © Charles Handy 1987, by permission of the author.

Let us look at two of these words and their implications. *Federalism* is a way of describing what we increasingly see as the necessary paradox of organizations – how to make something big while keeping it small. Paradox is something that *managers* abhor but which *leaders*, being more politically attuned, know is part of the grist of life, just as we hate the things we love, want both to be free and to belong, to have our cake and eat it.

Federalism manages the paradox of big and small by gathering into the centre only the things that really matter and letting go of the rest, by being 'tight–loose' in the new language. They are *reverse–thrust* organizations in that the energy and initiative comes from the bits not from the centre. The centre does not direct or command, it co-ordinates, facilitates, enables; and it is a centre not a head. These organizations at their best are living examples of *subsidiarity*, that moral principle enshrined in papal encyclicals which holds that a higher-order body should not do anything that can be done by a lower-order body. Subsidiarity is delegation turned moral imperative; it is trust in action because it means letting other people make decisions which may be mistakes, and having to forgive them, as long as they are genuine mistakes, lest that trust be destroyed. These organizations are fun to work in, they attract the best and are alive with energy, but when did you last read the words 'trust' and 'forgiveness' in a management manual? This is the language of leadership.

Trust, however, cannot be unbounded. Federal organizations keep ultimate control through the principle of *limited tenure* and the practice of *inverted doughnuts*. Limited tenure is a principle of political theory, which holds that real responsibility is given to a person only for a limited period of time, in case that responsibility is abused, or the decision to give it was wrong, or the individual turns out to be incapable or becomes corrupted. Unlimited tenure is a recipe for dictatorship, so democracies insist that presidents and prime ministers be re-elected, and organizations, when they give real power to people (by, for example, combining the roles of chairman and chief executive) do it only for a fixed period. In other words, fixed-term contracts are becoming more a feature of organizations as a necessary counterpart to increased responsibility and power.

The inverted doughnut is a pictorial way of describing the new job definition. Imagine an American doughnut which is a ring with a hole in the middle. In this picture the doughnut is inverted, so that the hole is filled in and the ring is empty but with a boundary to it. The new jobs are similar in that they have a core of essentials (if one doesn't do the core one has failed). But not to fail is not enough. The new jobs allow for discretion and require initiative ('intrapreneuring' if you like the jargon). The doughnut needs filling, but only up to the boundary. One is trusted – but to a limit. The job of the centre is to design the doughnuts so that the core is understood, there is room for discretion but the responsibility has clear boundaries. The new organizations work best with large doughnuts and small cores. Old organizations liked small doughnuts and large cores – that way they kept control, they 'managed'.

The other concept is *networks*. Networks depend on *making connections*. Organizations have always known about the so-called informal organization which lay behind the neat array of boxes on their organization charts but this informal organization was somehow seen as undesirable in well-run places, illicit even. Networks are now respectable. One is expected, if one is any good, to have one's own alliances and connections. Organizations act as 'gatekeepers' for people with connections to the world outside.

Networks, however, are unlike managed organizations. They depend on influence not authority. They are shifting and changing, more like a plant than a thing. They don't exist for you until you create or join them. They are like clubs, and like clubs they have a centre and a secretary rather than a head office and a manager. Some network organizations have even turned their office into a club, recognizing that networkers don't all work at the same place or necessarily at the same time. Why, after all, provide people with a private space, almost an apartment of their own, in an office block when often all they need is 'occasional' space and 'occasional' use of facilities. A club provides privileged access to resources not private spaces, and it's privileged access that is the key to a network.

It is a new language, this language of federations and networks, full of new images and metaphors. It requires us to learn new ways and habits, to live with more uncertainty but more trust, less control but more creativity. To those of us reared in another tradition it can be a strange and a frightening language, but we have to recognize that it is the *right* language. No one, after all, has ever liked being managed, even if they didn't mind being the manager, and anyone who has tried to run an organization has always known that it was more like running a small country than a machine. It was only the theorists who tried to apply the hard rules of number and logic and mechanics to an essentially soft system. Maybe the Irish were instinctively right to pay little heed to it until people like Peters and Waterman started talking the new language in their *In Search Of Excellence*, a book which obviously touched some chord.

As a result, leadership is now fashionable and the language of leadership increasingly important but, as Warren Bennis says in his book on *Leaders*, it remains the most studied and least understood topic in all the social sciences. Like beauty or love, we know it when we see it but cannot easily define it or produce it on demand. Again, like beauty and love, the writings on it are fun, sexy even, with their pictures of heroes and stories that can be our private fantasies. To read MacGregor Burns, Maccoby, Alistair Mant, Warren Bennis, Cary Cooper or Peters and Waterman is to escape into a private world of might-have-beens.

They may even do a disservice, these fun books, with their tales of heroes and their myths of the mighty, by suggesting that leadership is only for the new and the special. The significance of the new language is, I believe, that leadership has to be endemic in organizations, the fashion not the exception. Everyone with pretensions to be anyone must begin to think and act like a leader. Some will find it comes naturally and will blossom, some won't enjoy it at all, but unless you try, and are allowed to try, no one will ever know, for leadership is hard, if not impossible, to detect in embryo – it has to be seen in action to be recognized by oneself as much as by others.

So what is this mysterious thing and how does one acquire it? The studies agree on very little but what they do agree on is probably at the heart of things. It is this:

A leader shapes and shares a vision which gives point to the work of others.

Would that it were as easy to do as to say! Think on these aspects of that short sentence:

- *The vision must be different.* A plan or a strategy which is a projection of the present or a replica of what everyone else is doing is not a vision. A vision has to 're-frame' the known scene, to reconceptualize the obvious, connect the previously unconnected, dream a dream. Alistair Mant talks of the leader as 'builder' working with others towards a 'third corner', a goal. Those who are interested only in power or achievement for its own sake he calls 'raiders' or mere 'binary' people. MacGregor Burns talks of the 'transforming' leader as opposed to the mere 'transactional' one, the busy fixer.
- *The vision must make sense to others.* Ideally it should create the 'Aha Effect', as when everyone says 'aha – of course, now I see it', like wit perhaps – what oft was thought but ne'er so well expressed. To make sense it must stretch people's imaginations but still be within the bounds of possibility. To give point to the work of others it must be *related* to their work and not to some grand design in which they feel they have no use. If 'vision' is too grand a word, try 'goal' or even 'manifesto'.
- *The vision must be understandable.* No one can communicate a vision that takes two pages to read, or is too full of numbers and jargon. It has to be a vision that sticks in the mind. Metaphor and analogy can be keys because they provide us with vivid images with room for interpretation – low definition concepts as opposed to the more precise high definition words of engineering and management.
- *The leader must live the vision.* He or she must not only believe in it but must be seen to believe in it. It is tempting credulity to proclaim a crusade for the impoverished from a luxury apartment. Effective leaders, we are told, exude energy. Energy comes easily if you love your cause. Effective leaders have integrity. Integrity, being true to yourself, comes naturally if you live for your vision. In other words, the vision cannot be something thought up in the drawing office. To be real it has to come from the deepest parts of you, from an inner system of belief. The total pragmatist cannot be a transforming leader.

- *The leader must remember that the vision remains a dream without the work of others.* A leader with no followers is a voice in the wilderness. Leaders like to choose their teams but most inherit them and must then make them their own. Trust in others is repaid by trust from them. If it is to be *their* vision too, then their ideas should be heeded.

Such skills cannot, I think, be taught. But they can be learnt or, rather, discovered, fostered and allowed to grow. Leaders may well be born that way, or shaped by early experience, but how do we know whether or not we are leaders unless we try? Some say that the firstborn strive harder, or those who had to struggle more when young, or needed to prove something to parents or significant elders. But this is more about achievement than leadership.

For leadership to flower some things are necessary:

- *The room to move.* Space for responsibility and experiment is essential. Without freedom to change things there is no call for leadership. Without the room to make mistakes there is no point in experiment. Early responsibility is essential to the discovery of one's leadership; so is the readiness to *forgive* oneself, and be forgiven, for any mistakes made in the process. No one can learn from mistakes unless they are prepared to write them off to experience.
- *A belief in oneself.* No one with an inferiority complex is going to start creating visions or dreaming dreams. You have to believe that you can influence events and people. Carried too far this is arrogance, but unless you believe in yourself it is unlikely that others will. Warren Bennis describes how Wallenda the great tightrope walker never fell until he started to think about *not* falling and then he fell to his death. Belief in oneself is boosted by early success, but is also rooted in a greater belief which gives the individual some sense of the meaning of life and the purpose behind doing things. Those who see no point in things will see no need to change things, no need to make a difference.
- *An awareness of other worlds.* Re-framing is hard to do without perspectives from other worlds. People with long experience in one field have the blinkers of that experience. To see yourself and your situation as others see it, it is necessary to stand outside your world at times. To use metaphor, analogy and words effectively you need to know the metaphors and words. John Kennedy read history and biography; others travel, visit the theatre, listen to music, read novels or study literature. There must be time to live in other worlds.
- *A capacity for loneliness.* Leaders are, by definition, out front. They may be respected, trusted, believed in but they will not always be loved. It will often be lonely with only one's own convictions to hold on to. Furthermore, wise leaders take time to be by themselves, they understand about the need for retreats, stability zones and quiet times lest they lose themselves in activity

and become blinkered by their busyness – oscillation, Mant calls it, the withdrawing so that one may better re-enter. Cooper found that his leaders were, without exceptions, self-defined 'loners'.

Not all who have these features will end up leaders. They are necessary but not sufficient conditions. They are not the stuff of training courses but a highway code for those who would spend their lives in organizations. Pay heed to these things if you want to make a difference, or if you want to encourage others to make a difference.

It will not be without pain. Mistakes, even when forgiven, can hurt and cost. To be alone is often to be depressed. A belief in oneself goes with and comes from a constant doubt about oneself and about the point of things. Leaders are not invulnerable and should not be if they want the understanding of others. If organizations are to nurture the leaders they so badly need they must take more risks with more people, be more understanding and more forgiving. Only then will they discover what leadership talents are there.

But there is more to it than just spotting leaders. Organizations would be wise to embrace the new language of leadership, the language of politics, and begin to think of themselves as societies of citizens, societies with a point and a purpose, but to be run as societies not as machines, with leaders at their head. There is managing to be done, and it needs to be done effectively, but it is subordinate to the proper *leadership* of the bits that make up the whole.

References

Bennis, Warren and Nanus, Burt, *Leaders, the Strategies for Taking Charge* (Harper & Row, London, 1985).

Cooper, Cary and Kingley, Peter, *The Change Makers: Their Influence on British Business and Industry* (Harper & Row, London, 1985).

Maccoby, Michael, *The Leaders* (Simon & Schuster, New York, 1981).

MacGregor Burns, James, *Leadership* (Harper & Row, New York, 1978).

Mant, Alistair, *Leaders We Deserve* (Martin Robertson, Oxford, 1983).

Peters, Thomas and Waterman, Robert Jr, *In Search of Excellence* (Harper & Row, London, 1982).

2
Take Me to your Leader

'Business in America has lost its way, adrift in a sea of managerial mediocrity, desperately needing leadership to face worldwide economic competition'. So claims Mr Abraham Zaleznik, a professor at Harvard Business School, in his book *The Managerial Mystique*. Mr John Kotter, a fellow Harvard professor, agrees that most firms are 'overmanaged and underled'. An increasingly vocal group of management theorists asserts that what firms (especially American ones) need are leaders to steer them through the turbulent 1990s. But what is a leader? Can they be bred as well as born?

Born leaders are easy to identify. Mr Sam Walton, the founder of Wal-Mart Stores, America's third-biggest retail chain, Mr Lee Iacocca of Chrysler, Mr Jan Carlzon of Scandinavian Airlines System (SAS), Mr Akio Morita, founder of Sony, and Mr Richard Branson, founder of the Virgin Group – all have had the badge of natural leadership pinned on them. But what of Sir Peter Holmes, the modest chap who has turned Royal Dutch/Shell into the world's most successful oil company? Or Mr Yutaka Kume, who, as Nissan's president, is credited with revitalizing the Japanese carmaker? Neither fits the flamboyant, charismatic leadership mould. Nonetheless, companies seem to thrive under their 'leadership'.

One reason, says Mr Kotter, is that companies like Shell and Nissan know that being overled and undermanaged is just as dangerous as being underled and overmanaged – as Apple found out under Mr Steve Jobs, its founder. Their ideal, unsurprisingly, is a combination of strong management and firm leadership. But many firms find it hard to strike that balance because they fail to grasp the difference between management and leadership – and between the people who are good at each.

Reproduced from *The Economist*, 2 June 1990 © The Economist.

Mr Peter Drucker, a veteran at the guru game, says that the first task of a leader is to define a company's mission. In a world where product cycles are shrinking, new technologies have an ever-shorter shelf-life and customers demand faster delivery and higher quality, that increasingly means defining and inspiring change within a company. By setting a company's direction, communicating this to its workforce, motivating employees and taking a long-range perspective, a leader adapts the firm to whatever volatile environment it does business in.

This role is neatly contrasted with that of a manager's by Mr Warren Bennis, a professor at the University of Southern California. A leader, he says, challenges the status quo; a manager accepts it. A manager's primary role is to prevent the complexity of a modern company degenerating into chaos. Managers take details – like financial planning, quality, stock levels, staffing and market research – and bring order, consistency and control to them. To managers, systems and structure are all.

Because the abilities needed to lead and manage are so different, an aptitude for both roles is rarely found in one larger-than-life individual. Mr Jack Welch, chairman of General Electric (GE), and Mr Sam Walton appear to excel as both leaders and managers. But because their kind are so hard to find, companies cannot rely on locating a born leader-manager.

Instead, firms may find it easier to build 'leadership teams', combining the talents of their best leaders with those of their top managers. This does not mean simply lumping them all together on the company board and crossing corporate fingers – there must be a conscious effort to get leaders and managers to influence each other. In many firms, senior managers implement and administer, but rarely question a leader's mission. If they don't believe in it, the firm pulls in two directions at once. Leaders and managers have to be convinced that they have much to learn from each other – if, that is, they realize into which category each falls. Ideally, managers come to understand the problems of leadership and leaders the mechanics of management. A successful leadership team will outlive the visionary leader who put it together.

Take Compaq, an American computer company that has seen its annual sales grow from nothing to $2.9 billion in just seven years. From its formation Compaq nurtured a leadership team (guided by the vision of Mr Rod Canion, its president and co-founder) that mixed entrepreneurial flair with solid management talent and attention to detail.

Leadership in conventional, hierarchically structured firms can often be left to those at the top. But what of the sort of company many think will prosper in the 1990s – those run by a small workforce in a flat, unhierarchical structure? By being less complex, such firms need fewer managers and so have shorter, clearer lines of communication between their top leadership and their employees. That, however, makes the quality of leadership even more important to a firm's success.

This is particularly true of networked or global firms. The more fragmented a company – whether geographically or by activity – the more leaders it will need. The faster-changing a firm's markets, the more it will need 'changing' rather than 'running'. Success in the decentralized business of the 1990s may depend on finding leaders to inspire and motivate managers and employees at every level of a firm's network, and in each of the countries in which a firm operates (like SAS which, says Mr Carlzon, 'has 2,000 leaders').

Mr Kotter of Harvard believes that such a 'leadership network' can play a valuable role in selecting and nurturing future generations of a firm's top leadership. It can also help breed leader-managers. How? Spotting people with leadership potential is the easy bit; developing that potential much harder. Varying responsibility helps: the best leader-managers, says Mr Kotter, tend to have had a broad mix of different jobs and responsibilities early in their careers. Decentralization and networking also make the task easier, because they increase the number of jobs in a company that provide scope for leadership – and allow tomorrow's Jack Welchs to emerge.

References

Zalezik, Abraham 1989: *The Managerial Mystique.* Harper & Row, London.

3
What Leaders Really Do

John P. Kotter

Leadership is different from management, but not for the reasons most people think. Leadership isn't mystical and mysterious. It has nothing to do with having 'charisma' or other exotic personality traits. It is not the province of a chosen few. Nor is leadership necessarily better than management or a replacement for it.

Rather, leadership and management are two distinctinve and complementary systems of action. Each has its own function and characteristic activities. Both are necessary for success in an increasingly complex and volatile business environment.

Most US corporations today are overmanaged and underled. They need to develop their capacity to exercise leadership. Successful corporations don't wait for leaders to come along. They actively seek out people with leadership potential and expose them to career experiences designed to develop that potential. Indeed, with careful selection, nurturing, and encouragement, dozens of people can play important leadership roles in a business organization.

But while improving their ability to lead, companies should remember that strong leadership with weak management is no better, and is sometimes actually worse, than the reverse. The real challenge is to combine strong leadership and strong management and use each to balance the other.

Of course, not everyone can be good at both leading and managing. Some people have the capacity to become excellent managers but not strong leaders. Others have great leadership potential but, for a variety of reasons, have great difficulty becoming strong managers. Smart companies value both kinds of people and work hard to make them a part of the team.

'What Leaders Really Do', by John P. Kotter, *Harvard Business Review*, May–June 1990. Copyright © 1990 by the President and Fellows of Harvard College, by permission of *Harvard Business Review*.

But when it comes to preparing people for executive jobs, such companies rightly ignore the recent literature that says people cannot manage *and* lead. They try to develop leader-managers. Once companies understand the fundamental difference between leadership and management, they can begin to groom their top people to provide both.

Management is about coping with complexity. Its practices and procedures are largely a response to one of the most significant developments of the twentieth century: the emergence of large orgaizations. Without good management, complex enterprises tend to become chaotic in ways that threaten their very existence. Good management brings a degree of order and consistency to key dimensions like the quality and profitability of products.

Leadership, by contrast, is about coping with change. Part of the reason it has become so important in recent years is that the business world has become more competitive and more volatile. Faster technological change, greater international competition, the deregulation of markets, overcapacity in capital-intensive industries, an unstable oil cartel, raiders with junk bonds, and the changing demographics of the work force are among the many factors that have contributed to this shift. The net result is that doing what was done yesterday, or doing it 5% better, is no longer a formula for success. Major changes are more and more necessary to survive and compete effectively in this new environment. More change always demands more leadership.

Consider a simple military analogy: a peacetime army can usually survive with good administration and management up and down the hierarchy, coupled with good leadership concentrated at the very top. A wartime army, however, needs competent leadership at all levels. No one yet has figured out how to manage people effectively into battle; they must be *led*.

These different functions – coping with complexity and coping with change – shape the characteristic activities of management and leadership. Each system of action involves deciding what needs to be done, creating networks of people and relationships that can accomplish an agenda, and then trying to ensure that those people actually do the job. But each accomplishes these three tasks in different ways.

Companies manage complexity first by *planning and budgeting* – setting targets or goals for the future (typically for the next month or year), establishing detailed steps for achieving those targets, and then allocating resources to accomplish those plans. By contrast, leading an organization to constructive change begins by *setting a direction* – developing a vision of the future (often the distant future) along with strategies for producing the changes needed to achieve that vision.

Management develops the capacity to achive its plan by *organizing and staffing* – creating an organizational structure and set of jobs for accomplishing plan requirements, staffing the jobs with qualified individuals, communicating the plan to those people, delegating responsibility for carrying out the plan, and devising systems to monitor implementation. The equivalent leadership activity, however, is *aligning people*. This means communicating the new direction to those who can create coalitions that understand the vision and are committed to its achievement.

Finally, management ensures plan accomplishment by *controlling and problem solving* – monitoring results versus the plan in some detail, both formally and informally, by means of reports, meetings, and other tools; identifying deviations; and then planning and organizing to solve the problems. But for leadership, achieving a vision requires *motivating and inspiring* – keeping people moving in the right direction, despite major obstacles to change, by appealing to basic but often untapped human needs, values, and emotions.

A closer examination of each of these activities will help clarify the skills leaders need.

Setting a Direction vs. Planning and Budgeting

Since the function of leadership is to produce change, setting the direction of that change is fundamental to leadership.

Setting direction is never the same as planning or even long-term planning, although people often confuse the two. Planning is a management process, deductive in nature and designed to produce orderly results, not change. Setting a direction is more inductive. Leaders gather a broad range of data and look for patterns, relationships, and linkages that help explain things. What's more, the direction-setting aspect of leadership does not produce plans; it creates vision and strategies. These describe a business, technology, or corporate culture in terms of what it should become over the long term and articulate a feasible way of achieving this goal.

Most discussions of vision have a tendency to degenerate into the mystical. The implication is that a vision is something mysterious that mere mortals, even talented ones, could never hope to have. But developing good business direction isn't magic. It is a tough, sometimes exhausting process of gathering and analyzing information. People who articulate such visions aren't magicians but broad-based strategic thinkers who are willing to take risks.

Nor do visions and strategies have to be brilliantly innovative; in fact, some of the best are not. Effective business visions regularly have an almost mundane quality, usually consisting of ideas that are already well known. The particular combination or patterning of the ideas may be new, but sometimes even that is not the case.

For example, when CEO Jan Carlzon articulated his vision to make Scandinavian Airline Systems (SAS) the best airline in the world for the frequent business traveler, he was not saying anything that everyone in the airline industry didn't already know. Business travelers fly more consistently than other market segments and are generally willing to pay higher fares. Thus focusing on business customers offers an airline the possibility of high margins, steady business, and considerable growth. But in an industry known more for bureaucracy than vision, no company had ever put these simple ideas together and dedicated itself to implementing them. SAS did, and it worked.

What's crucial about a vision is not its originality but how well it serves the interests of important constituencies – customers, stockholders, employees – and how easily it can be translated into a realistic competitive strategy. Bad visions tend to ignore the legitimate needs and rights of important constituencies – favoring, say, employees over customers or stockholders. Or they are strategically unsound. When a company that has never been better than a weak competitor in an industry suddenly starts talking about becoming number one, that is a pipe dream, not a vision.

One of the most frequent mistakes that overmanaged and underled corporations make is to embrace 'long-term planning' as a panacea for their lack of direction and inability to adapt to an increasingly competitive and dynamic business environment. But such an approach misinterprets the nature of direction setting and can never work.

Long-term planning is always time consuming. Whenever something unexpected happens, plans have to be redone. In a dynamic business environment, the unexpected often becomes the norm, and long-term planning can become an extraordinarily burdensome activity. This is why most successful corporations limit the time frame of their planning activities. Indeed, some even consider 'long-term planning' a contradiction in terms.

In a company without direction, even short-term planning can become a black hole capable of absorbing an infinite amount of time and energy. With no vision and strategy to provide constraints around the planning process or to guide it, every eventuality deserves a plan. Under these circumstances, contingency planning can go on forever, draining time and attention from far more essential activities, yet without ever providing the clear sense of direction that a company desperately needs. After a while, managers inevitably become cynical about all this, and the planning process can degenerate into a highly politicized game.

Planning works best not as a substitute for direction setting but as a complement to it. A competent planning process serves as a useful reality check on direction-setting activities. Likewise, a competent direction-setting process provides a focus in which planning can then be realistically carried out. It helps clarify what kind of planning is essential and what kind is irrelevant.

Aligning People vs. Organizing and Staffing

A central feature of modern organizations is interdependence, where no one has complete autonomy, where most employees are tied to many others by their work, technology, management systems, and hierarchy. These linkages present a special challenge when organizations attempt to change. Unless many individuals line up and move together in the same direction, people will tend to fall over one another. To executives who are overeducated in management and undereducated in leadership, the idea of getting people moving in the same direction appears to be an organizational problem. What executives need to do, however, is not organize people but align them.

Managers 'organize' to create human systems that can implement plans as precisely and efficiently as possible. Typically, this requires a number of potentially complex decisions. A company must choose a structure of jobs and reporting relationships, staff it with individuals suited to the jobs, provide training for those who need it, communicate plans to the work force, and decide how much authority to delegate and to whom. Economic incentives also need to be constructed to accomplish the plan, as well as systems to monitor its implementation. These organizational judgments are much like architectural decisions. It's a question of fit within a particular context.

Aligning is different. It is more of a communications challenge than a design problem. First, aligning invariably involves talking to many more individuals than organizing does. The target population can involve not only a manager's subordinates but also bosses, peers, staff in other parts of the organization, as well as suppliers, governmental officials, or even customers. Anyone who can help implement the vision and strategies or who can block implementation is relevant.

Trying to get people to comprehend a vision of an alternative future is also a communications challenge of a completely different magnitude from organizing them to fulfull a short-term plan. It's much like the difference between a football quarterback attempting to describe to his team the next two or three plays versus his trying to explain to them a totally new approach to the game to be used in the second half of the season.

Whether delivered with many words or a few carefully chosen symbols, such messages are not necessarily accepted just because they are understood. Another big challenge in leadership efforts is credibility – getting people to believe the message. Many things contribute to credibility: the track record of the person delivering the message, the content of the message itself, the communicator's reputation for integrity and trustworthiness, and the consistency between words and deeds.

Finally, aligning leads to empowerment in a way that organizing rarely does. One of the reasons some organizations have difficulty adjusting to rapid changes in markets or technology is that so many people in those companies feel relatively powerless. They have learned from experience that even if they correctly perceive important external changes and then initiate appropriate actions, they are vulnerable to someone higher up who does not like what they have done. Reprimands can take many different forms: 'That's against policy' or 'We can't afford it' or 'Shut up and do as you're told.'

Alignment helps overcome this problem by empowering people in at least two ways. First, when a clear sense of direction has been communicated throughout an organization, lower level employees can initiate actions without the same degree of vulnerability. As long as their behavior is consistent with the vision, superiors will have more difficulty reprimanding them. Second, because everyone is aiming at the same target, the probability is less that one person's initiative will be stalled when it comes into conflict with someone else's.

Motivating People vs. Controlling and Problem Solving

Since change is the function of leadership, being able to generate highly energized behavior is important for coping with the inevitable barriers to change. Just as direction setting identifies an appropriate path for movement and just as effective alignment gets people moving down that path, successful motivation ensures that they will have the energy to overcome obstacles.

According to the logic of management, control mechanisms compare system behavior with the plan and take action when a deviation is detected. In a well-managed factory, for example, this means the planning process establishes sensible quality targets, the organizing process builds an organization that can achieve those targets, and a control process makes sure that quality lapses are spotted immediately, not in 30 or 60 days, and corrected.

For some of the same reasons that control is so central to management, highly motivated or inspired behavior is almost irrelevant. Managerial processes must be as close as possible to fail-safe and risk-free. That means they cannot be dependent on the unusual or hard to obtain. The whole purpose of systems and structures is to help normal people who behave in normal ways to complete routine jobs successfully, day after day. It's not exciting or glamorous. But that's management.

Leadership is different. Achieving grand visions always requires an occasional burst of energy. Motivation and inspiration energize people, not by pushing them in the right direction as control mechanisms do but by satisfying basic human needs for achievement, a sense of belonging, recognition, self-esteem, a feeling of control over one's life, and the ability to live up to one's ideals. Such feelings touch us deeply and elicit a powerful response.

Good leaders motivate people in a variety of ways. First, they always articulate the organization's vision in a manner that stresses the values of the audience they are addressing. This makes the work important to those individuals. Leaders also regularly involve people in deciding how to achieve the organization's vision (or the part most relevant to a particular individual). This gives people a sense of control. Another important motivational technique is to support employee efforts to realize the vision by providing coaching, feedback, and role modeling, thereby helping people grow professionally and enhancing their self-esteem. Finally, good leaders recognize and reward success, which not only gives people a sense of accomplishment but also makes them feel like they belong to an organization that cares about them. When all this is done, the work itself becomes intrinsically motivating.

The more that change characterizes the business environment, the more that leaders must motivate people to provide leadership as well. When this works, it tends to reproduce leadership across the entire organization, with people occupying multiple leadership roles throughout the hierarchy. This is highly valuable, because coping with change in any complex business demands initiatives from a multitude of people. Nothing less will work.

Of course, leadership from many sources does not necessarily converge. To the contrary, it can easily conflict. For multiple leadership roles to work together, people's actions must be carefully coordinated by mechanisms that differ from those coordinating traditional management roles.

Strong networks of informal relationships – the kind found in companies with healthy cultures – help coordinate leadership activities in much the same way that formal structure coordinates managerial activities. The key difference is that informal networks can deal with the greater demands for coordination associated with nonroutine activities and change. The multitude of communication channels and the trust among the individuals connected by those channels allow for an ongoing process of accommodation and adaptation. When conflicts arise among roles, those same relationships help resolve the conflicts. Perhaps most important, this process of dialogue and accommodation can produce visions that are linked and compatible instead of remote and competitive. All this requires a great deal more communication than is needed to coordinate managerial roles, but unlike formal structure, strong informal networks can handle it.

Of course, informal relations of some sort exist in all corporations. But too often these networks are either very weak – some people are well connected but most are not – or they are highly fragmented – a strong network exists inside the marketing group and inside R&D but not across the two departments. Such networks do not support multiple leadership initiatives well. In fact, extensive informal networks are so important that if they do not exist, creating them has to be the focus of activity early in a major leadership initiative.

Creating a Culture of Leadership

Despite the increasing importance of leadership to business success, the on-the-job experiences of most people actually seem to undermine the development of attributes needed for leadership. Nevertheless, some companies have consistently demonstrated an ability to develop people into outstanding leader-managers. Recruiting people with leadership potential is only the first step. Equally important is managing their career patterns. Individuals who are effective in large leadership roles often share a number of career experiences.

Perhaps the most typical and most important is significant challenge early in a career. Leaders almost always have had opportunities during their twenties and thirties actually to try to lead, to take a risk, and to learn from both triumphs and failures. Such learning seems essential in developing a wide range of leadership skills and perspectives. It also teaches people something about both the difficulty of leadership and its potential for producing change.

Later in their careers, something equally important happens that has to do with broadening. People who provide effective leadership in important jobs always have a chance, before they get into those jobs, to grow beyond the narrow base that characterizes most managerial careers. This is usually the result of lateral career moves or of early promotions to unusually broad job assignments. Sometimes other vehicles help, like special task-force assignments or a lengthy general management course. Whatever the case, the breadth of knowledge developed in this way seems to be helpful in all aspects of leadership. So does the network of relationships that is often acquired both inside and outside the company. When enough people get opportunities like this, the relationships that are built also help create the strong informal networks needed to support multiple leadership initiatives.

Corporations that do a better-than-average job of developing leaders put an emphasis on creating challenging opportunities for relatively young employees. In many businesses, decentralization is the key. By definition, it pushes responsibility lower in an organization and in the process creates more challenging jobs at lower levels. Johnson & Johnson, 3M, Hewlett-Packard, General Electric, and many other well-known companies have used that approach quite successfully. Some of those same companies also create as many small units as possible so there are a lot of challenging lower level general management jobs available.

Sometimes these businesses develop additional challenging opportunities by stressing growth through new products or services. Over the years, 3M has had a policy that at least 25% of its revenue should come from products introduced within the last five years. That encourages small new ventures, which in turn offer hundreds of opportunities to test and stretch young people with leadership potential.

Such practices can, almost by themselves, prepare people for small- and medium-sized leadership jobs. But developing people for important leadership positions requires more work on the part of senior executives, often over a long period of time. That work begins with efforts to spot people with great leadership potential early in their careers and to identify what will be needed to stretch and develop them.

Again, there is nothing magic about this process. The methods successful companies use are surprisingly straightforward. They go out of their way to make young employees and people at lower levels in their organizations visible to senior management. Senior managers then judge for themselves who has potential and what the development needs of those people are. Executives also discuss their tentative conclusions among themselves to draw more accurate judgments.

Armed with a clear sense of who has considerable leadership potential and what skills they need to develop, executives in these companies then spend time planning for that development. Sometimes that is done as part of a formal succession planning or high-potential development process; often it is more informal. In either case, the key ingredient appears to be an intelligent assessment of what feasible development opportunities fit each candidate's needs.

To encourage managers to participate in these activities, well-led businesses tend to recognize and reward people who successfully develop leaders. This is rarely done as part of a formal compensation or bonus formula, simply because it is so difficult to measure such achievements with precision. But it does become a factor in decisions about promotion, especially to the most senior levels, and that seems to make a big difference. When told that future promotions will depend to some degree on their ability to nurture leaders, even people who say that leadership cannot be developed somehow find ways to do it.

Such strategies help create a corporate culture where people value strong leadership and strive to create it. Just as we need more people to provide leadership in the complex organizations that dominate our world today, we also need more people to develop the cultures that will create that leadership. Institutionalizing a leadership-centered culture is the ultimate act of leadership.

4
Leadership, Management and the Seven Keys

Craig M. Watson

In recent years a good deal of excitement has grown around the implications and significance of the 7-S organizational framework,[1] stemming both from the insights the system yields into organizational effectiveness and from the explanation it provides for consistently outstanding performance by excellent companies.[2]

In brief, the theory holds that the traditional view of organizations pivots on three axes: *strategy*, which leads almost implicitly to organization *structure*, and *systems* which orchestrate complex functions resulting in performance. The 7-S construct, by contrast, suggests that four additional S's are critical to achieving and understanding the effectiveness of excellent management: *style*, the patterns of action, symbolic and actual, which top management communicates to the organization at large, and which the organization itself ultimately adopts as a cultural orientation; *staff*, meaning the people side of the organization equation, especially the socialization and development process which molds managers into effective, acculturated performers; *skills*, the company's unique competences and dominating attributes; and *superordinate* (or *shared*) *goals*, the set of values or aspirations which underpin what a company stands for and believes in.[3]

The significance of the new framework (as others have stated) is in the attention it draws to the 'soft' informal facets of organization which formerly were considered insufficiently systematic or 'hard' to be of interest. The traditional approach focuses on the relatively easy-to-change strategy, structure and systems, while the new approach alerts us to the crucial role played by the more elusive features.

From *Business Horizons*, March–April, 1983. Copyright 1983 by the Foundation for the School of Business at Indiana University, with permission.

The key factors distinguishing the 7-S framework from the traditional approach to organizational effectiveness, in fact, focus on the change levers which leaders, as distinct from managers, have always manipulated to effect organizational change and to achieve superior performance. By extension, much of what the 7-S approach embodies is the direct result of observing organizations run by leaders as opposed to managers.

The implications of this perspective are manifold. For example:

- If one believes that there is a difference between leadership and management, then there is some question as to whether managers can achieve 7-S performance at all.
- Society produces far fewer leaders than it does managers. The socialization process which cultivates managers also reinforces tradition, whereas leaders succeed in making change.
- Some cultures incline more naturally toward utilization of both the hard and the soft levers to effect change and achieve performance. This, in fact, has been called the 'art of Japanese management.' Does this imply that certain cultures are more naturally adept at creating leaders than others?
- Achieving 7-S management is a long-term undertaking. There is some question as to whether the predominantly short-term orientation of American management can be modified sufficiently to make the transition successfully.
- Finally, our management education system reinforces the traditional view of organization performance. The relative novelty of the 7-S framework makes it unlikely that the approach will be adopted quickly by the educational system.

These issues, while indeed speculative, are worth raising because it is easy to embrace new techniques and approaches as panaceas before fully appreciating their implications. Thus they are put forth as cautions.

Conflict, Convergence and Culture

Ironically, the 7-S framework offers two contrasting perspectives on the future potential of management.

- First, if the points made in this article are valid, 7-S management is the province of leaders, and managers per se will not ordinarily be capable of achieving sufficient mastery of all seven keys to attain consistently superb performance.
- Alternatively, the framework suggests that the effects of leadership (or, at least, its visible instruments) can possibly be *developed consciously and applied systematically by managers* to beneficial effect, by paying attention to the soft as well as the hard S's.

Proponents of the new framework say it is indeed possible to make managers more effective by focusing attention on the soft four keys. Conversely, the point can equally be made that leaders can become more effective managers by focusing more effort on the traditional strategy, structure and systems. In this sense, the 7-S framework underscores the importance of balance, of attention to style, shared values, systems, structure, and so forth equally, in the enlightened interplay of the hard and the soft. The whole can become larger than the sum of the parts; management and leadership can be made to converge.

In practice, the best-performing companies have, or have had, leaders at the top reinforcing values, lending style, molding staff and developing unique skills. At the same time, in rare cases, these leaders also possess superior traditional managerial skills. Where both facets are not present in the same individual, hierarchy assumes great significance. For example, where the leader occupies high position, managers below him are likely to be well motivated and the organization's performance correspondingly impressive. By contrast, when leader personalities work under traditional managers, there is likely to be friction and frustration, ultimately resulting in high turnover. The key complaints of those leading are an inability to get ideas heard, perception of threats or opportunities unheeded by the firm at large, and a prevailing managerial attitude prone to delusions about competitive realities or internal capabilities.

It is in countering the negative impact of these potential conflicts that particularly creative organizations are apparently successful. Excellent companies encourage ideas from all quarters. They keep structures lean and simple and encourage operational autonomy.[4]

On the issue of culture and its impact (whether Japan, for example, is more likely to produce leaders than the West), the 7-S framework offers important insights. First, good management does not depend on the presence of leadership, although in many cases it is enhanced by leadership qualities. What is crucial is the presence of the soft and the hard instruments in balance. Second, the Japanese are, apparently, more inclined to use the soft tests of management – as an extension of their cultural norms – than are Western managers whose culture stresses different values.[5] Third, managerial performance is multivariate. Culture certainly plays a part, but what is more significant is that excellent performance in organizations in Japan or in the West depends on achieving harmony among all seven keys to organization.

The awareness created by the 7-S approach to organizational effectiveness should benefit organizations run by either leaders or traditional managers, as we have used the terms. Outstanding companies are distinguished not by the leaders who head them or by the managers who run them, but rather by the manner in which leadership and management are harmonized to create a climate in which work is both uncommonly meaningful and unusually effective.

Notes

1   Robert H. Waterman Jr, Thomas J. Peters and Julien R. Phillips, 'Structure is not organization', *Business Horizons*, June 1980, p. 14; also *The McKinsey Quarterly*, Summer 1980, p. 2.
2   See, for example, Thomas J. Peters, 'Putting excellence into management', *The McKinsey Quarterly*, Autumn 1980, p. 31, and Anthony G. Athos and Richard Pascale, *The Art of Japanese Management* (New York, Simon & Schuster, 1981).
3   Each of the seven S's are defined more fully in Waterman et al. 'Structure is not organization'. Also see Robert H. Waterman Jr, 'The seven elements of strategic fit', *The Journal of Business Strategy*, Winter 1982, p. 69.
4   Peters, 'Putting excellence into management', p. 32.
5   Athos and Pascale, *The Art of Japanese Management*.

Chapter 2
Leadership: The Value of Military Precedents

Introduction

The need for better leadership in business has revived interest in examples set by military commanders of the past. The problems of inspiring a large armed force to fulfil a series of military objectives, usually in turbulent conditions, is the nearest equivalent we have to leading a modern business in a period of economic uncertainty. As John Kotter comments in chapter 1, 'A wartime army . . . needs competent leadership at all levels. No one yet has figured out how to manage people effectively into battle; they must be *led*.' The same, he says, applies in business where 'more change always demands more leadership'. Consequently, it has become fashionable to cite sources as wide as Lao-tzu, Alexander the Great, Gustavus Adolphus and Montgomery in supporting current theories about the nature and characteristics of good leadership.

But how valid is the analogy? The four articles below illustrate how modern experts on leadership have used military antecedents to highlight contemporary good practice. John Ridgeway (see chapter 17) thinks the analogy, particularly in terms of style, can only be taken so far and 'people with a long military experience are not suited for business leadership'.

John Adair in his book *Great Leaders* makes a serious attempt to place the theory and practices of past political and military leaders in the current framework of business thinking. The spread of characters is impressive – he quotes sources as wide as Xenophon, Jesus Christ, George Washington and Field-Marshal Montgomery – and he devotes a whole chapter to Nelson whom he sees as a particular exemplar of effective leadership. The extract included here relates to Nelson's ability to inspire and manage a team spirit throughout his command.

Nelson's ability to inspire trust and loyalty, like that of so many other military commanders, rested on what military historian John Keegan describes as 'the imperative of example' in his book *The Mask of Command*. The first and greatest imperative of command, he argues, is to be there in person. Although the extract reproduced here describes military crises that seem far removed from the modern business marketplace, the parallels are there in, for example, the fashion for 'management by walking about', the disapproval of chief executives who hide themselves away in plush twentieth-floor offices, and the approbation of Japanese, overall-clad MDs frequenting the shop-floor.

'Château generalship', based on elaborate military hierarchies, bears an uncanny resemblance to the bureaucratic style of management which grew up in the 1960s and 1970s. While it would be dangerous to take direct comparisons too far, close links exist between the issues facing modern military leaders and their industrial counterparts, particularly if armed forces and commercial enterprises are seen in the same organizational light.

Both have seen a steady devolvement of responsibility downwards, partially as a consequence of new technology and the removal of redundant middle-level hierarchies. Both have seen the need for a better trained and educated set of recruits – armed forces and Top 500 companies in most developed countries have been keen competitors for the same school-leavers and graduates. Both have seen an erosion of class and background as a key denominator of leadership in favour of a more highly educated meritocracy, with a consequent re-evaluation of the relationship between leader and led.

Thus the Israeli army, animated by a code of 'Follow me' and the triumph of the British army in the Falklands through heroic leadership is mirrored in the success of business leaders like John Harvey-Jones, Jan Carlzon, and Anita Roddick because all, as Keegan puts it 'insist on the closest personal identification of leaders with led'.

Norman Dixon's book *On the Psychology of Military Incompetence*, which looks at the wider organizational implications of leadership, is represented by an extract which examines the transformation of the Victorian colonial officer corps from an amateur to a professional body.

Some of the themes he touches on will be very familiar to modern managers. Officers were promoted beyond their ability (an obvious parallel with the 'Peter Principle' which operates in corporations) and were unable to manage 'combined operations' – something reflected directly in Bob Garratt's argument (see chapter 16) that specialists often fail to perform well in general management positions because they are able to fall back only on their past experience. Dixon's description of senior officers motivated by a fear of failure rather than hope of success also contrasts well with Jan Carlzon's description of ineffective delegation (see chapter 4).

Analogies between military and business leadership have been given a new piquancy because, in developed economies, business competition is gradually replacing war as 'state policy by other means'.

Edward Luttwak, top Pentagon adviser and professor of strategy at Washington's Centre for Strategic and International Studies, claimed in 1989 that economic rather than military prowess will be the principal denominator of future global influence. Professor Luttwak's optimism was premature. The world is not governed by economic logic. Within six months of his lecture, Iraq invaded Kuwait and the balmy prospect of a world free from major armed conflicts was shown to be an illusion.

However, it does seem likely that conflicts between the major trading powers – Japan, Europe, and the United States – will be fought over the money markets and through industrial competition; and that businesses rather than armies will be in front line.

Whatever the final outcome, there is much to be learned from the examination of excellent leadership, in whatever context it appears. Adair tells us Nelson 'gave clear directions; he built teams; and . . . he possessed a great leader's gift of drawing out the best from people', all abilities valued just as much in any of today's commercial organizations as in the eighteenth century Royal Navy. Wess Roberts also analyses the practical ways in which the study of historic military leadership can provide useful lessons to business leaders. He boils down the essential qualities of leadership to the very basics, identifying such attributes as loyalty, courage, physical stamina, required by leaders in all walks of life, military, political, social, or commercial. Since, until this century, so much of our experience of outstanding leadership has been military, to deny its relevance would be to deny a whole treasury of valuable lessons. It would be a tragic loss to the student of business leadership today.

1
Great Leaders: Nelson

John Adair

Perhaps once or twice in its history every nation produces a person with a genius for leadership. Horatio Nelson was such a genius. His leadership style was particularly remarkable given that it was being exercised in the Royal Navy in the conditions of the late eighteenth century, but of course Nelson, like all geniuses, transcends both his times and the limited military context. As long as the British are interested in leadership they will always study Nelson.

Nelson reveals almost all the core qualities of leadership. He had the authority of knowledge and personality, as well as of rank and position. He gave clear directions; he built teams; and he showed a real concern for the individual. As Nelson's career unfolded, it also became clear that he possessed a great leader's gift of drawing out the best from people. These are the reasons why Nelson's story is worth telling again in this context.

Early Life

Nelson's family and social background was relatively humble. His father, a country vicar in Norfolk, had eleven children. His paternal grandfather, another rector, who had been educated at Eton and Emmanuel College in Cambridge, had married the daughter of a butcher in Petty Cury. His mother, a relative of the Walpole family, kept up her links with the Walpoles, but she had other relatives nearer to home, notably the Suckling family. When Spain threatened the Falkland Islands and Horatio's uncle Captain Maurice Suckling was making ready for sea, he invited one of his Nelson nephews to accompany him. Horatio, the younger of the two, a well-spoken boy with a certain charm of

Excerpt from *Great Leaders* by John Adair, Talbot Adair Press. Copyright © John Adair 1989, by permission of the author.

manner, accepted with alacrity. As a midshipman, he sailed with Suckling to the West Indies. He also voyaged to the Arctic, and finally to the East Indies, where he was stricken by a fever.

On his way home to England in the *Dolphin* – the voyage took over six months – Nelson suffered a severe depression, caused first by his fever and then by his apparent lack of prospects. Under the kindly eye of the captain his health returned and his spirits revived. Nelson thought he perceived a radiant orb which beckoned him on. 'A sudden glow of patriotism was kindled within me,' he would tell his officers later, 'and presented my King and Country as my patron. My mind exulted in the idea. "Well, then," I exclaimed, "I will be a hero, and confiding in Providence, I will brave every danger." '

This simplicity of purpose remained his strength. Nelson's values were henceforth clear for the rest of his life – King and Country, God and the pursuit of glory. It was all straightforward. Later, in language appropriate to his age and rank, he advised a young midshipman to steer a similar course. 'There are three things, young gentleman,' said Nelson, 'you are constantly to bear in mind – first, you must always implicitly obey orders, without attempting to form any opinion of your own respecting their propriety; secondly, you must consider every man as your enemy who speaks ill of your King; and thirdly, you must hate a Frenchman as you do the devil. Although Nelson did not follow his own advice in the first respect, for he did not practise blind obedience, he knew that all entrants to the military profession must first learn to obey orders.

With Captain Suckling as his patron, Nelson rose fast in the service. Nelson was extremely ambitious; he had a gift for not only getting noticed by those who mattered in his career but also for establishing excellent relations with most of his superiors without any hint of subservience or servility. He was captain of a 32 gun frigate at the age of 21 years, but then he endured five years on the beach with half-pay in England, fretting for action. Like Alexander the Great, Nelson thirsted for battle. He desperately desired a great name and all the honours that accompanied success.

Nelson's impatience becomes more intelligible when it is remembered that he had yet to take part in a major sea battle. His enforced stay on land came to an end in 1793, when he was appointed to command the *Agamemnon* of 64 guns, under Lord Hood. Two days later England declared war on France. His new command brought him sudden glory, the loss of his right arm at Tenerife, and, from 1798 onwards – after the Battle of the Nile in Aboukir Bay – general fame. Such universal popularity might have been unwelcome to a man of different temperament, but Nelson loved it. He basked in the limelight of England's hero-worship. Nelson's enjoyment of his success was marred only by the effects of the nasty wound above the eyebrow he received in Aboukir Bay (Lady Emma Hamilton taught him later to cover up the scar by combing his hair forwards). He had lost his right eye in Corsica, and the sight in his remaining eye was beginning to fail.

The Man and the Legend

Later, Nelson took care to foster his own legend. He understood and practised the art of public relations. After actions at sea he excelled at writing what he called 'a famous account of your own actions.' He arranged for these despatches to be leaked immediately to the press, directing that where he had written 'I' and 'my' the third person should be substituted, to give the impression that some other hand had written them. He loved having his portrait painted. One of his mentors, the crusty old Lord St Vincent, told some ladies that Nelson, 'foolish little fellow, has sat to every artist in London.' (Nelson was only 5'2" in height.) Soon Nelson's image, drawn from these portraits, appeared everywhere: on souvenir jugs and mugs, patriotic handkerchiefs, and swinging inn-signs. In Yarmouth, when the landlady of the Wrestlers Inn asked leave of Nelson to rename her hostelry the Nelson Arms, he smiled and replied: 'That would be absurd, seeing that I have but one'!

People seldom forgot their first meeting with Nelson. It was in Admiral Hood's ship the *Barfleur* that Prince William, son of the reigning monarch and later England's eccentric sailor-king, met Nelson, then a 23 year-old frigate captain. His appearance made the straitlaced Prince stare. The Prince was midshipman of the watch on deck 'when Captain Nelson, of the *Albemarle*, came in his barge alongside, who appeared the merest boy of a Captain I ever beheld: and his dress was worthy of attention. He had on a full-laced uniform: his lank untidy hair was tied in a stiff hessian tail, of extraordinary length; the old fashioned flaps of his waistcoat added to the general quaintness of his figure, and produced an appearance which particularly attracted my notice; for I had never seen anything like it before, nor could I imagine who he was, nor what he came about. My doubts, however, removed when Lord Hood introduced me to him. There was something irresistibly pleasing in his address and conversation; and an enthusiasm, when speaking on professional subjects, that showed he was no common being.'

That youthfulness and enthusiasm never left Nelson. But in his later years his sandy-grey hair turned almost white. His face with its irregular features became lined with suffering, looked older than his years. Nelson improved his dress. In later life he customarily wore his blue naval uniform with gold epaulettes, adorned with his four orders of chivalry, the ribbons of two of them, and the gold medals awarded to all captains of ships-of-the-line after the battles of Cape St Vincent and the Nile.

During the long war with France, when at one point Britain was threatened by Napoleon's Grand Army, the nation needed a saviour. In fact it found two – Wellington and Nelson. The two men possessed very different backgrounds and characters.

Wellington came from the aristocracy. He had a certain aloofness about him, together with a lordly indifference to what people thought or felt about him – especially his social inferiors. He practised the virtue of self-control to the point of being taciturn. Wellington won victories and he won respect, but did he also win hearts? Wellington always seemed more at home with his officers, in their red-coats and gold epaulettes, than the rank-and-file, those scourings of society – the 'scum of the earth,' as he once called them. The British Army, he added, had turned these men into fine soldiers. Popular as 'Old Nosey' was for winning victories, for the good administration and even-handed discipline he maintained in his army, Wellington remained a commander rather than a leader.

In strange company Nelson usually said very little, although occasionally he could be boastful. He disliked any form of public speaking. Among friends Nelson spoke in a simple and unaffected way, his face animated. One of his nephews said that, 'at his table he was the last heard among the company, and so far from being the hero of his own tale, I never heard him allude voluntarily to any of the great actions of his life.'

Nelson could switch from one part to another with rapidity. Vanity and modesty fought for position in him. For Nelson's soaring ambition for glory and honour was confronted by a genuine humility before God – to whom he prayed night and morning – and before his fellow men. One of his captains, Sir Alexander Ball, tells the story that after the glorious battle of the Nile, he and his fellow captains commissioned an artist to paint Nelson's portrait. The artist had difficulty in even getting started. At last he admitted that the task was beyond his powers. 'There is such a mixture of humility and ambition in Lord Nelson's countenance,' he said, 'that I dare not risk the attempt.'

Achieving the Task

'Nothing can stop the courage of English seamen,' wrote Nelson exultantly after one fight against the French in the Mediterranean. Nelson exemplified physical courage. He gave evidence in childhood that he had little sense of fear. As we have noted, he had an abnormal thirst for action which recalls Alexander the Great. The odds against him seldom mattered. Luck and the devotion of his colleagues and subordinates saw him through – at least until Trafalgar. In the boat attack on Cadiz in 1797, he and a crew of thirteen men attacked a Spanish barge with a crew of thirty. They fought it out with swords and pistols. John Sykes, the coxswain, twice saved Nelson's life with his cutlass; a third time he dived forwards and received on his own head a slash meant for Nelson. 'We all saw it,' wrote one sailor. 'We were witnesses to the gallant deed, and we gave in revenge one cheer and one tremendous rally. Eighteen of the Spaniards were killed, and we boarded and carried her, there not being one man left on board who was not either dead or wounded. "Sykes," said Nelson as he caught the gallant fellow in his arms, "I cannot forget this." But my wounded shipmate only looked him in the face, and smiled as he said, "Thank God, Sir, you are safe." '

On 25 July 1797 Nelson attacked Santa Cruz and had his right elbow shattered. The amputation of his arm without an anaesthetic proved to be an agonizing ordeal, but according to an eyewitness Nelson bore it with 'firmness and courage.'

'Authority flows from the man who knows,' says the proverb. Having gone to sea at the age of twelve, after briefly attending three schools, Nelson had little formal education but he read voraciously while he was at sea. He applied himself, too, to mastering his profession, passing his Lieutenant's Certificate at 19, one year below the permitted age (it helped having his mentor, Captain Suckling, on the examining board!) 'I have been your scholar,' Nelson wrote to William Locker; captain of the *Lowestoffe* on which he served as lieutenant, 'it is you who taught me to board a Frenchman . . . and my sole merit in my profession is being a good scholar.'

Sea battles usually consisted of two long lines of stately white-sailed wooden ships sailing in parallel and pounding each other with broadsides. Nelson showed his flair and imagination in varying this theme. He spent much of his time thinking – thinking hard – about how best to use his 'grey-geese,' as he sometimes called his beloved ships. Off Cape St Vincent his self-confidence and flexibility of mind led him to ignore conventional tactics and turn his ship the *Captain* out of line and across the head of the enemy column. At the Battle of the Nile, Nelson surprised the French fleet by attacking them at anchor on the landward side where their gunports were inoperative. At Trafalgar he approached the French line at right angles with two columns of ships. 'What do you think of that?' he had asked one of his captains to whom he had explained the plan while they strolled in the gardens of his Merton house before leaving England. 'Such a question I felt required consideration, I paused,' recalled Captain Keats. 'Seeing it he said, "But I'll tell you what *I* think of it. I think it will surprise and confound the enemy! They won't know what I am about. It will bring forward a pell-mell battle, and that is what I want." '

Nelson was exceptionally good at communicating his ideas and plans to his officers. After joining the fleet off Cadiz before Trafalgar, he gave a dinner for fifteen commanding officers in his stateroom aboard the *Victory* on 29 September, his birthday, and to as many other captains on the succeeding day. 'I believe my arrival was most welcome, not only to the Commanders of the Fleet, but to almost every individual in it,' he wrote to Lady Hamilton, 'and when I came to explain to them the "Nelson touch" (his idea of bringing on a confused fight) it was like an electric shock. Some shed tears, all approved – "it was new – it was singular – it was simple!" and, from Admirals downwards it was repeated – "It must work, if ever they will allow us to get at them. You are, my Lord, surrounded by friends, whom you inspire with confidence." '

Bringer of Harmony

In all his command, Nelson both inspired confidence and created harmony. Whether it was with an individual ship, a squadron or a fleet, he demonstrated that he was a natural team builder. Nelson began with an unusually high opinion of his fellow officers and seamen. He trusted them and they in their turn resolved not to let him down. Months after the Nile, in a letter to him of congratulations, Lord Howe said how notable he thought it was that *every* captain had done his duty on that day. Alas, he added, in his long experience, that had not always been the case. Nelson replied: 'I had the happiness to command a Band of Brothers; therefore night was to my advantage. Each knew his duty, and I was sure each would feel for a French ship.'

This gift of creating or enhancing harmony wherever he went extended to the lower deck. He had the knack of finding the golden mean as far as discipline was concerned. The harshness of some naval commanders, who relied overmuch on fear and corporal punishment to enforce their orders, often caused dissension and even mutiny within the fleet. That unimaginative disciplinarian Prince William, when he commanded a ship under Nelson, was quite indiscriminate on occasion: he once had a visiting German journalist whipped with a cat-o'-nine-tails for some remarks which were not to his liking. Nelson eschewed such brutality. On one occasion in the West Indies, he courted unpopularity with his seniors for saving from the hangman's noose a drunken deserter called Able Seaman William Clark. Nelson had powers to suspend the court martial sentence, but not to pardon or discharge the man: he did both. Lord St Vincent, one of the old school, commented: 'he used a hatchet where I would have used a penknife.'

Once a crew was working as a team and was infected with the right spirit, Nelson gave them his whole-hearted and warm affection. 'Nobody can be ill with my ship's company,' he wrote of the *Agamemnon*, 'they are so fine a set.' He turned down the offer of a bigger ship in order to stay with them in what he regarded as 'the finest ship I ever sailed in.' During a time when Spain allied itself somewhat uncertainly to Britain, Nelson paid a friendly visit to the Spanish fleet in Cadiz. 'Very fine ships, but shockingly manned,' was his professional judgement. 'The Dons may make fine ships,' he remarked, 'but they cannot, however, make men.' By contrast, the Royal Navy, like Wellington's army, did make men out of unpromising and sometimes unwilling material. 'My seamen,' he once wrote to his wife, 'are now what British seamen ought to be . . . almost invincible: they really mind shot no more than peas.'

Nelson once told a friend that at the Battle of the Nile his daring plan rested upon the outstanding abilities of his captains and crews. 'Without knowing the men he had to trust, he would not have hazarded the attack: there was very little room, but he was sure each would find a hole to creep in at. 'Having caught sight of the French fleet,' Nelson added, 'I could not help popping my head every now and then out of the window (although I had a damned toothache) and once, as I was observing their position, I heard two seamen quartered at a gun near me, talking, and one said to the other, "Damn them, look at them. There they are, Jack, if we don't beat them they will beat us." I knew what stuff I had under me, so I went into the attack with a few ships only, perfectly sure the others would follow me, although it was nearly dark and they might have had every excuse for not doing it, yet they all in the course of two hours found a hole to poke in.'

Meeting Individual Needs

Nelson's early life in a country rectory in Norfolk had taught him to care for others. His financial generosity to those who had some claim on him was one expression of it. Nelson had plenty of that liberality which Sir Thomas Elyot had expected an English governor or leader to show. He was always an affectionate man, especially to children such as his youngest sister Kate or, later, to his future wife's 5-year-old son. A friend of hers once surprised the 'great little man of whom everyone is afraid,' at play under the dining room table with young Josiah.

Like any good naval officer of the day, Nelson concerned himself with the sailors' material needs, on one occasion providing one crew with fifty blankets at his own expense. He insisted that the men's quarters were properly ventilated and kept as free from damp as possible. He encouraged music and dancing, and any other activity which could help to sustain morale. He obtained Bibles and other Christian literature for the sailors. But such good works do not explain his extraordinary effect upon the lower deck. That was much more to do with his personality and charm.

Apart from Nelson's reputation, which preceded him like an ever mounting bow wave, the seamen loved him for his humanity and fellow-feeling. At Aboukir Bay, when a piece of iron shot ripped across his forehead above the eye leaving the bone white and skin hanging down over his face, Nelson was carried down to the cockpit. He was convinced that he was a dead man, for the spurting blood had blinded him. In spite of being in intense pain, when the surgeon broke away from a sailor he was attending in order to dress the wound, Nelson stopped him. 'No,' he said, 'I will take my turn with my brave fellow.'

After Nelson's early days as a lieutenant, the seamen of the *Lowestoffe* presented him with an ivory model of their frigate, filled with dominoes. Later it was a familiar sight in Nelson's cabin, a valued token of affection from his 'brave fellows.' In his despatch after that first major success off Cape St Vincent, Nelson added in a postscript that one sailor from his ship the *Captain* had come up to him on board the captured *San Joseph*, and shaken him warmly by the hand, saying he might not soon have such another place to do it in, and 'assuring me he was heartily glad to see me.'

As Captain of the *Boreas*, an officer on that ship recalled, he used to call the midshipmen his children. He never rebuked the more timid of them, but always wished to show them he desired nothing of them he would not instantly do himself. 'I have known him say – "Well, Sir, I am going a race to the mast-head, and I beg I may meet you there,"' The officer added that Nelson never seemed to notice the timid boy's lack of alacrity in climbing the mast, but 'when he met at the top, began instantly speaking in the most cheerful manner, and saying how much a person was to be pitied who could fancy there was any danger, or even anything disagreeable in the attempt.' Who could resist a Commander-in Chief who, asked by a fond mother to deliver a last-minute note to a midshipman on his first voyage, requested her to kiss it, so that he 'might take the kiss to him too'?

Trust in his colleagues and subordinates was the key to Nelson's leadership. It is summed up in the original form of his famous flag signal at Trafalgar. He ordered this signal to be hoised on to the *Victory* yardarm high above the amber-and-black sides of the ship as the two British columns inched towards the waiting French lines at an agonizingly slow speed of 2 knots. It was to read as follows: NELSON CONFIDES THAT EVERY MAN WILL DO HIS DUTY. He agreed to an officer's suggestion with commendable modesty – that NELSON should be changed to ENGLAND. As CONFIDES would have had to be spelt out letter by letter, Nelson also accepted the suggested substitution of EXPECTS. At least on one quarterdeck the response was characteristically British. 'What is Nelson signalling about?' grumbled Admiral Collingwood at the head of the other column, 'We all know what we have to do.'

After Nelson's death at Trafalgar the sense of elation which swept through the British fleet at its great victory was tempered by the great shock of losing such a leader. 'I never set eyes on him,' wrote a sailor in his letter home, 'for which I am both sorry and glad, for to be sure I should have liked to have seen him. But there, all the men in our ship who have seen him are such soft toads. They have done nothing but blast their eyes and cry since he was killed. God bless you! Chaps that fought like the Devil sit down and cry like a wench.'

•

Nelson's Legacy

Apart from his physical frailty, Nelson had other human weaknesses. Some would describe them as flaws of character. At Leghorn in 1794, for example, he is known to have shared his captain's cabin with an untidy and slovenly woman – 'he makes himself ridiculous with that woman,' wrote a brother officer. Some critics thought that Nelson had made a fool of himself with Lady Hamilton too, but there was a depth and permanence in their relationship which balanced his outward adoration of her and silenced all but a few critics. Among them, alas, was his sovereign, King George III, for whom he had ventured so much loyalty. According to a friend of Lady Hamilton's, she said that his besetting sins were 'venery and swearing,' but neither fault was untypical of the sailors of his, or any other, day. Besides, in the military, politcal and industrial fields, leaders have what has been called an 'idiosyncrasy credit': grateful for success, their colleagues discount human failings and peccadilloes. The British nation, and certainly the Navy, had no difficulty in overlooking his affair with Emma, for he was careful to observe the conventions of propriety. In this respect his charm helped him, for he remained on excellent terms with Emma's lawful husband, Sir William Hamilton, who actually died in Nelson's arms. Such faults may have made him less of a paragon, but paradoxically they make his virtues more accessible to those who would emulate him as a leader.

Of course Nelson had luck – lots of it. So many of his successes could have turned into disasters, and branded him forever as foolhardy. But most of the risks he took were carefully calculated. Nor could he have achieved his pinnacle of fame unless he was supported by other superb leaders, captains and commanders in the Royal Navy, who fell not far short of him in courage, professional knowledge and even leadership. Ovid's words in *Heroides* again come to mind: 'He was a leader of leaders.' Nor should his glory detract from the real heroes, those seamen who endured the long blockades at sea with him and fought their guns in the infernoes of smoke and flame between decks. What distinguished Nelson was his rare combination of leadership qualities and abilities. Fused together, and with a certain but indefinable personal charm, Nelson achieved excellence as a leader.

None of the portraits quite capture Nelson's personal magnetism, nor do any of the descriptions of him convey it. It is best deduced from the extraordinary effects he had upon others. Yet the memory of his inspirational leadership is central to the legacy he left to the British Navy. 'Not the least glory of the Navy is that it understood Nelson,' wrote Joseph Conrad. 'He brought heroism into the line of duty. Verily he is a terrible ancestor.' By that last remark Conrad meant that, for officers of the Royal Navy in particular, Nelson was a very hard act to follow.

2
The Imperative of Example

John Keegan

The first and greatest imperative of command is to be present in person. Those who impose risk must be seen to share it, and expect that their orders will be obeyed only as long as command's lesser imperatives require that they shall. Presence may with limited and temporary success be simulated – by frequent visits to the danger zone at moments of quiescence or by the invocation of a reputation for risk-taking in times past. Neither, however, guarantees that the seeming or one-time hero will thereby stimulate heroism in those he wishes to imbue with it. Legendary warriors like Churchill's Carton de Wiart, one-armed, one-eyed, seven times wounded on separate Sundays, or Franco's Millan d'Astray, founder of the Spanish Foreign Legion and also lacking an eye and an arm, may impel young soldiers to reckless deeds by the incontestable evidence of their own past contempt for danger; but few who have shown such contempt survive to infect others with their spirit. Old warriors who have survived risk intact seem to the young merely old; and would-be heroes not heroic at all. It is the spectacle of heroism, or its immediate report, that fires the blood.

Hence the collapse of so many armies whose commanders neglected to show themselves to their soldiers at the moment of danger. 'A rational army,' said Montesquieu, 'would run away.' And so, if we accept that self-preservation is the ultimate expression of rationality, we must agree it would. The thought is one that ought never to be far from any commander's mind. For the merest twitch of emotion stands between his exaltation and his descent to ignominy. At one moment he may, from his horse or headquarters, survey ten thousand, even a million men, ranked to heed his orders. At the next they may be streaming to

Extract from *The Mask of Command* by John Keegan, Jonathan Cape. Copyright © John Keegan 1987, by permission of Sheilhand Associates Ltd. on behalf of the author.

the rear, obeying no order but '*sauve qui peut*'. The transformation might sound over-dramatized; very large armies are as slow to disintegrate as they are to concentrate, since *panique-terreur*, the psychological state that eighteenth-century generals strove to create in the collective nervous systems of their opponents, can initally infect only those fractions of armies exposed to the enemy's main offensive effort. The rest will catch the infection indirectly, feeding their fears on rumour and sensation rather than the reality of rout at close hand, perhaps in consequence failing to find room on the roads to the rear, fighting rearguard actions willy-nilly or floundering in indecision until forced to offer their surrender when abandoned, encircled or marooned.

The sensation of defeat is, nevertheless, unmistakable and often uncontrollable. Few large modern armies have run with the instantaneity of Darius's at Issus or Gaugamela; parts of the Polish army preserved their integrity throughout the awful days of retreat from the frontier to Warsaw in September 1939, and the French defenders of Lille sustained such resistance in 1940 that their German opponents rendered them the honours of war when they eventually marched out to captivity. But when the germ of defeat takes a hold, even very large armies can fall apart with epidemic rapidity. Such was the fate of the Italian army at Caporetto in November 1917, of the bulk of the French army of the North-East in May 1940, of the German Army Group Centre in June 1944. The resulting humiliation of their commanders was pitiable. Cadorna, Georges, Busch had all been paladins; the first a general whose unapproachability struck fear into his subordinates, the second an Olympian of the generation of Foch, the third a victor of the French and Russian Blitzkriegs. Overnight they dwindled into despised nonetities. Cardorna was hurried into obscurity, Georges left weeping at his map table, Busch consigned to the pool of rejects unemployable even in the backwaters of Hitler's empire.

None wholly deserved his fate. The disorders which engulfed their armies were defeats that were waiting to happen, and perhaps no general could have averted them. But Cadorna and Georges had contrived to command in a fashion that ensured professional extinction would follow failure as night the day. Both were 'château generals' of the most extreme type, and though 'château generalship' was an understandable reaction to the recent appearance of long-range weapons, its effect on the relationship between leaders and led was so deadening that even the most arrogantly insensitive of generals should have taken steps to ameliorate it. By the time of Busch's disgrace in 1944 the more perceptive had already begun to do so. Cadorna and Georges appear never to have thought of attempting or even simulating heroic leadership themselves. To that extent they suffered their deserts.

Yet in their youth generals had shared risk with their soldiers as a matter of course, just as leaders had done for a hundred generations. Why the submergence of heroic leadership by château generalship, which was its antithesis? The answer is in part cultural and intellectual – and to this we shall return – but in greater measure technical. The trend of weapon development had for several centuries been acting to drive commanders away from the forward edge of the battlefield, but they had nevertheless resisted it. What occurred at the end of the nineteenth century was a sudden acceptance by the generals of all advanced armies that the trend could no longer be gainsaid and that they must abandon the post of honour to their followers.

The option of command from the rear had, nevertheless, always been open. Alexander had chosen not to exercise it because the values by which he lived and reigned forbade his incurring any taint of cowardice. Within 200 years of his death, however, his own society had advanced to a recognition that a general's station need not be fixed at the point of maximum danger, that he might indeed serve the cause of victory better from a place where he could observe and encourage rather than fire others by his example. But that recognition was not to extinguish the power of the heroic ethic altogether. On the contrary, what resulted was the marriage of the two, giving birth in turn to a code of compromise. By its dictates the general would seek to set as striking an example of risk-sharing as he could, consonant with the need to keep a distance from danger sufficient to allow his controlling the battle as a whole.

It was by those dictates that such commanders of professional armies as Caesar and Wellington adjusted their response to threat and crisis. Caesar, articulating a weapon system technically no different from Alexander's though superior to it by the index of drill and discipline, was often impelled to its frontier of contact with the enemy, and both dressed and behaved accordingly. He affected a distinctive red battle cloak and had ready prepared a repertoire of battlefield oratory with which to inspire and instruct his subordinates. The death of the legions with that of the Roman empire brought back the heroic style. But with the return of regular armies, of which Wellington's was the most perfected type, the compromise between prudence and exposure re-asserted itself. Wellington's close encounters with death were never haphazard, but the result of a mathematical calculation of the ebb and flow of danger. On the open battlefields where he and his opponents chose to give action, it was a consistent possibility, given the known ranges at which weapons took effect, to anticipate the fine tolerances when this position or that would become untenable by the commander and to move accordingly. Wellington did not represent his style of command in terms of the judgement of 'fight' and 'flight' distance by which a lion tamer exerts his mastery over his charges – and a spell over his audience; but it was calculated in almost exactly the same way. If one dimension of command is the theatrical, one would say that, while Alexander's performance was relentlessly Grand Guignol, Wellington's was brilliant melodrama, a succession of perfectly timed exits and entrances, each advancing the plot to its triumphant conclusion by spectacular and risk-fraught effect.

It was a performance, nevertheless, that literally diced with death, as his tally of minor wounds and disabled mounts testifies. Just forty years after his last appearance on the stage of battle, the pattern of risk-taking he had run would have swiftly exhausted an imitator's invulnerability. The tide of probability had then begun to run against anyone foolish enough to keep to the saddle within 500 yards of the firing line – he had survived long exposure at 100 yards or less – and wise generals reacted accordingly. Grant, as we have seen, was very wise. Confident in the power of other means to legitimize his authority, he unashamedly held himself rearward of all but the incalculable odds – stray shells, ambush – while sending his soldiers forward without compunction to face the danger he had decided it was not his duty to share.

Yet Grant did not think it proper to exempt himself from the environment of risk altogether. Though leaving the heroic role to his subordinates, he kept a place for himself on the stage of battle as a sort of actor-manager, prompting the principal players at need and intervening from the wings when crisis threatened the development of the action. The actor-manager role he created – few contemporaries learnt to function as he did – was to prove, however, a transient one, intermediate between Wellington's style, rooted as it was in the heroic tradition, and that of the château generals to come. Some commanders of the Prussian wars of 1866–71 would ride the battlefield as if none but a silver bullet could touch them. But the majority kept to or near their headquarters, communicating with the front by messenger and surveying it, if they could at all, by telescope. Fifty years later, their descendants – French and German indiscriminately – were not to think of quitting their headquarters at any time. Berthelot, Joffre's operation officer at the Marne in 1914, would indeed spend the whole of the battle literally *en pantoufles* – shod in carpet slippers – and sitting at his desk from which only the summons to a meal (he might have doubled as the fat man in a circus) could shift him. The hazards of the preceding Great Retreat had obliged him to set up his office in a succession of town halls and schoolhouses. With the stabilization of the front in October, however, he would be solidly established in château comfort at Chantilly and his opposite numbers in the allied and opposing armies likewise, the Germans having chosen Spa, a health resort in Belgium, and the British Montreuil, a charming little walled town close to the English Channel. It was from those secluded places that the great slaughter of the trenches would be directed, totally out of sight and, unless for a trick of the mind, also out of sound of all the headquarters responsible for it.

One of the inhabitants of British headquarters, Charteris, Haig's chief of intelligence, has left us a picture of life at Montreuil in 1916:

> Here at GHQ, in our own little town away back from the front line trenches [delicately put; Montreuil was fifty miles behind the lines], there are few visible signs of war. We might almost be in England . . . All the work in all the departments is now systematised into a routine. Most of it is done in office. One of the great difficulties of everyone at GHQ is to get away from the office often and long enough to get in close touch with the front. Few can ever get much

further forward than the HQ of Armies . . . Forward of Army Headquarters, one is nearer the fighting, but even they are now mostly in towns or villages several miles behind the front line. Further forward still are Corps Headquarters, where there is generally plenty of evidence of war . . . but even Corps Headquarters are now pretty big organisations and are almost always in a village. In front of the Corps Headquarters the Divisions are mostly in farmhouses, but well in the fighting line. One can almost always get one's car up to them. But that is about the limit, and visits forward of them consequently take up a good deal of time. We all manage, anyhow, to see something of a division headquarters, but it is only when there is some particular object, more than simply looking around, that one can give up the time to go beyond them. I have not even seen a Brigade Headquarters in the front line for the last month.

Since brigades stood a rank higher in the chain of command than battalions, which actually occupied the trenches, it may be seen that Charteris, whose duty was to form a picture of events at the front for transmission to his chief, did so at best largely second-hand. Haig himself, though his biographer, John Terraine, claims for him that he visited the trenches frequently, was rarely observed to do so by memoirists of the front line. Even at Montreuil he preserved an Olympian detachment from the work of the staff; one of them recalls that, as a special concession, staff officers were allowed to leave their desks to watch him ride in and out from his office provided they did not show themselves at the windows. Haig's residence was not even in Montreuil; he preferred to seclude himself from its relative hurly-burly at the château of Beaurepaire some ten miles away in the heart of the countryside.

The simulated absolute monarchy of château generalship ultimately provided the military equivalent of revolution in almost all the armies on which it was imposed. In May 1917, after the failure of some particularly heartless offensive plans, nearly half the divisions of the French army downed tools, announcing their unwillingness to attack the Germans again until their grievances were redressed. In October of that year the Russian army, disillusioned by the pointlessness of its sufferings, simply 'voted for peace with its feet', as Lenin put it, allowing him to transform the power vacuum which resulted into political revolution. In November the Italian army effectively gave up the fight to which Cadorna had relentlessly driven it, with consequences that almost brought Italy to defeat. It was a crisis of morale in the German army in September 1918 that prompted Ludendorff to tell the German government it must treat for peace. And even the British army, in the aftermath of the March retreat of 1918, suffered a collapse of morale so acute that Haig was impelled to subordinate his independence of command to the French, as the only means of securing reinforcements to shore up his shaken front.

At the root of all these spiritual crises lay a psychological revolt by the fighting soldiers against the demands of unshared risk. For two or three or, in the case of the German army in September 1918, four years, orders had emanated from an unseen source that demanded heroism of ordinary men while itself displaying heroism in no whit whatsoever. Far from it: the château generals had led the lives of country gentlemen, riding well-groomed horses between well-appointed offices and residences, keeping regular hours and eating regular meals, sleeping between clean sheets every night of campaign and rising to don burnished leather and uniforms decorated with the high awards of allied sovereigns. Meanwhile those under their discipline, junior officers and soldiers alike, had circulated between draughty billets and dangerous trenches, clad in verminous clothes and fed on hard rations, burying their friends in field corners when spells from the front allowed and kicking a football about farmyards by way of relaxation. The implication of such disparities can be suppressed in the short term; modern armies are, indeed, mechanisms of such suppression. Their elaborate hierarchies – fourteen ranks interpose between a private and general – act as a system of screens to camouflage the altitude at which dangerous orders are generated. Since the subordinates most exposed to the consequences, ordinary fighting men, receive those orders from someone scarcely less exposed than themselves, or perhaps even more so – the platoon or company leader – resulting dissatisfactions are dissipated at that level if they are indeed felt or expressed. It takes much time for a bad or inconsiderate general's qualities to diffuse downwards through the barrier layers of rank, and even more time for that diffusion to type him for what he is. Even when so typed, he continues to be protected by a parallel mechanism of suppression, the code of military law. Unlike civil society, military society makes dissatisfaction with a superior, once expressed in any form, a criminal offence; even 'dumb insolence' attracts confinement, while fomenting dissent is mutiny, in time of war an act punishable by death.

Yet, as even bad generals know, hierarchy and discipline cannot suppress the implications of risk disparities for ever. Even while the First World War raged, some armies had begun to recognize the deficiencies of château generalship and taken steps to alleviate them. Pétain, appointed to rehabilitate the French army after the mutiny of May 1917, not only instituted enlightened measures of welfare, more generous leave, better food, provision for entertainment – but also took care to design a series of limited operations against the Germans whose small scale ensured their success. By learning that their commanders could lead them to victory – and some French generals, like Marchand, had always been models of the exemplary style – the disheartened *poilus* were gradually weaned back to optimism.

That the commanders of citizen armies should have so gravely abused the reasonable expectations of their followers is evidence of how artificial and unreal was the general staff culture in which contemporary commanders had been raised. That culture was modern and its intensity a function precisely of its novelty. The perception by which it had been created was not false. The sudden heightening of danger on nineteenth-century battlefields quite properly required the commander to withdraw himself, and the consequent delay in the acquisition of 'real time' intelligence rightly demanded that subordinates should act for him at times and places when and where he could not be present. The cultural mistake lay in elevating those subordinates to the status of an élite and their function to superior expertise. General staff selection and training, based on fierce competitive examination, produced in the years 1870–1914 côteries of military specialists whose professional exclusivity was overweening. A social chasm was thereby opened between those who thought and those who fought; worse, thinking came to be deemed more important than fighting in the conduct of war, the emotions of ordinary soldiers subordinate to the perceptions of staff offices and the making of plans superordinate to their execution.

'Knowing', of a limited and theoretical sort, thus came to dominate 'seeing' in the system of military values, with results whose undesirability was to be concealed until the spiritual revolt of European armies in 1917–18 made them stand plain. The history of the emotional life of armies ever since has been one of a retreat from that disjunction. Staff officers who, even when general staff culture flourished at its most intense, had nominally been required to alternate between staff appointments and troop duty, were subsequently and with increasing strictness actually required to do so. Staff training, formerly restricted to a minority, has progressively been extended to the majority of officers. The dynamics of combat – its stresses and psychological climate – have come to form an ever larger subject of consideration in that training. Those who undergo it have demonstrated the military society's change of heart by the enthusiasm with which they cultivate intimacy with the man in the ranks and the frequency with which they seek his company. Leadership, of a style sufficiently heroic to satisfy Alexandrian exigencies, is the command mode to which modern generals now aspire. Their armies perform accordingly. The Israeli army, animated by a code of which 'Follow me' is the central tenet, defeated its Arab enemies with a consistency that seemed routine until in 1973 the Egyptian army, its leadership transformed by an internal revolution inspired by the heroic ethic, very nearly succeeded in reversing the pattern. The Chinese and Vietnamese armies, outstanding among victors in the post-war years, both insist on the closest personal identification of leaders with led. The British army, once infected as badly as any by general staff culture, demonstrated how completely it had cured itself of the disease by its victory in the Falklands, a triumph of heroic leadership against odds. And the American army, trammelled by a theoretical approach to warmaking though it tends to be, has elevated the management of small groups to so high a place in its operational doctrine that its general staff culture may now be judged to persist only in a benign form.

And yet the cure to which so many armies have successfully subjected themselves may, with perspective, now come to appear irrelevant to command's current central problem. For armies have, by the nuclear revolution of 1945, been set aside from that central place in the defence of nations they have occupied since time immemorial.

'In order that the men will be prepared for the fray in a manner they can comprehend easily,' advised Raimondo Montecuccoli,

> the commander will declare that it is not the army of the fatherland but the fatherland itself that is endangered because it will have nothing left if the army is beaten; that it has entrusted all its resources and power to the soldiers; that they are the repository of all its hopes that they surely do not wish to be destroyed.

Montecuccoli's assumption that the army in war epitomized the state, so that its commander was therefore burdened with essentially sovereign responsibilities, is one which would have held good at virtually any moment of the last twenty-four centuries. It holds good no longer. Armies are now but one means by which states of the first rank – those deploying nuclear weapons or belonging to an alliance which does – defend themselves, and not only that: they are a subordinate means. Truly critical command functions no longer belong to generals, but have emigrated to the centre of political power itself, have been returned into the hands of constitutionally sovereign authority itself and subject those who exercise them – president, prime minister, first secretary – to their burdens. Those burdens, always awesome, have been heightened by the dimensions of nuclear power, to the level of the almost unbearable. For it is not merely the 'resources and power' of the 'fatherland' – nation, *rodina, patrie*, call it what you will – that lie at risk should those exercising sovereign authority through nuclear weapons fail or miscalculate; it is the physical survival of the millions of human beings who have entrusted their wellbeing to him or her. Today the political leaders of the nuclear states have become Alexanders, the repositories of ultimate military as well as political responsibility in the polities they head, but with this unmanning – or unwomanning – difference: that those whose hands lie closest to the weapons by which society is defended are those who, in the eventuality of their use, would be placed furthest from the physical consequences of their impact. Nuclear war would expose every ordinary man, woman and child in every nuclear-armed nation to the risk of instantaneous disintegration or, failing that, to the inevitability of secondary irradiation. Presidents, prime ministers, first secretaries would, by contrast, belong to the only group – and that a tiny one – whose survival would in any way be assured against immediate or postponed nuclear extinction. The imperative of example would, in short, have been stood on its head; those at least involved in the prosecution of war and least equipped to protect themselves against its consequences – suckling babes, nursing mothers, the sick, the lame, the very old – would stand in the front line; heads of government, by definition also nuclear force commanders, would be sheltered in deep headquarter bunkers or sequestered in airborne control posts.

3
Leaders of Men

Norman F. Dixon

Discussion of leadership is so often overloaded with vague but emotive ideas that one is hard put to it to nail the concept down. To cut through the panoply of such quasi-moral and unexceptionable associations as 'patriotism', 'play up and play the game', the 'never-asking-your-men-to-do-something-you-wouldn't-do-yourself' formula, 'not giving in (or up)', the 'square-jaw-frank-eyes-steadfast-gaze' formula, and the 'if . . . you'll be a man' recipe, one comes to the simple truth that leadership is no more than exercising such an influence upon others that they tend to act in concert towards achieving a goal which they might not have achieved so readily had they been left to their own devices.

The ingredients which bring about this agreeable state of affairs are many and varied. At the most superficial level they are believed to include such factors as voice, stature and appearance, an impression of omniscience, trustworthiness, sincerity and bravery. At a deeper and rather more important level, leadership depends upon a proper understanding of the needs and opinions of those one hopes to lead, and the context in which the leadership occurs. It also depends on good timing. Hitler, who was neither omniscient, trustworthy nor sincere, whose stature was unremarkable and whose appearance verged on the repellent, understood these rules and exploited them to full advantage. The same may be said of many good comedians.

In short, there is nothing mysterious, romantic or necessarily laudable about leadership. Indeed, some of the most effective leaders have been those who, merely through having more than their fair share of psychopathic traits, were able to release antisocial behaviour in others. Their secret is that by setting an example they release a way of acting that is normally inhibited. This gives pleasure to their followers, thus reinforcing their leadership.

Excerpt from *On the Psychology of Military Incompetence*, by Norman Dixon, Jonathan Cape and Basic Books. Copyright © 1976 N. F. Dixon, by permission of Random Century Ltd. and Georges Borchhardt, Inc. on behalf of the author.

In military organizations leaders are usually of a rather different kind. For a start, they are appointed rather than emergent. That is to say, the needs of the individual soldier play almost no role in deciding the sort of leader that he gets. Secondly, the military leader possesses constitutional power of a magnitude which surpasses that of leaders in most other human groups. If he cannot pull his followers by force of character, he can at least push them by force of law.

The third and related feature of military leadership is that it is essentially autocratic and operates in what modern theorists call a 'wheel net' rather than an 'all-channel communication net'. In other words, the flow of essential information is to and fro between the leader and his subordinates rather than between all members of the group. Not very surprisingly, the wheel net, though no doubt gratifying to autocratic leaders, produces more errors, slower solutions to problems, and reduced gratification to the group than does the more democratic all-channel net.

In the light of these considerations it is perhaps strange that leadership in the British armed forces should have been as effective as it has. Indeed, on the assumption that the primary function of officers is to get the best out of their men, the curious alchemy wrought by the gentlemanly amateurs of the Victorian British officer corps, and even by the still relatively unprofessional officers of the First World War, deserves considerable respect. Since a salient feature of all the campaigns so far considered has been a remarkable absence of mutinous tendencies and a quite astonishing degree of tolerance, fortitude and bravery shown by the common soldier, we have to ask: was this despite or because of their leaders? And if the latter, how was it that even the most inept and reactionary of them could so touch the hearts of their men that they would give themselves to the fight with a cheerful and destructive energy that could, on occasions, rise to whirlwind proportions?

Even men like Elphinstone, Townshend and Buller, about whose flagrant incompetence in the role of decision-maker there can be no possible doubt, earned a loyalty and affection, albeit far beyond their deserts, which maintained the morale and fighting spirit of their men almost to the end.

By way of trying to explain these curiosities let us consider a few more findings from the extensive research on leadership. The first point to note is the distinction that has been drawn between two roles of a leader: 'task-specialist' and 'social specialist'. As task-specialist a leader's prime concern is to achieve the group's ostensible goal; in the case of the military, defeating the enemy. For such a role, being likeable is a rather less important trait than that of being more active, more intelligent and better informed than his followers. In his capacity as 'social specialist', however, a leader's main function is to preserve good personal relations within the group, thereby so maintaining morale as to keep the group in being. In the military milieu the function of a successful social specialist would prevent mutiny and reduce such symptoms of low morale as absenteeism, desertion, sickness and crime. Not very surprisingly, the most important attribute of such a leader is that he should be liked. Efficiency and task-ability are of rather secondary importance. While it is obvious that many leaders in the British armed forces have tended to be social rather than task-specialists, we have to ask why this should be.

It is easy to answer one part of this question. They were poor task-specialists because ours is traditionally an amateur army in which professional ability, knowledge and military flair have counted for little. But why good social specialists?

Again modern research has come up with some possible answers. It has been shown that whereas low-stressed groups, operating in situations that are devoid of painful uncertainties, do best under democratic leadership, organizations like the military in times of war that are subject to stressing ambiguities actually *prefer* autocratic leadership. In other words, the feelings of dependency induced by stress successfully neutralize a person's normal antipathy towards the autocratic leader.[1] While a man like Townshend would not be likely to survive for very long in a modern civilian firm, his autocratic mien was lovingly accepted by men whose lives were hanging by a thread.

But even if, given the right circumstances, an autocratic mien is no bar to being liked, we still need some more positive reasons for the extraordinary popularity of otherwise incompetent commanders. There are three such: 'riskiness', 'socio-economic' status and the past indulgence of the individuals concerned. Other things being equal, a man who is prepared to take risks makes a more popular leader than one not so inclined.[2] By taking a risk he metaphorically, if not literally, stands out in front of the group and is perhaps, by so doing, shouldering the responsibility for behaviour in which the group needs (and wants) to indulge but for which, if left on their own, they would lack the necessary moral stamina. The vicarious pleasure and feeling of admiration which we derive from contemplating big gamblers in any walk of life are components of this psychological phenomenon.

A less readily explicable factor is that of socio-economic status.[3] There are probably at least three components to the influence of wealth and position. Firstly there is the, sometimes no doubt erroneous, belief that 'he must be better than I am' which gives rise to the 'therefore-I-will-follow-him-to-the-grave-if-necessary' feeling. Secondly the traditional good manners and self-confidence of the financially and socially secure obviously makes for a more kindly and humane paternalism towards the underdog.

That officers of the old school earned the love of their men by behaving towards them as they might towards cherished pets was possible because of the real and enormous social gulf which the rank and file perceived between themselves and their rulers. The time-honoured distaste which other ranks have felt for officers who rose from the ranks is all part of the same picture.

Finally, the fact that the position was assured through their wealth meant a relative absence of those unpleasant traits which are associated with feelings of social inferiority.

Another obvious reason for the likeableness which eventuates in good social leadership has been researched by Greer.[4] This worker showed that successful leadership tended to occur if followers had been indulged by their leader. In this case the tractable nature of the group evidently reflects a wish to return past favours. By these lights it is hardly surprising that even the most incompetent generals were often effective social leaders. No one took greater risks than Townshend, no one was more concerned to indulge his troops than Buller, and few could outdo such notables as Lucan, Cardigan and Raglan when it came to a matter of displaying socio-economic status.

However, to someone who has not had the misfortune of serving under any of these officers it may seem scarcely credible that the riskiness of Townshend, the indulgence of Buller and the socio-economic status of the Crimean generals could have compensated for their other charactristics. How, for example, could troops overlook the palpable egocentricity of Townshend and the total 'unriskiness' and glaring incompetence of Buller; and how could they forgive the apparent negligence of Raglan? There are at least three related reasons. Firstly, in war, as in other situations of mortal threat, there is an understandable urge to clutch at straws – the good aspects of a leader are seized upon, the less good conveniently denied. We would guess that this anxiety-reduction will, moreover, be particularly likely to occur in a situation without degrees of choice. The situation of a soldier, in an organization which allows of no escape, confronted by the threat of imminent destruction, is just such. To put it very simply, he makes the best of a bad job, and this includes wholeheartedly accepting a leader even when the latter was not of his choosing.

Again, it is the nature of military organizations to recapitulate the psychodynamics of an authoritarian family group, one in which the paterfamilias can do no wrong. It is not necessary to be an ardent believer in psycho-analytic theory to realize that, in times of stress, there is a natural harking back to an earlier source of security.

But there is still one other reason for the extraordinary tolerance shown towards disastrous leaders – their 'invisibility'. The reputations of many bad generals have survived simply because the individuals concerned kept out of the way. Like God, they did not often reveal themselves. This analogy between belief in an earthly leader and belief in God may be carried further. Both are sometimes functions of experienced threat, and both may be enhanced by the surrounding mystery. Whether they are in fact good or bad, 'invisible' leaders like Raglan undoubtedly benefited from not being known and rarely seen by the rank and file.

The phenomenon is perhaps best illustrated by that most controversial of figures, Field-Marshal Haig, of whom it has been written: 'To write him down as a blundering, heartless incompetent in the prevailing fashion calls for considerable hardihood on the part of the critic. One fact remains that cannot be questioned: until the echo of the last shot had died away, no condemnation of Haig was ever voiced by the rank and file of the two-million-strong army under his command.'⁵ When it is considered that few of these two million ever saw their commander-in-chief but *were* confronted daily with the immediate, and fearful, consequences of his generalship, the parallel between blind acceptance of an 'invisible' military leader and the strengthening of religious convictions (regarding heavenly competence) which follows monumental natural disasters can hardly fail to be drawn.

The ideal military leader is, of course, one who manages to combine excellence as a task-specialist with an equal flair for the social or heroic aspects of leadership. Since the traits required for these two aspects of leadership are rather different, these so-called 'Great Man' leaders have been comparatively rare.⁶ Amongst the best examples were Wellington, Nelson, Lawrence and, in recent years, Field-Marshal Slim. Such leaders managed to combine extreme professionalism in the realizing of military goals with a warm humanity which earned them the lasting affection and loyalty of their men. There have, of course, been other 'Great Men' who, lacking the natural talents of a Nelson or a Slim for the role of social specialist, have deliberately simulated the necessary traits. The prime example of this genre is Field-Marshal Montgomery. By nature a rather cold, introverted and autocratic individual (a side of him seen by many of his officers), he nevertheless had the good sense to apply a somewhat contrived bonhomie, helped out with packets of cigarettes and numerous cap badges, which undoubtedly did much to ensure high morale and group-mindedness in the troops which he commanded. To many people, whether they like him or not, it must seem totally incomprehensible that Montogmery should have been actually criticized for his quite deliberate showmanship, which probably did more for civilian and military morale than any act by any other general since the beginning of warfare. Such jealous and unwarranted sniping exemplifies one of the more basic causes of military incompetence, namely the fatal confusion between the practical and symbolic roles of military organizations which results in the sacrificing of military efficiency for the sake of 'good form'.

The evident success of some British senior commanders in their role as social leaders does not mean that military mishaps have never been due to shortcomings in this respect. Three situations in particular have provided scope for military incompetence. The first hinges upon the fact that though the leadership qualities required at one level of command may result in promotion, they are often not those relevant to a higher level of command. Just as a brilliant general, such as the Australian Sir John Monash, may have been an indifferent brigadier, mediocre battalion commander and third-rate platoon commander, so, more seriously, there have been outstanding platoon and company commanders who, *promoted on the basis of their performance at these levels*, ended up as inept if beloved generals. Such examples of the Peter Principle, wherein people are raised to their own level of inefficiency, was never better illustrated than in the case of Sir Redvers Buller, who has been described as 'a superb major, a mediocre colonel and an abysmal general'. In this case, high-level military incompetence must be laid at the door of heroic leadership, for this was the quality which eventually put him where he could do the most damage to his own side.

The second situation in which the motivational as opposed to the intellectual aspects of leadership may lead to military disaster is where obedience, evoked by hero-worship, blunts reason and moral sensitivity to such an extent that the group may embark on behaviour which is little short of suicidal. A classic example is to be found in the psychopathic behaviour of some German units towards Soviet citizens during the invasion of Russia. It is certain that this behaviour helped seal the fate of Hitler's forces by turning potentially sympathetic Soviet peasants into vengeful saboteurs. It is possible that the discrepancy between 'military' behaviour under Hitler's leadership and the older, Prussian code of chivalry produced a sagging of morale and failure of soldierly pride from which the corps of officers could never totally recover. There is nothing so eroding of morale as to dislike oneself.

Happily, heroic leadership in the British military has usually been confined to younger officers. Senior military commanders, by reason of their unassailable rank and sheltering staff, have often remained so isolated from the rank and file that their possession, or lack, of heroic qualities has passed unnoticed.

There is, however, one further aspect of these more nebulous qualities of leadership which has played a not inconsiderable part in the story of military incompetence. It concerns the position which an individual occupies on two related continua: those of boldness to caution, and impulsiveness to indecision. Over the years military incompetence has resulted more from a dearth of boldness than from a lack of caution, and more from a pall of indecision than from an excess of impulsivity. The pusillanimity of Generals Warren and Buller at Spion Kop, which we looked at in a previous chapter, is a good example of this failure of leadership. Another is that of the Suvla operation in the Gallipoli campaign, where 'the greatest chance of the war was thrown away by the most abject collection of general officers ever congregated in one spot'.[7]

In more recent itmes, the Norway expedition of 1940 displayed not only similar shortcomings in high-level heroic leadership, but also the not infrequent contrast between the verve and initiative of junior commanders and the cautious indecision of those at higher levels of control. Donald Macintyre, writing of these events, records:

> The Commander in Chief, Home Fleet, after hesitating until nearly noon on 9 April, detached a cruiser squadron and destroyer to attack at Bergen, only to have his order annulled by the Admiralty who feared the shore defences might by then have been taken over by the enemy . . . What a different approach had been

that of Warburton-Lee [the destroyer flotilla leader whose spirited destruction of German naval forces at Narvik earned him a posthumous V.C.] – 'intend attacking at dawn!' His initiative and daring had turned Narvik into a mortal trap for nearly half the total German destroyer strength. Yet even now the harvest which Warburton-Lee's sowing had prepared was nearly lost to the British through indecision and hesitation.[8]

The same lack of forceful and decisive leadership at the highest levels of command was also evident in the fall of Singapore when caution, precipitated partly by the fear of injuring civilian morale, resulted in too little being done too late to avert the worst disaster of the Second World War.

One obvious explanation for the failure of the motivational aspects of leadership, in all these instances, is the relatively advanced age of the individuals concerned. Old men are more cautious than young men, and less able to make quick decisions than those whose arteries have not begun to harden. The refusal by the elderly General Burrard to exploit Wellington's crushing defeat of Junot at Vimeiro in 1808 is a classic example of this sort of failure in leadership.

> Thus in a loud voice clearly audible to his staff Wellesley exclaimed: 'Sir Harry, now is your time to advance. The enemy are completely beaten, we shall be in Lisbon in three days.' Sir Harry hesitated and Wellesley pressed him again, adding the bait of Sir Harry himself taking part in the victorious campaign . . . The French had in fact fled eastwards, leaving Torres Vedras and the road to Lisbon open. But Sir Harry had said No once and he said it again. Enough was enough. He had been created a baronet for doing nothing much at Copenhagen in 1807. Before Junot's attack he had said to Wellesley, 'Wait for Moore.' He repeated it. It was not a pun but a fatuity. Wellesley turned away in disgust, remarking to his officers that they might as well go and shoot red-legged partridges.[9]

Another possible factor is that many of these instances involved combined operations. Even Buller had a detachment of naval artillery which, with incorrigible and fatal obstinacy, he forbore to use against the enemy positions on Spion Kop. Are these perhaps cases where inter-service jealousy, like sibling rivalry, effectively deflated and used up the motivational energies of both the rivals? This was certainly true of the Singapore disaster, both in the Chiefs of Staff quarrels of 1925 and in the lack of effective liaison between Army, Navy and Air Force commanders during the Japanese invasion of Malaya in 1941 and 1942.

But there are other more fundamental and pervasive reasons for these failures in leadership which can be ascribed to the general psychopathology of military organizations. Their common denominator is anxiety. It is a feature of armed services that the penalty for error is very much more substantial than the reward for success. Whereas the naval officer who, through an error of judgment on the part of his subordinates, puts his ship aground will almost certainly be court-martialled and stands a fair chance of being heavily punished, the reward for taking a bold action which pays off may be no more than a mention in dispatches or some decoration with little or no effect upon promotional prospects. The net result of this bias towards *negative* reinforcement will be that *fear of failure* rather than *hope of success* tends to be the dominant motive force in decision-making, and the higher the rank the stronger this motive because there is farther to fall. There are of course other reasons for supposing that the anxiety which tends to curb bold initiative will be stronger in the higher levels of command than lower down the hierarchy. For one thing, responsibility is greater and, for another, perhaps for the first time, there is no one higher up to whom the senior commander can appeal.

Notes

1   See R. White and R. Lippitt, 'Leader behaviour and member reaction . . . '.
2   See R. Brown, *Social Psychology*.
3   See R. M. Stogdill, 'Personal factors associated with leadership'.
4   F. L. Greer, 'Leader indulgence and group performance'.
5   See A. J. Smithers, *Sir John Monash*, p. 178.
6   See E. F. Borgatta and others, 'Some findings relevant to the "great man" theory of leadership'.
7   Smithers, op. cit. p. 122.
8   Donald Macintyre, *The Naval War Against Hitler*, p. 35.
9   Elizabeth Longford, *Wellington: The Years of the Sword*, p. 199.

4
In the Roman Court: Leadership Qualities

Wess Roberts

Not yet in his teens, Attila was sent to the Roman court of Honorius. There, thought Rugila, the tutelage of the empire would surely develop characteristics in Attila that would make him a more compatible member of the Huns' royal family.

Attila personally rejected the fancy robes, pompous hairstyles, rich foods and perfumed quarters offered to him as a hostage, though such trappings intrigued his unsophisticated comrades. Attila attempted, but was unable, to ignite their spirit to resist this and other beguiling propaganda imposed by the empire. After failing to escape, Attila resolved to use passive resistance and to adapt to his temporary circumstances.

In the Roman court, he watched and listened. With each passing day he became more and more determined to rid the world of Roman and mysterious Christian influences. Attila was an extraordinary student of the internal and foreign policies of the empire. He grew in his awareness of their armies, weapons, order of battle and their lack of a strong navy. Attila used this period to spy on visiting ministers, to seek out the intrigues of the empire and to learn about policy making and diplomacy.

Life in the Roman court was a tremendous hardship for Attila. He was lonely for his people, for his family, and yearned to free them from the service of a strange and foreign nation that the Huns, once united, could surely defeat.

The boy who was sent as a hostage to the court of Honorius profited from his Asiatic virtue of patience. His attitude was one of stoicism and certitude. He learned that pushing events to happen before their time was less important than their ultimate achievement. He, therefore, set out to develop the personal

Excerpt from *The Leadership Secrets of Attila the Hun* by Wess Roberts, Bantam Press © Wess Roberts 1989, by permission of Transworld Publishers Ltd. and Arthur Pine Associates, Inc. on behalf of the author.

abilities that would ensure his success at the time that he would actively pursue his reign as King of Huns.

Attila on Leadership Qualities

As we gather in this counsel, I, Attila, have prepared my innermost thoughts regarding leadership qualities. These thoughts I give you so you and your subordinates might be better prepared to lead the Huns.

It is essential to the Hunnish nation that we have in our service leaders at every level who possess the skills, abilities and attitudes that will enable them successfully to carry out the responsibilities incumbent to their office.

There is no quick way to develop leaders. Huns must learn throughout their lives – never ceasing as students, never being above gaining new insights or studying innovative procedures or methods – whatever the source.

Our leaders must learn early in their service certain basic qualities and have opportunities to mature in them.

We must teach these qualities to our young warriors, if they are to develop into able chieftains. Basic instruction in horsemanship, with the lariat, bow and lance, is sufficient for our warriors but not for those who lead them.

In order to skilfully lead our nation, we must have chieftains who possess, among others, the following essential qualities, which through experience become mastered skills:

- *Loyalty* Above all things, a Hun must be loyal. Disagreement is not necessarily disloyalty. A Hun who, in the best interest of the tribe, disagrees, should be listened to. On the other hand, a Hun who actively participates in or encourages actions that are counter to the good of the tribe is disloyal. These Huns, whether warrior or chieftain, must be expeditiously removed. Their ability to influence and discourage loyal Huns is a contagious disease. In cases where disloyal actions and attitudes cannot be changed, harsh action must be taken to rid ourselves of those among us who see no value in and subvert our cause.
- *Courage* Chieftains who lead our Huns must have courage. They must be fearless and have the fortitude to carry out assignments given them – the gallantry to accept the risks of leadership. They must not balk at the sight of obstacles, nor must they become bewildered when in the presence of adversity. The role of a chieftain has inherent periods of loneliness, despair, ridicule and rejection. Chieftains must be long-suffering in their duties – they must have the courage to act with confidence and to excel in times of uncertainty or danger as well as in times of prosperity.
- *Desire* Few Huns will sustain themselves as chieftains without strong personal desire – an inherent commitment to influencing people, processes

and outcomes. Weak is the chieftain who does not want to be one. We must be careful to avoid placing capable warriors into positions of leadership that they have no desire to fulfill.

- *Emotional Stamina* Each succeedingly higher level of leadership places increasing demands on the emotions of chieftains. We must ensure that our leaders at every level have the stamina to recover rapidly from disappointment – to bounce back from discouragement, to carry out the responsibilities of their office without becoming distorted in their views – without losing clear perspective, as well as the emotional strength to persist in the face of seemingly difficult circumstances.

- *Physical stamina* Huns must have chieftains who can endure the physical demands of their leadership duties. Chieftains must nurture their bodies with the basic, healthful staples. Chieftains cannot lead from their bedside. They lack energy when filled with too much food or drink. The distorting potions of the Romans only confuse minds. A body not properly used becomes abused. A healthy body supports a healthy mind. Our chieftains must be strong in body in order to lead the charge.

- *Empathy* Chieftains must develop empathy – an appreciation for and an understanding of the values of others, a sensitivity for other cultures, beliefs and traditions. However, empathy must not be confused with sympathy, which may result in unwise consolation in times when, above all other things, the good of the tribe or nation must be pursued with adroit diplomacy or battlefield action.

- *Decisiveness* Young chieftains must learn to be decisive, knowing when to act and when not to act, taking into account all facts bearing on the situation and then responsibly carrying out their leadership role. Vacillation and procrastination confuse and discourage subordinates, peers and superiors and serve the enemy well.

- *Anticipation* Learning by observation and through instincts sharpened by tested experience, our chieftains must anticipate thoughts, actions and consequences. Anticipation bears a level of risk that is willingly accepted by a chieftain who will excel when others turn to the comfort of personal security.

- *Timing* Essential to all acts of leadership is the timing of recommendations and actions. There is no magic formula for developing a sense of timing. One often gains this leadership skill by applying the lessons learned through failure. Knowing whom you are dealing with, their motives, characters, priorities and ambitions are critical elements even when seeking approval of the simplest recommendation.

- *Competitiveness* An essential quality of leadership is an intrinsic desire to win. It is not necessary to win all the time; however, it is necessary to win the important contests. Chieftains must understand that the competition inside and outside our nation is strong and not to be taken lightly. A sense of competitive anger drives those who win on the battlefield, in negotiations and in situations of internal strife. A leader without a sense of competitiveness is weak and easily overcome by the slightest challenge.

- *Self-confidence*   Proper training and experience develops in chieftains a personal feeling of assurance with which to meet the inherent challenges of leadership. Those who portray a lack of self-confidence in their abilities to carry out leadership assignments give signs to their subordinates, peers and superiors that these duties are beyond their capabilities. They become, therefore, weak leaders and useless chieftains.

- *Accountability*   Learning to account for personal actions and those of subordinates is fundamental to leadership. Chieftains must never heap praise or lay blame on others for what they themselves achieve or fail to accomplish, no matter how glorious or grave the consequences.

- *Responsibility*   Leaders are necessary only when someone is to be responsible to see that actions are carried out and directions followed. No king, chieftain or subordinate leader should ever be allowed to serve who will not accept full responsibility for his actions.

- *Credibility*   Chieftains must be credible. Their words and actions must be believable to both friend and foe. They must be trusted to have the intelligence and integrity to provide correct information. Leaders lacking in credibility will not gain proper influence and are to be hastily removed from positions of responsibility, for they cannot be trusted.

- *Tenacity*   The quality of unyielding drive to accomplish assignments is a desirable and essential quality of leadership. The weak persist only when things go their way. The strong persist and pursue through discouragement, deception and even personal abandonment. Pertinacity is often the key to achieving difficult assignments or meeting challenging goals.

- *Dependability*   If a chieftain cannot be depended upon in all situations to carry out his roles and responsibilities, relieve him of them. A king cannot observe each and every action of his subordinate chieftains; therefore, he must depend upon them to get things done. Young chieftains should understand that Huns serving above and below them in the tribe and nation are counting on their ability to lead, and they should be proud of being entrusted with such responsibility.

- *Stewardship*   Our leaders must have the essential quality of stewardship, a caretaker quality. They must serve in a manner that encourages confidence, trust and loyalty. Subordinates are not to be abused; they are to be guided, developed and rewarded for their performance. Punishment is to be reserved as a consequence of last resort and sparingly applied only when all other attempts have failed to encourage the rebellious to comply. Without a flock there can be no shepherd. Without an army there can be no battle captains. Without subordinates there can be no leaders. Leaders are, therefore, caretakers of the interests and well-being of those and the purposes they serve.

Those of you who are overly ambitious may attempt to acquire these qualities over a short period. As I, Atilla, have found in my own life, these qualities of leadership simply take time, learning and experience to develop. There are few who will find short cuts. There are simply rare opportunities to accelerate competence, and without paying the price, no matter how great or small, none will become prepared to lead others.

Learn these leadership qualities well. Teach them to the Huns. Only then will we expand our ability to lead our vast nation in pursuit of world conquest.

[*Editors' note*: Readers will recognize, of course, that Wess Roberts uses the life and 'sayings' of Attila the Hun as a mouthpiece for his own views on modern business leadership. His book is intended as a lively allegory of contemporary business issues rather than a serious historical biography.]

Chapter 3
Leadership in Business:
The Modern Characteristics

Introduction

What qualities and characteristics do modern business leaders need or have in common? So much attention has been lavished on the subject by academics and psychologists that we could have picked a different account from every major management centre or international consultancy in the US and Europe.

The three in this chapter are fairly representative. The first, written for this book, looks at the characteristics of leadership from the perspective of the succession planner. The author, chairman and chief executive of a London-based management consultancy, highlights the 'common threads' in the characters of budding leaders during their academic and early professional career. Leaders, he argues, can be confused with 'charismatic egotists'. Great drive and a formidable intellect are not enough. Resourcefulness, astute decision making, and possession of the right knowledge are better indicators.

The second contribution is taken from Rosabeth Moss Kanter's blueprint for business strategy in the 1990s, *When Giants Learn to Dance*. Moss Kanter compares the characteristics of the two archetypes of modern business leaders – the 'corpocrat' hell-bent on conserving resources and the 'cowboy' entrepreneur living in the world of immediate action and unlimited risk. She concludes that neither provides the combination of discipline and entrepreneurial zeal needed to compete in global markets. Modern leaders need to draw on the better qualities of both, believing in themselves rather than in the power of their position, collaborating with a wide range of partners and showing a willingness to keep learning.

The final contribution summarizes the results of a survey of fast-track executives by psychologists Charles Cox and Cary Cooper at the University of Manchester's Institute of Science and Technology. Their findings, gleaned from research carried out in the latter half of the 1980s, leads one to wonder whether Moss Kanter's compromise 'business athlete' wasn't already well in place, and the 'cowboys' and 'corpocrats' more in the media imagination than in real life. Cox and Cooper's research revealed that 'Successful MDs were not high risk-takers . . . [they] saw themselves as "moderate risk-takers" . . . they were sure that they had the skills to cope with the situation they were entering, and so did not see it as particularly risky'.

Other characteristics to emerge from their study will not surprise – successful executives are good with people, have clear objectives, well-organized lives, and sound analytical skills. Interestingly though, the top people interviewed by Cox and Cooper are not intellectual, usually indulging in 'practical' spare time activities; and have few long-term career goals, believing that 'if you do well at what you are doing in the present, the future takes care of itself'.

Of the three, Moss Kanter's predictions are the most provocative. The laurels handed out to the mavericks of the 1980s have begun to wilt as the businesses they led to record heights went to the wall in rapid succession after the October crash. The models of good leadership which inspired journalists, academics, and commentators during the recent boom years are seen by Moss Kanter as entirely inappropriate to a global race for a dominant market share. Yet the list of characteristics she outlines – of executives who are focused yet multifaceted, self-confident yet humble, competitive yet collaborative, ethical yet pragmatic – seems a very tall order for any management development programme. And as we will see later in the book the concept of a global company may, in itself, be an illusionary goal.

1
That Red Light was just a Suggestion

Peter A. D. Giblin

As the car slowed at a red light in the outskirts of Milan late one autumn afternoon the driver, a prominent member of the Italian business community, quickly looked left and right and decided he could make it through the light with little risk of causing an accident. His passenger, a client from the UK, quietly suggested that this manoeuvre was perhaps inappropriate, to which the Italian responded 'That red light was just a suggestion'.

He went on to say that 'If we all followed the rules we would never get anything done around here'. It is perhaps appropriate in a discussion of the development of leadership potential and consequently the ability to spot future leaders, to consider this characteristic as exhibiting not only a willingness to take a chance but to bend the rules where possible. The driver of the car clearly had a flexible attitude towards the highway code and was certainly not prepared to be hemmed in by regulations or practices that he felt to be inhibiting. He was perhaps thinking that there must be a better way.

At a younger age such people are apt to demonstrate a capacity to learn the rules, in part to determine how to escape their strictures. It is entirely possible that future leaders are those who find themselves initiating, organizing and managing impromptu social events, captaining sports teams, producing a school play and the like, either because they are asked to do so by others – peers or an authority figure – or because they self-select based on strength of personality. In short they are viewed as winners, the right people to be around, and probably intuitively smart enough to recognize their own limitations and pick others to compensate.

It is deceptive, however, to assume that only the more visible, outspoken and perhaps pushy are destined for leadership. There are a number of others who

'That Red Light was just a Suggestion', by Peter A. D. Giblin. Original paper written for this publication © Axiom Advisers Ltd 1990.

have emerged from an environment where they were considered to be stubborn, withdrawn, intensely focused or controversially so full of energy and exuberance as to be disruptive and ineffective. The image of Winston Churchill comes to mind.

But, there is a thread common to all these individuals during their academic and early professional career; they almost always show a type of fanaticism coupled with physical energy, stamina and good health that enables them to move forward at a greater speed than their peers. Margaret Thatcher is an excellent example. The individual who is likely to be successful and recognized as a leader will be able to communicate his strongly held beliefs to others and ensure that they feel the intensity of conviction. As a result it is likely that the successful leader − even if he is not yet at the top of his professional career − will be viewed as a winner by his contemporaries either because he leads from the front or from behind in the sense that he goes to great lengths to support the people who work for him. He who coaches, delegates and supports and constantly communicates his objectives is likely to exhibit positive aspects of leadership.

While this may be obvious to many people, one of the biggest challenges to any individual who is responsible, for whatever reason, for identifying leadership potential and thus endorsing future leaders, is to try to reduce the subjective reaction to people and events to a type of objective standard against which many can be judged.

One approach is to form a series of questions related to judging an individual's superiority in four areas which, properly defined, cover most leadership characteristics. These areas are *resourcefulness, astuteness, compatibility* and *knowledge*. If the individual is constantly referred to by others as possessing these attributes there is a strong possibility that he has leadership potential or is an effective leader. A list of examples would include Lord Beaverbrook, Henry Ford and John F. Kennedy.

By *resourcefulness* it is meant that the individual focuses on achieving something dynamic and has the drive and inner will to accomplish his objective. It is likely that he is eager to make suggestions, to get deeply involved in what he is doing and prepared to take the risk that he may be wrong. He will have an element of entrepreneurship in his character, be intellectually curious and willing to innovate, seeking out new and better ways with original ideas despite criticism he may often receive.

He may also exhibit a certain restlessness manifested in a low boredom threshold and a fear of being too comfortable. A certain degree of impatience will translate into instinctive conclusions drawn when sizing up situations, and rapid responses. As indicated earlier, the resourceful person will have a high work capacity, be physically strong and determined to succeed. He will also exhibit strong will-power and a tenacity which is likely to wear down his colleagues. Although all this is extremely important, he will seek excellence and achievement rather than perfectionism which is often a harbinger of practical failure. He will make decisions and act.

With respect to *astuteness*, while it may be difficult to characterize, it is clear that the successful leader will have a sense of astuteness, an innate knowledge of when and how to act, a sense of timing and what is practical. In a business context this often reflects a certain instinctive reaction to what will work or indeed even what the effects may be in a particular situation. Perceptions are important and an acute feel will mean that the appropriate decision is more likely to be made. Coupled with these instincts are a series of characteristics which translate into focus. The astute individual tends to be ruthless with his team and knows what time and energy should be expended. As a consequence he is more likely to focus on three or four key issues which are essential to driving his business forward rather than going through a checklist from beginning to end. Assuming the above is correct, the astute individual is therefore more able to focus on a long-term vision, keeping sight of his goals and convincing others that the way forward is logical. Because of his instinct for doing the right thing, however, he is likely to balance personal execution with delegation as he realizes that the ends are more important than the means. Because he is flexible, he can deal with ambiguities, plan for contingencies and use common sense when facts and time are not available. In essence, he can deal with what is highly important and leave the trivia to pencil-pushers and bureaucrats.

Thirdly, the successful leader or potential leader must exhibit a highly developed sense of *compatibility* with those with whom he is associated. He must be skilled in dealing with others, recognizing that no two people are exactly the same and honestly taking the time to understand individual motivations. This means that he must be empathetic, seeking to comprehend a point of view, rather than necessarily sympathetic and agreeable; and genuinely open-minded to new ideas particularly if they come from less than favoured sources, allowing people to break the rules ('red light') without offence and lasting retribution. These attributes will enable him to communicate convincingly and also accept reversals without having his own confidence shattered. An acute understanding of others normally means respect and tact and often diplomacy to reach one's ends. This inevitably means that an individual is effective, creating team support and a sense of shared responsibility. In this environment it is also more possible to allow other individuals to develop their career so that they can reach their full potential. Compatibility also means, because of the above attributes, the ability to inspire others sucessfully, to motivate and to communicate an attitude that objectives can be reached.

The fourth important characteristic is *knowledge* in its broadest sense. It means undersanding the area of business concerned, perhaps not to extreme detail but in its true fundamentals. It is coupled with a type of intellectual curiosity that drives the individual to want to know what is happening in his field of concern and to demonstrate his ability to capture all necessary information and communicate it effectively to his colleagues. It also means the ability to analyse and dissect a problem to determine what is unimportant and therefore can perhaps be ignored. Clearly an individual with knowledge must have aptitude to think logically and understand, perhaps even rehearse the sequence of future events which may evolve because of his decision making. It is also particularly useful to have an excellent memory which allows one to accumulate experience and competence in a number of areas which inevitably leads to a knowledge-base, self-confidence and credibility. These characteristics in turn are likely to lead to effective organizational skills, a focus on what is practical and the capacity to seek out workable solutions to issues posed. Because the knowledgeable individual can truly sort out the wheat from the chaff he always has, or seems to find, the time to deal with matters that come up unexpectedly, and he normally handles stress effectively. Freneticism is not part of his life.

Selecting future leaders is a big responsibility and the matrix of qualities described above needs careful handling. Leaders can be confused with charismatic egotists. Individuals may have great drive and a formidable intellect which obscures their total inability to lead others and thus achieve a longer-term vision.

If an individual is perceived by others as being particularly *resourceful*, generally *astute* in his decision making, *compatible* with the vast majority of people with whom he comes into contact and *knowledgeable* in the areas under discussion, he is likely to be seen as a leader. If the individual is a true leader, has been *resourceful* in defining his objectives and separating the means from the ends, has been *astute* in recognizing that there are different priorities for the individuals in that meeting, has made an effort to be genuinely *compatible* with these people and *knows* what they want and what should be done, his chances of success are high.

An individual requires a combination of these qualities as the foundation for developing true leadership. It is not essential for him to possess all of them in equal proportion. But he must measure up significantly in each of the four areas. He will have the energy and the will to improve which enables him as the embryo leader to apply training and experience to fill any perceived gaps or inadequacies.

The true leader will therefore always ask himself whether that red light was an answer or a question. As Seneca said, 'There is nothing worse than living a long life and having nothing to show for it but old age'. That is what leadership is about.

2
In Search of the Post-Entrepreneurial Hero: Individual Skills for Success

Rosabeth Moss Kanter

If the post-entrepreneurial corporation requires a different kind of work system and career system, it also requires a very different set of individual skills. We need a new image of the hero in business – the kind of leader who can manage the balancing act and guide us to victory in the corporate Olympics.

Our archetypal images of business leadership have themselves derived from the two poles that define today's corporate balancing act. We could choose between the conservative resource preserver (what Howard Stevenson and David Gumpert called the 'trustee') and the insurgent entrepreneur (Stevenson and Gumpert's 'promoter').[1] In popular lore, the former was reflected in images of the 'organization man' or 'corpocrat,' while the latter was described as a 'maverick' or 'cowboy,' each character occupying one end of the conserve-or-build spectrum.

The corpocrat has long been the target of well-deserved criticism, and the corpocratic style is gradually disappearing from progressive businesses. But despite glorification of the maverick in the 1980s entrepreneurial revival, the cowboy is also too extreme to be entirely satisfactory as a leadership image – just as John Sculley found at Apple Computer. It is easy to see the weakness in both styles when cowboys and corpocrats clash. From Steve Jobs's problems at Apple to Ross Perot's clash with General Motors after GM purchased his company EDS, these are the typical sources of tension:

- The cowboy lives in a world of immediate action; the corporation manager wants review and deliberation. What the cowboy views as time-wasting,

Excerpt from *When Giants Learn to Dance* by Rosabeth Moss Kanter, 1989. Copyright © 1989 Rosabeth Moss Kanter, by permission of Simon and Schuster Ltd.

rear-covering conservatism the corporation manager may see as the consensus-building necessary to implement decisions that many people control.

- The cowboy wants to seize every opportunity, betting big – but if he loses he's wiped out. The corporation manager makes complex resource-allocation decisions balancing the protection of past investments with the pursuit of new opportunities; after all, the corporation is the trustee of other people's assets.

- The cowboy strains limits, but the corporation manager has to establish limits to guide the actions of multitudes of people efficiently. The cowboy breaks rules and gets away with it, but the corporation manager thrives on controls and the uniform application of rules. There are few worse morale-plungers in a corporation than the realization that some are more equal than others.

- The cowboy motivates by personal loyalty, surrounded as he is by just a few trusted cronies who love the work the way he does. The cowboy's direct control means that he can manage through impulse and whim, 'shooting from the hip.' But the corporation manager has to make complex and longer-term agreements that make whim out of place, and he or she seeks an impersonal commitment to the philosophy of go-anywhere-do-anything regardless of personal ties or feelings about the job.

- The cowboy rejects fancy 'citified' trappings, living simply at work – just one of the folks, regardless of wealth. But the corporation displays symbols of affluence to make people believe in its importance; it establishes gradations of privilege and perquisites to motivate people to seek the highest ranks.

The large corporate manager's suspicion of the cowboy, then, is not necessarily a politically motivated bias against mavericks who fight oppressive authority or speak unpleasant truths. It comes from a recognition that the cowboy personifies a challenge to the very premises on which a large corporation operates. Allow too many cowboys, and the foundations of hierarchy begin to crumble – but so does the basis for cooperation and discipline.

Without the bold impulses of take-action entrepreneurs and their constant questioning of the rules, we would miss one of the most potent sources of business revitalization and development. But without the discipline and coordination of conventional management, we could find waste instead of growth, unnecessary risk instead of revitalization. Just as Kodak and Pacific Telesis needed more cowboys, Apple and Digital needed more corporate discipline and cooperation.

Today's corporate balancing act requires a different style from either extreme, a post-entrepreneurial style better suited to playing in the corporate

Olympics. Our new heroic model should be the athlete who can manage the amazing feat of doing more with less, who can juggle the need to conserve resources and to pursue growth opportunities. This new kind of business hero avoids the excesses of both the corpocrat and the cowboy. Where the former rigidly conserves and protects, the latter relentlessly speculates and promotes. But the business athlete has the strength to balance somewhere in the middle, taking the best of the corpocrat's discipline and the cowboy's entrepreneurial zeal. Again the four F's come to mind: Focused, Fast, Friendly, and Flexible. Business athletes need to be intense, lean and limber, able to stretch, good at teamwork, and in shape all the time.

There are seven skills and sensibilities that must be cultivated if managers and professionals are to become true business athletes.

First, they must *learn to operate without the might of the hierarchy behind them*. The crutch of authority must be thrown away and replaced by their own personal ability to make relationships, use influence, and work with others to achieve results. Business athletes stand – and run – on their own two feet, rather than being propelled automatically by the power of their position, just as a member of any athletic team is revered not for wearing the uniform but for his or her own performance. The traditional corporate hierarchy is rapidly crumbling, and title or formal position count for less anyway, in a world of negotiations involving internal collaborations or strategic alliances or the formation of new ventures. In strategic partnerships, for example, there is no room for faceless bureaucrats sending impersonal memos. Partners become more exposed and available to one another as people, as the Grotech joint-venture participants and the Pacific Bell managers began to realize. Or in newstream ventures, the manager has little more to offer to potential members of the venture team than the excitement of trying because of the power of his or her vision. In many ways, business athletes have to count on their use of self, not their use of organizational status, to achieve results.

Second, business athletes must *know how to 'compete' in a way that enhances rather than undercuts cooperation*. They must be oriented to achieving the highest standard of excellence rather than to wiping out the competition. In the new game, today's competitors may find themselves on the same team tomorrow, and competitors in one sphere may also be collaborators in another. Even America's trade adversaries are potential partners, and it would be a mistake for the conduct of temporary competition to undermine the ability to cooperate later. Thus, business athletes must be skillful collaborators. Whether companies are seeking synergies through internal collaboration across business units or seeking leverage through strategic alliances and partnerships, the lesson is clear. Successful managers in the corporate Olympics must not only be good negotiators, seeking the best deal for 'their' unit, but also understand when and how to share resources, to combine forces, to do things that benefit another group – in the interests of superior overall performance. This relationship orientation means knowing how to assess and value what is good for all parties in the long run, not simply analyzing the 'fairness' of a single transaction.[2]

Third, and related, business athletes must *operate with the highest ethical standards*. While business ethics have always been important from a social and moral point of view, they also become a pragmatic requirement in the corporate Olympics. The doing-more-with-less strategies place an even greater premium on trust than did the adversarial-protective business practices of the traditional corporation. Business collaborations, joint ventures, labor-management partnerships, and other stakeholder alliances all involve the element of trust – a commitment of strategic information or key resources to the partners. But the partners have to rely on one another not to violate or misuse their trust. Even newstream ventures involve a high degree of trust, in the willingness to commit corporate resources to untried and uncertain activities with a minimum of monitoring. The trust required for all of these new business strategies is built and reinforced by a mutual understanding that each party to the relationship will behave ethically, taking the needs, interests, and concerns of all others into account.

A fourth asset for business athletes is to *have a dose of humility* sprinkled on their basic self-confidence, a humility that says that there are always new things to learn. Just as other kinds of athletes must be willing to learn, willing to accept the guidance of coaches, constantly in training, and always alert to the possibility of an improvement in their techniques, so must business athletes be willing to learn. A learning attitude is a clear necessity for swimming in newstreams, for exploring uncharted waters, but it is also a necessity for seeking synergies and for discovering the benefits of strategic alliances, many of which form so that partners can learn from one another.

I have seen this attitude emerge in companies and people that used to be closed in every sense. At Apple Computer in 1985, for example, I was often told that 'we have nothing to learn from anyone else;' but by 1988, Apple was actively creating strategic alliances for learning, and a major effort to reshape the finance function began with visits to other companies. Of course, to learn from others, people must – literally – learn to speak their language, whether Japanese, Spanish, or computer-ese.

Fifth, business athletes must *develop a process focus* – a respect for the process of implementation as well as the substance of what is implemented. They need to be aware that *how* things are done is every bit as important as *what* is done. My case studies and comparative data make it clear that execution may matter more than strategy. Whether restructuring builds synergies or leaves dead bodies in its path, whether alliances and partnerships indeed stretch capacity or simply stretch relationships to the breaking point, whether newstream investments lead to effective projects that produce results or to nothing – all this relies not only on the quality of the big strategic idea behind it but also on the concern for excellence of implementation.

Both Eastern Airlines and Western Airlines, for example, faced the same do-more-with-less pressures in the early 1980s, both made the bold strategic move of seeking wage concessions from employees in exchange for an announced 'business partnership,' and both were later acquired by other airlines. Yet the contrast in how each implemented its strategy could not be more striking. Eastern botched it by showing poor faith and not quite taking the steps that would make the employee partnership work, and since a hostile acquisition by Texas Air (resisted by management and sought by demoralized employee leaders), Eastern has been hurt financially by public displays of employee discontent, including claims of safety problems. Western, in contrast, as I showed earlier, managed the same strategic move by a careful attention to process and netted a more valuable company that merged smoothly with Delta to the benefit of employees, shareholders, and customers.

Sixth, business athletes must *gain satisfaction from results* and be willing to stake their own rewards on them. The accomplishment itself is really the only standard for the business athlete. With post-entrepreneurial pay-for-performance a growing reality, and with the middle management hierarchy dismantled, the measure of success must, in any case, shift from status to contribution, from attainment of a position to attainment of results. Promotion cannot be a reward at a time when there are fewer layers of management and employment security is being undermined or redefined. At the same time, the shift toward doing-more-with-less strategies opens up new kinds of opportunities for achievement and rewards – whether via participation on the frontiers of partnerships, where more power and responsibility fall upon partner representatives, or via involvement in newstream ventures that turn ordinary employees into entrepreneurs.

These seven managerial skills also point toward the individual skills required to manage a career at a time when climbing the corporate ladder has been replaced by hopping from opportunity to opportunity:

- A belief in self rather than in the power of position alone.
- The ability to collaborate and become connected with new teams in various ways.
- Commitment to the intrinsic excitement of achievement in a particular project that can show results.
- The willingness to keep learning.

All of these attributes constitute an investment in one's own human capital rather than a reliance on accumulating organizational capital. Ultimately, this new loyalty to project rather than to employer can be better for the company, too, because it produces results-oriented, entrepreneurially inclined employees who are dedicated to their activities instead of dedicated to corporate politics and position enhancement. And certainly it is better attuned to the workplace realities of the emerging business strategies.

Notes

1   Howard Stevenson and David Gumpert, 'The Heart of Entrepreneurship', *Harvard Business Review*, 64 (March–April 1985), pp. 84–94.
2   This attitude is related to the new feminist view of morality as encompassing not just analytic 'justness' or 'rightness' in the abstract but also maintenance of relationships.

3
Characteristics of the Successful Chief Executive

Charles J. Cox and Cary L. Cooper

The group of highly successful managing directors who form the basis of this study have a number of personal characteristics in common, which are certainly related to their success. While it may be possible to operate successfully at the top level without one or more of these, it clearly makes success more probable if all are present. Obviously not all of the MDs did have all the characteristics, and it may be that one method used to enable them to succeed was to select other members of the top team with compensating abilities. This makes it all the more important to know which characteristics are important and which of these one does, or does not, possess. These key characteristics are as follows.

Determination   These successful managers were all very determined and quite assertive individuals. This came through very clearly in the interviews and was reflected in the data from the 16PF questionnaire. This may well be a characteristic derived from their early experience, which for many of them involved situations (e.g. separation from their parents when very young) which required them to take responsibility for themselves at quite an early stage in their lives. When thrown on their resources while still very young, they needed quite a bit of determination to survive. If the individual succeeds, it may well set a pattern for later life.

Learning from adversity   Most MDs had experienced setbacks and problems during their careers, but had taken advantage of these as 'opportunities' for learning and development. Some, indeed, had knowingly taken on difficult jobs, partly for the challenge but also for the opportunities presented. Others had simply been 'thrown in at the deep end', finding themselves coping with

Excerpt from *High Flyers: An Anatomy of Managerial Success* by Charles J. Cox and Cary L. Cooper, 1988, by permission of Basil Blackwell Ltd.

situations which they had not anticipated. The common characteristic is that they survived and coped very successfully, learning a great deal in the process. This characteristic probably also derives from their early experience and is related to their determination.

Seizing chances when presented   All the MDs in our study were highly proactive and would respond to challenge. Most had been offered the opportunity of high levels of responsibility at a relatively early age and had taken this opportunity with enthusiasm. Often the challenges were quite daunting, such as taking over an ailing subsidiary or coping with an overseas operation in a strange culture far away from head-office support and encouragement.

Achievement orientation   They were all ambitious people with a need to achieve, but not in the rather narrow sense used by McClelland. They measured their success not by 'winning small battles' but by long-term achievement. They were also more concerned with the overall success of the organization than with short-term career aims. Related to this was a very *positive* approach to life. They were motivated very much by 'hope of success' rather than 'fear of failure'.

Internal locus of control   Part of their very positive approach to life was due to their high level of self-confidence, which in turn derived from clear 'internal reference-points', which were used to guide action. They had a very clear *internal* map of how the world is and ought to be. This facilitated positive action without self-doubt.

Well-integrated value system   Most of the chief executives interviewed had a clear set of values, which were well articulated. A key value was *integrity*, which implies being dependable and doing what you say you will do. Other values underpinned many of the points made above. They include the valuing of *achievement, independence* and *initiative*, but emphasis was also placed on *people and relationships*, which was felt to be important for individuals whose success is measured in organizational terms.

Effective management of risk   Successful MDs were not high risk-takers; this seems to be more a characteristic of the entrepreneur. The MDs in this study saw themselves as 'moderate risk-takers', and this fits with the evidence. Most had taken some risk, both at a personal level in, for example, career decisions, and at an organizational level in decisions taken in their job. The important element is that they were sure that they had the skills to cope with the situation they were entering, and so did not see it as particularly risky. In most instances, they appear to have been right.

Clear objectives   The successful MD knows where he is going. This is true at both the personal and the organizational level. They universally stressed the need to be clear about the long-term objectives of the organization, and the need to have the determination to achieve them. At the personal level, goals were rather short term and mainly concerned with doing the current job well. Most MDs, perhaps unexpectedly, denied having specific long-term career goals. The belief was that, if you do well at what you are doing in the present, the future takes care of itself. There seems an inherent contradiction here: if organizational success depends on clarity and determination in relation to long-term goals, why should personal success be any different?

High dedication to the job All the CEOs in this study worked very long hours and clearly regarded their job as by far the most important element of their lives, with the possible exception of their families. For a minority, even the family came second. Clearly, much of their personal fulfilment and confirmation of their worth as human beings came from their work.

Intrinsic motivation This is a corollary of their dedication to the job. If work is not intrinsically motivating, it is impossible to be dedicated to it. All the MDs in the study found their work completely 'involving and enjoyable'. One of the strongest impressions we gained concerned the universal *energy* and *enthusiasm* engendered by work.

Well-organized life We found very little evidence of serious conflict between work and home life. This is mainly because they were were well organized and used their time effectively both at work and at home. It must, however, also be admitted that this was because work nearly always took precedence. The wife looked after and organized the home and coped with her husband's 'unavoidable' absences due to the demands of work.

Pragmatic approach The approach to life of the successful top manager is essentially pragmatic, not intellectual. This shows very clearly in spare-time activities, which were almost entirely 'practical'. Very few individuals mentioned intellectual interests or pursuits.

Sound analytic and problem-solving skills Tine and time again MDs emphasized the importance of being able to analyse a problem and reach an effective solution. This was seen as an absolutely fundamental skill. This does not seem to be a highly intellectual process, but is rather the ability to recognize the factors involved and 'see the wood for the trees'. Quite often this would be 'intuitive' rather than strictly rational.

High level of 'people skills' Since all top managers, by definition, achieve their organizational objectives through other people, it follows that, to be successful, they must have a high level of interpersonal skills. Most MDs seem to operate an open and consultative style, but with a strong authoritarian back-up. However, whatever the style – from authoritarian to participative – the skills required are the same. These include the ability to select appropriate team members in the first place, communication skills, and the maintenance of motivation.

High level of innovation All the MDs who completed the Kirton Adaptation–Innovation Inventory were in the upper half of the distribution, i.e. they were 'innovators' rather than 'adapters', some of them very strongly so. In other words, they were the sort of people who in making changes would not be constrained by the existing system, but would challenge existing procedures and assumptions, thus producing something *new* rather than modification of what currently exists. This is a very important characteristic for someone who is responsible for the long-term development of a large organization.

Type A personality   The results of the Type A/B Behaviour Questionnaire showed very strong trends towards type A personality, which comprises a very aggressive, high-achieving, competitive and hard-driving lifestyle. The energy involved in this type of behaviour undoubtedly contributes to success, but it may be at a price. High type As are prone to coronary heart disease and other stress-related illnesses. However, an attempt to *manage* the extremes of this behaviour, and to promote healthy living to some extent, may mitigate the worst effects of this lifestyle.

Chapter 4
Leadership: A View from the Front

Introduction

The overwhelming majority of commentaries on leadership are vicarious – written by commentators, analysts, academics, and the like who examine its characteristics from a distance. But what do people in the top seat really feel about their own role? And how does their first-hand view differ from that of the objective observer?

It is surprisingly hard to find clear, well-written accounts by industrial captains. Like entrepreneurs, most of them find it difficult to define what sets them apart and makes them good at what they do. The majority of fashionable biographies that make it to the high street bookstands are unspeakably boring. Few add anything to the stock knowledge we have about good business practice, which is strange considering how important is the ability to communicate, as is consistently emphasized throughout this book, and in particular by Edwardes and Lorenz in this chapter.

Two of the authors in this chapter were among the best transformational leaders of the 1980s. Jan Carlzon, head of Scandinavian Airlines, turned SAS from an also-ran to a market leader in less than five years. In his book *Moments of Truth*, he cites the tenets of good leadership which helped him achieve this turnaround. These include, not surprisingly, creating and communicating a vision for the enterprise, encouraging creativity, using consultants effectively and developing 'feminine' traits of intuition and sensitivity to balance out traditional 'masculine' management styles – an issue explored in greater detail in chapter 12. Above all he stresses the importance of good delegation, so that business decisions are made as close as possible to the point where the tasks are carried out. As he comments: 'A leader is one who creates the right environment for business to be done . . . You have to give greater responsibility to people in the front line and then create a secure atmosphere where they will dare to use their new authority.'

John Harvey-Jones, who engineered a similar reversal in the fortunes of ICI in an equally short time, subsequently became a worldwide celebrity. He is one of the few managers bred from large corporations sufficiently articulate to discuss his work in terms that everyone understands. In his book on leadership

Making It Happen, he places the role of chief executive firmly in the wider context of the senior management team. 'There is no way that one man can manage an enormous company', he says. 'The job of the chairman, or chief executive, is to "manage" his colleagues on the board, and to manage the company through the board.'

This does not imply in any way that the CEO is constrained by colleagues over whom he or she has no control. In fact he or she is solely responsible for the delicate balance of the board, and thus for its success or otherwise as a governing body and source of leadership. This is a gargantuan task, which Harvey-Jones likens to 'trying to play three-dimensional chess'. Harvey-Jones also mirrors the views of Christopher Lorenz that even the best business leaders have a short life span: 'It is seldom that one finds individuals who are both "bad weather sailors" and "good weather sailors".'

Leaders who base their success on a style of management suited to one climate are liable to persist in this style well beyond the point where it is helpful to the company. Status and influence are powerful opiates and it is rare to find leaders as self-effacing as the Roman dictator Cincinnatus who returned to his farm after saving the Republic in the fifth century BC (see Kenneth Labich's article in chapter 9).

To find out whether this view is correct, we turned to Michael Edwardes' account of his years at British Leyland. Edwardes' leadership of BL in the late 1970s was seen in retrospect as exemplary at a time when the UK economy was heading for recession and the British car industry was crippled by militant trade unionism and government interference. If the keynote of leaders in periods of unbridled expansion is 'vision' the quality most needed when the bubble bursts, emphasized time and again by Edwardes, is 'courage'. A leader, Edwardes stresses, 'must be prepared to put his job on the line at regular intervals by pushing through contentious issues which could bring the business crashing down around his ears. And this last requirement leads to an attribute without which leadership cannot exist. Courage . . . This is not a job for compromisers, or for those who lean towards popularity.'

Another quality valued highly by Edwardes, as we have already commented, is the ability to communicate. Just as 'bull' leaders need to communicate their vision to the workforce to ensure it is taken up, so 'bear' leaders need to explain the reasons behind difficult and painful decisions such as factory closures and redundancies to prevent the orgaization becoming totally demoralized. Communication with the press and the general public is equally important. Just as Harvey-Jones and Carlzon are associated with their companies' success, so Edwardes was associated (often unjustly) with his company's failure. 'Inevitably', as he puts it, 'the media tends to concentrate on the individual making the noise'. 'At BL we have found that it does not pay to stick our heads in the sand.'

Edwardes also demonstrated that he had the rare judgement to recognize when the job was done, when it was time to go. In another part of his memoirs, he explains, 'Great management strength had been built at the top, and in depth; BL, which I believe needed me at one point, no longer needed me . . . The across-the-board improvement in the outlook for BL influenced my decision to move on when the five years was up – to create space for others.'

Commentators have a short memory. Edwardes probably would not appear on the list of the top business leaders of recent times. Harvey-Jones and Carlzon are assured their places. Yet many business leaders who were the darlings of the journalists and academics in the mid-1980s failed to save their businesses from the consequences of the October crash in 1987 and the recession that followed three years later. Business heroes, like those in politics or on the battlefield, reflect as well as influence the times they live in. Re-entrenching a large business in a recession is often unpopular and unglamorous. The role models of the early 1990s are likely to be less flamboyant and romantic than their entrepreneurial predecessors. But they will perform an equally valuable, if less lauded, function of leadership.

1
The Top Job

John Harvey-Jones

Of all the jobs that look different from an outside viewpoint, the top job must surely take the blue ribbon. It is only when you become aware of the range, scope, and incredible responsibility of the job that you realize that there is an almost limitless opportunity to be ineffective, unless you are totally clear about how you are going to set about it. The problem itself is manifestly an enormous one, which is not eased by the fact that it is a very fortunate chairman who has any significant hand-over from his predecessor, even if the incoming man is prepared to listen. After all, for many years you have watched the mistakes and blunders of your predecessors. You have always been aware of the things that have gone wrong, and have always believed that more could be done, or that things could have been done in different ways, or more effectively.

What you have not been aware of is the enormous scope, in a chairman's life, for diversity of attention, and the fact that, for the first time in your business life, there are no limitations of any sort on how you can spend your time, or to what you should address your attention. The people with whom you should work, the way in which the organization is set up, even the basic objectives and form of your company, ae all available to you as a clean sheet of paper for the first time. Well, not quite clean of course, because the company has already been moving in different directions, it already has a number of employees, a sense of values and so on. However, in reality there are practically no limitations to the ambitions and objectives which you can set yourself as the top man, and very few limitations to the objectives which you can set your company. You can borrow more money, change the people, buy and sell parts of the company, change the technical base, acquire other companies in other countries.

Excerpts from *Making It Happen: Reflections on Leadership* by John Harvey-Jones, Collins © John Harvey-Jones 1988, by permission of Harper Collins, Publishers Ltd.

Superficially at least, you have boundless opportunities, which match the boundless responsibility you now hold.

Moreover, to compound the problem, after long years of waiting you have suddenly reached the pinnacle of your ambition. Without the benefit of the full breadth of knowledge which can only be gained by holding the job, you have already formed a number of ideas about what you would like to do, almost invariably in terms of correcting what you see as being the mistakes of the past. You are conscious that you need to 'grasp' the organization immediately. You must move quickly if you are to convey the image of determination and clarity that you will need if you are to establish your leadership and achieve your ends. Furthermore, the responsibility lands on you suddenly, almost without warning. Neither you, your colleagues, nor your company are likely to take kindly to you spending your first three months in a secluded location, doing what you really ought to do, namely thinking. It is important to do as much thinking as you can before you get the job, but it is even more important to pace yourself and your workload, so that you allow yourself time to contemplate and reflect on what you wish to achieve, and how you intend to set about it.

The very first question that anybody asks the leader of a large corporation is how they do it. How can one man impress himself on people in eighty or ninety countries, numbering in all, perhaps, two hundred thousand? How can the influence of one individual actually make any difference to the company as a whole? How can one individual be responsible for, and have any worthwhile knowledge about, the sort of problems which are facing his people in areas as diffuse as Ecuador, Auckland, and Aberdeen? If he can't have any effect on the company as a whole, what on earth is he doing there anyway? All of these, and many more questions, have to be resolved to your own satisfaction if you are in fact to achieve what is expected of you.

You must be clear in your own mind that there is no way that one man can manage an enormous company. The job of the chairman, or chief executive, is to 'manage' his colleagues on the board, and to manage the company through the board. I have always believed in the concept of added value, in an organizational sense. Namely, that every level in the organization should exist only if it has some unique role, responsibility, or capability to add to that which people below it are capable of doing. The only job in the entire company where it is totally clear where the added value lies is probably that of the chairman and chief executive.

There are certain ineluctable responsibilities which lie upon him, but above everything the entire question of the board. Only he can develop the board as a collective organization, handle, select, and motivate its members, and manage its work. The style and way in which the board works will have an enormous effect on the group as a whole, and the content of what it addresses itself to will decide to a large extent whether it is successful in influencing a large organization. The actual way in which it works depends entirely on the chairman. There is an almost limitless range of behaviour in any board of directors, and, at one time or another, one experiences practically all of them. One has seen boards which are purely ritual dancing, dealing only with the legalistic boiler plate, where no decision has ever been taken, and where everything is 'fixed' before it ever appears. Equally well, one has seen boards at the other extreme, where the entire time is spent on seemingly endless, fruitless debate, which is never pulled together and turned into decisions. Indeed, if decisions were taken it is very doubtful whether there would be any mechanism to check on whether they were followed through.

In between these two extremes, board behaviour can cover every sort of note on the keyboard. Boards can be used to solve problems, although this is rare. It is, in fact, probably the best use of the combined talent you have, for remember that the board of directors of a company is very probably the most experienced, and almost certainly the best paid group that you have. If they can't solve problems it is a little difficult to see who can. In order to solve problems information has to be shared, and not only information, but doubts, fears, and questions. Boards can, in their ways of managing themselves, run the whole gamut between construction and conflict. Somebody has to intervene, to manage that balance.

These matters cannot be decided collectively. There may be a collective will, or precedents about the ways in which certain things are dealt with, but finally it is only the chairman who can decide the style. Only he can judge in what way the board can be most effective as a group, and how effective their influence will be on the company as a whole.

One of the areas about which I am still very uncertain is the never-ending argument about whether the top job should really be two jobs or not. I have seen successful examples both of a combination of chairman and chief executive in the one, and an admittedly smaller number but nevertheless very successful examples of a situation where a non-executive chairman has worked well and happily with a chief executive. Dalgetty, in the United Kingdom, is perhaps an extremely good example of a company that operated well with a non-executive and highly professional chairman in the shape of David Donne. Moreover, many of the companies that John Cuckney has run have had the same attributes. There is no doubt that if the top job of chairman and principal executive officer are combined in one, the job is a killer. The outside, representational role is immensely time-consuming, and tends to be an inescapable, self-accelerating function. The better known and more successful you are at projecting the image of your company, the more you are requested to do so. Time management and allocation between the representational and the executive roles is very difficult, since the latter requires very large amounts of time to be spent on the preparation of the work, and the management of the board as a whole.

There are real advantages to having the top job split between two people. It is easier to replace either one of them under such circumstances if some disaster happens, or if one or the other begins to be 'off the boil'. It is extremely difficult to replace a combined chairman and chief executive. You take a double risk for a start, and the actual mechanisms of replacement are difficult to effect. It is relatively easy to draw up the fields of responsibilities of two people who share the top job. The non-executive job should be primarily directed to the management of the actual board, and the external environment, as well as ensuring that mechanisms are in place to develop strategies and clear policies on the many issues for which a board has responsibility. The other, the executive role, is then responsible for seeing that these policies are carried out, and actually managing that process. The chairman is responsible for seeing that the board checks that their policies have been carried out by the chief executive.

The difficulty in such organizations is one of split responsibilities. An organization of this type calls for a degree of integration and understanding between the two top people which is often difficult to achieve. Moreover, it can fall into the trap which the Americans dislike so much, of a lack of clarity as to who is ultimately in charge, and where the buck actually stops. It is a fuzzier organization and, while it does have some highly desirable characteristics of flexibility, it lacks some of the crispness of having the whole thing tied into one person. Certainly such an approach is an unpopular one in America, where again organizational theory seems to be rather starker than in the United Kingdom.

Having tried to do the job as a solo effort for a number of, perhaps in retrospect, less good reasons than I thought at the time, I suspect that the strain of doing it on one's own may well not be worth the candle. If you have the job of chairman and chief executive in one you rely totally on your own sensitivities as to the real feelings of your colleagues. It is all too easy to lose the feel of the mood and to move into isolation without meaning to. At that stage the capacity for leadership is severely limited. If there are two of you, you have double the chance of evading this situation. However, I have even seen examples where both the chairman and the CEO have lost this feeling, and once it is lost it is very difficult to recover. On balance, in a UK environment, I think I prefer the top job to be split, but again this is a matter which rests with the chairman. He must decide what he thinks would be the best organization for the company and the board, after giving the matter careful thought. The difficulty of such an internal debate is that it is extremely difficult to understand clearly the pressures which one is imposing upon oneself, and there is a natural tendency to overestimate one's ability to handle things. . .

2
Profession: Leader

Jan Carlzon

In the summer of 1981, the first year I became president of SAS, I decided to take two weeks' vacation. But as soon as I arrived at my country house, the telephone began ringing. And it kept right on ringing with questions from people back at the office about the most mundane matters. Of course, sitting out in the country, I possessed less information than anyone at headquarters about what was going on, but they called me anyway. After a couple of days I gave up and returned to Stockholm. It was a waste of time to try to do my job long distance.

The following summer, a Swedish newspaper asked to interview me on the subject of 'taking it easy.' I agreed, but only on the condition that the article be published a week *before* my vacation. I wanted to make sure that everybody at SAS read what I had to say.

In the interview, I explained that I believed responsibility should be delegated within a company so that individual decisions are made at the point of responsibility, not far up the organizational chart. I said that we had created an organization designed to work in this manner and had appointed managers who were expected to operate this way. 'Now I intend to take four weeks' vacation,' I stated. 'If my telephone *doesn't* ring, that is proof that I have succeeded – people have accepted responsibility and are making decisions on their own. But if the phone rings, then I have failed – either in getting my message across or in recruiting managers who can accept responsibility.'

A few days later I left for vacation. And for four weeks, the telephone remained wonderfully silent.

That was the best evidence that the organization was, indeed, working the

Excerpt from *Moments of Truth* by Ian Carlzon. Copyright © 1987, by permission of Ballinger Division, Harper & Row, Publishers, Inc.

way it was designed to work – even if I had helped things along a little with the interview. Upon my return, I discovered that many decisions had been made in my absence. Some of them didn't thrill me – I probably would have chosen differently – but the significant accomplishment was that decisions had been made. Other people were taking responsibility based on accurate, up-to-date information.

That is the difference between the traditional business manager and the true leader in a customer-driven company. I like to think that the successes at Linjeflyg and SAS came about largely because I took to heart the important lessons I had learned early on at Vingresor. A leader is not appointed because he knows everything and can make every decision. He is appointed to bring together the knowledge that is available and then create the prerequisites for the work to be done. He creates the systems that enable him to delegate responsibility for day-to-day operations.

In the past, of course, it would have been inconceivable for the president of a company to cut himself off from the office completely for a month. A top manager was expected to make all the important decisions himself so he was always directly involved in operations. Important decisions had to be made constantly, and he therefore expected to work day and night, weekdays and weekends. Saying 'I haven't been able to take a real vacation in four years' showed his firm control and indispensability.

The typical chief executive was a decision-making machine. Employees supplied the raw data about a problem and presented their alternative solutions. The chief executive then processed this information and spewed forth the answer: 'We'll take Alternative 2B.' Since he was the only one who saw the overall picture, he was compelled to make important decisions himself. No one else was equipped to do so.

This system made it look as if the chief executive was taking full responsibility, but actually almost the opposite was true. He was not taking responsibility for the most crucial part of his job: making sure that the overall vision of the company was achieved. He was only making decisions about those issues that came to his attention. But even if all the important matters made their way up the pyramid, and even if the executive was a consummate decision-maker, he simply had *no time* to investigate every issue and render an informed judgement.

What were the results? Many decisions were simply never made. No one in the company was able to keep in mind the overall vision – the staff because they weren't privy to it, and the chief executive because he got too bogged down in decision-making. And many employees became passive, believing that even if they were to come up with a good idea, 'management wouldn't let us do it anyway.'

Many people consider it extremely demanding to manage in this classic fashion – they are constantly imposed upon by their staff, and they must work through nights, weekends, and vacations. But I believe the job of a true leader is actually much more difficult.

Nobody puts a proposal for a new comprehensive strategy on your desk and asks you to make a decision about it. You have to put it there yourself. And once you use your view of the big picture to formulate a strategy, you have to call on a wide range of skills to achieve a series of objectives. You must devise a business strategy tailored to your goal. You need to communicate the goal and strategy to the board of directors, the unions, and all the employees. You have to give greater responsibility to people at the front line and then create a secure atmosphere where they will dare to use their new authority. You must build an organization that can work to achieve the goal and establish measures that guarantee you are moving in the right direction. In short, you have to create the prerequisites for making the vision a reality.

This is a lot harder than implementing it yourself. I made exactly that mistake when I first became president of SAS. Though passenger business was our primary emphasis, we had also given our air cargo people responsibility for developing a new strategy. But it seemed to me that they were just coming up with general rallying cries like 'Go, Cargo, Go.' I was impatient and eager for some 'real' strategic thinking.

So I sat down with the head of cargo operations and said, 'This can't be so difficult. What the market wants, of course, is door-to-door service. Develop such a product and call it EuroCargo which will fit nicely with our EuroClass on the passenger end.'

He obeyed and, as you've probably guessed, it was a big flop. Why? Because I had made a decision from the top of the pyramid about an aspect of the business that was completely unfamiliar to me. I lacked a basic knowledge of the cargo market's special structure and division of labor. Coming from the passenger end, I did not understand that cargo was different – that it is a heavy industrial product sold to major manufacturing corporations through long-term contracts.

If I had created an atmosphere in which the cargo managers' own ideas flourished, of course, the mistake would not have been made. Instead, I took the easy way out, opting to decide myself, even though I didn't know what I was doing.

Many executives make that same choice, apparently believing that they cannot be good managers unless they know – or pretend to know – everything. Peoples' whispers that their immediate superior 'doesn't know anything – he couldn't even do my job,' are strong evidence that their boss thinks he has to know it all.

But a business executive need not have detailed specialized knowledge. I am the president of a large airline, but I can neither fly a plane nor repair one – and no one at SAS expects me to. A leader today must have much more general qualities: good business sense and a broad understanding of how things fit together – the relationships among individuals and groups inside and outside the company and the interplay among the various elements of the company's operations.

What is required is strategic thinking, or 'helicopter sense' – a talent for rising above the details to see the lay of the land. The ability to understand and direct change is crucial for effective leadership. Today's business leader must manage not only finances, production, technology, and the like but also human resources. By defining clear goals and strategies and then communicating them to his employees and training them to take responsibility for reaching those goals, the leader can create a secure working environment that fosters flexibility and innovation. Thus, the new leader is a listener, communicator, and educator – an emotionally expressive and inspiring person who can create the right atmosphere rather than make all the decisions himself.

These skills were once regarded as feminine, an association that goes back to women's roles in the old agricultural society when they took care of family and social relationships in the village. Their intuition and sensitivity to other people's situations are traits that are essential for any manager but cannot, unfortunately, be picked up overnight.

The new leadership role should open up many more possibilities for women in business. When we hired Birgitta Rydbeck as director of the SAS Flight Academy, we were looking for a professional *manager*, not a long-time pilot. Birgitta had a degree in business administration, and we were confident that she could create the proper conditions for flight training. Our move caused quite a stir among the pilots who believed that a specialist in aviation technology should have the position. They were quick to come around, though, as Birgitta demonstrated the perfect blend of leadership traits and proved herself a capable manager. I firmly believe that, in the long run, men and women alike will benefit from using 'feminine' and 'masculine' qualities in good combination.

In many respects, though, the leader has to be an enlightened dictator – one who is willing to disseminate the vision and goals throughout a large, decentralized organization but who will not brook active dissent to the underlying ideas. He must be able to present his vision convincingly so that the goals and strategies feel right to everyone in the company. Indeed, as my experience at Linjeflyg and SAS shows, the management's vision often corresponds with the employees' own ideas.

Some employees may not see or fully understand the vision and goals at the beginning. The leader must resist the urge to dismiss those people and, instead, work with them, give them additional information, and attempt again to make them understand.

Of course, there will always be those who refuse to be persuaded. From them, he must demand loyalty, if not emotional commitment, to the goals. Otherwise, they should be asked to leave.

At SAS we were able to convince almost every employee of the value of our vision. Everyone aligned and began moving enthusiastically in the same direction, and we were able to stir up a pretty strong wind, as our profit-and-loss statement showed. However, if one in ten had gone in a different direction, the countermovement would have slowed the momentum at a crucial moment in the company's history.

Therefore, when I say we must collapse the hierarchical structure in service-oriented businesses, I am not calling for corporate democracy in its purest form. Certainly, everyone – middle management, frontline employees, union leaders, and board members – must be given the opportunity to air their views and ideas. But they cannot all be involved in making every final decision.

The board of directors appoints the president and the top management team to design, present, and pursue a business strategy. Only after the leader has fully developed this strategy and communicated it to everyone else can he begin delegating responsibility – as he *must* do in a customer-driven company. A leader is one who creates the right environment for business to be done.

In the game of soccer, the coach is a leader whose job it is to select the right players. He must also ensure that his team goes onto the field in the best condition to play a good game. On the field, there is a team captain, analogous to a manager, with the authority to issue orders on the field and to change plays during the course of the game. But most important are the individual players, each of whom becomes his own boss during the game.

Imagine a situation in which a soccer player breaks away toward an open goal and suddenly abandons the ball to run back to the bench and ask the coach for the order to kick the ball into the goal. Before he can run back to the ball, he has lost not only the ball but also the game.

In changing a business environment, you can't wield total control from the top of a pyramid. You must give people authority far out on the line where the action is. They are the ones who can sense the changes in the market. By giving them security, authority, and the right to make decisions based on current market conditions, you put yourself in the best position to gain a competitive edge.

A leader, then, is a person who is oriented toward results more than power or social relations. Someone seeking power for its own sake may well sacrifice both personal relationships and results to obtain it. Someone who is too socially oriented might tend to compromise at every turn in order to avoid conflict. In the long run, this hurts results. But the results-oriented leader does not dictate the methods for achieving the results and, moreover, does not need to claim the victories as his own.

At times, the press in Scandinavia has 'divulged' that I personally have not originated all the ideas that have led to SAS's success. I welcome these revelations because they highlight exactly what I've been saying all along. The great triumph at SAS is that we have unleashed our employees' creativity through decentralization. Good ideas flow freely from every division of the company and are all channelled toward the same company-wide vision.

The same applies to my approach to outside consultants. I have frequently heard it whispered that in actuality a consultant thought up a particular idea. It seems to be a point of honor to be able to handle a situation without having to turn to outside consultants. That is someting that I have never really understood. It must spring from the traditional view that the manager has superior, infallible knowledge and must always retain total control.

To me, it cannot be anything other than sensible and responsible to bring a ship's pilot on board when you are steering your vessel into new and dangerous waters!

For a manager who wants to make all the decisions himself at all levels of the company, it may not be as prestigious to bring in an outside consultant who would then be involved in making some of these decisions. On the other hand, if you reorganize along the lines that I have set down here, then you may have to change the overall direction of the company. This is like trying to get a battleship to change course, a process that requires tremendous amounts of energy and very special skills.

If the leader now delegates responsibility to people throughout the company in order to bring about this change, then it would be unreasonable to expect that each could be a specialist in every aspect of it. Their job is to cope with long-term development far after the change has been completed. If I give them responsibility, then I also have to let them bring in the extra resources they need – a financial expert, an organizational consultant, or an advertising agency.

It makes no difference who comes up with good ideas. All that matters is that the ideas have worked, and today SAS is a strong organization that serves its customers well.

3
Leadership, Change and the Public Dimension

Michael Edwardes

One of the very encouraging aspects of change within BL has been the way line managers have accepted – not without some initial trepidation – a much broader view of their role. Their jobs used to be narrow and operational – get on with the job in hand, avoid trouble if possible, and if there is a dispute call in the employee relations people. Things are now very different. We established a proper communications channel which involves managers, supervisors, and foremen communicating with the workforce and the unions about issues within the company; this, instead of abdicating responsibility for information dissemination to shop stewards, who often worked in isolation.

The strategy of going direct to employees on matters of importance began within a few months of the new BL board and management being appointed. Issues such as job losses, restructuring, changes to working methods were too important to the recovery programme to be passed on through shop stewards at factory floor meetings; or at mass meetings where the objective was not careful deliberation, but a show of hands.

When the 720 employee representatives met the new management team at Kenilworth on 1st February 1978 to hear our plans for rescuing the Cars operations, every employee in each of the 36 factories and offices was handed a summary of the proposals before they left work on that day. We also wrote to employees at home and where there was an issue of wider public significance – like the Recovery Plan ballot in September/October 1979 – we used newspaper advertisements to get our message across. This was, of course, in addition to the face-to-face debate between managers and the workforce on the shop floor itself, and in briefing groups.

Highlights from chapter 12 of *Back from the Brink* by Michael Edwardes. Collins. Copyright © 1983 Harper Collins Publishers Ltd.

Inevitably, direct communication from management to individual employees was regarded with deep dismay and anger by some employee representatives, and even by some district, regional, and national officials. It was 'going over the heads' of the elected representatives. But it was, in our view, the only way in the early days of getting a fair hearing for management's plans and proposals. The existing process of establishing communication with employees in BL was not straightforward. The participation system of three tiers of consultative councils and committees had a momentum of its own and an ability to generate a paperchase up, down, and across the organization; it really was a wonder to behold. Furthermore, it did not achieve results: the direct message and urgency of action was lost in an administrative treacle.

The first step was to bring to bear on internal communications the skills which the company possessed through its external communications and public affairs people. The responsibilities for communicating both inside and outside the company were brought together. This had the immediate effect of shortening the internal communication chain, and of elevating its status and importance in the company structure. This was a major shift, for it became clear to people that communication in its widest sense was a matter of direct concern to the chief executive; management priorities started to reflect this. The signal had to be given from the top, and the regular weekly meetings I held with groups of managers, either in London or when I visited our various factories, helped to infuse the new direct style of communication into management behaviour. It was not always successful: at the time of the dispute at Longbridge over parity in early 1980 we were slow to react to the campaign of distortion by shop stewards. They quickly convinced the men that they had earned the right to productivity money, when the facts showed otherwise. It took immense efforts by local managers to recoup the situation, but once they got the truth across, the strike was short lived.

Since that time more and more attention has been given to making sure employees receive a balanced view of any particular issue – and not just a union interpretation. They have seen managers move out from behind their desks and go out into the production areas and defend the company's actions on issues like new working methods, the need to increase productivity, the risks inherent in taking unthought-out strike action – and so forth. It has placed extra strain and pressure on those managers, but my assessment is that they were relieved to be able to reassert their managerial role, and regain control of a situation that was in danger of going by default.

I would argue that the manager British industry needs is one whose contribution to his company is two-fold. First, he must be a talented practitioner of his own profession – be he design or production engineer, accountant, chemist, or metallurgist. He must have a thorough grasp and control of his direct functions and responsibilities (including his role as communicator) coupled with an appreciation of broad company strategy and direction. Second, if he is in a company which needs fundamental change to survive, he must be prepared to put his job on the line at regular intervals by pushing through contentious issues which could bring the business crashing down around his ears. And this last requirement leads to an attribute without which leadership cannot exist. Courage. If we are to bring British industry back to where it belongs, courage will be needed. This is not a job for compromisers, or for those who lean towards popularity – great courage will be needed, for this is a key attribute of leadership, for the problem solver of today and tomorrow. . .

In the wider context of opinion-forming, so many people rely on newspapers, television, and radio for news and for opinion that a very public – and newsworthy – company like BL has carefully to guard its reputation against unfair and inaccurate reporting. At BL we have found that it does not pay to stick our heads in the sand or even to be merely philosophical about errors of fact in the press. We have found that it pays to be vigilant, to act immediately to deal with an incorrect, biased, or malicious report, whether by phoning an editor or by moving quickly to field a spokesman on the BBC Radio 'Today' programme when they periodically unearth a militant shop steward who then undermines the credibility of the company.

One of the unhelpful by-products of becoming personally involved in public debate is that, inevitably, the media tends to concentrate on the individual making the noise. Once this happens there is this tendency 'to play the man, not the ball.' I've lost count of the number of times I've picked up a paper or watched a news bulletin to learn of a decision or an action I'm supposed to have taken; a decision that I haven't even been involved in. Of course personalization cuts two ways: it was perhaps not a bad thing during the period when unpleasant and painful decisions about job losses and factory closures had to be taken, that there was a single target for the flak – I've no personal complaints on that score. But a preoccupation with an individual can mask the wider considerations, as I explained at an Independent Broadcasting Association lecture in early 1982:

> What day-to-day coverage of industry there is, is often concerned with the negative; the disputes, the strikes and stoppages and even less directly the threats of strikes which may or may not materialise, and which are often portrayed as actually happening. I make the point not simply to try to convince you that BL is now a reformed character but because of the 'knock-on' effect BL has had on the image of British industry as a whole, particularly abroad.
>
> The plea I would make to you is that just as you wouldn't judge the whole of ITV by one specific period of poor programmes, please don't let your perceptions of British industry be coloured by BL's antecedents or judge BL today by British Leyland of yesterday.

To be fair, when the facts were pointed out, many of the commentators were quite ready to acknowledge that the change in our situation was not being adequately portrayed. We now get a more accurate press.

A key part of a successful manager's role is to communicate – first and foremost to his workforce, to explain and to motivate – but he should also be prepared to take his arguments and judgements to a wider audience, if the circumstances warrant. It is not always easy to persuade industrialists to fight publicly – indeed we had to work quite hard to persuade our own managers to speak up, on a local and regional basis, and we arranged for some 50 executives to have television and radio training, but it still took time to break down their reticence.

I do not expect a middle manager to expound on strategic policy issues, but there is a case for him being interviewed where he is the one with the knowledge and the responsibility. Conversely, you can't expect the top man to agree to be interviewed on a matter which is the proper preserve of an appropriately placed *less senior* executive. There is a disinclination among broadcasters and journalists to take anyone but the top man for interview. Many times the BL communications people have suggested that this or that executive would be more appropriate, but often the response has been a feeling of affront from journalists that their particular programme does not merit the man at the top. In doing this they often reject the very man who would have most to contribute. Industry has to work very hard at improving the communications skills of its managers. The more enlightened companies recognize this and are taking steps through courses and training to correct it as part of the overall need for better management of businesses.

4
The Staying Power of Visionary Leaders

Christopher Lorenz

If a poll were taken for the best European business leader of the 1980s, the vote would probably go to Mr Jan Carlzon, the head of Scandinavian Airlines. His remarkable turnaround of SAS, from an unpopular laggard to a model performer, set an example which countless other companies, in all sorts of industries, have since tried to emulate: one of the most successful is his arch-competitor British Airways.

In the political world, there is no doubt at all that most plaudits would go to Mrs Margaret Thatcher. She may not have turned her country into a model performer compared with its rivals – though she likes to think she has – but she has certainly made it more competitive than a decade ago.

Despite their very different styles – Mr Carlzon listening, consulting and always celebrating the successes of his staff, Mrs Thatcher cajoling, directing and keeping her ministers in their place – they epitomize the power of visionary leadership to revitalize an apparently moribund system.

But their staying power is questionable: Mrs Thatcher's because of her inability to adapt her style to changing circumstances, Mr Carlzon's because he faces a tougher task than a decade ago – not just externally, as SAS struggles against bigger rivals, but also within, as he tries to motivate a now confident, stable organization to submit itself to a new revolution.

Mr Carlzon's chances are helped by a vision broad enough to encompass new challenges: he is currently trying to transform SAS from a regional airline into an international travel service company. That involves a network of global alliances, and the replacement of an organization which is decentralized into small units with one in which operations are more integrated.

Reprinted with permission from the *Financial Times*, 12 February 1990.

Mrs Thatcher, on the other hand, is still fighting the same battles as a decade ago, even if they have already been won. Like Carlzon, she should be seizing on major changes in the external environment – such as eastern Europe – to develop new vision and a fresh set of challenges.

To some extent, the survivability of either of them is merely the familiar question of time: few leaders, whether in business or politics, last much beyond a decade. Those who have a one-track style usually quit very much sooner (or ought to): Sir Michael Edwardes was frank enough to admit when he left the British car maker BL (now Rover) in 1984 that if he had stayed for more than four years his value would have been only a third what it had been during the early period of his tenure.

More adaptable leaders – usually the more cerebral sort – can last much longer, and still add considerable value. Sir Christopher Hogg has now headed Courtaulds, the British fibres and chemicals group, for a decade, taking it through at least three different phases: a battle for survival in the early 1980s, revitalization in international markets for the rest of the decade, and revolution at the end of it, with a decision to unbundle the company by splitting off the company's original textile core from its more dynamic businesses.

Sir Christopher Hogg's track record challenges an otherwise powerful model of leadership and revitalization which was presented to the recent annual conference of the Strategic Management Society by two Canadian academics, Frances Westley and Henry Mintzberg. Stripping out the anthropological jargon, it suggests that most leaders find it hard to adjust more than once to the 'cycle of revitalization': once a revolution achieves its objective, a state of order develops in which all sorts of routines are required.

If the leader can adjust to this change, he or she loses the ability later to launch a new revolution, retreating instead into lofty distance at the top of the newly stable system – as some SAS insiders actually claim Mr Carlzon has done, despite his efforts to the contrary. By contrast, the one-track revolutionary who cannot adjust becomes a restless irritant, or worse.

Either way, the leader's days are numbered.

Chapter 5
Leadership and Creativity

Introduction

Creative leaders are often grouchy, crafty, dangerous, evangelical, contrary, inconsistent, and spineless, says Morgan McCall. Perhaps, to judge by the account of Michael Eisner, a man whose chief duty is to lead Disney creatively, and 'a CEO who is more hands-on than Mother Teresa', 'fanatical' and 'sporadically crazy' ought also to be added to the list. Mr Eisner's wife, a lady who often screens her husband's ideas, is a regular subscriber to the 'crazy' dimension. Eisner's own comment – 'To me the pursuit of ideas is the only thing that matters. You can always find capable people to do almost everything else' – confirms the 'fanatical'.

It is not surprising that creative leaders often appear to be rather unbalanced characters. They are the personification of an essential organizational dilemma outlined in the piece by Marsha Sinetar: 'just because big business wants entrepreneurs doesn't mean it is prepared to accept or appreciate their way of working . . . In reality, a substantial number of creatives are strangled within the orderly, systematic cultures of large companies: they can't work in these structured environments.'

Merely being 'creative' does not automatically qualify an individual for being a good leader. In fact, in many cases it is better if the 'creative' executive is a valued member of the CEO's élite support group; inspired entrepreneurs are all too frequently unsuccessful business leaders. In a short excerpt from Tudor Rickard's book *Creativity at Work* he points out that an overbearingly creative leader can have a very negative effect on the general corporate climate, giving out cues such as 'there's no need for you lot to be creative, just leave that to me'. Carlzon (in chapter 4) experienced at first hand just how destructive such 'creative' interference can be. On first becoming president of SAS, he identified a problem, jumped to a creative solution, and imposed it on his head of cargo operations. Carlzon admits, 'it was a big flop . . . If I had created an atmosphere in which the cargo managers' own ideas flourished, of course, the mistake would not have been made . . . The great triumph at SAS is that we have unleashed our employees' creativity through decentralization.' As

Rickards neatly puts it, 'Creative leaders make things happen, but their approach is subtle – more like a midwife than a surgeon.'

Peter Evans and Geoff Deehan illustrate the realistic approach needed to keep the creative leader's feet firmly on the ground by using an unexpected comparison between J. S. Bach and Sir Terence Conran. Bach's problem was to produce a concerto using well-established compositional rules without making them sound like formula music. 'The "genius" component only accounts for some of Bach's unique music', they explain, then going on to describe how 'Conran firmly believes that design is in a great degree problem-solving, especially when aimed at a mass market.'

In the end it is McCall who identifies the most significant paradox of the truly gifted leaders – to achieve their ends they have to draw on personal characteristics that are often contradictory, inconsistent, and grate against conventional views of how a public figure should behave (witness Harvey-Jones's long hair and loud ties).

Mirroring his conclusions, Marsha Sinetar comments that the price of encouraging creative entrepreneurs into senior management is a maverick attitude to how work gets done and what questions get asked. Their attitudes are often disruptive and may lack respect for conventional opinion and methods.

Both authors agree that creative leadership is undermined if it spends too much time living up to the expectations of others. A historical case in point is the contrast between Jefferson Davis and Abraham Lincoln, opposite heads of state in the American Civil War. Davis was the exemplar of Southern integrity. Correct to a fault, he would never have dreamed of dissembling or deliberate deceit to further his political goals. He was loyal to his friends and un-questionably patriotic. Yet he failed to inspire his people or his armies and succeeded only in alienating most of his Cabinet, government officials, and generals. Lincoln, the product of backwood politics, was crafty, inconsistent, and dishonest when it suited his purpose. A fervent abolitionist privately, he once commented that to achieve his main aim – preserving the Union – he would free all of the slaves or none of the slaves or free some and not others. He never let his personal morality – which by anyone's standards was very high – interfere with his role as a political and military leader. Yet he is now regarded as one of America's most inspired and effective leaders.

McCall points out that business leaders can be two-faced, manipulative and 'feisty'. They deal with people's emotions, not their rationality. Provided the cause is right, they will choose any means within the law to achieve it. Perhaps the biggest challenge facing senior executives in the coming decade is how to reconcile this seeming characteristic of creative leadership with the high ethical standards society now demands from its captains of industry (see chapter 7).

1
Entrepreneurs, Chaos and Creativity: Can Creative People Survive Large Company Structure?

Marsha Sinetar

I love chaos: it is the mysterious, unknown road. It is the ever-unexpected, the way out:
It is freedom, it is man's only hope. It is the poetic element in a dull and orderly world.

American artist, Ben Shahn, 1966

Suddenly, big business is in love with creativity. With the same fervor with which it courted MBAs in the 1970s, American industry is now trying to lure entrepreneurs into managerial positions. It has discovered that survival in today's volatile, global marketplace means finding, developing, and sustaining the very mavericks it rejected only a few years ago.

Why this dramatic shift in focus? One of the reasons is apparent as soon as we examine the entrepreneur's instinctive intelligence: entrepreneurs are better able to spot options and create new directions for an industry. Typically, they deal well with ambiguity and change, and that is a prerequisite for success in today's fast-paced business world. They can distinguish real from imaginary pitfalls, and the brightest among them can turn error into opportunity. Small wonder then that industry is scurrying to acquire creative thinkers.

Even current buzzwords point to the important place creativity holds in business. Intrapreneurial describes entrepreneurial characteristics when these turn inward, for organizational benefit. Entrepreneurialize is jargon used to describe any business activity that allows large, calcified organizations to

From *Sloan Management Review*, Winter, 1985. Copyright © 1985 by the Sloan Management Review Association, by permission of the publisher.

internalize the advantages of smaller, more nimble companies. But, whatever the terminology, progressive corporations are hiring entrepreneurs, sending managers to creativity seminars, and bringing in creativity specialists to teach executives how to think in original ways.

However, just because big business wants entrepreneurs doesn't mean it is prepared to accept or appreciate their way of working. There is much evidence suggesting that most large organizations are insensitive to the nuances and idiosyncratic work style of the creative personality. In reality, a substantial number of creatives are strangled within the orderly, systematic cultures of large companies: they can't work in these structured environments. Sometimes they leave, and sometimes their ideas just die, unused and unnoticed. But because business needs creative people, it must learn to understand – and support – this inventive breed of worker.

Who and What is a Creative Entrepreneur?

It is possible to distinguish two types of creative entrepreneurs: the activist and the creative thinker. Actually these two categories are not at all clear-cut, since all entrepreneurs if successful possess healthy doses of business acumen and original/resourceful thinking skills. What distinguishes one type from another is a subtle, almost elusive difference in thinking mode and in the manner of getting a job done. The activist is a doer. He has an innate understanding of what it takes to run, expand, reconceptualize, or create a business. This person's thought processes – the steady, incremental way of thinking, doing, communicating – fits into and naturally complement the core of organizational life. The activist is a natural dance partner to business, and activists have an intuitive, sixth sense when it comes to motivating personnel, marketing new products, and dealing with financial issues. They know, without having to learn through academic institutions or books, how to put business principles to use within organizations so that both principle and organization succeed.

Victor Kiam, president of Remington Products, Inc., serves as an excellent and well-known media model of the activist entrepreneur. With effectiveness and energy he participates in all facets of his company's operations. He markets and even sells the product: his ad campaign, 'I liked this shaver so much I bought the company,' is now nationally familiar. He meets regularly with employees to motivate and inspire them. Kiam has built an impressive, clear corporate identity. In fact, if media reports are accurate, this activist entrepreneur is doing so well he is currently moving his product into the Japanese marketplace, thus reversing a global trend of Japanese products encroaching on US markets. An impressive achievement.

The creative thinker, on the other hand, is more like an artist or inventor.

Primarily a thinker, he derives his greatest pleasure from the act of thinking itself, from the creative process in action. Achievement for him comes when mental abstractions are transformed into concrete forms – when idea becomes reality. Indeed, the creative thinker loves the conceptional work of his technical speciality so much that sometimes practical business needs get overshadowed by the images of his professional frame of reference (e.g. engineering, computer technology, genetics, mathematics, etc.). This person is totally absorbed in experimentation, investigation, and innovation. Money, status, the outcomes of business are secondary to the act of creation. It is thinking itself which provides deep, visceral satisfaction: a fact industry must not overlook or misinterpret.

For the creative thinker, problems are sorted out in a stylized, unpredictable, and often disorganized manner; herein lies the greatest conflict that creatives have within organized corporate structures. Often, creative thinkers are hard to get to know. As managers they frustrate and surprise people in their departments; as employees they don't conform. In any role their habits contradict organizational expectations and mores.

One such manager, a nationally respected visionary known best for his grasp and application of computer technology, arrives at work early each morning and makes coffee for everyone. Accustomed to working late into the night, he then cleans up the coffee room before the custodians can get to it. He is oblivious to his company's unwritten social law that says senior executives must not engage in such activities. Thus he unknowingly thwarts lower level employees' ego needs to do a job they feel is rightly theirs.

Another creative thinker, a corporate vice president, upsets subordinates and superiors alike by refusing all clerical help, including a secretary to answer his phone and type his letters. Instead, he scrawls all memos on yellow legal pads, unaware that his colleagues get irritated because of this and because they can't get in touch with him when he's away from his office.

For all that, the creative thinker is not a wild-eyed nonconformist. With respect to most of the small customs of life, innovators may be very ordinary, even boring, people. But these personalities thrive on freedom in three important areas of life:

- Freedom in the general area of their work and the way in which the work gets done.
- Freedom to ask novel or disturbing questions.
- Freedom to come up with unusual solutions to the things they're thinking about (sometimes in the form of what seems, to others, to be impractical ideas).

In other words, these types must have lots of room for experimentation and 'play.' Such license is like air for breathing to the bright, inventive mind, yet it is only the rare organization that can provide this.

Creativity Means Disturbing the *Status Quo*

Creativity means bringing into existence something that has never existed before. For the person who creates, thinking is play, and this becomes both his motive ('I desire to think') and his goal ('so that I can think some more'). Part of his recreation is experimentation: this is unsettling to others, and disruptive to organizational life. Courting error, taking a 'let's see what happens' stance, is natural to the creative thinker, but anathema to large organizations.

Because of size and structure, big companies are risk-averse, even though they may give lip service to being otherwise. Errors, mistakes, failures: these must be avoided because they destroy careers, departmental efficiency, record keeping, and the like. *Organizations are designed to administer, maintain, and protect what already exists; creative thinkers are designed to bring into existence that which has never been before.* The creative's need to think and invent disturbs the well-oiled machinery of organizational process; thus, creativity is experienced as chaotic in most business environments. Some examples will help illustrate this fact.

The head of a technical unit of a prosperous, multinational corporation thinks nothing of spending vast sums of money to experiment with state-of-the-art systems equipments. Colleagues who are responsible for the corporate bottom line wonder if he is sane. 'Just buy something reputable and stop playing games,' they plead in an effort to keep expenditures down, but he continues to load his offices and theirs with a variety of experimental equipment and spends freely. While his associates think he's irresponsible, he thinks about the future, and electronics, and how to bring his company to the forefront of technology. Because he cannot (or will not) communicate in terms familiar to others, a knowledge and goals gap grows between himself and those important to his success.

Another entrepreneur, hired to help a corporation reconceptualize itself into new markets, spent the majority of his first year wandering about the halls, asking people vague, unanswerable questions. His incomprehensible approach alarmed fellow executives; more action-oriented business colleagues considered his constant probing a waste of time. Months passed without formal meetings or the development of a strategic game plan. This creative thinker appeared to lack the logic and discipline of a businessman.

In time, the man successfully accomplished what he'd been hired to do. His style of handling the project, however, put him on thin ice even with those who'd hired him in the first place, again underscoring the difficulty that creatives have in a structured setting and the difficulty structured organizations have with the creative process.

What Do Creative Entrepreneurs Have in Common?

Every truly creative individual is a minority of one. There is no one else like him or her. It is difficult to group such persons into neat descriptive categories, except to say, as we have, that they don't fit the sterotypical way of doing business. However, the broadest area of their thinking skills and style of pursuing goals can be codified:

- they are easily bored, and would rather move into untried areas
- They are comfortable with ambiguity, at least when it comes to work
- they are neither risk-averse nor troubled by ambiguity
- they may be uninterested in social matters, and thus may not be socially 'well-rounded'
- they need to use their minds to solve difficult, personally fulfilling problems
- the healthier their personalities, the more likely it is that they experience their work as a calling or dedicated vocation.

When working in unexplored problem areas, creative entrepreneurs are able to cope without support or approval from others. According to research done by Paul Torrance, creativity researcher at the University of Georgia, Athens, creative people are happy with solitude, and they are less in need of discipline or order. Their dominant need may be to use their brains on complex problems, and this often overshadows their dependency on the approval or opinions of others.[1]

One such individual expressed his need to use his mind this way: 'I love to use my brain . . . it actually feels good in a physical sense. The best times for me are when I'm working, uninterrupted, on something that needs a solution. My ideal job would be if I could sit in a room with the door shut with no one to bother me, and the company would just slide problems it needs solved under the door.'

Such attitudes are disruptive to, if not disrespectful of, others. An all too familiar example is the creative entrepreneur who walks away from a successful business to work on a new project. His actions confuse family and colleagues alike. The energy, money, and time he must put into the new venture could so easily go into expanding the existing, profitable business. But, for a creative mind, moving on to a new challenge is natural, perhaps necessary. As a creative friend once told me, 'Show me something easy, and I'll show you something dull.'

How Can Organizations Sustain Creative Talent?

After all has been said about creative entrepreneurs, it must be clear that there are no instant answers, no quick-fix formulas that large organizations can use to

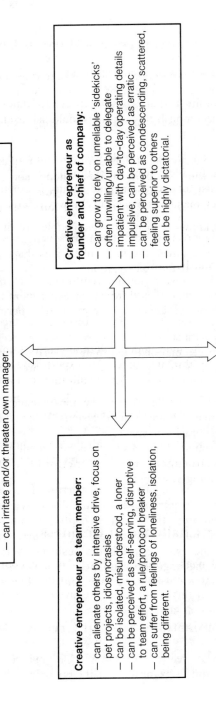

Creative entrepreneur as subordinate:

  — style, thinking, expectancies can clash when reporting to logical, linear thinker
  — can suffocate in rigid cultures
  — can suffer (or cause distress) when not managed (i.e. guided) into corporate culture
  — can experience management and/or the company as punitive to creative efforts
  — can be impatient to utilize brain, resulting in premature termination
  — can irritate and/or threaten own manager.

Creative entrepreneur as founder and chief of company:

  — can grow to rely on unreliable 'sidekicks'
  — often unwilling/unable to delegate
  — impatient with day-to-day operating details
  — impulsive, can be perceived as erratic
  — can be perceived as condescending, scattered, feeling superior to others
  — can be highly dictatorial.

Creative entrepreneur as team member:

  — can alienate others by intensive drive, focus on pet projects, idiosyncrasies
  — can be isolated, misunderstood, a loner
  — can be perceived as self-serving, disruptive to team effort, a rule/protocol breaker
  — can suffer from feelings of loneliness, isolation, being different.

Creative entrepreneur as manager:

  — can see management activities as uninteresting, irritating
  — can be perceived as 'ivory tower', impractical; lacking in short-range follow-through
  — can develop interpersonal communication barriers with subordinates (e.g. by avoiding coaching, corrective, appraisal-type conversations)
  — can be perceived as withdrawing and/or avoiding selected aspects of the job.

Figure 1 Common challenges facing the creative entrepreneur

harness the potential of creative people. There are, however, a few basic principles that can help businesses utilize the ideas and energy of entrepreneurs with more probability of success. (See figure 1 for analysis of the creative entrepreneur as subordinate, team member, manager, and founder of the company.)

First of all, management must be able to identify creative talent, then it must know how to use it. To accomplish this task, it should ask itself the following questions:

1   Who are our creative people, and how do we know they are creative? (This implies setting criteria for identifying innovators.)
2   What opportunities exist for creative people within this organization?
3   What barriers have key managers placed in the way of creative thinkers?

Once the organization knows who its creative people are, it must become introspective and ask itself:

1   In what way do we reward creativity?
2   Do we punish – that is, do we negatively reinforce, reject, or embarrass – those in the organization who look different or experiment freely?
3   In what specific ways do we encourage or promote experimentation and independent thinking?

Finally, in order to cultivate more independent, inventive thinking practices, organizations should audit thinking time. An expert isn't needed at this juncture, but opportunities to think are. An organization can ask itself:

1   What problem-solving opportunities exist for non-managers?
2   Do managers usually make all important decisions? What types of decisions are non-managers encouraged to make?
3   Are staff meetings, round table discussions, or small group meetings agenda-bound, tightly structured, or time-restricted? Or are these used, on occasion, as brainstorming sessions?

The Challenge to Business

One of the greatest challenges facing business today is encouraging creative people to express themselves innovatively while still maintaining the orderly functions of the company. If this is not done, creative entrepreneurs will leave generous salaries, incentives, and fringe benefits for more exciting and personally meaningful ventures.

In the words of one executive who left a large corporation to start his own company, 'I needed the basic kick of using my brain on things that really mattered. I was bored in my other job, even though I was handsomely paid.

There was no way of really thinking through the tough issues, no accountability or feedback in any immediate way. What I needed was the chance to use my mind. The company was too generous, but they didn't give me what I needed most – a real challenge.'

Note

1   E. P. Torrance, *Guiding Creative Talent* (Englewood Cliffs, N.J.: Prentice-Hall, 1962).

2
Creative Leadership

Tudor Rickards

Creativity can be managed and stimulated. The skills required, as in other areas, may not be evenly shared out around the population. They can develop through experience, application and learning (creative analysis). Or they can shrivel, become warped and misapplied. The obvious way to be a creative manager is through example – sparking off ideas which can be developed and implemented. Unfortunately, this strategy rarely succeeds. If the 'creative' leader is truly outstanding as a creative individual, he or she is rarely equally able to manage the creative ideas, and might therefore be better off as a team member producing an outstanding flow of stimuli. If, on the other hand, the leader is no better at producing ideas than the others, then the unconscious favouring given to the leader's ideas demotivates the others. It can send out cues that are negative for the creative climate – 'there's no need for you lot to be creative, just leave that to me.'

There is a quite different way of operating as a creative leader. It is to concentrate on 'ideas about ideas'. The concern should be how to get the best out of other people's talents, so that the emphasis is on the management of people. The style has been called a facilitating, or process-oriented, one. To develop this kind of leadership style you must learn to pay attention to the signals which people give out regarding their needs and beliefs. You must learn that sometimes the best way to help people solve problems is not to supply our own solutions – even if it is quite obvious to you what needs to be done. Creative leaders make things happen, but their approach is subtle – more like a midwife than a surgeon.

Excerpt from *Creativity at Work* by Tudor Rickards. Copyright © Tudor Rickards 1988, by permission of Gower Publishing Company Ltd.

This is how one successful businessman summed up creative leadership:

It's a kind of willingness to accept it when an employee says 'your way is not working'. It should make you really want to put thing right . . . Creative leaders develop procedures and practices which enable people to participate. When run properly, Quality Circles do that, for instance. The most successful leaders also are able to offer a precise shared understanding from time to time of their vision of the company leaving scope for those involved to own their part of the proceedings.

This style of leadership emerges in its most clear-cut form in group creativity sessions like brainstorming, where the leader concentrates on stimulating ideas and does not put in any of his or her own. And one of the spin-off benefits of practising such creative problem-solving sessions is that it helps develop the liberating leadership attitude, not just within the brainstorming session but in the wider work context.

3
Variations of Creativity

Peter Evans and Geoff Deehan

Perhaps the supreme example of the artist as problem-solver is the composer J. S. Bach. Bach worked at a period when rules of musical composition were quite rigid. There were specified ways of writing fugues or setting words to music of a religious nature. The composer had no freedom to establish his own guidelines – as is the case nowadays, say, with contemporary music – but had to accept the conventions of his day. The tools of his trade and the materials he could use were handed to him off the shelf. Indeed, in the case of Bach and his contemporaries, it was quite commonplace as well to borrow ideas from other composers. The music of Vivaldi figures quite prominently in Bach's output, albeit in an altered form.

Here then was Bach's problem: to produce a cantata or a concerto employing extremely well-used compositional rules and strategies without making them sound like formula music, a kind of aural painting by numbers. That he succeeded in doing so is indicative of the very special gifts of Bach compared to lesser composers of the day who were drawing on exactly the same toolkit. But these gifts are in part those of the practical problem-solver. The 'genius' component only accounts for some of Bach's unique music. In fact one might argue that it accounts for hardly any of it, perhaps even none at all.

Someone who would agree with that notion is the contemporary British designer Sir Terence Conran, the founder of the prodigiously successful Habitat chain of retail shops and subsequently the head of a massive empire of retail outlets worldwide. Conran firmly believes that design is in a great degree problem-solving, especially when aimed at a mass market. 'You're dealing,' he says, 'with a market where price is a constraint, you're trying always to squeeze a

Excerpt from *The Keys to Creativity* by Peter Evans and Geoff Deehan, Grafton Books Copyright © Peter Evans and Geoff Deehan 1988 by permission of Harper Collins Publishers Ltd.

quart from a pint pot. You know ideally what you would like to achieve, and you have so many restrictions of costs and marketing that, in order to achieve this, you have to work very carefully.'

Terence Conran also stresses that he sees a good deal of common ground between the two sides of his own work – as a designer and as a businessman. Both are founded on common sense. Just as the industrialist banker has to sort out his marketing, his cash flow, his financing, so too does the designer. The example he cites is Brunel, a brilliant engineer who had to sell his innovative ideas to railway and shipping companies and then control the costing and scheduling of their production. In the same league were the brothers Michelin who not only designed tyres but then thought up creative ways of marketing them, through publishing guides and maps, holding race meetings and touring events, and even making road signs. 'They were using creativity in the widest sense of the word to see that the smallish product had made actually inspired the world'.

Problem solving, in whatever field, is often a matter of perspective, of seeing the problem from the right angle. This is true of the artist and scientist as well as in more everyday circumstances. By altering your angle of vision or, as Dr Edward de Bono might put it, by contemplating a variety of 'information universes' you can often gain valuable insight.

4
Eisner on Creative Leadership

Christopher Knowlton

With childlike enthusiasm, Michael Eisner outlines a pet project over a bowl of frozen yogurt in the Walt Disney Studios commissary. He intends to combine a retail store selling Disney doodads with a restaurant serving healthy, low-cholesterol food. The cuisine, he gushes, will be 'fun, exciting, entertaining, and wonderful!' Then he admits that the concept doesn't tie in with Disney's other businesses and that most of his associates don't see much virtue in the plan. In a resigned voice he adds, 'I've been driving everybody crazy.'

Eisner is a CEO who is more hands-on than Mother Teresa. His chief duty at Disney is to lead creatively, to be a thinker, inventor, and cheerleader for new ideas – in founder Walt's own words, to be an Imagineer. Says Eisner, 'Every CEO has to spend an enormous amount of time shuffling papers. The question is, how much of your time can you leave free to think about ideas? To me the pursuit of ideas is the only thing that matters. You can always find capable people to do almost everything else.'

He uses a number of tactics to encourage, even induce, creativity in others. To come up with the layout for Euro Disneyland he called a meeting of a dozen of the world's most respected architects and had them brainstorm in a wildly creative session that became so heated, two of the architects began shoving each other and almost came to blows. 'I'll use meetings, company anniversaries, anything to create some kind of catalyst to get us all going,' says Eisner. He believes he must give his people free rein if he hopes to foster an entrepreneurial spirit within such a financially disciplined corporation.

As shepherd of the Disney flock, Eisner tries to promote a family-like camaraderie among his top managers. In late September he asked each division

Excerpt from 'Imagineer Eisner on Leadership' by Christopher Knowlton from *Fortune*, 4 December 1989. Copyright © 1989 The Time Inc. Magazine Company, by permission of the publisher.

head to perform a skit for the anniversary dinner celebrating the team's first five years at the company. The skits peppered Eisner and President Frank Wells with barbed jokes about their management styles and big pay-checks. At the end of this roast, instead of giving tit for tat, Eisner, Wells, Roy Disney, and their wives danced out onto the stage and performed a raucous kick line while booming out their spoof of 'We Are the World.'

Befitting a former English major at Denison University in Ohio who once had a passion for writing plays, Eisner thinks in terms of story lines. He applies that thinking to all the company's activities, whether he is building a $200 million hotel or a $10 million theme park attraction. 'We ask, "What is the story we want to tell when people walk into one of our new buildings? What are they going to feel? What is going to happen next? And how will it end?"' He is using movie storyboards to create a chronology and schedule for the construction of his Colorado vacation home.

The ideas that grab him – and often he can't remember if they are his own or embellishments of someone else's – are those that surprise him and tease his imagination. He disdains ideas that seem too familiar. On the other hand, for an idea to succeed at Disney it can't be so avant-garde that it ceases to be commercial. The *Making of Me* attraction in Epcot Center's new Wonders of Life pavilion, which features footage of the birth of a baby, had its genesis in Eisner's own emotionally charged experiences at the delivery of his three sons. His tastes are mainstream and all-American, combined with a gut instinct for what new flavor might be popular next.

Appropriately for the chief of America's leading peddler of wholesome entertainment, Eisner sees his family as his inspiration. He follows the tastes, interests, and activities of his children with the vigilance of a police-beat reporter. His wife, Jane, often screens his ideas. Says he: '98.5% of my ideas revolve around things that we are both involved in. With the stuff that is really on the edge, I will ask her if I'm crazy. Of course she usually thinks I am.'

5
Captains Outrageous

Morgan W. McCall Jr

Managers are the glue that keeps systems from flying apart, from running down, from spinning out of control. Because organizations expect them to maintain stability, many managers see creativity as a threat to control. What kind of creative leader can thrive in this environment?

Some obvious and clearly valuable traits come to mind: Creative leaders may be reflective, strategic, organized, and methodical. But they may also possess – and benefit greatly from – some characteristics not often thought of as virtues: An effective manager may be, at least at times, crafty, grouchy, dangerous, feisty, contrary, inconsistent, evangelical, discriminatory, and spineless.

The basic dilemma in the manager's role was illustrated by a study done in 1974 by two social scientists. Michael Cohen and James March studied the presidents of 42 universities, and found them to be reactive, parochial, conventional, and naïve. By reactive, Cohen and March meant that much of the presidents' work consisted of responding to the demands and concerns of other people. By parochial, they meant that the presidents were a homogeneous group with similar experiences and relatively similar views of the world. They were conventional because they had to live up to the expectations of others: Many people expect a university president to be traditional and conservative. Cohen and March found the presidents naïve in that, although they thought they had a great deal of control over events, they really had only modest control. Many of the biggest influences on universities – say, the birth rate 20 years ago – were far beyond the power of any college president to change.

Though lacking full control over events, business leaders, too, must guard

Excerpts from 'Captains Outrageous', by Morgan W. McCall Jr, from *Across the Board*, November 1989, The Conference Board Inc., by permission of the author.

against becoming too reactive and parochial. They need to generate – or stimulate others to generate – original, creative ideas, new ways of doing things, new processes and products. They have to seek out those ideas, collect them, evaluate them. Then, having selected a few, they must convince large numbers of people that the new ideas are worth investing in and implementing. In such an inherently contradictory setting, being crafty, grouchy, dangerous, and the like can have advantages.

Take craftiness. In a political environment, a good deal of cunning is necessary to create something or to help others create something. When colleagues disagree, good leaders are able to negotiate well and circumvent constraints, and they're very sensitive to tactical issues in the use of power.

Furthermore, managers have to be able to survive failures. In *Whatever It Takes*, a book on managerial decision-making, Robert Kaplan and I examined the potential consequences of making risky decisions. We found that a high-level manager is usually permitted one or two boners. If creative leaders are to survive, they must at times dissociate themselves from failures and hook up with successes. They may write and rewrite history. They may manipulate and use people. They have to be effective in a political world, and that means crafty.

If complacency is the enemy of creativity, grouchiness can be its spur. Some people believe that satisfied employees are more productive, but research has not demonstrated a consistent relationship between satisfaction and performance. In fact, though productive employees tend to be more satisfied, satisfied employees are not necessarily more productive.

If a happy employee is not always a productive one, it follows that creative leaders need not be warm and fuzzy. If they push hard for improving productivity, they may well be grouchy at times. And their subordinates may be expected to complain a lot about their grouchy boss.

Abraham Maslow, the well-known psychologist, once made the interesting suggestion that the number of complaints in an organization is relatively constant; no matter how good a company is to its employees, the number of complaints will remain about the same. Instead of focusing on the number of complaints, Maslow said, we should look at their nature. Complaints about safety, working conditions, or security are of a lower order than complaints about not getting enough praise, or threats to self-esteem. Karl Weick, an organizational psychologist, has even suggested that in an effective organization, a large proportion of complaints focus on the desire for perfection, truth, beauty, and other ideals. These, of course, are issues of the highest order that are seldom addressed when more immediate, physical problems exist.

So we may have grouches out there who are trying to jostle people out of complacency, to move them out to a higher level of complaint, if such a thing is possible. I suspect that creative leaders are, in fact, a bit grouchy, that they do prod people, and that they probably don't worry as much about the satisfaction of their people as their people would like.

It should come as no surprise that creative leaders can be dangerous: They tend to take risks first and ask questions later. From an organizational point of view, the unpredictability of this can be disturbing. New ideas represent a threat to organizational survival, and carrying them out may call for a commitment years into the future and cost millions of dollars.

At times, creative leaders must appear feisty because they deliberately generate conflict, not necessarily to increase competition, but to spark creative thinking. The real challenge, of course, is not only to generate conflict, but to make it useful; so creative leaders often try to control and direct it as well. Non-creative managers prefer to compromise, possibly the worst strategy. What remains is usually the least interesting part of each idea – the part that everyone agrees on.

Another reason that creative leaders may be feisty is that in an organization it is tough to get resources. They must battle for resources and for the power to implement their ideas. In addition, to protect people who have 'weird' ideas takes a lot of work – it takes fighting. Some of the managers we talked to, those who struck us as creative, loved to straighten out messes, get involved in conflicts, and make conflicts productive.

Some creative leaders out there are contrary in the sense that their behavior seems to defy common sense and even violate social norms. In their study of college presidents, Cohen and March found that creative leaders treat goals as hypotheses, intuition as reality, hypocrisy as transition, memory as an enemy, and experience as a theory.

Most people like to have a concrete goal, something to work toward. But those who are more creative apparently treat goals as mere hypotheses. They are not wedded to a particular point of view, and are ready to throw it over quickly when presented with convincing evidence against it.

Many people view 'intuitition' as an excuse for doing something that they can't justify on logical grounds. But creative leaders see their hunches as valid reasons to try something new. They will take a risk and see what happens; they learn from experience.

They also 'treat hypocrisy as transition.' Now there's a thought-provoking idea. Most of us try to achieve consistency between our attitudes and values on the one hand and our actions on the other. Cohen and March argue that when people behave in a manner that is different from what they believe, they are ripe for change.

Research suggests that behavior creates attitudes, not the reverse; what people do is an excellent predictor of what they will eventually believe. Creative leaders may encourage people to behave differently, and, in so doing, may get them to think differently and create new values.

They tend to treat memory as an enemy. Habit, folklore, and myth are as prevalent in organizations as anywhere else, so creative leaders are suspicious of them.

Finally, creative leaders may treat experience as a theory. The danger of learning from experience is that we come to believe only our own experience. Creativity requires suspension of belief, a willingness to test other possibilities.

Effective managers keep things highly integrated, with lots of rules, processes, and control. Creative leaders, however, recognize that over-integration can mean rigidity, and they struggle to understand what Peters and Waterman called 'loose–tight controls.' Their goal is to keep the system flexible. As we integrate organizations – make them more interdependent, more controlled – we drive out the possibility that the different parts can do things in new and better ways. Creative leaders fight the urge to integrate, to solidify, to make everything interdependent. They want to keep the pieces loose enough so that if they lose a few the organization will survive.

'Leaders are evangelists, not accountants,' the psychologist Karl Weick once said. By that he meant that creative leaders manipulate symbols and ideals for the rest of the organization. In that sense, they are evangelists, the spiritual leaders of the organization, preaching a cause, saying that it is all right to be creative, using a reward system to make people who do something bizarre but effective a symbol for the whole organization.

George Graen, who studies leadership, showed that leaders rarely treat all of their subordinates the same way. They have in-groups and out-groups, and are discriminatory in their relationships with individual subordinates.

When I suggest that creative leaders are discriminatory, I don't mean sex or race bias; they may or may not be prejudiced in those ways. What I mean is that creative leaders are adamant about competence. They recognize and use it, and discriminate with it. They protect the creative ones from the Philistines.

Perhaps the best example of this obsession with competence is a laboratory director who described himself as follows: 'At work, I'm a very difficult SOB, and that's not a character recommendation I'm particularly proud of. I feel guilty very often, but I'm so difficult that no one works for me unless they're good enough and tough enough. I explode all the time. I'm like the office plague: I snoop into everything and everyone wishes I'd stay out so I don't screw it up. But that lab is my baby.'

When living in a complex organizational environment, it helps to be a listener, an absorber, a monitor. In its broadest sense, being open to information means being able to set aside one's own preconceptions, biases, and rigidities to let other points of view enter. What's intriguing about leaders is that they can be spineless when appropriate, yet can act and persevere against criticism. They can turn their absorbing, monitoring functions around and suddenly begin to make things happen.

Many creative leaders would probably appear two-faced to an outsider. On the one hand they are playing the traditional organizational game so that they can stay in the system and continue to do something with it. On the other, they are moving ahead, gaining credits, and being generally outrageous.

The inherent complexity of the creative leader – the inconsistencies, paradox, and contradictions – are starkly portrayed in *American Caesar*, William Manchester's biography of General Douglas MacArthur: 'He was a great thundering paradox of a man, noble and ignoble, inspiring and outrageous, arrogant and shy, the best of men and the worst of men, the most protean, most ridiculous, and most sublime.'

Creative leaders get things done. In these times of change we need them desperately. While their virtues may not be obvious, all their apparent vices will not always be counterproductive. But one thing is sure . . . not everyone will always like them!

References

Kaplan, Robert and McCall, Morgan 1985: *Whatever It Takes*. Prentis-Hall.
Manchester, William 1978: *American Caesar*. Dell, New York.

Chapter 6
Crisis Leadership

Introduction

In his book *The Mask of Command* John Keegan asks whether military commanders should lead from the front and concludes: 'Sometimes a commander's proper place will be at headquarters and at his map table, where calm and seclusion accord him the opportunity to reflect on the information that intelligence brings him . . . Other times, when crisis presents itself, his place is at the front where he can see for himself, make direct and immediate judgements, watch them taking effect and reconsider his options as events change under his hand.'

The same applies to business. If there is one overriding message from the recent series of corporate 'disasters' – from the Exxon oil spillage in Alaska to the sinking of the British ferry, the *Herald of Free Enterprise* – it is that swift intervention from the top is essential, and the quality of leadership displayed will largely determine whether the crisis becomes terminal or is stopped in its tracks.

Failure to respond quickly and effectively to the sinking of the *Herald* proved fatal to Townsend Thoreson. As Simon Caulkin explains: 'The unforgettable public image of corporate unpreparedness was one factor in a cumulative destruction of credibility . . . Townsend Thoreson began 1987 as market leader. Today . . . the company no longer exists.'

The two contemporary crises considered in this chapter – the Perrier 'benzene scare' and the US government's opening responses to the invasion of Kuwait by Iraq – may be poles apart in context, but the actions taken by senior management in both cases are remarkably similar: a swift reaction, a clear strategy followed consistently, a well-thought-out communications strategy, proper delegation to a crisis management team, and, above all, the direct and visible involvement of the chief executive in shaping and articulating the response.

The most striking factor linking both accounts is the way in which the two organizations rose to the sudden demands made on them. Bush failed to anticipate the events leading up to the Gulf crisis just as Perrier's senior management clearly overlooked the possibility of contamination in their bottling processes. But once the crisis occurred, the ability of top teams to take and respond to tough decisions, the quality of communications, and the existence of tried and tested procedures to deal with unexpected trauma were all key factors in helping senior executives regain control over events. The fact that this culture and back-up were already in place is as much a reflection of good leadership as speed and quality of the response.

Neither crisis has been resolved. The long-term effects of Perrier's public confession of 'impurity' on both their market share and stock market value is still unclear; and although the outcome of the Gulf War was a decisive allied victory, America's interests in the Middle East may be worsened unless Saddam Hussein is removed from power and a lasting peace is brought to the whole region.

Nevertheless, the textbook responses of both organizations supports our earlier contention that the basics of good leadership are unaltered regardless of context (see chapter 2). The most effective business captains, like their military counterparts, are those that combine backroom reflection in periods of stability with active intervention when the situation demands it.

1
Dangerous Exposure

Simon Caulkin

'Eau Neau', chorused headline writers everywhere when minute quantities of benzene, a carcinogen, were found in bottles of Perrier, the world's best-selling mineral water, in early February 1990. For Perrier, a French dairy-products and beverages company whose table-waters and soft drinks account for half its $2.9 billion in annual sales, the discovery of the impurity was not a joking matter. Rather, it was the beginning of an episode which challenged every aspect of the company's operation: its management, its production processes, its relationship with consumers and its credibility with investors. Eventually, Perrier withdrew 160 million bottles of water from 110 national markets in the largest consumer-product recall ever. The cost of the crisis so far: $140 million, plus a 40 percent fall in market share. On February 14, Gustave Leven, Perrier's publicity-shy chairman – who later retired, at the age of 76 – emerged from his habitual silence to explain at a turbulent press conference in Paris that 'Even if it is madness, we decided to take Perrier off the market everywhere in the world. I don't want the least doubt, however small, to tarnish our product's image of quality and purity. That image, and the respect and confidence of our customers, have no price for me.'

Perrier's experience demonstrates why crisis management and investor relations have become two of the fastest-growing management disciplines. Even if, as analysts believe, the company itself was never at risk of takeover or collapse because 40 percent of its stock is held by Leven and his allies and because Perrier water is not its main profit-maker, the distinctive green Indian-club-shaped bottle is effectively its trademark and Perrier water is its flagship product. So, as well as risking its leading share of major growth markets for bottled water such as the US and the UK, the recall put the reputation of the

'Dangerous Exposure', by Simon Caulkin, from *Best of Business International*, Autumn 1990.

entire company at stake. The implications have not been lost on investors, and the subsequent performance of Perrier's shares on the Paris bourse reflects fears that the full costs of February's events have yet to be counted. Alain Kerfourn, an analyst at Sellier, a French stockbroker, applauds Perrier's prompt action to contain the crisis but cautions that 'The company's image has been dented. The affair has weighed heavily on the company's shares – and may continue to do so.'

Although it faces the expensive long-term task of re-establishing itself on the shelves of some of its major customers, Perrier survived. It has learnt the lesson that many of the companies that were takeover targets in the 1980s woke up to a mite too late: today, more than ever before, the investors, customers, governments and public at large who are the stakeholders in companies can make or break them. That is why communicating effectively with all these corporate audiences promises to become as critical a management task for every company as it was for Perrier during those fraught months of 1990. Says Jon White, director in charge of public-affairs courses at Cranfield School of Management, in England: 'It is essential to manage a company's important relationships and anticipate events or issues which may arise to disrupt them. What plans does the company need to make for this or that eventuality, in terms of key relationships? How is it going to explain itself to the media, its customers, the marketplace and government regulators?' Tim Bell, chairman of Lowe-Bell Communications, a UK specialist in financial and crisis communications, puts it more baldly: 'The question is simple,' he says. 'Can the company remain in control of its own destiny?'

Perrier's ordeal by water began when its subsidiary in the United States, the Perrier Group of America, learnt that some bottles in North Carolina had been found to contain small quantities of benzene. The company's own tests confirmed the impurity, and on February 9, Perrier announced the immediate withdrawal of 72 million bottles in the US, then rapidly extended the recall to include Canada. The Perrier bottling line in Vergèze, in the South of France, was shut down for investigation. Ronald Davis, Perrier's chief executive in America, affirmed that the health risks were minimal and that the company was taking drastic action to maintain the product's reputation. 'When you sell purity, you can't compromise,' he said later.

Meanwhile, in Europe, the price of Perrier's shares had tumbled 16 percent, and the company was struggling to prevent the crisis becoming a rout. Initial investigation, Perrier said, attributed the problem to human error in the cleaning of the equipment used for bottling water for the US. The spring which provides the water was not under suspicion. Armed with this reassurance, Perrier resumed bottling at the same time that it was authorizing all its subsidiaries to recall existing product if consumers or distributors demanded it. They did. Successively, Japan, Hong Kong, Switzerland, Denmark and West Germany followed America's lead in withdrawing Perrier from sale.

Problems occurred in particularly acute form in the UK market. Perrier had increased annual sales there from 12 million to 200 million bottles over the previous decade, and in 1989 supplies had run out during a long, hot summer. In 1990 Perrier was taking no chances, so, ironically, by February stocks were at record levels. The first that Perrier's chairman in the UK, Wenche Marshall Foster, knew of the problem in the US was when her daughter picked up a radio news bulletin as she returned from a party in the early hours of Sunday, February 11. Perrier (UK)'s four-person disaster team, consisting of the chairman, the marketing director, and their public-relations and advertising advisers, met that same morning to set in motion an established emergency plan. Events then went like this:

Monday, February 12   Perrier (UK) instructs an independent analyst to test bottles. It alerts the Ministry of Agriculture, which also begins tests. Perrier (UK)'s PR agency, Infoplan, puts into operation its 10-line emergency telephone switchboard, to which Perrier's London staff divert all crisis calls. More than 25,000 such calls will be handled over the next few weeks, 1,700 of them on the first day.

Wednesday, February 14   St. Valentine's Day. Independent analysis finds traces of benzene in some bottles. Marshall Foster decides on the immediate recall of 40 million bottles. She is asked to delay her statement to coincide with Gustave Leven's Paris press conference at 4 p.m., at which he announces the definitive cause of the contamination and the unconditional worldwide withdrawal of the product. Half-measures, says Leven, were not possible.

In the new version of events, the cause is still human error – but now in failing to replace dirty filters on the bottling line. This will cause a secondary wave of emotion in the US when it is established that (a) the problem has gone unnoticed for six months, and (b) instead of having been introduced by accident, the benzene occurs naturally and routinely has to be screened out. What other noxious elements have to be removed before Perrier can call itself pure? the press asks sarcastically.

In the UK, all major trade customers are contacted by telephone, fax or hand-delivered letter. Deciding against a press conference, Marshall Foster spends much of the night conducting 20 one-to-one interviews with leading journalists.

Tuesday, February 20   After sympathetic initial treatment by the UK media, Marshall Foster faces an unexpected new problem: what to do with 40 million unwanted bottles. The British glass industry is not equipped for large-scale recycling of green glass, and environmental-protection groups are quickly up in arms over the possibility that the bottles might be dumped rather than recycled. Meanwhile, they continue to pile up at four UK centres.

Monday, February 26   A solution. Marshall Foster announces that Perrier (UK) will take the environmentally preferable option: it has found two companies that, for a price, will crush and store the glass and recycle it over a year.

Wednesday, March 14   New stock begins to arrive in the UK. By the end of March, come-back advertising campaigns are in full swing in France, the US and the UK. Despite a bill of $32 million for the UK operation, Marshall Foster is optimistic: 'It will take time to get back our market, but I think in years to come we will go into the textbooks for the way we managed this crisis and came back.' In the US Ronald Davis adds that 'Ten years from now, a couple of days of confusion will be forgotten.'

It is still too soon to be sure. In both the US and the UK, the media latched on to a new angle to the story. When Perrier is produced, the media discovered, water and gas at the source are tapped separately from different parts of the same rock formation before being combined at the bottling line. What price, then, the 'naturally carbonated' description on the label? Perrier argued that it was entitled to use the term. Regulators in the US and a major retailer in the UK, J. Sainsbury, were not convinced, which delayed full reintroduction of the product. The total cost of the 15 parts per billion of benzene that triggered the crisis will not be known for months, perhaps years, to come.

Twenty years ago, Perrier's drama might never have occurred. Pressure on the single production source and the workers manning it was less fierce, environmental groups were less well mobilized, consumers less sensitive to health issues. Except for a few prescient examples, the notion of managing a company's reputation as a corporate asset barely existed. That seems a distant, primitive age. Since then, a combination of the technical complexity of products and processes, the long world stock-market boom with its feverish trade in corporate control, and the fragility of a dangerously loaded environment have made operating conditions for management ever more hazardous. At the same time, more efficient communication has formed a better-educated public increasingly inclined to call companies to account when things seem to be wrong. The result: more opportunities for disruptions to occur, greater cost to overcome them and more demanding audiences to satisfy that the right thing has been done. 'When things happen nowadays, they certainly *do* happen,' observes Cranfield's Jon White.

Perrier probably got the big decisions right. Crucially, the company adopted a worst-case scenario, acted fast and accepted the consequences. There was no hard evidence, after all, that the product was harmful. 'Perrier could have decided to keep quiet and correct the problem internally, in the hope that there wouldn't be any damage,' says White. 'In fact, it took what seems to be the full-honesty approach: *We have a problem, there's nothing to worry about, but we want to be sure – so as a company we'll take the loss.*' In retrospect, the size of that loss reinforces the impression of responsibility given by the company's behaviour.

The acceptance of responsibility is one reason for Perrier's generally sympathetic treatment by the media. It acted right. A second reason – and not the same thing at all – was that it was seen to act right.

In the age of instant communications, perception is reality and the media reaction can tip the balance between success and failure. That is why perception must be managed. Perrier did control it, at least in London – where Infoplan had drawn up its client's first crisis-management plan five years before. It had a trial run during the UK's Perrier drought in 1989. When the real crisis struck, by sticking undeviatingly to the agreed communications procedures, Perrier was able to remain in charge of events and retain a vital measure of initiative.

Crisis is a threat combined with acute time pressures. Thus, reasons the Dutch journalist Dieudonnée ten Berge in her book *The First 24 Hours*, 'The cardinal rule of crisis communications is to get the bad news out fast and to get it out completely. If you are aware that bad news is coming, you must stay in control of the information. If you don't feed journalists the information they need or you don't feed it swiftly enough, they will look for other, less reliable sources.'

Having done that, Perrier could address the special requirements of its different audiences: the need of consumers for guidance on refunds and the return of bottles, the need of the retail trade for information on supply, the need of government bodies and pressure groups for updates on environmental and health issues, and the need of the media for interviews and a continuous supply of information. Looking back, Infoplan's chairman, Daphne Barrett, agrees that the first 24 hours were critical and highlights the role of the emergency switchboard in the UK: 'Because we had the hot lines, we could set the tone with the media and expose the chairman for interviews later.

As the UK operation established itself as an effective source of information, it began to be seen as a point of contact for English-speaking journalists all over the world, and it logged inquiries from the United States, Scandinavia and even France, as well as from the UK.

Perrier did make mistakes. In its eagerness to say something – anything – the French management committed the common error of speaking before it was certain of the cause of the crisis, later having to retract and risk the 'continuing-history effect' described by ten Berge. 'Once you are wounded, the outcome is similar to the way sharks are attracted by the first drops of blood in the ocean – the media will not rest until they get the prey,' she observes. Even worse, in the US the story at one stage threatened to shift from the incident itself to the company's change of mind, with the implicit suggestion of a cover-up: the Watergate syndrome.

Secondly, incomprehension and doubt surrounded the surprising complexities of mineral-water production and bottling, emphasizing the need for detailed product information to be available to the media and other interested audiences. A British crisis-management expert, Michael Regester, notes that the early stage of an incident is often the hardest to deal with precisely because little real information is available. Whenever possible, he counsels, 'fill the void by issuing background information about the company and the installation involved, to demonstrate that you are willing to co-operate and communicate with the outside world. Doing so will establish you as the authoritative source of information about what has gone wrong.'

This technical inquest should not disguise the fundamental fact that Perrier's biggest mistake was needing to handle the crisis in the first place. Perrier lost money, and risked its market and reputation, as the result of avoidable error. The company's experience underscores the principle that crisis cure, whether on the stock market or on the floor of the factory, begins with crisis prevention. Once a crisis happens, the issue is damage limitation. For all the melding corporate spirit that a crisis can engender – Barrett speaks of a company being 'forged in the fire' – no company would choose to live its trauma a second time.

For some companies, there never will be a second time. These are the ones which discover that, in a crisis, there is no luxury of a management-learning curve. Instead, there can be just one brief glare of exposure that bares to the public gaze not only the organization's technical competence, but its heart and soul: and if they are found wanting, there may be no way back. Few onlookers will forget the televised torment of a beleaguered PR official of the UK Channel-ferry operator Townsend Thoresen on the night of March 6, 1987. *I don't know. These things don't happen,* was her helpless response to frantic callers demanding news of the *Herald of Free Enterprise*, which had capsized outside Zeebrugge harbour. Captured on prime-time television news, the words would stand as a cruel corporate epitaph. Manifestly ill-equipped to deal with either the disaster or its communications aftermath, the company never recovered from the effects of the tragedy, in which 190 people lost their lives. The unforgettable public image of corporate unpreparedness was one factor in a cumulative destruction of credibility which obliged the parent company, P&O – itself heavily criticized for lack of sensitivity – to paint out the Townsend Thoresen name on the side of its ships. Townsend Thoresen began 1987 as market leader. Today, although the court cases continue, the company no longer exists.

At least half of all crises are predictable, in nature if not in timing. Food companies will experience a poisoning scare, oil companies will face an oil spill or a drilling accident. But although managers know the risks, they are strangely loth to act. In the UK, suggests Daphne Barrett, no more than a quarter of companies have made preparations to handle a crisis. Even in the sensitive area of investor relations, where crisis can most often be seen coming and where the most interested parties happen to be the companies' owners, most fail to contain risks by keeping their stakeholders adequately informed.

After the explosion in mergers and acquisitions, no company can say that it has not been warned. Don't think that the impetus has died with junk finance and the slowing of the stock-market boom. The globalization of markets for capital and products, the tighter regulation of securities, the concentration of corporate ownership in fewer hands, the increasing sophistication of investors: all have made the marketing of the corporate brand to financial consumers as central to management as the marketing of the product to end-users. 'Investor relations has come out of the anteroom and into the boardroom,' declares Roddy Dewe, chairman of the Dewe Rogerson consultancy and a pioneer of the discipline in the UK. 'The PR person who does investor relations now sits alongside the lawyer and accountant as an adviser to the chief executive in any bid or initial public offering.'

At the extreme, imagine a venture in which the maintenance of credibility among investors is the single most important factor in determining the company's success or failure. This is the position of Eurotunnel, the Franco-British enterprise that is constructing an undersea link between the UK and France. For Eurotunnel, completing the enormous job of construction is just half the management task. Its technical competence is irrelevant if it cannot maintain government confidence that the multibillion-dollar project is viable, uphold the faith of investors and persuade banks to continue to provide its huge overdraft. Right now, this vast venture stands or falls by its investor relations.

Eurotunnel's high visibility and acute dependence on the providers of its funds make it a special case. Yet despite the lip-service of annual reports to shareholders, many managers ignore the reality that, when the chips are down, they are subject to the same facts of life. For Eurotunnel or any company, the ultimate arbiters of its future are its owners, not its managers. John Makinson, a former financial journalist who counsels companies in the UK on investor relations, notes that to many this thought is oddly unfamiliar. 'The graveyard of UK public companies', says Makinson, 'is littered with tombstones bearing the legend I IGNORED MY SHAREHOLDERS or, more often, I REMEMBERED MY SHAREHOLDERS TOO LATE.' One such belongs to Rowntree Mackintosh, a British confectioner that succumbed to a $4 billion takeover bid by Nestlé, the Swiss multinational, in 1988.

With annual sales of $22 billion and net profits of $1.1 billion, Nestlé was already the biggest food company in the world. Size was therefore on its side, as was initiative. But Nestlé also suffered from several disadvantages at the start of its campaign to win over investors in the City of London. It had not wanted to bid, and did so only to counter the opportunism of a fierce Swiss rival, Jacobs Suchard, which had bought 15 percent of Rowntree's shares in a raid on the London stock exchange. In the UK, Nestlé was seen as Swiss (foreign), invulnerable itself to takeover (unfair), and secretive (suspicious).

Rowntree, on the other hand, was a respected UK company with well-known brands in an industry dear to British hearts and stomachs. It had an excellent basket of brands – notably Smarties, Kit-Kat and Quality Street – and a good marketing name. It had a reputation as a caring employer. True, distribution of the company's products outside the UK was not good, and, in a licensing deal, it had effectively given away its franchise in the US. But Rowntree wanted to remain independent, and it surely had a platform from which to argue its case. Yet despite a potent ground swell of British economic nationalism which Rowntree sought to exploit, in the three-cornered fight that developed, Nestlé quickly won every argument. How?

By having a strategy and sticking to it, is the simple answer. A takeover bid may not be won on the first day, says Tony Carlisle, the managing director of Dewe Rogerson, Nestlé's PR adviser, but the commanding heights often are. Preparation is vital. Notes Carlisle: 'One of the very great dangers in mergers and acquisitions is that in the heat of the moment, you lose sight of strategy and pursue tactics and noise. What the people who really matter want to know is why you are interested in the company and how you will operate it afterwards. In Nestlé's case, the broad strategies and synergies were all identified in advance, and never altered.'

The core requirement, says Carlisle, was for Nestlé to do two things: make a sensible case to Rowntree's shareholders for their company's passing into Nestlé's control, and offer them an effective package. Undeniably, Nestlé won half the battle by appealing directly to shareholders' pockets. Before the battle the price of Rowntree's shares was 480p, or $7.68. Nestlé's opening bid was 890p a share, and it finally paid 1050p. In other words, the value that the Swiss put on Rowntree's brands was double the stock market's valuation under the existing management. That the bid was in cash helped. But Nestlé walked away with the communications medals.

Nestlé had considered the message it needed to put across to each of the audiences that could have a direct or indirect influence on the outcome of its bid for Rowntree. There was a persuasive financial message for investment analysts and the financial press, a reassuring message on competitiveness and reciprocity for political audiences both in the UK and elsewhere in the European Community, a message of professionalism and expansion for Rowntree's managers and employees, and a message of good citizenship for the public. During a two-month war of words, Nestlé's managers seemed to be unfailingly available, polite and reassuring to each audience in turn. Thus, Nestlé's managing director, Helmut Maucher, took time to point out that his company had 19 British-managed factories with 10,000 employees in the UK – where the company had been present since its founding in 1866. He spelt out plans for developing Rowntree's sales abroad, where the British company, Maucher observed, did not have 'the resources to compete effectively in increasingly competitive world markets'.

Most damagingly, it leaked out – but apparently not from the Swiss camp – that the year before Nestlé had warned Rowntree that it was vulnerable, and had proposed a friendly association rather than an outright purchase. Rowntree had turned the offer down. (It transpired later that Suchard, likewise in vain, had also originally offered collaboration.)

Rowntree had little to offer against Nestlé's persuasion. Unlike the Swiss company's top management, Rowntree's chairman, Kenneth Dixon, was rarely available to speak to the press, and this itself drew critical comment. On the issues of commercial strategy posed by Nestlé – the distribution synergies evident between the two companies and the previous offer of long-term co-operation – Dixon had very little to say. This reinforced the impression that there was not only no communications strategy, but no strategy to communicate. Short of hard fact, the press began to speculate about boardroom dissension. Rowntree was reduced to complaining about short-termism among institutional investors (which was hardly likely to win their friendship), objecting in principle to foreign ownership and trying to capitalize on the goodwill attached to its familiar brands. Not only was most of this mere noise, irrelevant to the key audiences which would decide the outcome; the immediate leap to a political rather than commercial defence was a very dangerous tactic. As Tony Carlisle points out, if that gambit fails, 'there's nothing left to fall back on'.

One of Rowntree's more dismal ploys was to hire a brass band to play outside the Houses of Parliament, to drum up political support. But perhaps the most telling witness to the company's lack of realism came when union officials among its own employees urged Dixon to meet the rival Swiss bidders and arrange a friendly merger with the one that offered the best prospects. 'The Rowntree board does not seem to have digested the inevitable outcome of this auction,' noted the *Sunday Times*, underlining the view that Rowntree's management should have been concentrating on obtaining the best deal for its workforce and shareholders, rather than fighting a forlorn rear-guard action against its Swiss invaders. Observing the irrelevance of Rowntree's appeals to economic nationalism in a modern world of regional and global consumer markets, one commentator summed up: 'The problem is that Rowntree has conducted an old-style defence in a new-style battle.'

The essence of investor relations is the matching of investors' expectations with a company's real prospects. Or, as Neil Ryder and Michael Regester put it in their book *Investor Relations*, 'the maintenance of demand for the company's securities at a price which accurately reflects its true potential among investors whose investment horizons match those of the company'. Note that this is not the same as maintaining the highest possible share price. The once high-flying UK advertising-agency group Saatchi & Saatchi has learnt painfully, on the way down, that an unrealistically high share price can ultimately be almost as damaging to a company's reputation as Rowntree's unrealistically low share price proved to be.

'It was never clear', says Carlisle, 'that Rowntree had looked on the marketing of its capital as an adjunct and a support for the manufacturing of confectionery.' Rowntree compounded this strategic failure by ignoring Nestlé's explicit warning that it could be a takeover target, passing up the chance to form an amicable alliance and neglecting to put other defences in place. Says Regester: 'Rowntree thought that everyone who bought Smarties would be a supporter. But investors had never been told about the long-term future of the brands, until along came Nestlé saying exactly what would happen. Rowntree deserved to go under.'

Investor relations and crisis management share important characteristics. Often – as Rowntree and Perrier found – they fuse into the same thing. Crucially, they both involve prevention as much as cure, the long term as much as the short term, and strategic as well as tactical considerations. A company with a carefully constructed reputation has an important corporate resource to draw on in a time of need so that, as Jon White puts it, 'You don't suddenly have to build relationships with the media or your investors if things go badly wrong: you've been working with them over time. If you've been honest and open with them before, they'll give you a breathing space. If you haven't, they won't.'

Organizations are no longer the self-contained, self-sufficient entities that they once appeared to be. In an increasingly transparent world, they can be seen as elements in a network of relationships, bound into society by links not only with business partners but also – directly or indirectly – with governments, interest groups, the media, and local, national and international communities. So here's the choice. Tell these audiences nothing. Or turn the company inside out, sensitize its management to the wide world outside and address its audiences for what they are: from now on, strategic players in the company's future success or failure.

Appendix: Crisis Checklist

All companies face crisis, but those that are prepared for the worst have a better chance of survival. To devise a strategy for managing crisis, start by asking these questions:

- *What are the most obvious areas of risk?* Some, like fraud and computer failure, are common to all companies; others, such as toxic spillage or consumer boycott, may be specific to an industry or even to a company.
- *Do you have procedures for preventing these risks becoming a crisis?* They should be agreed, written and rehearsed, like a fire-drill.
- *Have you got a crisis-management team ready to go into action?* To set one up after a crisis has occurred will simply be too late.
- *When a crisis happens, who will be affected and how?* Identify your audiences: workforce, customers, suppliers, investors, media, government and regulatory bodies, the public at large.

- *How will you communicate with them?*   Each audience has a different concern that requires a different message. Have you prepared information on the company's products, processes and finances? How will you handle a flood of media interest and telephone calls?
- *Do you have a communications strategy?*   In a crisis, assume the worst (half-measures may increase the damage); take the initiative; establish the company as the authoritative source of information; and stick to agreed procedures.
- *Do you routinely communicate with your audiences?*   When you need their goodwill, it'll help if you were already treating them as partners in the enterprise.
- *Still think it takes too much time, manpower and money to prepare for a hypothetical crisis?*   Then what value do you put on survival?

2
George Bush as Crisis Manager

Ann Reilly Dowd

React swiftly. Be decisive. Take charge, then don't be afraid to delegate. Set a clear strategy and stick to it. Communicate, communicate, communicate.

Those are the kinds of guidelines consultants lay down when they advise corporate executives on how to handle a crisis. And they define the way George Bush has responded to one of the toughest management challenges in recent times. As the confrontation with Iraq moves into what may be a prolonged second act, the President could yet make mistakes. But his performance to date has been, in the words of former Defense Secretary and CIA director James Schlesinger, 'splendid.'

Sure, Bush has been lucky. The end of the Cold War gave him maneuvering room to orchestrate an unprecedented international response to Iraqi aggression. Saddam Hussein made that task easier by first attacking another Arab state and then calling for popular uprisings in the region, actions likely to send some nervous Arab leaders running into the American tent. But like any skillful manager, Bush has made the most of his breaks.

Experience helps. After three decades as an oilman, UN Ambassador, CIA director, and Vice President, Bush has a more sophisticated grasp of the Middle East – and closer ties to its leaders – than any previous US President. Says David Sadd, an Arab-American investment banker who met with Bush six days after the invasion: 'He was even aware of a border dispute between Saudi Arabia and Yemen that was giving the Saudis pause about moving troops from the Yemen border to the Kuwaiti border. And he had already spoken to Yemen's President Saleh about it. He's very well versed.'

In this crisis, as in so many others, the response during the first 24 hours was crucial. Says former US diplomat Robert Hormats, now vice chairman of

'George Bush as Crisis Manager', by Ann Reilly Dowd, from *Fortune*, September 1990 © 1990 The Time Inc. Magazine Company, by permission of the publisher.

Goldman Sachs International: 'The fact that Bush moved so quickly to freeze Iraqi and Kuwaiti assets, block trade, and rally the west immediately to do the same was the key to foiling the great bank robbery of 1990.'

Through the early days, Bush focused his prodigious energy – another useful quality in a crunch – on rallying support among foreign leaders for his decisions. At the height of the crisis, he was averaging a telephone call an hour, often rising very early in the morning to straddle time zones. 'I'm going to have a very big phone bill,' he joked to reporters.

During this initial round of high-level salesmanship, the President targeted his message to his audience. With Arab leaders he played on legitimate fears that Saddam could not be trusted, sharing US satellite intelligence data showing a threatening buildup of Iraqi forces along the Saudi border. He also offered US military support. In a gesture aimed at reassuring King Fahd, he used a national security loophole to waive the Metzenbaum amendment, legislation that normally limits US deliveries of jets to the Saudis.

With European leaders and Japan's Prime Minister Toshiki Kaifu, Bush focused on the devastating economic costs of an Iraqi invasion of Saudi Arabia. To reassure Turkish President Ozal, whose country is in the front line, he sent Secretary of State James Baker to Ankara with promises of US military backing. The common goal in all these contacts was swiftly to weave the tightest possible net around Iraq.

Confident of the ability and loyalty of his top lieutenants, Bush also delegated effectively. When the crisis broke, Jim Baker, who was already with Soviet Foreign Minister Eduard Shevardnadze in Siberia, helped persuade his counterpart to cut off arms sales to the Soviets' longtime client and then flew to Moscow to issue a historic joint condemnation of Iraq's aggression. Later, Assistant Secretary of State Richard Solomon broke away for a less public visit to Beijing, where he helped get the Chinese, key members of the Security Council, to back a UN embargo. Other aides flew to Riyadh, Alexandria, Rabat, and Damascus to build support for sending US troops to Saudi Arabia. Throughout, Bush kept in close touch by phone.

At first Bush focused on diplomatic and economic sanctions. But two days after the invasion, with reports that Saddam had rounded up American oil workers and was massing troops along the Saudi border, the former Navy pilot gathered his advisers and gave them 24 hours to come up with military options. The next day at Camp David, after further consultation, he made the crucial decision to commit American troops to the Middle East.

According to aides, Bush didn't agonize once the necessity for this tough call became apparent. Says one: 'It's his style to ask lots of questions and work his way through complicated issues. On this one, he was very calm, measured. There was no hand-wringing.'

Once he decided to send troops, however, Bush recognized the need to lay out his goals and rally the American public. On Tuesday, August 7, having received a formal invitation from the Saudis to send help, Bush told his aides to start working on a speech. That night, Middle East expert Richard Haass and National Security Adviser Brent Scowcroft discussed a draft with Bush in the White House residence. The President made some suggestions, and Haass and Scowcroft stayed in the West Wing to refine the piece until around 2.30 a.m. The next morning Bush fiddled with the prose until minutes before his performance at 9 a.m. Afterward, aides applauded. Then the President went off to more meetings, phone calls, a press conference, and – well, why not? – some tennis.

Maintaining what reporters have dubbed the 'aerobic presidency,' despite the threat of war, is how this hyperactive 66-year-old copes with the stress of long, demanding days. Confident that no one can question who's running the show, Bush makes no apologies for his occasional breaks. 'I am determined that life goes on,' he told reporters. So when Saddam issued his call for a 'holy war,' Bush responded by doffing his tie and hitting the links – as well as the waves, tennis courts, and jogging paths – of Kennebunkport, Maine.

Throughout the crisis the President has so far managed to maintain balance and perspective – no easy feat. The morning after Saddam's troops swept south into Kuwait City, Bush squeezed in a congratulatory call to the parents of Timothy Swanson, a just-released Peace Corps worker who had been held captive in the Philippines. Later he visited Republican National Committee Chairman Lee Atwater, who is still fighting a brain tumor, and wrote an apology to a reporter whom he felt he had mistreated at a press briefing.

While he concentrates on countering Saddam, Bush has also been moving to defuse a related crisis – the threat of recession. Says a top White House adviser: 'Even before we presented any formal analysis, Bush grasped the implications for the budget, monetary policy, and energy policy. He knew the Iraqi invasion would slow growth and complicate policy making.'

The Bush team's biggest worry is that rising inflation, brought on by higher oil prices, will give Federal Reserve Board Chairman Alan Greenspan an even stronger reason not to lower interest rates. Soon after the invasion, Treasury Secretary Nicholas Brady and chief economist Michael Boskin visited the Fed chief to convey, in great detail and no uncertain terms, their desire for easier money. Meanwhile, to get a budget deal the President has recently launched a vocal attack on congressional Democrats in hopes of pushing them back to the negotiating table. Nothing would give Bush a freer hand in dealing with his longstanding problems back home than a swift and successful end to the dangerous showdown he faces in the Persian Gulf.

Chapter 7
Leadership, Ethics and the Environment

Introduction

One of the most important attributes of post-entrepreneurial leaders identified by Rosabeth Moss Kanter in chapter 3 was the ability to operate 'with the highest ethical standards'. The complexity of cross-national business relationships, involving collaborative partnerships, joint ventures, and other stakeholder alliances, requires a high degree of trust and 'a mutual understanding that each party to the relationship will behave ethically, taking the needs, interests, and concerns of all others into account'.

Moss Kanter's premise is borne out by the views of front-line practitioners. Recent surveys on the qualities required by chief executives in the future (see article 5) show that ethical standards come high on the list. Respondents to a Korn Ferry report on leadership in the twenty-first century (see chapter 13, article 2) expected their chief executive to be 'above reproach' and recognized that 'the CEO's ethical standards are indispensable to internal and external credibility.' A canvass of business leaders' views by *Fortune* magazine showed the same concern.

This would not have been the case ten years ago. That ethics is now a serious boardroom issue reflects not only the higher demands of a global market but a change in society's attitude to business practice in the wake of stock exchange scandals, growing concern over the environment, and the increasing number of industrial accidents involving the public.

Previously, ethics was discussed in the wider context of equal opportunities and corporate social policy. In the 1960s and 1970s Top 500 companies were encouraged to indulge in 'good works' of the kind pioneered by Joseph Rowntree in the late nineteenth century. This includes charitable giving, secondment of senior personnel to community projects, arts sponsorship, and the support of educational initiatives. Generous tax concessions on both sides of the Atlantic made it easy for organizations to show their benevolent intentions cost-effectively. America's long-standing lead in corporate benevolence was taken up in Europe through bodies like the UK's Per Cent Club, whose members pledge to donate 1 per cent of their annual profits to charity and community aid.

The debate over ethics that surfaced in the late 1980s is wholly different from this form of corporate paternalism. It centres on the personal behaviour of the individual and not just the image of the organization. It implies not only that relationships between organizations are governed by implicit or explicit codes of behaviour but that the constituents of businesses extend beyond the customer and shareholder to encompass all those who work for the organization, local communities and, in effect, everyone directly affected by the organization's activities.

Any attempt to quantify business ethics runs into immediate problems. The first is whether the exercise is self-defeating. In chapter 5, Morgan McCall points out that creative leaders (and thus effective leaders) are often inconsistent, devious, and two-faced. His implication – that the direction of commerce has little to do with social morality – is shared by F. G. Bailey in the introduction to his book *Humbuggery and Manipulation: The Art of Leadership*. After considering the role of leaders in society, Bailey concludes: 'leaders are often villains, and . . . it is very difficult to be an effective leader and at the same time a good person . . . one does better to look dispassionately at the institution [of leadership] itself and admit that it has no place for those who practice nothing but the right and the good.'

Bailey's cynicism is rebutted by Sir Geoffrey Chandler in a letter written to the British newspaper *The Independent* in the wake of the Guinness scandal. Sir Geoffrey stresses the dangers of separating business morality and individual morality. 'The trouble is that too many business leaders proclaim simplistically that they are in business "to make money,"' he says. 'So too are burglars and brothel keepers . . . You cannot tack on ethics or "social responsibility" to business behaviour like an unrelated musical cadenza. They must be inherent in all that a business does.'

Yet the borderline between what constitutes ethical and unethical behaviour is often little more than a hair's breadth. It varies from one society and one company to another, 'making it difficult to regulate through any universal social or legal code. The British Member of Parliament Frank Field, in a letter replying to Sir Geoffrey, sees ethics as an extension of Christian doctrine. 'No industrial society seeking agreed means of regulating all forms of human behaviour can operate . . . unless some basic beliefs are not only agreed but regularly reaffirmed', he concludes. What he fails to add is that for beliefs to be agreed they have to be shared. In global markets led by business executives from different cultural backgrounds and spiritual persuasions, this is hardly easy to achieve. A survey of 300 US and European companies conducted in 1987 (article 5) shows how ambiguous ethical considerations become once they are extended beyond narrow social boundaries.

Most of the respondents agreed that sexual harassment, inappropriate corporate gifts, and environmental protection were 'ethical' issues; but only a small majority included the security of company records, workplace safety, product safety standards, disinvestment, advertising content, 'whistle-blowing', and the way in which companies won government contracts.

This ambiguity is also illustrated in 'Ethics in the Trenches'. A panel of 56 business practitioners and commentators respond to four common ethical dilemmas – accepting bribes in developing countries, trading in South Africa, offering corporate freebies, and disposing of toxic waste. Although there is universal condemnation of the acceptance of luxury trips in return for favourable advertising and bribes in Turkey, respondents are noticeably more divided in the attitudes to South African trade and the disposal of harmful chemicals.

However a company chooses to define ethical bench-marks, the behaviour and leadership of senior managers is likely to be critical. The attitude of the chief executive and top directors will determine whether ethics feature strongly in the organization's mission, operations, and culture.

Upholding animal rights, protecting the environment, and helping the community are not just the publicly expressed personal priorities of Anita Roddick, chief executive and founder of the Body Shop: they are built into the company's recruitment policy, training schemes, and relationship with suppliers. The Body Shop's human resource strategy aims to attract people with the right values and builds ethical business practices into every part of the company's activities.

Anita Roddick was held up by Tom Peters as an example of how chief executives can 'green and clean' their companies in a presentation to an international conference on 'The Greening of European Business', held in Munich in October 1990. Peters argues that, far from being a threat, environmental concern provides businesses with the opportunity to achieve 'massive' cost savings and breakthroughs in process and technology improvements. Employee involvement is essential, he argues, and the role of chief executives is to 'talk up' the issue and get greening and environmental concern 'in the air'.

This approach is mirrored in the way business schools tackle ethics and the management of environmental resources in ethical education. Pioneering centres such as Harvard, Georgetown, Manchester, and King's College, London weave ethical issues into every functional discipline rather than hiving it off into a separate department. A similar approach is taken by the new crop of centres devoted specifically to environmental issues, including those based at London Business School and INSEAD. The article by Clare Lorenz explores these methods in greater detail.

1
Understanding Leadership: A Question of Virtue

F. G. Bailey

This essay is about how leaders control followers, not about what they do to the world with the power that followers give them. Of course statesmanship – doing things to the world – is important. But for my purposes, it matters only insofar as success (or failure) as a statesman affects the capacity to be a politician – to control followers.

I once spent a year studying politicians. This was in the Indian state of Orissa and most of my subjects were members or would-be members of the Legislative Assembly. Independence had been gained only twelve years before, and there was a very strong sense that this was a new age, there was much to be done, and the lead in doing it must come from the politicians. They – at least, the elite among them – presented themselves not as politicians (as I have just defined that word) but as statesmen, as enlightened and virtuous leaders, giving guidance so that the many problems posed by the new environment would be solved; so that, to use a phrase commonly heard at that time, 'the Plan could be implemented.' Some also saw themselves, to borrow Philip Selznick's phrase (1957:28), as experts 'in the promotion and protection of values.' They were guardians of an Indian heritage; they were the creators of new traditions on which would be founded a better society. Above all, their task was to do good, to be virtuous; they would have missed the irony in Christ's message: 'and they that exercise authority . . . are called benefactors' (Luke 22:25).

Since then I have read biographies and autobiographies of leaders in various countries and at various times. I have also studied small men in local politics in a backward rural area in Orissa and others, somewhat more powerful, in a north Italian province. More recently I have observed leadership in formal

From F. G. Bailey, *Humbuggery and Manipulation: The Art of Leadership*. Copyright © 1988 by Cornell University, by permission of Cornell University Press.

organizations, especially in universities in several parts of the English-speaking world. Finally, as is the case with everyone else, my daily life is awash with propaganda and commentary about our present leaders. In time and place, there is much diversity; in what I see as the trap in which leaders are caught, it is all very much the same.

For a leader every resource has a constraint; and every constraint is potentially a resource. There is little that is easy and straightforward, and the leader who really lets things drift along (as distinct from the one who only appears to do so, affecting nonchalance) has forfeited the title. The human condition is very complicated and very messy. To cope with it, one must simplify, and the simplifications should be neat and logical. But in fact they are very often neither, first because they may be arrived at under pressure, when there is urgent need to take action; and second because they are often the product not of disinterested logical thought but of a compromise between interests. So the simplifications turn out to be messy and complicated like the reality from which they sprang.

Leadership, in one of its aspects, is the art of cutting into this chaos and imposing a simplified definition on the situation, that is, making people act as if the simplified picture were the reality. This cannot be done in any honest, open, reasoned, dispassionate, and scientific fashion. The leader must be partisan. He must use rhetoric. He must be ruthless, be ready to subvert values while appearing to support them, and be clever enough to move the discourse up to a level where opportunism can be successfully hidden behind a screen of sermonizing about the eternal verities. Leadership is a form of cultivating ignorance, of stopping doubts and stifling questions.

Most leaders would reject this assertion about the requirements of their art. If their opponents do happen to behave in that way, it is not because such behavior is inevitable (they themselves never do such things) but because those particular persons lack virtue. Montgomery of Alamein (1961:104) writes that successful leadership requires 'conviction, transparent honesty and sincerity, tenacity, political courage.' Elsewhere (1961:153) he writes admiringly of Sir James Grigg: 'There are two faults in others which he will never forgive – one is insincerity and deceit of any kind, and included in this is, of course, intrigue; the other is any inclination to immorality of any sort.' Those, one is invited to suppose, are the qualities necessary to command devotion from subordinates. With such vigorous defensive smoke, there has to be a fire somewhere.

Indeed there is. It is astonishing how much patent falsehood there is in public life. This is an expression not of regret that people are dishonest but of surprise that politicians appear to get away with dishonesty so easily and so often. Is there not something strange about a culture such as ours which condemns lies but at the same time condones them with such categories as 'campaign promises' and 'mere rhetoric'?

No less striking is the ready cynicism of the politicans themselves. A man who has divorced and remarried, who is widely believed to be quite uninterested in his children and grandchildren, and who rarely goes to church on Sundays presents himself and is apparently accepted as an exemplar of Christian family living. The same man lends his benignant television presence to the opening of the Special Olympics, having first done his utmost to cut financial aid for the handicapped. Another candidate (this is the 1984 election in the United States) issues a false report that her rival is to be indicted for the misuse of public money and does so on the eve of the election when there is no opportunity for a rebuttal. Of course she may not have known that the report was false. My third example, however, is one of quite explicitly cynical dishonesty. According to a story in the *New York Times*, the vice-president's press secretary, when questioned about the accuracy of something said by George Bush in a television debate, remarked that 80 million people heard the debate, and if journalists correctly report him as lying, 'So what? Maybe two hundred people read it or two thousand or twenty thousand.'

A newspaper that carried this story (*Washington Post*, reported in *Manchester Guardian Weekly*, October 28, 1984) stigmatized this remark not only as 'an open and unembarrassed expression of cynicism' but also as 'contempt' for the electorate. A lie is sometimes a sign of disrespect. Presumably also the contempt was for the public's implied lack of critical intelligence. But more than contempt is involved. Behind all three examples is an unspoken conviction that whatever is said about standards of truthfulness, accuracy, and decency, such standards do not really apply in politics. Although they must certainly be taken into account in the formulation of strategies, these standards are not seen as ethical imperatives.

The disquiet one feels when leaders play tricks with the truth is not prompted only by ethical feelings. It also concerns rationality. Why do people not take the trouble to find out if what they are being told is true? Why do leaders assume that no one will bother to search out the truth? Whatever happened to the scientific attitude? Does no one care about objective truth? The answer will be that the essence of leadership is a capacity to go beyond rationality, to operate by intuition, and to obliterate a scientific search for objective fact (except in certain enclaves of the operation) and at the same time to convince the followers that the leader knows what he is doing. If the educated mind is the mind that entertains doubt and asks for evidence, then the art of leadership is (among other things) also the art of diseducation.

A significant part of the audience that looks in on leaders is not at all critical and is ready to believe anything, or so it appears from the stuff that is laid out for its edification. I will quote a few vivid and extreme examples of diseducation.

Here is Nkrumah brusquely closing the mouths of potential critics: 'All Africans know that I represent Africa and that I speak in her name. Therefore no Africans can have an opinion that differs from mine. If one of them acts against my better judgment, he must be doing it because he wants to fight because he has been paid' (Lacouture 1970:256). Hitler was not quite so crass: 'With us the Führer and the ideas are one and the same, and every party comrade has to do what the Führer commands, for he embodies the idea and he alone knows its ultimate goal' (Fest 1975:279). Commentary by a third party can be utterly unbelievable: 'All operations of the Great Fatherland War were planned by Comrade Stalin and executed under his guidance. There was not a single operation in the working out of which he did not participate' (quoted in Leithes 1977:104). It can also be poetic:

> All rivers flow into the sea and every Red heart turns towards the sun. Oh Chairman Mao, Chairman Mao, the mountains are tall, but not as tall as the blue sky. Rivers are deep but not as deep as the ocean. Lamps are bright, but not as bright as the sun and moon. Your kindness is taller than the sky, deeper than the ocean, and brighter than the sun and moon. It is possible to count the stars in the highest heavens, but it is impossible to count your contributions to mankind. (Urban 1971:139
>
> Mai Hsien-teh was unconscious or semi-conscious for quite a long time after being admitted to hospital. People anxiously awaited his regaining consciousness, the nurse tested his reactions by showing him a pictorial magazine. As she turned the pages she noticed his lips quivering. His eyes were concentrated on a picture of Chairman Mao. With great effort he managed to raise his left hand, which had remained useless since his admission to hospital, and with trembling fingers he touched the picture. He suddenly exclaimed 'Chairman Mao!' It was the first time since he had been in hospital that he had spoken so clearly. The image of the great Chairman Mao and his brilliant thought roused Mai Hsien-teh from his stupor. He became fully conscious and able to think clearly. (Urban 1971:44)
>
> Poor Herdsman Chao Tzu-ching eventually survived following a successful operation on his brain which was injured during an accident at his work site. Who enabled him to bring back his life from threatening death? It was our great leader Chairman Mao, the red sun in our hearts, the invincible thought of Mao Tse-tung, and Chairman Mao's revolutionary line. These brought him back to life again and gave those who fought for his life the inexhaustible strength and infinite wisdom needed to make such a miracle. (Urban 1971:157)

How such claims could be made, let alone apparently accepted, defeats my imagination. The most charitable interpretation of such statements, if we are too refined to call them plain lies, is to say that they are metaphorical and expressive, telling us how the writers or speakers feel rather than about actual attributes or accomplishments.

No doubt there is comfort to be got from the idea that by and large leaders are virtuous and intelligent and can work miracles. I want to bring more into the light the opposite case: that leaders are often villains, and that it is very difficult to be an effective leader and at the same time a good person. Leaders are not saints, not even the 'saintly' ones such as Gandhi; and when some story comes out that makes the halo fall down around the leader's neck, instead of talking about clay feet and the frailty of human beings, one does better to look dispassionately at the institution itself and admit that it has no place for those who practice nothing but the right and the good. 'If we had done for ourselves the things that we are doing for Italy, we should be great rascals,' said Cavour, getting some way toward the truth (Trevelyan 1948:23).

Leadership is the art of controlling followers. It is presented as an art because to practice it successfully, one needs to have a talent. That is what is meant when a leader's intuitions are praised as evidence of 'divine guidance' or condemned as 'the devil's own luck.' In more mundane terms a leader must have 'leadership quality,' and leadership is too complicated or too subtle an activity to be reduced entirely to rules and procedures that could be taught in a classroom. That is what leaders say, and, notwithstanding their vested interest in having that idea believed, they are correct (given the present state of our analytical capacities). At least they are correct if one is envisaging a definitive and exhaustive theory of leadership. But, short of that logical perfection, there are certainly known (and communicable) regularities in the way leaders behave in their efforts to control their followers, certain calculations that they make, and these calculations can be stated as rules or the collections of rules that constitute strategies.

What are the calculations about? Strategies available to a leader and appropriate for the task at hand depend on several variables (including, of course, the task itself and the actions taken by opponents, real or invented): first, the psychological disposition of the followers; second, values and beliefs and third, institutions. These three variables constitute resources for a leader: they are also constraints on his actions. He can use them, but they also limit what he can do. Strategies, in other words, are like lunches; a payment is always required. The leader can, however, entertain the possibility that psychological, cultural, or institutional items that are unsuitable may be altered so as to give him better control over his followers. That too will have a cost.

Strategies vary not only according to the disposition of followers but also according to their relationship with the leader. One of the few people to whom General Montgomery gave ungrudging admiration was his superior officer, chief of the Imperial General Staff, Alan Brooke. The latter, it seems, was the perfect staff officer, commanding the loyalty and respect of all who served under him. But, Montgomery thought, he would not have done so well as a commander in the field because he 'wouldn't have got himself across to the soldiers in the right way' (1961:124). Two categories are evident: first, the soldiers in the field; second, the staff. The same distinction applies in all kinds of leadership. For the statesman who controls a nation there is the mass who vote for him, serve in his armies, pay their taxes, and know their leader only as an image; second, there is an entourage, the 'official family' (as it was called in Franklin Roosevelt's time), who help him formulate and implement policies and who know him face to face.

Each category requires its own techniques for control. For the mass, although there is certainly a threshold of material satisfaction and another threshold of repressive action, the principal device for control is not bread, circuses, and police but one or another form of charisma. I have cheapened that much-used term to include media-induced charm; and if in his actual person the leader has all the magnetism of a withered carrot, that is of no significance if he can afford to pay advertising experts to put him across to the mass as sprightly and inspired. Historians, one suspects, are also given to writing in the charisma for anyone who has made a mark, and only such defiantly drab leaders as Clement Attlee and General Franco seem to be proof against puffery. That is, after all, a conclusion to be deduced from the generally accepted notion that a leader's charisma is to be recognized only in the beliefs and actions of his followers. Members of the entourage, on the other hand, are close enough to see the carrot's lack of grace. Furthermore, they could not do their job unless they dispensed with make-believe and worked hard to deal with reality. For this and other reasons they cannot be controlled by an image of the leader's miracle-working capacities. Other techniques are needed, and some of them, surprisingly, require the leader to create disorder and uncertainty among them. Only in rare instances does a leader remain a hero for his entourage; for the mass he is nothing if he lacks heroic attributes.

Leaders do have one quality in heroic measure. It is not virtue. Rather it is a readiness to transcend (that is, to defy or ignore or distort), the rules that constrain lesser people in their reasoning and in their ethical standards. The quality, in a word, is audacity (which is a combination of boldness, impudence, and shamelessness).

References

Fest, Joachim C. 1975: *Hitler*. New York: Random House.
Lacouture, Jean 1970: *The Demigods: Charismatic Leadership in the Third World*. New York: Knopf.
Leithes, Nathan 1977: *Psychopolitical Analysis: Selected Writings of Nathan Leithes*, ed. Elizabeth Wirth Marvick. New York: Sage.
Montgomery of Alamein 1961: *The Path to Leadership*. London: Collins.
Selznick, Philip 1957: *Leadership in Administration: A Sociological Interpretation*. New York: Harper & Row.
Trevelyan, G. M. 1948: *Garibaldi and the Making of Modern Italy*. London: Longmans.
Urban, George (ed.) 1971: *The Miracles of Chairman Mao: A Compendium of Devotional Literature 1966–1970*. London, Stacey.

2
The Principle of the Thing

Clare Lorenz

The wave of scandals that has broken upon the business world in the past few years has dismayed managers just as much as it has fascinated members of the general public, and often served to confirm some of their worst suspicions. Instances of fraud, bribery, insider dealing and other financial shenanigans have left many thousands of people poorer than they should be, and rocked the business establishment on both sides of the Atlantic. To the pressures that these events have imposed on managements can be added others of an environmental nature. It's little wonder that many companies are increasingly concerned that if they don't lay down – very clearly – how they and their employees should behave, then they themselves could be among the prime losers – of both reputation and wealth.

In the worst case they could find themselves in court. The sinking of the *Herald of Free Enterprise*, with terrible loss of life, raised the question of corporate responsibility for safety for the first time in a British court of law, and left P&O facing a corporate manslaughter charge. In the US, pollution of Alaskan waters by Exxon also landed employees in court, and heaped universal condemnation upon the oil company. The implications for any business which makes, processes or transports a product are all too obvious.

The debate about 'ethical' standards which has been launched by such incidents is likely to be longer lasting than the corporate and social responsibility programmes which preoccupied European business in the 1970s. This time round companies are treating the subject in a more hard-nosed manner. They have more insistent cause for worry. They are also seeking an economic – as well as a moral – justification for their investment of time and

'The Principle of the Thing', by Clare Lorenz, *Management Today*, September 1990, by permission of Management Publications Ltd, London.

energy. Yet their approaches to the problem are often lacking both in direction and in effective follow-through. A few companies have been attempting to formulate codes of behaviour. Others are rethinking their value and mission statements to take account of all 'stakeholders'. Most are in a state of some confusion as to how to proceed. Nor are Europe's business schools much help, since their thinking on the subject is frequently over-academic.

The picture is very different in the US. There the subject has been under continuous research for 20 years. Over 600 books on business ethics have been published in the US, compared to only 60 in Europe. The level of business interest can be judged from the statement of the chairman of IBM that corporate responsibility is 'central to business competitiveness'. (Incidentally, the expression 'business ethics', which came into vogue in the 1980s, is now used almost interchangeably with 'corporate responsibility', although an individual's behaviour within a corporation is rarely regarded as part of the latter.) But right across the board there is a degree of public awareness about business ethics which is seldom matched in Europe.

The subject first surfaced in US universities in the late 1960s, in the context of social responsibility programmes. The following two decades were the time of equal opportunities legislation and environmental concerns, and interest in the subject never quite died away. It was often hidden, however, among human resource or legal framework courses. Alternatively it was offered as an 'elective', an optional course, and therefore ignored by many students and frequently disregarded as being of doubtful importance by teachers.

In the late 1980s business ethics received a shot in the arm when John Shad, ex-chairman of the Securities and Exchange Commission, personally donated $20 million to Harvard Business School, on the strict understanding that MBA students would be instructed in ethical business practice during their two-year stay. In 1989 Harvard responded to this financial windfall by introducing a compulsory crash course in ethics into the initial three months of the programme.

Thomas Piper, the finance professor – significantly – who was made responsible for developing ethics teaching, reported on the students' reaction in the December 1989 issue of the HBS *Bulletin*: 'Our MBA students watch us very carefully during the first few months of the programme, gauging whether or not we feel that these issues are central to management and to management education. If our students are ever open to suggestion from us it is certainly in the first few months of the first year. So, if these issues are not legitimized and addressed effectively during this period, our students may well conclude – unfortunately and inaccurately – that ethics and values are not relevant to the programme, or worse yet, to business. This danger is especially severe in a school whose teaching technology is closely related to practice.'

It's worth remarking, in view of America's long-standing interest in the subject, that some European companies have been among the pioneers in setting scrupulous standards of business behaviour. Rowntree and Pilkington are two notable British examples. However, the type of paternalism for which these companies were famous in the early years of this century is no longer appropriate in its closing decades.

In recent years new kinds of 'good works' have evolved in the UK, which allow companies to demonstrate their benevolent intentions: charitable giving through the Charities Aid Foundation or the Per Cent Club (perhaps surprisingly this has never yet been challenged by shareholders); involvement in one or more of the 400 Business in the Community schemes; secondment of senior personnel to community projects or to educational initiatives such as the Education 2000 trust. But none of this is enough to guarantee a company's good relations with the rest of the world. It is, indeed, rather typical of the European approach to business ethics: treating the matter as peripheral, as a 'soft' addition to the normal affairs of business.

So what should companies do to prove their devotion to high standards and protect themselves against accusing fingers? At its simplest, an ethical code sets out to provide a framework which will allow an organization, and all the individuals within it, to deal with issues which have a moral dimension. It encourages people to feel that they can do as they would be done by when they walk through the office door. It calls on companies to listen, and to react positively to what they hear within and around them.

Before going much further than that, and in order to appreciate what distinguishes business ethics from personal morality, it is obviously wise to look across the Atlantic. Writing last year in California State University's *Business Insights*, Michael Hoffman, professor of philosophy and director of the centre for business ethics at Bentley College, Massachusetts, argues that business ethics arose out of the ashes of unfulfilling twentieth-century philosophies. 'Our present century has been weaned on relativism [denial of ethical absolutes], on pragmatism [the belief that something is right if it works], on positivism [equating knowledge with observable experience] and on behaviourism [interpreting human actions as totally determined and predictable]. The unifying thread of all this is the reduction of everything considered true and meaningful to material reality or physical experience . . . science and materialism have flourished and ethics and values have been relegated to matters of emotion, attitude and feeling.

'Such an ideology permits no . . . significant development of the non-material, non-measurable aspects of our lives, such as freedom, morality and divinity. However, there is something about the human spirit which resists this sterile picture and cries out for a different ideology which will preserve our humanity and provide our lives with a value system.'

Hoffman pleads for recognition of what he regards as non-quantifiable input. The role of the employee within a company and the ethical demands put upon it as a corporate entity – these are matters of business ethics. The stakeholder concept is central to any discussion of the subject. A stakeholder is, of course, any person or group with a special interest in a company: not only shareholders but employees, customers, suppliers, unions, the local community in which it operates.

Further out lie more interested parties, all of which exert pressures on the company – society's expectations, legal requirements, government influence. These pressures are increasing all the time: the growth of multinational groups, and of international trade generally, imposes extra obligations upon businesses. All the same, there are limitations, as Professor Jack Mahoney, director of the King's College Business Ethics Centre, London, has pointed out – in a week when one company was asked to sponsor a nearby hospital ward. Business cannot be expected to shoulder all society's needs; government has responsibilities too.

The existence of the King's College centre is one of the many signs that Europeans are at last getting to grips with business ethics as a matter for serious study. Courses on the subject have also been introduced at London Business School and at Strathclyde University Business School, Glasgow. The 1989 academic year saw the start of several programmes at Continental universities. Most of these European courses are 'elective'. On the other hand, many of them were launched (as at LBS where professor of finance Andrew Likierman played a major role in establishing the course) in response to requests from the student population.

The academic nexus is growing stronger. The second conference of the European Business Ethics Network, held in Barcelona in October 1989, attracted twice as many people as the first meeting two years earlier, most of them from the European and American academic worlds. Now European academics are becoming concerned that, while they may be providing in some measure for students, they are not getting through to practising managers. However, business participation in the Barcelona conference was also up. And the Network has signalled its intention of seeking greater business involvement by electing a director of Barclays Bank to its governing body.

One UK institution which considers business ethics a difficult subject to sell to industry was nevertheless happy to undertake a study of company codes of behaviour. There have been previous studies of this phenomenon since European companies began formulating corporate codes around the mid-1980s. In a 1988 survey of 600 European companies, Professor Bodo Schlegelmilch of the European Management School, Swansea, found that 41% of respondents confessed to a written code. Germany recorded the highest score at 51%, France the lowest at 30%. The UK came midway between. Two years earlier, in 1986, a similar survey by the American Centre for Business Ethics suggested that 75% of US companies operated a written code.

More revealing than the bald comparison, however, the Swansea study showed that many European companies are strangely coy about admitting to a code. Schlegelmilch observed that numbers of the more open companies had American parents, so were quite likely to have caught the ethical bug from the US.

It goes without saying that possession of a code of conduct does not necessarily mean that a company behaves 'ethically' – or vice versa. But it does indicate a willingness to face up to the issue of corporate responsibility. More than one European company has expressed a fear that, by publishing its code, it could be exposing itself to attack. On the other hand, a secretive attitude inevitably implies that the company could have something to lose by being open.

Two British researchers, Sheena Carmichael and John Drummond of Strathclyde Business School (authors of *Good Business: A Guide to Corporate Responsibility and Business Ethics*, Business Books, 1989), believe strongly that open communications are a vital defence against disasters – far more vital than a slick PR agency. They also argue that managements should benefit by paying attention to ethical concerns. 'Ethics are an excellent tool for predicting social issues that will affect organizations in the coming years,' they maintain. 'Many of the social changes which have affected companies in the last couple of decades have been preceded by intense ethical discussion . . . which was virtually ignored by business.'

These social changes include demands for black and ethnic minority rights, environmental pressures, the growing power of women in the workforce, health and safety. If business fails to take account of such factors, it will find the law brought to bear. Carmichael and Drummond further contend that companies which stay one step ahead of the law gain economically over those which have to drag themselves into line. The point has obviously been taken by numbers of companies fearful of being bumped into unplanned action.

More controversial is Carmichael and Drummond's contention that 'a weak [corporate] culture contains the seeds of ethical success. Among many examples to the contrary, the behaviour of the pharmaceutical house Johnson & Johnson in the Tylenol affair stands out. Johnson, one of America's best known strong culture organizations, was able to overcome the lacing of Tylenol with arsenic by openly admitting the problem, which it then dealt with in an efficient and coherent fashion. The company's excellent public image remained intact.

Cultures, like codes, come in different styles but one clearly influences the other. Kirk Hansen, a former Stanford teacher who has set up a fund to award 'Nobel prizes' to companies able to show ethical change for the better, points out that change only comes about through leadership from the top. This might earn a nomination for BP, whose code was directed and issued by its recently retired chairman, Sir Peter Walters. BP's 'Policy on Business Conduct and Code of Business Ethics', published in 1988, repeatedly reminds employees that they must operate inside both the local legal framework *and* the code: the company is well aware of the dangers attached to bribery.

The extent to which BP's code actually influences individual conduct – or prevents the spillages to which the oil industry is so prone – may never be clear. As to the latter threat, the company has initiated talks with competitors in places where they have installations in close proximity, such as Alaska, the aim being to reach agreement on joint safety measures. This may fall some way short of academic proposals that international industries should agree on worldwide codes, but it certainly indicates progress.

The call for agreements between multinationals has been sounded with particular force by Professor Richard T. de George, one of America's most respected teachers of business ethics. Even so, like others who have studied the subject over many years, de George is sceptical whether a lot of existing codes really mean a great deal. There must also be some doubt about those that have been handed down from on high, as at BP, and which are not based on agreement at all levels.

The fact is that it is usually middle managers who are the first to notice that all is not well, yet they are seldom free to take remedial action. Whistle blowers tend to fare badly at the hands of their employers. An employee of Guardian Royal Exchange was dismissed after revealing that the company had avoided giving accurate figures to the Inland Revenue. In the US, Roger Boisjoly, an expert on gasket seals, pointed out to his employer that NASA's Challenger shuttle had a potential problem. He was downgraded for his trouble, and eventually left the company. The astronauts died.

3
Business Ethics after Guinness

Geoffrey Chandler

Sir: The comment in your leading article (28 August) that the Guinness trial is a 'victory for the whole system by which the City of London is now regulated' has, I suspect, only dubious validity. A later sentence

> The new system's danger is that whatever the law does not explicitly forbid will be considered tolerable

points to a far more fundamental truth.

If corporate behaviour is to be based primarily on a framework of external regulation rather than on a clear internal perception of the purpose of a company and the duties of the managers who serve, then we will divorce business morality from individual morality and encourage the belief that law and regulation constitute the whole, not the minimum, guide to practice.

The trouble is that too many business leaders proclaim simplistically that they are in business 'to make money'. So too are burglars and brothel keepers. It is therefore small wonder that these activities may be confused in the minds of those who make the common assumption that idealism and business are incompatible, and that we see many of our most talented young deterred from entering this fundamentally important activity.

This perception is encouraged by a company law which gives almost exclusive primacy to the interests of shareholders, which are too often interpreted as lying in a short-term share price rather than in the enrichment of the human and technical capability vital to long-term corporate prosperity.

There is now in this country an embryonic business-ethics business. It is wholly to be encouraged, since, with the commitment of business and academe,

Letter from Sir Geoffrey Chandler published in the UK national newspaper *The Independent*, 5 September 1990, by permission of the author.

it could enrich thinking and practice as it has in the United States, But it is no substitute for individual corporate action.

You cannot tack on ethics or 'social responsibility' to business behaviour like an unrelated musical cadenza. They must be inherent in all that a business does. And until business people articulate clearly that their prime function is to serve their customers by the provision of products or services, and that profit is a condition of survival and, in a competitive world, an indicator of social utility; and until they spell out to their various constituents or 'stakeholders' – employees, customers and community, as well as shareholders – what principles guide their conduct, then they will, despite many shining individual examples, remain collectively suspect.

Today business is being asked to undertake a wide range of responsibilities – in education and the community in general – conventionally regarded as external to its central activities. That it should play its part as a corporate citizen is absolutely right, but what it does should be dictated by a coherent philosophy which will both contain the pressures and persuasions brought to bear by politicians for their own pet projects and also ensure that these activities are no more vulnerable to business fluctuations than are shareholders' interests. They need moreover to be part of a philosophy which embraces the whole of the business.

If the Guinness affair is to be any good for us it will only be if it leads to boardrooms thinking about the purpose, practice and principles of their own businesses, not about the construction of further external safeguards.

Yours faithfully,
GEOFFREY CHANDLER
London, SE10
2 September

4
Christianity as the Basis for Business Ethics

Frank Field

Sir: On 5 September you printed Sir Geoffrey Chandler's important letter on the lack of an agreed set of business ethics. Writing in the wake of the Guinness affair Sir Geoffrey comments:

> If corporate behaviour is to be based primarily on a framework of external regulation rather than on a clear internal perception of the purpose of a company and the duties of the managers who serve it, then we will divorce business morality from individual morality and encourage the belief that law and regulation constitute the whole, not the minimum, guide to practice.

Later in his letter Sir Geoffrey again makes the valid point on the impossibility of letting businesses go about their own affairs and then including social responsibility or business ethics as a last item on a board-meeting agenda.

Sir Geoffrey concludes his letter by commenting that what businesses do should be influenced by a 'coherent philosophy' but he is silent on the basis of this consistent philosophy.

This is not a new problem. Although Christian belief amongst some intellectuals in the last century was replaced by doubt, these great Victorian agnostics believed that all people of goodwill wished to maintain a framework of Christian ethics, governing both our individual and public actions. They thought it would be possible to retain Christian ethics while putting to one side, or even rejecting Christian doctrine.

For a time the agnostic lobby appeared to be successful although now, with hindsight, the record looks rather different. For a considerable period of time commonly shared Christian ethics survived on what can be described as an ever

Letter from Frank Field, Member of the British House of Commons in reply to Sir Geoffrey Chandler, published in *The Independent* on 10 September 1990. Reprinted by permission of the author.

diminishing bank deposit of Christian belief. We are now in a position where the basis of belief on which the ethics were constructed has all but disappeared.

At one time opponents of Christianity were confident that an alternative source of civic morality could be taught through the schools. That theory has not proved successful. Neither has the belief that the urge to do good is so deep rooted that we do not require a commonly agreed morality to control private and corporate activity. That view is increasingly in tatters.

A third option is now being tried. Political parties have moved beyond common and statute law to attempt a new form of institutional business regulation. As most of the new fortunes have sprung from speculation no one can be surprised that the political debate has centred on regulating the City. The present system is, no doubt, imperfect and will be improved step by step in the light of experience. But how else can we, in the immediate future, begin to build a consensus to govern the corporate sector than by this approach?

A longer term option is however still available and this offers the churches an enormous opportunity. We can now see that those over-confident Victorian agnostics were wrong in their stance that it is possible to raid the Christian hive, carry off the honey of Christian ethics and yet not be prepared to feed the bees through the winter. Similarly, no industrial society seeking agreed means of regulating all forms of human behaviour can operate in the long run unless some basic beliefs are not only agreed but regularly reaffirmed.

Yours faithfully,
FRANK FIELD
MP for Birkenhead
(Lab)
House of Commons
London, SW1
7 September

5
Defining Corporate Ethics

Ronald E. Berenbeim

US and European CEOs and senior managers view corporate ethics as a subject to be dealt with at three levels, each more specific than the last: (1) the corporate mission, (2) constituency relations and (3) policies and practices.

The most easily recognized and universally applicable category is the *corporate mission*. Executives interviewed say that the enterprise in which they are engaged, and the products or services that they market, ought to serve an inherently ethical purpose. They believe that a company's primary ethical responsibilities are defined by the nature of its corporate objectives. Thus, a pharmaceutical concern will see its objectives as serving ethical purposes – promoting better health and saving lives. Food companies see their ethical mission as improving nutritional standards, while maintaining price levels that their poorest customers can afford.

Corporate managers speak of *constituency relations* in formulating their company's ethical standards. This effort usually entails statements of corporate responsibility to any or all of the following: employees, local communities, customers, suppliers, shareholders, home-country and foreign governments, and in some cases, the general public. The majority of the corporate codes of conduct examined describe the company's commitment to these groups, rather than prescribe ethical conduct for specific situations.

The former Chairman of a large Japanese company summarizes this view of constituency relations: 'Our responsibility is not only to our stockholders, but to our clients, our employees and their families, our local community residents, and indeed all of society at large. Our profit comes about through our effort to promote the prosperity of the community as a whole.'

'Defining Corporate Ethics', by Ronald E. Berenbeim. Conference Board Report 900, 1987.

There are significant differences of opinion in the role that ethics ought to play at the third level – in evaluating *policies and practices*. Ethics, as the Vice President of Public Affairs of a Swiss multinational notes, can be 'a key that opens all doors,' the guiding principle behind every decision. But there is no widespread agreement among business leaders that this should always be the case. Some executives argue that ethical considerations are inappropriate for many management decisions and policies because, under certain circumstances, public commitments to ethical principles can give way to business and administrative priorities; or the potential connection between ethical commitments and broad social policies can make the company a target for pressure groups.

For example, while assigning ethics a place in business deliberations, an aerospace executive voices reservations: 'The broad definition of ethics may permit the media, special interest groups, and the government to increase pressure on business to address areas that they are currently not equipped to handle. Companies should be concerned with business ethics in dealing with employees, suppliers and customers. They should not be involved in social, political or moral issues such as abortion, South Africa, sexual preference, and other personal moral issues.'

Other executives are uneasy about the potential conflict between corporate ethics programs and management roles. The Director of a corporate ethics program commented that, among high level executives, 'Discussion of the subject generates discomfort. The word suggests a mass confessional. It raises issues that are thought to be more relevant to philosophical discussions. People wonder what sort of new demands an ethics program will make on them. Will they be expected to act as judge, detective, guru, teacher, grand inquisitor, or guiding light to the employees that they supervise?' These roles and the tasks that go with them all imply new, difficult and uncomfortable supervisory requirements for executives.

Current Issues in Corporate Ethics: The View from the Top

A corporation develops its ethical standards in response to the issues it confronts in pursuit of its business objectives. Viewed in this light, a profile of a company's ethical concerns sheds light on how it reconciles management and business priorities with public policy questions. The Conference Board asked CEOs of major companies which of 27 highly visible issues – in their personal opinion – also involve ethical considerations for business, how important each issue will be for business over the next five years, and which problems require further attention in their own companies.

Table 1 Ethical categories of current corporate issues

Equity	Rights	Honesty	Exercise of corporate power
Executive Salaries	Corporate Due Process	Employee Conflicts of Interest	Political Action Committees
Comparable Worth	Employee Health Screening	Security of Company Records	Workplace Safety
Product Pricing	Employee Privacy	Inappropriate Gifts	Product Safety
	Sexual Harassment	Unauthorized Payment to Foreign Officials	Environmental Issues
	Affirmative Action Equal Employment Opportunity	Advertising Content	Disinvestment
	Shareholder Interests	Government Contract Issues	Corporate Contributions
	Employment at Will	Financial and Cash Management Procedures	Social Issues Raised by Religious Organizations
	Whistle Blowing	Conflicts between the Corporation's Ethical System and Accepted Business Practices in Foreign Countries	Plant/Facility Closures and Downsizing

RONALD E. BERENBEIM 171

These 27 problems generally fall into four basic (and somewhat overlapping) categories (table 1).

1 *Equity* is generally used to mean basic fairness, apart from any established legal or human right. For example, executive salary scales are sometimes the subject of controversy when critics say that it is inequitable for certain employees to receive annually thirty or forty times more than the lowest paid worker in the firm.[1] Some arguments for comparable worth are also rooted in an ethical appeal to greater fairness in determining the material rewards for work.

Equity issues are not limited to salary and pay considerations, however. They can also arise in the pricing discretion companies are permitted under applicable law. As is the case with compensation practices, ethical questions can be raised with regard to either results or the means used to attain them.

2 *Rights* are treatments to which a person has a just claim. The origin of the claim may be legislation, legal precedent or community notions of dignity. Modern views of rights are generally protective in nature. They seek to defend individual autonomy from encroachment by powerful institutions or the community at large.

Societies accept the concept of rights to varying degrees. The Japanese, for example, rely heavily on their traditional concept of reciprocal obligation, which mandates discussion, conciliation, and adjustment of differences instead of an appeal to abstract concepts of justification. Rather than filing lawsuits, Japanese who allege discrimination usually form a 'victims group' that negotiates with company representatives. The resulting accommodation does not set a precedent, but it establishes a basis for an ongoing dialogue.[2]

Corporate due process, protection for 'whistle-blowers' and shareholders, and erosion of the employment-at-will doctrine are examples of 'rights' issues that arise in the corporate context. Equal employment opportunity began as an equity problem, but has achieved the status of a 'right' to some degree in the United States.

Dignity is a subcategory of rights, where protection is rooted in the community's sense of elemental decency rather than regulated by specific constitutional, judicial or legislative mandates. For example, employee privacy and sexual harassment are issues subject to increasing legislative and judicial activity, but the legislative and judicial systems have yet to find an absolute formula for extending these rights to employees.

One of the more difficult dignity issues is employee health screening, because it can involve a conflict of ethical principles. Some see it as invading employee privacy in the interest of social responsibility. The CEO of a US manufacturing company raised this issue when he said: 'The right to screen, particularly for drug abuse, is essential to maintaining a safe, competitive work place. To the extent that there is inherent conflict between screening and employee privacy rights, the issue should be resolved in favor of safety and competitiveness.'

3   *Honesty* in corporate ethics relates to the integrity and truthfulness of a company's actions or policies. Issues of honesty arise both in connection with corporate behavior and with employees acting under the company's nominal supervision. Misleading advertising, questionable financial and cash management procedures, 'gifts' for foreign officials, and waste or fraud in the performance of government contracts are examples of corporate behavior that may be labeled dishonest.

Other honesty issues arise in connection with the company's responsibility to supervise those who act in its name, and the reciprocal obligation of employees to observe company and community standards in their business dealings. The misappropriation of proprietary information for personal enrichment, or to help a competitor, is an abuse of trust. Acceptance of inappropriate gifts can corrupt the purchasing process. Conflicts of interest between employee activities outside the workplace and company interests can create situations of divided loyalty. In all of these circumstances it is the employee who has an ethical responsibility, but a company cannot escape the consequences of lack of proper supervision.

4   *Exercise of corporate power.* Corporations recognize a responsibility to contribute to community enterprises that are consistent with their mission and with their commitments to the various constituencies they serve. Corporate financial and executive assistance and efforts to generate public support for programs are believed to be an important element of the company's ethical profile. Decisions of US companies to support policy positions though political action committees are recognized as a responsible exercise of corporate power; but depending on the individual or policy supported, these activities may raise ethical questions.

Business organizations also acknowledge the ethical component of adhering to standards for workplace, product and environmental safety. Workplace concerns appear to have given rise to a second generation of issues. For example, the CEO of a Canadian bank noted that there was some concern (which he believed to be unfounded) regarding 'the longer term effects of CRT screens on physical or psychological health.' A group of Swiss executives anticipate pressures in their company to restrict smoking to certain areas.

Beyond generally accepted responsibilities, more controversial positions advocated by religious or political groups may raise ethical questions that have an impact on corporate policy and practices. In recent years, companies have faced external pressures to disinvest from South Africa. The business community has been divided on this issue. Some companies have withdrawn from South Africa; but in interviews, one CEO and several top managers argued that the ethical position is to remain in South Africa, because they believe foreign investment is a critical lever for social change in that country.

Is This an Ethical Issue for Business?

Each of the 27 survey issues in table 1 was identified by a substantial number of respondents as posing ethical issues for business, but some topics were cited more often than others. The range among individual problems assessed as 'ethical' varies from 37 to 91 per cent (see table 2). At the top of the list, with

Table 2 Is this an ethical issue for business? (300 companies worldwide)

Issue	%
Widespread agreement (80% or more say yes)	
Employee conflicts of interest	91
Inappropriate gifts to corporate personnel	91
Sexual harassment	91
Unauthorized payments	85
Affirmative action	84
Employee privacy	84
Environmental issues	82
Moderate level of agreement (50–79% say yes)	
Employee health screening	79
Conflicts between company's ethics and foreign business practices	77
Security of company records	76
Workplace safety	76
Advertising content	74
Product safety standards	74
Corporate contributions	68
Shareholder interests	68
Corporate due process	65
Whistle-blowing	63
Employment at will	62
Disinvestment	59
Government contract issues	59
Financial and cash management procedures	55
Plant/facility closures and downsizing	55
Political action committees	55
No consensus (less than 50% say yes)	
Social issues raised by religious organizations	47
Comparable worth	43
Product pricing	42
Executive salaries	37

over 90 per cent agreeing that the subject raised ethical questions for business, are *employee conflicts of interest, inappropriate gifts to corporate personnel* and *sexual harassment*. At the other end of the spectrum are the three equity issues – *comparable worth* (43 per cent), *product pricing* (42 per cent) and *executive salaries* (37 per cent).

US and non-US companies were in substantial accord as to the ethical content of all but four issues – affirmative action, sexual harassment and whistle-blowing were regarded as more important by US corporations; plant closures were of greater concern to the non-US participants. Although 76 per cent of the companies studied have a code of ethics, there was little difference between the responses of companies with and without codes.

Which Issues will be Most Important over the Next Five Years?

CEOs who identified an issue as ethical in nature were also asked how serious they thought the problem would be for business in the next five years. *Environmental issues, product and workplace safety, employee health screening, security of company records* and *shareholder interests* were cited by more than two-thirds of these participants as critical or serious concerns for business in the next five years (see table 3). Companies with official codes of ethics regarded employee conflicts of interest and unauthorized payments to foreign governmental or business officials with greater concern.

US and non-US companies agreed substantially about the potential impact on business of 21 of the 27 issues. US concern was considerably higher with regard to five of the six remaining subjects: sexual harassment, political action committees, social issues raised by religious organizations, employment at will and employee health screening. Non-US companies viewed only one problem with greater seriousness than did their US counterparts – comparable worth.

Which Issues Require Further Attention?

Only eight issues were regarded by at least 10 per cent of the participants as requiring additional attention (figure 1). *Employee health screening* was mentioned most often: nearly half of the participants (122) said that their companies need to develop policies in this area, more than twice the number of respondents for the next most urgent issue, security of company records.

US and non-US companies have significant differences in outlook on health screening. Nearly 60 per cent of the US respondents thought their companies ought to pay more attention to it, while slightly less than one-third of the non-US companies held that view. The issue is also regarded more seriously by US

Table 3   How important will this issue be for business in the next five years?

Issue	No of respondents who said issue gives rise to ethical considerations for business	% of this group who think issue will be 'critical' or 'serious'
Very important (70% or more checked 'critical' or 'serious')		
Environmental issues	221	86
Product safety	192	78
Employee health screening	230	77
Security of company records	216	73
Shareholder interests	194	70
Workplace safety	214	70
Moderately important (40–69 % checked 'critical' or 'serious')		
Affirmative action/EEOC	250	66
Disinvestment	137	64
Plant/facility closures and downsizing	149	64
Sexual harassment	179	59
Financial and cash management procedures	157	56
Corporate due process	188	51
Employee privacy	244	50
Governmental contract issues	132	49
Unauthorized payments	218	47
Conflicts between company's ethics and foreign business practices	193	46
Employee conflicts of interest	267	44
Product pricing	115	44
Political action committees	152	43
Comparable worth	121	41
Low level of concern (less than 40% checked 'critical' or 'serious')		
Advertising content	200	37
Inappropriate gifts to corporate personnel	260	36
Executive salaries	107	32
Corporate contributions	202	31
Whistle-blowing	174	29
Social issues raised by religious organiza- tions	119	21

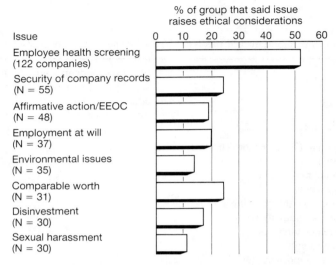

Issues checked by fewer than 30 companies are not listed

Figure 1   Ethical issues that require additional attention

companies – over 80 per cent of them think it is a critical or serious problem, while only 37 per cent of the non-US firms see it in this light. Other differences between US and non-US companies include the greater concern of US respondents with employment-at-will issues and the emphasis of non-US participants on product safety.

Notes

1   For a good example of opinion for and against high executive salaries and bonuses, see Robert C. Solomon and Kristine Hanson, *It's Good Business* (Harper & Row, 1985), p. 205.
2   Allen R. Janger and Ronald E. Berenbeim, *External Challenges to Management Decisions: A Growing International Business Problem*. The Conference Board, 1981, Report no. 808, pp. 48–68.

6
Ethics in the Trenches

John Delaney and Donna Sockell

That Hermes was the Greek god of commerce and thieves is historical evidence that business behavior and ethical behavior are not always synonymous. Recent scandals, including misconduct on Wall Street and the savings and loan debacle, confirm that businesses and business people must daily confront the double life of Hermes. The dark side of business behavior looms large today because competition has reduced margins, forcing companies to cut costs and possibly corners to meet financial projections.

Wrongdoing has inspired a dialogue about ethical behavior in business and a heightened consciousness about how businesses behave. Executives are regularly urged to pledge allegiance to 'ethical conduct' – it is argued that ethical firms are spared the public backlash and reduced profits that accompany the disclosure of immoral behavior.

But what is ethical behavior? Countless articles, speeches, and surveys testify to the attempts made to answer that question. Indeed, just last year, we surveyed more than 1,000 graduates of Columbia Business School classes of 1953–1987, asking them whether they had faced ethical dilemmas during their business careers. More than four-fifths reported they had. On average, they confronted four dilemmas (defined as actions or decisions that did not feel right) in 1988 alone. More than 100 of the respondents described in detail ethical dilemmas that they had faced.

We chose seven of these dilemmas as the basis for a new survey of ethics. What makes our new survey distinctive is that it's rooted in the real world as much as could be. Specific scenarios are described in the exact words of the executives who experienced them. We asked 247 people – all prominent in

'Ethics in the Trenches', by John Delaney and Donna Sockell, from *Across the Board*, October 1990, by permission of The Conference Board, New York.

business, academia, and public life – to deal with each situation as helpfully as possible. From this group we developed a panel of 56, who each gave advice for two or three scenarios. In total, we received about 127 separate answers.

How should the responses be interpreted and what can be learned from them? This is a difficult question to answer. Do conflicting responses to a scenario indicate, for instance, that ethical expertise is non-existent? Certainly not. Just as stockbrokers might give conflicting recommendations after examining a financial scenario, so might ethicists give inconsistent advice for an ethical scenario. Moreover, responses might differ because of inferences about additional aspects of the dilemmas; stated simply, scenarios did not include all of the information that our panelists would have taken into account in a real-life situation.

This month's scenarios concern the ethical issues involved with operating a business abroad, economic relations with South African companies, corporate junkets, and the disposal of hazardous waste.

The 'price' of doing business outside the United States. It is often said that business ethics differ inside and outside of the United States. In some places it is necessary to pay commissions to gain business. Is it an 'unrealistic American moralism,' as Geoffrey Hazard, a Yale University professor of law and business, writes in his response, to prohibit such payments? Or is it moral courage? And if it is, is that moral courage akin to business stupidity? On the other hand, writes John F. Budd Jr, vice chairman of Carl Byoir and Associates, 'integrity has no national limitations.' Increasingly, firms must deal with this issue because many expanding markets lie outside of America.

Economic ties to South Africa. The decision to do business in South Africa or with South African firms is one of the most difficult a company must make. Indeed, one Columbia graduate reported to us that his firm created an independent subsidiary to operate its South African businesses so that it could claim to have divested. The scenario presented to our panelists raises the issue of how best to support the oppressed people of South Africa. Is operation in South Africa, even following the Sullivan principles, tacitly supporting the immorality of apartheid? Is divestment just running away from a problem?

More broadly, firms face the 'South African question' in deliberations concerning investment in any country with a record of human-rights violations. For example, is it right to divest South African ties for moral reasons while seeking markets in China, which has its own record of human-rights violations?

Corporate junkets. How lavish should the trappings of corporate life be and who should pay for them? The perks routinely provided to executives in some firms can give rise to ethical problems, as the third scenario illustrates. Few would disagree with William E. Simon, the former Treasury Secretary, that a variety of forms of entertainment constitute a legitimate portion of a business relationship. But some companies' legitimate business expenses can be other companies' junkets, and it is sometimes difficult to distinguish the two. Jeffrey M.

Kaplan, an attorney who has defended individuals accused of white-collar crimes, writes, 'It is critically important to keep attention focused on the risks because at first blush they appear minimal.' Prosecutors could make a corporate junket into an executive's nightmare.

Disposal of hazardous waste. While our panelists are unanimous in condemning the dumping of hazardous waste in violation of the law, their comments expose some of the more subtle ethical questions that arise in day-to-day business. Is it ethically correct for firms to lobby government with the intention of influencing environmental laws? Is the notion that legal rules provide the proper bounds for ethical activities valid? Any comfort we take in legal rules guiding ethical conduct is dashed by the reality that we face a global economy, and laws vary across nations. Some products banned in America may be legally sold in other countries. Does that make the sale of those products unethical here but ethical elsewhere? It is not possible or wise to define every ethical and unethical activity through law. It is up to all companies and individuals to define their own ethical standards.

The advice given by our panelists clearly shows that there is no 'one best way' to solve ethical dilemmas. Often, it is the character of the corporation that ultimately determines how a dilemma will be solved. Even if we feel an action is wrong, we can rationalize it as a decision in the best interest of our firm – in part because we are taught that bureaucratic decisions and economic decisions are 'value free.' But one of our panelists, Thomas C. Kohler, a Boston College law school professor, points out that, no matter how much we would like to be 'moral bureaucrats,' there is no code of ethical behavior that releases us from living with the decisions that we make.

Whether concern about business ethics is enduring or merely today's hot topic, business executives will continue to be faced with ethical dilemmas. We hope that our panel's responses to these four scenarios will help the individuals in the trenches weather their ethical storms.

One Man's Baksheesh . . .

I am CEO of an international trading company in Turkey. One state-owned manufacturing company (Company A) in one of the Middle East countries opened a tender for 15,000 tons PVC granule K value 70. Company A makes all its purchases through tenders. For seven years in that market my company has never been able to do any business with Company A (though we have sold many bulk materials to other state-owned companies in that market). One of our new managers had a connection with the purchasing manager of Company A, who promised to supply us with all of our competitors' bids if we pay him a 2 per cent commission on all of our sales to his company. Our area manager accepted this arrangement. He got the competing bids, made our offer, and we got the tender. I learned of this situation when reviewing our income and expenses chart, which showed the 2 per cent commission.

What shall I do, given the following: (1) If I refuse to accept the business without any legitimate reasons (presently there are none) my company will be blacklisted in that country – where we get about 20 per cent of our gross yearly profit. (2) If I accept the business and do not pay the 2 per cent commission, the purchasing manager will make much trouble for us when he receives our shipment. I am sure that he will not release our 5 per cent bank guarantee letter about the quality and quantity of the material. (3) If I accept the business and pay the 2 per cent commission, it will go against everything I have achieved in the 30 years of my career.

You have three ethical problems here: first, your company has won a rigged bid; second, you must pay the person who rigged it or he will make life miserable for you; and third, you have to decide what to do with the area manager who accepted this arrangement. In alternative (1), you assume that there are no 'legitimate' reasons for turning down the bid. If you're smart enough to be the CEO of this company, then you ought to be smart enough to construct some sort of explanation for why you can't accept the business – how about miscalculations in the initial bid? If this sort of white lie makes you squeamish, then how about a half-truth – the manager in charge did not follow company procedures and you have reason to believe that he made the bid with knowledge of the competitors' bids. This may sound silly and naïve to a Middle Easterner, but that's okay, you aren't one of them. What is legitimate to us may be different from what is legitimate to them; you must respect each other's right to have values. Here it's important to impress upon them the fact that *you* think your reason is legitimate.

Gasp! An ethics professor recommending lies and half-truths! Let us remember that you have two sets of moral obligations, one to do what is morally right and another to fulfill your duty to employees and shareholders. Using some moral imagination here might allow you to fill both. Moral courage doesn't always require martyrdom. In all of the alternatives you give up too easily. Only when every possibility is exhausted should you simply give in, turn down the business, and prepare for the consequences.

Joanne Ciulla
Senior Fellow
Legal Studies Department
The Wharton School
University of Pennsylvania

Pay the commission; your firm has fiduciary obligations to its stockholders. You are competing with other firms, which presumably pay baksheesh, in a country where baksheesh is, we are assuming, standard practice. 'Baksheesh' may be wrong in the United States, where it is not tolerated and is illegal, and where bribery would confer an unfair advantage. No so in Turkey. If Company A pays its workers less than the American minimum wage, do we stop doing business with it?

Michael Levin
Professor of Philosophy
City College of New York

Part of this decision is easy – the manager needs to go – quickly, dramatically, and publicly. You can't tolerate that behavior – and you need to send that clear message to each and every person in your company. As for what you do with this order, that is more complex. Try honesty. Arrange to talk with the CEO of Company A. Even in Turkey, asking for a 2 per cent commission to reveal company confidential information is not kosher. In that conversation I'd ask the CEO what he would do and what he'd like you to do. I'd follow his advice unless it also violates your standard of ethics. If he advised paying the commission and being quiet, I'd fulfill this one contract – being certain that my board knew about the situation and concurred – and then not bid again with that company. They can't pay you enough to sacrifice what you believe.

Jim Belasco
Professor of Management
San Diego State University

Does your company have a code of conduct? Does the code deal with payoffs overseas? Would you be undermining your own ethics code by making such a payoff? Would not that, in turn, undermine the seriousness with which the code is taken by others in the company? These should be considerations in your decision. Can you confer with your general counsel? Ethics officer? (I am assuming that such a payoff is *not* in violation of the Foreign Corrupt Practices Act.)

Andrew W. Singer
Editor of Ethikos
New York City

The arrangement violates the Foreign Corrupt Practices Act. Under the Internal Revenue Code the 2 per cent commission is a non-deductible outlay. Since the amount apparently was deducted from the company's tax return, the CEO should require a consultation with legal counsel about filing an amended return and whether reference to the matter has to be made in disclosure statements required by the SEC. Counsel may conclude that amendments are not necessary because the discrepancy is not material. If so, the cleanup work can be limited to internal measures within the company.

In confronting a past transaction as distinct from a future one, there are ethical 'sunk costs.' The new manager probably thought he was doing the right thing in paying the commission. The restrictions in the Foreign Corrupt Practices Act are widely regarded as unrealistic American moralisms. The fact that the law is unrealistic does not diminish the illegality of the transaction, but, in my opinion, it affects the ethical significance of employee participation in the transaction. It makes no sense to 'hang' the manager, even as an incident to making a change in company policy. Severe sanctions may backfire in future employee relationships.

I would ask whether there is not a way in which an amount equal to the commissions can be legally paid for the benefit of the purchasing agent even though that would violate the purpose of the Foreign Corrupt Practices Act. Adhering to the spirit of a foolish law is not ethically obligatory. For example, a consulting company could be formed as a channel. The CEO's company is doing business in Turkey and the world at large, not in the supposedly clean business environment in the United States.

Geoffrey Hazard
Professor of Law and Business
Yale University

If the company is a US firm, the CEO has no choice. [The arrangement] is a violation of the US Foreign Corrupt Practices Act. The CEO should discuss the matter with the CEO of Company A and let the chips fall where they may. [Do not] pay the commission, even this once.

Bruce Smart
Former Undersecretary of Commerce for International Trade
Upperville, Virginia

Confront your area manager who made the deal. Explain and emphasize your policy on appropriate ethical arrangements and clarify your expectations for ethical behavior. Contact the CEO of Company A, inform him of the arrangement made and the 2 per cent commission. Offer him one of two choices: (1) He may reopen the bidding with full knowledge of the actions that have taken place, or (2) if he wishes to continue the business with us, Company A will receive a discount equivalent to the 2 per cent that was to be paid to the Company A purchasing manager, with full knowledge that our future dealings would be conducted in fairness and candor. Finally, reassert your expectations for ethical behavior – specifically in foreign countries – with all staff members operating abroad.

Anonymous
Los Angeles

Since the CEO has knowledge of the transaction and its unethical nature, he should choose alternative (1) [refuse to accept the business]. He should also talk with the area manager about ethical standards. This might be a difficult decision in light of the importance of the transaction. However, it will take acts of courage in business decision-making to raise the moral and ethical standards in the business community.

Douglas A. Fraser
Former President
United Automobile Workers
Detroit

Some would be tempted to shrug the situation off and chalk the personal discomfort up to cultural differences. They would be wrong to do so, on at least two counts. The first is pragmatic: Where will the bribery stop? Will the purchasing agent decide to let some of his cronies in on the action? Will he decide next year that 3 per cent is better than 2, or 4 better than 3? In the bribery game, once you are in you are always in and you never get out gracefully.

The second consideration is the example you are setting for your company if you turn a blind eye to the sales manager's behavior. You decided that what he did is a transgression of your principles. If you overlook this transgression, you telegraph a loud message to your company: 'What I say isn't what I do. Sometimes you have to break the rules.' Can you afford to send that message?

With your sales manager in tow, meet with your counterpart in Company A and make a clean breast of the incident. Explain that bribery is unacceptable in your company. Let him know that you want Company A's business, but not at that price. And yes, you will probably need to dump the sales manager to prove to your people that you mean what you say about business practices.

Ron Zemke
President
Performance Research Associates
Minneapolis

The proper procedure would be a variation of alternative (1), whereby I would refuse to accept the business and would explain to the purchasing agent our reasons for considering [the rigged bidding process] to be an unethical procedure. I would indicate to the purchasing agent that we would like to continue doing business in a normal, honest way but that, if that wasn't possible, it would be necessary for me to explain to his supervisor why we could no longer supply him with our products and how this was denying his country products of best quality and value.

James M. Biggar
Chairman and CEO
Nestlé Enterprises
Solon, Ohio

Bringing South Africa Home

I have my own construction consulting company. I was hired nine months ago to consult on a project involving some of my former co-workers. After I was hired, I discovered that the developer received significant funding from the general contractor, a business based in South Africa. I feel strongly about human rights and equality. However, I could see no positive result of resigning this assignment. It would hurt my colleagues and my own struggling business and certainly it would have had no effect on the plight of workers in South Africa. All this is true, but I still feel uncomfortable with my decision.

The owner of this firm assumes that resigning from the assignment would hurt his colleagues. Are there no others who could do the project equally well? Is it possible that he could 'help' his colleagues in another by resigning – help them to understand how important human rights and equality are? Is it really true that his decision would have no effect on the plight of workers in South Africa, or is this simply an easy way out for him? There were millions of people in Germany who used the assumption that their individual actions 'would have had no effect' on the German Government between 1933 and 1945 to justify their inaction.

John H. Barcroft
Executive Director
James S. Kemper Foundation
Long Grove, Illinois

[If the developer did not deceive you about] his South African Association and you did not specifically make 'no South African' association a condition of accepting the job, you are obliged to carry out and fulfill your contract's terms. Then you should no longer accept any work from this particular developer. If your work is very good – so that the developer will want you on his team again – then your refusal to work for his company in the future will have an impact.

Anonymous
New York City

You need to do what will make you respect yourself. If you cannot do so by continuing in this project, then abandon it. But if you have an open conscience, then my advice is: Although some practices in South Africa clearly are repugnant, one should not condemn the nation and all of its people because of them. Better than turning away, one should decide what action best accomplishes what should be done in South Africa. If the general contractor is a company working toward constructive change, the leaders of the firm merit support.

Curtis Tarr
Dean of Johnson Graduate School of Management
Cornell University
Ithaca, New York

What to do about South Africa is an issue on which reasonable people may well disagree. They key point may be that if black South Africans want economic sanctions applied, they can apply those sanctions themselves simply by withdrawing their labor. At this writing, they have not done so. Your policy is as defensible as resigning the assignment would be, I think more so.

Edwin Newman
Journalist
New York City

Simply to assume that a business based in South Africa is opposed to human rights and equality is morally irresponsible. Companies supporting the Sullivan accords have done business in South Africa for years. This construction consultant [should] get exact information about the South African contractor. It may be the case that the contractor is diverting business funding abroad because he is dissatisfied that potential building projects in South Africa would further the development of human rights in the home country.

Robert L. Dilenschneider
CEO
Hill and Knowlton Inc.
New York City

If you're uncomfortable, let your conscience be your guide, and resign the assignment. But I do not believe in some sort of presumed institutional response to every situation. The question here is not how the Government of South Africa treats its citizens or what its official policies are. The question is, 'How does the business that is providing the funding treat its employees, and what are the views of the business's executives and leaders? Do they support the Government policies? Or have they taken a stand against those policies?

Let's make decisions based on the beliefs, policies, and practices of the people with whom we are doing business. To refuse to support the 'good' people in South Africa would be tantamount to having refused to support the American white Southerners who worked so hard in the '50s and '60s for the cause of equal rights in the South, or tantamount to having suggested that all white Southerners were 'bad.' The 'let's not do any business in South Africa or with any South Africans' attitude is simplistic at best, destructive to the cause of human rights at worst.

James A. Autry
President of Magazine Group
Meredith Corporation
Des Moines

Because ethics is 'obedience to the unenforceable' it requires judgment, which makes it relative and subjective. One's personal ethics can be more sensitive than the ethics of the general population. I would say that this is the present case.

Our society has not reached consensus regarding South African business relationships. Your sensitivities here need to be better informed regarding the South African contractor's record regarding human rights. He may be a supporter of the African National Congress and actively working to end apartheid. Or he might be a real abuser. I would make my final decision based on what I found out. Ethical concerns frequently force us to choose between being uncomfortably somewhat richer and comfortably somewhat poorer.

James E. Liebig
Author of Business Ethics: Profiles in Civic Virtue
Green Bay

A Perk or Shady Business

I was the senior finance person in a major division of a *Fortune*-rated company. The president of the division invited me to attend a focus marketing group in Utah to improve my understanding of the business. We took the company Lear Jet to Utah with the advertising representative. We spent one week in Utah, ate at lavish restaurants, and had all our skiing and private lessons paid for by the advertising company. We spent one hour one evening behind a one-way mirror watching the focus group panel. Nobody took notes. The president of the division didn't even bother to watch; he just had a beer and chatted with the ad person.

I felt uneasy and did not find out until two years later how my company paid for that week. We were spending millions on advertising, and sometimes ads were dropped or delayed, although all ads had to be prepaid. The ad agency would 'reduce' the credit to the company . . . By the way, one month after the trip I received a pair of $500 handmade Lucese [*sic*] boots shipped to my door. The president of the division had a pair but no one ever talked about how these boots appeared or who paid for them. Other 'focus' trips to Utah continue. Only 'up and coming' people in the company are invited to attend.

My advice would be to 'imagine the real' (a phrase coined by Robert Jay Lifton, the psychiatrist). I would urge questioners to imagine what it would like to be investigated by Federal prosecutors and agents, indicted, found guilty, and sent to prison. I would ask them to imagine, for example, how it would feel to hear their children crying themselves to sleep night after night, filled with fear, anger, and profound uncertainty for the future. In scenarios like these, it is critically important to keep attention focused on the risks because at first blush they appear minimal. In [this] scenario, the crime is not immediately apparent (and thus easy to avoid thinking about) and it seems to have been going along for quite some time, and thus to be somehow accepted.

[It] seems to be the very opposite of the sort of willful, malevolent, greedy conduct usually associated with business crime. In fact, [this is] precisely the type of situation that the government is, increasingly, turning its attention to, and, quite possibly, none of these comforting factors would deter a prosecutor in the slightest. Only by understanding and internalizing what is really at risk will members of the business community find the strength to resist the types of pressures and temptations identified in the scenario.

Jeffrey M. Kaplan
Partner
Chadbourne & Parke
New York City

First, I would return the $500 boots with a note saying you do not accept expensive gifts. Next, I would never participate in another junket like this. Then I would document the instances when ads were dropped or delayed and when credits to the company were reduced. With this information, I would go to the CEO and relay the whole story.

K. F. Mountcastle
Executive Senior Vice President
Dean Witter Reynolds
New York City

This is simply theft from the owners of the company just as if the money were taken out of the till by the employee.

Benjamin Stein
Columnist
Los Angeles

Obviously there's monkey business here. This is almost so blatant as to qualify for an anti-business Hollywood movie script. Corporate ethics are the integrated sum of the ethical behavior of all members of the company. Common knowledge recognizes 'TANSTAAFL' (there ain't no such thing as a free lunch), and somewhere there'll be a quid pro quo. It's a slippery slope and the [scenario] suggests a corporation where 'me-ism' is rife and every employee is at some risk of falling afoul of its practices. Get out of this situation. It will not be worth it.

Fred L. Wilson
Professor
College of Liberal Arts
Rochester Institute of Technology

Don't practice in business what you would not be comfortable explaining to your wife, children, and down-line employees. You should mount a major drive to dump the ad agency and get one that has your account based on the merit of its work, not favors to your top people. Were I on the board of your company and found that your allegations were correct, I would: (a) be on management like a blanket to find out how in the world they would justify their behavior to the shareholders, and (b) be after you specifically in your role as financial watchdog for not bringing this sort of thing to my attention.

Would blowing the whistle put your job in jeopardy? Of course. But these things have a way of coming out sooner or later anyway. The longer this sort of thing goes on with your knowledge and compliance, the worse you are apt to feel about yourself, and the worse trouble you may be in when the yogurt really does hit the fan.

Robert H. Waterman Jr
Co-author with Thomas J. Peters of In Search of Excellence:
Lessons from America's Best-Run Companies
San Francisco

There is misappropriation of company funds going on here plus a too-cozy relationship with an ad agency. As a senior official, you ought to bring up this matter with the division president. If he is unwilling to stop the practice, a communication to top corproate management is appropriate. In any case, send back the boots.

Daniel J. B. Mitchell
Professor of Business and Management
John E. Anderson Graduate School of Management
UCLA

It is scandalous and morally repugnant to condone or to take part in a charade in which a high-priced holiday is paid for partly by shareholders, partly by taxpayers, and not at all by the beneficiaries of the luxury and largess. The vision of North American executives lollygagging around the ski slopes of Utah on their companies' time while the Japanese and others are attacking our markets is hardly a recipe for economic success.

William A. Dimma
Deputy Chairman
Royal LePage
Toronto

In my experience, the genuine professionals who are good at their craft do not need to engage in the kind of behavior described in this scenario. These people know they are competent at their profession. They understand the proper services to provide a client, and they let the results do the talking for them.

There are, to be sure, forms of entertainment that are a legitimate part of a business relationship – such as a dinner or a lunch or a round of golf. But the activities described in this scenario go well beyond this. I would be suspicious of a client who felt it necessary to provide expensive gifts and trips to my senior executives as a means of keeping an account. It would suggest to me that they are not serving the company effectively or honestly.

William E. Simon
Chairman
William E. Simon & Sons
and former Treasury Secretary
Morristown, New Jersey

Purists would say: Blow the whistle or quit. I think we spend too much energy and make too much commotion over nickel-and-dime 'ethical' transgressions, so my recommendation is: stay with it, work hard, keep your nose clean (send the $500 boots to Goodwill), and as you rise, let there spread out behind you a wake of no-nonsense ethical standards.

Michael M. Thomas
Author of Hanover Place
New York City

This situation is very close to, if not, theft of the company's funds. If I were a superior manager I would admonish all involved and make clear to the vendor and the managers that they would lose their jobs or contracts if it ever occurred again. I hate the thought of attempting to buy influence. Earn the damned contract on the basis of competence and performance! Period!

What should the finance manager do? First, there are some tax questions here. [He should] inform everyone that these gifts must be reported as income. Second, he should return the boots, informing the vendor, with a copy of the letter to the president, that he feels such gifts are inappropriate.

Lawrence M. Miller
President The Miller Consulting Group

This scenario is a painful example of the type of activity that gets 'business' a bad name. Certain social interactions in the line of business are essential. But this expensive boondoggling, based on account manipulation, only serves to increase the costs of operation, raise invidious comparisons among staff, and decrease productivity. This kind of action often excludes women and minorities – individuals who would benefit most from the social interactions.

Jing Lyman
Founder
National Coalition for Women's Enterprise
Palo Alto, California

To Flush or not to Flush

I am currently in a business regulated by the Environmental Protection Agency. It deals with hazardous waste, not toxic waste, although I guess that various combinations of our wastes could probably be fatal. The question here is that of disposal. The cost of proper disposal is very expensive. How do you dispose of waste, bear the cost, and remain competitive, knowing that your competitors are dumping their waste illegally. You see, I can simply flush the waste, and a city investigator said that I wouldn't have to worry whether some of the waste dumped accidentally because even if everyone dumped everything they had, the city system could handle it. So if the city system can handle it, why should I bear the cost? Why can't I flush it down the tap? The EPA does check the tap every now and then but it doesn't do so at midnight or 5 a.m. Should I dispose of this waste at a great expense or should I dump it down the drain?

I would encourage the questioner to consider the probable results if all persons in his industry (and other generators of hazardous wastes) were to ignore EPA requirements. This reflection, moreover, says nothing about the fact that 'flushing it down the tap' appears to be illegal. Proper ethical behavior in this case does not seem obscure. Would the questioner have a similar dilemma if the city investigator offered to provide a 'clean' report for the payment of a fee?

Stanley R. Klion
Executive in Residence
Columbia Business School
New York City

Rather than worry about being caught (and eventually the chances are good that you will be), you should determine what is right for you to do. I cannot believe that any city system will be able to handle all the hazardous waste that might be discharged into the sewerage lines. But if it can, temporarily, it is not fair for you to ask all those people who use the city system to pay more so that your illegal use of the lines can be accommodated. So do not do it. Figure out the least expensive, sound way to handle the waste, and dispose of it in that manner. Of course, some of your competitors will use illegal means. Being moral may not always be the least expensive alternative, even in the long run. But it is the way to live best with yourself and those around you.

Curtis Tarr
Dean of Johnson Graduate School of Management
Cornell University
Ithaca, New York

EPA regulations require the proper disposal of hazardous waste. These regulations should be followed. If the waste can be handled by the city system, its disposal should not be that expensive and possible other sources of disposal should be explored. On the question of your competitors' illegal dumping, this may be more perception than reality. Requests for stricter enforcement may offer relief. It is good business to avoid illegal dumping because, in the long run, those who do so will be held responsible for clearing up the problems dumping causes.

William G. McCreery
Assistant General Counsel
Pfizer Inc.
New York City

What others are doing or getting away with in no way affects this ethical situation. You either compete in business under the rules of the game or get out. If you can see this situation any other way and can sleep at night, you should be sleeping in a jail cell.

Jack Falvey
Consultant
Intermark
Londonderry, New Hampshire

One's ethics are how one acts based on the values and principles that one believes in. If you believe that the environment needs to be protected, you will not dump the wastes. If you believe that the law should be obeyed, you will not dump the wastes. If you believe the environment should be protected, you will work for enforcement of the EPA regulations. What a city investigator said or implied is immaterial should the EPA find you in violation of its regulations, and your reputation could suffer significantly if the violations were to become public.

James E. Liebig
Author of Business Ethics: Profiles in Civic Virtue
Green Bay

If ethics is the search for a principle of right or good conduct, I do not see the 'ethical dilemma' posed in this scenario. Complying fully with the legal boundaries established by the EPA for disposing of waste properly is the only ethical course. Any expedient to illegally dispose of the waste, although profitable, cannot be justified.

Holly J. Gregory
Attorney
Weil, Gotshal & Manges
New York City

7
Anita Roddick: The Holistic Manager

Michel Syrett

Walk into The Body Shop's international headquarters in Littlehampton, West Sussex, and you are confronted by a large mural stressing the company's commitment to environmental conservation. On the opposite wall is a vivid painting of a mother holding her child out to the world. Both are symbolic of The Body Shop's concern to use naturally based ingredients in their products, untainted by the exploitation of animals as a source of raw materials or cosmetic testing. It 's a theme which is also writ large in its mission statement, publicity and financial reports.

This is not fashionable lip service at a time when 'green' philosophy has finally slipped into mainstream political and commercial thought. Community and environmental concerns have been central to The Body Shop since Anita and Gordon Roddick founded the company in 1976. Phenomenal financial growth has not compromised their values-led management style. Rather it has provided the resources to reinforce and further develop ethical and conscious-raising business practices which underpin not only day-to-day operations inside the company but external relations with suppliers, customers and public relations advisers.

The Roddicks' ability to sustain philanthropic values with undiminished commercial expansion has confounded cynics who predicted they would have to water down their holistic philosophy when The Body Shop joined the Stock Exchange in 1984.

'Our great mentors are the Quakers,' says Anita Roddick, now 46 and dressed in her habitual board-room dress of jeans and a short-sleeved shirt. 'They made a lot of money but were honest in themselves, sold honest products

'Anita Roddick: The Holistic Manager', by Michel Syrett, from *Ashridge Management Review*, Winter 1988/9 © Ashridge College Association, by permission of Ashridge Management College.

and being honest, told no lies about their products. Business should be about innovation and nurturing the spirit in people. Business should look after the back street as well as the high street. The instigators of change have got to be business people. They've got to be listened to.'

'Work Out' Schemes

Many of the ways in which Roddick has chosen to put this philosophy into practice have been well-publicized. The Body Shop is a corporate member of Friends of the Earth. Packaging, publicity material and corporate communication literature are printed on re-cycled paper.

Anyone taking up a Body Shop franchise is required to support at least one community project. The choice of the project is left entirely to the franchisee and staff. Body Shops support anything from 'work-out' schemes for the young unemployed to old people's homes and handicapped children's centres. No Body Shop employee is expected to undertake the extra work in their spare time, although many do. All projects are undertaken officially on company time. As The Body Shop has spread its commercial activities into other countries, the Roddicks have exported this approach. She sees social values as an integral part of the company, ranking on an equal footing with its ability to expand commercially. Community action is a mainstream corporate priority, not a sideline, and Roddick has invested a substantial amount of time and resources into recruitment and training systems which ensure that The Body Shop's 'core' values are sustained throughout the organization.

A central issue is the choice of suitable franchisees. All but 13 of the company's 340 shops worldwide are franchised. Roddick and her key directors are now re-evaluating the way in which they are selected.

'Our choice in the past has been dominated by gut feeling and instinct and this is not enough,' she comments, 'We haven't got the process right for the 1990s. The biggest internal debate we are having is how we are going to select franchisees for the next ten years and the yardsticks we are going to apply.'

Underpinning this debate is Roddick's view that basic business skills can be provided by the company but the right attitude and values cannot. 'We have the back-up to teach almost anyone to run a Body Shop,' she says. 'What we can't control is the soul.' To this end, the strict vetting all applicants receive is balanced by seemingly offbeat questions like: How would you like to die? What is your favourite flower? Who's your heroine in history or poetry – all questions that give Roddick a feel for whether the applicant is someone she can work with comfortably.

This holistic approach is also built into The Body Shop's training schemes. Roddick deeply mistrusts conventional training – a process she believes 'drives every ounce of individuality' from participants and imposes a business language and attitude of mind which places them out of touch with the majority of people whose interests they are supposed to be serving.

Increased financial resources enabled her to set up The Body Shop Training School in London three years ago. This now provides the base for in-house staff training in business and retailing skills such as product knowledge, customer care, communication and presentation skills.

'The courses do not simply tell our people how to keep a customer or stock up their shelves,' Roddick comments. 'We have courses on the chemistry of cosmetics covering issues such as skin biology and ageing in society. We have courses on acid rain for example, where franchisees and staff are invited to take part in environmental campaigns. We have lectures from design people who discuss values and aesthetics on the High Street. We therefore run in the opposite direction to the rest of the cosmetics industry. They train for a sale. We train for knowledge.'

The Right Stuff

The Body Shop is set aside from its competitors, because 70 per cent of the company's product range is manufactured by outside suppliers but Roddick goes to great lengths to ensure the ingredients are drawn from natural products. She still spends about two months of each year travelling the world to look for new, modern approaches to the manufacture of cosmetics based on traditional practices in rural communities in the Third World.

Her relationship with suppliers is every bit as rigorous as those of Marks & Spencer and other retailers producing own-name brands – each supplier, for example, is required to sign a declaration guaranteeing none of the ingredients has been tested on animals during the previous five years. But she picks collaborative ventures that emphasize the interdependence of developed, developing and underdeveloped economies, and which aid rather than undermine environmental balance.

Benefits Two-Way

The benefits are two-way. Her funding of the International Boys' Town Trust in India gave her a new source of Body Shop products. The boys now supply soap bags and 'footsie rollers' (wooden massagers) as well as silk-screen print summer uniforms for the staff. 'We wanted to teach the kids a trade but we also wanted a source of products which did not use cheap labour or cheap materials. They've made 100,000 footsie rollers this year and production has now spread from the Boys' Town to the local villages. The point about cheap labour is important. The scheme has made something like £100,000 profit and I wanted to know exactly where it went.'

Her use of external business support services has been equally discerning, a fact best illustrated by her choice of PR firm Munro and Forster. Good public relations is fundamental to The Body Shop's marketing strategy. Roddick quickly learned the same lesson as Marks & Spencer – that product advertising is unnecessary when a company has built up a strong and continuing public image.

Roddick courts publicity. She makes herself deliberately available to the Press and is a constant source of good copy. 'The Press like me,' she commented at the CBI last year, 'I'm always available and I'm loudmouthed and quotable.' Her views on health care, environmental issues and the callousness of big business are not manufactured and are entirely consistent with the aims and philosophy on which The Body Shop has been founded.

Astute PR

But they also form part of an astute PR campaign which guarantees coverage in the lifestyle section of women's magazines and the Sunday supplements, and which results in editorial coverage which Roddick recently estimated is worth £2 million a year.

Roddick's personal relationship with Munro and Forster plays an important part in how the campaign is managed. The company was picked after The Body Shop was launched on the Unlisted Securities Market when it became clear to Roddick that the company was beyond the survival stage and was in a position to promote a broader corporate message based on holistic business philosophy.

'My original PR company was product-based,' she explains. 'I knew we were going beyond the beauty press and would be discussing much larger issues. These needed to be communicated sensitively and accurately. So when I looked around for a new company, I had a number of requirements. I wanted a small, female company. I wanted the account run by a female team. I didn't want them to have any other account with cosmetic companies. I also wanted them to be versed in the medical world. I wanted them to be erudite and I wanted them to be great writers. If they liked us, so much the better.'

The choice worked. Munro and Forster has grown with The Body Shop and acted as a vital support in Roddick's choice of publicity. 'They have become a very good sounding board and a great buffer,' she says. 'They've succeeded because we've succeeded. We're not just client and consultant. We're family.'

Hearts and Minds

This personal approach to work relationships is still the foundation on which The Body Shop's management style is based. Roddick controls the company and its culture because she has won the 'hearts and minds' of Body Shop staff working for the company directly and in the franchised outlets. She spends at least another two months of each year touring Body Shop outlets where she encourages staff involvement in product development through good employee communication literature and a well-managed system of 'suggestion-boxes'.

She is notoriously heretical when it comes to management methods and is not above using her personal standing with Body Shop to go over the heads of her franchisees and middle managers when she encounters obstruction.

'Middle managers have always been my bugbear,' she says. 'The directors of the company are progressive and the ground staff are progressive. But middle managers are more territorial, more protective of their own position and infinitely more conservative than anyone else. There are times when I get tired of playing the benign dictator. I can't convince them if the soul isn't there. I go to the staff direct and this is probably the best way of implementing change.'

Given this approach it is hardly surprising that business school graduates do not fare well in The Body Shop. Anita Roddick comments: 'We are a bizarre company because we have annual gross increases of 50–70 per cent. There's no book on how to manage that. We are writing our own rules. We are developing our own standards. We are certainly policing ourselves better than any auditor could.' However, problems of consolidation and future direction are now beginning to trouble her. She would like to see recruitment procedures which spread the net to younger people who are 'disfranchised' from the business community. Despite the fact that well over half of her franchisees are women, she is concerned at the lack of female participation in senior management (Roddick is still the only woman on her company's board) and is trying to lay the right foundations by encouraging more women into middle management positions.

Above all, she is aware that the pivotal position she continues to play in both the marketing and day-to-day management of the company is placing her under more and more stress and could end as a liability rather than an asset. 'Everybody worries about what would happen if something happened to me,' she comments:

> You wind up absolutely weak with frustration because you know you're doing what you are doing best, but you can't split yourself several ways. At the end of the day you're tired and it is difficult to sustain that sense of energy for young kids who see you as a mentor and a role model. The pressure is enormous.
>
> The company is continually improving and could be even better at doing what it does well now. A priority is therefore to get systems and people in place that can

keep this improvement moving. I'm surrounding myself with people in their mid-20s and mid-30s who are not professionally trained and do not have a background in mainstream retailing or cosmetics, but who have energy and intelligence, a good eye and a good ear. They will be the custodians.

And it is The Body Shop's performance rather than her own position that Anita Roddick talks about most when interviewed, something that is reflected in her reaction to the steady stream of awards showered on her by the business community in recent years.

The CBI Business Enterprise Award in 1987 is something I'm really proud of because it reflected on the company rather than me. The stated reason for the choice of Body Shop was that it combined business success with the creation of wealth for the community. I think it was bloody well deserved.

Individual awards I take more lightly. I'm not trying to be controversial for its own sake nor am I trying to down the business community as a matter of principle. It's just that in 12 years I have met so few people who make my blood zing. There's actually an unfulfilled and frustrated part of me that wants to say to the business establishment, 'Hey I want some help and advice. I want to be your groupie and get some short cuts through life.' But I can't because most of the tired, worn out, business solutions don't work at The Body Shop.

8
Green = Opportunity

Tom Peters

The greening of Europe (North America, Asia) is a matchless opportunity for the wise corporation. It is not a threat.

First consider a simple question. By coincidence, the European edition of the *Wall Street Journal* (1 October 1990) featured a list of the world's 100 largest companies, as measured by stock market value. My 'quiz': Which company is 'biggest' – Nissan, Dow Chemical, ICI . . . or America's Waste Management? The way I've presented the case makes the answer obvious: It's Waste Management! Though the company has only $4.4 billion in sales, compared to Nissan's $33 billion, the stock market made Waste Management more valuable ($19 billion) than Nissan ($18 billion), Dow ($15 billion of market worth from $18 billion in sales) or ICI ($14 billion in worth from $21 billion in sales). That is, the beady-eyed, emotionless evaluators of securities see the dollars and cents potential of the environmental movement. Though this is anecdotal evidence, I contend that it is a dramatic and fair indication of the case for opportunity.

The evidence, of course, stretches far beyond this. For example, the direct US environmental market is now estimated to be $56 billion; it's ticketed by experts to grow at 30 per cent to 40 per cent per annum for the next three to five years. There is, quite simply, the most extraordinary opportunity for market growth in areas associated with protection of the environment. (Only information technology is in the same league.)

Another dimension of opportunity is the reaction of corporations to new regulations; it will cause (is already causing) the greatest burst of process-technology improvement breakthroughs this century. While the product-improvement arena is not so far advanced, I predict that we will be able to say the same thing about it very soon. Periods of dramatically changing regulation

Excerpt from *Lean, Green and Clean: The Profitable Company of the Year 2000* by Tom Peters. Copyright © 1991 TPG Communications, by permission of the Tom Peters Group.

and turbulence, always cause phenomenal bursts of innovation – it's no different relative to the environment.

There is simply a massive competitive advantage for those who get there the 'firstest with the mostest.' That is, investments in cleaning up today will pay off many times over when regulations tighten – which they will. There is no way that I could overstate this case: this is a remarkable, perhaps once-a-century opportunity to be roughly 'first' in a huge game. *The Economist*, in a special report published earlier this year, suggests that only 100 to 200 sizeable firms are going after the green issue in a big way. Whether the number is 50 or 350 is not important. In brief, darned few outfits are seriously 'getting on with it.' Thus those who start – in a very straightforward fashion – as late as today, still have a chance to be on the leading edge. Such chances don't traipse by very often.

Again, the environmental opportunity is a chance to achieve massive cost savings. Most effective environmental action will result from doing 'it' simpler. To do it simpler will mean doing it cheaper, as the quality and time-based movements have shown. Beyond that, it's a pay now or pay later proposition. Looking at future liabilities associated with meeting as yet unwritten environmental regulations will cause your capital budgeting rituals to be turned upside down.

Simple compliance is never enough. Consider a couple of cases in the US. Our 'Superfund' legislation, associated with the cleaning up of toxic wastes, is unmistakably retroactive. Even if a company obeyed the letter of the law 30 years ago, now that the law has toughened, it is just tough luck for the company. 'Retro-activism' has become, and increasingly will become, the regulators' watchword: you will be judged tomorrow for today's, yesterday's and the day before's sins. And you will be charged for them with compound interest (or punitive damages)! In a related vein, look at the market for hazardous waste disposal in the US: The price has surged from about $80 a ton to $255 a ton in the last ten years; expect a tenfold increase in the next ten years: A few pennies spent reducing hazardous waste from newly designed processes and products today will mean many tons of dimes saved five years, ten years and fifteen years hence.

Call it opportunity or threat as you wish, being clean and green is the only basis for future expansion, plant or product. The NIMBYs (not in my backyarders) are out in force! And they've no plans to go quietly back into their caves. If you are a dirty company, or even have a dirty past, there is no chance, whatsoever, that the NIMBYs will allow you to site a new facility, or expand an old one, near their playpen. Could the message be any plainer?

Being green and clean will increasingly be a major selling point for attracting the best graduates and workers to boot. The new generation looks at green far differently than the past generation. Being demonstrably on the 'right' side of this issue will be of great significance in this, the age of the brain worker.

The essence of implementing anything big, such as a top-to-bottom passion for greening, is altering the attention pattern of the organization. That means environmental audits, performance-appraisal schemes, measurements, compensation, board-level environmental representation, unit-level environmental representation, catch programs (such as 3P at 3M). But above all it translates into chief executive leadership – via her or his calendar. In short, while detailed programs and procedures are critical, it's the boss, at the factory or division or corporate level, spending time (or 'hanging out around the issue' as I like to call it), that makes all the difference.

When I look at supreme quality programs, at textile-maker Milliken & Company in the US, for example, I most clearly see a top boss and chief lieutenants who constantly 'talk up the issue.' It's in their language. It's in the stories that they repeat day after day. It's in every newsletter. Yes, it's in the charts and graphs and compensation schemes, too – but these are almost afterthoughts. Getting the greening/cleaning/environmental issue 'in the air' in a million ways is really the name of the game.

Ed Woolard, Du Pont's chairman, takes every opportunity to jawbone zero pollution. Anita Roddick of the Body Shop is a walking chatterbox/billboard for environmentally sound products and management. Each of these chieftains' firms, even the relatively informal Body Shop, has a mass of formal programs for bringing the message to bear; but it is the spirit and repetitiveness of the leaders' walk, talk and time spent that count most.

Chapter 8
Leadership and the Non-Profit Organization

Introduction

It is no coincidence that one of the most prolific writers on management issues, Peter Drucker, recently turned his attention to the needs of the non-profit organization.

The progressive rolling back of the state in both the US and Europe has resulted in a wider and more significant role for charities, educational trusts, health care institutions, and community bodies of all kinds. Many undertake sophisticated services and manage considerable resources requiring professional skills previously associated solely with their commercial counterparts.

But while the need for professionalism is as acute, the objectives of non-profit organizations require a distinct style of leadership. As Drucker points out, hospitals, churches, charities, schools, and colleges do not have a conventional 'bottom line'. Their objectives and 'constituents' are wider and more complex. Their sources of finance are acquired through very different means. They are often committed to religious, moral, or vocational causes which cannot be abandoned because the organization's efforts are not producing results.

Above all, the people who work for non-profit organizations are frequently motivated by a different work ethic and have a less straightforward attitude to authority. They will be inspired and motivated by example to a far greater extent than employees in commercial companies. Leaders of these organizations need strong character and integrity, Drucker stresses. They have less time in which to establish themselves, and their mediocrity, if it exists, shows up almost immediately.

Drucker addresses the subject purely from the perspective of the organization itself. Other authors such as the UK's Charles Handy have begun to realize that the special qualities required of non-profit leaders provide models that can be drawn on by their commercial counterparts.

Senior managers in the private sector also have to address wider constituents such as how social concern over business ethics and the environment affects their ability to recruit staff and the consumer demand for their products or services. They also have to inspire and manage workers who are not purely motivated (as they were assumed to be in the past) by promotion or a bigger salary. The ambiguity that the non-profit manager has always confronted in defining objectives and implementing strategy is now matched by turbulence and uncertainty in business markets.

Thus non-profit and commercial organizations have a lot to exchange in the 1990s. Charities, educational bodies, and voluntary agencies need the functional skills and disciplines of the private sector better to fulfil their objectives – such as marketing, finance, and technological expertise. Business leaders can draw usefully on the multidimensional and motivational leadership of the voluntary sector to meet the wider demands of the modern boardroom agenda.

1
Leadership is a Foul-Weather Job

Peter Drucker

The most successful leader of this century was Winston Churchill. But for twelve years, from 1928 until Dunkirk in 1940, he was totally on the sidelines, almost discredited – because there was no need for a Churchill. Things were routine or, at any rate, looked routine. When the catastrophe came, thank goodness, he was available. Fortunately or unfortunately, the one predictable thing in any organization is the crisis. That always comes. That's when you *do* depend on the leader.

The most important task of an organization's leader is to anticipate crisis. Perhaps not to avert it, but to anticipate it. To wait until the crisis hits is already abdication. One has to make the organization capable of anticipating the storm, weathering it, and in fact, being ahead of it. That is called innovation, constant renewal. You cannot prevent a major catastrophe, but you can build an organization that is battle-ready, that has high morale, and also has been through a crisis, knows how to behave, trusts itself, and where people trust one another. In military training, the first rule is to instil soldiers with trust in their officers, because without trust they won't fight.

The Problems of Success

Problems of success have ruined more organizations than has failure, partly because if things go wrong, everybody knows they have to go to work. Success creates its own euphoria. You outrun your resources. And you retire on the job, which may be the most difficult thing to fight. I'm now in California instead of

Excerpt from *Managing the Non-Profit Organization* by Peter Drucker. Copyright © Peter F. Drucker 1990, by permission of Butterworth-Heinemann, Oxford.

New York University, where I was for twenty years, in part because the Graduate Business School at NYU decided to cut back rather than grow with the growing student demand. That's why I left. When I started to build a management school at Claremont, I made sure that we did not overextend ourselves. I was very careful to ensure that we kept the faculty first rate but small, and that we used adjuncts, part-time people, then built a strong administration. And then we could run with success. If the market grows, you have to grow with it, or you become marginal.

I am arguing these days with our pastor, who wants to keep our church small. This is in a community where we have a lot of young people, students, and a lot of people in retirement homes who want to come to church. My very nice and able pastor likes to keep it small so that he knows everybody. I said to him, 'Look, Father Michael, it won't work.' Five years after he had come in, the church began to shrink. The lesson for the leaders of non-profits is that one has to grow with success. But one also has to make sure that one doesn't become unable to adjust. Sooner or later, growth slows down and the institution plateaus. Then it has to be able to maintain its momentum, its flexibility, its vitality, and its vision. Otherwise it becomes frozen.

Hard Choices

Non-profit organizations have no 'bottom line.' They are prone to consider everything they do to be righteous and moral and to serve a cause, so they are not willing to say, if it doesn't produce results then maybe we should direct our resources elsewhere. Non-profit organizations need the discipline of organized abandonment perhaps even more than a business does. They need to face up to critical choices.

Some of these choices are very difficult. I have a friend, a Catholic priest, who is Vicar General of a large diocese. The bishop called him in to deal with the shortage of priests. Which services should they keep and which should they abandon? There is the terrible dilemma of Catholic schools in a big metropolitan archdiocese where 97 per cent of the kids are not Catholics and aren't going to be Catholics; they're fleeing the misery of the public schools. I've been arguing with the diocese for years. Some of the priests say, 'Our first task is to save souls; it's not to educate people. Let's put our few priests and nuns on our first priority.' And I say, 'Look, it says in the Bible, "But the greatest of these is Charity," and that's what you are doing. You cannot possibly leave those kids in the lurch. That's a value choice, and it's critical that it's faced up to and not pushed under the rug, as we like to do.'

Once you acknowledge that, you can then innovate – provided you organize yourself to look for innovation. Non-profit institutions need innovation as much as businesses or governments. And we know how to do it.

The starting point is to recognize that change is not a threat. It's an opportunity. We know where to look for changes.[1] Here are a few examples:

Unexpected Success in your Own Organization

Some institutions of higher education, for instance, have learned that continuing education of already highly educated adults is not a luxury, or something to bring in additional money, or good public relations. It is becoming the central thrust of our knowledge society. So, they have organized themselves and their faculties to attract the doctors, engineers, and executives who want and need to go back to school.

Population Changes

About twelve years ago, the Girl Scouts of the USA realized that demographic shifts in the United States, with the fast growth of minorities, were creating a new frontier for the organization – new needs and the opportunity to change. They now have a 15 per cent enrolment of minority kinds, which explains why they kept growing even though the total number of girls of scouting age fell quite steadily during that period.

Changes in Mind-Set and Mentality

Very few things have so altered our view of society as the women's movement of the last twenty years. What opportunities does it create? About fifteen years ago, one of our largest volunteer organizations, the American Heart Association, realized that, even though its original big job – research – was not yet accomplished, a new opportunity had opened to take advantage of the tremendous growth in health awareness by the American public. It decided to redirect its national forces.

The lesson is, Don't wait. Organize yourself for systematic innovation. Build the search for opportunities, inside and outside, into your organization. Look for changes as indications of an opportunity for innovation. To build all this into your system, you, as the leader of the organization, have to set the example. How can we set up systems to release energy that will allow the proper innovative decisions to be made and implemented and, at the same time, encourage the operation to go on at the necessary level while it is being changed? Let me try to outline a simple series of steps.

First, organize yourself to see the opportunity. If you don't look out the window, you won't see it. What makes this particularly important is that most of our current reporting systems don't reveal opportunities; they report problems. They report the past. Most answer questions we have already asked. So, we have to go beyond our reporting systems. And whenever you need a change, ask: If this were an opportunity for us, what would it be?

Then, to implement the innovation effectively, there are a few points you must be aware of. First, the most common mistake – the one that kills more innovations than anything else – is the attempt to build too much reinsurance into the change, to cover your flank, not to alienate yesterday. The Japanese made that mistake in the one area where their export drive failed significantly: telephones. They had the technology but tried to hedge their bets by selling switchboards that were both electromechanical (and therefore could be plugged into existing old systems) *and* electronic. The electronic switchboards force customers to tear out their old equipment, even though it may be perfectly good. But those who did go into either expansion or improvement of their existing system decided to pull out the old and go straight to the state-of-the-art.

The same sort of mistakes can be found in the pharmaceutical industry and in educational programmes. Twenty years ago, a good many hospitals, seeing the trend toward taking care of patients outside the hospital, built outpatient clinics into the hospital. That didn't work. The free-standing surgical clinic, however, *did* work because it was not in the hospital.

Next, you have the problem of organizing the new. It must be organized separately. Babies don't belong in the living room, they belong in the nursery. If you put new ideas into operating units – whether it's a theological seminary or an automobile plant – the solving of the daily crisis will always take precedence over introducing tomorrow. So, when you try to develop the new within an existing operation, you are always postponing tomorrow. It must be set up separately. And yet you have to make sure the existing operations don't lose the excitement of the new entirely. Otherwise, they become not only hostile but paralyzed.

The Innovative Strategy

Next, you need an innovative strategy: a way to bring the new to the marketplace. Successful innovation finds a target of opportunity. Somebody who is receptive, who welcomes the new, who wants to succeed and, at the same time, has enough stature, enough clout in the organization so that, if it works for him or her, the rest of the organization will say, Well, there must be something to it.

I am always being asked, 'If you were running a metropolitan museum, or a major public library, or a relief or service agency in a community, would you have part of your organization set up some kind of small task force committed to R&D or to marketing? Some group working within the organization that would be weighing the possibilities of innovation for the organization?'

Well, the answer is yes and the answer is no. Yes, because you need a few people who do the work, who have the time to do it. It's hard work. No, because if you isolate the planning, you're going to end up overlooking perhaps the small but crucial things. Let me give you a very simple example. The executives of a big museum decided to move from the old-time museum, whch kept the art works in and the people out, to the modern kind of museum, which is basically an educational community. They set up a separate planning group, which did a magnificent job planning exhibitions and publicity and so on. But being isolated from operations, the planners overlooked a few 'housekeeping' details. They forgot, for instance, that you need a much bigger parking lot. Also, if you suddenly have 300 fourth graders in, you need toilets. When they opened, you cannot imagine the pandemonium. And that's typical.

If you first plan and then try to sell, you're going to miss the important things. But you also waste years of time. Selling has to be built into planning, and that means involving the operating people. But don't forget one thing: everything new requires hard work on the part of true believers – and true believers are *not* available part time.

The Churchills may be very rare. But another group is, fortunately, quite common. These are the people who can look at a situation and say: This is not what I was hired to do or what I expected to do, but this is what the job requires – and then roll up their sleeves and go to work. I know a college president who was conned into taking his job with the usual promises by the board that it would raise the money. He came out of tax-supported state universities. He arrived with a wonderful programme of faculty recruitment and educational reform, took one good look, and came to me, very unhappy. Somebody has to raise money, he said, otherwise that institution won't be there in five or ten years. And I said, You know, there is only one person who can raise money in a college – the president. And he said, I'm afraid you're right. He found an exceedingly able man on his faculty who for five years ran the school, while the president concentrated on raising money, in which he proved himself incredibly able. He saved that institution.

Let me give you another example of a rural electric cooperative, one of the large ones, founded during the 1930s when the American farmer couldn't get any power. Well, by now everybody has power, so the question is: What do we do now? There was strong sentiment on the board and in the membership for selling out to the nearest large power company. A new chief executive came in, took a look, and said: 'Yes, as an electric cooperative we have fulfilled our mission, but as a community development organization, it has only begun. Here is a tremendous farm crisis [this was in the early eighties]. All kinds of basic social services need to be supplied to our farm members, and they can only be supplied by somebody with a distribution system.'

He made all the difference. Farm prices are still low and depressed, but this six-county system is one of the few farm areas we have that is, I wouldn't say prosperous, but doing well because of the action this man took, seeing the opportunity. And it's not that uncommon. *This* is effective crisis leadership.

How to Pick a Leader

If I were on a selection committee to choose a leader for a non-profit organization and there were a roster of men and women as candidates, what would I look for? First, I would look at what the individuals have done, what their strengths are. Most selection committees, I know, are overly concerned with how *poor* the candidate is. Most of the questions I get are not: What is he or she good at, but we think this person is not too good at dealing with students, or what have you. The first thing to look for is strength – you can only perform with strength – and what they have done with it.

Second, I would look at the institution and ask: What is the one immediate key challenge? It may be raising money. It may be rebuilding the morale of the organization. It may be redefining its mission. It may be bringing in new technology. If I looked today for an administrator of a large hospital I might look for someone to convert the hospital from a provider of sickness care to a manager of sickness-care providers, because more and more will be done outside the hospital. I would try to match the strengths with the needs.

Then I would look for – call it character or integrity. A leader sets an example, especially a strong leader. He or she is somebody on whom people, especially younger people, in the organization model themselves. Many years ago I learned from a very wise old man, who was head of a large, worldwide organization. I was about twenty, not even that – and he was in his late seventies, famous for putting the right people into the right enterprises all over the globe. I asked him: 'What do you look for?' And he said: 'I always ask myself, would I want one of my sons to work under that person? If he is successful, then young people will imitate him. Would I want my son to look like this?' This, I think, is the ultimate question.

I've seen lots of businesses and all of us have seen lots of governments survive with mediocre leaders for quite a long time. In the non-profit agency, mediocrity in leadership shows up almost immediately. One difference clearly is that the non-profit has a number of bottom lines – not just one. In business, you can debate whether profit is really an adequate measuring stick; it may not be over the short term, but it is the ultimate one over the long term. In government, in the last analysis, you've got to get re-elected. But in non-profit management, there is no such one determinant. You deal with balance, synthesis, a combination of bottom lines for performance.

Certainly, the non-profit executive does not have the luxury of dealing with one dominant constituency either. In a publicly listed company, the shareholder is the ultimate constituent. In government, it is the voter. When you look at the school board, a public service agency, or a church, however, you have a multiplicity of constituencies – each of which can say no and none of which can say yes. The multiplicity of constituencies is reflected in your boards, your trustees, who are likely to be intensely involved in running the agency. You could say public schools are governmental, but the school board is not governmental. It has the constituency role. That's what causes all the difficulty for school superintendents. They are really public services agencies rather than government agencies.

You can't be satisfied in non-profit organizations with doing adequately as a leader. You have to do exceptionally well, because your agency is committed to a cause. You want people as leaders who take a great view of the agency's functions, people who take their roles seriously – not *themselves* seriously. Anybody in that leadership position who thinks he's a great man or a great woman will kill himself – and the agency.

Your Personal Leadership Role

The new leader of a non-profit doesn't have much time to establish himself or herself. Maybe a year. To be effective in that short a time, the role the leader takes has to fit in terms of the mission of the institution and its values. All of us play roles – as parents, as teachers, and as leaders. To work, the role has to fit in three dimensions. First, the role has to fit you – who you are. No comic actor has ever been able to play Hamlet. The role you take also has to fit the task. And, finally, the role has to fit expectations.

One of the more brilliant young men I ever hired as a teacher completely failed in the college classroom. In teaching freshmen, he abdicated his authority, and the kids revolted. He didn't understand that nineteen-year-old freshmen in an undergraduate college expect a teacher to have authority.

You have two things to build on: the quality of the people in the organization, and the new demands you make on them. What those new demands will be can be determined by analysis, or by perception, or by a combination of both. That depends on how you operate. I am a perceptual person. I look. But I've also seen very able and effective people who are totally paper-oriented. They take a sharp pencil and come out right.

There are simply no such things as 'leadership traits' or 'leadership characteristics.' Of course, some people are better leaders than others. By and large, though, we are talking about skills that perhaps cannot be taught but they can be learned by most of us. True, some people genuinely cannot learn the skills. They may not be important to them; or they'd rather be followers. But most of us can learn them.

The leaders who work most effectively, it seems to me, never say 'I.' And that's not because they have trained themselves not to say 'I.' They don't *think*

'I.' They think 'we'; they think 'team.' They understand their job to be to make the team function. They accept the responsibility and don't sidestep it, but 'we' gets the credit. There is an identification (very often, quite unconscious) with the task and with the group. This is what creates trust, what enables you to get the task done.

In Shakespeare's *Henry V*, the young prince whose father just died – he's now king – rides out. Falstaff, the old disreputable knight who has been the prince's boon companion in drinking and wenching, calls up to his 'Sweet Prince Hal,' and the new king rides by without even a look at him. Falstaff is cruelly hurt. He raised the prince because the old king was a very poor father and a cold one, and the young man found warmth only with that disreptuable drunkard. Yet Henry is now king and has to set different standards for himself because he is visible. As a leader, you are visible; incredibly visible. And you have expectations to fulfill.

Then there is the story of the one leading German statesman before World War I who saw the catastrophe Europe was sliding into and tried desperately to reverse the trend. He was the ambassador to London in the early days of the century – a leading dove. But he resigned his ambassadorship because the new English king, Edward VII, was a notorious womanizer who liked the diplomatic corps to give him stag parties at which the most popular London courtesans would pop naked out of cakes. The ambassador said he was not willing to be a pimp when he saw himself in a mirror shaving in the morning. I don't think he could have averted World War I. Still, politically, he may have made the wrong decision. And yet, I think, it was the essence of leadership. You are visible; you'd better realize that you are constantly on trial. The rule is: I don't want to see a pimp in the mirror when I shave in the morning. If you do see one, then your people will see one too.

'To every leader there is a season.' There is profundity in that statement, but it's not quite that simple. Winston Churchill in ordinary, peaceful, normal times would not have been very effective. He needed the challenge. Probably the same is true of Franklin D. Roosevelt, who was basically a lazy man. I don't think that FDR would have been a good president in the 1920s. His adrenalin wouldn't have produced. On the other hand, there are people who are very good when things are pretty routine, but who can't take the stress of an emergency. Most organizations need somebody who can lead regardless of the weather. What matters is that he or she works on the basic competences.

As the first such basic competence, I would put the willingness, ability, and self-discipline to listen. Listening is not a skill; it's a discipline. Anybody can do it. All you have to do is keep your mouth shut. The second essential competence is the willingness to communicate, to make yourself understood. That requires infinite patience. We never outgrow age three in that respect. You have to tell us again and again and again. And demonstrate what you mean. The next important competence is not to alibi yourself. Say: 'This doesn't work as well as it should. Let's take it back and re-engineer it.' We either do things to perfection, or we don't do them. We don't do things to get by. Working that way creates pride in the organization.

The last basic competence is the willingness to realize how unimportant you are compared to the task. Leaders need objectivity, a certain detachment. They subordinate themselves to the task, but don't identify themselves with the task. The task remains both bigger than they are, and different. The worst thing you can say about a leader is that on the day he or she left, the organization collapsed. When that happens, it means the so-called leader has sucked the place dry. He or she hasn't built. They may have been effective operators, but they have not created vision. Louix XIV was supposed to have said, '*L'état, c'est moi!*' (The state, that's me!). He died in the early eighteenth century and the long, no-so-slow slide into the French Revolution immediately began.

When effective non-profit leaders have the capacity to maintain their personality and individuality, even though they are totally dedicated, the task will go on after them. They also have a human existence ouside the task. Otherwise they do things for personal aggrandizement, in the belief that this furthers the cause. They become self-centred and vain. And above all, they become jealous. One of the great strengths of Churchill and one of the great weaknesses of FDR was that Churchill, to the very end, when he was in his nineties, pushed and furthered young politicians. That is a hallmark of the truly effective leader, who doesn't feel threatened by strength. In his last years, FDR systematically cut down everybody who showed any signs of independence.

I would not want any person to give his or her life to an organization. One gives one's very best efforts. What attracts people to an organization is high standards, because high standards create self-respect and pride. Most of us want to contribute. When you look at schools where kids learn and schools where kids don't, it's not the quality of the teaching that's different. The school in which kids learn expects them to learn. Many years ago, I did a survey of Boy Scout Councils with tremendous differences in performance. In the performing ones, they expected the volunteers, the scoutmasters, and so on, to put in very hard work. And I mean hard work, not just appearing Friday night for a couple of hours. The ones with high demands attracted the volunteers and attracted and kept the boys. So it is the job of the leaders to set high standards on one condition – that they be performance-focused.

Most leaders I've seen were neither born nor made. They were self-made. We need far too many leaders to depend only on the naturals. The best example of one who surely was not born a leader, had no training, and made himself into a very effective one, was Harry Truman. When Truman became President, he was totally unprepared. An ordinary politician, he was chosen as Vice President because he presented no threat to FDR. Truman not only said, 'I am President now and the buck stops here,' but he also asked, 'What are the key tasks?' His entire preparation had been in domestic affairs. He forced himself to accept the fact that the key tasks for his administration were outside the United States and not the New Deal (much to the disappointment of the New Deal liberals, beginning with Mrs Roosevelt). He forced himself to take a cram course in foreign affairs and to focus – painfully – on what he considered to be key tasks.

In a way, the hospital as we know it today is the creation of a totally obscure and forgotten Catholic hospital administrator of the 1930s and 1940s (who taught me all I know), Sister Justina in Evanston, Indiana. She was the first person to think through what patient care is. For her contributions she got very few thanks in her life, especially not from the physicians, but she was a born leader. She was retiring, shy, understated, very conscious of the fact that her formal education had stopped in first grade in an Irish country school. But there was a job to be done. And that, again and again, is what really makes the leaders. They are self-made.

Douglas MacArthur was a brilliant man and probably the last great strategist, but that wasn't his great strength. He built a team second to none because he put the task first. He was also unbelievably vain, with a tremendous contempt for humanity, because he was certain that no one came close to him in intelligence. Nevertheless, he forced himself in every single staff conference to start the presentation with the most junior officer. He did not allow anybody to interrupt. This contributed incredibly to his ability to build an organization that was willing to fight against the vastly superior enemy and win. It is very clear from his letters that this didn't come easily to him, never. He always had to force himself. It wasn't his nature, but it *was* the key task, and so it had to be done.

Tom Watson Sr, the creator of IBM, began as a self-centred, imperious man – vain, with a very short fuse. He forced himself to build a team, a winning team. He once let somebody go who I thought was very able and I asked why. Watson told me: 'He is not willing to educate me. I am not a technical man, I am a salesman. But this is a technical company, and if they don't educate me in technology, I can't give them the leadership they need.' It's that willingness to make yourself competent in the task that's needed that creates leaders.

When Ted Houser took over in the early 1950s, Sears, Roebuck had had twenty-five years of unbroken success. Houser had been a buying strategist and a statistician, purely a figures man. He looked at the company and asked: What does it need so that it can be successful *another* twenty-five years? He concluded that it needed managers. So he forced himself into taking the leadership of Sears' manager development in a very effective and yet very quiet way. Everybody down to the manager of the smallest store knew that the chairman in Chicago was watching him, and would know whether he was developing people. Sears hasn't had a new idea since 1950, yet it remained very successful for twenty-five or thirty years, almost up to 1980, because it had the people. That's what Ted Houser built.

The Balance Decision

One of the key tasks of the leader is to balance up the long range and the short range, the big picture and the pesky little details. You are always paddling a canoe with two outriggers – balancing – while managing a non-profit. One is the balance between seeing only the big picture and forgetting the individual person who sits there – one lonely young man in need of help. I've heard of hospitals that talk health-care statistics and forget the mother with a crying baby in the emergency room. That kind of failing is fairly easy to correct. Being on the firing line a few days, a few weeks a year, usually does it. The opposite danger is becoming the prisoner of operations. That's much harder to avoid. The effective people do it very largely through their work in associations and other organizations. The successful chief executive of one of our major community service organizations, one of the very large Scout Councils, sits on three boards of which only one is a community service organization – quite intentionally. And she also sits on an advisory committee of the city government. That way she is forced to see the same issues she faces in her own organization through the other end of the telescope. That works.

I've also seen it done on a smaller, much smaller, scale. A dean I worked with for many years, whom I considered singularly successful, went on the American council of Deans. I said to him, 'Paul, you are so busy, why do you do it?' And he said, 'I'm too close to the details. Once a month, I need to see what the overall issues really are.' That, too, is a fairly effective way.

Let me say there are always balancing problems in managing non-profits. This is only one example. Another, which I think is even harder to handle, is the balance between concentrating resources on one goal and enough diversification. If you concentrate, you will get maximum results. But it's also very risky. Not only may you have chosen the wrong concentration, but – in military terms – you leave your flanks totally uncovered. And there's not enough playfulness; it doesn't stir the imagination. You need that, so that there will be diversity, especially as any single task eventually becomes obsolete. But diversity can easily degenerate into splintering.

The even more critical balance, and the toughest to handle, is between being too cautious and being rash. Finally, there is timing – and this is always of the essence. You know the people who always expect results too soon and pull up the radishes to see whether they've set root, and the ones who never pull up the radishes because they're sure they're never ripe enough. Those are, in philosophical terms, Aristotelian Prudences, so to speak. How to find the right Mean.

It's actually fairly easy to deal with people who want results too soon. I'm one of them. And I've taught myself that if I expect something to happen in three months, I say, make it five. But I've also seen people who say three years when they should say three months. That's very hard to counteract. As in all Aristotelian means, the first law is 'Know thyself.' Know what is your degenerative tendency.

I've seen more institutions damaged by too much caution than by rashness, though I've seen both. Maybe I'm conscious of it because I was over-cautious when I ran institutions, or was part of the running. I did not take risks, especially financial risks, I should have taken. On the other hand, I've seen one of the country's universities almost ruined – Pittsburgh, in the 1950s – by a brilliant man who came in and tried to convert what was a fair metropolitan university into a world-class research institution in three years. He thought money would do it. Instead, he almost killed the university, and it has never quite recovered. I've seen the same thing in a museum and the same thing in a symphony orchestra. So, one has to have balance, and again the only advice I can give is to make sure you know your degenerative tendency and try to counteract it.

Then there is the balance decision between opportunity and risk. One asks first: is the decision reversible? If it is, one usually can take even considerable risks. In the non-profit institution, you must constantly gauge whether the financial dimension of a risk is too great. That's all I can say. One looks back at the decision: Is it reversible? And what kind of risk is it? Then one asks: Is it a risk we can afford? All right if it goes wrong, it hurts a little. Or is it a risk that, if things go wrong, will kill us? Or the trickiest of them all, the risk we can't afford not to take. I've been in a similar situation recently. I sit on a museum board – and a big collection was offered to us, way beyond our means. I said, Damn the torpedoes, let's buy it. It's the last chance we have. It'll make us a world-class museum. We'll get the money somehow. The balance decisions are what we need non-profit leaders for, whether they are paid or volunteer.

The Don'ts of Leadership

Finally, there are a few major don'ts for leaders. Far too many leaders believe that what they do and why they do it must be obvious to everyone in the organization. It never is. Far too many believe that when they announce things, everyone understands. No one does, as a rule. Yet very often one can't bring in people before the decision; there just isn't enough time for discussion or participation. Effective leaders have to spend a little time on making themselves understood. They sit down with their people and say: This is what we were faced with. These are the alternatives we saw, the alternatives we considered. They ask: What is your opinion? Otherwise the organization will say: 'Don't these dummies at the top know anything? What's going on here? Why haven't they considered this or that? But if you can say, Yes, we considered it, but still reached this decision, people will understand and will go along. They may say we wouldn't have decided that way, but at least upstairs, they just didn't shoot from the hip.

And the second don't. Don't be afraid of strengths in your organization. This is the besetting sin of people who run organizations. Of course, able people are ambitious. But you run far less risk of having able people around who want to push you out than you risk by being served by mediocrity. And finally, don't pick your successor alone. We tend to pick people who remind us of ourselves when we were twenty years younger. First, this is pure delusion. Second, you end up with carbon copies, and carbon copies are weak. The old rule both in military organizations and in the Catholic Church is that leaders don't pick their own successors. They're consulted, but they don't make the decision. I've seen many cases in business – but even more in non-profit institutions – where able people picked a good number two to succeed them. Somebody who is very able – provided you tell him or her what to do. It doesn't work. Partly out of emotional commitment, partly out of habit, the perfect number two is put into the top spot, and the whole organization suffers. The last time I saw this was in one of the world's largest community chests. Fortunately the number two who was picked by his predecessor because he was so much like her realized after a year that he didn't belong in the top job and was utterly miserable in it – and he left before either he or the organization had been badly damaged. But that is a rare exception. The last don'ts are: Don't hog the credit, and Don't knock your subordinates. One of the very ablest men I've seen do this headed one of the most challenging new tasks in a non-profit organization I know. His alumni now work for everybody else but his organization, because the moment they went to work for him he saw nothing but their weaknesses. He didn't promote any of his people and never sang their praises. A leader has responsibility to his subordinates, to his associates.

Those are the don'ts.

The most important do, I have said again and again already: Keep your eye on the task, not on yourself. The task matters, and you are a servant.

Note

1   See my *Innovation and Entrepreneurship* (Oxford, Butterworth-Heinemann, 1985).

Chapter 9
National Attitudes to Leadership

Introduction

With the growing attention given to global diversification, it is easy to forget that the management of many large multinationals, as well as domestic companies entering overseas markets, is often grounded in a national or regional culture. Companies like the Swiss firm Forbo, which have board directors from every country where it has factories, are the exception. Business colonialism may be frowned upon, but in terms of the attitudes and perspective of top managers it still rules.

Given the dominance of the United States in the post-war years, it is hardly surprising that parochialism remains a feature of North American business. The most striking indication is the recent Korn Ferry survey of 1,500 chief executives worldwide (article 4) which asked what qualities CEOs in the year 2000 should ideally possess. In a dramatic contrast with respondents from Europe and Japan, Americans rated the need to have an international outlook as a low priority. US executives also gave by far the lowest rating to linguistic ability and attached little importance to foreign business experience.

Domestic confidence also underlines the surveys of American executives conducted by *Fortune* in 1988 (article 1). Top US CEOs dismiss allegations that there is a leadership crisis in America. They claim modern leaders in their country are more effective and present a bullish confidence in their abilities to cope with the challenges of a global marketplace – their way. It would be interesting to see if they would answer in the same way now.

Turn to Europe and the picture is very different. In the survey of 1,500 managers conducted by Management Centre Europe (article 3), CEOs 'fail miserably in meeting the ideal criteria of leadership'. Admittedly, we are not comparing like with like. The US surveys show CEOs' opinions of themselves. The European report highlights the views of their subordinates. But the tenor of the two pieces of research shows a level of self-doubt among European businesses that does not seem to exist in the US. Asked where the best leadership is found most respondents in the survey pointed to the US and Japan.

This may well be a product of Europe's emerging identity crisis. The widely heralded emergence of the 'Euromanager' presupposes a management or leadership style distinct from approaches adopted in America or Asia. Yet there is little evidence to support this. The paucity of research into the supposed characteristics of European management, and the lack of good company case-studies to compare with those of US and Japanese enterprises, is a major handicap in an attempt to define any collective traits resulting from the Single Market.

What about Japan? The Japanese are notorious for keeping control of their subsidiaries. Local CEOs are, more often than not, Japanese and have a higher proportion of expatriate middle managers than companies with other national origins. Yet the Korn Ferry survey shows that many more Japanese executives have an international outlook than their counterparts across the Pacific, and speak a second or third language.

The surveys in this chapter also highlight significant differences in the importance executives from each region place on the various facets of their jobs. US executives put particular store on a direct experience of marketing, finance, and production. In a media-conscious country, they need to be good public speakers and know how to handle the media. Japanese executives, as one might expect, rate technological expertise as one of the future keys to success, particularly when combined with product design or research and development (R&D) skills. They also expect senior management to play a more direct role in day-to-day decisions.

Europeans tend to be split in their adherence to either US or Japanese approaches to leadership. In the survey of executives by Management Centre Europe, the Germans, Austrians, Swiss, and Scandinavians felt Japan fostered the best leadership. The French, Italians, Spanish, and British pointed to the U.S.

There are some aspects which all seem agreed on: although broad generalizations may be based on national stereotypes, in fact there are as many leadership styles as there are individuals aspiring to such a role; and even among the Americans, there is rising concern about the supply of good leadership skills among the next generation. As J. Peter Grace of W. R. Grace despondently predicts, 'I've been in business through the Thirties, Forties, Fifties, Sixties, and Seventies, and I have never seen such rapid-fire and pressure-filled changes in technology, in tempo of workplace, and in business fundamentals as in the past eight years or so. We do not have a big supply of the quality of leadership required in this new, competitive, global environment.'

1
The Seven Keys to Business Leadership

Kenneth Labich

The Barbarian hordes were descending on Rome, mayhem in their loathsome souls. There was only one man to take charge of the republic in its hour of need, and the call went out to a humble farmer named Cincinnatus. He came, he saw, he conquered. Then barely pausing for the laying on of laurels and the odd victory orgy, he went home and resumed tilling the lower XL. What a guy!

Cincinnatus lived in the fifth century BC, but his tale seems especially apt in this season. A presidential election quadrennially teases out the American public's deep longing for a selfless savior of heroic proportions, and the candidates unsurprisingly play to the crowd. George Bush earlier in his campaign confessed the need to display his grasp of 'the vision thing.' Michael Dukakis says the real issue before America is what he calls 'the L word,' the leadership thing.

Harry Truman, who turned out to be a much more effective leader than most had expected, defined the terms as well as anyone. Leadership, he said, is 'the ability to get other people to do what they don't want to, and like it.' An unprecedented array of complex problems in US business – overseas competition, rapid technological change, deregulation of markets, a revolution in management–labor relations – has greatly increased the need for corporations to evolve and adapt. Accordingly, the need for unusually creative leaders to propel their companies through major change has never been greater. John P. Kotter, a professor at the Harvard Business School, contends, 'It is not hyperbole to say that there is a leadership crisis in the US today.' The CEOs of America's largest companies disagree, saying the quality and quantity of leadership is sufficient to meet today's challenges (see article 2). But then it

'The Seven Keys to Business Leadership', by Kenneth Labich, *Fortune*, 24 October 1988. Copyright © Time Life Inc. 1988, by permission of the publishers.

shouldn't be surprising that the top business leaders think business leadership is in good hands.

Quite a bit can be done to make the most of leaders we have and develop the leaders of the future. While the best leaders seem to possess a God-given spark, anyone can become a better leader. Management consultants, business school professors, and corporate CEOs largely agree on seven guidelines that, in aggregate, produce effective leadership:

1   *Trust your subordinates.* You can't expect them to go all out for you if they think you don't believe in them.
2   *Develop a vision.* Some executives' suspicions to the contrary, planning for the long term pays off. And people want to follow someone who knows where he or she is going.
3   *Keep your cool.* The best leaders show their mettle under fire.
4   *Encourage risk.* Nothing demoralizes the troops like knowing that the slightest failure could jeopardize their entire career.
5   *Be an expert.* From boardroom to mail room, everyone had better understand that you know what you're talking about.
6   *Invite dissent.* Your people aren't giving you their best or learning how to lead if they are afraid to speak up.
7   *Simplify.* You need to see the big picture in order to set a course, communicate it, and maintain it. Keep the details at bay.

Trust subordinates

Managers have been hearing it for years, yet many of them still don't believe that the corporate command-and-control structure, with virtually all authority and responsibility residing in a chief executive at the top of a management pyramid, is fast giving way. The model that management consultants and B-school professors advocate instead is one they call the high-commitment organization. It requires pushing responsibilty down the ladder and relying far more on the energy and talent of the entire work force. Your workers haven't been evincing much energy and talent? Maybe that's because they don't trust the company to reward those qualities, and perhaps that's because the company doesn't trust the workers to exhibit them.

Management experts say the key to making a high-commitment organization work is mutual trust between top executives and employees. The ability to engender that trusting relationship has become the No. 1 leadership test. Says Steven F. Dichter, a partner at management consulting firm McKinsey & Co.: 'You can no longer afford to manage for average performance, and if you want to get that extra margin from employees you have to loosen all the boundaries.'

Beth Pritchard tried it, and it worked. She heads S. C. Johnson Wax's insect control division, which markets products such as Raid ant and roach spray and Off mosquito repellent. The division was already the leader in the field when Pritchard, 40, took over two years ago. But she has set it on an even more successful course, radically changing formulas for key products, revamping packaging, and redeploying her top staff to zero in on the needs of customers in each region of the US (the rationale being that Northeastern bugs are quite different from Southwestern ones). She accomplished all that by recognizing the potential of the people working for her and delegating as much authority as possible. Says she: 'My philosophy is that you can't do anything yourself. Your people have to do it.'

An important initial step toward giving more authority to lower-level employees is letting them have a voice in decisions. Ford Motor chief Donald E. Petersen, 62, was among the first CEOs of giant American companies to recognize this. To freshen the sense of teamwork at Ford, he established a company conference center where small groups of executives from around the world receive information and discuss basic strategies. 'Employee involvement requires participative management,' says Petersen. 'Anyone who has a legitimate reason, who will be affected by a decision, ought to have the feeling that people want to know how he or she feels.' Such worker involvement was a major factor in the improved quality of Ford's cars in the 1980s, which played a large role in its financial turnaround. Industry veterans who remember the company a decade ago say the change in attitude among employees is almost palpable. CEOs polled for the following article consider Petersen America's most effective business leader.

Giving subordinates more freedom hardly requires turning the organization into a free-for-all. McDonald's, famous as the company that leaves nothing to chance (always salt the bin of French fries from *back* to *front*), in many ways encourages employees in the field to function autonomously. Top management likes operators of individual restaurants to tinker with menu items and ways of serving customers. A cherished chapter of company history tells how a franchisee in Pittsburgh invented the Big Mac. CEO Michael R. Quinlan, 43, has no wish to change the system. As he says, 'We've got a 10,000-restaurant laboratory out there.'

Another benefit of giving subordinates lots of authority: The policy helps them become leaders who may one day take charge of the company. Is it any wonder that such detail-obsessed CEOs as Harold Geneen of ITT and Harry Gray of United Technologies left messy succession problems in their wake? By contrast, look at Johnson & Johnson's James E. Burke, who is passionate about decentralized management and partly for that reason is often cited as one of the most effective leaders in business. He says, 'We spend time with our managers but we tell them it is their responsibility to run their company.' One reason: 'Leaders are developed by challenges.'

Develop a Vision

Many executives complain that they can't afford to be visionary as long as Wall Street analysts and restive shareholders continue to press for higher earnings quarter by quarter. Impressive evidence suggests that investors actually pay attention to long-term planning by management; for example, a study by a Pennsylvania State University researcher of companies that announced large investments not expected to pay off for years found that the companies' stocks generally rose on the news.

Certainly employees keep an eye on the long term. Like anyone being led, they like to know where they're going and why, and they hate to be whipsawed by changing goals. Steve S. Chen, 44, left Cray Research last year because he had a vision of a super-computer that Cray decided not to build. 'This machine *will* be built, it *has* to be built,' says Chen. 'The future of technology in this country is at stake.' Evidence of a vision's potency to inspire: About 40 colleagues followed Chen out the door.

Don't understimate the power of a vision. McDonald's founder, Ray Kroc, pictured his empire long before it existed, and he saw how to get there. He invented the company motto – 'Quality, service, cleanliness, and value' – and kept repeating it to employees for the rest of his life. When Stanley C. Gault took over as CEO of Rubbermaid in 1980, the then staid producer of household items was slogging toward the recession, sure to get hammered. But Gault, who had recently lost out in a race for the top job at General Electric, came aboard and let the troops know what he was aiming for: 15% average annual growth of sales, profits, and earnings per share, plus $1 billion sales by 1990. He slashed staff, sold off divisions, and made some timely acquisitions, and Rubbermaid has exceeded those ambitious goals. Gault sailed through the recession and since 1981 has posted 31 consecutive quarters of record sales and profits. The Wooster, Ohio company has become one of the nation's fastest-growing, most innovative manufacturers, introducing over 1,000 new products in the past five years. Says Gault: 'You have to set the tone and pace, define objectives and strategies, demonstrate through personal example what you expect from others.' One thing Gault expects is plenty of hard work. His personal schedule often includes ten-hour workdays, seven days a week.

Of course a leader must be able to sell his vision, and that can be difficult. The instantly classic example: Richard Ferris's attempt to assemble a vast travel conglomerate of United Airlines, Hertz rental cars, and Westin and Hilton International hotels under the Allegis name. The projected synergies would have taken a long time to develop, and investors were not persuaded to follow Ferris to the payoff. Last year, rather than give Allegis allegiance, they decided the company was more valuable in pieces.

Keep your Cool

While crisis isn't the only test of leadership, it's the acid test. By demonstrating grace under pressure, the best leaders inspire those around them to stay calm and act intelligently. Example: John J. Phelan Jr, 57, chairman of the New York Stock Exchange, who was particularly graceful even as stock prices plunged around him last October. Under powerful urging to shut the exchange and halt the bloodletting, Phelan stood fast and kept his doors open. He held a series of crucial press conferences, helping to prevent more panic selling by displaying dispassionate decisiveness. He maintains that genuine leadership necessarily involves stepping forward in a crisis. 'You have to take a position, whether you like it or not,' he says. 'The natural inclination is to hide in a hole for a while. But if you don't talk about some of the problems, you create a credibility gap.'

Sometimes a crisis lasts far more than a day or two. Organized labor has been under assault for nearly a decade in the US, and no union has been savaged more brutally than the United Steelworkers. The combination of restructuring and new technology has cut membership rolls in half, to about 640,000, and managements throughout the basic industries have sought deep wage cuts and benefit givebacks. That the Steelworkers remain a cohesive unit with reasonably favorable contracts stands as testimony to the crisis management skills of union head Lynn R. Williams, 64, arguably the most effective leader in US organized labor. 'You deliberately try to work by committee, by consensus, but there are times when a leader simply has to take charge,' he says. 'I am willing to assume responsibility in a critical moment.' For example, after LTV declared bankruptcy and stopped paying insurance premiums for retirees in 1986, Williams faced down management, calling a strike at one of the company's Indiana plants and then threatening to expand the job action. LTV eventually resumed the payments.

Thanks in large measure to Williams's negotiating skills, steelworkers received an innovative profit-sharing plan in exchange for wage concessions. If their employer is sufficiently profitable, workers get back cash. If not, they receive stock. Union members also have a greater voice in strategic company decisions and enjoy additional job security. Williams asserts that the basic industries have stabilized enough to enable the union to begin organizing again to rebuild its membership.

Encourage Risks

Effective corporate leaders encourage employees not only to take chances but also to readily accept error. They make clear to one and all that the future of the enterprise rests on a willingness to experiment, to push in new and untested directions.

The best way for a leader to convey that message – or any message – is by leading the charge personally. Frederick W. Smith, 44, set an entrepreneurial tone for Federal Express when he founded the company 15 years ago. A former Marine Corps officer back from Vietnam, Smith risked several million dollars he had inherited from his father on a longtime dream of starting up an overnight air delivery service. At the time no obvious nationwide market for such a service existed, and few industry experts thought one would develop quickly. Smith persisted and assembled an international delivery empire that earned $188 million on revenues of $3.9 billion in fiscal 1988. Even with all his success, Smith continues to resist the safe route; sometimes he stumbles. He introduced an electronic message transmission service called ZapMail in 1984 and lost $233 million on it. His philosophy of risk is succinctly stated in the *Federal Express Manager's Guide*, a folksy compendium of leadership tips that functions as a sort of company bible. 'Fear of failure must never be a reason not to try something different,' it says. Employees know that Smith lives by it.

Be an Expert

Another hallmark of successful corporate leaders is that they do their homework. The troops will follow a lot more willingly if they are confident that the man or woman in front knows at least as much as they.

What August Busch of Anheuser-Busch doesn't know about beer probably isn't worth knowing; ditto with Corning's Jamie Houghton on the subject of glass. Both run companies that dominate the competition.

Both CEOs also run family-dominated companies and were educated in their respective industries virtually from birth. Most executives don't have that advantage, and many have parachuted into companies with which they are only passingly familiar. Apple Computer Chairman John Sculley has achieved much-noted success as a corporate leader, even though he knew almost nothing about personal computers when he came to Apple in 1983 after years as a marketer at PepsiCo. Aware of his problem, he immediately set about solving it. 'I'm essentially an intuitive leader, and you can only be intuitive about something you understand,' Sculley told *Fortune* this summer. 'When I first came to Apple, I didn't know enough to be intuitive.'

Armed with the proper mind-set, Sculley quickly filled in the gaps, and his mastery of the personal computer business became obvious during his famous showdown with company founder Steve Jobs in 1985. Given a choice between the two, top executives and board members who had once harbored suspicions about Sculley because of his lack of technical background rallied round him.

The Apple chief continues to explore the further reaches of his industry and business life in general. This summer he embarked on a nine-week sabbatical to pursue studies of futuristic technologies and the changing structure of American corporations.

Invite Dissent

A company run by an effective leader is a place where dissent is desirable. Says Warren Bennis, a professor of business administration at the University of Southern California and longtime leadership scholar: 'The smart ones tend to hire people of youth and vitality, people who are chronic grumblers about the status quo.' James Burke of Johnson & Johnson is a boss who actively courts fractious types. 'My style is to encourage controversy and encourage people to say what they think,' he says.

That practice paid off during J&J's extended crisis over Tylenol poisoning. Relying on his staff's sometimes noisy advice, Burke seized the initiative when seven people died from cyanide-laced Tylenol capsules in 1982. He recalled some 30 million Tylenol packages and sent out new ones with elaborate safety seals. When a poisoner struck again in 1986, Burke pulled all capsules off the market and sold the pain reliever only in tamper-resistant tablet and caplet form. Following Key No. 3, he stayed cool in numerous media appearances in which he explained his efforts and soothed anxious consumers. All the while he was entertaining often sharply differing opinions about what he should do, and he believes he made better decisions as a result. Recalls Burke: 'People yelled and said what they thought, and I synthesized it all. We had a tremendous fight over whether we should go on *60 Minutes*.' Burke allowed CBS cameras into crucial strategy sessions, winning further public support of his efforts to contain the crisis.

As president of Xerox's 33,000-person US marketing group, Addison Barry Rand, 43, has amassed an impressive reputation for inspiring his staff. An important element of his success has been an unqualified willingness to accept a variety of opinions and integrate them into his management strategy. Says Rand, who has risen steadily at Xerox since joining the company 20 years ago: 'The higher you get in an organization, the more important it is to have people who will tell you when you are right or wrong. If you have 'yes' people, then either you or they are redundant.'

Simplify

Effective leaders possess an extraordinary ability to focus on what is important and reach elegant, simple answers to complex questions. It's not a matter of settling for an easy answer or quick fix, but of zeroing in on essentials. Drew

Lewis, 56, now chairman of Union Pacific, has built his career on an exceptional knack for locking on to the most vital parts of a problem and executing deceptively simple solutions. In the 1970s he helped rescue a gaggle of faltering Eastern railroads by forming Conrail. As chairman of Warner Amex, he renegotiated major cable contracts and thereby greatly reduced the company's huge losses. He's at it again with Union Pacific, restructuring and streamlining a company with a big railroad and other diverse holdings. He has already sold assets, entered the waste management business, and reduced a 52,000-person work force by 6,000. Characteristically, he has attacked bureaucracy with special vigor, directing a reduction of management layers in the railroad from nine to four.

Lewis is currently involved in perhaps his most difficult and frustrating leadership challenge. As co-chairman, with Robert S. Strauss, of the National Economic Commission, he must help produce a plan for reducing the $150 billion budget deficit. One way would be to cut interest payments, defense outlays, or entitlement programs like Social Security – which together make up 89% of the federal budget. Another tack: raise taxes. Congress is sure to resist both and Lewis's leadership will be on the line.

Leaders shake things up, which may be one reason we don't have more of them. 'A lot of top executives simply don't want to cope with change, and it becomes harder to move them the more successful their company has been,' says Eric R. Zausner, a managing director at the consulting firm Booz Allen & Hamilton. The problem can be especially severe at a large corporation, which may have an entrenched bureaucracy with no recognition of its stake in making change work. Some leadership experts say that is one of the many woes facing top management at General Motors. Chief Executive Roger Smith has fought the problem, trying to inject some spirit into middle managers. But the bureaucracy has fought back.

An entire industry can benefit from the brisk shaking up that a leader can provide. If it can happen to a public utility it can happen anywhere – and it is happening to a public utility. William W. Berry, 56, chief executive of Virginia's Dominion Resources, sensed early in the Reagan Administration that deregulation would provide expansion opportunities beyond his company's core utility business. So he acquired shares in 14 power plants and projects from Maine to California and is selling electricity to local utilities while seeking to buy cheap power from various sources. Berry continues to push for fewer restrictive federal power regulations, and his efforts may soon change the system to encourage competitive bidding in the buying and selling of power. Why? He answers with the leader's creed: 'I have had a certain reluctance to accept things as they are. The status quo isn't acceptable here.' The change that Berry advocates would transform this tired monopoly business.

Management experts identify other characteristics of leadership that apparently can't be taught, at least not to adults. Today's effective leaders really do care about dealing honestly with the various stakeholders in their company – employees, shareholders, customers, suppliers. 'This is the type of person who is as good as his word,' says Frederick D. Sturdivant, senior vice president of the Massachusetts consulting firm MAC Group. 'You would like to think this quality is pervasive, but it's not.' Drew Lewis, for example, has earned a reputation for displaying a highly refined sense of justice. By all accounts he upheld it during the most controversial chapter of his career, the strike and subsequent firing of air traffic controllers early in the Reagan era, when he was Transportation Secretary. Lewis recommended that the controllers be fired – yet Robert Poli, head of the defunct union, has singled out Lewis as one of the 'administration' heavies who took no pleasure from the workers' distress.

The leaders we most admire have a sense of balance in their lives. They know when to close the door and go home. Says Sturdivant: 'They simply do not exploit their families. They have real lives away from the office.' In the end, these personal qualities count heavily when we assess those who present themselves as leaders in business, the political arena, or any other field. When we ask ourselves if someone is worth following, what comes to mind sooner or later is the C word, the character thing.

2
The No. 1 Leader

Kate Ballen

Whom do America's top business leaders consider the most effective members of their brotherhood? When asked in the latest *Fortune* 500/CNN Moneyline CEO poll, executives mentioned more than 100 names. The winner, Ford Motor chief Donald E. Petersen, was a bit of surprise, considering the vast amount of favorable publicity that has surrounded Detroit rival Lee A. Iacocca – whom Petersen beat by five votes. While these results suggest that no US business chief currently towers above his peers, the outpouring of names is consistent with the poll's finding that eight out of ten CEOs consider American business in good hands. This sanguine bunch is also nearly unanimous in believing that their companies are bringing along at least as many productive leaders as a decade ago. Don't worry about finding natural-born leaders; these CEOs think it's possible to teach what it takes.

An independent opinion research firm, Clark Martire & Bartolomeo, conducted the survey from September 14 to 23. The respondents were 206 CEOs of *Fortune* 500 and Service 500 companies.

In voting for the most effective business leaders, the CEOs named a troika: Petersen, Iacocca, and GE's Jack Welch. After those three the number of votes for any candidate fell off sharply; another drop followed No. 10, Johnson & Johnson's James E. Burke. A significant number of CEOs (27%) didn't nominate anyone to the roster. Lawrence O. Kitchen of Lockheed probably speaks for many in this group when he says, 'I don't want to shortchange anyone. Iacocca is obviously an effective leader, for example, but I know there are so many others out there who just don't have that publicity.'

A few CEOs seemed to have the opposite problem – thinking of anyone to mention. One cited the head of Alcoa but couldn't recall his name (it's Paul H.

'The No. 1 Leader is Petersen of Ford' from *Fortune*, 24 October 1988. Copyright © Time Life Inc. 1988, by permission of the publisher.

Q Whom do you consider the most effective leaders in US business?

A	Don Petersen, Ford	25%
	Lee Iacocca, Chrysler	23%
	Jack Welch, GE	20%
	John Reed, Citicorp	11%
	John Akers, IBM	11%
	Roy Vagelos, Merck	7%
	Charles Knight, Emerson	6%
	Ken Olsen, DEC	5%
	John Young, Hewlett-Packard	5%
	James Burke, J&J	5%

O'Neill); another had the same trouble remembering who runs Monsanto (Richard J. Mahoney). Two CEOs nominated Walter B. Wriston, even though he retired as chief of Citicorp in 1984. One cited Drew Lewis of Union Pacific, but another cited Drew Lewis of Warner Amex, a company Lewis left two years ago. And one chief nominated AT&T's James E. Olson, who died last April.

On the whole, of course, the CEOs are well acquainted with their counterparts, almost always referring to them familiarly – as Stan Gault of Rubbermaid, for example, or Larry Rawl of Exxon. The overwhelming majority (84%) say US business does not face a leadership crisis, and they often cite this familiarity in explaining their views. 'The colleagues I know have the qualities, intelligence, desire, and ability to move industry ahead,' says Roger W. Johnson of Western Digital, a supplier of computer components. While many consultants and scholars worry that today's business chiefs aren't up to such challenges as global competition, takeover attempts, and restructurings, the CEOs interviewed often argue that these problems are making them tougher, more seasoned leaders. Says Stephen D. Hassenfeld of Hasbro: 'It always takes events to push people.'

The CEOs of highflying companies are especially confident about the state of business leadership. Says Jack Twyman of Super Food Services, a distributor whose profits have more than tripled since 1980: 'American enterprise has never been stronger.' Howard P. Allen of Southern California Edison runs a standout utility in a sometimes troubled industry. 'Sure, you have a number of utilities that are in financial difficulty with nuclear plants,' he says. 'Maybe the managers haven't done as good a job as they should have, but the majority of utilities are in good shape charging reasonable rates to the public.'

Q Some expert critics claim there is a leadership crisis in US business. Do you agree or disagree?

A	Agree	12%
	Disagree	84%
	Not sure	4%

So why the talk about a business leadership crisis? Ask these CEOs and some of their responses verge on the passionate. Says Stanley M. Howe of HON Industries, an office furniture manufacturer: 'Seldom does television show business leaders in a good light. We always seem to be characterized as crooks.' Richard H. Deihl of savings and loan holding company H. F. Ahmanson adds, 'We've got better management than ever. They may not be so visible, but it's more because they're afraid of what the media will do to them.' Other CEOs chalk up the criticism to human nature. 'People just like to criticize,' says Edmunt T. Pratt Jr of Pfizer. Or as Edmund M. Carpenter of General Signal says, 'It's always traditional to have curmudgeons say there's no one to lead us.'

Q　Does your company employ as many effective leaders today as it did ten years ago?

A　Yes　　　　97%
　　No　　　　0%
　　Not sure　3%

Some of those curmudgeons are in executive suites. Of the CEOs polled, 12% believe US business does face a leadership crisis. Among the reasons: managers' inability to compete in a global economy, too much focus on short-term results, and insufficient investment in plants. 'The rest of the world is passing us by,' says Kenneth W. Perry of American Petrofina. 'I don't see any emerging leaders with the guidance to see us through the 1990s.' Even optimists might shudder at what lies ahead after hearing W. R. Grace's J. Peter Grace: 'I've been in business through the Thirties, Forties, Fifties, Sixties, and Seventies, and I have never seen such rapid-fire and pressure-filled changes in technology, in tempo of workplace, and in business fundamentals as in the past eight years or so. We do not have a big supply of the quality of leadership required in this new, competitive, global environment.'

Nearly all the CEOs polled, 97%, think the quality of leaders in the pipeline is terrific. They say their companies employ as many effective business leaders as ten years ago, and 40% volunteered without any prompting from the pollsters that they think their companies have *more* effective leaders than a decade ago. 'The young people we continue to attract are more intelligent, interesting, and willing to work than their predecessors,' says Jerry V. Jarrett of Ameritrust. Observes David H. Swanson of Central Soya: 'There are more quiet, more efficient people. There's more production and less flash.'

Companies that have been liberated from regulations see a particularly dramatic change. John C. Canepa of Old Kent Financial says, 'When we were a highly regulated industry, being a banker was a no-brainer. The government made all the decisions for you. Now, because we've grown so much, we've decentralized and diffused management. There are leaders at every level.' CEOs that have rethought corporate values also believe they have produced stronger leaders. 'My company has more effective leaders as we've promoted the importance of long-range thinking,' says Josh Weston of Automatic Data Processing. Adds William J. O'Brien of Hanover Insurance: 'Building a company on vision and value fosters better leaders.'

Q   Can effective business leadership qualities be taught?

A   Yes   73%
    No   10%
    Some can, some can't   7%
    Not sure   10%

Almost three out of four CEOs agree that effective leadership can be taught. They cite rotating assignments, internal training, and increasing responsibilities as important schooling. 'If you are born with reasonable skills, a real leader can emerge,' says Hassenfeld of Hasbro. Arnold B. McKinnon of Norfolk Southern ebulliently explains how leader development has progressed at his company: 'We've got a group of younger people coming along who have had a higher level of experience than we had, who were given major responsibility sooner than we were, and who are better prepared to take over.' Lawrence Kitchen of Lockheed will retire this year and is spending his last few months on the job preparing his successor, Daniel M. Tellep. Says Kitchen: 'One of a CEO's primary duties is to develop people who can move into the leadership position.'

And by the way, just what does leadership mean? Some of the CEOs polled grow impatient when discussion lingers on the intangibles. Twyman of Super Food says, 'You can cut through all the malarkey – performance is what determines whether you are effective.' Raider Irwin L. Jacobs of Minstar concludes somewhat ominously: 'Sooner or later, if a leader is not performing, it catches up with him. Shareholders no longer stand ineffectiveness.'

3
Leadership: The Attitudes and Opinions of European Managers

They may not know it, and perhaps they'll never find out, but today's so-called business leader doesn't nearly meet the qualities expected of him by his management. In a carefully structured survey of over 1,500 top and middle managers, chief executives are found seriously wanting in critical areas that have been defined as key parts of the leadership equation for decades.

Europe's CEOs fail miserably in meeting the ideal criteria of leadership. Indeed the ideal is so far from day-to-day reality that one wonders who reads all those management books and attends all those conferences and seminars; clearly there is a lot of catching up to do on the part of the man at the top. While we wouldn't go so far as to say that today's CEO has – on average – got it all wrong, there is certainly something of a managerial black hole out there in organizational space, where much of the thinking and writing of the last two decades has vanished without trace.

Analysing the personal opinions of over 1,000 of our respondents from all over Europe throws up startling evidence that 'Mr Chief Executive' of the management fairy-tale doesn't exist, and that all of us have a lot of work to do in developing and educating the next generation of top people.

Consider the evidence. The respondents believe that the ideal CEO needs five top qualities

- the ability to build effective teams
- the ability to listen
- the capability to make decisions on his own
- the ability to retain good people
- the ability to surround himself with good people.

Excerpt from *Leadership: The Attitudes and Opinions of European Managers* 1988, by permission of Management Centre Europe, Brussels.

In only one of these key leadership attributes (the capability to make decisions on their own) do today's CEOs score more than 50 per cent, when measured by real 'on the job' performance.

Worse still, the true picture that emerges is of the lonely, strong-willed autocrat (65%) making solo decisions (66%), who is ambitious (65%) and in many cases motivated by power (59%) or money (40%).

Taking the leadership recipe apart, and mixing in the results of our survey, we find that two leaders have emerged. One, the result of our respondent's impressions of what a business leader should be; the other, today's imperfect reality.

One key difference separates the ideal from the reality – *people*.

As Peter Drucker says, 'The manager's first task is to make effective the strength of people.'

This viewpoint – which colours much of his and other professional management watcher's writings – is supported by a former head of multinational oil-company Shell, 'Leadership is a natural, unforced ability to inspire people. The influence that emanantes from a good leader is unspecifiable, but cannot be effective without the following combined qualities being present: natural drive and a fundamental respect for, as well as a genuine interest in, people.'

Indefinable, unspecifiable, and yet 1,500 managers, working through a list of likely criteria, managed to put together the leadership recipe for our times. Since it is widely agreed that the term is indefinable who is to say they're wrong? And their definition, their secret richness, involves people: motivating them, listening to them, caring for them.

Sadly, according to their reports from the business battle-front, many of today's CEOs haven't been reading Mr Drucker, or any other management guru for that matter.

Analysing the results of their subordinates' perceptions, too many of today's leaders are tough, solo-fliers, who have never heard of participative management or team building.

Consider the top five attributes (as scored in the survey) of the real European CEO:

- capable of making decisions on his own   66%
- strong-willed   65%
- ambitious   65%
- energetic   62%
- motivated by power   59%

There's not a lot of people management or team effort in that line-up.

Looking across the organizational void to where management's Sir Galahad defends the corporate Camelot and the round-table of consensus, we find that the 'ideal' leadership attributes hinge on the 'interest and respect' of people.

- Effective teams need people.
- Listening shows concern with people.
- Retaining good people needs skill.
- Surrounding yourself with good people at the top takes time and energy.

Only one key attribute of the ideal and the perceived stands up – the capability to make decisions of his own. But whether that means when all else has failed, or this solo act is part of the usual corporate ethic, we can't say.

Listen and Learn

A total of 93 per cent of the respondents put the ability to listen as the second important attribute of a true leader, but only 44 per cent of the sample said that *their* CEO knew how to listen – yet management pioneers have been writing about this for years.

Fred Harmon in his book *The Vital Difference* counsels, 'Listening is a skill and an art. The most important skill for a manager is being able to deal with people, a good people person knows how to listen.'

Bill Marriot of the hotel and catering giant: 'Managers get into trouble when they stop listening to their staff.'

Bob Gattie of international executive search firm TASA, in his publication, *The Manager of the Year 2000*: 'Although the successful manager will have a great personal impatience to get on, both in terms of the job and his personal success curve, he will have to have infinite patience to listen, to tell and to help.'

Louvain's de Woot says of his ideal CEO, 'Fifty to eighty per cent of his time will be spent in communication – listening, talking, negotiating, interviewing. Yet many managers are poor communicators; many so-called leaders are incapable of listening.'

Perhaps a lot of CEOs just pay lip service to the people factor in organizations, but a great deal of the perceived qualities of a leader show a huge need for management development organizations to increase their influence in the top levels of Europe's corporations.

Whatever Happened to Business Ethics?

Seventy-six per cent of the surveyed managers said that 'high ethical standards' were a vital attribute in the ideal leader. Commenting on their own CEO, only 53 per cent said he had this attribute.

This seems surprising. As Dr Tom Horton, President and CEO of the American Management Association, says, 'Underlying the skills and capabilities of successful chief executives is the essential quality of integrity. Without integrity there can be no trust. Leadership is based on trust and effective management is fuelled by it.'

Indeed, if the CEO's integrity or business ethics are called into question, or just not recognized, this pervades the whole corporation. Perhaps the film-star ideal of the white-haired patriarch should be put to rest forever in the cold light of reality.

Protecting the Personal Power-Base:

But it is to the personal power-base that the survey keeps returning with the searchlight. Further down our attribute list – at the level where our sample feels things are less important – interesting corporate cans of worms are being opened.

The respondents believe that to be a leader 'motivated by power' is not a vital factor (only 35 per cent scored it as important), but 59 per cent said that this was a key factor of their own CEO's leadership.

Perhaps worse still, 'motivated by money' was seen as an important factor by just 17 per cent of the sample, but four out of every ten (40%) ascribed this trait to their own top executive. Furthermore, being 'ruthless' in business was seen as one of the least important characteristics (10%), but according to Europe's managers almost a third of CEO's (28%) are ruthless in their day-to-day dealings with their people.

In fact the Leadership Study shows that the captain of industry as defined by Hollywood and the fiction writers is totally wrong, except those that seem to get onto the covers of business books. Short, bald and disliked may be a little too strong, but few executives in the lower ranks expect him to look like a leader (30%), be an industry figure (26%), or be admired by employees (20%).

However, in reality, although only 51 per cent think that their CEO is physically fit, 44 per cent think he looks like a leader, 38 per cent say he is an industry figure and just 29 per cent are able to admit that he is admired by employees at all levels.

There is not doubt that – according to the sample – Europe's managers believe that their CEOs are pretty authoritarian, and the picture is a lot bleaker – in the team building and participative management departments – than many of us would have thought.

Although we will be going back to survey the business community again – and charting any changes – we should, in Europe at least, not be too disappointed. Let's leave the leadership debate with a comment from Phillippe de Woot of Louvain:

When the first American stepped on the moon, the director of NASA, James Webb, did not burst into the national anthem, as many a European would have been tempted to do. He simply spoke of, 'the power of method. The method which has enabled ordinary people to do an extraordinary thing'. He was referring to 400,000 people, 20,000 companies and 200 universities.

De Woot concludes:

> This is a valid philosophy. What counts is the balance between the talent, character and power of conviction of the born leader on the one hand, and on the other the methods, processes and delegation of tasks that enable a vast number of people to play their part in a collective effort. We Europeans, without our long tradition of feudalism, are still tempted to put too much faith in personal power alone.

In addition to the survey Management Centre Europe held parallel discussions and interviews with managers, business professors, consultants and commentators on their views of leadership and how the ideal matched reality. One thing these conversations clearly underlined was that management and leadership are a moving target. No sooner have you got the range than the subject moves. As society changes, as new technologies develop, the job of the leader changes. In this section of our report we address some of the issues that influence leadership today and tomorrow.

For example, Pat Canavan, who presides over the worldwide human resource operations of electronic component giant Motorola, emphasized the importance of the first quality, the ability to build effective teams. His view is that corporations are already at the stage of being so complicated that the traditional organizational approach of a single leader at the top needs questioning closely. 'It is difficult', he says, 'to imagine what we think of as leadership all residing in one man in the future.' His vision is 'of two, three, even four people directly involved with operating at the top'.

Professor Henk Thierry, an organizational psychologist with the University of Amsterdam, agrees, quoting a former Dutch CEO. 'Most of the time as a leader I spent seeing people and being a public relations figure, and that's what I regret. My *real* job was to see to it that the 210 people who reported to me were the best there were.' Thierry adds, 'We must remember that in any organization there are levels of leadership, reaching up to the top. The problem as I see it is that corporate systems won't work the higher you go. Expertise is to a certain extent measurable, but how will you measure a sense of mission?'

This innate ability to build effective teams also links up with the ability to listen (the second most important attribute cited by Europe's executives). Professor Ed Shien of the Sloan School at MIT suggests, 'Some of the most effective leaders are those who sit for hours in meetings and never say a word, but when they see things not developing they get very active. They prime the pump and push and tug and haul and the group gets working again – then they drop into the background.'

Laying further emphasis on the need for good people and good teams, Bill Mainguy, managing director of MCE says: 'You get good people around you and you get them working on the issue, then you don't have to make the decision, because unless they all believe it it's not going to happen anyway.' He concludes, 'If the leader makes the decision and they don't believe it, they will subvert it somehow.'

Indeed, according to a Swedish top management respondent: 'A leader always structures as much as he feels he needs to when the structure is absent.' Perhaps it is more than that. Some 85 per cent of MCE's poll cited 'surrounding himself with the right people at the top' as a key ideal factor, and that means more than just finding supermen. John Evans, managing director of insurance company London Life comments, 'The leader's role is to enable his functional heads to function and not interfere. In a sense you have to allow them the freedom to make their own mistakes. If they are good enough to be appointed they are good enough to make their own mistakes.'

Developing the 'Right Stuff'

But will the leader of today and the leader of tomorrow be very different? Changing patterns in society mean that for an increasing number of people there are dual careers for man and wife and these have to be taken into consideration.

For those interviewed, the motivation to be a leader seems to transcend this changing societal role. Motorola's Canavan explains: 'You say to someone, "We are going to promote you to manufacturing manager. You have got to relocate, take on 84 new responsibilities, work 60 to 70 hours a week and have to lead a group of people whom you've never met." Most people say, "Thank you for this wonderful opportunity to ruin my personal life, to relocate my family and become boss of a group of people who don't even know who I am." You could say that given these circumstances "No" is an infrequently heard response.'

The power factor – although cited as something inherent in their boss by a majority of the respondents – does not, or should not, really come into play. Says a German CEO, responding to the survey, 'Power is maybe not as important to the people who strive for the top as the need to be responsible for more and more and more.'

This opinion is qualified my MCE's Mainguy: 'What is the leader really after? It's the bigger responsibility, longer time horizons, bigger pieces of something. There will always be executives for whom that is a critical part of their life/career pattern.'

This motivational factor could be important. Jac Fitz-Enz, president of California's Saratoga Institute, comments: 'Having the best isn't the only answer, it's having leaders with the right stuff!' But what is the right stuff? Certainly, on the basis of this survey, the executive jury is out on whether their business leaders have it all – too many think they don't. More interesting

For Europeans, the US and Japan grows the best

Margaret Thatcher and a slurry of political and religious leaders may be regarded as the tops – possibly because, outside of their own countries, few managers can name heads of corporations – but the European sample have very clear ideas where the best leadership is found: in the US and Japan.

Just over a third of the sample (34%) voted for the US and a quarter (24%) for Japan. Other countries, quite frankly didn't count as there was a definite case of managerial chauvinism creeping into the statistics; the French, Germans, British and Italians voting heavily for themselves. Taking out those 'home' votes reduced European leadership to practically nil, with only Germany making any impression at all with a tiny five per cent.

Interestingly enough the Germans, Austrians, Swiss and Scandinavians all put Japan ahead of the US by two per cent, while the French, Italians, Spanish and British gave the US a massive lead in this indefinable of all management characteristics.

perhaps is whether these down-the-organization executives think they have the ability to make it to CEO status. And if they do, will the reality and the ideal finally meet, or will their subordinates, in turn, expose the poor leadership qualities of the next generation of CEOs?

What of the future? Many of the people interviewed repeated the same themes, the same needs in a leader as today. One issue above all asserted itself. What about all those women coming into the executive suite? Are they going to change the way leaders are perceived in the way they manage people?

Comments from (male) executives indicate that this question is still awaiting an answer. One respondent says: 'It is bound to happen, but will they be entirely different in the role of CEO, or are they just going to be the same old thing in a different sexual club?'

However you twist the equation and interpret these results, it is clear that the reality of being a leader, and the theory are very often different. It all comes down to how you deal with people. And perhaps as the business world changes and people become more important – rather than just a commodity – it is those men and women who know how to motiviate to build consensus and develop tomorrow's product or tomorrow's market who will be seen as the successful leaders.

As MCE's Mainguy says: 'That's what distinguishes a leader from a manager – an intuition, a sense of what the critical issues are within the group that they are trying to lead at that time.'

4
Reinventing the CEO: Regional Differences

The ideal American CEO in the year 2000 will:

- *have experience in marketing – and probably in finance and production/operations*. After a period of widely recognized neglect by top management in many American corporations, respondents indicated a need to re-emphasize production and operations. US executives consider experience in production/operations to be much more important to the ideal CEO than do executives in Latin America, Western Europe, and particularly Japan. (Our Japanese respondents rate production/operations significantly lower than do executives in all other regions).
- *be a good public speaker with media skills*. This may reflect the media-conscious environment in which US executives routinely function.
- *have a domestic outlook*. Of all the nationalities to respond to our questionnaire, Americans gave the lowest rating to the CEO's need to emphasize the international outlook of the organization.
- *speak English (in Tucson, Tokyo, Tangier, and Timbuktu)*. In light of the low value attributed to an international outlook, it was not surprising that US executives gave by far the lowest rating to the importance of expertise in foreign languages. In the year 2000, only the rare American CEO will speak French in Paris or Japanese in Tokyo.
- *not to have foreign business experience*. Consistent with other items in our survey that measured international skills, American executives attached significantly less importance to foreign business experience for their ideal CEO than did executives elsewhere. A well-known problem among

Excerpt from *Reinventing the CEO*, a global study of 1,500 chief executives conducted jointly by Korn Ferry International and Columbia University Graduate School of Business, 1988, by permission of Korn Ferry International.

American human resources staff is their difficulty in persuading US managers to accept international assignments, which are frequently considered expensive, dangerous, and damaging to careers. While these attitudes may reflect tax structures and political climates, they are also an outgrowth of American corporate views and policies. Unlike their counterparts in other countries, senior US executives do not place a premium on international experience when making decisions about an executive's suitability for advancement.

- *not have experience in diverse types of business.* American executives rated experience in diverse types of business lower than did respondents from other regions. This may suggest an American belief that managerial experience in one setting is fully germane to other settings.

The ideal Japanese CEO in the year 2000 will:

- *be a technologist.* The Japanese perceive technology, in its many manifestations, as the key to success in the 21st century. In line with their emphasis on new product development, our Japanese respondents rated such areas as research and development and technical education more highly than their counterparts in other regions.
- *have an international outlook.* This is one more indication of a Japanese commitment to globalization. For instance, many more Japanese than American executives speak second and third languages (see figure 1).

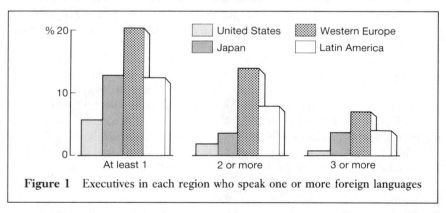

Figure 1   Executives in each region who speak one or more foreign languages

- *personally make all decisions.* The CEO's involvement in all decision-making processes has long been a distinguishing feature of Japan's corporate structure. Although Japanese respondents predict a slight decrease in this trait between now and the year 2000, they still consider it more important for the CEO than do any of our other respondents. While responsibilities in the Japanese corporation are invariably delegated, the CEO will still have to approve all significant plans and decisions. In this way, the Japanese CEO of tomorrow, like today's CEO, will maintain immediate connections to key managers and corporate developments.

- *be well educated.* Japanese executives rated all areas of education to be of higher importance for their future CEOs than did our respondents from other nations. In addition to a good undergraduate degree, the Japanese CEO in the year 2000 may have graduate education in business, engineering, science, liberal arts, or law.

The ideal Western European CEO in the year 2000 will:

- *be multilingual.* Respondents from Western Europe rank expertise in foreign languages highly, as do the Japanese. This ranking reflects the multilingualism that characterizes the European continent and the consequent emphasis that European schools typically place on languages.
- *have a specialized education.* Western European executives rate liberal arts education, both at the undergraduate and graduate levels, as far less important for their future CEOs than do respondents from other regions. This may be an expression of ideological and political schisms that divide European liberal intellectuals and corporate executives.
- *be excellent in just one area.* Western European executives rate experience in diverse functions lower than do other respondents; fewer than half of the executives from Western Europe considered such experience very important for the CEO of the year 2000, compared to about two-thirds of executives from other regions. These figures suggest a European bias toward functional excellence in a single area as an important criterion for executive advancement.
- *be less concerned about ethics and community affairs.* Our Western European respondents give relatively low ratings to the CEO's emphasis on ethics and involvement in community affairs. This may be a result of Europeans' tight focus on specific aspects of business; perhaps more general concerns are believed to fall outside the purview of the corporation.

The ideal Latin American CEO in the year 2000 will:

- *be skilled in international economics and politics.* Latin American executives anticipate the greatest need for expertise in international economics and politics; a higher percentage of respondents rated this area 'very important' for the year 2000 in Latin America than in any other region, including Japan. In a region largely characterized by shaky governments and precarious monetary systems, such expertise will be indispensable.
- *incorporate an international outlook into the company's management style.* Latin Americans rated an emphasis on an international outlook far more highly as a component of management style than did European or American executives (though not as highly as Japan), thus reaffirming the Latin American commitment to a strategy of geographic expansion.

- *reward loyalty and length of service.* A higher percentage of executives from Latin America than from any other region rated loyalty 'very important' as a personal characteristic for the ideal CEO. Accordingly, they place greater emphasis on rewarding loyalty and length of service as an aspect of management style.
- *be concerned with acquiring computer skills.* Executives in Latin America gave the highest rating to the importance of formal training in personal computers and telecommunications for the future CEO.

Commentary on Regional Variations

These results provide a poignant indication of national differences that promise to influence profoundly the success of American corporations. The insularity of US attitudes toward international business and international communication, while neither unexpected nor new, points to a continuation of America's lagging competitiveness.

By discounting the importance of an international outlook, of multilingualism, and of foreign assignments, our US respondents gave expression to a parochialism that can only inhibit opportunity. The global economy is becoming ever more integrated. Today, products and production 'transcend national borders.' How much more so tomorrow? Surely, the outstanding CEO in the year 2000 must be a citizen of the world, with a firm grasp of international politics and economics.

Unlike the US executives, our Japanese and Latin American respondents gave high marks to the importance of an international outlook. Of course, to a certain extent, they have no choice. Japan is an island nation with a large population and negligible natural resources; much of Latin America is plagued by debt and political instability. Both regions must look outward for business opportunities.

Conversely, the USA, with the world's biggest GNP and a diverse domestic marketplace, has not been driven into the international arena by the same forces that have helped to make Japan a key player in global trade. Nonetheless, it is troubling that the executives of most US corporations, perhaps by virtue of minimal international exposure, discount the importance of an international outlook. What is most disturbing is that they do not acknowledge this liability, and so risk selecting a successor with the same narrow vision.

Chapter 10
Leadership and the Global Marketplace

Introduction

If management in most countries is still parochial, what role can business leaders play in breaking down the barriers? And how are their own roles altered by the expanded scope of the company's markets and operations?

The contributions in this chapter offer two perspectives by chief executives who led 'international' companies during the 1980s. John Harvey-Jones concentrates on the cultural aspects of globalization. He stresses, rightly, that a management team of polyglots is no solution unless they possess an understanding of the national cultures in which the business operates, founded on the experience of living and working with the local population.

The superficial 'sameness' of business methods around the world hides differences in attitudes and values which emerge only in the course of day-to-day operations. A common company culture will reap benefits only if it assimilates rather than attempts to dissolve the tapestry of cultural heritages at its disposal; and if it is fuelled by the international grass roots of the organization rather than imposed from a headquarters staffed by nationals from a single parent country.

John Elliott, chief executive of the Australian brewing giant Elders, focuses on operations. A worldwide presence can be maintained only if the company is prepared to shift its capital resources, corporate headquarters, and strategic functions (marketing, R&D, human resources, etc.) to locations that best suit its international needs. Multinational companies run colonially from a single location will not provide the strategic focus and front-line feedback necessary to keep track of what is happening in its various territories.

Elliott's comments are off the cuff – they were made during a lecture to MBA students at the UK's Cranfield School of Management – but they raise interesting implications for the business leader of a newly international business. The range of options of how to run an international business is immense. José de la Torré of the University of California, Los Angeles distinguishes companies with strong central authority – who may run their marketing, R&D, and even human resource management from the top – from those who run a series of national businesses from a small headquarters; and the even looser businesses that rely on franchises, joint ventures, and 'grand alliances' to maintain a presence in disparate markets around the world. Nor are these options mutually exclusive. A company may keep tight control over one region and maintain a presence in another through a variety of collaborative ventures.

None of these options emerges as being significantly better than any of the others. The structure adopted by the organization will depend on the nature of its business and the extent to which it needs direct control over its front-line operations to exploit new markets in different business environments. But regardless of the structure, chief executives will fail to provide the right direction for the business unless their decisions are based on a direct understanding of the territories in which they are trading, and the right balance of direct supervision and delegated control.

The expansion of business into new territories, separated by large distances and even greater contrasts in culture and market conditions, presents a real dilemma to the 'global' chief executive. No one individual has the capacity to collect and digest the volume of information needed to make strategic decisions for a multinational business on his or her own. Yet unless chief executives regularly acquire front-line information, they will be unable to respond quickly and effectively to changing market conditions and to sift and analyse the information placed in front of them.

Both contributors stress this. John Elliott talks about the importance of networks as a source of future business opportunities and the difficulties of keeping in touch with the senior 'communities' of more than three countries at a time.

John Harvey-Jones cites his early upbringing in India and the command of a boat crewed entirely by Germans as important precursors to his business career. His ability to draw on this inner understanding of the two countries, which both boast a substantial ICI presence, helped him guide the local strategy more effectively.

It is not surprising, therefore, to find Harvey-Jones advocating the early exposure of key managers to other cultures through international postings. Cross-boundary job rotation forms the heart of the senior management development programmes in most successful multinational companies. This approach is explored in more detail in chapter 20.

1
Do We Want to be International?

John Harvey-Jones

One of the great paradoxes of business today is that superficially the world is becoming more and more a single market, while in reality national differences are becoming accentuated. The sheer cost scale of modern business is such that in almost every case we need to attempt to sell in world markets. This is particularly so in Europe, where the single markets of each country are quite inadequate to support a world competitive business, and where history has already developed in each country a degree of self-sufficiency which would be quite unthinkable in any single American state or province of Japan.

Nevertheless, the differences between nations are as great as they ever have been and for British or American businessmen there is a particular trap, which is the growing use of English as the main language of international business. It is interesting, for example, that even in Peking the language of the International Business School is English. Operating in this milieu requires much greater sensitivity to national differences than we are accustomed to having. The mere fact that one stays in the same sort of hotel almost anywhere in the world, that one drives in the same sort of car, that it is now possible to call by telephone or telex directly from almost anywhere in the world, all give a superficial feeling of sameness. A sameness which is desperately misleading, and which must never be taken for granted.

The comment that Britain and America are two countries separated by a common language is uncomfortably true. I am always amazed at how admiring American people are of the verbal facility of many Britons, the wider range of vocabulary and the, to them, more elegant construction of the language. But the British using more words in a more elegant way does not make for better

Excerpt from *Making It Happen: Reflections on Leadership* by John Harvey-Jones, Collins © John Harvey-Jones 1988 by permission of HarperCollins, Publishers Ltd.

understanding between our nations. Even in companies which pride themselves on their internationalism, and ICI is one, it is amazing how frequently misunderstandings arise between the British and the American branches. Because we apparently speak the same language we tend to believe that we think in the same way and that the words convey the same messages. It is, of course, a peculiarly British characteristic to think that every man is the same under the skin, and that Eskimos are really only would-be Old Etonians wearing fur coats. The realization that Americans use language in a different way, that they are motivated by different things, that they apply a different perspective of history, and that they are the prisoners of different prejudices from ourselves, is something that we find very difficult to understand.

The main task of business is a long-term one. Overwhelmingly the prime responsibility is to try to ensure that the business that we have built up endures, and it can only endure by changing. The sort of business that I ran involves the deployment of very large amounts of capital, in rather inflexible plants, designed to serve particular markets. A fly-by-night approach to commerce is quite hopeless, not only because of the nature of the plants themselves, but also because of the commitment to research and the development of new products. Our aim has to be to try to develop a sense of mutual interdependence. We all know that in private life such relationships can only be built on trust, and a very full understanding and tolerance of individual motives and behaviour. The same is true in business. Under pressure for short-term performance there is an increasing tendency to forget this simple fact. But businesses are not disembodied entities; they consist of people. The individual banker who has lost money on a deal which you have made too keen will learn from that experience, and will seek to recoup on a later occasion. Good business should contain something for both parties, and people who seek continuously to disadvantage the other partner soon run out of potential partners, in just the same way as the pyramid-seller never achieves the nirvana promised by his theory. I am always worried when we do a deal which is too favourable to us at the expense of our business partner, because I know that the day will inevitably come when the position is reversed.

The point I am trying to make is that commercial matters involve a great deal of rather sophisticated clarity of purpose, which individuals who act in these areas often do not think their way through. People do not always look far enough ahead to see the conseqeunces of a particular course of commercial action. It requires understanding, sensitivity and perception to know what the long-term consequences of one's actions may be. For example, if you constantly seek to beat the market, it is almost inevitable that somebody is going to try to beat you, which may ultimately be very damaging to your company. If you try merely to match the market there is a clarity of aim and purpose behind your activities which may seem unadventurous but which actually will affect all the myriad commercial decisions which you take. This sort of ruthless clarity of analysis in the background of the way in which one approaches things is difficult enough to permeate through an organization of the same nationality, but it becomes much more difficult when applied to people of other nationalities and other backgrounds. Having a true company philosophy requires great patience, sensitivity and understanding. Most of us feel that in learning to speak another lanaguage we automatically gain with it a deeper understanding of the people. Nothing could be further from the truth. Some of the best-trained interpreters in the world exist in the Soviet Union, but their actual knowledge and understanding of the different ways of thinking in other countries, and the national characteristics which lie behind the mere translation of the exact word, is a much rarer attribute, unless they have had the opportunity of living overseas. To develop the ability to work in a truly international sense it is highly desirable to have lived in a number of different countries and to have experienced at first hand the differences in them. Differences in small but significant things like shopping, diet, social behaviour and so on.

Language is not a computer program, and indeed the actual literal translation of words can cause offence out of all proportion to the actual intent. To the Anglo-Saxon there is a world of difference between being called a liar on the one hand, and being asked to verify the figures since they are at variance with those tabled by the other side, on the other. In other countries these distinctions are not so obvious, and offence can be given quite unwittingly if translation is too precise. Moreover, dealing with other nationals through a translator or an interpreter is no substitute for direct discussion, even if one's use of language is poor. Nothing is more frustrating than holding a meeting with a Japanese, and giving a short one-sentence reply which, when interpreted, takes six or seven minutes to communicate. At this stage one not only begins to lose confidence but can easily lose the train of what one has been saying, even though the interpretation may have been sound. It is very much easier, even if the language is imperfect, to be communicating directly. But above everything the task is to ensure that the individuals who are making the decisions understand what they are committing themselves to, or at least what you think they are committing themselves to. If the wording is imprecise or capable of two interpretations you can be sure it will be misinterpreted, and the only way to avoid subsequent differences is to test the agreement you have against a number of hypothetical examples. I can think of many cases where sitting down together and saying, 'Let us just see how the contract would stand up if the oil price fell to X, or if we found that we could not sustain our market position', will unearth either deliberate obfuscations or, more frequently, ambiguities which one may spend enormous amounts of time trying to resolve in the long term. It is necessary to check and recheck from every angle that one can think of, because business is based upon trust and trust is based, in turn, on clarity and understanding. It is particularly necessary to check ruthlessly in an internationally operating company because, in addition to the pursuit of a common business aim, large companies have an overlay of values and behaviour which makes it easy to believe that everyone understands perfectly what you have tried to communicate when in fact they may not.

ICI operates on a substantial scale in India, a country where I was brought up as a boy, and there are many examples of the way in which ICI values and approaches have influenced the behaviour in our companies there, even though for many years there has been only one Englishman in a company with at least ten thousand employees. Indeed, the company has not been headed by an Englishman since the early 1970s. Shortly after the war we built a large explosives factory at a place called Gomia in the state of Bihar to serve the Indian coal fields nearby. The centre of expertise in our industrial explosives area was at Ardeer in Scotland. The plant was built, and the Indian engineers and work people trained by a wonderful team of Scots managers and work people, who spent a small number of years in this remote part of the world. To this day that factory in India, which has not employed a single Scotsman there, to my certain knowledge, for the last fifteen years, still solemnly celebrates Burns' Night every year. They pipe in the haggis and drink to the blessed memory in exactly the way that our expatriate Scotsmen did when they were there in the late 1940s. Such customs, which are of immense value in promoting feelings of unity in a large company are too easily taken to mean that the method of working and the use of language will be exactly the same in both Britain and India. In reality nothing could be further from the truth. Indian people love to talk, discuss, examine and debate. The short, crisp discussion and decision makes them feel uncomfortable. They do not feel that the many ramifications that they would wish to pursue have been properly explored, while to a Scottish or English manager prolonged debate is taken as a sign of non-compliance, doubt and lack of enthusiasm.

Appalling problems can stem from this lack of understanding. For example, Americans tend to be very much more literal in their interpretation of language than British people are. A statement that nothing will be changed in a business relationship means just literally that to an American and the smallest deviation on unimportant matters, even if the deviations themselves are agreed as being desirable, is taken as betrayal of the original concept. British people tend to be more pragmatic and when they say that nothing will change, mean that nothing of substance will change, but that individual adjustments may be necessary to meet changing circumstances. Again, failure to examine what both parties thought they heard can lead not only to mistrust, but even worse, to the view that one party is not having adequate regard for the interests of the other and is treating them with contempt. That is no way to run a railway, let alone a multinational company.

These problems become of particular interest and concern when you get representatives of many different countries attending, for example, a senior staff training course. No matter how hard you try, the likelihood is that staff training courses will be devised and presented very largely by the staff of your head office or your headquarters, and therefore in ICI's case they tend to be held in Britain. It is constantly surprising to find how different are the things that have been heard and remarked on by the people of different nationalities attending such a course, despite their apparent command of English, knowledge of the workings of the company, devotion to the values of the business, and their intimate knowledge, liking and respect for each other. I can think of courses where we have had a very specific aim to increase awareness of commercial opportunities, or to provoke discussion of our concerns about capital expenditure, which have been attended by overseas people who have thought that the objective of the course was in the first case personnel policy, and in the second one business strategy.

To deal with these problems in an international company requires a number of actions which we seldom take. I have already laid some stress on the desirability of having lived and worked in more than one country. Understanding the real differences between countries is much easier if these cross-postings can be made earlier in your career rather than later. They are also helped a great deal if the whole of your family moves with you because then the learning becomes a shared process. There is, however, some danger when families move as a whole unit, and it is perfectly possible to live in Japan for example, and make the whole of your life around the American Club, and the Country Club, never developing the friendships and understanding of the country which are after all the object of the exercise. When my wife and I lived in Germany while I was still with the Navy, and I commanded a ship which was crewed entirely by Germans with the exception of one other British colleague, I developed an understanding and liking for Germans and Germany which has enriched the rest of my life. I do not believe that this would have happened if I had just visited the country, no matter how often.

The wise decision that I took at the time (although in reality it didn't seem much of a decision since there didn't seem to be many other options), was to run the ship on exactly the lines of a German naval vessel rather than trying to get my twenty-five sailors to learn British ways. The ship was commanded and run in German, we served German rations and ate in the German manner. The officers and the crew all ate together, an excellent habit, but one which I had not seen anywhere else. Discipline was conducted in a very different way from the navy I knew. Sailors are sailors the world over and have a remarkable ability to find totally implausible and unlikely reasons for arriving back late and drunk from shore leave. The difference lay not in the ingenuity of the story which was comparable, but in the response expected from the officer. The story usually went along the lines of, 'I was coming back on board in good time, absolutely sober, when I saw an old lady who had fallen into the harbour. Without thought

I dived in, dragged her ashore, and was lying exhausted by my efforts when a friendly passer-by revived me with rum, brandy, schnapps or whatever. Entirely due to this heroic act, I unfortunately arrived back late.'

In the case of the British sailor any sign that you had accepted such an implausible story was immediately taken as a clear indication that you were not fit to be an officer. You therefore applied a fairly mild punishment and an admonishment along the lines of, 'If you think I believe that you must think I was born yesterday!' In the case of the German sailor, questioning such a story was taken as being a matter of bad taste. The correct way of handling the incident was invariably to say something along the lines of, 'I greatly admire your dedication to the good name of the ship; however, as you know, orders are orders, and discipline is discipline.' You then proceeded to punish him with approximately twice the sentence that you would have given to the British sailor. The interesting lessons that I learnt during this experience were of far greater value to me in later life than any amount of reading or theory could possibly have been, and I was lucky enough to learn them while I was still young.

2
Managing an International Business

John D. Elliott

We think there are a number of important characteristics that are essential if you are going to build an international business and have a proper strategy. The first one is that you do need good systems. If you are going to run a major international business you have no other option. I have observed many of the American corporations who in the 1950s and 1960s expanded round the world and got it all wrong because all the budgets, all the data, had to flow back to the corporate headquarters, wherever it was, in New York or Chicago or wherever. The frustration of the people working out in the field was so great that they lost many of their staff, and many of those organizations retreated – they said, 'We can't handle the French, we can't handle the British, we can't handle Europe – as for Australia, well it's just too far away. And the reason was that they weren't using nationals, many of them, and they weren't prepared to delegate the decision-making. I think that is a very important part of it.

Another characteristic in developing the strategy of your business is that you've got to have people questioning all the time what you're doing. Senior management should not be worried about people questioning. If you do not have an executive and a management philosophy that requires people to raise questions and to test the quality of your own thinking then you're really not involving the orgaization at all. You have to talk things through. We have arguments and debates in our place and we all enjoy it; it gets a bit ferocious at times but it's usually done in a good spirit. You've got to be acting as a team and not competing against each other. Again, take the example of American organizations – in many of them there is an enormous amount of competition within the organization, there's a lot of back-stabbing and a lot of people trying

Excerpt from the Henry Ford II Scholar Award Lecture given by John D. Elliott, Chairman of the Elders Group, on Wednesday 19 April 1989 at Cranfield School of Management, UK. Copyright © John Elliott, by permission of the author.

to get to the top. We at Elders try all the time to build much more of a team-work approach. That's essential and the way you do that is not to hide things from people and not to have too much formality in your organization.

When I started at Elders I found that everybody put their coat on when they came in to see me and that these bits of paper kept coming in every day. I just sat at the desk for the first day. Nobody was allowed to travel around Australia – where they had 500 branches of their pastoral business – without permission from the Chief Executive of the whole group. So he had to be there every day signing these bits of paper. I told them to throw them out and if anybody came in with a coat on they'd be fired. I got that philosophy through quite quickly. But you do need to involve people and to make them feel that they can contribute. That is the only way.

As I travel around the world and sit down with people I get a feeling that people are contributing. People talk about the Elderization process – we do Elderize people, we do get them into that culture. We also make sure that everybody understands the strategy. After it has evolved you've got to make sure everybody understands it. What are they really trying to do? And it's amazing – it's a bit like a football team, or a cricket team – once you've got everybody going in the same direction, once you've got them all motivated to try to accomplish the same thing, the chance of getting it achieved is obviously a lot better. And finally, we reward people. We do think they should have a stake in the company. Your laws here in Britain do not make it easy for employees to have shares in the organization. I think it's an essential part of business. If management and employees right up and down the scale can have some form of stake in the company they work for and can get some of the rewards from good performance, it commits them more to the company, they take a much greater interest. We find this a very good process.

The other matter that is important if you're going to build an international strategy is that you do need networks around the world. In our agribusiness we built networks to trade in agricultural products in 40 countries, in finance in 15 countries, and our metals trade in 23. Now the reason you need networks to build an international business is that is where the opportunities come to. That's where you build contacts. That's where you see and learn what's going on in a country. The only problem is that senior executives in companies cannot, in my view, operate in more than about three countries, because if you are the Chairman, as I am, or you are running one of our big businesses, you have to get to know the senior people in that community in order to operate in that country successfully. Therefore, there is a limit to how many countries you can focus on and say, This is going to be one of our major bases in the world.

You've also got to be prepared to shift major blocks of your business if you are going to be successful internationally. For example, we moved our whole strategy group for the corporate group of Elders IXL to London some three years ago because in Australia there were no other brewers we could buy, the agribusiness could grow only by good performance, there was the odd mine we could acquire; but there was nothing there we could do to develop the business. So we came to London, which has proved to be an outstanding decision because one can travel across the Atlantic, and we do see Europe and the United States as the big key areas of opportunity, much more so than Asia.

We also moved our treasury function here to Britain. We raise large sums of money, we keep lines of over $10 billion in Elders to handle all our finance business, our lending, foreign exchange, and also to finance all our agribusiness for customers and clients. You need big lines of credit – where do the banks come to you? You've either got to be in New York or you've got to be in London. So we moved that to London.

That's why we were prepared, if we bought S&N, to go to Scotland. People said, 'they won't go' – all that nonsense, when you're in a battle. Of course we'd go, it doesn't make any difference – you've got to go where the right place for that business should be. For example, as a result of building the fledgling grain-handling business in the United States (which started off the back of our small Australian company) into the seventh biggest grain trader in the United States, we took the decision three months ago to move the whole of the head office of that business into Kansas City.

So, what about all the people? you say. Well the funny thing about all the people is we don't tell them they all have to go and live in Kansas City. We tell the most senior ones they can live where they like. I mean this quite seriously – don't disrupt your family, don't disrupt all the kids' schooling – you just have to be prepared to travel. I would say that the top 15 in the Elders group are continually travelling, and if they don't like their work, well, they don't want the job and you've got to do that by example yourself. In a sense, where people live becomes quite irrelevant and we don't disrupt people's lives. The most senior people have to travel because if they move all their family to Kansas City, you'll find that the man who's running that business will still be travelling back to Australia and into Europe – he's not home in Kansas City either, and his wife gets even more upset, because at least if she lived in Melbourne or London she would have her friends and the family. I think it is quite an important point, but you've got to be prepared to shift pieces of your business to the right place, and the people have got to be prepared to go with them.

So there are a number of things that are necessary to develop an international strategy. You've got to have good systems, the people working together well to develop the strategy, you've got to have your connections and networks around the world to make sure the opportunities come to you, you've got to be prepared to shift and modify where your business runs from, and you've got to have people who are prepared to be international.

In conclusion, let me just say that our philosophy is there is no such thing as a problem, only an opportunity, and that is a very important catch-cry in our company. Change always provides opportunities, and obstacles are there to be overcome. We see tremendous scope for growth not only in the brewing business, but in our finance business, which will probably make about $100 million this year from a base of $4 million about five years ago.

Our future, however, is tied up with attracting and retaining good young people. We go around the world to the universities in the United States, we're starting to buld our relationship here, as well as in Asia and Australia, to try and explain the philosophy of Elders, which the press certainly doesn't get right. Our culture and our commitment is to building a major well-run global business that rewards all the shareholders and provides exciting opportunities for people to grow, not only in their job but in what they see in life.

Chapter 11
Leadership and the Senior Management Team

Introduction

The cult of leadership in the 1980s was almost entirely centred around the individual. Business journals and books are saturated with case-studies of how one solo figure founded and expanded their own business (Alan Sugar, Anita Roddick) or turned around a major corporation that was moribund or in decline (Harvey-Jones, Carlzon, Eisner). Usually there is a hidden partner who is seen to contribute to the success (Roddick's husband, Frank Wells in the case of Eisner), occasionally the partnership is equal (Saatchi and Saatchi), but the spotlight of glory remains narrow.

The harsher perspective of economic recession has robbed this fertile source of journalistic and academic copy of some of its glamour. Businesses founded on the crest of an unparalleled post-war boom have floundered in less friendly markets; and where the success has proved more enduring, the single vision of a charismatic leader has created difficult succession problems (see chapter 15).

The greatest danger, which Meredith Belbin points out, is that single-vision leadership is a two-edged sword. If the 'big' leader loses touch or is corrupted by power, no one will have the status or influence to stop the slide or pick up the pieces. As the recent economic fortunes of Amstrad, Blue Arrow, and the Saatchi brothers in the UK show, few people possess 'all-weather' abilities.

The 'excellent' leader, therefore, ensures that his or her skills are balanced by a strong senior team. Yet a recent survey of top teams by Cranfield's Andrew Kakabadse suggests that a majority of chief executives feel uncomfortable about the performance of their team and their ability to address sensitive issues or achieve important corporate objectives.

The three contributions to this chapter examine various aspects of senior teams and how they operate.

The case for a team approach is put by Meridith Belbin, probably the world authority on team building. He points to the dangers of 'solo' leaders 'acting as though they have no weakness'. The more macho the leader, he argues, the more submissive the followers, something which undermines 'the very culture of the company'. Belbin goes on to argue that information technology opens up new opportunities for senior team building and the ability of organizations to spot and integrate managers with the right balance of skills. His views are reinforced by Andrew Kakabadse who breaks down the characteristics of senior managers into six 'types'. Effective teams, he says, are those where members learn to work well together and accept differences in style and approach. Does this make the solo leader redundant? No, says Antony Jay, popular BBC producer and co-writer of *Yes, Minister*. Creative teams still need to be 'led'. If the creative leader is removed, the group becomes 'an extinct volcano'.

Balancing individual and collective approaches to leadership is therefore essential. The pay-off is not just consistency in corporate performance that can weather recession as well as exploit a bull market; good teamwork is vital in a crisis. The case studies in Chapter 6 show with dazzling clarity, how individual leadership and team charisma combined to help two very different organizations respond to unexpected crisis.

1
Solo Leader/Team Leader: Antithesis in Style and Structure

Meredith Belbin

When Margaret Thatcher and Ronald Reagan established a close personal and political relationship the whole world soon became aware of one difference between them: few political allies of the period displayed such a contrast in leadership styles.

Thatcher was the most formidable female leader of her nation since Boudicca and Queen Elizabeth I. By reputation she ran 'a one person Cabinet' and commenced meetings with an announcement of the decisions she favoured before proceedings began. She was imbued with a keen sense of the divide between friends and enemies, and a key question about political colleagues was whether they were 'one of us'; the stamp of her authority was rendered by her famed phrase, 'There is no alternative.' As a firm decision-maker who could deliver what she promised she was unequalled. Yet it was not enough. She was ultimately removed from office not by her enemies but by friends, or, more exactly, by the wishes in the last resort of those with whom she worked.

Reagan, on the other hand, was a person who confessed to trusting almost everyone. His folksy approach made him much loved by large sections of the American public. Given a good script he could communicate it more appealingly than anyone else on the American political stage. The risk was always that his spontaneous response to some unexpected event or question might commit his administration to an untenable line of policy. When the specific danger occurred in the Iran/Contra affair and the erstwhile actor decided to create his own lines, it was a role for which he was ill-fitted, and the outcome was correspondingly ill-fated. On that issue anyone other than Reagan might have met his political demise. But he was forgiven, and his fame is likely to endure in history for the part he played in ending the cold war – he was the

'Solo Leader/Team Leader: Antithesis in Style and Structure' by Meredith Belbin. Original paper written for this publication © Meredith Belbin 1991.

man who, given the approving nod from staff behind the scenes, could take Gorbachev off on a friendly walk and convey to the world with smiles and gestures of the arm that old enemies were now reconciled.

The sharp differences in style and contribution between leading world figures are readily perceived by the public due to the media being quick to divulge even the smallest scraps of information. From that it is clear that well-known political leaders do not need the same given check-list of personal attributes in order to make their mark.

The same sharp contrast in style of leadership is less acknowledged in management, for since it became a taught subject the rise in management orthodoxy has persuaded many that there is a 'correct' way of doing everything. Particular leaders are apt to become models for others who, by studying and copying them, hope to turn out the same way.

The misconception is that such a single model exists. Those who have had the chance to see business leaders at close quarters will observe that the differences in *modus operandi* are just as great as those between renowned political leaders. The basic reason is that leadership style is inseparable from the nature of the person. And people turn out to be remarkably different from one another, especially in the higher reaches of accomplishment. Understanding what these differences are has an important bearing on the type of organization that needs to be built up to serve a range of given leadership styles.

Team Roles Revealed by Research

The opportunity to become more familiar with this area came my way some years ago when I had the good fortune to be invited to conduct what became known as the Henley studies. These focused on the factors separating successful and unsuccessful teams in a college business game and therefore dealt with a situation in which leadership has to be shared.

The composition of the teams proved to be one of the biggest determinants of the business outcome. With the aid of a battery of psychometric tests it was possible to predict the collective role behaviour of teams made up of certain types of individuals, which indeed proved easier than predicting individual behaviour.

Balanced teams composed of persons likely to engage in complementary role behaviour performed better than unbalanced teams. That performance could be further enhanced by both individual and team self-knowledge. The practical implication was that individual differences in style, role, and contribution, far from underlining personal weaknesses, became a source of potential team strength.

Nine distinctive roles were identified in the study with most people being prone to encompass two or three of them and almost as conspicuously to avoid

Roles and descriptions team-role contribution	Allowable weaknesses
PLANT Creative, imaginative, unorthodox; solves difficult problems	Weak in communicating with and managing ordinary people
RESOURCE INVESTIGATOR Extrovert, enthusiastic, communicative; explores opportunities; develops contacts	Loses interest once initial enthusiasm has passed
CO-ORDINATOR Mature, confident, and trusting; a good chairman; clarifies goals, promotes decision-making	Not necessarily the most clever or creative member of a group
SHAPER Dynamic, outgoing, highly strung; challenges, pressurizes, finds ways round obstacles	Prone to provocation and short-lived bursts of temper
MONITOR EVALUATOR Sober, strategic, and discerning; sees all options; judges accurately	Lacks drive and ability to inspire others
TEAMWORKER Social, mild, perceptive, and accommodating; listens, builds, averts friction	Indecisive in crunch situations
IMPLEMENTER Disciplined, reliable, conservative, and efficient; turns ideas into practical actions	Somewhat inflexible, slow to respond to new possibilities
COMPLETER Painstaking, conscientious, anxious; searches out errors and omissions; delivers on time	Inclined to worry unduly, reluctant to delegate
SPECIALIST Single-minded, self-starting, dedicated; provides knowledge or technical skills in rare supply	Contributes on only a narrow front

Figure 1   Team-role profiles

certain others in which they were not comfortable performers. These team roles involving clusters of executive-type behaviour are set out in figure 1.

The effective team member was seldom seen as the ideal would have it – an all-round individual performing well in each of the roles. The picture was rather of someone with clear, useful, and much appreciated atrributes fitting into a valued team niche. Further, those possessing very salient team-role strengths often had a corresponding weakness that belonged to the same cluster of characteristics as the strength itself. For example, the clever, innovative *Plant*, being somewhat up-in-the-air in thoughts, often failed to put the finishing touches to an idea or did not always express the practical significance of what was being suggested in a way that others could understand. In practice such a recognized shortcoming need prove no disadvantage since it would open up the opportunity for another. So in this instance a natural *Implementer* or a *Completer* could find role fulfilment. Greater diversity in the team leads to more synergy. Complex issues were tackled creatively and with greater efficiency. If a certain deficiency in an adjacent attribute is the price that has to be paid for a particular strength, that price is often worth paying. Which is why we are inclined to refer to it as 'an allowable weakness'.

A Polarity in Leader Types

Here we come up against a dilemma. Leaders are not notable for admitting their weaknesses, whether allowable or otherwise. They act as though they have no weaknesses. The more macho the leader the more submissive the followers tend to be. It is a consequence that continuously reinforces the dominant nature of the solo leader. This effect can be so powerful that the very culture of the company may shift to reflect the solo leader's favoured style of managing.

The team leader, who because of the nature of the exercise came more to the fore at Henley, forms a sharp contrast to the solo leader in many respects. Perhaps one key though seldom recognized factor is a willingness to acknowledge some personal role limitation.

Here the concept of the team role has a central relevance. Because people are so different, team leaders do not slot automatically into any given team role. They come in all shapes and sizes. For example, some team leaders have a very social quality (being *Co-ordinator/Resource Investigator*), or are distinguished by their practical drive (*Shaper/Implementer*), or may be shy but intellectually very able strategists (typically *Monitor/Evaluator/Plants*). Each team leader may develop an idiosyncratic style.

Despite the differences what team leaders have in common is a belief in the interdependence of members of the team. The pattern within the team may vary according to the nature of the group. The differences are of course important but not nearly as important as the basic division in approach between the solo leader and the team leader (see figure 2). The outgrowths of their contrasting strategies are liable to give rise, as we shall see later, to very different forms of organization, and these have an added importance due to their tendency to stabilize.

Overcoming the Information Barrier

At this point it may be worthwhile to switch our attention to the team leader and the concerns that have begun to develop from this concept.

Team-role theory, based on the Henley research and as expounded in my book *Management Teams: Why They Succeed Or Fail* (Heinemann, 1981), took

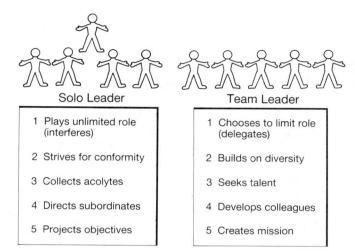

Figure 2 The solo leader and the team leader

some time to percolate into the mainstream of management education before becoming well established worldwide. The theory and its associated practices have had a good run in serving to enhance the self-awareness both of the team member and of the team itself. But, clearly, if team leaders are to share power and to divide roles equitably, good information about other team members is an essential requirement.

It was on this score that the concept began to encounter operational problems. The difficulty is commonplace wherever methodologies rely on self-reporting: individuals are inclined to see themselves as they would like to be and not necessarily as they really are. There is no point in sharing information about mutual strengths if that information is suspect. For example, one often finds an individual claiming to be 'very creative' when that view runs counter to the general opinion of colleagues.

It was a problem that had to be overcome. We did it by developing a sophisticated computer-based system that could handle a large amount of miscellaneous information about people and job characteristics. The system included an information filter that separated useful from suspect information and applied both to the self-assessment inventory (into which a control scale was introduced) and to an additional measure that utilized observer assessments. The total body of data about a person was then scanned and statistically integrated to give the optimum team-role profile. This ouput then triggered off a range of computer advice on placement in jobs, teams, and so on.

The system known as Interplace is now being used widely in different parts of the world. In some places bold changes in personnel practices have followed, and the impact is also starting to impinge on the structure of organizations.

How Solo Leaders Handle Information and the Organization

Effective leadership depends on receiving and managing information about those who are to be led. Before we begin to map out an approach that applies to shared leadership it would be as well to consider how conventional leadership of the one-person variety tends to operate.

For the purpose of both knowing and managing the troops it has long been an accepted premiss that it is necessary and desirable to have reasonably frequent face-to-face relations. The Romans considered that one commander would ideally manage ten subordinates. They could all be addressed without raising the voice and could be counted on the fingers and thumbs of two hands. Thus the Roman army was built up on multiple units of ten. In effect each officer knew his exact place in a well-ordered mathematical series.

Management hierarchies have much in common with the Roman army. The main difference is that for any given complement size the span of control is reduced and the number of levels is increased. The basic reason for this reduced span, which has the effect of multiplying levels, is that the information flow in the industrial and commercial field between bosses and subordinates is more complicated and less standardized than in military operations.

The solo leader comes into his own under most types of command system whether of a military or politically autocratic nature. Where strong decisions are needed there are obvious advantages to be gained from having a clear-cut top/down organization. With a big boss the information flow is largely downwards. However, for this streamlined advantage a price has to be paid – or rather two prices.

The first arises from the fact that no one is perfect. The big leader may lack the talent or become corrupted by power or both. Should gross mistakes be made underlings are in no position to rectify them. The danger is greatest in totalitarian states whose leaders wield unfettered power. The collapse of the command economies of the USSR and Eastern Europe indicate the vulnerability of multi-tiered bureaucracies run by big bosses whose elevation has owed more to ruthlessness or political connections than anything else.

In the industrial and commercial world solo leaders with flair have had more success. Yet pride and prestige have preceded the downfall of many once dazzling business stars. As a result of painful experience financial institutions are becoming increasingly wary of the charismatic *arriviste*. A good management team is being seen increasingly as being a sound vehicle for investment. The comparison is as between a well-tried saloon car versus a racing model with faulty or suspect brakes. The latter may be fast off the mark, yet may fail to finish the course.

The second big price that has to be paid for the enthronement of a solo leader lies in the effect on the organization. Solo leaders by nature are reluctant to delegate. They are ever ready to spot rivals or potential usurpers. To keep control they have to ensure that what is conceived on high is transmitted without any loss of message to the lowest point in the hierarchy. This can be done only through the appointment of trusted underlings who can be personally supervised. Such a formula reduces the span of control and, due to the reduction of face-to-face relations, multiplies the number of levels in a hierarchy. The consequence is the growth of multilevel bureaucracies, well designed for carrying out very specific courses of action but ill-equipped for adapting to the requirements of an ever-changing world. Such organizations almost audibly groan under their own weight.

Organizations without Solo Leaders

There is another and safer way of using talent other than by finding the big leader. It is to find and develop the balanced management team. The central point is that if such talent is to be used it requires a special blend of people. Each member needs to be talented in his or her own right but in a different way. Some team-role shapes may be more suited to team work than others. For example, it may be more difficult for a pure *Shaper* or *Specialist* to belong to such a team. But it is by no means impossible, for teamworking depends not only on personal style characteristics but on a philosophy of outlook which can be passed on through education.

In principle balanced teams need a liberal regime. In authoritarian cultures teamworking cannot really thrive. Even formal job boundaries in functional responsibility can interfere with teamworking. That fact alone makes it difficult to understand and represent the nature of the management team by means of an organization chart. Yet organization charts have a special value. Without them discipline can be lost and people not know where they stand.

That is why I have thought it worthwhile to set out here my views on the sort of organization that team leaders are likely to set in motion in the near future and to differentiate such an organization from the more familiar organizations that solo leaders favour.

Teams in industry and commerce come into their own only when transfunctional issues have to be dealt with. Typical applications cover new ventures and special projects. But the issues discussed mainly at top level nearly always turn out to be interactive. Marketing, production, sales, finance, and distribution impinge on one another and cannot satisfactorily be disentangled and treated as separate provinces of responsibility. Combination, on the other hand, takes us straight into the realms of strategy. So there is a case for arguing that most top management key issues demand team treatment.

At middle and junior levels a different situation prevails. Lateral consultation becomes less important while a sharper separation of personal responsibilities makes for an efficient service based on individual accountability.

On this reckoning no uniform structure adequately covers all levels of management. If there is to be a basic division somewhere it lies between strategic management and operational management.

Strategic management always entails complexity. Its demands emphasize consultation, the development of ideas, and the weighing up of options. The higher the level of complexity, the greater the likelihood of making a mistake. That is why strategic management benefits from the varied contributions made from members of a balanced management team. Equality or near equality of status helps to ensure that the contributions of each will be judged on merit rather than on the power of rank. The typically successful team is a relaxed and typically jolly affair. Anybody is prepared to say anything. Leg-pulling underlines the relative absence of status. On an organization chart the true representation of this body must be depicted by its flatness (see figure 3).

Operational management works best by following different principles. The procedures and methods are largely agreed. And even if they were not the competence of the manager in charge should ensure that any problems and contingencies are adequately dealt with by personal decision and action. Here the command structure of the solo leader may be entirely appropriate. The operational manager needs to be left to get on with it. So one observation that has been repeated a number of times is not altogether surprising – namely that the person who wields most authority in management is the foreman on a large building site.

What is now left for our consideration is how strategic management should relate to operational management. That embraces the associated issue of how a team leader should relate to a junior solo leader.

The answer is to provide targets, standards, and guidelines rather than to issue detailed commands and supervise the work carried out. Operational managers need to be self-managing. They benefit little from hearing words of advice or command from those who know less about the job than they do.

Traditional hierarchies are becoming, so we have argued, less and less relevant to the management of a complex modern business. In its place we propose a two-tier management structure comprising strategic management and operational management. As a corollary there is a need to 'de-layer' – that is, remove middle-management tiers. It is not merely that extra layers raise costs but more especially because they generate 'noise' in the system while also reducing the discretionary powers of operational management.

During the course of my industrial experience over the years I have been struck by the effects, in times of recession, of introducing a manpower cut-back 'across the board'. In hard times this sometimes meant reducing the number of managerial posts. The results, however, have invariably been associated with an

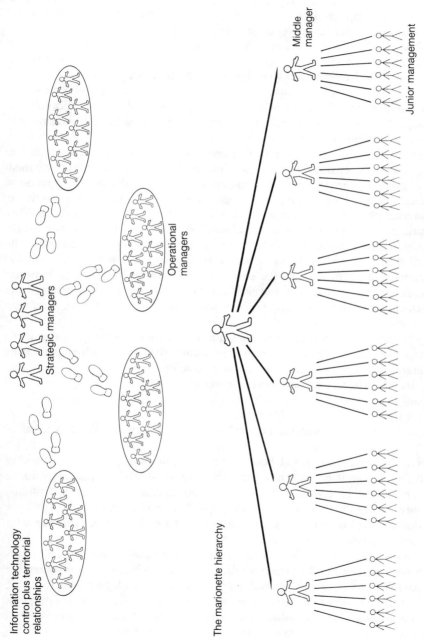

Information technology
control plus territorial
relationships

Strategic managers

Operational
managers

The marionette hierarchy

Middle
manager

Junior management

Figure 3 Team leadership model

increased level of managerial efficiency. Overmanaging the job is evidently a bigger handicap to industrial competitiveness than simple overmanning. Overmanaging and 'overlayering' are interlinked.

The Impacts of Information Technology

My contention, based especially on our experience of user applications of Interplace, is that information technology is now changing the management scene in two important ways.

First, there has been sharpened appreciation from senior managers of the distinctive contribution they can expect from colleagues based on the information now readily available to them and willingly shared. Secondly, the development is having an important bearing on how different levels of management interface with each other. Because senior managers have computer advice that allows them to gain intimate knowledge about an almost infinitely large number of individuals along with the jobs on which they are engaged, old-fashioned eyeball-to-eyeball contact no longer plays the same part. It is becoming less and less relevant for strategic management. Yet the requirement remains for different reasons. People expect it. Morale demands it. There is no other way in which workers and foremen can communicate upwards to top management. So where does that leave us?

The dilemma is one that few companies have adequately faced. The issue cannot be fudged. It requires a radical solution. What is clear at least is that top management has a dimension of responsibility that is tangential to the mechanism whereby key decisions are made.

Can Strategic Management and Visibility be Reconciled?

For reasons stated earlier, I believe that the immediate priority in improving managerial effectiveness is to reduce the number of levels of management, to widen the span of control, and to delegate responsibility. The gains in flexibility, vitality, and in due course, no doubt, profitability will be enormous.

But the risk is a lack of human contact together with all the ills that can stem from remoteness.

We may live in an age when we are still agog at the wonders that computers can offer us. But I believe that the solution to our problem calls for something remarkably old-fashioned. Walkabout management provides a means for being on the spot at a desirable level of frquency. It matters little if, for this purpose, the top manager is not competent technically to supervise. The objective is not command or downward communication but upward communication.

The team leader of the future will have a strategic role to play in a management team which may be unknown and of little concern to those outside it. But leadership also entails an important different dimension. Team leaders need a quality of approachability. That means being regularly seen and available, preferably in informal situations. To make this possible in practice team leaders need territorial responsibilities irrespective of their distinctive professional roles so that in visiting operational stations they are empowered to act as representatives of top management.

A Leadership Trend in Prospect

The concept of team leadership is relatively new. It has yet to establish practices that in the perceptions of work-staff differentiate it from solo leadership. But that change, I believe, is under way. And if it achieves its full potential, we may see developing in the near future some organization charts that bear little resemblance to those we have been used to in the past. Reconciling the roles that managers play at senior level and further down the line is the nub of the problem, and the whole area invites fresh thought.

To summarize, there are signs that large organizations are close to renewing their organization structures so as to render themselves more enterprising and flexible. In the opinion of the author, much will depend on the extent to which the theory of team leadership overtakes and replaces the quest for the solo leader – the once acclaimed saviour of businesses and of empires.

2
Managing Senior Management Teams

Andrew Kakabadse et al.

Teams are necessary for the continued growth, development and daily management of a business. Yet, in how many teams have individuals experienced positive, forward looking, fruitful, added value experiences, whereby, even if the work load may be immense, the professional pride and personal satisfaction from being a member of that team is a significant and memorable experience in one's working life?

The survey response is 'uncomfortably few'.

- 40% of British General Managers feel negative about their immediate bosses in the senior team.
- 58% of chairmen, CEOs, MDs feel uncomfortable about the effectiveness of the senior team and the performance of its members.
- 51% of CEOs, MDs, GMs feel there are important sensitive issues at top level which remain unaddressed.
- 63% of senior management recognize substantial hindrances exist in the senior team to achieving objectives.

In the survey, a question was asked of top management: 'If matters do not improve in the top team, will the business be affected?' The answer given is yes, the business will be affected. The three key issues identified are: the people in the company, the future of the company and business performance in general (see table 1).

The reason teams are so important at senior management level is that teams are the prime mechanism for the consideration and implementation of policies and strategies. Senior executives need a forum in which they can discuss the

Excerpt from *Boardroom Skills: The Top Executive Survey* by Andrew Kakabadse, Siobhan Alderson, Andrew Myers, and Mairi Bryce, a report published by Cranfield School of Management. Copyright © Andrew Kakabadse 1990, by permission of the author.

Table 1 Top team impact on the business

Issue	% of respondents
Business will be affected	26
Organization will be affected	18
People in the company will be affected	27
Members of the top team will be affected	21
Future of the company will be affected	25

fundamental issues that face the organization and identify and agree to implement approaches that will address current and future concerns and challenges.

Manufacturing cannot produce products of which Sales and Marketing have absolutely no knowledge or experience. Some consideration, even crude, will have taken place so as to co-ordinate the production with the market exploitation of products. Finance and Human Resources need to interact with the other functions simply to justify their existence. It would be difficult to obtain and understand figures representing commercial performance without the finance function interrelating with the line functions. It is impossible to recruit, develop, pay and make redundant people if the Human Resource function does not co-ordinate with the line functions.

In effect, senior executives work in groups.

Top British managers were asked: 'How much better would the company be if the top team performed better and resolved key issues?' The key issues to emerge are the people and strategic issues, namely increased profitability through improved sales and marketing, improved employee morale, better internal relations and overall better performance from employees (see table 2).

Table 2 Improved business performance

Issues	% of respondents
Increased profitability through improved sales/marketing	20.2
Greater trust	18.1
Focus on key customer groups	16.0
Improved employee morale	20.6
Better internal relations	21.2
Fewer resignations – people leaving	11.7
Better understanding of the structure	12.2
Improved response to new initiatives	18.1
Overall, better performance from employees	21.5

In the short to medium term, people and organizations can muddle through, considerably dependent on the professionalism, will and endeavour of supervisors and middle managers. In certain organizations, it is surprising just how long short to medium term really is, as the pride, expertise and standards of quality of the lower and middle ranks of management, which keeps the place going, is admirable.

However, time does catch up and catch one out. The people and strategic issues insidiously present themselves as operational problems in terms of staff turnover, low morale, loss of market share, increasing costs and poor product/service quality. What seemed like an irritant yesterday can become an inability to induce added value today.

Therefore, what is a team? A team is both a forum for discussion, decision-making, identifying strategies for policy/operational implementation, and an environment – ambience – which is enabling or disabling to the processes of discussion, decision-making and implementation.

If the members of the top management group feel that the quality of relationships, the openness of discussion, the commitment to the decisions reached and the discipline to implement the decisions made are positive, they would probably term their group a team – a stimulating, positive, enabling environment within which to work.

If the members of the top management group identify the relationships and decision-making and implementation processes as tolerable, but need to create a degree of formality and order in order to ensure that the agenda is addressed, that group may be termed a committee by its members.

If the members of the top management group consider the quality of their relationships to be negative, their decision-making to be poor, with little commitment to implementation, the group may be seen as 'those so and sos that I have to work with on a regular basis' – at best just a forum where certain essential meetings take place.

Poor-quality relationships need not occur. The creation of an effective team at the top is entirely in the hands of the members of the top management of the organization. From the surveys and case studies, shaping a disparate group of executives into a more cohesive team involves utilizing a philosophy and style of management conducive to enhancing positive relationships and addressing serious issues.

Styles and Philosophy of Management

Executives evolve, over time, a style and philosophy of management. They underpin the more fundamental views each executive holds concerning how the organization should be managed, how people should be handled and with which other executives the individual easily identifies.

Style(s) and philosophy of management reflects its beliefs as to how people wish to be managed, addressed and how they should interact with others. For example, managements may be open and want others to be open, to speak their mind, to be team players, individualists and entrepreneurs. For others, communication is not so important, or discipline in terms of identifying with the policies and procedures of the company may be a deeply held philosophy.

The quality of interaction between the members of the senior group is crucially influenced by the mix and match of the style and philosophy held by the members of the senior team. The skill is to manage the people in the senior team in a manner conducive to focusing each person's attention on the key issues, and to nurturing in them a sense of commitment and ownership towards the organization. Managing people effectively, handling different personalities, addressing beliefs and values in a way acceptable to them, whilst still keeping them, as people, focused on the business is a fraught process.

A key determinant of the quality of executive relationships is the style(s) and philosophy of the members of the executive. If the underlying views and attitudes held are conducive to in-depth discussion about the business, its problems and its progress, then such discussion will take place. If the views and philosophy negate satisfactory business conversations, then issues are likely to remain unaddressed and fester. Managing the people in a way that is acceptable to them but also conducive to the business is a rare and highly valued attribute.

The difference between an effective and an ineffective team is not a matter of fundamental compatibility between its members, but that serious consideration has been given to how the personalities in the team interrelate. In an effective team, attempts will have been made to create an environment conducive to generating meaningful discussion about the business. This may involve inducing a certain amount of tension in the group, but not to the point of being debilitating.

Those executives who do not seriously consider the impact of the interrelationships of the personalities on the top team are not likely to have thought about the impact they personally make on the group. The ones who have considered their impact on their team colleagues and have made attempts to adjust their approach, and as such have developed a style and a philosophy conducive to the team and the business, have *thought* about what they are doing. Those who have not tend to *react* to their colleagues on the team.

Six distinct styles and philosophies of management emerged from the research data. Two come under the *thinker* category and four the *reactor* category.

The Thinkers

Integrator

The capacity to recognize the problems, needs and challenges facing people within the organization, together with the sensitivity to respond to the demands of the market, are fundamental values to the integrator. The integrator tries to match the needs of the business with the level of capacity, and the maturity of senior management with the demands of the market place. As one highly successful executive remarked, 'I see the business through the eyes of my direct reports.'

The integrator makes the time to learn about the business. The individual has learnt how to withstand external pressure to act (and can control the temptation to respond and act), until he reaches a balanced view. The integrator is likely to spend time walking the floor, getting to know the problems and issues facing his immediate subordinates, appreciating what the processes of sales and marketing mean for the business, whether converging or divergent views exist as to how to improve performance in the market place and the implications for the business if such convergence or divergence of view is allowed to continue. Essentially, the integrator becomes intimately acquainted with the details of the business, the people running the business and developments in the market place.

Such drive to learn emanates from an understanding that *ownership* of the strategies being pursued and *identity* with the organization are crucial.

Ownership of the policies and strategies being pursued must exist within the senior team. If senior management do not identify with what they have decided, what hope is there of anything being effectively implemented? Once the top team have truly appreciated the nature of the problems and challenges they face, the actions and practices required to improve, then it is possible to stimulate a shared commitment to progress. The approach of the integrator is to invest time and effort to stimulate a climate of commitment and if necessary hold back from implementing important decisions until such commitment is apparent.

Obtaining agreement, however, does not mean gaining commitment. Gaining commitment involves feeling confident that colleagues, bosses and subordinates are going to act upon what has been decided, in fact observing *coherence* and *consistency*. Coherence means being able to express clearly the concepts, issues and strategies to be pursued. If an individual cannot talk about the issues at hand or express what they think or feel, they may not really understand the issues in question or feel too uncomfortable or threatened to express what they believe.

Consistency refers to the behaviour exhibited in implementing strategies or decisions. If the members of the senior team do not carry out what they have agreed, if policies and strategies are inconsistently implemented across the function and department, the behaviour of those executives indicates a lack of ownership. The acid test is always – will people do what they say?

To ensure that issues of coherence and consistency are fully addressed, the integrator attempts to create an environment where full and open discussion of people and business issues can occur. The integrator will have recognized that debate about issues is insufficient. Discussing issues and giving feedback to individuals on their behaviour and comments have to go hand in hand in order to overcome barriers and generate the necessary levels of commitment.

In order to offer feedback with the intention that that feedback be sincerely considered, the integrator needs to show that he can receive and handle feedback by having nurtured relationships within the top team in order to create a level of comfort for focused and intense business conversation to take place. Relationships need to be sufficiently robust for a healthy feedback process to take place. Feedback is not just about expressing one's views and feelings clearly. It is also about building up other people to receive the message.

The capacity to see what is required and then pragmatically work out what to do, especially in terms of predicting time, underlies the qualities of the integration-oriented executive. The need for flexibility is paramount. In certain circumstances the individual may have to adopt a softer, supportive, comfort-oriented style with colleagues and direct reports due to the low level of morale in the organization – people need building up. But the senior team could become too comfortable to appreciate, or respond to, demands from the market. In response, a tension-oriented style may be necessary to remove the lethargy.

The integrator recognizes that the manner in which issues are addressed – the process – is as important as the issues to be addressed.

Discipline-oriented

Discipline-oriented executives have a high respect for the structure of the organization, for the formal relationships within the structure and for ensuring that the administration, systems and procedures are efficiently applied. In effect, the individual identifies with the current establishment and strives to improve the efficiency of the administration.

At times accused of being bureaucratic for identifying with the administrative *status quo*, such individuals have recognized that a well-run, disciplined organization is fundamental to success. Consequently, it is imortant for them and others to follow established but meaningful work procedures. In so doing, discipline-oriented individuals pay attention to detail and demand that others do likewise. They desire that others be well disciplined and respect people who stick to the rules.

By showing personal discipline and attention to detail, the individual is more likely to ensure that decisions made and agreements reached are implemented and tracked in order to ensure efficient application.

Executives who hold discipline-oriented values are most effective when they realize that their natural attributes of efficiency and attention to detail need to be coupled with an understanding of market circumstance, and the personal impact they make on the organization. Further, they need to establish effective internal and external communication, which does not come naturally to that sort of person. Once discipline-oriented executives recognize that they need to develop themselves on the job, they are likely to emerge as high-calibre top managers.

The Reactors

Self-Made Syndrome

Executives who behave as self-made men, value independence – they feel they need to manage relationships, undertake and manage work activities and make decisions their way. The need for considerable personal space and for the expression of their own views and needs are predominant concerns. Perceived encroachment of one's personal space is viewed negatively. Suggestions and ideas that seem to contradict their ideas, inputs that are seen to interrupt their flow of thought, are perceived as irritants, which may need to be removed. Only compliance with their own ideas is viewed as positive.

The reason the individual has evolved this self-oriented approach is that they may consider themselves to be self-made. The owner/manager entrepreneur whose drive, ideas and charm with customers/clients, suppliers, distributors, financiers (i.e. crucial external contacts) built up the business and made it successful, may not learn to adjust to running a more sophisticated and larger organizational entity. He has still to appreciate that he does not always have to come up with the 'right' ideas; he does not need to be the only driving force in the organization.

In practice, the term 'delegation' is not understood by the self-made person. The concept of the team is interpreted as an extension of themselves, their ideas and their ego, not as a mechanism for attending to the needs of a more complex structure operating, probably, in a number of markets. The individual has not learnt that the self-made way of the past is no longer relevant – and in fact is now a disadvantage.

Only What They Need To Know

Executives who communicate with others on an only what they need to know basis have evolved a style and philosophy of low disclosures – they give away little about how they think and feel and communicate the minimum necessary for others to complete tasks.

This more closed or limited communication style is unlikely to arise simply as a result of lack of skill to communicate or interact with people. It is more likely to arise because communication is not seen to be necessary. People and the organization are viewed as parts of a system that simply need instruction in order to perform: people should do just what is required of them.

What accounts for this way of thinking? The individual may have become used to the doing of tasks on his own, either because of his specialism or because of inability to delegate. As a specialist, there may have been little need for him to delegate, or there may not have been the trained staff available in the past to form a team. Whatever the reasons, the executive has become used to working on his own, an attribute which emerges as an inability to communicate once he is appointed to general management.

Alternatively, the individual has not appreciated the processes of encouraging others to be sufficiently capable and mature to accept delegation. His experience has been that he achieves more on his own than with others. Checking out plans or ideas is viewed as slowing him down rather than adding anything of value and that the mistakes of others can be avoided if he undertakes the task himself.

The person is possibly still task-oriented in his approach – he just wants to get jobs done and no one can do them as fast or as well as he. He has not matured into high office or appreciated that policies and strategies must be implemented through others. He does not appreciate that communication does not involve just telling others what to do. Time needs to be spent in nurturing relationships so that others feel comfortable with him and can discuss and question what he wants in order to implement what is required. Without that, individuals are unlikely to enter into a dialogue as to the most appropriate ways of achieving objectives or meeting the boss's requirements.

Over-Sensitive Executive

Some executives display an over-sensitivity as to how they are and should be addressed. They can become quite emotional, allowing their mood to influence their judgement of people and situations. They also judge others by their manner, their overall interpersonal conduct and whether they seem to be on the same wavelength as themselves. Bosses, colleagues and subordinates who seem optimistic and pleasant are favoured. Others who seem cold and distant may be viewed as unacceptable. Judging people by what they seem and not by what they do is far from accurate. Interactions that are perceived as supportive are viewed positively and could form the basis for rewarding, or agreeing to the policies and strategies favoured by, the other person. Behaviour or interaction perceived as inappropriate or even distasteful are likely to be rejected and the people disregarded or put to one side.

Ironically, the individual may see himself as effective at managing people, with a capacity to relate to others and to be supportive when it counts. He would think it positive that he is guided by feelings about others and may openly claim to use his heart as much as his head when deciding what to do next. Undoubtedly, such sensitivity is a virtue. To know how to handle others, relate to them and recognize before others the problems that are likely to arise with particular individuals is a positive feature.

However, what distinguishes a sensitive individual from one who is over-sensitive is that the latter is likely to take criticism personally, regardless of the intention. His emotionalism can be a handicap in his appreciation of the contribution of his colleagues and subordinates, or of the pressures and problems they face. It may be difficult for him to distinguish between the role demands, challenges, constraints and functional requirements facing them, and the personal performance of any one manager. Individuals who find themselves in a difficult position for business reasons, or because they are overexposed in a poorly configured structure, may be accused of poor performance simply because their behaviour irritates or threatens the over-sensitive executive. Little thought would have been given to why the other person is behaving poorly or underperforming. Hence, for the over-sensitive senior manager, one response is to blame others.

Another is to blame himself. The over-sensitive senior manager may see the problems of the organization, the poor performance of others, as his fault. He overestimates the degree to which he should be held responsible for problems that arise.

Such emotions not only cloud the professional judgement of the senior manager, but have a strong impact on their performance and contribution. After a while, they simply feel drained, stressed or even depressed, and perform below par.

Specialist

Executives who are specialists identify with a particular profession, discipline or expertise. They tend to understand those who are like them. Communication is considerably easier amongst those of a similar professional orientation.

Communication problems can arise with people who do not identify with or understand the values of that profession or professional. The specialist has been overexposed to very particular ways of thinking, a particular language and approach, and so may be out of touch with the vagaries of life. They have ceased to think and communicate as generalists. In the words of one CEO 'Those guys that have spent all their life in one function have had their general management street skills kicked out of them.'

He may have been too long in a particular specialist function such as finance, or line function such as manufacturing. Hence he finds it difficult to appreciate the overall general management implications of a situation and may not be able to appreciate the nature of the problems facing colleagues. The single-minded focus, the high standards and at times critical approach of the specialist can leave colleagues cold. Even if the ideas are brilliant, the way they are sold could be off-putting to the point of rejecting both the person and the recommendations made.

The following statements highlight the attitudes of top executives who are also specialists:

- More specialists are needed in positions of authority in this organization.
- Work satisfaction comes from understanding the technical/specialist side of my job.
- Members of the top team should identify more with function/department rather than the body corporate.

Their emphasis is on promoting functional specialism. Strategic direction and communication are little regarded.

Specialists appointed to general management positions but with little or no general management experience or training are seen as problematic. Too many specialists of a particular kind at the top can create fundamental strategic problems. British manufacturing has long faced the problem of being product-driven and not market-led. Lack of understanding as to the needs of customers and an over-emphasis on the technicalities of the project easily occur when too many experts are involved at strategic decision-making levels.

In many specialist operations the specialists tend not to value business management skills. The meaning of terms like sales and marketing, become confused in practice. The skills of managing people are not given prominence. He is likely to make assumptions regarding the degree of shared values and vision amongst the members of the top team. The emphasis is on product and product technology, not on branding, on specialist project teams, not on pulling the organization together to hit the market. One frustrated senior executive, in discussing how to change the nature of the top team in a serious attempt to stem diminishing revenues, said, 'It's simple! This place is run by our engineers and we all know what that means.'

3
Creative Groups

Antony Jay

Despite the importance of creativeness in industry, it would be foolish and dangerous to assume that it is the only desirable quality, or that the ideal firm would consist exclusively of creative people. Today's success usually comes from yesterday's creativeness, and there will always be a need for the efficient manager of a going concern who has no original ideas to contribute, but who can keep things running happily and profitably once they have been devised and started. This is the kind of manager for whom the vast majority of the management books are written, and I have nothing to add. Indeed the need is not for addition but subtraction. However, the top management of a firm should be concerned about tomorrow's success – on the night before Alamein, Montgomery was thinking hard about the invasion of Italy – and tomorrow's success comes from today's creativeness. It is therefore important to know if you can arrange for the right sort of creativeness to happen, or if you just have to try and recruit the right sort of people and then cross your fingers and pray.

Perhaps one day it will be possible to formulate scientific laws for the generating of creative ideas, but that day has not yet come. Nevertheless, if you look back on a number of creative movements there is one pattern which seems to repeat itself, the pattern of a leader who is himself a highly creative person working with a small nucleus around him, a creative group. It is by no means the only way to bring about change, or to seize and fashion to your own ends change which is happening, but it seems to have been consistently successful. There are numerous examples ranging from Charlemagne and Henry II to Lenin and John F. Kennedy. Sometimes, if the group is successful, it may grow until it appears to be very large; but if you look closely you find that only a small

Excerpt from *Management and Machiavelli: Power and Authority in Business Life*, by Antony Jay, Century Hutchinson. Copyright © Antony Jay 1967, 1987, by permission of the Random Century Group Ltd. and Curtis Brown Ltd. on behalf of the author.

number belong to the central nucleus, however much power and responsibility other people may have in particular but limited areas of the enterprise. Groups of this same kind can be found in art, in science, in military history, in social reform and other areas of life. They also happen in industry; not all that often in my experience, but if you have ever worked in or close to one, you recognize others at once; and if you observe them and talk to people inside and outside them, you find they share a number of important characteristics which also seem to have been shared by the creative groups of the past.

1 *The authority of the leader himself is unquestioned and unchallenged.* In fact in a successful group he is often spoken of with an uncritical admiration which borders on reverence, and infuriates outsiders. Just what makes a creative leader is so important that it must be dealt with separately; for the moment it is sufficient to say that without one the creative group does not exist. He is the stallion; there must also be his mares though they themselves may become stallions (substallions?) so to speak, with their own subordinates. Obviously you cannot lay down an exact number for this group, but I would be surprised to find a leader with more than five people who formed the central nucleus and I would think that three is closer to the norm; this is not to say that there cannot be many more trusted and able members of the group, only that the central nucleus must be small.

2 *Within the central nucleus there is dialogue.* This is a difficult concept to describe to those who have not experienced it, but an important one. It seems to be the product of long thrashing-out sessions – call them debates or discussion if you prefer, but they are usually very informal – at which attitudes, ideas, policies and critical standards are hammered out until there is a body of shared convictions about methods and products and markets or whatever the group's business is concerned with. The emotional impulse is usually dissatisfaction with what is being done, or not being done, by other people in the business; this of course happens outside creative groups as well, and the distinguishing factor of a creative group is that it produces a positive, constructive and original idea. It may be a bad idea, but it is an idea and not just an anthology of gripes. And once this is hammered out, over the months, it forms a basis for a continuing dialogue, discussions which rest on such a broad base of shared convictions that they usually end with agreement, improved understanding of the group's business (or art), perhaps new ideas to investigate or develop, and a broader base for further dialogue to spring from. This makes it difficult for newcomers to reach the central nucleus, since there are so many shared convictions which in time become underlying assumptions and often take a lot of discovering. It also tends to make the group unpopular with people outside it, since they nearly always side with each other in argument and appear deliberately exclusive.

3 *Creative groups and output.* They do not work at their best when spirited away to a country house and told to 'have some ideas'. It is not remarkable that

Shakespeare wrote his plays while he was an active member of the Lord Chamberlain's players; it is exactly what you would expect. They were a creative group (led by Richard Burbage) from which a considerable output was demanded in the shape of new productions for new occasions, and the group's success, as so often, was in proportion not only to the qualities of its members but also to the demands made upon it. Any creative group belongs where the work is being done, in the quick forge and working-house of thought.

Output is necessary in the first instance as a spur to ideas: the knowledge that a deadline is approaching, that something has to be done urgently, is a wonderful liberator of the creative impulse. That is why the 'wastage' principle does not work with creative groups. The idea of getting ten groups all to put in an idea from which one will be selected and nine discarded does not get the best out of these groups: the sense of urgency is divided by ten. It is much better, very often, for the one group to bear the responsibility alone, to know that everything depends on what they come up with, and that good or bad it will go into production because there is nothing else. Leonides and his Spartans would not have fought so bravely at Thermopylae if they had known that there were nine more regiments from other cities waiting in reserve.

Output is also important for morale. Creative groups use up a lot of energy. Often they work hard and long and late, and they cannot be supervised, checked on for punctuality and efficiency, as the more routine performers can. It is often impossible anyway, but when morale is high it is also unnecessary because the work becomes a great source of satisfaction. For this reason, they respond better to encouragement and enthusiasm than many others. But most of all they respond to success, to the visible, objective success of what they are doing. This is the only real morale-raiser, and since high morale is vital to a successful creative group, a regular, indeed an exceptionally high, demand on their output is vital as well.

The third need for output is as feedback. If the dialogue is to continue, then there must be a continuous supply of new data, a continuous learning process. Only by continuing to produce can improvements be made, new facts revealed and the body of shared convictions augmented or revised or refined by new evidence.

4   *The leader of a creative group must have as much autonomy as possible.* He must be able to implement the ideas of the group on his own responsibility. If they have to be passed up to someone else, they will not be put into effect with the same understanding, nor with the same confidence and enthusiasm. And of course the group works with all the more willingness if it knows that the leader is the man who will actually implement the idea himself and not just go off and try to sell it to someone else.

5   *Creative groups have to grow, or they die.* If they devise and launch a new and successful project, they are unlikely to be satisfied with the running of it once it is established. Indeed the mere fact of being good enough to launch it is

proof that they are too good to run it – at least as a full-time job. They need the constant stimulus of bigger challenges and responsibilities, better resources, larger budget, more staff, as well as sufficient personal promotion and increase of salary to keep their morale high. Given this, they seem to be able to go on for a very long time, perhaps growing from a small section into a department and then into a division or a subsidiary company, and perhaps finally becoming the management group of the corporation.

It is an attractive idea to think that the members of a creative group can be removed and turned into creative leaders with groups of their own. It does not seem to work. They can make good executives, but it seems that the simple fact that they work well under a creative leader is evidence that they are not creative leaders themselves. There are, however, two qualities they must have, in addition to a sound knowledge of the group's business. One is creativeness, originality of mind, the ability to have ideas of their own that are not just copies of other people's. In selecting people it is less important whether these are in fact good ideas, so long as they are original. The second quality is judgement, the ability to weed out the good ideas from the bad; this develops later, as a result of learning what works and what doesn't in market terms. Of course a creative leader must have both these qualities, but he also needs the further quality of leadership, the capacity to inspire other creative people, and this is what a member of a group is unlikely to have.

6 *If the creative leader is removed from a group, it becomes an extinct volcano.* As with real volcanoes, it takes time to realize that it has become extinct, but it gradually becomes clear that although it is still efficient, the thing isn't bubbling any more. Our society has many extinct volcanoes – societies, magazines, political groups, television programmes, etc. – which were once exciting and important, and now carry on a staid and routine existence after the glory has departed. The Reform Bill of 1831–2 created a ferment in English society, but the resulting Reform Club, while still in existence, is not now pullulating with outrageous modern ideas. An interesting corollary is that if a firm wants to weaken a competitor, one of the cheapest and most effective ways is to identify the creative groups and offer the leaders, or better still the leaders and a couple of their closest colleagues each, lucrative and attractive jobs on its own staff. It is not important that it should need them itself, although they ought to prove an invaluable addition to the strength, only that the competitor should be deprived of them.

7 *Creative groups define their own projects.* This is not to say they do not need projects given to them – they must have some details of what product is required, how big the budget is, what plant and labour are available, what the time scale is, etc. But the more freedom they are given within those broad limits, the more successful they are likely to be. People tend to devise what they can achieve themselves, and projects devised by creative groups are likely to draw on the skills and expertise and interests which the group possesses. They

will not devise a product whose success hinges on metallurgical factors if they have no one with metallurgical qualifications in the group. It therefore follows that there will be more variety in the results of the creative coupling, the 'bisociation' within the group, if the members of the group have different backgrounds. Of course if they belong to different species they may not mate at all; but if they all have an almost identical background and experience the intercourse is likely to be incestuous and the offspring eugenically unsound.

I am well aware that listing some of the shared characterisitcs of creative groups is not the same as providing a formula for starting them. I am equally aware that some of the most important creative ideas have come, without any particular external stimulus, to people working entirely on their own. But great industrial enterprises, although they need the brilliant invention, also need the robust continuing supply of smaller-scale creative ideas harnessed to a productive drive in order to turn the invention into a product. It was in the 1930s that Chester Carlson 'bisociated' his production knowledge of photoconductivity gained as a physicist with his 'market' knowledge of the demand for document copying gained as a patent lawyer, to produce the idea of Xerography, and he did the experiments privately in his own back kitchen. But it was not until 1960 that Xerox copying started to revolutionize the world's offices and libraries. It was the creative group under Joseph C. Wilson of the Haloid Corporation which transformed a bright idea into a revolution, and made Xerocopying one of the great industrial success stories of a decade. At the moment – such is the speed of advance in science and technology – there may well be a greater number of inventions and discoveries lying around than there are groups capable of exploiting them. There is, after all, no inevitability about the exploitation of inventions: the Byzantines invented clockwork and used it only for levitating the emperor to impress visitors, the Chinese invented gunpowder and used it largely for firework displays, the Tibetans discovered turbine movement and exploited it only for the rotation of prayer wheels. The link between the invention, or the discovery of a principle, and its use to increase the well-being of man (whether as user or shareholder) is usually an industrial firm, and within the firm it is the creative group which sees and exploits the possibilities. And if you combine a unique principle like Xerocopying with a creative manufacturing group, you no longer need creative advertising people or creative packaging people or creative public relations people. All you need is a thick order book and a big switchboard.

Chapter 12
Women as Leaders

Introduction

Few aspects of leadership have attracted more attention than the role and development of women. In this book we examine two issues. The first, examined in chapter 19, concerns numbers. Throughout the 1970s, academic research and popular debate concentrated on the paucity (then) of women professionals and managers. As women were recruited into junior management in greater numbers, attention shifted to the 'glass ceiling' which prevents women reaching senior positions. As Valerie Hammond argues in chapter 19, this is due to poor career management and training as much as explicit bigotry, although other contributors stress that male attitudes to women in the boardroom still create formidable barriers to female advancement.

By contrast, the articles in this chapter focus on the 'qualities' of female leadership and whether these differ markedly from those displayed by men. As the number of women leaders increases, albeit far too slowly, this issue has become important not only to feminists and sociologists but to board members planning their successors and the growing army of organization behaviourists who advise them.

The writers in this chapter look at the issue from a variety of viewpoints, but their arguments boil down to three contrasting strands of thought. The first is that women, by their very gender, bring to their work qualities that men often lack. Jan Grant describes the change that took place in feminist thought between the 1960s, when people felt that women needed to achieve equal opportunities, and the 1980s when women's ways of behaving, feeling, and thinking were seen to be valuable in themselves. Grant looks at a variety of 'female' attributes, including collaboration, affiliation, and nurturing, and argues that these characterisitcs are particularly relevant to modern business, with its emphasis on people skills and more collaborative business strategies. The article by Roz Morris shows how popular this view has become. Professor Cary Cooper, for example, comments: 'men manage by punishment and women manage by rewards. Women are socialized to manage people and relationships in the home, and now they're taking their skills from the home and transferring them to the workplace. Our studies have shown that women tend to be more participatory in their management style and they are seen by both male and female subordinates to be much more caring than their male counterparts.' Rennie Fritchie also comments that women are great 'Right Brain Thinkers' and thus more creative and flexible than men.

This argument is supported by John Harvey-Jones in his book *Making it Happen*: 'The emergence of more women at senior positions will, I believe, be of immense help to industry . . . Women seem to me to have better intuitive capabilities and a deeper, inbuilt, sense of fundamental responsibility. They are prepared to stick with details longer than men, and to ensure that things are actually done right. They also have a different perception of other people's reactions and, by and large, are more sensitive to them.'

The second concept is more subtle. Both sexes have a masculine and a feminine side to their nature, which is reflected in their management style. 'Feminine' characteristics – co-operation, affiliation, nurturing, intuition, etc. – exist in both men and women, and organizations need to create a climate in which everyone feels free to express them.

Jan Carlzon expresses this view in his book *Moments of Truth* (see chapter 4): 'the new leader is a listener, communicator, an educator – an emotionally expressive and inspiring person who can create the right atmosphere rather than make all the decisions himself. These skills were once regarded as feminine, an association that goes back to women's roles in the old agricultural society when they took care of family and social relationships in the village . . . I firmly believe that, in the long run, men and women alike will benefit from using "feminine" and "masculine" qualities in good combination.'

But if men are capable of exhibiting 'feminine' qualities, the converse proposition – that women are capable of exhibiting 'masculine' qualities must also be true. The article by Jaclyn Fierman in chapter 19 argues that successful female executives in the United States need to 'look like a lady; act like a man'. Hard experience tends to support this. While some female leaders like Anita Roddick personify the caring collaborative image of feminine management, others do not. The best case we have – Margaret Thatcher's premiership – confounds all theoretical analysis. In Hugo Young's analysis of her leadership style, she is more aggressive and competitive than any man in her Cabinet when tackling the task of government; yet her personal relationships with colleagues, friends, and family are marked by a traditional feminity which few modern career women would think seemly.

Where does this leave us? A third viewpoint is emerging which is expressed most forcibly by John Adair in his book *Great Leaders*: 'There is no evidence . . . that male and female qualities exist. There are women, for example, who lack both intuition and a sense of responsibility. Courage and aggressiveness, on the other hand, are by no means uniquely male characteristics. All attempts to generalise about the leadership qualities or abilities that women possess, as opposed to men, upon closer examination seem to collapse like a house of cards. There seems little point in labelling certain attitudes or characteristics – such as compassion, warmth, gentleness and humility – as being "feminine" and other qualities as being "masculine". For these qualities are to be found in both sexes in different measures or combinations.'

Maybe this is too cynical. Maybe people of both sexes react to and are conditioned by their working environment, so that women in businesses dominated by men act like men and men in businesses shaped by women act like women. Maybe there are biological, genetic differences that determine different management styles. Until the trickle of women reaching the boardroom becomes a flow, the jury is out on this issue.

1
Women as Managers: What They can Offer Organizations

Jan Grant

An ancient Chinese story taken from Sun Tse's manual on strategy for warriors is presented as an allegory by the leading French feminist Hélène Cixous in her article 'Castration or Decapitation' (*Signs: Journal of Women in Culture and Society*, vol. 7, no. 1, 1981). According to this story, the King commanded General Sun Tse to make soldiers out of all 180 of his wives. As a start, Sun Tse arranged the women in two rows, each headed by the King's favorite wives, and taught them the language of the drumbeat. This language was very simple – but instead of learning it quickly, the ladies started laughing and chatting and paid no attention to the instructions. Even though Sun Tse repeated the instructions several times over, the women simply laughed all the more. The Chinese military code of the time deemed such behavior mutinous, so the women were condemned to death. The king was not happy about losing so many wives; however, Sun Tse, being a man of absolute principle, said that the Absolute Law forbade one from going back on a king's order. He beheaded the two women commanders; they were replaced, and the lesson was started over. As if they had never done anything but practice the art of war, the women turned right, left, and about in silence without making a single mistake.

According to Cixous, the moral of the story is that women must conform to the masculine model if they want to keep their heads. However, 'they keep them on the condition that they lose them – lose them, that is, to complete silence, turned into automatons.'

'Women as Managers: What They can Offer Organizations', by Jan Grant, from *Organizational Dynamics*, Winter 1988. Copyright © American Management Association, by permission of the publishers.

This article will address the following question: Is it possible for women to enter organizations (particularly their power structures) without losing their heads – that is, without losing their ability to speak as, for, and with women? Further, if this is possible, what are the ramifications for the organizations themselves?

Women Managers: A Shifting Emphasis

Organizations clearly reproduce themselves. People in power (who are mostly men) mentor, encourage, and advance people who are most like themselves. Not surprisingly, then, the handful of women who actually do achieve senior rank in organizations usually resemble the men in power. They have had to identify with and emulate the model in order to progress in the organization. Thus numerous recent studies in organizational behavior have shown that there are apparently very few, if any, personality or behavioral differences between male and female managers. For example, a number of studies have shown that as women move up the organizational hierarchy, their identification with the male model of managerial success becomes so important that they end up rejecting even the few valued feminine managerial traits they may have earlier endorsed. For many women, then, being successful in an organization means suppressing or eliminating attitudes and behaviors that would identify them as 'typically female,' and therefore as ill-suited for leadership roles (as those roles are currently defined). Even in terms of needs, motives, and values, no differences emerge between male and female managers.

Thus, although organizations have been successful in creating the 'she-male,' there are arguably negative consequences for both the individual women concerned and the organizations themselves if this pattern continues to be followed. These negative consequences occur because the very characteristics that are undervalued, repressed, or considered unimportant in positions of power are the ones necessary to make organizations more responsive to human needs for a sense of connectedness, community, purpose, affiliation, and nurturing.

Before considering these characteristics, we should briefly review the shifting emphasis in feminist theory to give a framework and sociopolitical context to the arguments that follow. During the late 1960s and early 1970s, feminist authors such as Shulasmith Firestone, Betty Friedan, Germaine Greer, and Kate Millet attempted to minimize differences between men and women in order to achieve equality of opportunity. The critique of patriarchy led initially to a notion of androgyny in which male and female sex-role traits were amalgamated into one personality. This androgynous personality would be a balance between the male sex-role traits of 'agency' and the female sex-role traits of 'communion.' Agency refers to such characteristics as independence, self-reliance, autonomy, aggression, leadership, initiative, competitiveness, ambition, analytical thinking, dominance, forcefulness, competence, and instrumentalism. Communion refers to such qualities as nurturing, compassion, sensitivity, cooperativeness, affection, gentleness, empathy, interpersonal sensitivity, and interdependence. The analysis of power in sexual politics, however, became diffused during this period, and the emphasis moved to how women could be resocialized to compete on an equal basis with men. This resulted in the emergence of workshops on the assertive woman, women and success, dressing for success, and women in management. However, as Jeanne E. Gullahorn has pointed out in her book *Psychology and Women* (Winston and Sons, 1979), 'Becoming experts on slave psychology involves the danger of overlooking the fact that the ultimate problem is not the slave victim but the institution of slavery.' Thus, although it is laudable that seminars, self-help groups, and workshops are oriented toward making women more assertive and more agenic, the focus of these activities is still on women as victims with deficits that should be corrected. There has also been a backlash against the androgynous ideal as being intrinsically sexist. For example, some findings show that it is the masculine attributes of androgyny that are correlated with self-esteem and adjustment.

The concept of androgyny also ignores issues of power and social structure in its promise of social change through individual psychological transformation. The qualities that are actually valued in organizations apparently do not endorse these androgynous ideals either. In a national survey taken in 1972 of male and female managers in the United States, D. C. Basil found that the five most highly valued personal characteristics are decisiveness, consistency, objectivity, emotional stability, and analytical ability.

Accordingly, from the late 1970s to the present, feminists began to emphasize a perspective that actually valued women's experience, traditional values, and ways of behaving, feeling, and thinking. This woman-centered perspective celebrates and exonerates female difference, instead of suggesting that women imitate male agenic features with an androgynous sprinkling of communal qualities. Thus feminists such as Adrienne Rich, Nancy Chodorow, Jean Baker Miller, Dale Spender, and Dorothy Dinnerstein have written lyrically about the positive values of female difference and the possibility of social change through a revaluing of these differences.

Six Psychological Qualities

In her book *Toward a New Psychology of Women* (Penguin, 1976) Jean Baker Miller argues convincingly that the dominant culture projects onto the subordinate culture (or cultures) all aspects of life that are physically and psychologically too unpleasant to deal with. By doing this, however, the male-led society:

> may have also, simultaneously and unwittingly, delegated to women not humanity's 'lowest needs' but its 'highest necessities' – that is, the intense, emotionally connected cooperation and creativity necessary for human life and growth . . . Because women have filled in these essentials, they have developed a foundation of extremely valuable psychological qualities.

Although biology has played a part, it is mostly women's experiences in the family, the community, and the economic and political structure that have led to this development.

What are some of these qualities, and how are they relevant for organizations? There are six important areas to consider: communication and cooperation, affiliation and attachment, power, physicality, emotionality, vulnerability and lack of self-confidence, and intimacy and nurturing.

Communication and Cooperation

Because women have had a lot of practice from an early age at communicating with and caring for others, they are often good at it. They can often find a means of conciliation with others instead of getting involved in a confrontation. Research has shown that in most societies the communication networks among women serve as the foundation for social interaction. When a group of men are talking, part of the process is 'gaining the floor' – a competition in which the winner is the one who speaks. Women, on the other hand, tend to take turns in group discussion. This more cooperative behavior is important in terms of consultation and democratic decision-making processes that should lead to higher morale and greater commitment from people in an organization. The recent emphasis on 'quality circles,' which encourage worker participation, herald the importance of communication and cooperation in organizations.

Affiliation and Attachment

There is very strong evidence that women have developed a different psychic 'starting point' at which affiliation is valued as highly as, or more highly than, self-enhancement. In psychological theory, women may be described as 'dependent' – as needing others too much because they have not individuated, separated, or developed autonomy. However, this strong sense of ties to and concern for others can be a real resource in organizations that often create feelings of alienation and lack of community.

The importance of attachments and connectedness for women has often been seen as a deficit. The developmental cycles described by Sigmund Freud, Erik Erikson, Jean Piaget, and Lawrence Kohlberg all celebrate the growth of separation, autonomy, individuation, and natural rights. Consider, for example, Erikson's stages of development: trust versus mistrust, autonomy versus shame, initiative versus guilt, industry versus inferiority, identity versus identity confusion, intimacy versus isolation, and generativity versus stagnation. Apart from the first stage, all the following stages are oriented toward separation until adulthood, when intimacy reemerges. However, as Carol Gilligan has shown so well in her book *In a Different Voice: Psychological Theory and Women's Development* (Harvard University Press, 1982), there is apparently a fusion of identity and intimacy for women, rather than a situation in which identity precedes intimacy, as it does in men. Although most models of human development applaud the truth of separation, they give a back seat to the reality of continuing connection. Contributors to the life-cycle literature should start including women's developmental patterns as they are experienced by *women* – not as deficient in comparison with those of men. The strong emphasis on individuation in the models 'for a healthy life cycle' apparently leads to a lack of mutuality and interdependence in spite of the claim that intimacy is built upon separation. Consider, for instance, Harry Levinson's conclusions (as quoted in Gilligan's book) about aspects of his life-cycle research based on a small group of men:

> In our interviews, friendship was largely noticeable by its absence. As a tentative generalization we would say that close friendship with a man or woman is rarely experienced . . . We need to understand why friendship is so rare and what consequences this deprivation has for adult life.

Or alternatively:

> At 45, he enjoyed one of the best marriages in the study, but probably not as perfect as he implied when he wrote, 'You may not believe me when I say we've never had a disagreement, large or small.'

Just as the woman's voice and experience are missing in the developmental theories, so are they absent in the hierarchy of organizations. The emphasis on productivity, competition, egocentricity, self-reliance, independence, and success is out of balance and creates 'disease.' Women's greater ease with the relational world could help make organizations places in which affiliation, friendship, connection, and personhood could be valued in a more integrated manner.

The members of a departmental workshop were recently exploring some of the difficulties they had experienced in communication as a department. It was intriguing that the women's perception of the process was quite different from that of their male colleagues. Although the women felt that the process had cleared some interpersonal constraints and allowed people to link more productively, most of the males felt that the time would have been much better spent in concentrating on departmental philosophy, goals, and tasks. It is true that productivity should be valued in work, but it is equally true that process should be valued as well. An overemphasis on either one leads to a distorted view and eventually to a distorted organization.

Power

Women clearly experience, use, and view power in a fashion different from that of men. An investigation of the inner experience of power shows that women's power fantasies are more concerned with both sides of an interdependent relationship and are more likely to acknowledge women's own interdependence than are men's fantasies. Women also tend to equate power with giving and caring or with nurturing and strength, whereas men tend to equate it with aggression and assertion.

In her book *Money, Sex and Power* (Longman Inc., 1983) Nancy Hartsock shows how women writing about power describe it not as domination or ability to control, but rather as capacity, particularly as capacity of and for the entire community. In other words, women's experience of connection and relation also has implications for their use and understanding of power that may hold 'resources for a more liberatory understanding.' When power is conceptualized as power over others, it means that one must spend much psychic energy in limiting and controlling the power of others in order to advance oneself. The notions associated with female values of power as a transforming force from within, or with power as a liberating force in the community, could produce radical changes in organizations that currently support a hierarchical notion of power over others.

In her study of political women entitled *Political Women* (Basic Books, 1975), Jeane Kirkpatrick supports this notion that women perceive power differently from the way men perceive it. She found that the women politicians resembled their male colleagues in their willingness to fight for their convictions, but that the women saw power as an instrument of public purpose rather than as a tool for personal ambition. Thus their communal qualities are emphasized even in a very agenic profession.

Physicality

In her book *Of Woman Born: Motherhood as Experience and Institution* (W. W. Norton, 1976) Adrienne Rich argues beautifully for the notion of biology as a resource rather than biology as destiny:

> In order to live a fully human life, we require not only control of our bodies (although control is a prerequisite); we must touch the unity and resonance of our physicality, our bond with the natural order, the corporeal ground of our intelligence . . . It is no wonder that women have minimized their physicality.

Their body has been made so problematic for women that it has often seemed easier to shrug it off and travel as a disembodied spirit.

Thus the very physicality of women, tied as it is to nature's images of birth, blood, pregnancy, lactation, and nurturing of growth, becomes an asset in the way it grounds women in the day-to-day realities of growth and development. The experience of female biology can lead to an earthiness and concreteness – a kind of 'gumboot involvement' in life that is immensely helpful to organizations.

Emotionality, Vulnerability, and Lack of Self-Confidence

In a graduate course on counselling skills I taught in 1987, there were six male and six female adult students from a range of professions. I was intrigued at their different responses to an experiment in which they were asked to assess their strengths and weaknesses in ten developmental tasks of life that stressed such traits as autonomy, relationships, and identity. It was emphasized that the review was private and would be kept confidential. A number of the males (but none of the females) had difficulty in identifying any weaknesses in any developmental areas. When the group was encouraged to express their difficulties, one man eventually encapsulated the fear of the whole male sub-group:

> It's a dog-eat-dog world out there, and I wouldn't dare admit any weaknesses because I don't know how they'll be used against me. I wouldn't even like to identify my weaknesses to myself. It is too dangerous.

Women seem to have far greater ease in expressing their vulnerability, their lack of self-confidence, and their emotions. Jean Baker Miller in particular has reframed these so-called 'weaknesses' in women as very solid strengths. By having to defend themselves less and deny less, women are in a strong position to work productively with their feelings of weakness and to eventually build new strengths on a sturdier psychic basis than denial allows.

This also allows for a more accurate assessment of self and of one's strengths and weaknesses – an assessment that would ultimately be more beneficial to organizational behavior. Instead of viewing these qualities as strengths, however, there is rather an exhortation for women to change, to become more self-confident and less emotional. Whereas women may in fact benefit from acknowledging and building on their strengths, to follow the models presented in management seminars and literature is again to exhort women to improve themselves, to change so that they may fit the system and therefore be successful in it. That women's ability to express emotionality, vulnerability, and helplessness may actually add a humanizing dimension to organizations is not a notion that is much in evidence in the management literature. However, this humanizing dimension could have a very positive effect on the quality of life in organizations.

Even in psychological research and achievement, there is an overemphasis on occupational and academic achievement and a conspicuous absence of references to interpersonal accomplishments. This high valuation of instrumental qualities leads to a devaluation of expressive concerns, even in a discipline that is heavily involved with concerns of relations and expression.

Intimacy and Nurturing

In her book *The Reproduction of Mothering: Psychoanalysis and the Sociology of Gender* (University of California Press, 1978) Nancy Chodorow argues that girls emerge from the pre-oedipal period with greater 'relational potential, retaining a greater capacity for empathy with others and with the experience of themselves as less separated from others and as more connected to the world.' This sense of continuity with others leads women to value closeness and to nurture intimacy in others in a way that has often been seen as pathological – for instance, the role of the suffocating or overinvolved mother or the overly dependent employee. Yet these values actually bring a great challenge to the exaggerated autonomy and separateness of male psychology. Feminists have recently made very radical and deep challenges to the very structures of knowledge.

A number of authors have shown how the excesses of the scientific world view are connected to the exaggerated male psychology of autonomy and separateness; these excesses lead in turn to an overvaluing of rationality, objectivity, and analysis and, again, to an undervaluing of nurturing, skill in interpersonal relations, and creativity. The ideals that govern science, philosophy, or organizational theory will be necessarily restrictive, partial, and limited if they still refuse to acknowledge the important skills associated with the more reproductive processes of society.

Conclusions

It remains to be seen whether women can use the insights of the woman-centered perspective to 'keep their heads' while working in male-dominated hierarchical organizations. There are undoubtedly practical and philosophical difficulties in such an approach. To begin with, the very qualities that are elucidated are those that are least important for success as it is currently defined in such organizations. To hold on to the values that one feels are important while simultaneously working in organizations that undermine those values is to travel a lonely and difficult path. In addition, the argument must not be for keeping women in solely nurturing, expressive, and communal roles; rather, it must be for building upon these qualities as strengths rather than denying their value because they do not fit into the upper echelons of organizations.

These 'human resources' skills are critical in helping to stop the tide of alienation, apathy, cynicism, and low morale in organizations. The arguments are ultimately relevant not only from the perspective of women's identity, but from the organizational perspective as well. If organizations are to become more humane, less alienating, and more responsive to the individuals who work for them, they will probably need to learn to value process as well as product.

Women have an extensive involvement in the processes of our society – an involvement that derives from their greater participation in the reproduction process and their early experience of family life; both of these activities, so different from the activities of men, lead to the development of different psychic structures. Thus women may indeed be the most radical force available in bringing about organizational change; however, they cannot do this as isolated tokens. Further, women must learn to value their own experiences, believe in their own values, and listen to their own inner voices and the voices of other women if indeed they are to speak 'in a different voice' in the organizations for which they work. If women can find ways of bringing their whole selves into the organization, not as saintly mothers or dutiful daughters but as mature women, the result will be both liberating for women and humanizing for organizations.

2
Management: Why Women are Leading the Way

Roz Morris

American author and sex survey queen Shere Hite summed it up this way recently: 'Women had to knock on the door of the masculine world. They had to say, "Let us in. We can do it." They had to be like men, use power dressing. Now women have found that this is very unsatisfactory and they're saying it's not enough. Relationships are central. They should be central for everybody.'

Congresswoman Pat Schroeder, heavily criticized for weeping in public when she gave up her bid for the US Presidency, fought back afterwards saying, 'I was told you don't want someone's finger on the nuclear button who cries. And I say you don't want someone to have their finger on that button who doesn't cry.'

Emotional, illogical, butterfly minds. Remember all that? For years women were kept at a distance from real power by men constantly ready to scoff at female behaviour. Gradually in the 20th century, a few isolated stereotypes were allowed into the male world on male terms. The Token Woman, the Queen Bee, The Only Woman in the Cabinet. Strong, exceptional women like Margaret Thatcher, Golda Meier and Indira Gandhi.

Now though, the perpetually irritating Rex Harrison Approach (Why can't a woman be more like a man?) is definitely old hat. Suddenly it's very OK to *vive la différence*. Butterfly minds are suddenly in demand and there are now courses for men to learn how to use women's mnagement styles. Whatever next? The Industrial Society calls its course 'The Benefits of Difference'.

In fact the differences between the attitudes and assumptions of men and women are now so untaboo after years of Women's Lib non-mentioning of any differences at all, that some people are making a very good living out of training people to spot the differences and use them to run their businesses successfully.

'Management: Why Women are Leading the Way', by Roz Morris, *Options*, December 1988, by permission of Rozmo Productions.

And nowadays it's not just the exceptionally successful women like Anita Roddick of The Body Shop or Steve Shirley, the founder of the FI group who are able to do their own thing in their own way.

Now that there are more women than ever in middle management positions, they are helping to change the style of British business. 'The values that women are bringing to the workplace are the values that industry is supporting today,' says Val Hammond, the director of research at Ashridge Management College, and also president of the European Women's Management Development Network:

> Obviously there are some women leaders who use confrontational, male styles of leadership, but studies have shown that far more women choose to lead their groups in a more co-operative way. And this is the coming management style. The manager as hero, the general ordering the troops around, is out. It's no longer possible to stand on the bank and shout at the people in the boat. Nowadays the manager is a developer who steers the group and is right there in the boat with them.

So how do men and women differ in business? The received wisdom seems to be that, in general, men tend to be far more competitive than women, more interested in winning than in doing the best job possible, more interested in office politics, more career conscious, and far more willing to boss people about.

The perceived view is that women, in general, are more interested in doing a good job than in career advancement, more interested in the health and personal worries of their employees, more concerned to get agreement at meetings, and more concerned to give back to the community as well as taking out.

'Now this doesn't mean that all men are Attila the Hun and all women are Mother Theresa,' says management consultant Rennie Fritchie, who last year made a big impact at the CBI's first ever conference for businesswomen and whose book, *Working Choices* offers professional guidance to encourage women to find an occupation to suit their age and lifestyle. 'But it is true that there are general differences of approach between men and women and they can each gain from the other.'

Bridget Litchfield, who at 39 is the managing director of FOCUS, a company operating in Britain and Holland, set up to provide new jobs and counselling for both non-management and management groups, believes that men and women have different philosophies of business. A percentage of profits from FOCUS goes to community and charity work:

> I think it's essential that you should support your local community. Just to make profits for profit's sake isn't enough. You must put something back. My business philosophy is that people come first. But I think it's easier for a woman to express

personal interest in an employee than for a man. Also, it's more acceptable for a woman to show emotion.

Professor Cary Cooper of the University of Manchester Institute of Science and Technology at the head of one of the biggest occupational stress units in Britain believes that it is the women managers who have the human skills needed to take British industry into the 21st century. In general, 'men manage by punishment and women manage by rewards,' he says.

> Women are socialized to manage people and relationships in the home, and now they're taking their skills from the home and are transferring them to the workplace. Our studies have shown that women tend to be more participatory in their management style and they are seen by both male and female subordinates to be much more caring than male counterparts. In practical terms this means that men's style of management contributes to stress, by putting to much pressure on people and stopping them from producing their best. Stress at work costs Britain between five and 10 per cent of the Gross National Product every year, through a combination of ill health, disease and death. The GNP is about £300 billion per annum, so stress caused by male managers is quite obviously costing the country billions of pounds every year. Stress at work is closely related to the amount of control people feel they have over their area of responsibility. British managers, mostly men, are not in general too good at allowing their subordinates this kind of freedom, because they are too sensitive about their own power.

The first senior women had to be more like men than men. Now there's a larger group of women, in middle management at least, they can develop their own style. Well, I don't know how other people do things, how they motivate their staff, because I run my own company, so I don't have the problems that women have in large organizations where a lot of men just sit on the rungs of the ladder. They're not *against* women, they're just not *for* them,' says Anita Roddick, one of the most high profile examples of a different management style Britain has ever produced.

Roddick has a modern version of philanthropy that involves a deliberate concentration on Third World products and ingredients, and the positive involvement of her staff in charity work. All Body Shops are franchised and one of the rules of the franchise is that each shop has a community project. 'We've got girls in our shops going to hospices every week,' she says. 'Some visit drug dependency units. They all have local charities. And they do this in company time. Women are very good at saying, "Why is altruism anathema to business?" Captains of industry are too scared of love. They'd rather say fuck than love. They're more shocked by it. Love and compassion are more easy for women to deal with, so women can understand the holistic approach. That means putting a lot back as well as taking out.' The dictionary definition of holism is 'a philosophy in which the whole is greater than the sum of its parts'. It's a concept that came out of the Sixties and Seventies and Anita Roddick admits that she is still heavily influenced by the Make Love Not War philosophy:

How can you not motivate people when you have products you believe in? How big companies keep their staff if they have no principles baffles me. The thing that gives this company its morals is the constant search for a better way. The cynics say this is just good public relations. They're just lazy and lethargic. I could make far more money not doing things this way, but I am making money by putting in as well as taking out. For instance, we have a foot roller. It's made in southern India. We could get this made anywhere, so we pay the market rate. We don't pay a Third World rate, so we're helping these villages directly. Now I don't hear too many men talking like this. Altruism isn't fashionable. But there's nothing wrong with the pursuit of honest profits combined with social awareness, and women should be shouting out to lead the way to a better life.

'Organizations used to look for bright, biddable people. People with brains, but who would fit in and do what they were told. Now they want "intrapreneurs",' explains Rennie Fritchie:

Intrapreneurs are people who can be enterprising and individualistic and challenge old ideas, but within an organization. Traditionally such people were discouraged in large organizations and had to go off and set up their own thing and become entrepreneurs. Now we need enterprising people within organizations, the yeast that leavens the dough. And women fit the bill for this kind of creativity. There are now management courses in Helicopter Thinking (that's the old-fashioned Butterfly Mind) and Right Brain Thinking (that's emotional, illogical, intuitive and creative). You see, research has shown that women are tremendous Right Brain Thinkers. That's the creative side of the brain, while men use the left side more, that's the part that analyses and uses logic. Obviously both men and women use both sides of the brain, but research indicates that women have more ideas transferring from one side of the brain to the other. So women are clearly more flexible than men. And you can forget about the old criticism that women don't want to work long hours like men, so they can't be real workers, can they? There's no need to work flat out all the time and get stale and tired. The attitude that real men work 16 hours a day, six days a week and never stop thinking about work is what has brought British industry to where it is today, which still could be a lot better, couldn't it?

Basically we've always noticed that men are more competitive and status conscious than we are,' says Sandra Milner. Sandra and Pauline Matthews, two sisters in their early thirties, run the Milner Group, a design company specializing in pub design:

Because we're in a business which is very unusual for women, as most women designers are not working on pubs at all, we've always noticed the differences in approach between men and ourselves. No job is too menial for us. We often vacuum a place before we hand it over to the client, but a man would not dream of doing that himself. He'd pay to get someone to do it. We care more about detail and if we see someone else has improved their standards we think it's great for the industry, but men are likely to be much more competitive, ready to stab each other in the back and do each other down. And one thing that really gets us down is unnecessary meetings. We sit in a lot of meetings where what could be said can be sorted out in a few minutes. But men like meetings so they can strut about like peacocks. Part of the deal for them is having long, boring meetings.

'Men think meetings are essential,' says Rennie Fritchie:

They're important for finding out how to defeat rivals, the latest office politics and so on. They can escape to meetings and then stay late to get the real work done. Women have a very different attitude. If you have to get home to look after your children, you certainly won't see meetings as useful. You want to get your work done during the eight hour day. In fact, you'll be more efficient. I've often sat in meetings and costed them. How much are they actually costing the company? Travel, salaries, waste of time and so on. It can run into hundreds of pounds an hour to have meetings and there's no doubt that many of them are just part of men's office politics.

'Men tend to think women running meetings are very unstructured because they are not so rigid as men in sticking to the agenda,' says Val Hammond:

We've done comparative research into men and women in management since 1977, and it's clear that meetings show up a lot of differences. At the end of meetings, women tend to have reached agreement. The men can be very sharp with each other, and the real meeting takes place afterwards. In the average business meeting with either all men or mostly men, the people present give verbal agreement but in actual fact they often don't agree in their hearts. This means they walk away from the table at the end of the meeting without really agreeing. They are quite likely to try to undermine the decisions instead of trying to make them work. So the meeting hasn't really achieved its ultimate objective of making some progress towards an agreed idea. Women use a different style which takes on board everyone's position and moves the whole group ahead. This can be very effective and in fact it's the method used by the Japanese. They have a management style in which the whole group agrees. By the time they get to a meeting they have all been approached beforehand and the meeting is a formality.

Professor Cooper at UMIST has no doubts at all that the future belongs to women:

In the next decade there will be more technological and social change and Britain will have to accept this to survive. More women will be needed in senior positions because it's obvious they can manage change better. Men tend to look at problems technically and they're trained to be macho and decisive. They say to a worker, 'Here's a change, now get on with it.' Women tend to be much more particpatory in their management style; both male and female employees say that women bosses tend to think about people as individuals. Now men have patently been very bad at accepting technological change. To observe this, you only have to take a look at some of the obvious examples such as the coal industry or printing. Male managers have tried to impose change and it didn't work without a lot of struggle. Male workers have also shown great inflexibility.

One of the biggest challenges facing British industry is the challenge of adapting to new technology, and in future we are going to need more women managers in the workplace to help us do that. Men will have to swallow their pride and let women get on with the job because men's style of management by punishment contributes to stress in workers and stops them producing their best. Studies have shown that women are better at coping with change themselves and at encouraigng others to cope with it.

Professor Cooper points out that one in every four new businesses is being set up by a woman and more women than ever are now leaving universities looking for a career in management, yet still more than 95 per cent of company directors and 90 per cent of managers are men. However, business schools and management departments now have an average of 40 per cent women and his own department is up to 45 per cent, so that much needed change is really on the way at last.

Management consultant John Langford, who runs courses for men about women managers, (within the framework of the law) points to banks as a sector of business where male domination in a very male orientated world is already changing fast. 'The banks used to do all their business with men and they used to base all their annual staff interviews on exams passed, mistakes in work, time-keeping and so on,' he says. 'Now they're changing their emphasis and concentrating on monitoring communications skills and presentation of ideas. In simple terms they want their people to be pleasant and welcoming to customers and they've realized that women are better at this than men. Men haven't been culturally encouraged to communicate and talk about feelings, but these are the skills that are going to be needed in the future.'

Anita Roddick makes a similar point:

Recently the money business, exemplified by the City yuppies, has been a great growth area for women and if there you have to take on all the old hard-edged values, and think like a man to succeed. But this isn't typical of where women are at present. Women are definitely flooding the office market and humanizing business by creating crèches and flexitime, job sharing and part-time work, and many people now recognize that the old rigid rules of business are extremely outdated. I believe the old system is completely falling apart. I see all these middle-aged tired executives struggling in a tired system and I am convinced it's definitely doomed. Our staff believe in our company so we don't lose them. We're training people to challenge the old system. At present we're a very, very different company, but I think our style will be the norm by the end of the century.

3
Ambition and Leadership in Men and Women

Virginia O'Leary

It is a truth universally acknowledged that there are fewer women than men in positions of power and authority – in the business world, in the professions, in the arts, in politics. Women are not the anomaly in the corporate boardroom that they once were, but they are not represented in proportion to their numbers or their talents. For example, in the United States women hold only 3 to 4 per cent of the directorships of the top 1,000 firms, and only 25 per cent of those companies with women directors have more than one token woman. Why this is so remains a matter of some controversy, and two very different routes have been taken by those who would explain the situation. On the one hand, 'person-centered explanations' try to discover what there might be in the 'female personality' that would make women less ambitious, or otherwise less suited for leadership roles. 'Environmental explanations,' on the other hand, emphasize the psychological barriers to female advancement found in the makeup of those who select and encourage new leaders – not just personnel officers, but all of us – for example, as voters and as patrons of arts.

Do Women Fear Success?

One person-centered explanation – taken as demonstrated, until quite recently – is that women simply lack the motivation to compete. A number of studies have compared how much difference there is in the achievement of men and women at set tasks, when given 'relaxed instruction' and 'competitive instruction.' When giving competitive instruction researchers tell those who

Excerpt by Virginia O'Leary from *The Opposite Sex*, ed. Anne Campbell, Ebury Press, 1989, by permission of Andromeda Oxford Ltd.

have volunteered for the experiment such things as that the results will be used to measure their 'intellectual and leadership capacities.' Men's rate of achievement tends to increase substantially when this element of competition is introduced, whereas women's does not. However, close scrutiny of the findings has revealed that although competition fails to increase the women's achievement, this is already much higher than the men's under relaxed instruction. What is revealed is not female absence of a desire to achieve but lower male achivment when men are not given a special motivation.

Researchers have also suggested that women are frightened of success, especially if they see it as incompatible with femininity. According to this theory, fear of success is aroused in those situations in which the emphasis is on competitive success, and the woman feels anxious about the aggressive overtones of competitiveness. It is assumed to be especially acute for women if the competition is against males. For example, a bright young woman who aspires to be a lawyer might settle for a career as a legal secretary because she fears that success as a lawyer might diminish her image as a desirable woman and wife.

A high female fear of success was first recorded in an experiment in which women university students were asked to write completions to the following statement: 'After first term finals, Anne finds herself at the top of her medical school class.' The completions were analyzed for the presence or absence of imagery implying that success seems a frightening prospect. The following are typical of those regarded as expressing such fear:

- No one will marry her. She has lots of friends but no dates.
- Unfortunately, Anne suddenly no longer feels so certain that she really wants to be a doctor. She wonders if perhaps it is not normal.
- Anne is a code name for a nonexistent person created by a group of medical students.
- She starts proclaiming her surprise and joy. Her fellow classmates are so disgusted with her behaviour that they jump on her body and beat her. She is maimed for life.

Male students wrote responses to the same statement, but for them the central character was named John instead of Anne. The difference between the responses of males and those of females was dramatic. In contrast to the females' 65 per cent, fewer than 10 per cent of the male respondents wrote stories implying fear of success.

This study was conducted in the 1960s, but strong evidence soon emerged that this male–female difference reflected the mood of the times rather than nature. Several American surveys conducted in the early 1970s found the fear of success among males to be as high or higher than that of females. This was a time when the rejection by young men of traditional American values – a trend which had only begin in the mid-1960s – had reached its climax. In particular, large numbers of young American men of the early 1970s had come to see a drive for success (especially success in the business world) as making a person seem insensitive to issues ranging from egalitarianism to international peace.

Now that success is back in fashion, male fear-of-success scores are once again lower, although not so much lower, than women's. It seems that women are not naturally less motivated than men, but in our present social climate some may be less likely to appear hungry for success in situations in which they view competitive success as incompatible with femininity.

Another person-centered explanation, based on research in 1977, is that women have not been brought up to compete or to play on teams. Because of this, they lack the requisite managerial skills or traits necessary for success in the corporate jungle. According to this theory, men more optimistically balance the chances of success against the possibility of failure, whereas for women the consequences of failure loom larger. However, since this view was put forward there has been a dramatic increase in the number of women starting their own businesses. Starting a business on your own has long been regarded as a high risk because of the high rate of failure (80 percent). Yet, contemporary American women are three to five times more likely than men to go into business for themselves. Women may be less likely than men to learn to play on teams, but that does not seem to provide an adequate explanation for their absence from high-status positions.

A Good Environment for Ambition?

A common environmental explanation for the small numbers of women business executives is that the distribution of opportunity and power, and the social composition of groups at work, result in boundaries that inhibit women from succeeding. According to this view, a critical factor holding women back is the fact that there are far fewer women than men in full-time work. As a minority of the workforce, women are consequently scrutinized more closely, are under pressure to prove that they are not partisan to feminist views and are expected to conform both to their traditional social position and to the prevailing sex-role stereotypes. The same is true of many other kinds of organizations, such as political parties and government agencies.

Women's social position, in comparison to men's, is secondary. This means that, without knowing anything else about two individuals, we tend to accord a higher status to the one simply because he is a man, and a lower status to the other simply because she is a woman. Women are stereotyped as more emotional, nurturing, passive and sensitive than men. Secretaries therefore are implicitly expected to 'understand' their bosses (usually male) by responding to moods, whims, needs, and personal quirks much as a wife would.

As a result, managers tend to assume that a secretary's nurturing and submissive behavior reflects her personality rather than requirements of her job, and they are unlikely to recommend her for promotion to positions of greater responsibility on the assumption that she lacks the necessary traits to succeed.

One very subtle form of sex discrimination at work lies in the very different ways in which the performance of men and women is assessed and rewarded. Experiments and interviews have indicated that in business a man's successful performance of a task is generally attributed to his skill, whereas a woman's successful performance of the same task is attributed either to luck or exceptional effort. On the other hand, a man's failure is attributed to bad luck, a woman's failure to low ability.

It has also been found that such distinctions can have a dramatic impact on personnel decisions. Business students were asked what recommendations they would make on a number of equally successful employees. Four different causes – skill, effort, luck, and task ease – were offered to account for different employees' successes. The only ones the students recommended for promotion were those whose success was attributed to skill. Competence was in every case viewed more favorably than a reputation for hard work. These findings imply that women who are assumed more often than men to be successful because of effort are apt to be bypassed when the most favored organizational rewards – promotions – are distributed.

In view of this it is hardly surprising that any employer interested in maximizing productivity will believe that it is far more cost-effective to encourage the men rather than the women with generous pay rises and promotion. Why waste valuable resources trying to increase the output of the women, who are already apparently working as hard as they can to compensate for their lack of ability?

The fact is that despite the persistence of this belief that male and female behavior indicates that, as individuals, executive men and women seem to be virtually identical psychologically, intellectually and emotionally. In one study of men and women ecologists, a difference was found in the scientific productivity of the male group and the female group – more of the men's research was published and later referred to by other researchers in their publications. However, a meager 4 per cent of the men in the study accounted for this difference; 96 per cent were no more productive than the average woman ecologist. Many of the women had heavier family responsibilities than any other the men, and their lower average productivity probably reflects this.

Why Women Opt out of Competition

Misunderstandings in the workplace help to preserve the status quo. Women have made inroads into lower and middle management, but the difficulties they face are themselves a deterrent to ambition. The 'glass ceiling' beyond which they have difficulty ascending has led many women to opt out altogether. Some seek to pursue power and influence through entrepreneurial channels, others to redirect the motherhood–work balance in favor of motherhood. For it is motherhood that, for most women, ultimately takes priority over their other ambitions.

Men, of course, want to be fathers, but our cultural outlook is only gradually shifting the expectation that although this should create no career conflicts for them, a woman must choose between a serious commitment to her job and serious commitment to her family. Employers ask prospective female employees what their husband's work is and whether the husband is likely to be transferred, and they want to assess whether a new employee is likely to start having babies. If there are children, it is expected that the mother rather than the father will stay with them when they are ill and be the first one home in the evening to relieve the nanny or the childminder. All of this ties one hand behind a woman's back when she is competing to get ahead in the corporate world, in scientific research, or in the professions. Many a 'supermom' drops out exhausted. Others redefine their roles to exclude goals that are incompatible with family responsibilities. Not because they are unable to meet the challenge, but because they are unwilling to pay the high price of traditionally defined success.

In spite of the barriers, women can be expected to arrive in increasingly greater numbers in positions of power. As they do, we may also expect to see changes in the environment in which men and women pursue their ambitions. There is no consistent picture of what happens when women are in power, but in Norway, where the Prime Minister is a woman, as are seven of seventeen members of the Cabinet, and over 40 per cent of the members of the Parliament, child-care subsidies have increased, as well as the number of weeks in the paid parental leave scheme resembling Sweden's.

4
Elected Unopposed

Hugo Young

Margaret Thatcher had proved it was possible to be a woman and be prime minister, and live to fight for a second term. In the 1979 election, she ran far behind her party, and even further behind her chief opponent, James Callaghan. At the end if 1982, with 1983 certain to be the next election year, her popularity remained, after its brief post-Falklands resuscitation, well behind the party's. But her situation was nonetheless transformed. She was established in political leadership. Around this burgeoning personality, nothing wove a more complex web than her femininity.

Its importance was then, and has remained, a matter of some dispute. This is not surprising. There were competing and contradictory aspects of her gender, as it related both to her rise to the top and to the way she handled herself when she got there.

One school of thought, perhaps the most voluble, held that she actually discarded most of the significant gender traits and became, for all practical purposes, an honorary man. This was an intelligible analysis. Politics is a male world, and nobody can succeed in it without some of the qualities commonly associated with masculinity. In one sense, she could not help becoming an honorary man from the moment she became leader of the party, a condition aptly symbolized by her admission, after considerable grumbling among the baffled clubmen, to honorary membership of the all-male Conservative stronghold, the Carlton Club. Since all previous party leaders had belonged, there seemed no way of excluding the present one, although her installation was not followed by any further concessions to female Tories.

Some of this leader's most prominent characteristics were not obviously womanly. She set great store by domination and executive command. In public

Excerpt from *One of Us: A Biography of Margaret Thatcher*, by Hugo Young, Macmillan London Ltd. Copyright © Hugo Young 1989, 1900 by permission of Curtis Brown Ltd. on behalf of the author and Farrar, Straus & Ciroux, Inc.

she rarely showed emollience. Her approach to most situations turned them into a struggle which she had to win. In peace and war, she prided herself on her toughness. Her speech was often harsh, her demeanour self-consciously severe.

At best, on this view, while plainly remaining a woman, she used womanhood merely as a helpful device. 'She shows how much femininity is a production,' Beatrix Campbell writes. 'Femininity is what she wears, masculinity is what she admires.'[1]

Campbell distinguishes between gender and sexuality, judging that while the former is important the latter, the real heart of the feminine, is concealed to the point of conscious insignificance. 'Is this a function of age?' Campbell enquires. 'That a middle-aged suburban woman is not represented as sexual in white Anglo-Saxon culture? Is it because she is a married woman and a mother, facts which both express sexuality and make it inaccessible? Is it because the arsenal of criticism fired at Margaret Thatcher, surely one of the most personally disliked politicians since the war, de-eroticises her?' A condition summarized in one common verdict: 'She's not a real woman.' Or, as Jimmy Carter's national security adviser, Zbigniew Brzezinski, once said: 'In her presence you pretty quickly forget that she's a woman. She doesn't strike me as being a very female type.'[2]

Campbell's preferred explanation is the lady's preoccupation with maleness and manly virtues. This, according to the enquiring feminist, made itself clear in some of her favourite reiterations. 'It is not femininity but buccaneering masculinity which is evoked in her celebration of Victorian values, of the prime ministers who came before her, of "merchant venturers".'

Another, subtler, feminist perspective is offered by Marina Warner. Warner notes the role of the media, especially the cartoonists in the tabloid press, in conferring on this female leader an intimate identification with Britannia.[3] Especially after the Falklands war, the traditional allegory, which casts queen as country, attached itself in popular mythology to the person of the prime minister: a device which did not deny femininity but exalted it.

Warner also emphasizes a de-eroticized quality. The sexual woman, she suggests, has been replaced by the nanny, the matron, the governess. 'Margaret Thatcher has tapped an enormous source of female power: the right of prohibition.' Her toughness, her 'flintiness', her 'piercing' quality are not designed, according to Warner, to prove that she is as good as a man 'but that she is not under the governance of Venus, that she is a stranger to the exactions and weaknesses of the heart, that her most private organ is her gut'.

What is certainly not disputable is the reluctance of this controlled and controlling woman to treat women, politically, as any different from men. She was against this on principle, apparently seeing nothing in her own rise to power which might prompt her to single women out for special attention, or consciously single out herself and her sex and the special effects this might have on her political strategy. Women as a separate category of voters were not of special interest. Patrick Cosgrave, who worked for her, once proposed to do some private polling to investigate this relationship with a view to seeing how it could be further exploited. He later recorded her put-down: 'Since my draft idea for a poll depended on an emphasis on her sexual identity, she turned the scheme down flat.'[4]

A woman whom some fondly expected to give women and their advancement priority in fact did exactly the opposite. Although she had always had a job herself, whether working for Joe Lyons or reading for the Bar or becoming an MP, she led no sort of crusade for others to do the same. Before she got anywhere in politics, she was, as we have seen, strident in her assertion that women were as entitled as men to succeed in public life. She was saying this as early as 1953. When she had reached the top, a change came over the balance of her rhetoric. She became a lot more ready to praise the Conservative model of the housewife and mother. As for positive discrimination or anything which smacked of feminism, she was derisive.

Both prejudices were epitomized in a lecture she gave in July 1982, commemorating, rather oddly, a revered Liberal feminist, Margery Ashby. First there was praise for domesticity. Contemplating the suffragettes, Mrs Thatcher noted that 'they had the inestimable privilege of being wives and mothers and they pursued their public work against the background of full and happy domestic lives. They neglected no detail of those lives . . . The home should be the centre but not the boundary of a woman's life.' But then there was the assertion that nothing more was needed to change the condition of women. 'The battle for women's rights has largely been won,' she said. 'The days when they were demanded and discussed in strident tones should be gone for ever. I hate those strident tones we hear from some Women's Libbers.'[5]

Even to less demanding feminists, her attitudes actually looked worse than that. Never mind her incomprehension of women's liberation, she declined, they thought, to be sensitive in more elementary matters. Barbara Castle, who as a Labour cabinet minister in the 1960s preceded her as leading woman in this male world, thought she could have been far more perceptive about the particular difficulties ordinary women faced. Her attitude to the social services, Mrs Castle contended, showed that 'she's had no compassion at all for the working woman struggling to deal with a home, earn a wage, deal with an elderly parent, perhaps a mentally handicapped child, and sickness in the family.'[6]

So several outward signs, from the severity of her manner to the aggression of her anti-feminist ideology, argue for taking her at what seemed like her own valuation: as a woman in a man's world neither demanding nor receiving concessions to her feminity. Yet that account left a gap in her manifest personality. It might have quite aptly described some other women politicians. Shirley Williams, Social Democrat and near-contemporary, was free of these disabling prejudices, being a healer not a warrior by temperament and more of an egalitarian feminist by conviction. In Mrs Thatcher's case, leaving sex out of the picture became, as time went by, a steadily more misleading violation of the truth.

First, it so obviously mattered very much to her. What Campbell diminishes as a femininity concerned merely with 'what she wears' was, nonetheless, very feminine. Barbara Castle noticed this from the beginning. Her diary at the time the Thatcher leadership started is full of private solidarity with this amazing opponent who had risen to the top ahead of every man. At an early Question Time, Mrs Castle noted her appearance: 'She sat with bowed head and detached primness . . . hair immaculately groomed, smart dress crowned by a string of pearls.' At the same time, the diarist writes, she brought out a kind of male gallantry which she obviously enjoyed. 'Margaret's election has stirred up her own side wonderfully: all her backbenchers perform like knights jousting at a tourney for a lady's favours, showing off their paces by making an unholy row at every opportunity over everything the government does.'

Throughout her public life, she gave the greatest care to her appearance. Mrs Castle used to find that Mrs Thatcher's wardrobe had virtually taken over the lady MPs' room in the Commons. 'The row of pegs was always filled with her clothes,' she recalled. 'There would be half-a-dozen garments hanging up there and underneath them a tidy row of at least eight pairs of shoes. I can only assume that she slipped there from the opposition front bench, nipped into this little room and did her quick-change act between great parliamentary scenes.'[7]

The only woman to be admitted to her cabinet, Janet Young, who was leader of the House of Lords from 1981 to 1983, noted how attentive she was to her skin and complexion. 'When you meet her, you know this is a woman,' Lady Young once remarked to me. Nor did she trouble to conceal her detailed interest in these feminine concerns in the interviews she gave to women's magazines, which appeared so frequently, year in and year out, as to indicate that behind her refusal to permit Cosgrave's scientific inquiry there in fact lay a shrewd understanding of her particular female constituency.

She sometimes did the same on television. Only someone at least partly a woman's woman could have agreed to show her wardrobe to the viewing masses, as Mrs Thatcher once did on the BBC.[8] She had arranged for the camera a rack of favourite clothes, and went through them with quite innocent pleasure. 'This black one came through the Falklands war all right,' she enthused over one suit. 'Clothes should be a background not a foreground,' she decreed as a general rule of public dressing. Black and blue were best, because brighter colours tended to distract attention, and frills should always be avoided. Her underclothes, she announced, came from Marks & Spencer.

Only a woman, surely, would have enthusiastically collaborated in such an invasion of her privacy, and by no means every woman at that. Certainly it would be hard to imagine any of her predecessors in Downing Street publicizing the name of his tailor, still less the supplier of his hosiery.

It was not just by her keenness on womanish things, however, that she showed herself to be different from a male prime minister. There were other outward signs. For example, she wasn't ashamed to weep in public. This could happen on occasions devoid of sentiment. 'I once saw Margaret Thatcher weep. It was in Lusaka in 1979,' wrote Owen Harries, at the time an adviser and speech-writer to the Australian prime minister, Malcolm Fraser. It happened, he said, when she failed to get her way over a detail in the preliminaries to the Rhodesian settlement.[9] But more usually the tears flowed in moments of personal emotion: when bad news came in from the Falklands, or after an IRA atrocity. When her son, Mark, disappeared during a trans-Sahara motor rally in January 1982, she spent six days in a state of extreme anxiety, frequently weeping, sometimes in public. Reporters who caught her off guard before she addressed a lunchtime meeting at a London hotel found her in the foyer crying quite openly when there was still no news.[10]

Nor was she above deploying such emotion in what seemed a more calculated way. Once, on television, the very memory of what happened to her father was enough to summon it up. She was describing how Alfred had been thrown off the Grantham council when the office of alderman was abolished. Plainly this had eaten into her heart. She recalled how he had laid down his aldermanic robe. 'I remember when my father was turned off that council, including his speech for the last time. Very emotional. "In honour I took up this gown and in honour I lay it down." That's how he felt.' Almost theatrically, she produced a handkerchief and brushed away a tear at the thought of it.[11]

But tears weren't the only manifestation that she was indeed a woman and, as a woman, different. There was also her role as hostess, pursued with as much tireless dedication on small occasions as on large. After her trip to China she held a small reception for everyone on her plane, including cabin staff and journalists as well as officials. Arriving late, I was immediately led on my own private journey round the public rooms. Number 10 Downing Street had been 'a furnished flat to rent' when she took it over, she briskly chattered: nothing on the surfaces, other people's choices on the walls. She'd changed it all. Here was the silver from Lord Brownlow (descendant of Alfred's aldermanic colleague), there the portraits she'd personally chosen: a good Nelson, a better Pitt, a special corner for scientists including a bust of Grantham's own Isaac Newton, one or two Turners, one or two Romneys, and only one solitary foreign painting, a small Corot landscape. Now it was more like the public home she wanted. Obviously she had given hundreds of visitors the same tour, the tour of a house-proud tenant which few people had enjoyed from Callaghan, Wilson, Heath, Douglas-Home, Macmillan or Churchill.

Her sex, however, went beyond her private consciousness and instinctive behaviour. It was an unavoidably important element of her relationship with her public, noticed by all and commented on by many. We have seen, for example, how awe-struck she rendered the male-dominated society of Japan. But the French, more sophisticated in such matters, were hardly less ready to speak of her in tones of submissive adulation, for her femininity if not her political behaviour. Before a visit to France, in March 1980, she was interviewed for French television. The interviewer emerged from Downing Street and told *Le Figaro* that he kept the memory of a woman 'full of charm and seduction whose radiating presence conceals a great authority and a deep-seated desire to infuse some warmth into the climate of Franco-British relations'.

Le Quotidien de Paris, still more lyrically, permitted itself to speak of this political leader in terms it could not have begun to employ about a man, even one it admired to distraction. Mrs Thatcher, it said, should not be called the Iron Lady, 'for that metal is too vile, too obscure'. She was, instead, 'a woman of uranium, with peculiar irradiations. Compared to her, how leaden appear most of our leaders, opaque masses of flesh, austere fortresses without windows, save for the loopholes of deceit and the skylights of hidden pride. Power corrupts a man but liberates a woman and reveals her for what she is.'

Not all foreigners were so enchanted. The closer they got, the more vexed they often became. 'You must tell your prime minister', a German official told EEC Commissioner Chistopher Tugendhat, after the interim settlement of the British budget contribution in May 1980, 'that she hurt my Chancellor (Helmut Schmidt] in his male pride. If things are to be put right between our two countries, she must find a way of making it up to him.'[12]

To European statesmen, the female in their midst presented a double problem. It evidently hurt them in their maleness if she beat them. But she also to some extent disabled them before the issue was determined. Viscount Davignon, a vice-president of the European Commission from 1977 to 1984, observed the process as a man of the world. 'They felt it was more difficult to be rough with a woman than with another man,' he said. 'And so being challenged by a woman disconcerted them. If it had been a man they could have said "Shut up".'[13]

By 1985, Davignon thought, it was no longer a problem. The Europeans had got used to her, and gave no quarter. Whether the same was ever true of the Conservative Party is another matter. There the gender factor came up against the indestructible psychic conditioning of the English middle-class male. This was not well adapted to dealing with an aggressive woman. Julian Critchley, discussing the received opinion that the best way to deal with their leader was to 'stand up for yourself, shout back, argue the toss, and then she will respect you', also noted the drawback to this course of action. 'We've always been brought up to believe that it's extremely rude to shout back at women,' he said.[14]

Critchley, who was never a minister, spoke somewhat theoretically. Jim Prior saw things at close quarters and confirms the difficulties he could never surmount. The Thatcher method, he reports in his doleful autobiography, the confessions of a beaten man, depended heavily on challenge: seemingly incessant confrontations based on detailed briefing and a desire to press her antagonist, who could be any minister or official, to the limit. Prior found that such constant aggression exposed his own weaknesses. 'It is not a style which endears, and perhaps even less so when the challenger is a woman and the challenged a man,' he writes. 'I have to confess that I found it very difficult to stomach and this form of male chauvinism was obviously one of my failings.[15]

But there was another side to the virago, her capacity to allure. Visitors calling on her for the first time attested to the sex appeal she could project in a private conversation. She was reckoned by her ministers to have a particular weakness for handsome men of a certain age, who stood up straight and wore well-cut suits: a preference of which the most conspicuous beneficiary was widely agreed to have been Humphrey Atkins, chief whip throughout her leadership of the Opposition and later Northern Ireland Secretary. Robert Armstrong had a small encounter which he never forgot. At a cabinet meeting her earrings were obviously pinching her. 'As the meeting went on, she removed one of them,' he once told me, 'and as she did so she gave me a sidelong look of total amused complicity. It was a completely male–female moment.'

Jim Prior, equally, records one moment when he was not being beaten about the head. A newspaper had commented on the 'sexy' voice she had developed on a radio programme. In fact this was the result of a cold. When Prior next saw her, he said, 'Margaret, I read in my paper that you have developed a sexy voice.' Back came her reply: 'What makes you think I wasn't sexy before?'

The fact is that sex, if not sexiness, was incontestably a conscious part of the Thatcher personality as a political leader.It always had been, and could not have been otherwise. She couldn't fail to be acutely aware of the disability under which it placed her, especially in her early days – as the constant references in her speeches showed 'If you want something said, ask a man. If you want something done, ask a woman,' she trumpeted to the Townswomen's Guilds in 1965. At the 1969 party conference she quoted Sophocles: 'Once a woman is made equal to a man, she becomes his superior.'

When this woman had become superior to the men, she remained a woman. If she was best known for male qualities, such as aggression and domination, these were doubtless explicable by her feminine predicament: they were necessary, in large quantity, to combat the aggression and domination to which the surrounding males would otherwise subject her. Has any woman deficient in hardness ever succeeeded in politics, anywhere in the world? Has any man, come to that? Margaret Thatcher possessed this universally necessary ingredient, but it coexisted with attributes men could not in fact lay claim to.

Janet Young, sensitive to the woman's strange place in this circle, thought there were two particular ways in which femininity and political leadership intermingled. 'Being a woman makes her decisive,' she reflected, when still observing Mrs Thatcher at close quarters in government.

> Women have to make instant decisions, admittedly of a minor kind, like what shoes to buy for the children and what to have for supper. This gives them a natural decisiveness which applies itself to larger fields. But there is also a great caution, again very feminine. An anxiety in human terms about the effects of an action. It could be seen in Mrs Thatcher during the Falklands. The men were discussing the casualties in cold figures, but you could see that wasn't the way she was thinking about them. This made her cautious.

Caution, in fact, was not the quality most commonly associated with her as the first electoral test of her leadership approached. Strength and lack of compassion were much more widely perceived. And as for anxiety about the effects of her actions, cold indifference to the misery of unemployment was an essential accompaniment to the economic policy, and the evidence suggests that she possessed more of this than any prime minister of the twentieth century. But her ratings had risen on most of the measures that mattered, and she was now judged predominantly as a leader and nothing else. Without discarding womanhood, she had transcended it. A Mori opinion poll told the story of what had changed between April 1979 and April 1983. Four years before, only 34 per cent of voters thought she 'understands the problems facing Britain'. Now the figure was up to 40. Then, 30 per cent thought she 'has a lot of personality' and 21 per cent that she was 'more honest than most politicians'. These, too, had now risen to 41 and 30 respectively. Where 26 per cent used to think her 'a capable leader', four years' experience put this up to 56 per cent. As for being 'rather inexperienced', the figure was now statistically insignificant, down from 28 per cent in 1979 to 3 per cent in 1983.

Her most glaring weakness was a strange one. It showed perhaps the limitations of a feminine nature when hoisted into the highest place: not its lack of central importance but the way in which it was seen by many people to elevate the prime minister too far above the masses. She did, after all, make great play with her role as housewife. The image was used repeatedly to illustrate how the national economy should be run and how this woman, unlike any man, could apply the household economist's down-to-earth experience of making ends meet. It came out in many an interview: repeated tales of making Denis his morning cup of tea, tidying the kitchen in her private flat, sorting out her linen. But for some reason these bids for ordinariness stubbornly failed to reflect themselves in her reptuation with the voters. On her rating as 'down to earth', the Mori poll showed a decline from 24 to 18 per cent. Her tendency to 'talk down to people' was noted by 53 per cent where only 31 per cent had mentioned it before.

This worried her handlers, now readying themselves for the most expensive sales campaign in the history of British politics. Maurice Saatchi, salesman in chief, saw a flaw in the product and it bothered him. Every poll said in one way or another that she was 'out of touch with real life', he told me in early 1983. She had most of the other virtues. But somehow her very uniqueness had caused her to ascend inconveniently towards the stratosphere.

Notes

1 Beatrix Campbell, *The Iron Ladies* (London, 1987). Subtitled 'Why Do Women Vote Tory?', this is a study, not seriously deformed by its Marxist perspective, of women and their role in the Conservative Party as well as of the female Tory voter.
2 Young and Sloman, *The Thatcher Phenomenon*, p. 36.
3 Marina Warner, *Monuments and Maidens* (London,1985), pp. 51 ff.
4 Cosgrave, *Thatcher*.
5 The first Dame Margery Ashby memorial lecture, 26 July 1982, quoted in Campbell, *The Iron Ladies*.
6 Young and Sloman, *The Thatcher Phenomenon*, p. 132.
7 Ibid., p. 38.
8 'The Englishwoman's Wardrobe', BBC Television, 10 November 1986.
9 *The Times*, 29 July 1986.
10 See Junor, *Margaret Thatcher*. This remains the best account available of Mrs Thatcher's personal life.
11 Interview with Miriam Stoppard, Yorkshire Television, 18 November 1985.
12 Tugendhat, *Making Sense of Europe*, p. 122.
13 Young and Sloman, *The Thatcher Phenomenon*, p. 39.
14 Ibid., p. 41.
15 Prior, *A Balance of Power*, p. 138.

Chapter 13
Leadership: Past, Present and Future

Introduction

What skills and attributes will business leaders need in the coming decades? What issues do today's CEOs feel their organizations will face?

Two recent studies, conducted in very different ways, give fascinating insights into chief executives' vision of the future. Korn Ferry consultants and Columbia University combined their resources in 1988 to survey over 1,500 chief executives, asking them (among other things) to rate the skills and personal characteristics they felt CEOs would need by the year 2000; and *Fortune* magazine celebrated its sixtieth birthday by asking a variety of US, Japanese, and European executives to comment on the future.

Common issues emerge from this interesting blend of statistical data and personal opinion. People skills – the ability to influence, motivate, and empower one's staff – are the fastest growing priority for many CEOs. According to respondents in the Korn Ferry study, the business leader of the twenty-first century will need to be creative, enthusiastic, open-minded, energetic, and encouraging rather than dignified and conservative. Effective delegation is seen as part and parcel of good people management. One of the chairmen interviewed in *Fortune* comments: 'A primary issue . . . will be helping managers to understand that it's not their job to supervise or to motivate, but to liberate and enable.'

The other increasing concern in both studies is ethics. Respondents in the Korn Ferry study 'expect their chief executive to be above approach' and 'recognize that the CEO's ethical standards are indispensable to internal and external credibility'. Another *Fortune* interviewee stresses that individual opportunity is not the same as 'unrestrained privilege. When you see what Donald Trump has become known for, it's very difficult to explain to a 25-year-old plant worker that capitalism is really a good system.'

Ethics is seen by both sets of respondents as not only related to personal standards of morality. Employee involvement in business decision-making, personnel policies reflecting racial diversity and equal opportunity, and greater collaboration between businesses permeates many of the comments. 'We must learn to evolve from a contractually oriented business culture where if it's not in the contract we do whatever the hell we want', says one expert in negotiation.

Peter Benton, delving into the past, is more cautious. 'In Athens', he points out, 'the Agora, fraught with every citizen, paralysed the power of Demosthenes to resist Philip of Macedon, who could make his own decisions fast.' 'Success', he predicts, 'will go now to the *impresario*, skilled in generating the enthusiasm and focusing the aspirations of many individuals with distinct talents.' The ability to delegate effectively, combined with judgement, leading to the security of an admirably phlegmatic approach are two qualities which Benton sees as a requirement for the future leader in turbulence. Ironically, he takes the trouble to scan history for examples, and presents the Duke of Marlborough as one who may be emulated with particular success: 'he . . . rides in the whirlwind, and directs the storm.'

In the end it is the leader's vision which still predominates. 'Business leadership in the 21st century will entail fighting wars before they occur', states the Korn Ferry study in a commentary to which Napoleon or Hannibal would immediately respond. 'The new leader will identify enemies before they themselves realize they are adversaries, anticipate weapons before they have been invented and attack before anyone realizes that there is a battle to be fought.'

Yet this vision will be useless if it remains on the boardroom table. As John Welch Jr of General Electric concludes in the *Fortune* survey: 'The Eighties had no shortage of individual business heroes. In the Nineties the heroes, the winners, will be entire companies that have developed cultures that instead of fearing the pace of change *relish* it.'

1
Today's Leaders Look to Tomorrow

Toss out your old assumptions. Rarely has a decade started with so many fresh prospects. Global revolutions are under way in managing, in politics, in technology, in communications. We are entering an age of boundless mobility and competition for business, for ideas, for people – truly an unparalleled era of possibilities. Perhaps this is the dawning of the *real* Age of Aquarius.

What will business be like? How will science change our lives? Who will create wealth? How will the world's old and new powers compete – and cooperate? What values are likely to guide our societies? In the pages that follow, some of the world's most thoughtful and stimulating leaders tell what to expect.

We've Got to Simplify and Delegate More

John F. Welch Jr, 54, CEO of General Electric, has transformed the company from a stodgy bureaucracy to one of the most forward-looking corporations around. He spoke with Stratford P. Sherman.

'The pace of change in the Nineties will make the Eighties look like a picnic – a walk in the park. Competition will be relentless. The bar of excellence in everything we do will be raised every day.

'The pace of change will be felt in several areas. Globalization is now no longer an objective but an imperative, as markets open and geographic barriers become increasingly blurred and even irrelevant. Corporate alliances, whether joint ventures or acquisitions, will increasingly be driven by competitive

'Today's Leaders Look to Tomorrow' from *Fortune* 26 March 1990. Copyright © 1990, The Time Inc. Magazine Company, permission of the publishers.

pressures and strategies rather than financial structuring. Technological innovation and the translation of that innovation into marketplace advantage will be accelerating ever faster. And in the coming decade, we're going to see increasing demands for sensitivity to the environment. Only a total commitment of everyone in the company can provide the level of responsibility that will be acceptable to governments, employees, and customers.

'Simply doing more of what worked in the Eighties – the restructuring, the delayering, the mechanical, top-down measures that we took – will be too incremental. More than that, it will be too slow. The winners of the Nineties will be those who can develop a culture that allows them to move faster, communicate more clearly, and involve everyone in a focused effort to serve ever more demanding customers.

'To move toward that winning culture we've got to create what we call a "boundryless" company. We no longer have the time to climb over barriers between functions like engineering and marketing, or between people – hourly, salaried, management, and the like. Geographic barriers must evaporate. Our people must be as comfortable in Delhi and Seoul as they are in Louisville or Schenectady. The lines between the company and its vendors and customers must be blurred into a smooth, fluid process with no other objective than satisfying the customer and winning in the marketplace.

'If we are to get the reflexes and speed we need, we've got to simplify and delegate more – simply trust more. We need to drive self-confidence deep into the organization. A company can't distribute self-confidence, but it can foster it by removing layers and giving people a chance to win. We have to undo a 100-year-old concept and convince our managers that their role is not to control people and stay 'on top' of things, but rather to guide, energize, and excite.

'But with all that must come the intellectual tools, which will mean continuous education of every individual at every level of the company. At GE we spend nearly $500 million a year on training and education. We see that not as an expense but as an investment in continuous renewal, the key to productivity growth. Continuous education drives everyone to find a better way, everyday. We used to make a circuit breaker – nothing fancy, the sort you'd find in any commercial building – that traveled 15,000 miles on its route to market and took 20 weeks to make. It spent ten of those weeks in transit between the eight different plants that worked on it. Could we find a better way? Of course. And we did. We're asking questions like that about *everything* we do, and we're beginning to find the answers.

'The Eighties had no shortage of individual business heroes. In the Nineties the heroes, the winners, will be entire companies that have developed cultures that instead of fearing the pace of change relish it.'

A New Ethic: Get Back to Basics, Get Good

Restless and blunt, Chrysler CEO Lee Iacocca, 65, is one of the mythic figures of US industry. Alex Taylor III interviewed him.

'American business has got to perform differently in the 1990s. The 1980s were a time of quick bucks, greed, and a lot of corruption. Sanctity isn't making a comeback. We'll still have human beings who are lustful and greedy. But there's an ethic developing that we've got to get back to basics; we've got to work and pull this country up by its bootstraps. We can't sit around and commiserate with one another – we've got to get good, we've got to compete, we've got to be world class. We can't just shout it, we've got to be it.

'You win or lose on the factory floor. If you don't build a car right, then you don't have quality and you don't have costs in line. What good is anything else? You've got to understand processing as well as design, and you better know about CAD/CAM [computer-aided design and manufacturing]. Then you have to comprehend exchange rates and how the world ticks. Our kids have to learn that if they want to compete.

'So much of our brain power has been siphoned off into the defense establishment. If you look at it in total, R&D in this country is terrific, but if you take out defense, there's none left. That's when we look bad against Japan. The military-industrial complex, which I've often believed exists, is not going away. But as you start to take it down, you can free up some of those brains to do commercial work. Instead of building black boxes and missile silos, they'll be working on instrument panels.

'We can get good again. I think that's going to happen with our company, the auto business, and I hope industry in general. I don't subscribe to the notion that we'll become a service nation. We have to stand for something. I think you are going to see a change. Why? The alternative is to say, 'Well, the hell with it. We'll just become a nation of consumers and we'll become second-rate. We'll depend on somebody else.' I don't think that's going to happen.'

Partnerships Will be the Thrust of the 1990s

Colgate-Palmolive gets 64% of its revenues from outside the US. CEO Reuben Mark, 51, spoke to David Kirkpatrick about how to build a global company.

'The essence of business as we move into the 21st century is going to be tapping the talent of good people. It's not about where you locate the plants, it's how you locate the best people and motivate them. How do you trust them and have them trust you.

'It's certainly not easy, but communication and bridging cultural gaps is the top priority. You've got to be honest and straightforward: What you tell the outside world has to be the same thing you tell your senior people, and the same thing you tell your factory workers. Pardon the high school coach stuff, but if everyone is working on a team basis and sees a specific set of goals, it's going to happen. The one-man band doesn't exist.

'Partnerships of all kinds will be the thrust of the Nineties and beyond: increasingly strategic interdependencies between companies, governments, people. A few years ago we fired all 13 of our advertising agencies and formed a partnership with two worldwide agencies and told them: 'You set up wherever we do business. You don't have to worry short term about losing our business.' We give employees of the agencies stock in our company. If they make a few mistakes in one country, it's not a tragedy. It's a long-term relationship, and they are probably doing great work elsewhere.

'Setting up in new countries is different from how it used to be. Once, you dropped an American off in Venezuela or Thailand with a boatload of toothpaste and had him build a business. Now we go into partnership with local business people or the local government. The fundamental difficulty is how to execute a global strategy and still allow those leading the local entity to feel they are controlling their own destiny. We encourage them to be entrepreneurial so they can feel responsible for the results.

'When it comes to managing people, I see business moving away from the authoritarian approach and toward a shared decision-making approach. After that, it's a very small jump to actual ownership. People at even a fairly low level in Colgate have stock or options – part of our way of making partnerships with our own people.

'We have all kinds of programs to identify and reward our most productive employees. Believe me, it is far more difficult to engineer that kind of encouragement consistently worldwide than you would ever expect. If it can get screwed up, it will. Some managers don't want to do it, and you have to sort of force them. It's easy to make videotapes about the company's strategy and vision. What's tough is to make sure they're showing the tapes in the plant in Turkey.'

It's Not What You Preach but How You Behave

Max DePree, 65, is chairman and retired CEO of Herman Miller, the office furniture company his father founded. He talked with David Kirkpatrick.

'Most people come to work well prepared, well motivated, and wanting to reach their potential. A primary issue for the Nineties will be helping managers to understand that it's not their job to supervise or to motivate, but to liberate and enable.

'Take a 33-year-old man who assembles chairs. He's been doing it several years. He has a wife and two children. He knows what to do when the children have earaches, and how to get them through school. He probably serves on a volunteer board. And when he comes to work we give him a supervisor.

'He doesn't need one. His problem isn't to be supervised, it's to continue toward reaching his potential. How can he get the opportunities that are important to him and his family? Also, how can we protect him from poor work he gets from the third shift? Or from people who give him too many computer forms to deal with?

'The Nineties will require a much more cross-cultural attitude on the part of managers. They need to have deeper insight into the strengths that women, ethnic minorities, and immigrants can bring. In our plant in Irvine, California, we have to communicate in English, Spanish, and Vietnamese. We also have four female vice presidents and two black vice presidents.

'We've had a bit of a backlash to deal with. A few white men said they didn't want to work for one of these new managers. We said transfer or leave, diversity is here to stay. It's morally right – and it happens to be pragmatically right. A number of our women and minority managers are absolutely outstanding.

'One thing that's gotten a little out of hand in our capitalist system is the idea that individual opportunity somehow is the same thing as unrestrained privilege. When you see what Donald Trump has become known for, it's very difficult to explain to a 25-year-old plant worker that capitalism is really a good system.

'Boards of directors need to become both more deeply involved in companies and much more accountable. Directors need to take away from management the initiative for things like setting the board's agenda. Our directors decided that the CEO may not collect more than 20 times the $25,000 that the average factory worker gets, so we've got a half-million-dollar cap.

'You have to look at leadership through the eyes of followers. Lech Walesa told Congress that there is a declining world market for words. He's right. The only thing the world believes is behavior, because we all see it instantaneously. None of us may preach any more. We must behave.'

Let the Manager Do his Thing – or Replace Him

Jean-Marie Descarpentries, 54, is presedent of CMB Packaging, Europe's largest container company. Shawn Tully interviewed him.

'The management style of the future is the flattened pyramid of SAS President Jan Carlzon. It's not a trick, but a fantastic invention: You don't order people from the top, you lead them. You give them vision and help. In the past, if a business unit were in trouble, the people at the top dictated the action to be taken. Today, we first help the business unit manager to try to overcome the difficulties. There's only one key decision: whether to replace him. You must let the manager do his own thing. If you do not, the company cannot run fast enough. You have a lot of highly motivated people in the flattened pyramid because you give them more responsibility and confidence.

'At this company, we are a community of entrepreneurs. The best of them come from small and medium-size companies – they're used to going fast and creating new products. Normally, you get people trying to improve the existing assets. But you don't run fast that way. We want 90% entrepreneurs and 10% optimizers. In most companies you have the opposite.'

'I Would Abandon Business Contracts'

Leonard Greenhalgh, 45, teaches a highly popular course on negotiation at Dartmouth's Amos Tuck School of Business Administration. He spoke with Brian Dumaine.

'US businesses have an antiquated notion of what competition is all about. When we Americans think of competition we think in adversary terms: You dump a supplier if you can find one with a cheaper product. You abandon the customer if you can find a more profitable one.

'But now we're dealing in a global market, where other people are in collaborative business cultures. Americans don't have a really fine sense of what collaboration is all about. You can't have an adversary, me-first mentality and get a just-in-time production program or an R&D joint venture to work. We must learn to evolve from a contractually oriented business culture where if it's not in the contract we do whatever the hell we want. What's missing is good will, trust, and a genuine concern for the other person's welfare. We need to do business based on relationships.

'That's how the Japanese do it. A Japanese contract is so vague it's unenforceable in US courts. It says, well, the two of us will get together, and we think we're going to do this product, but if that doesn't work for us, then we'll have to change the terms of the agreement, because why would we want to go ahead with it and do it if it was killing us?

'If your partner isn't living up to the terms of the agreement, that tells you the agreement isn't good for your partner. Why not make the terms so good that the person would agree to do it so you wouldn't need a contract? Managers should be resolving these conflicts, not lawyers. If I could, I would abandon business contracts.'

Let the Workers Make White-Knuckle Decisions

Edward E. Lawler III, 51, professor of management at the University of Southern California's business school, specializes in organizational change. Jeremy Main interviewed him.

'In the 1990s we will reinvent management – and constantly modify our invention. I expect all varieties of participative management and employee involvement to spread, partly because the traditional systems of managing are failing. There's a recognized need to change and that is the major difference from ten years ago, when the big corporations would not admit they were sick. Look now at the fallen icons – the IBMs, the GMs, the Kodaks – who have become too bureaucratic to compete globally in industries we thought we had locked up.

'Employee involvement offers management the things it needs to compete globally – better quality, a focus on the customer, fast response time – while reducing overhead and flattening the organizational structure. Maybe 50% to 60% of large corporations use quality circles, problem-solving groups, and other ways to get employee suggestions. Another 5% to 10% have work teams that push power down so workers themselves are making white-knuckle decisions about hiring, firing, and pay.

'The radical jump coming now in employee involvement will give workers resposibility in the total business process. For example, work teams at the new Volvo plant in Uddevalla, Sweden, will take customers' orders, communicate with dealers, and indeed relate to the cars throughout their lives because they will get quality and maintenance data on the cars they build. Eventually a customer may come to watch the team build his car – and perhaps even help built it.

'The key issue, the unknown, about employee involvement is how much support we can count on long term from senior executives. We can rant all we want that we're going to die if we don't change, but it's up to management to restructure itself and to utilize the work force. Top managers are not focusing enough on how organizations are really managed. They are more concerned with dramatic short-term events. They are becoming increasingly detached from what is going on in their own organizations.'

It's Time to Train your Generalists

Steven C. Wheelwright, 46, a Harvard business school management professor, is one of the country's foremost experts on manufacturing. Brian Dumaine interviewed him.

Just about everyone agrees that to develop new products it's smart to form teams made up of people from manufacturing, engineering, marketing, and finance. But we're going to see dramatic changes in how such teams operate in the coming decade.

'When companies establish cross-functional teams, most don't truly change the *way* they work. The add another layer – people whose only authority is to keep their eye on the schedule. These companies are merely maintaining their stodgy hierarchies and using teams as a last-ditch attempt to salvage old ways of managing.

'What's required is a team led by a manager who is a business champion, instead of someone who favors his own area of expertise. Today's team leader has to champion the *product*, which means breaking down the walls between functions and getting people to compromise. To persuade them to think this way, we have to start training people to be generalists before they accumulate 20 years as specialists. It may mean rotating them through jobs. Teams don't need just great design engineers but engineers who also understand marketing and manufacturing.'

Employees Must Reflect the Diverse World

CEO James R. Houghton, 53, has made a practice of advancing women and minorities at Corning. He spoke with Kenneth Labich.

'Any company that helps women and minorities play a fuller role can expect some salutary results in the coming years. For one, I think these companies will be more ethical. I do not mean to imply that women and minorities are more ethical than white males, but rather that their presence will encourage all employees to be more accommodating and considerate in their contact with customers – and by customers I'm talking about everyone with whom they work.

'Companies simply can't prosper in a diverse, multicultural world unless they reflect that diversity to some degree. It's like the Darwinian ideal that diversity in the gene pool creates strength and survivabilility in any species. A corporation that successfully draws on the talents and abilities of all its employees as individuals will be best positioned for success.

'As companies reflect more cultural diversity, they will become more tolerant, more willing to use differences, rather than sameness, as criteria for individual success within the organization. Any business climate in which broadly different indivduals may succeed will be a climate where the whole organization prospers.'

Wanted: Eight Million Educated Workers

Stephen A. Garrison, 49, is CEO of Ward Howell International, an executive search firm. Thomas A. Stewart interviewed him.

'If we maintain today's ratio of employees to population, we will have 15.6 million new workers in the year 2000. That's not enough: Assuming a moderate GNP growth rate of 2.9%, we will have 23.8 million jobs by then. Improved productivity can't close that gap. So where will we find all these people?

'Let's start with women. To retain those who opt out of corporate life, we clearly need benefits like day care and spousal relocation, but there should be more. Clothing allowances, for example. It costs a woman, in my estimate, two or three times as much as a man to dress for the executive workplace. Or – try this on your human resource people – a 'hassle bonus.' Having children while maintaining a job is one hell of a hassle. How about a $10,000 annual bonus for a woman between the ages of 35 and 45? It would vest after 10 years, when she would get $100,000 plus any capital appreciation – a good start toward educating those children.

'Then let's talk about minorities. There is practically a zero growth rate in US jobs that don't require high school diplomas. Yet we have 26 million functionally illiterate people and 46 million borderline illiterates, many of them black or other minorities. Corporations spend $25 billion a year for remedial literacy programs, a drop in the bucket compared with what's needed. We will see many programs for people who come early to work or stay late to learn to read, using operating manuals and word processors. Let's contribute $5,000 a year to the pension plan of employees who succeed in workplace literacy programs. Corporations should consider sending minorities to college. They could do this with loans, which the employee repays or works off.

'We must also open the gates to immigration. If a person has a college degree and knows English, we ought to bring him or her in. We can use that strength. In my view, a college education should be tantamount to getting a green card, which allows foreign citizens to live and work here.'

To Compete Globally, Look at the World Map

Percy Barnevik, 49, is president of Asea Brown Boveri, a leading supplier of big electrical equipment, including power generators. Shawn Tully interviewed him.

'There is a tendency in the Western world to talk about only one region at a time. Ten years ago, people talked about Latin America as a great opportunity. Now everyone talks about Eastern Europe. Instead, we should look *everywhere*, including the fast-moving Far East, the forgotten Africa and Latin America, all of Europe, and the subcontinent of India. To meet global competition, you have to be global yourself and meet your competitors on their home ground.

'Industrial America is coming back as an international competitor. We need a more competitive Europe and US to meet the challenge from the Far East. Japanese companies are extremely dangerous and forceful competitors. We all have to compare ourselves to the best, not to our neighbors.

'Who could have imagined ten years ago what people would sacrifice for a cleaner environment? Almost half of our $25 billion annual sales is directly or indirectly related to environmental issues. The greenhouse effect, global warming, and the ozone layer are high on the political agenda in Western Europe. In Eastern Europe, the environmental destruction is horrifying. Its countries need to totally rebuild their energy systems. That means even more opportunity.

'Americans have a different view of the world from us [Asea Brown Boveri is a Swedish-Swiss joint venture]. They sit on that huge continent that takes about 80% of its own products. In contrast, we just look at the world map. You find all nationalities in this headquarters building, and that's a big advantage. Our official language is now English, but every day you have to remember whether to call somebody 'Doctor' or 'Joe.' You have to live with this cultural mixture. It's a real education.'

2
The Leader of the Twenty-first Century Corporation: A Profile

Like an artist swiftly changing one portrait into another with a few carefully chosen lines, our completed questionnaires provide a sharp, compelling image of *change* in the attributes of executive leaders. The following discussions offer a selection of some of the salient perceptions that emerged from our investigation.

Areas of Expertise

The four areas of CEO expertise rated most highly by our respondents demand a comprehensive understanding of individual and market psychology (see figures 1 and 2).

1 *Strategy formulation.* Our respondents told us that strategy formulation is the area in which the ideal CEO must exhibit the most expertise. The CEO of the twenty-first century will have to be able to create strategic plans and know precisely how and when to initiate them.

2 *Human resource management.* Management of people is an indispensable component of sustained corporate performance and competitive advantage. Accordingly, human resource management as an area of CEO expertise rises from the third most important ranking in 1988 to the number two position in 2000 (see table 1).

3 *Marketing/sales.* The growth strategies and competitive tactics predicted for the year 2000 will require a strong market orientation and customer responsiveness. Therefore, the future CEO will need to possess a knowledge of marketing. The fact that this area falls to third place in the

Excerpt from *Reinventing the CEO*, a global study of 1,500 chief executives conducted jointly by Korn Ferry International and Columbia University Graduate School of Business, 1988, by permission of Korn/Ferry International.

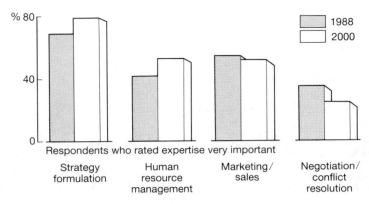

Figure 1 The changing need for expertise

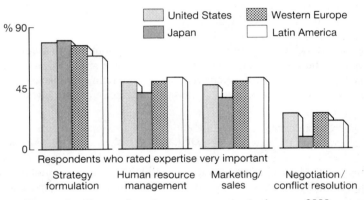

Figure 2 How each region rates expertise in the year 2000

Table 1 Ranking ten areas of CEO expertise

Rank	1988	2000
1	Strategy formulation	Strategy formulation
2	Marketing/sales	Human resource management
3	Human resource management	Marketing/sales
4	Negotiation/conflict resolution	Negotiation/conflict resolution
5	Accounting/finance	Accounting/finance
6	Media skills	International economics and politics
7	Production/operations	Media skills
8	International economics and politics	Science/technology/R&D
9	Science/techology/R&D	Production/operations
10	Foreign languages	Computer literacy

year 2000, while human resource expertise rises to second, suggests a slight shift in emphasis from understanding customers, the people *outside* the company, to developing and retaining personnel, the people *inside* the company.

4   *Negotiation/conflict resolution.* The twenty-first century will be not only a period of rapid change, but an era of perpetual conflict. From hostile acquisitions to litigation, from protectionism to corporate espionage, the CEO of the year 2000 will be confronted with a constellation of complex challenges. Furthermore, the delicate balance of multiple stakeholders and the need to deal with more diverse groups of people will heighten the importance of skill in negotiation and conflict resolution.

Bottom of the barrel were foreign languages and computer literacy. Despite the globalization of the past decade and the substantial impact that computers have had on the work place, our respondents gave these two areas the lowest ranking for the CEO of today *and* tomorrow.

The overall ranking for foreign languages is heavily influenced by our American respondents, who rate this area far lower than anyone else. (Surprisingly, Latin Americans foresee the greatest *decline* in its importance; Western European and Japanese executives both expect it to become more important.)

All our respondents predict modest increases in the importance of computer literacy, however. Thus, while they do not believe computer expertise will be an essential skill for the CEO of the twenty-first century, they do seem to anticipate that future conditions will marginally increase the CEO's need for direct computer access.

Despite the relatively low value given to computer literacy, it seems likely that the level of direct computer interaction by CEOs will continue to increase, especially among younger executives who have grown up with PCs. Technological advances are facilitating the use of computers at top levels of management; executives, as well as CEOs, can access and analyze corporate data with only minimal interaction with the computer, and without relying on employees for support.

The CEO who can freely explore the global revenue, profit, and employment data available in the firm's central computer system will have the opportunity to be more creative in assessing the company's direction. CEOs can, in fact, have a computer system available at all times – in the office, at home, in the car, on the plane – providing instant access to critical data with the touch of a finger. Furthermore, instant access to data saves considerable time. Because of these features, effective use of computer information systems is likely to become one of the most vital weapons in every CEO's personal arsenal.

Personal Characteristics

Our respondents emphasized the symbolic role of the chief executive. They believe that CEOs of the twenty-first century must be *leaders*, inspiring managers to implement the optimistic visions of the corporation. The effective CEO will imbue the organization with energy and inspire employees to realize their potential. According to respondents, the ideal CEO of the year 2000 will not be able to meet the new demands by abandoning proven traits. The ratings for only one characteristic decreased substantially from 1988 to 2000: it is expected that the ideal chief executive of the future will be substantially *less conservative* than the chief executive of today.

Ethics are rated most highly among the personal characteristics needed by the ideal CEO in the year 2000. Respondents expect their chief executive to be above reproach. They recognize that the CEO's ethical standards are indispensable to internal and external credibility, to setting admirable standards for the organization, and to keeping the firm out of court.

CEO also stands for creative, enthusiastic, and open-minded. Rated just below ethics are a series of elusive, intangible, but meaningful attributes:

- creative
- enthusiastic
- open-minded
- intelligent
- inspiring
- energetic
- encouraging.

Another group of similarly intangible attributes was also rated highly (though lower than the previous group):

- analytic
- loyal
- physically fit
- organized
- risk-taking
- diplomatic
- intuitive
- collaborative.

While these characteristics are rated lower than those in the first group, the ratings are still high in an absolute sense – well above 'moderately important.' This suggests that the respondents expect the ideal chief executive to have the diversity of complementary characteristics (such as both 'analytic' and 'intuitive') required by a complex environment.

The characteristics rated lowest were:

– tough
– personable
– patient
– dignified
– conservative.

Most of these characteristics can be used to describe the CEO who ushered in the twentieth century. Respondents believe that a radically new type of leader will be needed in the volatile business environment of the twenty-first century.

Management Style

Although the position of chief executive officer is an extremely demanding job today, tomorrow it will be more so. In comparing the management style of today's CEO with that of the ideal CEO for the year 2000, respondents indicated the heightened importance of a host of key behaviors (see figure 3).

Vision

The CEO in the year 2000 must 'see' the future of the corporation and its place in international business, and must have a clear vision of how managers can achieve corporate goals. The CEO, embodying the distinctive mission of the organization, must imbue the corporation with a sense of purpose and direction. This task will be a particularly crucial and difficult challenge for the CEOs of large, geographically dispersed companies.

Succession Planning and Other Forms of Executive Wisdom

The vital importance of good *succession planning* is now well known, and the CEO in the year 2000 will carefully plan smooth successions. Our respondents identified several important components of such a plan. *Management training and development* are essential for preparing and retaining talented executives, and *linking compensation to individual performance* encourages the best players to stay on the team. While establishing high standards for employees, and gearing rewards to those standards, the future CEO will also *readily reassign or terminate individuals* who do not meet objectives, neglecting such sentimental considerations as loyalty and length of service. The ideal business leader will *delegate authority*, not only because of severe personal time constraints, but because top managers flourish when given responsibility for important decisions. And this new chief executive will eschew waste by maintaining a *lean staff* and by *setting a personal example of cost-consciousness.*

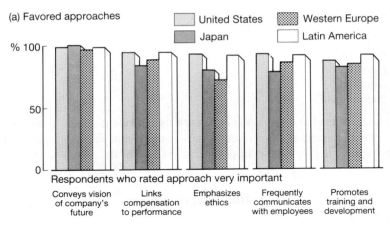

(a) Favored approaches

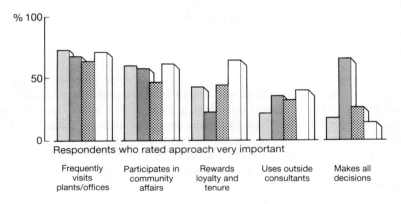

Figure 3 Management style of the future CEO
(a) Favored approaches
(b) Least important approaches

The Ultimate Communicator

The CEO of the twenty-first century will be a superb communicator, eloquently exchanging views with employees, customers, and the media. For all regions but Japan, which already rates it most highly, frequent communication with customers was one of the aspects of management style expected to increase most in importance. In addition, public speaking and dealing with media were rated the most important areas of formal training by our overall respondent sample.

3
Riding the Whirlwind: The New Leadership

Peter Benton

The Passing of Autocracy

The feudal world, with its strong sense of structure and reverence for the authority of its leaders, certainly did not encourage debate on their dicta. Just as Marcus Terentius sardonically remarked to the Emperor Tiberius, the glory of obedience characterized that social form. In 1655, Louis XIV could say 'L'état c'est moi'; but while the divine right of kings held sway, it was for most fear that forced that conformity, as Vaclav Havel helps us to appreciate, in his wry satires on the communist social cage.

But it was not like that in the heroic age: Agamemnon, about to lift the siege of Troy, faced this onslaught from young Diomedes, in Homer's words, translated by Alexander Pope.[1]

> If I oppose thee, Prince! thy Wrath with-hold,
> The Laws of Council bid my Tongue be bold . . .
> The Gods have made thee but by halves a King;
> They gave thee Sceptres, and a wide Command,
> They gave dominion o'er the Seas and Land,
> The noblest Pow'r that might the world controul
> They gave thee not – a brave and virtuous Soul.

A rather tolerant chief executive to bear with that outburst; perhaps his pleasure in finding a fighting spirit in his army compensated for the offence to his *amour propre*.

In that age of the individual, even Olympus saw questioning of the supreme authority, reflecting the values of men. Jove had his problems. In a full board

Excerpt from *Riding the Whirlwind: Benton on Managing Turbulence*, by Peter Benton, 1990 Basil Blackwell Ltd.

meeting of the gods he laid down corporate policy: no interference with either side in the battle for Troy, under penalty of being fixed with burning chains to brazen floors in hell. To no effect. His own wife, Juno, 'headstrong and imperious still, she claims some title to transgress his will,' wheedles the head of a major subsidiary – Neptune – to join the war on the side of her favourite Greeks; she borrows Venus' marvellous girdle to infatuate her husband. The old chairman, moved by the unaccustomed caress nods off, waking in fury to find that some of his directors have launched an enterprise while he dozed. Neptune leading the Greeks in battle, and the Trojans in full retreat. A corporate aide is sent hot foot to insist on instant compliance with board policy, to be met with:[2]

> What means the haughty Sov'reign of the Skies,
> (The King of Ocean thus, incens'd, replies)
> Rule as he will his portion'd Realms on high;
> No Vassal God, nor of his Train am I.

How reminiscent of a modern boardroom! Does not Neptune's reply have its echo in the Crocker president's reaction to control from the Midland Bank in London, or Sohio's chairman and BP?

That breezy contest for power survived only in pockets when feudal structures dominated a society that was terrified by incessant marauding after the collapse of the Roman Empire; then, when people hungered after order, the sacred authority of the appointed ruler was held to justify passive obedience in some very disagreeable regimes. Even the great William the Silent, founder of Holland out of the empire of Philip II, was deeply concerned at the illegitimacy of his new state. It took three revolutions to bury that concept in the West: 1688, 1766, and 1789. A regrowth of absolutism after the defeat of Napoleon was finally routed in 1848, when all Europe rose against the remaining feudalists, with remarkably coincident uprisings in Paris, Rome, Vienna, Cracow, Naples, and Turkey. The United States gained Texas, California, and much else from a Mexico troubled by the instability of the old world.

Set Them Free!

The rigidity of the feudal world started to crack much earlier where individual freedom was well rooted. First in Italy, then in the Low Countries and in Britain, the Renaissance saw new styles of leadership emerge, after the long centuries of autocratic and unquestioned authority. In the turbulent sixteenth century, Queen Elizabeth sent men and ships out with only the most general objectives – relying on initiative and a healthy instinct for self-enrichment. Britain's huge empire made its most dramatic advances under the inspiration of the elder Pitt. In that *annus mirabilis* 1759, fleets and armies thousands of miles apart scored victory after victory, within the strategy of a supreme command, but through the creative aggression of individual leaders close to the opportunity, with the power to act on their own judgement. James Wolfe at Quebec, Boscawen at Quiberon Bay, the battles of Minden and Madras, saw victories inconceivable if planned in detail from above or directed from the centre. Forty years later, Nelson's 'perfect and generous confidence' in his captains made his victories possible too.

Of course those changes, in the balance of individual freedom and in the structure of society, took decades to evolve. In our corporate world, the swift onset of turbulence has caught some leaders on the hop; they have found the pace too fast. When giants like ITT and GEC have won stock market praise for twenty years through tight control of costs and contracts, it cannot be easy to find new ways of leading.

The New Agenda

New conditions demand a fresh approach. As the monoliths and structured hierarchies prove arthritic in the fast new game, empowering the individual is the new requirement, to act with personal initiative, close to the opportunity. No longer is it sound for the leader to insist that all is done his way; delegation means that others will find ways of doing things that may seem odd to the rule-maker, but, if relevant, prompt and energetic, more likely to win. Perhaps de Tocqueville's observation will console, 'La liberté démocratique . . . fait moins bien chaque chose, mais elle fait plus de choses.'[3]

No longer can the general hope to see every detail of the battle from his command post; it just is not feasible for even the most active leader of a complex business to have a hand on every lever. Not possible to do so and yet vitalize the team; not practical to juggle with a fast-moving present and judge calmly the imponderable forces affecting the future. When direct action by the leader himself is more rarely appropriate, the new man must achieve through the will of others. Success will go now to the *impresario*, skilled in generating the enthusiasm and focusing the aspirations of many individuals with distinct talents. He listens, sensitive to the breath of new influence; he shapes, aware that people need a vision and a structure; he inspires in each an urge to excel, when the criteria of that excellence are relative to external standards, specific in each case. Leadership in turbulence is an affair of the whole human being, with the statistics and the specialists on tap but not on top, as the saying goes.

When the leader has devolved the authority to decide, and can no longer see all the action; when the proven rulebook may be obsolete before it is printed; he must find new ways to achieve his goals. The direct order is replaced by a framework – a set of values to guide the independent actions of many individuals. Devising that framework needs sympathetic thought, specific to the objective, because the crucial concern is what people will do under the influence of those formulae. Principles that look sound from the boardroom, or have been proved valid in different circumstances, may cause strange effects in other conditions, or when other personal criteria operate. Frameworks formed for a predictable world can hold fallacies in turbulence.

The Well-Tempered Leader

Above all, in a turbulent age the new leader needs judgement. When the past is only an uncertain guide to the future, he needs the intellect to conceive what forces bear upon his future, and the personality to judge soberly the capability for action. Those must be crucial characteristics in a leader who can take his enterprise consistently to victory. Joseph Addison gives us the sublime picture of the Duke of Marlborough at Blenheim, 'he . . . rides in the whirlwind, and directs the storm'.[4] That image of the sure-footed leader, vital yet serene amidst turbulence, all-seeing and calm in judgement, certainly won the loyalty of those mixed battalions of Dutch, German, and British soldiers who stemmed the power of the Sun King. 'Marlborough never lost a battle, because he never fought a battle he could not win.' That was the phrase I used to modify the eagerness of some rash telecommunications managers in challenging the piecemeal aggression of our trade unions in the 1979 'winter of discontent'.

The Roman Empire found itself embroiled in serious wars through local folly – the arrogance of young Appius Claudius in Armenia, for example, or Crassus' avarice for Parthian gold.[5] Controlling the hotheads is more crucial in some instances than in others – certainly no wise leader is happy to find energies locked in needless battles, which may be lost. How to prevent such follies has vexed empires, and should concern also the wise leader of a disaggregated organization, though Wu Ch'i perhaps went too far, in ordering the execution of the warrior who dashed forward from the line of battle and slew the enemy's champion in single combat.[6]

More admirable is that combination of tactical skill, judgement, and the ability to coalesce the intentions of individuals that Marlborough demonstrated on the battlefields of Europe in the first decade of the eighteenth century. Time and again he manœuvred to present the allies with an opportunity for victory, only to find that one element or another of his force held back: the Dutch field deputies, the Margrave of Baden, or perhaps one of his own units arrived too late. Without complaint, where he judged the force available was not sufficient to achieve his objective, he withdrew, regrouped, and manœuvred for another opportunity. When the tactical position was sound, and he judged that his forces were coherent and sufficient for victory, he struck hard. I found those precepts helpful in the less glorious task of wresting the control of Britain's international telephone service from union activists. A careful campaign of measures, developed over eighteen months and more, agreed with James Hodgson, head of the international executive, and his colleages, seized the initiative and kept it. When the time was right, the frontline management acted firmly to put the new procedures in place, secure in the knowledge that my signature had authorized their stand, and that this time, they would not be abandoned under pressure. The union called a stoppage: they walked as far as the door, and turned back. The confidence of victory in firstline management settled the issue. A confidence that was not derived from the reckless 'do your worst' defiance; confidence that was built on the sure knowledge of necessary actions soundly conceived and solidly backed.

The First Victory is Sweetest

Every leader of free men and women needs to establish that he brings victory with him. Field Marshal Bramall, one of Britain's most thoughtful soldiers, urges a general in a new command to organize victory as the first priority. Even setting a brigade against a company position may be justified, if it brings that first sense that the new leader is a winner. Certainly Montgomery, criticized by some for excessive caution, knew that the mystique of Field Marshal Rommel could only be cleared from the minds of the Eighth Army if his own initial actions resulted in solid victories. At Alam Halfa, and then Alamein, he certainly produced those. In 1979, Sainsbury's Depot Replenishment program set their corporate computer system on the path to success.

Marlborough had shown his generation of leaders that it was not cowardly to refuse battle in which defeat was probable; providing that the will to re-engage was there. Sir Richard Grenville's suicidal attack in the *Revenge* on the mass Spanish fleet in Queen Elizabeth's time, may have made for stirring ballads, but would have destroyed his country, had he a fleet to commit, rather than a single small ship. One of the great heroes in Rome's wars with Hannibal, Fabius Maximus Cunctator, was given his cognomen – The Delayer – in admiration for the series of indecisive actions in which he weakened the power of his adversary while never exposing his own forces to destruction. Marshal Kutuzoff's controlled retreat before Napoleon led to the destruction of that disturber of mankind.

Another Way

A very modern leader who developed his style from left-wing views in youth is Sir Peter Thompson, of the British National Freight Consortium. The extraordinary growth of that rag-bag of nationalized transportation businesses is one of the epics of our time. Bought from the government by its employees in

1980, the next eight years saw share prices increase a hundredfold, making truck drivers into millionaires. How was it done? Structure, strategy, and style. With his 30,000 employees grouped into 700 business units, no one feels very far from the customer or from the profit and loss account. With thousands of substantial employee shareholders, poor performers get short shrift. Protesters from a disbanded unit at the Annual General Meeting were disconcerted to find that their protests were not met by brotherly support in the union spirit, but by critical rejection. 'You've had your come-uppance', from fellow workers who had observed slack performance and disapproved.

Peter Thompson, though, brought something more; he brought a strategy founded on values perceived by the customer, rather than the traditional introverted concern with internal transport functions. 'Sell solutions not features' is said to be the IBM cry. Certainly, selling solutions – the whole task, end to end – has paid off well for National Freight. Nowhere more so than in moving business families around the world, where the transfer of a household, entire and breakage-free, looks very much like value; usually each element in the complex process just looks like hassle. In distributing the *Financial Times*, taking responsibility for the whole chain – printer to newsagent – looks like value too, particularly when the system seems free of union sanctions.

Recognizing that employing shareholders is fine while stock prices rise but disagreeable in retreat, National Freight starts its mission statement with 'we'll seek to become a company for all seasons'. Structure and strategy, but perhaps most important, style. With main board members each nursing a constituency of employee shareholders, with good performance seen as a social duty, National Freight's remarkable financial achievement can only have come from superb development of individual capabilities. A humane style with practical economic benefits: why, it even pays off in making acquisitions, when owners accept a lower price from a congenial suitor. Quite a formula! Generous bonuses each year, related to achievement against budget, are a feature of the style too; focusing attention on the business unit rather than the remote corporation. Twelve and a half per cent on basic pay for achieving quality, and 30 per cent more for getting the financials right, gives some balance between the short term, and building the long-term assets of goodwill and reputation.

Does this all sound a bit like a Yugoslavian co-operative? Is it a formula that only works on the way up, a frustrating encumbrance when Icarus heads for the water? Perhaps, but maybe not. After all, the power of those worker shareholders lies in the Annual General Meeting, and in the election of directors. Once named, they can be backed or sacked. While in the saddle, they are free to act, unlike those unfortunate leaders in the communist world who have to fight individual issues through an Athenian democracy. In Athens the agora, fraught with every citizen, paralysed the power of Demosthenes to resist Philip of Macedon, who could make his own decisions fast. Democracy has its many forms; some give the inspiration of freedom while harnessing the individual to the common good; others debilitate.

Notes

1 Homer, *The Iliad*, vol. III, tr. Alexander Pope (Lintott, London, 1717), p. 5.
2 Ibid., vol. IV, p. 170.
3 Alexis de Tocqueville, *De la Démocratie en Amérique*, vol. II (Gosselin, Paris, 1835), p. 131.
4 Joseph Addison, *The Campaign* (1705).
5 A. N. Sherwin-White, *Roman Foreign Policy in the East* (Duckworth, London, 1984), pp. 174 and 279–290.
6 Sun Tzu, *The Art of War*, tr. Samuel B. Griffith (Oxford University Press, Oxford, 1971), p. 107.

Part II
Development

Chapter 14
Leaders: Born or Bred?

Introduction

Recognizing that leadership is more important at a time of continual uncertainty and change raises dilemmas for the management educator.

As we argued earlier, traditional business education founded around narrow functional specialisms is clearly unsuited to providing managers with the personal and intellectual attributes commonly associated with leadership. Vision, charisma, creativity, multilateral thinking, openness to other cultures, respect for other viewpoints, and an ability to listen and communicate are not acquired purely through formal teaching. But can they be acquired at all through intervention by the company trainer or the business-school tutor?

By the time young people are recruited into junior management, are the formative influences that shape their leadership potential – childhood experiences, upbringing, school and university education, travel or early life in a variety of environments and countries – already in place? Furthermore, are there genetic factors at play which pre-empt any preparatory process and present educators and employers with a *fait accompli*?

And if intervention by the employer or business school has a direct bearing, what methods are available or appropriate to shape leadership potential in managers who, in contrast with their predecessors of another age, have not been bred into the role by early education and upbringing? What formative experiences can be built into their career progression and how can these be enhanced, if at all, by formal business-school education?

The contributions to this second half of the book tackle these issues in depth. The overwhelming view is that, although genetics and upbringing are important factors that should not be ignored, leadership potential can be shaped by company and business-school intervention. But formal training and education needs to interweave with imaginative internal career development involving action learning, projects and secondments, assignments in a variety of different locations, and the imaginative use of sabbaticals – all measures which build on the experiential learning and multifaceted experiences of early life.

Above all, as more than one contributor stresses, organizations should be less élitist and narrow in where they look for their future leaders and more tolerant of behaviour that denotes leadership potential such as an ability to take risks, unconventional outlook, and even eccentric behaviour. Who could have predicted that the man best able to turn ICI around in the early 1980s would be a Belbin 'plant' with a ghastly taste in ties and a hairstyle that makes him look like a geriatric hippy?

John Adair delves deep into history by examining the view of Xenophon, concluding that leadership is learned through a combination of on-the-job experiment coupled with periods of reflection and reading to help them set their experiences into context. Nevertheless, Adair himself comments, 'It is a common fallacy that leadership is learned only through experience. Experience only teaches the teachable, and it is a school which charges large fees.'

This contrasts with two other perspectives on the contribution to leadership by genetics, early upbringing, education, and formal management development. Charles Cox and Cary Cooper stress the formative influences of childhood and education in a survey of forty-five chief executives which formed the basis of their book *High Flyers*, published in 1988. Jay Conger touches on the research carried out by William James, resulting in a world divided into 'once borns', whose life is harmonious and peaceful, and 'twice borns', who are faced 'with great struggles'. This theory ties in with Cox and Coopers' CEO who is revealed to have been often thrown 'on to his own resources very early in life, forcing him to take responsibility for himself and possibly others'. Conger, a self-confessed behaviourist, is not convinced by the usefulness of the generalized results of this research, and argues that if students can be taught tennis they can be taught leadership. To take the analogy further, tennis stars may be born with the latent potential to be 'stars' (although even this is arguable) but will not realize this potential without systematic, continuous, and gruelling tuition.

Conger's view sets the scene for this section of the book. Each chapter examines one aspect of how leadership is taught and explores related issues in detail. In this chapter Peter Benton somewhat reluctantly concludes that while the connection between 'the playing fields of Eton and mastery of the British Empire may be a little strained, leadership does seem to be a skill that works best when unselfconscious'. Self-confidence is considered by Philip Sadler to be 'absolutely fundamental, because to take on a leadership role is a courageous thing to do'. Both Conger and Sadler are agreed that much can be done to develop already present leadership potential, but the common facile approach is vastly inadequate. As Conger sardonically comments, 'Leadership is reduced to an essence that can be bought and sold like an enticing cologne. The assumption that a week-long session on leadership will turn someone into a leader is, of course, nonsense.'

The most striking conclusion is that organizations will succeed in developing leaders only if they understand how people learn as well what to teach them.

1
Leaders: Born or Bred?

Jay A. Conger

From ancient Greek philosophers to contemporary business executives, the issue of whether leaders are born or bred has been hotly debated. Some argue that the origins of leadership are largely mysterious and a matter of birthright. By early childhood, its seeds are already sown, and only the select will be blessed with such opportunity. Others believe that leadership is not a gift of birth or parentage but rather a set of skills that can be taught and acquired. Leadership talent, they feel, exists in most of us; it only waits to be tapped. Either perspective has profound implications. In the first case, we are relatively powerless to develop greater leadership ability in our organizations. Instead, we must assume a passive and hopeful attitude that at the 'right moment' a leader will appear or else we must carefully design our recruiting procedures to identify the select few. In the second case, we can direct resources and structure experiences to encourage individuals to become leaders. This is a more optimistic scenario and one that many institutions embrace given their annual expenditures on leadership training and development. But while the debate is a thorny one, there are indications that leadership is indeed more a matter of development and experience than of genes or family dynamics. In this chapter, we will try to discover why this is so. But first, let us look more closely at the arguments of these two schools of thought.

If we begin with the perspective that leaders are born and not bred, we discover that this is argued largely by psychologists and, specifically, by psychiatrists. By orientation and training, they trace a leader's drives and motivations to certain early childhood experiences. Without these, they argue, it is almost impossible to attain leadership status. Fundamental to their thinking is the work of American psychologist William James who formulated a theory of

'Leaders: Born or Bred?' by Jay A. Conger. Original paper written for this publication © Jay A. Conger 1989.

basic personality types – the 'once-borns' and the 'twice-borns'. The 'once-borns', James argued, were individuals who experienced the flow of life as reasonably straightforward from the moment of birth. Their family life was harmonious and peaceful. 'Twice-borns', on the other hand, were faced with great struggles. Their lives were never easy, and unlike 'once-borns', they could take little for granted. As a result of these differences, the two personalities developed very distinct world-views. For the 'once-borns', their sense of themselves was derived from a feeling of relative harmony and oneness with their environment. They felt little compulsion to be different from others or to act in ways that departed from the norm. For the 'twice-borns', there was instead a sense of profound separateness and one that would later foster leadership ability. Because of it, these individuals felt little dependence on their organizations, their work roles, or on others, and as such had no desire to adhere to the status quo or to follow others' directives. Instead, the 'twice-borns' were free to promote change and to lead people in new directions. Along with certain aptitudes and personal expectations of achievement, their self-reliance would set them in motion to become a leader. With the selective influence of mentors and others later in life, they would gain a foothold into positions of leadership (Zaleznik, 1984).

While such arguments are intuitively appealing, there are aspects of this 'childhood-origins' philosophy that are troubling. For example, proponents of this school provide few details about the exact character of these family situations. We know that the child develops a feeling of being special and a sense of having to struggle – but what types of parent–child relations are necessary to create this condition? I suspect there are so many permutations that it is impossible to specify them. Secondly, a life of struggle would seem to suggest that children of the impoverished and the criminal would be the most likely candidates for leadership. Yet most of our leaders come from the more educated and financially secure classes. So what is meant by 'struggle'? Some specify the struggle as one of 'inner conflict', but again the type of inner conflict is left vague. Inner conflict is a universal phenomenon, so how do we distinguish between the inner conflict that facilitates the development of leadership and that which necessitates a visit to the psychiatrist? And even proponents of the 'born-leader' school argue that childhood experiences alone are not sufficient; later developmental experiences such as mentors can be equally important (Zaleznik, 1984).

In thinking about the 'once-born' and 'twice born' distinction, remember also that its originator James was a social scientist. His theory of personality types was not meant as an accurate picture of reality but as a conceptual tool. In the real world, most of us lie somewhere along a continuum between these two types. It is not possible, therefore, for such a model to capture accurately the complexity of human life. Thus the arguments of those who believe leadership to be the product of childhood is far from satisfactory.

Let us shift our attention to those who favor the argument that leadership can be trained and developed, which viewpoint I share. Proponents of this view argue that many more forces are at play in the development of a leader, that events and experiences later in life are just as important as those of childhood. For them, other sources of leadership development include teachers, hardships, opportunity, education, and role models. Underlying their argument is the assumption that the potential to lead is far more widely present. Its rarity is a reflection of neglected development rather than of the scarcity of certain abilities.

It may be useful to employ an analogy from the world of art. Assume, for a moment, that leadership and artistic ability are similar in that both require creativity, unconventionality (to become, ultimately, great), a set of distinct skills and behaviors, and certain aptitudes. If we apply the question 'Is an artist born or bred?' to an artist like Claude Monet, we are asking whether his ability to paint comes from an innate ability or from talents that were developed over time. Biographies of Monet indicate that, while he possessed artistic ability at a early age, it was not until he came under influence of other artists that he began to formulate his own style. His technique was refined over time and with considerable effort. It was not a matter of special genes but rather one of abilities developed over time. Leadership skills involve much the same process: they are the result of important interactions with others and developmental experiences. Granted, some may develop a greater aptitude for art or leadership than the general population, and some may even have certain natural talents. These individuals become the Monets, the Winston Churchills, and the John F. Kennedys of the world. But while these aptitudes are present to a greater extent in some individuals, the basic abilities nonetheless are more widely present among the general populace.

At the same time, it must be said that not everyone can become a leader. Some simply do not possess enough of the basic skills or the cognitive orientation. So while aptitudes to lead exist widely, they are not present in every individual. Also, the aptitude may be present, but not the desire; some may not have the motivation to lead. Furthermore, leadership depends on special dynamics that evolve between leaders and their subordinates, which cannot be duplicated textbook-style. Finally, from a practical standpoint, we may not want too many leaders in our organizations. Imagine a company comprising all bosses and no subordinates.

It would be more constructive, therefore, to approach the issue with the view not of creating an army of leaders but rather of enhancing general managerial skills, in other words, focusing on creating better managers by developing in them some of the skills of effective leaders. For instance, we might draw lessons from the strategy skills of exemplary leaders to enhance a manager's strategic abilities, using our best leaders as models in the areas where we feel our managers to be weakest. Leadership development programs then become one of a variety of means to assist in developing an individual's ability to manage effectively. Assuming that leadership can be developed, let us now see how it could be done.

Developing Leaders

A tragedy of management today is the lack of leadership in many of our organizations. The ability and desire to lead are often lacking because of an absence of opportunity and investment in the processes and rewards that foster its growth. Rather than tapping, developing and encouraging these dormant abilities, many organizations, however, often discourage leadership skills by their benign neglect of 'managing' and concern to preserve the status quo. They pay the price of lost leadership potential and, in turn, organizational ineffectiveness.

The problem is also a matter of focus. Companies and government agencies have devoted much energy to training programs – typically offering simple leadership models with feedback sessions to provide managers with greater self-awareness on a series of 'leadership' dimensions. This approach has serious flaws. First, what many training programs call leadership is actually 'managership.' These programs perpetuate administrative rather than leadership skills. They teach simple goal-setting, managing by objectives, participative decision-making, and so on, and while these skills are vital to effective managership, other capabilities, such as strategic vision, tactical abilities, persuasion, motivational skills, determination, are more critical to effective leadership.

The second problem is that many stop with the training program. Leadership is reduced to an essence that can be bought and sold like an enticing cologne. The assumption that a week-long session on leadership will turn someone into a leader is, of course, nonsense. To develop a leader takes more than a training program. It is an important step, but only one of many. Instead, companies must begin leadership development at the point of recruiting. Thereafter, job experiences, rewards, organizational cultures, and training must all work together to reinforce and promote the skills of leading. The organization itself must encourage expressions of leadership. Companies must take a more integrated, lifelong approach if they are to begin tapping the potential of today's managers. They must use the many experiences a manager faces in his or her career as opportunities to train and promote leadership.

Finally, our present approaches to leadership development fail to see that part of the problem is tied to our business culture and to our educational system. Our business culture, notable for its creativity and vision in the entrepreneurial sector, is woefully unsupportive of these qualities in large corporations. This attitude is changing thanks to fierce competitive pressures, but there is still limited awareness of the need for managers to develop greater strategic powers, to become more effective communicators, to enhance their motivational skills, and to master the processes of organizational change and renewal. Corporations must actively encourage and reward these skills if they want them. At present, trainees from the company's once-a-year leadership seminar find themselves returning to an office where opportunities to practise their new leading skills are rare, and their initiatives go unrewarded or ignored.

Our business schools and even our university programmes are also part of the problem. In some ways, we are failing to train young people in the very subjects that may later help them to think more creatively and comprehend the broad implications of market trends – certain topics in the social sciences and humanities, for example. To illustrate the predicament and, at the same time, offer us hope that the creative skills of leadership can be taught, we turn to the results of an unusual research study conducted at Carnegie-Mellon University a number of years ago, which suggests how it is possible to learn and unlearn skills such as imagination through course-work.

Bob Altemeyer, a Carnegie-Mellon researcher, decided to test two groups of students over their four years of university to see if they would develop different styles of thinking. One group was selected from the College of Fine Arts where they majored in architecture, art, design, or music; the other group was from the College of Engineering and Science where they majored in engineering, maths, or the hard sciences. Before, and then during each of their four undergraduate years, they were tested for analytic and logic skills and for imagination and intuition skills. Some of the results were surprising. But first, the not so surprising results. The engineering and science students significantly improved their scores on the analytic tests as they moved from their freshman to senior years. The fine arts students significantly improved their scores, as well, but on imagination. The surprise was that on tests measuring imagination the engineering and science students showed a consistent *decrease* in imagination as they moved from the freshman year to the sophomore year and so on to the senior year. The fine arts students showed the same decline in their analytic skills. Four years of education in the fine arts had improved imaginative thinking but with a loss in analytic problem-solving skills, while education in engineering had improved proficiency in analytic ability but at the cost of imagination. The learning of one style of thinking alone, it appears, may cause the active unlearning of the other (Altemeyer, 1966).

While these findings illustrate the power that education plays in promoting or inhibiting certain abilities, they also seem to suggest that we can actively train and learn such skills. On this optimistic note, let us look at one of the most important skill areas of great leaders – strategic vision – to see what can be taught and developed.

Developing a Leadership Skill: Strategic Vision

One of the hallmarks of great business leaders has been their ability to see strategic opportunities others have not perceived. It is a vital talent in an era marked by intense global competition. While we may not be able to train visioning per se, we can certainly facilitate the processes that enable it to occur. Organizations can do this through four means: selection procedures, job experiences, supervisory styles, and specific training programs. Since selection is a critical step in developing organizational leaders, we begin with recruiting.

Selecting people for creativity, vision, and unconventional insight is no easy task. Who knows what to look for? Indeed, corporate recruiters may actually go out of their way to avoid such characters: 'To go after the occasional interesting oddball, the out-of-step type, is risky for recruiters' own careers. It's dangerous to be blamed for hiring weirdos, loners, and nerds, and that's the way some managers will see such unusual recruits. People like that will be irritants, disturbers of the peace. Besides, if they are hired but not supported by appropriate backup, they'll soon go away' (Leavitt, 1986, p. 158).

So we have a dilemma: while we may think we want more unconventional types, we really do not. But suppose your organization has had a change of heart and decides to take the risk and hire a few people who are imaginative and visionary. What would you look for? Most of the criteria we currently use in selection involve straightforward analytical skills. If you want to find people who by nature and experience are more likely to be pathfinding creative types, you will have to develop new criteria. You might begin by searching for individuals with stronger than average conceptual and creativity skills. In interviews, you might ask candidates to solve hypothetical case studies of strategic dilemmas or other problems requiring creative solutions. There are tests and questionnaires to measure creativity (Kirton, 1976) as well as ability to think and plan over long time-spans (Jacques, 1982, 1986). Certain needs might also be tested, for example, it appears that individuals who have strong power needs (McClelland, 1985) are likely to become more successful and possibly more effective leaders (House, 1988; Miner, 1978). Such measures could be used in initial selection procedures.

Organizations might also try to ascertain whether candidates have a sense of determination and a passionate interest in their product or service. A degree of prior experience in their industry (especially diverse experience) might help since creativity is enhanced by a depth-and-breadth of knowledge and experience. Candidates with a strong intrinsic motivation for their work may ultimately have the most potential to become visionaries. Interview questions focusing on the candidate's favorite tasks and projects in the past may be revealing in this respect. Once recruited, junior managers should be matched to tasks that stimulate their intrinsic motivation as this appears to enhance their ability to be innovative (Amabile and Gryskiewicz, 1987).

Job experiences may be particularly vital to enhancing the development of visionary leaders. One reason why we have more tactical managers than visionary leaders is surely because of excessive functional specialization. When executives are promoted through the ranks of a single function, it is hard for them to lead from a generalist's perspective. This is the type of experience that may often be required (preferably during the early stages of one's career). Moreover, there should be far greater exposure to all the dimensions of a particular function, for example manufacturing trainees should have experience in most areas of their company's production process. Such experiences should include job rotation with considerable line-and-field experience, which all heighten sensitivity to markets and to the organization's character. As a person's experience widens, so does his ability to perceive the breadth of issues needed to understand his operation strategically. Such experiences should involve considerable opportunities to experiment with leadership.

Decentralization is especially critical to this process. Companies skilled at creating leaders push responsibility downward and, in turn, create more challenging jobs. Many of these companies create as many small units as possible or else develop challenging opportunities by emphasizing growth through new products and new ventures or by using temporary and frequently restructured teams and task forces. In this way, chances are increased that managers will develop a broad conception of their organization's role and have greater opportunities to lead.

Supervisory style may also play a role in the creative abilities associated with visioning. In R&D laboratories, for instance, a high measure of individual autonomy is critical for creativity. While the project manager retains 'strategic autonomy' for a project's overall direction, he or she allows 'operational autonomy' regarding the means by which the overall goal will be achieved. In one study of especially creative R&D groups, it was found that

> the best managers are those who ask questions. The role of the manager is to make clear what the objective, directions, and purpose are, to set up a picture or long-term objective that a person will be working toward. Once the operation is under way, the managers should then provide an environment where a lot of questions are asked. He should be non-judgemental – the people working on the project, or their peers, should make the judgements (Amabile and Gryskiewicz, 1987, p. 27).

These management practices helped to promote creative approaches to problems. Marketing managers or manufacturing managers could adopt a similar process – setting overall objectives but leaving the creative business of getting to those objectives up to subordinates.

Training visioning skills, however, is a more difficult task. In the first place, some have certain 'cognitive personalities' that lend themselves to imagination and creativity, but others do not. This is the right and left brain argument. Moreover, vision is a much more complex and personal experience than a workshop could ever hope to capture and train. Our focus, then, should begin with the basic skills of creativity and problem-solving. Techniques such as 'synectics' (Gordon, 1961) and 'Janusian thinking' (Rothenburg, 1979) may aid managers in developing such skills. There are also programs offered by organizations such as the Center for Creative Leadership (Greensboro, N.C.) that focus specifically on helping managers to develop their creative abilities and corporations to identify aspects of the environment that inhibit creativity. Sessions such as the Quick Environment Scanning Technique (QUEST) (See Bennis and Nanus, 1985) may be useful in stimulating vision. In such programs, managers come together to brainstorm about future opportunities and threats in the marketplace and to determine the implications for their organization's strategy. The brainstorming nature of these sessions forces managers to explore strategic and tactical options that the conventions of their organizations would normally preclude.

But training in creativity will take root only if organizations support the experimentation it takes to unlearn less creative approaches. For the fastest way to kill incipient creativity skills is to place them in an organization that demands uncreative ways of thinking and has few rewards for initiative (Leavitt, 1986). Learning creativity demands individual effort supported by certain organizational factors. Stanford psychologist Harold Leavitt (1986) argues that the teaching methods most helpful for creative problem solving are mostly enabling methods like relaxation. Essentially they involve turning off the 'rules of reason' we rely on every day. Organizations can encourage this dynamic in several ways. They can promote 'planned playfulness' – a day of unconventional activities, or a retreat to an unusual site. Rewards, especially intrinsic rewards, can be powerful stimulants. Extrinsic rewards, however, are dangerous because they can drive out intrinsic motivation. If I'm paid to do something, it may lose some of its appeal.

But the most important thing organizations can do is to approve of creativity. Social disapproval is the most powerful killer of creativity, for social fears block the expression of ideas. Companies should instead provide support for innovative champions and back them against opponents. They should also avoid punishing certain types of innovative failure. Efforts based on quality, perserverance, and energy, for instance, should not be penalized (Leavitt, 1986).

These are a number of means that organizations can use to develop abilities associated with strategic vision. To ensure that such skills effectively take root in an organization, it is necessary to devise selection procedures, rewards, jobs, supervision, and structures that reinforce each other and support the flourishing of creative strategic insight within the firm.

Conclusion

In summary, leaders are bred not born. Many managers today possess the basic aptitudes to become leaders. It is a matter of encouraging and developing their motivation and skills and of creating organizations that are more supportive of individuals with an unconventional perspective, a sense of passion, or a willingness to take great risks. This is perhaps the larger challenge facing us – creating organizations that demand leadership from their employees rather than simply good managership.

References

Altemeyer, R. 1966: Education in the arts and sciences: divergent paths. Unpublished Ph.D. dissertation, Carnegie Institute of Technology.

Amabile, T. M. and Gryskiewicz, S. S. 1987: Creativity in the R&D Laboratory. Technical report no. 30. Greensboro, N.C.: Center for Creative Leadership.

Bennis, W. and Nanus, B. 1985: *Leaders*, New York: Harper & Row.

Gordon, W. J. J. 1961: *Synectics: The Development of Creative Capacity*. New York: Collier.

House, R. J. 1988: Power and personality in complex organizations. In L. L. Cummings and B. M. Staw (eds), *Research in Organizational Behavior: An Annual Review of Critical Essays and Reviews*, 10. Greenwich, Conn.: JAI Press.

Jacques, E. 1982: *The Form of Time*. London: Heinemann.

—— 1986: The development of intellectual capability: A discussion of stratified systems theory. *Journal of Applied Behavioral Science*, 22, 361–83.

James, W. 1988: *Varieties of Religious Experience*. New York: Mentor Books.

Kirton, M. 1976: Adaptors and innovators: a description and measure. *Journal of Applied Psychology*, 61 (5), 622–9.

Leavitt, H. J. 1986: *Corporate Pathfinders*. Homewood, Ill.: Dow Jones-Irwin.

McClelland, D. C. 1985: *Human Motivation*. Glenview, Ill.: Scott Foresman.

Miner, J. B. 1978: Twenty years of research on role-motivation theory of managerial effectiveness. *Personnel Psychology*, 31, 739–60.

Rothenburg, A. 1979: *The Emerging Goddess*. Chicago: University of Chicago Press.

Zaleznik, A. 1984: Managers and leaders: are they different? In W. E. Rosenbach and R. L. Taylor (eds), *Contemporary Issues in Leadership*, Boulder, Col.: Westview Press.

2
Leadership Skills

John Adair

Are Leaders Born or Made?

If leaders are made in the sense that they can acquire the authority of knowledge, are they born as far as the capacity to inspire is concerned? It is tempting to conclude so. The ability to give people the intellectual and moral strength to venture or persevere in the presence of danger, fear or difficulty is not the common endowment of all men and women. Xenophon, however, did believe that it could be acquired through education, though not 'at sight or at a single hearing.' He was not specific about the content or methods of such an education for leadership, but Socratic discussion must have been one strand.

As Xenophon implied, some degree of leadership potential has to be there in the first place. Many people possess it without being aware of the fact. Given the need or opportunity to lead, some encouragement and perhaps a leadership course or programme, most people can develop this potential. Those with a greater amount of natural potential can correspondingly become greater leaders within their spheres, providing that they are willing to work hard at becoming leaders.

Learning about leadership happens when sparks of relevance jump in between experience or practice on the one hand, and principles or theory on the other hand. One without the other tends to be sterile. It is a common fallacy that leadership is learned only through experience. Experience only teaches the teachable, and it is a school which charges large fees. Sometimes people graduate from it when they are too old to apply the lessons. Leadership is far

Excerpt from *Great Leaders* by John Adair, Talbot Adair Press. Copyright © John Adair 1989, by permission of the author.

better learned by experience *and* reflection or thought, which, in turn, informs or guides future action. Other people, as examples or models, teachers or mentors, have an important part to play in this process. Socrates, for example, most probably acted as Xenophon's own mentor.

The belief that theories or principles imbibed from books or courses can by themselves teach a person to lead, is equally a half-truth. All the academic study of leadership does is to teach one *about* leadership, not how to lead. It is certainly useful for people to clarify their concepts of leadership, either as a prelude or as an interlude in the practical work of leading others. But leadership is learnt primarily through doing, and nothing can replace that necessary cycle of experiment, trial-and-error, success and failure, followed by reflection and reading. Following this path of self-development, a person may become so effective as a leader that others will say 'He or she was born to it.' Little will they know the work it took!

3
The Anatomy of Managerial Success

Charles J. Cox and Cary L. Cooper

The Development of the Successful Managerial Personality

As with all psychoanalytic theories, it is assumed within transactional analysis that one of the main determinants of adult personality is early childhood experience. This can, of course, be modified by later experience. In the case of successful top managers (and others), two important developmental influences are education and work experience.

Early Childhood

There is quite strong evidence from this study and others that there are in the early childhood of successful top managers a variety of events which have the effect of throwing the individual on to his own resources very early in life, forcing him to take responsibility for himself and possibly others (e.g. siblings). These events are often associated with separation from the parents, either through death or being sent away from home for some reason. Other important influences are parental attitudes, particularly in relation to achievement and work.

Education

Obviously, school and further education must contribute to some extent to the individual's development, but we found it difficult in this study to discern any clearly identifiable trends. There is a tendency for those with public school and

Excerpt from *High Flyers* by Charles J. Cox and Cary L. Cooper, 1988, by permission of Basil Blackwell Ltd.

Oxbridge backgrounds to be in the larger 'blue chip' organizations, and those with grammar school and professional training to be in smaller, more local companies. However, the school that one goes to is largely determined by parental influence and social background, so this may simply be a further manifestation of early experience. The main influence of school is probably in the development of logical abilities (the *Adult*) and social skills. Several MDs did say that they first began to recognize and develop 'leadership' and 'influence' skills at school. There is no evidence that any one type of school is better than another in this respect. It seems to be very much determined by individual teachers and the opportunities they create. For the current generation of successful top managers, formal management education appears to be largely irrelevant.

Career Experience

Along with early childhood, the other area of experience which does seem to be vitally important is what happens early in the individual's career. To reach the top, one must have a wide variety of experience and must avoid narrow specialization. Most MDs in the study had experienced quite high levels of responsibility at a very young age, and had been confronted with 'make or break' opportunities to which they had responded with confidence and even enthusiasm. What is particularly important is that they were successful in dealing with these opportunities. Significantly, we do not know what happens to individuals who fail in these situations. That a good 'track record' is essential is confirmed by many studies. Another important influence is whom the individual works for during his career. Many MDs recorded their debt to earlier bosses who had facilitated their development. The reciprocal of this is that the successful manager is good at learning from his experience.

4
The New Leadership: Born or Made?

Peter Benton

If successful leadership comes in so many forms, how should leaders be developed? And developed they must be, though some romantics may believe leadership falls like divine grace on a blessed few; or, in Montgomery's sardonic phrase, like dew from heaven. First, as he showed, great leaders need to be competent. Great charisma will get men or women to follow you once; but perhaps next time they will remember whether their trust was fruitful, or ended in chaos and tears. Competence brings too that sense of capability and resource that can foster resilience and creativity. Just as Poincaré told us,[1] facts need to be in the subconscious to feed the imagination.

Most successful leaders, in a world that requires so much of them, will be individuals with rather broader capabilities than their predecessors. No longer just committee-men, for as Donald Petersen of Ford Motor Company put it to a Californian audience in 1988, intuition and emotion must count in successful market judgements. For that, formation needs to start early; open to mathematics, science, and technology, but also to the humane studies. That the obviously practical subjects are not enough is a cause that needs more defenders. Corelli Barnett may be winning too great a victory.

Leadership, though, is more than just a matter of the intellect. While the connection between the playing fields of Eton and mastery of the British Empire may be a little strained, leadership does seem to be a skill that works best when unselfconscious. And if unselfconscious, best surely learnt in early youth. Squash and fencing may stir the competitive instincts, but for leadership the team game is the thing – and the newest team game of all for the young is the business venture. In Britain, 25,000 teenagers join together each year in

Excerpt from *Riding the Whirlwind: Benton on Managing Turbulence* by Peter Benton, by permission of Basil Blackwell Ltd.

groups of ten or so to form a business, float the shares, prosper or stagnate, and then back to base, liquidation and final dividends. Young Enterprise is an extraordinary national movement with incalculable benefits for the leadership talents of young people. Football, hockey, and cricket nurture leaders too, and sparkling individualists. But the thousands of young people trying their hand at a commercial enterprise perhaps learn something more: they learn the art of the balanced judgement.

For most, the power to lead is one developed over years, inspired by others, reassured by success. Not, I think, an affair exclusively for the training department or the classroom. Leaders develop leaders. In the days of Organization Man, there was a specialist for everything: even for management development. Paradoxically, in the era of delegation there are some things the prudent chief executive takes to himself; he is not just the conductor of an orchestra, for example, playing off another man's score. Corporate strategy used to be an affair for the specialists; now no prudent leader leaves that task to others. Organization structure and appointments used to be the preserve of the personnel function: but not, I think, in today's most successful companies. Financial controls were devised by accountants; but look at the appalling consequences of fallacies in misguided zeal. But of all the tasks that truly belong to the new chief executive, the development of leaders can least be left to the *apparatchiks*. Leaders must develop leaders.

Notes

1   Henri Poincaré, *Science et Méthode* (Paris, Flammarion, 1908).

5
Managerial Leaders: Developing People with Charisma and Competence

Philip Sadler

Given the increasingly turbulent and challenging nature of the business environment, characterized by rapid technological change, global competition, deregulation of markets and new consumer aspirations and expectations, there is a growing need for a new breed of manager. He or she must not only be competent in such things as planning, problem solving, decision-making and controlling but must at the same time be capable of bringing about radical change in organizational cultures. In other words he or she must be able to exercise leadership as well as manage competently.

Leadership – Exercising Power or Empowering?

An act of leadership has two elements. First, the person providing leadership knows what he or she wants to happen; secondly, he or she successfully influences others so that they help bring the desired change about. There is no essential difference between one child saying to others 'Let's play hide and seek', an infantry officer who, without issuing a word of command, leads his platoon by example in an attack on an enemy position, and a supervisor at work saying 'Shall we stay on until the job is finished?' Leadership takes place in each case if the desired behaviour follows. Effective leaders, then, are people who can get others to do things without having to exercise power, authority or force. Many people carry the title 'leader' but do not exercise leadership in this sense.

'Managerial Leaders: Developing People with Charisma and Competence' by Philip Sadler. Original paper written for this publication © Philip Sadler 1988.

Leadership and Management

Decisions about the training and development needs of managers and about the competences they need to acquire should be based on a clear understanding of the distinction between management and leadership. There is some common ground between management and leadership but not all managers lead and not all leaders manage. For instance, a manager may be competent in administration, be able to plan, make sound decisions through analysing facts, use various management tools and techniques, yet still be ineffective as a leader. Such managers must rely on the power and authority vested in their office to get other people to do things.

The reverse problem is that not all leaders can cope with administrative tasks – many cannot grasp even the simplest set of figures. They may fail to analyse information rationally when reaching decisions; they may be bad managers. In consequence they may lead their organizations into loss-making ventures or even into liquidation.

Ideally we need *managerial leaders*, people who can combine the charisma of leadership with managerial competence, whose vision not only inspires others but can be translated into practical reality.

Different Forms of Leadership in Organizations

Just as plans for developing managers must take into account differences in the nature of the management task at different organizational levels – supervisory, middle, and top management – so it is also important to take into account that the demands of the leader's role also vary.

It is possible to distinguish three types of leadership.

1 *Face-to-face leadership*. This is the supervisory kind of leadership appropriate to small groups. It is primarily provided by first-line managers to groups of shop-floor workers, but all leaders give this kind of leadership to their own face-to-face groups. For example, the company chairman is not a first-line supervisor, but the leadership he gives to his fellow directors on the Board is face-to-face leadership.
2 *Organizational leadership*. This is the kind that middle managers have to provide for people who are typically two or three levels below them. It is their job to get the whole team working together – people in different functions, with different attitudes and different jobs to do. Organizational leaders are rarely face-to-face with all their staff – perhaps only once or twice a year. Although the people concerned all know the boss, the boss does not necessarily know all of them, particularly if he or she is dealing

with a dispersed workforce. Despite this, he or she still has to be the leader. This makes organizational leadership more complex and difficult than face-to-face leadership.

3 *Institutional leadership*, as when the leader is chairman or chief executive, running an entire company. At the extreme he or she could be managing operations as large and dispersed as ICI with 180,000 employees worldwide. How does the institutional leader provide effective leadership given that he or she is never going to see 95% of the employees? This challenge makes institutional leadership the most difficult of all.

It is important to think about those differences in the leadership role when planning the development of managers in relation to career stages and determining the qualities which need to be developed.

Building a Picture of Leadership Competence

Two examples of recent empirical research into leadership competence illustrate the kinds of behaviour that are associated with competence as a leader. Both were described at a conference sponsored by the European Foundation for Management Development in Rome in 1988. One was some interesting work being done at IMEDE (now, having merged with IMI, known as IMD) in Switzerland with Citibank. They matched two groups of managers, 39 managers in each, who had been assessed as either *outstanding* or *average* leaders. The two samples were matched by nationality, age, service and sex. Through talking to people about leadership behaviour, the researchers identified 750 separate leadership practices. They then reduced these by semantic differentiation (i.e. looking at the meaning of something rather than the words used to describe it) to 59 practices.

The researchers then issued a questionnaire to the subordinates of the 78 managers to see how many of these 59 leadership practices differentiated between the highly successful and the merely average leaders. They found that of the 59, 39 actually differentiated. They were able further to reduce those 39 down to five by combining them into broad categories. From the IMEDE study, therefore, emerged a picture of leadership competence defined in terms of the following five behaviours:

- obtaining commitment to the organization and the task
- coaching – working with someone to improve his or her performance on the task
- appraising
- rewarding
- managing groups (which might be called team leadership).

The next step was to endeavour to develop the ability of Citibank managers to carry out these five activities.

The second presentation at the EFMD Conference was from a representative of United Technologies, who described how, following a somewhat less rigorous route, they had identified the following factors as the key leadership competences:

- creating a shared vision
- empowering others
- developing people
- recognizing merit.

In both cases the behaviour patterns or competences are quite different from those traditionally associated with the techniques and tools of management.

The Qualities Underlying Effective Leadership

In order to develop people's competence to carry out these types of activities (and these are offered as examples rather than definitive lists), it is important to clarify what it is we are trying to change, develop or nurture.

The literature on leadership distinguishes between what are termed *innate* and *acquired* qualities of leadership. Some examples of innate qualities are listed below:

- *Energy and stamina* are certainly likely to be required.
- *Vision*, the ability to look up and beyond the immediate future and create a picture of what could be, is also frequently cited.
- With regard to *intelligence*, however, research studies (usually with American undergraduates in psychology) show that when people pick leaders they tend not to choose the most intelligent people in the group.
- *Self-confidence* can be regarded as absolutely fundamental, because to take on a leadership role is a courageous thing to do, and people can do it effectively only if they actually believe in themselves. People of quite moderate ability can believe in themselves so strongly that other people come to believe in them also. Such people are often extremely effective as leaders. However if that self-confidence ever goes, then the whole edifice of their leadership collapses like a punctured balloon.
- *Assertiveness and dominance* are rather more controversial, particularly in the light of more recent theories about a post-heroic type of leader and the abandonment of the macho style of management. It is true that in the past many effective leaders were extremely assertive and dominant, yet some of the most successful business leaders of recent years have been extremely quiet and reserved, even shy.
- *Integrity* is also arguable because there have been many successful leaders who have quite clearly lacked integrity, yet who manage to have quite a strong following even when their lack of integrity has been publicly exposed.

- It is important to be *creative and imaginative* and to be brave. If you work in physically dangerous circumstances it may actually be essential.
- To be *able to tolerate stress* is also important – there is a lot of stress in being out front; the leader has to be able to live with that and to cope with it.
- *Adaptability and flexibility* are also possibly important.

Although these qualities are largely innate, they are still capable of development, though to differing degrees. In the case of intelligence, for example, we are told that after about the age of 17 intelligence starts to decay rather than to improve. What training can do is to help people use their intelligence more effectively rather than develop it further. Training and development can also result in people becoming stronger in terms of self-confidence; they can learn assertive behaviour; they can acquire a new set of values and beliefs; they can expand their imaginative and creative ability by engaging in more creative types of activity, and so on. While these qualities may be innate they are certainly not stillborn; they can be developed.

There are other qualities which people can be helped to acquire. Task competence, however, is rather different from the others. In some situations it is essential, in others merely useful. The leader of a squadron of fighter pilots has to be a good pilot before he is accepted in the role. On the other hand, in a different situation there is a role for the mobile general manager with 'portable' managerial leadership skills who can move into a situation, where he knows nothing about the technology or the task, yet by virtue of his leadership he can take over and make things happen.

A Holistic Approach to Leadership Development

Leadership development programmes are mainly concerned with the following five themes:

- conceptual knowledge
- skills and techniques
- role-modelling
- values
- self-awareness

The weakness of most leadership course, is that they focus principally on skills rather than on the other factors. It is important, however, to bring these other factors into programmes of training and development, particularly values, self-awareness, and role-modelling. It is also important to integrate all these factors into a holistic approach to leadership development.

Conceptual Knowledge

The most obvious form that this takes is providing potential and actual leaders with a greater understanding of human behaviour. It is useful for a leader to have some conceptual ideas about motivation, the factors which make for effective teamwork, organization structures and other theories derived from psychology and social psychology.

Some years ago, at Ashridge Management College there was a popular course called 'Management and the Behavioural Sciences', which provided a survey of this whole conceptual field. The course did not give participants any skills, it did not set out to challenge their attitudes or values, it just gave them conceptual knowledge. Ten to fifteen years ago people were quite hungry for that knowledge which was very new and very exciting.

The other factors under this heading are languages and knowledge of cultural differences. Today's business leaders frequently operate in an international framework in which they have to be able to speak foreign languages and operate in cultures other than their own.

Skills and Techniques

These have been the main focus of leadership training. There are courses in interpersonal skills, negotiating skills, influencing skills, counselling skills, group process skills and teamworking skills. The demand for this type of training is virtually insatiable and there is a relatively standard way of doing it. Under the guidance of a very skilled coach, participants practice the skill using closed circuit television. They receive feedback from the coach and from the other participants. They can achieve a very significant improvement in performance at the end of about five days. People go away from such courses convinced that they can now exercise these skills better than before. Again this is straightforward. The problem is to integrate skills development with the other learning processes.

Role-Modelling

This involves identifying effective leadership behaviour and trying to emulate it. A simple example is time-keeping. The leader who is the first one in the office or the factory each day sets an example and provides a pattern of behaviour which others can follow. Colin Marshall of British Airways, for example, sets the pattern for his management team in this way.

Management by walking about is frequently advocated. It implies a real interest in how the job is going rather than sitting behind a desk and reading computer print-outs. Again, this is a behaviour pattern which can serve as a model.

Young managers naturally observe how leaders behave, and a large part of this is unconscious. They build into their own patterns of behaviour the things that they sense are effective. In the past a frequent lead in to leadership training was to watch a film, such as *12 Angry Men*, or *12.00 O'clock High*. The instructor would ask 'Now what did we get out of that in terms of the leader's behaviour?' A more modern approach involves making videos of real-life situtions. Managers are shadowed by camera teams to record and study what they do in a working day. There are obviously some pitfalls in this approach because if a manager has a camera man, a sound man and an observer team following him around every day, he or she will tend to change behaviour. Even more important, the people he or she interacts with would change their behaviour even more so, not only because they are being filmed but also because the rest of the organization will one day see the end-result.

At the very least, however, this technique starts people talking. The evidence is that people move immediately into an animated discussion about such videos. As a catalyst they are probably very good, even though they are not necessarily valid portraits of actual leader behaviour.

Values

These are virtually totally ignored in leadership development and yet are fundamentally important. Values can be defined as the things characteristic of the leader which evoke feelings like trust, respect, admiration or the reverse. We acquire these early in life, in family, in school, from various mentors and role models that we come into contact with. However, the bundle of values that people bring into adult life has to be sorted out and consciously rethought and reordered when taking on a leadership role. This is because assuming a leadership role involves wielding a considerable amount of power. It is possible to get by with a certain set of values as long as an individual's role in life is more passive and he or she is less likely to be faced with choices and decisions which affect other people's lives.

Those who have been through the process will know that officer training in the armed services is very much a process of inculcating an appropriate set of values. It is about learning the obligations which are associated with being an officer and a leader. This degree of concern with values is markedly lacking in the preparation of leaders in industry and this is reflected in the ethical issues and problems that so many organizations are now facing. There is an urgent need to do something about these issues, difficult as it is, and face that challenge.

Self-Awareness

This involves an individual knowing what he or she is capable of, stretching himself or herself to attain this but also accepting limitations and weaknesses.

A lot of work in this area goes on during the Leadership Development Programme which Ashridge Management College runs under licence from the Center for Creative Leadership in Greensboro, N.C. It involves bringing to the course or sending in advance questionnaires about leadership which have been filled in by peers and subordinates back at work. This is one of the most revealing experiences that any person can undergo. People sometimes come close to tears when getting this feedback. The course tutors build on to this with their own comments and observations, and there is yet more feedback from the other people attending the programme. Feedback from psychometric tests is also used.

Self-awareness can also be developed through the Outward Bound approach, where individuals get to know themselves by facing danger and deprivation and testing and challenging themselves in situations demanding physical courage and endurance. Increasingly, however, there is a school of thought which argues that the stress created by such exercises is appropriate to learning to lead in physically dangerous or demanding situations but has less relevance for managerial leadership in industry, where a different kind of stress is generated. For example, a more appropriate challenge for managers might involve collecting 20 or 30 mentally disabled children, taking them out for the day and giving them a good time. This might actually be more challenging and more stressful than climbing down a rock-face, particularly for the person who abseils down the rock-face every other weekend and does not, therefore, find it particularly stressful. In other words there is a strong case for using socially challenging situations alongside the physically challenging ones.

These five aspects of leadership are all important. Somehow we have to find an approach to leadership development which manages to weave all these threads together. While it remains important to provide a certain grounding in conceptual knowledge and it is clearly essential to impart or improve interpersonal skills, more needs to be done to help leaders develop more effective patterns of overall behaviour, to sort out their values, and provide opportunities for enhancing self awareness.

The Special Needs of Institutional Leaders

The key leadership roles in society are played by those occupying jobs such as chairmen or managing directors of business enterprises, hospital general managers, chief officers in local government, chief constables, university vice-chancellors and the like. Allowing for some obvious differences between the nature of the precise duties involved there are some important common elements in such jobs.

The main requirements of leaders at this level include the following:

- the ability to visualize some desired future for the organization which, if achieved, will result in its prosperity, growth or enhanced reputation
- the ability to instil in many more people than can be personally known a sense of common purpose
- the ability to act for long periods without guidance or instruction from superiors and without support from a peer group
- the ability to sustain the isolation – even loneliness – that goes with occupying such a position
- the ability to use very considerable power with integrity and with fairness
- the ability to carry a burden of responsibility of a different order from that carried by senior functional executives – and to do so in such a way that it does not seem to others to be burdensome.

How can people be prepared for the role of institutional leader? How can tomorrow's chief executives best be developed for industry?

There is clearly no simple answer. However, a useful starting point is to provide opportunities for interaction and exchange of ideas with practising chief executives or leaders in other spheres – politics, religion and the arts, for example. Another is to provide support groups to facilitate learning. Since 1980 a series of programmes called 'Action Learning for Chief Executives' have been held at Ashridge Management College. Participants in these programmes meet in 'sets' of four to six persons together with a set adviser or facilitater. They meet for one day at a time at monthly intervals, usually for six months. No attempt is made to feed them any functional knowledge or to teach them any techniques. Instead, they become involved in a quite different learning process. The starting point is for each member of the group to expose to the others a real-life issue or problem he or she is facing in the role of institutional leader. In the interaction which follows these issues or problems get redefined – sometimes even lost sight of altogether – but in the process the chief executives gain insight into their own behaviour and attitudes and those of others. In the words of one participant: 'I think it helped me get through a period where I certainly realized that probably nobody ever knew what to do anyway – the fact that you get a title like managing director shouldn't actually mean that all the answers are there.'

The Leadership Challenge

We live in a rapidly changing world and have to learn to cope with the uncertainty and anxiety which change provokes. At such times people feel a need for leadership – they seek reassurance and a sense of direction from people whom they can trust. Increasingly, people at work, especially the younger and more highly educated, will respond to leadership but reject attempts to exercise power or impose authority. Also, if organizations are to adapt to change and survive, they need innovation – not just new ideas but the ability to translate new ideas into action – new products or services delivered in new ways. Here again leadership is essential. For all these reasons we need to pay much more attention in the future to developing leadership competence. This is the most important challenge facing industry and the business schools – and one which increasingly they are tackling by working together.

Note

1   Henri Poincaré, *Science et Méthode* (Paris, Flammarion, 1908).

Chapter 15

Selecting Leaders: The Role of Fast Tracks and Succession Planning

Introduction

If the conclusion of the last chapter is that leaders are bred not born, the strong implication is that they need to be bred at an early age. A variety of contributors in this book, including John Harvey-Jones, Cary Cooper, and Jay Conger, stress that the formative influences of successful executives took place when they were young and more receptive to a variety of different influences, experiences, and attitudes.

This conclusion forms the rationale for the 'fast-track' schemes that are now commonplace in most large multinational companies. As Lynda Gratton observes in her contribution to this chapter, selecting leaders 'is little more than an act of faith enveloped with unknowables'. For this reason, companies may be tempted to leave the decision until the last moment, but 'This is not an option available in . . . large companies . . . [where] success . . . is frequently associated with the early acquisition of management accountability and a breadth of functional and business experiences . . . [which] has to be gained over decades.' As Gratton goes on to explain, the creation of élite cadres has numerous historic precedents, including the mandarin class of ancient China and more recently the British civil service. The modern version of the high-flying scheme was shaped in the 1960s by UK and Dutch multinationals like BP, Shell, and Unilever, and is grounded in a systematic combination of formal training and early job rotation over a period of ten years or more to provide broad-based work experience across different functions and national boundaries. The purpose is not to select candidates for specific vacancies up to twenty years in advance, but to create a pool of management talent with general management skills who can be groomed for specific vacancies when the exact parameters of the position can be identified more clearly.

This model for developing senior executives is still seen as state of the art. Yet there are a number of potential flaws, which are pointed out in subsequent articles. Diversification into different markets or activities, frequently involving mergers, acquisitions, and joint ventures, have resulted in organizations that are far more complex, made up of a variety of sub-businesses, each with different and sometimes conflicting needs.

As Gratton concludes in her second contribution, there is no one universal approach to succession planning that works equally well across all companies. Organizations should match their succession strategies to their business plans. They should also take into account the changing career aspirations and expectations of managers who are normally selected for fast-track development.

The second issue is whether the élitism of fast-track schemes is justified. Wendy Hirsh, in an article that plays devil's advocate to the executive development community, questions some of the basic assumptions made by high-flyer strategies. She points out that these schemes can be self-fulfilling, over-rigid, and time-consuming; and discriminate against female candidates (who may wish to start a family at precisely the time the development process reaches its peak) and older managers who do not usually get a look-in. She concludes: 'high-flyer schemes are inflexible in terms of size, and often in terms of the qualities of the people they produce. They seep deep into the culture of the organization and are bound to produce élitist beliefs about what kinds of development are valued, and for whom. They are not easily adaptable in times of rapid organizational change, and can be damaging for the high-flyers (when their ambitions are unfulfilled) as well as for others.'

Hirsh is not arguing for the abandonment of the fast track. But she does plead convincingly for schemes that are more flexible and less narrow in the way candidates are selected. Gratton also sounds a few cautionary notes about the selection processes used to identify potential, but her worries are more concerned with the obsessive way new technology is being used to try to pin-point what exactly leaders do and how this can be built into modern assessment techniques – something she regards as 'little more than a search for the holy grail'.

This kind of grail-quest has been engaging search consultants for some time, and the final contribution by Bernard Bass provides a good example of the academic work that has shaped their thinking. He cites some interesting generalizations concerning the charismatic leader: 'Their facial expressions are animated' and 'the magnetic attraction of the charismatic leader's eyes is often commented upon'. As a breed they are 'great actors' and 'always on-stage'. According to one academic, they must be 'able to present themselves as workers of miracles likely to succeed where others would fail', a characteristic cited in chapter 21 as representing a pressure that causes many never to make it quite to the top. Charismatic leaders have an innate confidence which lends them the courage to 'say things publicly that followers feel privately but cannot express'. Of course, successful leaders can be non-charismatic, but they tend not to be so successful.

Do Bass's revelations render the elusive grail less elusive, or do they merely offer further information just to confuse? The reader must make his or her own judgement.

1
Selecting Leaders: Practices and Trends

Lynda Gratton

Selecting business leaders or those with a potential to lead is a complex operation. In part, the complexity reflects the difficulties of understanding what it is leaders actually do, and of identifying the characteristics that distinguish those who triumph from those who fail. Leaders such as Iacocca have argued that they play an essential role in determining the performance of the company, and many academics have supported this view (Chandler, 1962). Others have doubted the efficacy of leaders and argue that their impact is overrated (Salancik and Pfeffer, 1977) and limited by many factors which are outside their control.

While issues of efficacy are not central to a debate on the selection of leaders, they provide an insight into some of the ambiguities with which it is beset. Simply stated, if we are unaware of what it is leaders do, or what influence they have on a company's prosperity, what basis do we have for selecting them?

It could be argued that selecting leaders or those with potential for leadership is little more than an act of faith enveloped with unknowables. Perhaps it would be best to leave decisions about leadership selection until the last possible moment, when the contestants are approaching the pinnacle of their career. This is not an option available in the many large complex companies in which leaders and senior executive cadres are drawn from the internal labour force. For, as researchers like Margerison (1980) have shown, success at this level is frequently associated with the early acquisition of management accountability and a breadth of functional and business experiences. The acquisition of these broad career events is unusual for employees in hierarchical, highly structured, or complex organizations. For the majority, experience is limited to a single

Original paper written for this publication © Lynda Gratton 1990.

business scenario and a narrow functional 'chimney stack', where they gain depth but not breadth of knowledge.

Consequently, the breadth of experience which forms the base of subsequent achievement has to be gained over decades. In many large companies it is not possible, nor cost effective, nor even beneficial to engineer breadth-of-job experiences for all employees. They can be given only to a minority of young employees, those who will significantly benefit from them, and who will probably assume senior executive and leadership roles in the future. While fine-tuned selection judgements are made just before an individual assumes a senior executive role, the decision about whether they should be in the pool of candidates for that role is made many years earlier. In effect, the crucial leadership selection decision does not take place when the leader or senior executive is elected; it takes place many years earlier during the identification of the pool of talent from which the individual will be drawn.

The principle of selecting and creating élite cadres has many historic precedents. For example, in ancient China the mandarin class were identified at an early age through a series of examinations. On a more contemporary note, the British civil service has for many years used relatively sophisticated processes to make early decisions about leadership potential. The progression of this group of fast-trackers is accelerated up the organization.

The principle of the fast track was enthusiastically seized on by some Dutch and UK multinationals in the 1960s. It was during the following decade that companies such as Shell, Unilever, and BP launched their programmes. They were devised to produce executives and leaders who could represent the company in the numerous business environments and cultures in which they operated. The programmes achieved this by supplying participants with breadth and depth gained from early and significant experiences across diverse businesses of the company, and most importantly, across international boundaries.

The phenomenon is by no means limited to Dutch or UK multinational companies. Fast-track career schemes are currently operating in companies around the world. For example, they are the cornerstone of leadership selection and development in many substantial Japanese companies such as Matsushita, Sanyo, and Nissan. In large French companies early leadership selection is based on a competitive tournament of élite educational qualifications (Evans, Lank, and Farquhar, 1989).

Features of the Fast Track

Companies create fast-track processes to meet their specific requirements, but most have at least five features in common;

- Selection is made at a relatively early age, from entry as a graduate to mid-thirties, with mid-twenties as a norm. Selection decisions can be based on executives' view of their subordinates' suitability, performance on personality and aptitude tests or in assessment centres. These are typically one- to five-day events in which potential fast-trackers engage in situations designed to simulate aspects of the role of the executive. These can include working through an executive in-tray, engaging in group problem-solving, or making a presentation.
- Once selected, fast-trackers can be assured of attention from senior executives. This can be informal but is frequently formalized through mentoring and sponsorship. They are also privy to powerful networks and decision-making forums. For example, many multinationals operate high level committees which meet frequently to discuss the careers of this group.
- Members have preferential access to external and internal training opportunities, for example programmes such as the Sloan and other international prestigious programmes.
- Provision of a rapid series of job experiences across a range of situations which typically include various business scenarios, functions and countries.
- Access to consideration for the leadership roles as they become vacant. Senior executive vacancies are rarely advertised on the open market. Instead selection is made from a predetermined pool of potential candidates. As suggested earlier, this pool can be in existence for many years.

A repercussion of these features is that many schemes are supported by a range of sophisticated techniques and processes. Some are devised to aid initial selection, for example assessment centres and psychometric appraisal. Others assist placement decisions through the use of multidisciplinary committees and complex computer systems carrying information about people and jobs.

Growing Popularity of Fast-Track Processes

Initially the development of pools of potential leadership talent was the cornerstone of the human resource policies of multinationals. By the mid-1980s it was becoming increasingly popular in companies in many sectors. A professional firm like the accountants Deloitte Haskins & Sells for example, implemented a process called 'focused development' which accelerated high-potential people into partnership status with the aid of consultants steering them through a four-phase programme (Cunningham and Leon, 1986). Similarly, the international computer firm Olivetti introduced their 'no frontiers' programme, designed to accelerate the development of a cadre of international technical graduates. In the financial sector National Westminster Bank identified a series of levels of potential from a relatively early age, whilst in retail, Marks & Spencer screened graduate recruits for the fast track.

The trend has grown despite some rather spirited attacks on the value of the process (for example, Hirsh, 1985). To understand what has contributed to the popularity of fast-track schemes we need to take both the rational and the more intuitive view.

At the most rational level one can argue that fast-track schemes ensure that limited resources such as executive time, job opportunities, and training are targeted at those who will benefit most. Specifically, jobs that provide significant work experience are safeguarded for those with the highest potential. The widespread and international job moves which are a part of fast-tracking facilitate the growth of informal networks, increase participants' identification with the organization, and develop an organizational environment in which cross-fertilization of ideas can occur (Edstrom and Galbraith, 1977). As a consequence they reduce the problems associated with *laissez-faire* development such as important jobs blocked by mediocre performers, and preponderance of people with 'chimney-stack' careers, too specialized to operate in a general management context.

But they also serve other, less apparent, more 'intuitive' objectives. One could argue that the existence of a visible élite cadre reduces the current leaders' concern about the future of the company, and through the formalized mechanisms of sponsorship and mentoring, ensures a continuation of the old order. Additionally, the sophistication of the mechanisms afford an obvious role for the human resource function.

Fast-tracking leadership potential has clear rational and intuitive benefits for an organization. However, there can be drawbacks for those on the fast track. For example, rapid job moves provide limited opportunity to come to terms with the impact of their decisions, can severely limit their chance to taste failure, and result in over-emphasis on short-term performance (Kovach, 1986). Some fast-track processes assume a switch in the early twenties from a technical to a generalist career path. This can be a high risk for the participant who fails to establish himself in a generalist role, having lost his technical edge, and is thus cut adrift.

While these drawbacks are significant, in my view there are more fundamental organizational issues. These are associated with the restricted flexibility and adaptability of many fast-track schemes. The sophisticated complexity of fast-track schemes can lead both to success and to defeat. The lack of flexibility has two repercussions, in the type of individuals selected for the scheme, and the mechanisms of the scheme itself.

By closely targeting specific high-potential characteristics, the organization severely limits the range of styles and aspirations which could later emerge at senior level. Implicit is the danger of cadres of 'me too' clones, with a reduction, to use a Darwinian analogy, of the potential 'gene pool' and hence the future senior group's ability to adapt and cope with situations not yet envisaged.

The lack of adaptability is also evident in the mechanisms of fast-track schemes. Most are designed to accelerate the development of men who join the company after university and remain in it through their careers, progressing through the hierarchy. Most are not designed to accommodate the different career needs of women, those who want to enter the company at a later stage in their career, or who prefer a 'spiral' to a vertical progression. The processes have become institutionalized, unable to adapt to changing attitudes and aspirations.

Trends Emerging in the 1990s

What of the future? We are seeing trends of increasing specificity and flexibility, a realignment of some basic philosophies, and further developments in the technology.

Increasing Specificity

The fast-track schemes created in the 1960s were frequently seen as industry standards. The strategic human resource roles they created were the envy of human resource professionals, many of whom operated in their own companies not as architects, but as clerks of works. The schemes' sophistication and apparent reliability and validity accounted in part for their growing popularity. However, as I have argued elsewhere, the complex fast-track processes are not beneficial to all companies. Most obviously, they are of limited use in highly diversified business scenarios where businesses are operating in distinctive product and market sectors. Under such conditions there may be little advantage from providing executives with cross-business experience.

There is a growing realization that, to be successful, human resource processes must mirror and fulfil the demands of the business strategy and be more than an amalgam of 'nice to have' techniques (Fombrun, Tichy and Devanna, 1984). I would expect to see the identification and development of leaders more consciously designed to meet the demands of the business strategy. The specificity is already surfacing in debates about general versus business-specific leadership characteristics. Some argue that the competency associated with successful leadership performance differs across business strategies, a hypothesis explored in some depth by practitioners such as Gerstein and Reisman (1983).

Increasing Flexibility

A second area of debate has centred on the recognition that the inflexibility of many fast-track schemes will seriously impact on their ability to deliver. Handy (1989), amongst others, has argued against lifetime employment in a single company, and for self-determination and career mobility, which would mean fundamental modifications to the current fast-track schemes. Perhaps most importantly self-determination will minimize the pay-backs from 'delayed gratification' which has been the cornerstone of the emotional contract between employer and fast-track employee. Robbed of the ability to deliver, delayed-gratification companies must build into their schemes greater flexibility and increased focus on the individual and his particular skills and abilities.

From Paternalism to Partnership

Many fast-track schemes have embedded concepts of paternalism and organizational control. Career development is seen essentially as a demand driven activity, designed to ensure a continual supply of individuals to fill vacant positions. This is manifested, for example, where succession plans are devised with limited consultation with the individual or where the existence of a fast track is implicit rather than explicit.

Since the mid-1980s some companies have endeavoured to be less paternalistic by involving individuals in the development of their own career plans. In a well-documented illustration, the computer company ICL created a five-day assessment centre in which participants assessed themselves and their peers and from this information generated personal development plans (Pouah, 1986). By the 1990s these trends are beginning to make themselves felt with well-established fast-track schemes of multinationals. In the case of BP the initiative came in part from organizational surveys which demonstrated the negative consequences of the fast track. In a programme launched in 1991, fast-track individuals enter into a series of self-diagnosis and 'reality checking' before producing their own personal development plans.

This individual-centred approach to identifying and developing senior executives diminishes the traditional paternalistic and controlling role, and fosters a mature and relatively open dialogue. It is likely that this focus will be an increasingly important part of fast-track processes of the 1990s.

Developments in the Technology

The above trends illustrate progress in the concepts and nature of the fast-track schemes, but there have also been advances in the technology of competency profiling and potential assessment.

The advances in competency profiling have addressed an issue debated earlier in this paper: what do leaders and executives actually do? Shell were one of the first companies seriously to confront this question in a large study in which the much quoted 'helicopter' quality emerged. Twenty years later the question is still being asked, and by the 1990s many companies are devoting significant resources to the solution. So much so that in a review published in 1989 Storey writes of a 'massive expenditure of resources' on generating competency descriptors. Why the growth in interest, and is it little more than a search for the holy grail?

The growth in interest coincides with the culmination of research in the field, particularly that of Boyatzi, who in 1982, reported on research sponsored by the American Management Association. The resulting model of competency has been influencing concepts of leadership development in both Britain and America.

The benefits of competency profiling arise from a shared language which describes what it is that executives do; but is this 'massive expenditure' creating added value? I would sound two cautionary notes. First on the academic basis of competency profiling. As Storey (1989) has argued, there is currently a lack of empirical research to support the competency model. This is compounded by the complication of describing, in a single model, the complexities and varieties of executive tasks as described by observers such as Mintzberg (1973) and Stewart (1976). Secondly, on more cynical note, one could argue that the 'massive expenditure' is a direct consequence of human resource consulting practices over selling the benefits. In effect, the decision is led by strong marketing rather than by clearly articulated organizational needs.

Advances in the assessment of potential have come through greater use of a range of techniques from cognitive ability and analytical reasoning tests to assessment centres (Robertson and Makin, 1986). This has been a significant trend, since interviews, although historically the most popular technique of executive selection, have very low accuracy (Reilly and Chao, 1982). Many companies have used assessment centres for graduate entry but some, such as the UK insurance company, Legal & General, are using the technique at the most senior levels in the company to assist in immediate executive selection decisions.

Assessment centres have the advantage of accuracy but they are intensely resource-hungry. More cost effective are peer and self-assessments, which broaden the range of information collection and involve the individual in the diagnostic process. Both the Prudential Corporation and BP have introduced peer appraisal into their leadership development programmes while General Electric have been using this type of information for some time (Friedman and LeVino, 1984).

Clearly we will see further technological developments over the next decade. But they can benefit the company only if they meet the demands of the business strategy rather than reflect the latest consulting hype. There is no doubt in my mind that the greatest challenges arise from developing more flexible and individual-centred processes. The resolution of these challenges will come through fundamental changes in culture and structure, not necessarily through more sophisticated technology.

References

Boyatzi, R. 1982: *The Competent Manager: A Model for Effective Performance.* New York: Wiley.

Chandler, A. 1962: *Strategy and Structure.* Cambridge, Mass.: MIT Press.

Cunningham, I. and Leon, P. 1986: Focusing managerial development. *Journal of European Industrial Training,* 10 (8).

Edstrom, A. and Galbraith, J. 1977: Transfer of managers as a coordination and control strategy in multinational organisations. *Administrative Science Quarterly,* 22 (June), 248–63.

Evans, P., Lank, and Farquhar, A. 1989: Managing human resources in the international firm: lessons from practice In P. Evans, Y. Doz, and A. Laurent (eds), *Human Resource Management in International Firms.* London: Macmillan.

Friedman, S. and LeVino, T. 1984: Strategic appraisal and development at General Electric Company. In C. Fombrun, N. Tichy, and M. Devanna (eds), *Strategic Human Resource Management.* New York: Wiley.

Fombrun, C., Tichy, N. and Devanna, M. 1984: *Strategic Human Resource Management.* New York: Wiley.

Gerstein, M. and Reisman, H. 1983: Strategic selection: matching executives to business conditions. *Sloan Management Review,* (winter),

Handy, C. 1989: Are jobs for life killing enterprise? *Director* October, 29–30.

Hirsh, W. 1985: Flying too high for comfort. *Manpower Policy and Practice,* (summer), 14–17.

Kovach, B. E. 1986: The derailment of fast track managers. *Organisational Dynamics.* 15 (2).

Margerison, C. 1980: How chief executives succeed. *Journal of European Industrial Training,* 4 (5), 1–32.

Mintzberg, H. 1973: *The Nature of Managerial Work.* New York: Harper & Row.

Pfeffer, J. and Salancik, C. 1978: *The External Control of Organisations: A Resource Dependent Perspective.* New York: Harper & Row.

Pouah, N. 1986: Assessment centres for self development. *Industrial and Commercial Training,* 18 (2).

Reilly, R. and Chao, G. 1982: Reliability and fairness in some alternative employee selection processes. *Personnel Psychology,* 35, 1962.

Robertson, I. and Makin, P. 1986: Management selection in Britain: a survey and critique. *Journal of Occupational Psychology,* 52, 45–57.

Schmitt, N., Gooding, R. Z., Noe, R. and Kirsch, M. 1984: Meta-analyses of validity studies published between 1964 and 1982 and the investigation of study characteristics. *Personnel Psychology,* 37, 407–22.

Stewart, R. 1976: *Contrasts in Management.* London: McGraw.

Storey, J. 1989: Management development: a literature review and implications for future research, part 1: conceptualisations and practices. *Personnel Review,* 18 (6), 2–18.

2
Heirs Apparent: Succession Strategies for the Future

Lynda Gratton and Michel Syrett

Managing succession to senior executive positions has been high on the list of the HR director's priorities throughout the 1980s, not least because it is the one personnel responsibility which is guaranteed to attract the wholehearted involvement of the board.

For some time many personnel executives have been worried that they have not been getting the process right. This is fuelled by economic and social developments which are undermining traditional approaches that require an organizational structure and stability of markets which many organizations no longer experience. Traditional approaches also assume a relationship between the individual and the organization that is often no longer in place.

Before beginning a discussion about succession strategies, there are two important things to say. First, there is no one universal approach that works equally well across all companies; rather, effective companies match their succession strategies to their business strategies. Secondly, above and beyond the shaping of succession, there are a number of key trends, both within companies and among individuals, which necessitate a fundamental re-think of many of our assumptions about succession. Of course, both issues have profound implications for the role of the human resource specialist.

Business Strategy

Much of our thinking on succession, as in other personnel processes, has been focused (almost to the point of myopia) on the complex and often elegant

'Heirs Apparent: Succession Strategies for the Future', by Lynda Gratton and Michel Syrett, from *Personnel Management*, January 1990, by permission of *Personnel Management*, official journal of the Institute of Personnel Management.

systems of the multinationals. It is a salutary thought that some, such as Shell, IBM and Unilever, have been taking a planned and ordered approach to their succession needs for the best part of 20 years. From the coveting of these systems have arisen numerous clones – what one might call 'son of Shell' or 'IBM mark 2'. In particular, they have used the more glamorous aspects of succession technology, for example, career-tracking computer systems and assessment centres. In this rush for 'me too look-alikes', we have on occasions forgotten that the succession processes of Shell or IBM have been influenced by a number of assumptions and needs:

- The need for a cadre of top executives capable of operating and resourcing the company's requirements across the globe.
- The assumption that the complexity of senior management posts demands in-depth functional, international and general management experience.
- The need for a development programme based on rotating placements in different parts of the organization worldwide network, often lasting two years or more, which carries with it the requirement that individuals are prepared and willing to be mobile to gain promotion.
- An emphasis on the needs of the job and an assumption that executive roles are relatively stable and predictable over time.
- The requirement that individuals become 'corporate men' (for men they inevitably are!), prepared to identify with and remain in permanent employment with the organization for most of their early and middle career.
- The assumption that the board is the custodian of the organization and that one of its principal aims is to pass this custodianship to the next generation.

While these needs and assumptions may be true for the complex multi-nationals, there are many organizations for whom this is patently not the case. These multinational models of succession break down in those companies which are young and growing rapidly and in those which have diversified into a number of marketplaces.

To illustrate the breadth of succession strategies, we describe the strategies of four very different but equally successful companies. The complex multinational is represented by IBM, the computer giant. Its succession strategies are contrasted with the equally effective, though very different, Amstrad. Both operate in the competitive computer sector, yet they differ markedly in culture and maturity.

Both IBM and Amstrad are essentially 'single sector', focusing on the production, manufacturing and sales of computers. What of those companies which are diversified and operate in many markets, each with different needs and forces? Some, like BAT, operate what Goold and Campbell have termed a 'strategic planning model',[1] others, like Hanson and BTR, operate a 'financial control business model'.

The fundamental variations in the succession strategies of these very different but equally successful companies are set out below. The succession strategies are described with emphasis on the types of executives they require, the succession systems currently in place and the process of orchestration which supports the strategy.

IBM: Mature, Single Business

IBM's succession strategy is a classic example of the traditional model of good practice. The company operates on a global basis, employing over 380,000 people across 130 countries, with an organizational structure reflecting both its geographic and functional groups.

Executive needs   IBM's principal succession needs are for an international cadre of executives with in-depth understanding of the company's products, marketplace and the specialist support functions. This necessitates a complex career path involving both cross-functional and international experience. The early identification of talent and a series of planned job moves is therefore a prerequisite.

Succession systems   Candidates are developed from within – very limited external recruitment occurs after the early stages of the succession programme.

- Potential is identified early on, usually in an individual's late 20s. Assessment of potential is usually based on current performance by line managers, who operate on a clear and agreed understanding of 'what makes for success round here'. This is supplemented by a series of assessment centres.
- 'Heirs apparent' are coached and developed for each senior post, with up to nine jobs being identified in advance. Development of individuals is based on 'testing work experiences', supplemented by both internal and external development and training activities.
- Integration between career plans of individuals and succession plans for top jobs involves complex computer-based matching. This 'hard data' is supported by a central succession role, reporting to the most senior levels of IBM, which is responsible for ensuring that the group of candidates have development and job opportunities.

Orchestration of the development of individuals is undertaken by the manager of executive resources. Job assignments last a maximum of three years and are supported by a process in which positions earmarked for the development of fast-track individuals cannot be filled by people who are unpromotable. The whole process of career advancement is supported by a culture created by the senior management team, who got to the top in the same manner. Their involvement and interest in the succession processes is channelled through a corporate management committee, which spends up to a quarter of its time on executive resourcing.

Summary of key aspects

- The importance placed on developing 'heirs apparent' for each senior post.
- The focus on continuity.
- The focus on depth and complexity.
- The emphasis on data integration.

Amstrad: Young, Single Business

Amstrad was built up by Alan Sugar from a £10 million supplier of stereos and videos to an organization with a current revenue of £600 million.

Executive needs Amstrad's succession needs focus on the development of a cadre of executives with similar objectives, aspirations and views; and the need to complement the skills of the founding partners with a more balanced management team from a range of disciplines.

Succession systems In the fast-growing corporate structure, which is constantly changing, succession processes are more *ad hoc* and subject to revision. The most important aspects are:

- *The chief executive's 'span of control'* With a workforce which has only just begun to top 1,000 people, Amstrad's chief executive can take personal responsibility for the development of high-potential people and ensure they receive the right kinds of job experience.
- *Internal, job-focused development* Most members of the current board were promoted from within the organization particularly from the sales and marketing functions. They were initially close friends or members of personal networks.
- *Short-term objectives* In contrast to the 'market gardening' approach of IBM, Amstrad's succession policies are usually short-term 'fixes', with promotion based on performance and a candidate's understanding of the 'here and now'.

Summary of key aspects

- The need to develop a multi-functional senior management team, balancing the skills and expertise of the founding group.
- The current transition from founder members to second generation, achievable only by defining the skills and weaknesses of founders so that skill gaps can be filled.
- The role of the chief executive in gathering people around him and bringing in new talent, while letting go of power at the appropriate time.
- The difficulty of succession planning at a time when the company is expanding and changing rapidly.

BAT: Diversified Company/Strategic Planning

BAT is a leading global conglomerate with a £17 billion turnover which has diversified from tobacco into finance (Eagle Star, Allied Dunbar) and retail (Argos, Marshall Field).

Executive needs   The major succession challenge confronting BAT is to allow autonomy to its various businesses, which are at different stages of maturity and face different business scenarios, while ensuring executives with the highest potential have experience of more than one company. Its succession needs are therefore to develop a cadre of executives capable of operating each business; to 'add value' from the corporate group to the businesses from the synergy and integration between the businesses (and between subsidiaries and the centre); and rapidly to assimilate talented executives entering through the acquisition process.

Succession systems   BAT aims to balance the individual needs of each business with those of the corporate group. Succession systems are based in the individual businesses and as such reflect their specific needs and corporate strategy. So succession ranges from the orderly approach of mature businesses in stable marketplaces (see IBM above) to more *ad hoc* strategies adopted by start-up companies and those in rapid growth (as with Amstrad).

The centre takes a direct interest in people with director-level potential, both in terms of developing appropriate work experience and through internal and external training. Movement across businesses is an important feature and takes place on an individual basis.

Orchestration   For diversified companies like BAT, the emphasis in achieving succession is on negotiation and persuasion rather than rules and procedures. Having said that, the corporate group takes an active role in reviewing the succession lists of individual businesses. The annual meeting of the chairman's policy committee is the focus of this monitoring activity. The review and influencing process is assisted by a senior corporate resource and a corporate management training centre.

Hanson plc: Diversified Company/Financial Control Strategy

Hanson is a major diversified company with interest in a range of business, including typewriters (SCM), cigarettes (Imperial) and London Brick.

Executive needs   In these companies the need is to develop a highly competent group of corporate staff (which in Hanson numbers 20 in the London centre, 15 in New York). The emphasis in the business is on the acquisition and development of basic under-performing business.

Succession systems   Acquisition of poorly managed businesses is crucial to the growth strategy and provides a continual pool of management talent. Following acquisition, the top managers invariably leave, to be replaced by a senior

Hanson director previously involved in the acquisition. The 'liberation' of middle managers, through increased responsibility and the provision of clear feedback and rewards, is crucial.

Development and identification of talent is in the hands of senior management. High-potential people are rapidly given responsibility and their performance tested by this process.

Cross-business development or international experience is not an imperative unless it directly mirrors the marketplace of the business.

Orchestration   There are no corporate human resource specialists in Hanson; indeed, corporate staff are kept to a minimum. Succession is seen as the responsibility of the individual business and is not monitored. The major monitoring is through financial returns. However, one of the main responsibilities of the group chairman is to assess, motivate and monitor management.

These case studies serve as a useful reminder that there is no one way to approach the succession of senior executives. What they do is to demonstrate how effective companies mirror their business strategy with succession strategies. More particularly the business strategy influences:

Sources of talent   from the internal 'market gardening' approach of IBM to the acquisition source of Hanson.

Succession planning processes   At Amstrad the chief executive can 'reach out to talent'; for companies like Shell, complex, extensive systems based on systematic job movement are required.

Co-ordination and integration   In smaller companies, flexible people-centred approaches work best. Integration is a real issue for diversified companies. At BAT the synergy between businesses is reflected in integrating succession systems; at Hanson, with no cross-business synergy, integration is minimal.

Role of HR

It has been argued frequently by commentators, such as Guest and Tyson, that the role of HR practitioners needs to change from that of 'systems administrators' and 'clerks of works' to internal consultants and architects of best practice.[2]

Nowhere is this more important than in managing succession. HR executives have vital roles to play as change agents, recognizing the impact of internal corporate planning and external developments on future senior management roles and developing programmes flexible enough to be adjustable to the rigours of a turbulent business environment.

Succession is a highly political and inexact process. Many young people currently entering organizations with high-flying talent will fail to reach positions of seniority in 15–20 years' time because development programmes have provided them with the wrong skills or the career framework is too rigid to let them grow in the way they would like. Working more closely with the board, and with an accurate understanding of the future corporate direction. HR executives have a critical role to play in helping their organizations develop the business leaders it requires.

Many of our long-held assumptions about succession are appearing increasingly fragile. The two main challenges which confront HR practitioners when designing an effective succession strategy are the changes in organizations and changes in individuals.

The stream of mergers, acquisitions and international alliances which have taken place since the mid-1980s has destroyed much of the old order and resulted in new structures and organizational demands. Many companies, for example, are now made up of a variety of 'sub-businesses', each of which has different and often conflicting management needs.

These needs are difficult to predict in advance, thus creating executive jobs with future parameters and demands that are often unknown. In fast-moving markets, involving shorter product life-cycles, shorter consumer time-spans, rapid changes in technology and unpredictable demand, the planned and orderly approach dictated by traditional succession policies may be difficult or impossible to achieve.

Succession policies have also failed to take into account changing perceptions of organizational behaviour and structure. Commentators such as Handy and Moss Kanter have highlighted the move towards smaller, less hierarchical working structures and styles of management, based on concepts of the organization as a human organism to be motivated, influenced and led, rather than units to be managed and administered.[3]

One of the most important implications is that senior jobs, particularly in smaller fluid organizations, tend to be built around the individual's needs and attributes. Yet many companies still base succession on career structures that are imposed on participants rather than developed with them.

The failure to build the needs of the individual into succession programmes is particularly damaging in a climate where the problems of retaining and making the maximum use of existing professional staff has become a key personnel issue.

Many organizations still rely on graduate trainees as the main source of fast-track candidates. Yet the current drop in school-leavers will result in a fall of up to 10,000 graduates a year in the UK by the mid-1990s and similar reductions in the United States, Germany, Denmark and the Netherlands.

Different Aspirations

Those suitably qualified for fast-track development that do emerge from higher education may have attitudes to work and career aspirations that differ markedly from their predecessors'.

Up to half will be women, many of whom will want at some point of their career to take time off to start a family, often precisely at the point when succession programmes reach their most critical stages. Research by the Institute of Manpower Studies suggests that professionally qualified women are far less likely to return to their employer after statutory maternity leave.[4] Many find themselves choosing between maternity leave followed by an immediate return to full-time work, or no work at all. Most give up work altogether and hope to resume their careers later on, something easy to accommodate in specialist roles but almost impossible to allow for in succession programmes.

A growing proportion of new candidates will be from minority ethnic communities, one of the fastest-growing parts of the UK, US and European populations. They may well prefer to work in organizations and communities with a long tradition in ethnic minority recruiting, and eschew large, established businesses, with a culture and approaches to development still shaped by a white male workforce.

Regardless of sex and race, those suited to fast-track development may not aspire to traditional vertical career development. Many may wish to take time off in mid-career to further their education, travel or work in the community. Others may choose to become advisers, consultants or independent contractors rather than slogging up the corporate ladder to take up positions as managers of large businesses. And in an era when business leaders are no longer seen as folk heroes and community values are replacing the individualistic 'can do' assumptions of the 1980s, others still may reject business-related careers in favour of less currently fashionable occupations like teaching or health care.

New Assumptions

All these factors mean that we cannot simply impose the best practice of our most successful companies in an indiscriminate manner. HR practitioners must draw on a new set of less definable assumptions and requirements. For example, senior jobs may exist in a radically different context and involve significantly altered skills and knowledge. As a consequence organizations will have to:

- work harder developing mechanisms which link succession practice to future requirements

- be far more sensitive to change in the needs for succession
- be adaptable and flexible in their assumptions.

Also, succession will have to be based more on the needs of the individual rather than exclusively on the requirements of the job. Successful succession programmes, therefore, may have to incorporate:

- better career counselling and appraisal based on a two-way exchange of ideas and requirements
- more flexibility in terms of the way organizations see career development, and in the provision of career breaks, job-sharing and access to professional part-time work.
- imaginative use of secondments, sabbaticals and assignments, which allow high-flying individuals the opportunity to pursue broader personal and professional interests, while equipping them with skills and experience which will benefit them in general management positions.

Succession is one of the top items on the agenda of most chief executives and personnel directors. It cannot be left to chance, but on the other hand, buying in 'clones' of the multinationals' approaches is equally unrealistic. What is needed is a strategy designed to meet the needs of the company; a strategy which pays due regard to the internationalism of the company, its product mix, complexity and culture; a strategy which builds on what is possible rather than attempting to develop the realistic; and finally, a strategy which appreciates that the world is changing and that trends both within and outside companies will necessitate new and creative approaches.

Notes

1   Michael Goold and Andrew Campbell, *Strategies and Style: The Role of the Centre in Managing Diversified Companies*, Basil Blackwell, 1987.
2   David Guest, 'Human resource management and industrial relations', *Journal of Management Studies*, Sept. 1987. Sean Tyson and Alan Fell, *Evaluating the Personnel Function*, Hutchinson, 1986.
3   Charles Handy, *The Age of Reason*, Hutchinson, 1989. Rosabeth Moss Kanter, *When Giants Learn to Dance: Mastering the Challenge of Strategy, Management and Careers in the 1990s*, Simon & Schuster 1989.
4   Wendy Hirsh, *Women, Career Breaks and Re-entry*, Institute of Manpower Studies, 1985.

3
Flying too High for Comfort

Wendy Hirsh

Ask personnel managers or indeed senior executives what issues are on their minds and you will find that something concerning 'management talent' and how to develop it crops up with surprising regularity. The level of concern about management development has been significantly increasing over the past two or three years and has led to sustained research programmes in this field.[1]

A recent review of management resources found

> A dearth of top flight managerial talent in all sectors of industry – this is the strongest complaint to emerge from the interviews with the 100 top managers in the survey[2]

Although it does not give details of particular organizations, this article is based on extensive personal observation and analysis of the problems of 'management talent' in major employing organizations, and seeks to generalize from common experiences observed. If it appears unduly critical, this derives from a deep-seated unease about the way in which issues of management development are currently perceived and handled.

Not far behind the terms 'management talent', 'developing managers' or 'managers for the future' seems to come 'high flyer'. Most self-respecting UK companies seem to feel they need 'high-flyers' (whatever they are) and structured schemes or programmes with which to develop them.

What is a High-Flyer?

Different organizations assume different things by the term 'high-flyer', but there are some key common aspects which are usually implied.

'Flying too High for Comfort', by Wendy Hirsh, from *Manpower Policy and Practice*, Summer 1985, by permission of the author.

Let us imagine a substantial UK company and a typical high-flyer – we'll call him Icarus. What is special about him? (It goes without saying, that Icarus is a 'him' for reasons which will be mentioned later.)

- Icarus is *young* (under 40) and probably still in middle management or below – high-flyers are seldom seen to exist past the age of 40, and those who have reached the top either were not high-flyers or have usually lost the label.
- Icarus has 'talent', although this is likely to be seen in general terms (bright, ambitious, 'our kind of man', right personality profile) rather than in terms of track record, skills or knowledge. 'Potential' is the trendy word for talent.
- His 'talent' is the kind the company believes necessary for senior management. High-flyers are destined for the top.
- Icarus has been identified early on in his career as a high-flyer. He will be moved quickly and deliberately up the career structure.
- Icarus is on a high-flyer scheme which will ensure that he achieves rapid career development. He will be assessed carefully and special processes will review his progress so that he can be 'groomed for stardom'.

The early identification of potential, youth and speed of progression, the destination of senior management, and the conscious management of a high-flyer's career are all common attributes of 'talent-spotting' company policy.

What do High-Flyer Schemes Look Like?

Conscious career management implies the presence of processes within the company to achieve two main aims: to identify high-flyers within the company and to provide them with planned career development.

Icarus may have entered the company as a high-flyer. This would probably be through a *graduate entry scheme* with selection processes (often assessment centres, psychological tests, etc.) designed to spot potential for senior management. Identification of high-flyers can also be achieved by *selection from those already inside the company*. However, as this has to be done early on (25–30 at the latest), it tends to use techniques not dissimilar to those of graduate recruitment. This sifting is often restricted to certain groups, usually defined by entry schemes or educational/professional qualifications.

Once defined as a high-flyer, Icarus will not lose his label for quite a while. Although many companies claim that they move people in and out of the high-flyer group, there is little evidence that this occurs in practice. Icarus will have his details entered on a special record system in the management development executive's office, and he will be carefully watched. If Icarus does not reach senior management by the time he is 40, he will relabelled as 'dead wood'.

Other systems, however, are supposed to make sure that he does get there. Early in his career *planned progression* will be organized through a series of attractive assignments. This usually lasts for about five years; or until it proves harder to find vacant assignments at higher levels.

The card index of high-flyers will be pulled out whenever a succession chart is being drawn up or a senior job is being filled. These processes may or may not be enough to ensure that Icarus actually progresses – it depends on whether the managrement development manager has any influence over appointments, and whether there are enough opportunities for promotion. The high-flyer scheme will however, ensure that his name appears regularly on personnel short-lists.

He is likely to be sent off on a prestigious *management training course*, preferably abroad. If his company does not believe in these, he will be assigned action-learning, and climb mountains on an action-learning programme.

If the card index, luck and plentiful promotion opportunities work in unison, Icarus will find himself within sight of senior management positions by his mid-30s. At this stage, phase two of high-flying takes over and he is *groomed for particular senior posts*. (This will usually be done by moving him between functions to broaden his business appreciation.) As before, luck and opportunity, plus company politics, will determine whether he finally makes it.

If at 35 Icarus is stuck in a career blockage at the lower levels of management in a dead-end function (like personnel), he can safely assume that he never was a high-flyer and that he must have done something wrong.

Why are High-Flyer Schemes Attractive?

Although the description above is a thumb-nail caricature, the appeal of high-flyer schemes is deep-seated. The rapid growth of organizations in the past made them a practical way of speeding up the development of a stock of managers for companies who could not keep pace with their own expansion. Today, however, their appeal appears to be based on:

- profound anxieties about the next generation of senior managers. Because these schemes are visible, they are a comfort.
- fears that in organizations with career blockages, good people will get 'lost' and never reach the top
- the desire for young managers, which is passionate, although nobody seems to know why. It is apparent, however, that current senior managers reached the top quite young, borne on a tide of 1960s growth.
- the fact that they may be attractive to certain recruits – particularly graduates. Some sectors (manufacturing, retail and finance) have used schemes offering rapid careers to attract graduates into new kinds of careers.
- Their tremendous appeal to personnel specialists, because they look active,

sophisticated and modern; tell people they are talented; and provide lots of 'fun' training activities with only small groups of bright participants.

What are Such Schemes Assuming?

All the motivations above are understandable, and some are very important. However, when we try to relate what senior managers, personnel specialists or employees think they will get out of high-flyer schemes there are some hidden traps.

High-flyer schemes are based on a number of important assumptions:

- Management potential can be spotted very early.
- This definition of potential will still be relevant in 20 years' time when Icarus has reached the top.
- Getting to the top young is good for the business.
- If you get senior management right, it will help the business. This is obviously true, but is senior management performance really the most important personnel problem?
- Career moves can be planned and achieved.
- The concept of systematic development is sound, and should be managed by the company.
- Icarus is a willing pawn in the game.

Some of these points are highly debatable. It is regrettable that companies with high-flyer schemes rarely ask themselves uncomfortable questions about whether any or all of these assumptions can be justified.

The Unintentional Impact of High-Flyer Schemes

The biggest traps in the high-flyer model are probably its inadvertent consequences. The high-flyer concept is a strong drug for the organization. These are some of its side effects:

Once Icarus is selected, he and everyone else think that he is wonderful. He reaches senior management entirely as a self-fulfilling prophecy.

The mechanisms for spotting high-flyers select people like Icarus. They are all very similar and a homogeneous senior management results. This spells trouble if the business environment changes to one in which Icarus and his friends do not perform well.

All these people have careers which reach certain levels by certain ages. The ages of 30–35 are particularly important. This leads to a high incidence of stress in young managers. It is also, incidentally, why Icarus is a man. This singular timing of careers will not allow women into senior management unless they choose between career and family.

The size of the high-flyer group tends to become inflexible. If the business expands quickly there are too few high-flyers. If blockages develop, how do you give Icarus the career he expects?

High-flyers concentrate on looking good (which is assessed) rather than performing (which is not). They do not stay in tough management jobs long enough at middle levels to have to live with thorny problems over an extended period of time. They can also cause havoc by moving into departments which they do not fully understand.

Those recruited later in their careers are normally too late to be on the high-flyer track, although they might vary the pool of talent. Those in peripheral careers within the company (technology, research, data processing) are also passed over.

For every Icarus who may be turned on by the scheme, there are ten other managers (or potential managers) who are not. Telling a small part of the workforce it has talent appears very like telling the rest that they lack it. Even if the scheme is supposed to be confidential, employees are not blind.

The personnel function gives much time and attention to high-flyers. It is difficult to sustain a serious commitment to the development of other employees when you are busy with action-learning and succession charts.

All in all, high-flyer schemes are inflexible in terms of size, and often in terms of the qualities of the people they produce. They seep deep into the culture of the organization and are bound to produce élitist beliefs about what kinds of development are valued, and for whom. They are not easily adaptable in times of rapid organizational change, and can be damaging for the high-flyers (when their ambitions are unfulfilled) as well as for others.

Alternative Strategies

The wisdom of the high-flyer picture of senior management should, at best, be seriously questioned. In the author's personal view, most organizations which have established such schemes would have performed equally well or better without them. Some have used more varied and widespread mechanisms for selection and development and produced managers at all levels, who appear to perform at least as well.

Before assuming that a high-flyer scheme is vital, these questions should be considered:

• What different kinds of people do we need in various levels and functions? How are these levels and functions changing over time?

- Can we maintain a pool of talent varied in both size and nature so that we can respond to uncertainty?
- How quickly do people need to move through the structure and how long spent at one level is developmentally valuable? How long do we want people to stay in the top jobs? Do we really want them there at 40, and if so, why?
- Do we need additional mechanical processes to make career development happen? How can our ordinary promotion and development systems do this for us?
- What part will Icarus play in his own development? If he's that good, couldn't he get to the top anyway? If he isn't that good, what is he doing on the high-flyer scheme?

Notes

1   Wendy Hirsh, *Career Management in the Organisation: A Guide for Developing Policy and Practice* (IMS Report No 96, Institute of Manpower Studies, 1984).
2   *Management Resources? Present Problems and Future Trends*, London Business School and Egon Zehnder, 1984.

4
Assessing the Charismatic Leader

Bernard M. Bass

Charismatic leaders have an extraordinary impact on the performance of their followers as well as many virtues and vices similar to what we found in the samples of managers and military officers we assessed. It was thought that charisma was limited to the Gandhis and Martin Luther Kings at the world-class level, rather than a matter of quantifiable individual differences among people in general, and managers in particular. However, empirical and survey validation research has shown it to be one of the most powerful predictors of success as a manager or executive in business, as a military officer, as a religious minister, and as a champion of innovation in industry.

Max Weber saw the concept as bestowed by colleagues and subordinates rather than by God, and applied it to understanding the development and maintenance of complex organizations. In Weber's view, there are five components to charisma:

- a person with extraordinary gifts
- a crisis
- a radical solution to the crisis
- followers attracted to the exceptional person believing that they are linked through him to transcedent powers
- validation of the person's gifts and transcendence in repeated experiences of success.

In the charismatic relationship, two of these components seem essential. First, there is a pattern of abilities, interests, and personal traits common to most charismatic leaders. Ordinarily, charismatics have much expertise. Second,

Abstract of a presentation given at a conference on Contemporary Trends in Assessment by Professor Bernard M. Bass, organized by Saville and Holdsworth at Warwick University, UK in September 1990, by permission of Saville and Holdsworth Ltd. and Professor Bass.

there is a strong desire by followers to identify with the leader. Both these characteristics seem particularly capable of being assessed.

Requisite abilities, interests and personality of the charismatic leader include the following: emotional expressiveness, self-confidence, self-determination and freedom from internal conflict. They are likely to have a strong conviction in the moral righteousness of their own beliefs, to be radical, unconventional, risk-taking, visionary, entrepreneurial and exemplary.

Charismatic leaders project a powerful, confident, dynamic presence. Their tone of voice is engaging and captivating. Their facial expressions are animated, yet they remain relaxed. Eye contact is direct. As Ann Willner has noted, the magnetic attraction of the charismatic leader's eyes is often commented upon.

Charismatic leaders display complete confidence in the correctness of their position and in their capabilities. They make this a clear aspect of their public image. Even when personally discouraged and facing failure, they are unlikely to make public such feelings. Charismatic leaders' elevated self-esteem helps them to avoid defensiveness in conflicting interpersonal situations. It also helps to maintain the confidence that their subordinates have in them. Charismatics tend to project on to likeminded loyal followers their continuing confident opinions of themselves. Charismatic leaders are great actors. They are always on-stage. They are always projecting to their followers their extreme self-confidence and convictions, so that they become larger than life. According to Robert House, charismatics must be able to present themselves as workers of miracles likely to succeed where others would fall.

For Weber, charisma was firstly a personal attribute of leaders whose purposes, powers, and extraordinary determination set them apart from other people. Nietzsche's Superman had some of the same characteristics: inner direction, orginality, self-determination, sense of duty, and responsibility for the unique self. For Nietzsche ordinary men conformed to the expectations of others; Superman could free himself from the expected. He was a point of contact with the future who created new values and goals. But Superman was also a highly self-oriented narcissist.

In a consideration of self-determination, there are methods for assessing self-efficacy, self-monitoring, self-reinforcement, and locus of control.

Charismatic leaders can say things publicly that followers feel privately but cannot express. As noted by David McClelland, charismatics have an insight into the needs, values, and hopes of their followers and the ability to build on them through dramatic and persuasive words and deeds; they have the ability both to 'conceive and articulate goals that lift people out of their petty preoccupations'. Such leaders, John Gardner has pointed out, can unite people to seek objectives 'worthy of their best efforts'.

The assessment of insight is complicated because it is correlated with projection, empathy, as well as real and assumed similarity to the subjects of the insight.

Charismatic leaders maintain their confidence and determination despite serious setbacks and defeats, through self-assurance which is 'at one with their inner images', according to Manfred Kets de Vries. The confidence and determination of charismatic leaders stem from a greater freedom from internal conflict between their emotions, impressions, and feelings (Freud's id) and their controlling conscience (Freud's superego). Freedom from the id–superego conflict makes for strong ego ideals and assuredness about what the leaders value as good, right, and important. Convinced of the goodness, rightness, and importance of their point of view, charismatic leaders are likely to be more forthright and candid in reprimanding subordinates. They can maintain a clear conscience if they feel they need to sack them, whereas the ordinary manager would be plagued by self-doubt.

In their speeches, whether or not written by themselves, charismatic leaders use high-action verbs, short pauses between phrases and sentences, and reiteration. They evoke audience response. Their messages are simple and focus on the collective identity of speaker and audience. Jesse Jackson carries the approach to its extremes. Standardized psychometric measurements of eloquence are possible.

According to previously collected opinions of political historians, charismatic US presidents were more active and took significantly stronger actions than non-charismatic presidents. They were also judged more highly esteemed and able to accomplish more in their administrations. Standardized self-reports of general activity level are available in personality inventories.

There is an intense emotional attraction to charismatic leaders by their followers beyond ordinary esteem, affection, admiration, and trust. It involves devotion, awe, reverence, and blind faith. There is unqualified belief in the charismatic and his mission. It is an absolute emotional and cognitive identification with the leader. This is best measured by surveys of followers with, for example, the Multifactor Leadership Questionnaire (MLQ).

Charismatic leader–follower relations are widely found in complex organizations as well as in political life. Charisma surfaced as the most important element in quantitative studies by myself and colleagues since 1985 of leadership effectiveness in educational institutions, the armed forces, business, industry, hospitals, and other non-profit organizations.

Charisma has been found at all organizational levels, admittedly more at the top than bottom or middle levels. In the MLQ surveys many followers described their military or industrial superior as someone who made them enthusiastic about assignments, inspired loyalty to the organization, commanded respect from everyone, had a special gift of seeing what was really important, had a sense of mission, and excited subordinates. Some of these subordinates had complete faith in their leader and felt good to be near him. They were proud to be associated with the charismatic leader and trusted his capacity to overcome any obstacle. The charismatic leader served as a symbol of success and accomplishment for his followers.

In the 1990s the challenges of rapidly changing workforces, markets, and technologies have to be met. Efforts must be increased to avoid bureaucratic and traditional rigidities by recourse to *ad hoc* groups, temporary systems, and organicism.

Subordinates in lower ranks who described their immediate supervisors as charismatic also saw their units and their organization as more productive. And the opinions about the lower- and middle-level charismatic leaders' effectiveness is shared by their superiors.

In field surveys the charismatic leaders were seen by subordinates to be more dynamic (emphatic, active, fast, aggressive, bold, extroverted, energetic, and frank). Subordinates developed more self-assurance under such leaders in contrast to those working for non-charismatic leaders. They said their work was more meaningful if their leader was publicly acknowledged as charismatic. The subordinates of charismatics worked longer hours per week, which suggested the heightened motivation of subordinates under a charismatic leader. They revealed a higher level of trust and acceptance of the charismatic leader compared to the non-charismatic in their ratings of 'self-disclosure' to the charismatic leader.

Sixty-six percent of the covariance of 143 leadership items from which the MLQ was derived could be accounted for by a factor of charismatic leadership. Managers identified by their superiors as 'top performers' earned a significantly higher charismatic leadership score from their subordinates than a random sample of 'ordinary' performers.

High correlations were found between subordinates' ratings of the charisma of their leaders and the effectiveness of their leadership. This was in contrast to the correlations found between how much contingent reinforcement the manager practised and his or her rated effectiveness. Similar results were obtained in a computer firm and for samples of New Zealand educational administrators and professional personnel as well as in another dozen studies. The high correlation of charismatic leadership with effectiveness was in contrast to the considerably lower correlations found for other measures of leadership behaviour such as consideration and initiation of structure. A similar pattern emerged in determining how much stress and burn-out was avoided in subordinates of charismatic leaders. Leaders with high scores on the MLQ charismatic scale were also seen to encourage self-actualization among subordinates.

MLQ ratings to assess charismatic leadership can be obtained from three or more co-workers and/or subordinates. These assessments by others are usually more valid as predictors of subsequent success than self-ratings. Secondly, standardized self-report instruments are available to test for likely components of charisma. These include: expressive behaviour, self-confidence, determination, insight, freedom from internal conflict, eloquence, energy level, and social boldness.

Charisma an important and useful concept, providing valid assessment of actual and potential leaders.

Chapter 16
How Leaders Learn

Introduction

The implicit assumption behind this book is that good leaders are bred rather than born and that, as a consequence, continuous development of leadership skills is part of any senior manager's job remit. Sadly, this is not always the case. The articles in this chapter highlight a number of concerns about the quality of learning that takes place, collectively and individually, within organizations and the extent to which business leaders encourage this to happen and benefit from the process.

Charles Hampden-Turner stresses the need for a constant, conscious learning process. He argues that we are in an international learning race where the stakes are restricted to the rise and fall not just of individual businesses but also of nations and whole regions of the world. The process of continuous learning not only achieves the short-term aims of immediate commercial advantage but the longer-term advantages of creating individuals and thus organizations with a healthy will to broaden the bounds of their knowledge and experience.

The concept of the learning organization is explored further by Bob Garratt. Initially, the climate within the organization needs to be conducive to learning. As he says, 'The simplistic belief that, typically, an across-the-board reduction of n percent of the cost base will somehow bring corporate health and happiness is highly seductive and very unwise.' This point is echoed by Benton in his book *Riding the Whirlwind*: 'In our corporate world, the swift onset of turbulence has caught some leaders on the hop; they have found the pace too fast. When giants like ITT and GEC have won stock market praise for twenty years through tight control of costs and contracts, it cannot be easy to find new ways of leading.' Perhaps as Hampden-Turner asks, even more succinctly, in a part of *Charting the Corporate Mind* not published here: 'Is the West's unquestioned pursuit of "the bottom line" its Achilles' heel? Of course, profitability must be one objective of an organization, but should it be *the only* one, or is not profitability one horn of several dilemmas? In that case, are we sacrificing the values necessary to the learning race to short-term profitability?'

Garratt argues that not only are many specialist managers promoted into senior positions without training in general management and appropriate career experience, but little time or money is available to them to develop themselves into their direction-giving role and so they remain constrained by responsibilities outside their 'comfort-zone'.

Lack of time for continuous learning is also a common complaint of senior managers who have profited from general management development earlier in their careers. Once in position, it is *all too easy* for business leaders to focus entirely on the day-to-day running of their enterprise and lose touch with events in the world around them that will have a direct impact on their corporate strategies. Their ability to create and foster a new vision for the company suffers accordingly.

But Garratt goes on to suggest that a further role for senior managers is to 'lead the learning' in the organization – and that the chief executive should help the top team to position itself so that it forms a centre of learning and thus a climate in which all employees see self-development as an integral part of their job. In an extension of the principle that 'leaders should lead from the front', he stresses that the need for senior corporate managers to find time to further their learning not only broadens their own direction-setting abilities but provides an important model for everyone else in the organization.

Both Hampden-Turner and Garratt establish the inextricable link that now exists between leadership and learning. Leadership skills can be developed and built on through systematic training and development, but these skills will be maintained only if senior managers update and widen their knowledge through continuous learning.

Peter Williamson of the London Business School takes a more pragmatic view as to what can be done to draw out the leadership skills of those attending MBA courses. He begins by assessing the leadership role and how it is changing, quite properly since an MBA education aims to equip participants for the future. Williamson quotes Dick Giordano's description of a successful future leader in his 1990 Stockton Lecture as 'a person who can live with above average ambiguity and manage sometimes conflicting objectives'. Williamson's examination of a new kind of learning environment suggests that 'tomorrow's business leaders [will] learn their required skills through play'.

The direction set by a corporation's leaders, in times of expansion or recession, is more critical to its commercial survival than it has ever been. But the leader's ability to set the right course, and the company's collective and individual ability to follow, depend on its ability to acquire and update new knowledge and skills. Leading this process of learning may prove to be the most important role of the modern business manager.

1
Standing at the Helm

Charles Hampden-Turner

If the 'corporate mind' is to plan a successful strategy it must learn to steer in the direction chosen. Apart from the need to create value, a business organization has patterns and dynamics of its own.

Kubernetes is the Greek word meaning 'helmsman' or 'steersman' and from this we get cybernetics as a field of study. If we want to understand leadership we need to consider what it means to take the helm. Let us consider the very simple circle in figure 1. This figure is known as a cybernetic loop or a recursive system. It goes endlessly around, yet changes all the time because every gust or pull of the tide calls for a different response from the helmsman. There are also within this circle at least two tensions or dilemmas, indicated by the painfully stretched ropes crossing at the centre. The tensions occur because the course steered by the helmsman is resisted by the wind and current which pull in other directions, while the direction in which the wheel points is in tension with, and is different from, the drift of the ship as caused by the elements.

Between 12 o'clock and 6 o'clock on this circle and between 3 o'clock and 9 o'clock are two related dilemmas. The helmsman must be simultaneously aware of the course being steered and the deviations occurring, and must keep on correcting his course. The skill of the helmsman or that of anyone who tries to lead a group or organization is to resolve these tensions or dilemmas, in this case to use wind and current together with wheel and rudder to bring the ship to its destination. Depending on the helmsman's skill, the wind and tide, despite their seeming opposition, can be used in ways that further, and combine with, the course that has been charted.

In fact, there are many more dilemmas present in any basic loop, and to make

Excerpt from *Charting the Corporate Mind* by Charles Hampden-Turner 1990, by permission of Basil Blackwell Ltd.

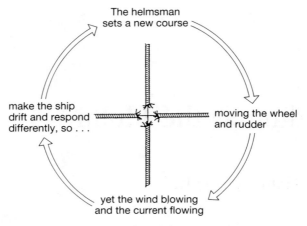

Figure 1

this clearer let us empty the figure of content and make it even simpler: figure 2. From the helmsman's viewpoint he is engaged in a process of

- *leading* so that he can *learn* and *learning* so that he can *lead*.

His ship keeps

- *erring* so that it must be *corrected*.

Steering this ship involves

- maintaining *continuity* in the midst of *change*.

In holding to his course he is both

- the *cause* of the ship's position, yet *affected* by it.

Each element in the system, i.e. wind, rudder, etc., is

- *independent* of the other, yet *dependent* on it.

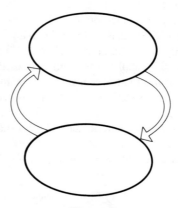

Figure 2

All elements in the system can be
- *analysed* as *parts*, yet they *combine* as a *whole*.

And how would we recognize excellence in a helmsman? Surely the outstanding skipper spots an error fast and corrects it, can change course rapidly while maintaining the continuity of his/her purpose and is the cause of his craft's superior performance because he/she takes every disturbance into account in determining the course of action. He/she knows the independent influence of each element and how the ship depends on each and all of these, and he/she can analyse any problem quickly to yield a better performance from the whole enterprise.

What makes the nautical metaphor particularly apt is that the 'seas' of international commerce have become more and more turbulent of late. Time was when the only waves were made by large, mostly American, corporations, but today there are so many actors plying so busy a trade that every craft must navigate the choppy waters created by the unpredictable combinations of half a dozen bow-waves, and all manner of mutual adjustments must be made to avoid destructive collisions, especially head on.

But there is another reason why cybernetic thinking cannot be avoided by even the most determined leader ready to defy the elements. An organization, its markets, employees and customers are living systems; that means that several elements in that system have their own energy, purpose and direction. You can drop-kick a football made with leather from a dead bull. But you cannot drop-kick a live bull because it has its own preferences and will prefer that you be the one to fly through the air. No sooner do we introduce another living system or human organism into a cybernetic loop than these will go their own ways, like the wind and the current, and we at once face the dilemma of resolving at least two directions in tension with one another.[1]

If we assume that our ship is a living system then there are dilemmas which arise from this reality as well.

- Any biological or social system is *differentiated* in its function, yet these need to be *integrated* if the whole is to develop.
- Its members must have some local *freedom* and *discretion*, yet all remain subject to the captain's *authority* and *command*.
- Orders must go from the *top down*, yet these cannot maintain their quality unless information goes from the *bottom up* to educate decision-makers.
- The captain *empowers* his subordinates to make certain judgements and decisions, yet expects their exercise of such responsibility to confirm his *own power* and influence in the ship.
- All crew members may legitimately *compete* with each other to achieve the skills of seamanship but all must *cooperate* in furthering the effectiveness of the ship itself.

We could multiply such tensions indefinitely.

Virtuous and Vicious Circles

But not all cybernetic systems are benign and not all result in leaders' or organizations' learning. Systems can grow 'virtuously' or they can regress 'viciously', and it can mean life itself to recognize the difference. In a vicious circle the tensions between opposing 'sides' of the circle (or horns of the dilemmas) become so severe that 'the rope snaps'. In other words, the mutually constraining influence of values-in-tension is lost and the system 'runs away'.[2] Let us return to our nautical metaphor and consider the case of Captain Queeg on the bridge of the USS *Caine* at the height of the typhoon, described in Herman Wouk's *The Caine Mutiny*. Because the storm is clearly in charge of the situation I have begun with the unruly elements (figure 3).

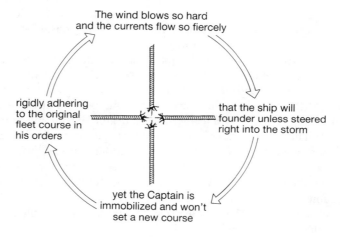

The wind blows so hard
and the currents flow so fiercely

rigidly adhering
to the original
fleet course in
his orders

that the ship will
founder unless steered
right into the storm

yet the Captain is
immobilized and won't
set a new course

Figure 3

Note what happens when the 'tensions snap'. The Captain no longer responds to the typhoon, and the ship's course no longer responds to the danger of capsizing. Yet the arrows feeding *around* the circle continue their vortex of mutual intensification. The more the storm rages, the more the Captain is immobilized, and the more the ship is inundated by the waves, the more rigidly the Captain repeats 'Fleet course is 110°!' Each opposed element is escalating the force of its opposition. The storm and the ship's increasing danger is immobilizing and rigidifying the Captain, while the latter's rigidity is increasing the peril of his ship and the dire effects of the storm, with a vicious circle resulting.

The anthropologist Gregory Bateson called the process *schismogenesis*, 'a growing split in the structure of ideas'. In this example 'the wind blowing' gets *split apart from* 'how the Captain should steer the ship', and the ship's 'imminent foundering' gets split apart from 'the best direction to steer'. The splitting in this story occurred within the paranoid mind of the captain. The Navy dealt with this split by court-martialling the officers who relieved him but finding them innocent.

Note that only an organization that *heals its split* can learn as the US Navy learned in this story. Split systems 'run away' until they self-destruct. This is what would have happened to the *Caine* had not Lieutenant Maryk relieved Captain Queeg and then headed the ship into the wind so as to give its screw some purchase in the water. This action reconnected the snapped nerves of the ship's social system and it survived.

Vicious circles are not usually the products of a psychotic break within a leader or the disintegration of his/her mind. It is more common for leaders to prevent their own disintegration by siding with one clique or faction against the others. In this way they 'save' themselves, yet the organization is severed. Whether or not a leader has personally contributed to the 'growing split in the structure of ideas', the dynamic has a momentum of its own, and the leader may be as one 'tied between wild horses' and is pulled apart psychologically by the 'snapping ropes' at the centre of the vicious circle. Because dilemma is so painful, many managers prefer to rend the system rather than rend themselves, yet this will blind the managers to the polarity they have rejected and may fatally cripple the organization's capacity to learn.

Splitting, then, which precipitates a vicious circle, is an often inadvertent response to painful stress and anxiety from which the individual flees to find support within a clique. This can happen in all kinds of corporate conflict. Automobiles designed and made by even the most dedicated producers will not necessarily delight their intended customers. Workers will not necessarily see the purpose of the organization as identical with their own purposes. Rather than assume a unanimity which is not there, or an ideological antagonism which is everlasting, why not recognize a dilemma whose pain must be endured so that it can be resolved? Resolve means to solve again and again. Just as the helmsman keeps noting errors and correcting them, so dilemmas do not go away but perpetually re-present themselves in changing forms and varieties. Employees may develop (or regress) in their levels of skill. Shareholders may prefer the bid of a corporate raider. Customers may change their tastes or grow more sophisticated with the help of your product. The environment may suddenly deteriorate, the community clamour, the government interfere. The struggle to resolve the claims of different stakeholders in the organization never ends.

Yet, the cybernetic 'virtuous circle' presented here is above all else a form of organizational learning which can accelerate to help us win the learning race or can lag and lose us a prosperous and creative future. It is not just leaders or helmsmen who learn. The whole 'ship' can organize its experience to perform more effectively. Some lessons can be automated, much as a stabilizer corrects for disturbance or a compass shows the course that must now be steered if the original destination is to be attained. But other types of learning are relational, as when the crew of a racing yacht learns to act as one.

Notes

1 Gregory Bateson likened such dilemmas to the croquet party in *Alice in Wonderland* in which Alice had to use a live flamingo as a mallet, hedgehogs as balls and men stooping as hoops. The consequence of using live creatures as instruments was chaotic; see *Steps to an Ecology of Mind*. New York: Ballantine, 1975, p. 256.
2 A good description of systems dynamics is in Draper L. Kauffman, *Systems 1: An Introduction to Systems Thinking*. Minneapolis, Minn.: Future Systems, 1980. A writer who takes 'paradox' very seriously is Robert E. Quinn; see *Beyond Rational Management*. San Francisco, Calif.: Jossey-Bass, 1988.

2
Creating the Culture of the Learning Organization: The Challenge for Learning Leaders

Bob Garratt

The need for a culture of learning in organizations has rarely been greater. Recent man-made disasters show, at public inquiry, that the knowledge, skills, and attitudes necessary to avert such tragedies as the King's Cross Underground fire, or the *Herald of Free Enterprise* ferry sinking, existed within the organization. What did not seem to exist were three crucial elements needed for the organization to collate and use the acquired learning. First, there was no agreed process for codifying and diffusing the learning from one part of the organization to another. Second, there was no climate created in which learning could be encouraged and celebrated. Third, there was little leadership or moral courage from the top managers to exemplify the behaviours necessary for learning to flourish. In short, there was no system, nor culture, by which the organization could learn.

This paper is designed to achieve two ends. First, it reviews the changing scene of the increasingly fashionable topic of 'The Learning Organization' over the past three years since my book of that title. I take as a basic assumption that it is possible and necessary for organizations to learn. In an increasingly turbulent world the ability to learn rapidly and continuously is the key to survival and growth. It is not just the headline-hitting man-made disasters which show the need for this. In business both the rate of corporate collapse and the growth of hostile takeover bids have caused managers to feel the need to create a system of rapid learning for their organizations. Public sector organizations have similar needs as both local and central government agencies

'Creating the Culture of the Learning Organization: The Challenge for Learning Leaders' by Bob Garratt. Original paper written for this publication © Bob Garratt 1988.

are increasingly subjected to the unfamiliar pressure of competition and markets. They too are aware that without the ability to learn rigorously and regularly they will be corporately dead in the foreseeable future.

But the people now becoming aware of the need to learn are often the very people who have created the Non-Learning Organization in the first place. The second objective of this paper looks at the work which is helping transform non-learning top managers into Learning Leaders – the people who can give continuing strategic direction to their organizations because they are capturing its learning fast enough to stay in the game.

This paper is in two parts: first, a reflection on my model of the Learning Organization; second, a look at current trends in developing such organizations, together with some speculation on trends as 'Learning' becomes, literally, a capital issue in organizations. The latter signals to me that 'management' and management education are at the cusp of a catastrophe theory curve, after which it will never be the same. And a good thing too, if the old ways led so easily to those man-made tragedies.

Towards a Climate for the Learning Organization

I am interested in top managers' thinking about the balance between effectiveness and efficiency in organizations. For a long time there has been a dominant trait in management thinking which prized efficiency, above all through cost reduction. I am especially aware of this in the UK companies that have been publicly floated in the last five years. Their strategic thinking has followed a remarkably similar pattern at least with regard to efficiency. Those in the top team have told themselves and others that their prime objective is to 'prove themselves to the City'. This is usually interpreted as the need to increase earnings per share rapidly, by a huge cutting of the business's cost base. This often has a temporarily beneficial effect on the share price, which does not affect it greatly, and then a larger, negative, effect on the customers who start complaining about the deteriorating quality of service or product. Efficiency has routed effectiveness, and public perception of the organization plummets. This is the beginning of another type of man-made disaster and one which will have a much bigger negative effect on earnings per share. One thing needs stressing: it is entirely man-made and can therefore be solved by the same people.

The simplistic belief that, typically, an across-the-board reduction of n percent of the cost base will somehow bring corporate health and happiness is highly seductive and very unwise. Organizations comprise complexes of systems, structures, rules, processes, values, history, cultures, values, symbols, and visions which are to an extent integrated into a whole. A full frontal attack on the cost base alone can easily destroy this integration although this will not necessarily show up in the financial performance figures. These may well improve in the short term, but the ability of divisions and departments to talk to each other and transfer learning will have been reduced or lost entirely. Such lack of communication shows up clearly where the customer meets the organization – at the sales or service point. That is where the complaints start to mount. This is especially true if the newly floated corporation has pushed its corporate advertising hard. Customers are not easily fooled by words if the service performance drops noticeably. They subscribe to Michael Frayn's maxim that 'more means less'. The irony is that the customers learn but the organization rarely does. These are the first steps on the primrose path to the everlasting bonfire.

I am not advocating that costs should never be reduced. That would be absurd. In extreme circumstances it is necessary to prune drastically to encourage new and healthier growth. But most circumstances are not extreme – they sound so only if an unwise top team and its people panic. It is a sounder approach for them to seek a dynamic balance – a gyroscope rather than a seesaw – between effectiveness and efficiency.

Why worry so much about effectiveness? There are two main reasons. First, it is the perceived effectiveness, rather than perceived efficiency, for which the customer pays willingly. This is true of private and public organizations. A perceived highly effective organization will be able to rely on reasonable customer loyalty, and be able to sustain its claim of good value for money long after its perceived cheap competitors are in commercial trouble. Moreover, an organization perceived as effective by its customers (doing the right thing rather than doing things right) will often be able to charge a premium price for its goods or services. This takes time to establish but it is at this point that subtle refining of the service through a focus on efficiency can lead to greater things in terms of products, services, and brands. The most healthy conditions in which to grow a customer-friendly organization are when the effectiveness has been developed first and only then has efficiency been introduced, sensitively so not to upset the customer's perception of quality. This seems to me a sound approach for developing the Learning Organization.

Customer Service and the Learning Organization

The best current examples of learning organizations are those who have faced up to the need to improve dramatically their quality of customer service to ensure their corporate survival and growth. Early examples like Unipart have given way to present role models like SAS and British Airways. What interests me most in these cases is that the top teams created first very clear and simple visions and objectives for their organizations. They have robust bench-marks and measurement systems which the staff can understand and judge themselves against, and they spend hard cash on creating the culture and environment in which the whole organization can learn how to improve effectiveness and efficiency simultaneously.

Characteristic of a successful learning process is that the top team is seen to behave continuously in the way they advocate others should behave – sadly a rare event in my experience. It is easy to mouth the words, much harder to live them. Success derives from the redirection of much top-team time over years, not weeks, into being with and learning from the customer-facing staff. This is crucial as it is where the deep-rooted learning on the operational side of the organization is stored. It is the role of the top managers to encourage learning for codification and diffusion around the organization. When these moments of truth are tapped and turned into a rigorous and regular system of learning, then one goes on to achieve the strategic positioning desired. If it is not tapped and used, authentic learning is cut short in the organization and becomes based on illusions and myths rather than on information. This is the route back the man-made disaster.

Most of the successful 'culture change' (they are much more than that) programmes use a learning process which starts with high-profile, energy- and consciousness-raising processes with the top-team commitment made clear through their continuing presence. They ask for, and get, staff commitment to the vision and objectives of the 'new' organization and then, importantly, delegate the responsibility to learn to the small teams working in real time at their workplaces. This delegation of the responsibility for learning how to do the job effectively and efficiently is highly energizing for individuals and teams. Its business objective is to secure and retain the type of customer needed for the survival of the business. In achieving this the staff roles change from being a passive agent of 'the corporation' to become an active problem-solver working on behalf of the corporation to satisfy the customer's needs. The usually passive employment contract is transformed into a series of changing psychological 'emotional' contracts with both the customer and the organization. This enriches the nature of the work itself.

The processes by which the small teams work and learn in real time to support and criticize themselves constructively rely heavily on Action Learning. This is so well proven that I shall not expand on it here except to say that it is remarkably cost-effective and keeps the staff's energy and commitment levels high over long periods because they become their own organizational problem-solvers. Such enthusiasm can be harmful to an organization if it is not integrated with the learning of the senior managers and the top team. And there's the rub . . .

Developing the Learning Leaders

My work has shown that those who become directors rarely have developed the ability to give direction to their organizations. It is a sad fact that a directorship is often seen by both the bestower and the receiver as a reward for past performance rather than in anticipation of future performance. The directorship is a key role change from the specialist, operational role to a more generalist, strategic one. A director has to have the ability to rise above the daily round of operations and view the changes and the horizon so that he can reframe the direction of the organization to meet those changes. Sadly, this is rarely done in a systematic way and so one ends up with underdeveloped directors.

This is understandable but not excusable. Directors are rarely given any induction into their new role or inclusion into their work-teams. No time or money is usually made available for them to develop themselves into their direction-giving role, so after a six- to nine-month struggle, feeling very uncomfortable in the process, they do what any person would do and return to their previous position of comfort. To be precise, they abdicate the direction-giving role and return, albeit unofficially, to their old, specialist job. They feel great, if somewhat guilty. This has two negative consequences for their organization. On the one hand it means that there is not enough energy, time, or diversity of thinking going into the direction-giving policies and strategies of the organization. A vacuum is created where the focus of organizational learning should be. This means that it cannot cope with the rate of change in its external environment and, consequently, cannot be effective. It will then be perceived as user-unfriendly by the customers and the vicious downward spiral of corporate collapse will be under way.

On the other hand the unofficial return to the comfort of the director's old, specialist, operational job (while keeping all the perks of the directorship) means that the person promoted into that job finds their development blocked by their old boss now sitting on their shoulders. This creates frustration and obstructs learning. In turn, the person so blocked may well regress unofficially to their old job, the regression continues down through the organization. So the search for comfort rather than role at the top of an organization can create the perfect conditions for the non-learning organization. This is unhealthy for both the corporation and individuals involved.

Helping the top team to position itself so that it forms a centre of learning for the organization is a key to creating the climate for the Learning Organization. This focus of learning needs to be at the junction of the realms of effectiveness and efficiency in the organization. My model (figure 1) shows this as the interface between the inner-directed (first-order change) operational cycle of learning – where the focus is on efficiency – and the outer-directed (second-order change) policy cycle of learning – where the focus is on effectiveness.

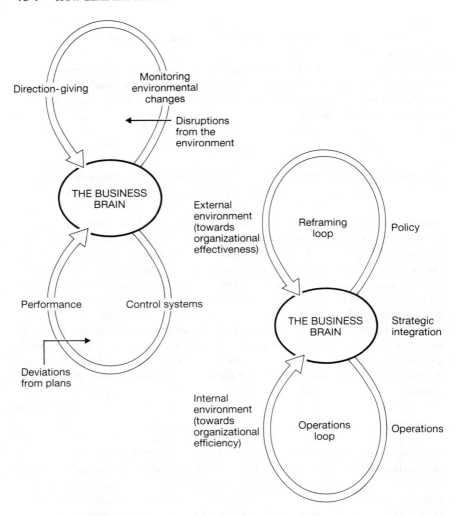

Figure 1 (a) The Learning Organization model
(b) The Learning Organization and the three-level hierarchy

This effectiveness-creating cycle of learning is not just the province of the directors. To survive it is necessary for them to subscribe to Professor Reg Evans's maxim that for any organism to thrive its rate of learning has to be equal to, or greater than, the rate of change in its environment ($L \geqslant C$). As much of the learning is done during those customer-facing 'moments of truth' it is important that the staff are able to contribute to the debate about what is being learned in the organization. In my view the strategic effectiveness/operational efficiency interface, what I call 'The Business Brain', needs regular and rigorous learning inputs from as diverse a community as possible – staff, customers, and total outsiders.

This is not necessarily a comfortable process, particularly in the early stages, so the tendency is to let go of the rigour and regularity and claim that this is not an efficient use of time and money. This is where we came in, and it leads us back to man-made disasters.

Some Ways Forward as the Climate Becomes More Receptive

The top management scene depicted above may seem depressing. It is, and since the publication of my book I have been saddened by the number of directors around the world who have said that the description of the underdeveloped director 'fits me exactly'. However, there is good news in that they are now willing to make such a statement, and to ask for help in developing themselves and their team. Better news is that the tools necessary to create that developmental process already exist, or are under development.

Before I look at the tools I want to talk about the changes in the economic and social climates which are making it easier for directors to pay serious attention to learning in all its aspects in organizations, including their own development. I think there are three discernible trends which are reframing the climate.

Culture Change Pressures

First, the success of culture change programmes are causing many top teams to be questioned by stakeholders and customers as to how they intend to raise the service levels of their organization. This can cause an unhelpful 'me too' reaction which launches pale imitations of the successful interventions. These facile 'Have a nice day' fixed, superficial smile type of programmes give directors the impression of action without the pay-off in customer satisfaction. They fool no one and can create even more negative customer reaction. Interestingly, they are being invested in heavily. The changes wrought in the successful programmes use a complex web of thoughts and processes which require a great deal of time and role-restructuring at the top of an organization. They also need the installation of true management information systems, as distinct from data-generating systems, by which to monitor changes and trends in real time. By doing both it is possible to focus learning and to take strategic action rapidly so that the operations folk can learn how to transfer these directions into efficient service and product.

The Implosion of Middle Management and the Rise of IT

I think we are seeing the end of the 'fat middle' in most of our organizations. During the late 1970s and early 1980s we saw an implosion of the workforce as the nature of future work was redefined. Simultaneously, but much less clearly, we saw the same implosion of the direction-givers. My crude guess is that between 40 and 50 per cent of these went in the decade 1978–88. Unfortunately, we have not been as precise in determining their future work and currently have a messy residue of non-teams trying to run most of our organizations. This type of director changes job every two years on average in search of comfort and advancement, and seems to be the lifeblood of many head-hunters. The consequence of this continuous job-hopping is to further the non-learning organization because they are rarely around when the consequences of their plans come home to roost.

The implosion of the middle management level has taken a long time to come but is now under way, and this will help with the underdeveloped directors as the trend will push them and the customer-facing staff closer together to mutual advantage. This is happening in two ways. First, the culture change programmes are causing the top and bottom levels to talk, debate, and learn from each other in novel ways. The resulting feedback systems mean that each level has a vested interest in playing their role better. Interestingly, the delegation of the responsibility to learn back to the work-face calls for a level of first-line management to take rapid decisions and live with them. So we are seeing the renaissance of the supervisor along with the loss of many middle managers. Second, the rise and rise of Information Technology systems is making the desire of top managers to monitor real-time trends at the customer interface a reality. It is possible in manufacturing industry, retailing, or financial services to track trends in real time. In some industries it has gone much further so that it is possible to see individual performance clearly. In financial services one can view the performance of, say, traders on a computer screen which can be seen by other traders. Such bylines of good traders are celebrated or criticized semi-publicly and can form the basis for powerful learning individually and corporately. The continuing installation of IT equipment would suggest that this will be a growing trend for better or worse in organizations.

The most noticeable aspect of both changes are that they diminish the present role of middle managers dramatically. If they are in the organization to amplify or attenuate messages vertically or horizontally, then the changes mentioned suggest redundancy as the top and bottom come together to learn. This process changes the perception of the shape of organizations. If the standard view of an organization is as a pyramid (with the customer hanging somewhere off the end of the pyramid), the customer-service view is of an inverted pyramid with the customer paramount above it (figure 2). To link

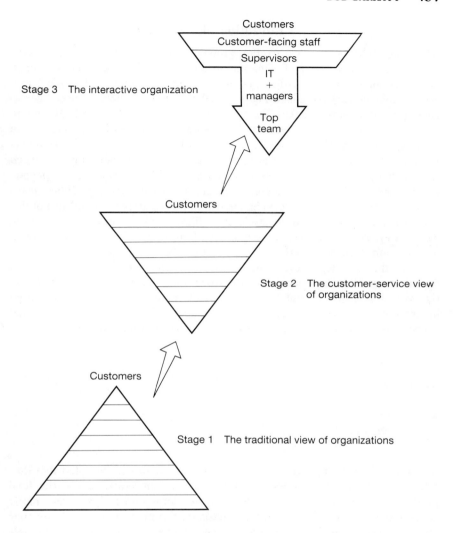

Figure 2 The transformation of the organization hierarchy

effectively the direction-givers with the customer-facing staff it is necessary to reduce the number of levels in the hierarchy, usually to four including the supervisors. When true Information Technology is added to this mix then the final shape of the organization is more like a squat arrow rather than the traditional elongated pyramid. So far this does seem to lead to much more effective and efficient organizations.

The Revaluing of Learning

The third change relates to the growing awareness of the commercial importance of capturing and using the products of the learning processes in an organization. I am not talking specifically about education and training as I assume that all work has a learning potential. The issue is that it is rarely seen as such and so investment payback is not expected of it. Matters are beginning to move quickly here. Most organizations are unbelievably lax in the codification of what they learn. Even in the R&D laboratories it is the product or service at the end of the process which is valued rather than the many things learned during that process. The only asset we have capable of learning is our people, regardless of what the artificial intelligence proponents say. They learn continuously unless we create a climate where this is not rewarded. Most of this learning is discarded or stored carelessly in files, portfolios, or disks beyond the light of day. Yet in these lies the accumulated problem-solving experience of an organization. Can one codify and capitalize on them?

Seen through legal eyes these are the 'intellectual property' of an organization. The very mention of the word 'intellectual' can frighten the life out of business people, but that is a measure of just how far we have to go before the notion of the Learning Organization takes root. This intellectual property is made manifest through five major types of legal device:

- patent
- copyright
- registered design
- trademark
- servicemark.

These form the trade secrets of an organization. It should be noted that they rely as much on the processes of learning (the know-why) as on the final product or service (made manifest as the know-how). They are rarely considered on a regular and rigorous basis on top management, nor are they often protected legally. Yet rights can be established over an organization's investment in its learning and these – its intellectual property rights – are a source of increasing interest and action by forward-thinking directors.

This growth of interest in the intellectual property of an organization is seen currently in the excitement over the acquisition and protection of brands. The establishment of brands, particularly global brands, is a long-term investment in the learning processes and products of a business. But it is rarely seen like that. Now that companies like Grand Metropolitan and RHM have valued their brands at £588 million and £678 million respectively, there seems to be a race to get brands valued as assets on the balance sheet. The wisdom of this has yet to be tested but its highlighting of organizational learning and development processes is enlightening.

It is also reflected in the growing interest in valuing information in relation to markets. As the worlds of trade, commerce, and manufacture become real-time dependent and, consequently, highly interactive, the need for high-quality information grows apace. But this demands an ability to have time to think, and then ask discriminating questions. Put another way, the top team needs to have time to be wise. There are many people around who are clever but few who are wise. The clever ones can come up with the answers, but it is the wise ones who ask the discriminating questions on which they can be clever. The subtle use of information to gain strategic and competitive advantage will be of growing interest to top managers in their learning organizations.

Learning as a Capital Investment

I hope I have shown that the climate in which it is possible for organizations to learn has changed for the better. The breakthrough in valuing brands and intellectual property is leading slowly to a re-evaluation of education and training within the organization. Traditionally these have been seen as an annual budget spend which could be adjusted rapidly depending on trading conditions. Now there are signs of some organizations thinking of their learning as a capital spend. This makes sense of the current thinking on brands and intellectual property and can be extended into the growing need for creative researchers and developers. If all of this is then set in the demographic context of a negative birth rate for the last twenty years, the need to put a high priority on investing in organizational learning is seen to be urgently necessary. Moreover, it is far beyond the present world of training and personnel management as it is now becoming a prime responsibility of line managers from top to bottom of the organization. The need to reframe our expectations of training and personnel management is being forced by the growing demand for Learning Organizations.

The Development of the Top Managers to Free the Organizational Learning

My recent work has encouraged me greatly in the belief that top managers are increasingly keen to accept their policy-formulating and strategy-implementing roles, with the reciprocal that they keep their hands out of the operational, day-to-day, world. Persuading top managers to be comfortable with having time to think, observe, reflect, travel, and talk with customers and competitors, rather than to keep taking action is possible. It is often difficult, but it can be done. It is tricky because top managers often have invested twenty of thirty years of their working life doing things that do not require a great deal of generalist thinking. To be expected to spend most of one's time observing trends and thinking strategically is a learnable skill, but it does require a lot of behavioural unlearning (of perhaps decades) before the new role can be learned.

The good news is that there is a growing body of knowledge, particularly in the UK, about how to help such people become comfortable with their more thoughtful role. This ranges from the careful identification of thinking processes appropriate for particular types of problem-solving, such as Jerry Rhodes and Sue Thame's work, through to the high-tech use of interactive computers to allow intuition and logic to help model creative policy and strategy-making, such as Tony Hodgson's work. At the broader organizational level Gunnar Walstam and Rolf Hickmann are pursuing intriguing ways of redescribing the organization's learning in terms of the patterns of sales and development within it.

The field of management and management education seems to be in the process of being redefined so that survival and regrowth through focusing on systems of rapid and public learning are given greater importance. This is why we need Learning Leaders in the 1990s. I am happy to say that I think we will have them.

3
Developing Tomorrow's Leaders: What Role for the MBA?

Peter J. Williamson

Imagine yourself standing on top of the Empire State Building, trying to direct the New York traffic. It is through this exercise that I have asked a class of MBAs sitting in a 100-seat lecture theatre, eyes closed, to begin to understand what being at the top of a company can feel like. Full of ideas and energy, responsible for corporate survival as well as success, the top managers are all-powerful, yet powerless. They can only dimly perceive what individuals are doing on the ground. They can't make much of a contribution by doing it themselves. They must choose between communication via a huge sign with few specifics (we sometimes call it a 'mission statement'), or through the many layers of management on each successive floor below. The latter carries the well-known risks of reinterpretation and degradation of the signals at every stage.

These problems exist, albeit sometimes with lesser severity, at many levels of managment. They arise from the fact that, as the old adage goes, 'management is the art of getting other people to do all the work'. This paper explores the role of MBA education in better equipping managers to deal with these leadership issues. It does so in the context of the changing leadership requirements as we move through the 1990s into the twenty-first century.

'Developing Tomorrow's Leaders: What Role for the MBA?' by Peter Williamson. Original paper written for this publication © Peter Williamson 1991.

Yesterday's Heroes

The turn of the decade has seen the collapse of many of the highest-profile corporate 'successes' of the 1980s. These fast-growing, warm-weather flowers succumbed to the first cold snap. With them went many of their leaders, disappearing into the ranks of yesterday's heroes.

Of course there have always been corporate leaders on the rise and fall. Looking back, however, it is clear that the cult of individualism was a hallmark of a large section of the corporate world in the 1980s. Individuals loomed larger than life from the covers of popular business and news magazines, the companies they led often left behind in the shadows. In a frenzy of buying and selling, the identity of the company was often unclear anyway. Some of them represented little more than financial shells for borrowed funds.

These leaders were men and women with financial prowess, backed by the power of money. Their skills were not those of the patient paddy-farmer. Instead, they were experts at identifying undervalued assets and underutilized resources. They 'ran the numbers' and then made the next acquisition. Their challenge was not so much directing the traffic from the top of the Empire State, but piloting their helicopter, landing on the next corporate edifice to plant their flag. Their leadership style was tough and independent. 'Give me a business, any business, and I'll make its assets sweat' was their catch-cry.

These individuals did play an important role in improving corporate efficiency. They shook out much of the waste of unnecessary co-ordination and compromise which had resulted from unwieldy diversification during the 1970s. They scaled back the cosy corporate headquarters with their huge staffs. They were highly effective in leading small paratrooper teams, avoiding or cutting through the mass of bureaucracy below.

For business schools they threw down the challenge that academics had vastly over-complicated the task of management. What the leader required was a few simple rules and the decisiveness of the 'one-minute manager'. They had the advantage that these basic messages were easier to communicate: people believed and backed them.

For all this, the 'lone-gun' leadership concept turned out to have flaws. Probably the most obvious was the discontinuity of succession when the lone gun tired. Problems also accumulated over time as the organization lost empathy with its leader or was left behind in the pace of change. Even more important, however, was that the powerful ideas of the lone guns proved fragile to a change in the environment. While perfectly adapted to the needs of the Wild West expansion phase, this kind of leadership was ill-suited to sort out the tangled traffic congestion in the complex, interconnected corporate city it had so successfully sprouted.

The Era of the Network Leader

In September 1989 *The Economist* published the results of a survey that asked British executives which companies they most admired. At the top of the list was Shell Transport and Trading, followed by Glaxo, Marks & Spencer, J. Sainsbury, and Bass.

Generalization is always hazardous. It is fair to say, however, that one of the characteristics all these companies share is their well-developed and complex teams of interdependent management. They are led by some outstanding people, who emphasize the building of teams, and share an understanding of and commitment to the product and the business. Financial controls are important, but they are carefully designed to achieve the right balance of control, decentralized responsibility, and motivation. These companies are not in the business of lone-gun financial engineering; if anything the criticism is that they are more conservative than their bankers.

Looking back into the history of corporate America, Germany, and Britain, Alfred Chandler finds that the most successful enterprises have been those who have developed mechanisms to exploit 'system-based' advantages. These come from co-ordinating a complex managerial network to exploit the potential benefits of scale across a company's total sales volume worldwide and share the accumulated learning from all their activities and sites without sinking the organization under a burden of excess overhead.[1]

Leadership capabilities to manage this complex co-ordination are now more important than ever. The linkages between a company and it subcontractors, suppliers, and distributors are steadily becoming more important as firms strive for increased focus and the cost flexibility of outworking, while trying to improve the speed of response to their customers. International companies are seeking to get greater leverage from global reach by transferring learning across the organization and concentrating research and development in a series of 'centres of excellence' within their firm. The rise of a wide variety of strategic alliances is even blurring the definition of competitors and partners; sometimes a single outsider can be both friend and foe in respect of different arms of the same company. Companies are also being asked to take more account of their responsibility to the natural environment and the local communities of which they are part, and to match these with the sometimes conflicting pressures from shareholders. In short, boundaries within and outside the firm are becoming increasingly less well defined.

With these needs in mind, Dick Giordano, chairman and chief executive of the BOC Group, in his 1990 Stockton Lecture at the London Business School, summed up the successful leader-manager as we move through the 1990s and beyond as 'a person who can live with above average ambiguity and manage sometimes conflicting objectives'. He spoke of tomorrow's leaders as people with the skills to encourage networking inside and outside their companies, who could engender an organization where management teams actively contributed to other parts of the company even where this had no immediate reward in their own profit numbers, while at the same time accepting decentralized responsibility for delivering against their business unit's bottom line.

This new kind of network leader will ned to be comfortable with the idea of replacing 'I' with 'We'. They will be individuals with excellent process and people skills. They will not only need to be able to live with ambiguity, but to manage it proactively. They will not be conquerors, but rather experts in building a network to access a wide range of specialist capabilities and developing the co-ordination necessary to deliver quality and service reliably to the customer without things falling through the cracks.

Perhaps above all, the network leader will need to have a broadly based and integrated view of how the parts of a business fit together, where the frictions are likely to arise and how the interfaces can be profitably managed. A knowledge of the interaction between different functional perspectives, rather than specialist expertise in one of them, will be key. The ability to step into the shoes of an American, European, or Japanese businessman, instead of being bound to a single cultural norm, will be critical. Finally, there will be a premium on managers who can put all of this complex, interlocking detail into a strategic perspective on where the corporate colony of individual cells should be trying to go.

Enter the MBA

The desire to improve business leadership through formal management education goes back a long way. Forerunners of the modern MBA appeared in the late 1890s in the *Handelshochschulen* in Germany and schools of business in the USA. Cologne established a school concentrating on the basic tools of accounting, finance, and business economics in 1898. The Wharton School of Commerce and Finance had already begun offering undergraduate courses in these subjects in 1891.

The first graduate business degree was launched by Dartmouth's Amos Tuck School of Administration and Finance in 1900. Harvard opened its Graduate School of Business Administration in 1908 and by 1914 had gone beyond accounting, finance, and economics to offer courses in marketing and business policy, the latter aiming to 'develop an approach to business from the top-management point of view.'[2]

During the 1950s and 1960s the number of American MBA graduates doubled and then tripled, and with rapid growth in enrolments and new institutions entering the fray, concerns were expressed about quality assurance. A systematic review of both undergraduate and graduate programmes was sponsored by the Ford and Carnegie foundations in 1959. These reports contained scathing criticisms of lax standards and 'remedial' courses. They called for all students to take a core including 'rigorous analytical, quantitative, and behavioural components' and for the elimination of industry-specific and vocational electives. Backed by the funding of their major foundations, these recommendations were to set the direction of management education for the next twenty-five years.[3]

It was into the aftermath of Ford and Carnegie that business education in Britain was launched. Lord Franks in 1963 recommended the establishment of two business schools: one associated with the University of London, the other with the University of Manchester. They naturally took care to incorporate the lessons of American experience in their curricula and approaches.

What kind of influence, then, did an MBA à la Ford and Carnegie have in shaping the potential leaders who passed through? Certainly a solid grounding in analytical, quantitative, and behavioural approaches can't have been a bad thing. There was, however, an inherent danger. As the functions and disciplines further developed their own individual bodies of business theory and technique, they might grow apart. The integrated 'top management perspective', which Harvard so clearly set as an objective as far back as 1914, might be lost. There was also a risk that, in a world of examinations and 'right answers', the development of process skills and the exercise of imprecise judgement might get short shrift; that in the process of equipping highly competent business analysts a generation of lone guns might be produced, people who would rather solve a problem themselves instead of managing the efforts of others to solve an interconnected set of problems, people who were more comfortable 'running the numbers' than managing ambiguity.

As we entered the 1990s, there was growing criticism that business schools were turning out individuals more suited to backroom analysis than business leadership. In Europe in particular, where the MBA will not be a widespread middle-management qualification for the foreseeable future, its contribution to shaping potential top managers is critical. Given its history, the new capabilities required of tomorrow's network leaders are presenting the MBA with a major challenge. None the less, it is a challenge leading business schools are preparing to meet.

Rising to the Educational Challenge

No course of education or training can create some of the basic qualities required in a leader. Nor can it provide a substitute for the most realistic of all management learning laboratories, the company. In recent interviews I conducted with senior executives, however, many pointed out that some of the core skills and perspectives required of tomorrow's leaders are very difficult to acquire in a day-to-day corporate environment.

Despite increasing use of cross-functional postings by leading companies, it is difficult for most managers to develop a true breadth of vision: an appreciation of the full range of managerial issues and an understanding of how activities and functions fit together conflict and require trade-offs. Most are promoted through the lower and middle ranks by demonstrating task-orientated success. By the time they recognize the need to acquire a broader, integrated perspective, the Peter Principle is already at work.

Successful managers generally develop strong empathy with the company culture and a natural commitment to 'the way we do things around here'. If they have learned only by immersion and have known no other way, it is difficult to maintain an awareness of alternative approaches and successfully to nurture experimentation and debate when they come to lead an organization. Managing change is not a skill that is well developed during a career climbing the ladder in most organizations.

Finally, it is sometimes difficult in the corporate environment to find low-risk opportunities to develop some of the necessary practical skills. As one manager put it, 'There aren't too many risk-free opportunities to develop the necessary negotiation skills in our business; you can hardly let them practice on an acquisition or with 4,000 staff at Heathrow.'

One of the important contributions of an effective MBA, therefore, will be in helping to fill these gaps, complementing the leadership skills which high-potential individuals can develop through day-to-day management experience.

I believe that, to achieve its full potential contribution to building the capabilities required by the business leaders of tomorrow, an MBA best starts out, not with ready-packaged solutions, but by building awareness of a broad range of emerging managerial issues. These issues, like managing international linkages and diverse cultures, thriving amid the ambiguity of modern network organizations, delivering total quality and service, and managing change then provide context within which rigorous concepts and management tools can be developed. While the issues will evolve and change over time, an MBA graduate who has learned the tool-kit in the context of realistic applications will have the motivation and confidence to apply it in the future. By releasing concepts and techniques from their textbook confines, they can become part of the day-to-day management approach. By developing the different perspectives of individual functions and disciplines within the context of common issues, the integrated and strategic viewpoint required by tomorrow's leaders will be seen by MBA graduates as the norm.

In parallel, the needs of the network leader will demand from MBA education greater emphasis on a range of process skills. These range from negotiation and presentation to building teams and designing budgeting systems which properly motivate as well as measure.

Last, though far from least, an MBA for the business leaders of tomorrow will have to be unashamedly international in its outlook: international in its materials, drawing on internationally experienced faculty, and with the opportunity for students to study and work overseas during the course.

This is a tall order, and yet, one further ingredient is required: a change in the way tomorrow's potential leaders learn.

Tomorrow's Leaders at Play

Given the many years most of us have spent in classrooms, recent research suggesting that teaching is a very inefficient means of communication comes as quite a shock. An important study in the early 1980s, for example, found that at best 40 per cent of the material taught was received by the student and in most situations it was only 25 per cent.[4]

With the need to expose future leaders to ways of structuring the complex issues of the modern, international organization where cause and effect are separated in time and place, traditional teaching methods look even more inadequate. Successful initiatives with a new breed of learning environments at the Royal Dutch Shell Group, London Business School, and MIT suggest that tomorrow's business leaders will learn through play.[5]

A popular game is the People's Express Airline Simulator, which is a chance to run the discount airline through computer, rather than simulate flight. In the hands of a team of functional experts – marketing, operations, finance, personnel – successive day-to-day decisions are made, supported by a wealth of management information on every aspect of the business, the kind of data most executives only dream about. After eight to ten simulated quarterly periods this crack team has usually achieved a spectacular corporate collapse; spiralling down in a vicious cycle of past decisions coming home to roost, marketing promises which operations can't deliver, competitor retaliation, financial constraints, and rookie flight and cabin crews working untenable hours.

The lessons are salutary. After rethinking their strategy, their interaction as a team, the necessity of interpreting short-term data in context, and the need to take an overview of the entire business and its competition, the players gradually learn to run this company successfully and to embed their functional viewpoints in a viable growth plan. They have taken the first steps towards becoming the kind of network leaders future business will demand.

New learning techniques of this kind continue to be developed. They are deploying new technology and multi-media approaches to relax the classroom constraints in simulating reality. They are enabling more 'learner-directed learning' where the participants have an increased say in the agenda. They provide settings for team rather than individualistic learning. Finally, they are putting the tools for learning in the hands of the learners so that these can be used to explore issues and concepts outside the formal sessions.

Conclusion

Tomorrow's leaders will need a different mix of capabilities than yesterday's lone-gun heros. The era of the network leader is unfolding. The premium will be on managers with the capabilities to exploit the benefits of international co-ordination of activities, build interdependent management teams, and manage above-average ambiguity. Excellent process and people skills be rewarded: the catch-cry will be 'We' not 'I'. Rather than being outstanding functional specialists, leaders will be distinguished by their understanding of how to integrate the different parts of a complex business and profitably manage the frictions and interfaces. As internal and external boundaries of the firm start to merge, they will need to be able to give strategic direction to a loose corporate colony of internal business units, external suppliers, and distributors, franchisees, alliance partners, governments, and local communities who respond to persuasion and negotiation rather than decree. As if that were not enough, tomorrow's business leader will need to see the world through the eyes of cultures other than his or her own.

The MBA has an important role to play in complementing the capabilities that can be acquired through day-to-day business experience. It can contribute to building awareness of a broad range of managerial issues, developing rigorous concepts and functional tools within the context of these issues so that an integrated perspective becomes the natural way of thinking among its graduates, and laying down a solid grounding in process skills. At an international business school the individual can also begin to process of stepping outside a single culture to develop a facility to cross borders and cultures with the intellectual freedom too few have so far achieved.

To fulfil this potential the MBA too must change. Leading business schools are taking up the challenge. But change is never easy. Integration and specialization need to be carefully balanced, and for instititutions with proud teaching traditions it is difficult to come to terms with the idea that, after all, our most effective contributions may lie in using new technologies to help tomorrow's business leaders learn their required skills through play.

Notes

1   A. D. Chandler, *Scale and Scope: The Dynamics of Industrial Capitalism* (Belknap, Cambridge, Mass., 1990).

2 M. Copeland, *And Mark an Era: The Story of Harvard Business School* (Harvard University Press, Boston, 1958), p. 43.
3 R. Gordon and B. Howell, *Higher Education for Business* (Columbia University Press, New York, 1959).
4 J. Holt, *How Children Learn*, rev. edn (Delacorte, New York, 1983).
5 See A. P. De Geus, 'Planning as learning', *Harvard Business Review*, March–April 1988, pp. 70–4.

Chapter 17
Leadership through Outdoor Training

Introduction

Jay Conger's earlier comment that creativity is best inculcated through 'planned playfulness' and days of unconventional activity (see chapter 14) applies also to many other attributes of leadership such as initiative, motivation, and risk-taking, and rapid decision-making.

Outdoor training is the best and most widely used example of the 'unconventional' options open to the management trainer. It provides an experience so far well outside the scope of most managers and professionals, which promotes not only individual intiative but effective team-building. As John Ridgeway comments in the profile provided by INSEAD's Manfred Kets de Vries: 'Inhibitions break down and people talk, real person to real person, rather than the fellow who looks in the shaving mirror in the morning and puts on the face he wants the world to see.' This leads to a better self-awareness, and thence the vital confidence so valued by Benton and Sadler (see chapter 14).

Yet the natural benefits of exposing potential leaders to 'yet another huge set of variables to the overall larder of experience' does not let the programme designer off the hook. David Charlton warns that outdoor training is pretty useless as a development aid unless linked to learning objectives and realistic expectations agreed between the provider, participant, and sponsoring organization.

In this sense, outdoor training is not distinct from any other of the imaginative learning activities in the management trainer's portfolio including secondments, sabbaticals, and distance learning. All have a huge potential to change attitudes, shift values, open the mind, and encourage lateral thinking. But the transference of this learning will benefit the company only if it is built into a logical and very carefully conceived career-development plan.

As Charlton concludes: 'A manager who returns with a nugget of useful learning . . . and then finds himself denied the opportunity, authority, and resources to implement his learning, will be disappointed . . . The experience will devalue the message as well as the medium and will discredit the management development department.'

1
Developing Leaders Using the Outdoors

David C. Charlton

The use of the outdoors as an educational 'resource' has a long and complex history in Western culture. From Rousseau to Kurt Hahn, from Baden-Powell to Sir John Hunt's recently published *In Search of Adventure*, the belief is strong that there is scarcely a single social ill or physical problem which would not respond to a course of treatment in the 'outdoors'. Two distinct and contradictory views of nature seem to be apparent in this. According to one view, the natural environment is seen as threatening and dangerous: something to be conquered and overcome. Some providers of outdoor education still claim that 'if you can climb that rock, my son, you'll be a leader of men'. The other view emphasizes our affinity with nature and stresses empathy with rather than struggle against, collaboration rather than competition. Both attitudes are deeply rooted and appear in many instances to be not contradictory but complementary.

As long ago as 1762 Rousseau was urging parents to send their children into the countryside 'so that they may regain, amid the fields, the vigour they have lost in the unwholesome air of places too thickly populated'. (Emile pp. 13–14) He believed that exposure to the natural world and its extremes would 'harden [children's] bodies to the changes of the seasons, climates, and elements, as well as to hunger, thirst, and fatigue'. Later in the same century Wordsworth said that he grew up in Cumberland 'fostered alike by beauty and by fear' (Prelude line 301). Reverence and awe in the face of nature seems to have led 'muscular Christians' like Robert Baden-Powell to see exposure to the risks of the natural world as potentially character-forming. In Scouting, as in Kurt Hahn's Outward Bound schools, a dose of exposure to untamed wilderness was

'Developing Leaders Using the Outdoors' by David Charlton. Original paper written for this publication © David Charlton 1990.

suggested as a cure for everything from masturbation to flat-footedness and 'bad citizenship'.

It is the empathetic rather than the combative approach to the natural environment that I wish to stress, an approach perhaps more in sympathy with future leadership requirements. For present purposes I will define the outdoors simply in terms of the United Kingdom, although I am aware that outdoor development, expeditions and programmes for young people as well as senior management to high mountain and wilderness areas are available around the world and will become more so in the future as our environmental awareness increases towards managed action.

Consider the geography of the UK: bordering the Atlantic and the Euro-Asian land mass, sitting midway between the North Pole and the Equator and influenced by a variety of climate, geology, and topography without equal in so small an area. Our large cities are all within a short drive of a national park (though we might remember that even city centres can provide a rich and varied outdoor experience). No nursery, theatre, laboratory, or classroom was ever thus equipped for learning.

However, if we are thinking about the potential of this environment for the development of leadership, we have something more in mind than a holiday in beautiful surroundings. It is on the imaginative and managed use of this environment for development that I want to focus. Other variables can be added to the potential of the outdoors each capable of significantly changing outdoor environments and thus the opportunity for learning:

- the changing seasons and the weather
- the ebb and flow of tides
- the timetables of day and night, the sun and the moon
- the habits of living creatures and the rhythm of growing things.

Now we have increased the index of possibilities many times over.
Two further variables may be added. The conditions and rhythms of the outdoors can be modified infinitely for learning purposes by:

- the orchestration of structured intervention and creativity
- the human reaction to the unfolding experience.

The Orchestration

We can manage the experience to reflect any required emphasis to heighten or soften the learning from the most obtuse to the most obscure or subtle. It is the business of outdoor experience providers to orchestrate the material to greatest effect. We can do this through a multiplicity of rules, constraints, conditions, games and exercises involving new circumstances, changing one goal-post for

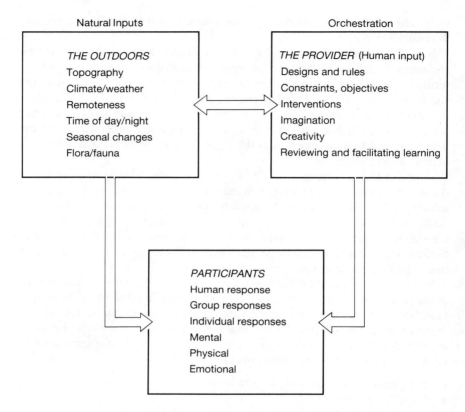

Figure 1   Inputs to outdoor experiential learning

another while shifting objectives and emphasis by regulating data. But it is not just the orchestrated interventions that enhance the use of the outdoor for leadership development. The orchestration of creativity and imagination applied carefully can transform experience into an indelible memory. The use of theatre and the creative arts can support the passage of learning by harnessing the imagination. The perceptive provider will always want to be on the look-out for opportunities to synthesize the naturally variable outdoors, the regulatory interventions of management designs, and the synergy of serendipity.

An example may illustrate the point. Pairs of walkers during a leadership programme met members of a circus who encountered the paired participants on the walk route in a geomantic setting and started to demonstrate their skills (juggling, clowning, acrobatics, conjuring, fire-eating, etc.). Before long the participants became students in the separate skills. Within a very short time and with no threat or appraisal they quickly mastered the rudiments of some circus skills. Later the delegates combined their new-found skills and, joining with the circus people, became a troupe which entertained late-night revellers as they left the cinema and pubs in Exeter. As a start to a leadership development programme it was a spontaneous success. Confidence and risk-taking developed among the trainees until a first step towards public performance was taken in new skills. Mistakes were made, but the significance of these went unnoticed. This event was partly orchestrated but illustrates the effective use of creative synergy in learning.

The Human Response

Whatever way the outdoors is managed for experiential learning and leadership development the human response will add yet another huge set of variables to the overall larder of experience. The intellectual, emotional, and physical response of an individual will change and change again in relation to other individuals' changing responses, or as groups interact with other groups. The permutations of the learning experience are as endless as they are powerful in outdoor programmes.

Reviews

At appropriate stages reviews are usually held after completion of various stages of the outdoor experience. This is often followed by replanning and then retesting. The test vehicles change but the behaviour attitudes and style of leadership are diversely tested throughout the cyclical model. Providers conduct their reviews in a variety of ways. At Celmi we spend most of our review time looking at the good news so that good practice can be actioned, assessed, and amplified.

Poor practice is certainly not ducked but dwelling on the downside becomes unnecessary and counter-productive in a well-managed learning experience. It is more important to identify strengths that can be built on rather than review perceived weaknesses. Too many groups are led by leaders who focus on failure and fallibility rather than identify the good intent and successes of subordinates so that these may be nurtured.

Celmi utilizes imagination and drama not least in its simple venues (farmhouse, sailing barges) but in its interpretation of the outdoors and the creative enhancement of the total experience. The effect is to cause clients to be comfortably surprised away from more structured thinking and experiment with their own creativity and behaviour in a non-threatening and supportive environment as they learn.

This is a subliminal and effective process for developing creative leadership and is essential if leaders are going to have a chance of creating new futures and goals towards holistic values.

Learning is carried by experience into the mind via a number of routes. Learning that enters by two or more routes is likely to be enriched by a better understanding. Stereo music is better than mono recordings but neither is as good as being at the Festival Hall. The routes include:

the mouth – for things we drink and eat
the ears – for the sounds we hear (words, music)
the eyes – for the visible things and movement we see
the nose – for the things we smell
the nerves – for the things we touch
the sixth sense for the intuitive insights.

The more routes to the mind the better, so learning in multiple combinations will be enriched. If a piece of awareness is not comfortably accommodated or stored in the mind it may go on to the heart to become part of our emotions. Sensitive facilitating should minimize the destructive potential of emotion while maximizing the positive attributes and enabling emotion to be separated from content.

What is described here is essentially a holistic approach to leadership development using the outdoors. Future leaders will certainly need to be aware of wider issues rather than simply addressing the bottom line, and people will come to expect leadership from those whose values address the individual, the task, the group, and the environment.

It is not sufficient to the aware; awareness itself needs to be managed. The stockbroker in Tokyo may be aware of the movements of international commodities while having insufficient understanding of the effects such movements have on the lives of others or how they may finally respond.

The Learning Experience

Just as the managed outdoor experience itself is rich with learning opportunities so the skilled facilitator will enable participants to discover things for themselves. Discovery born of one's own curiosity is more relevant to learning and leadership if one is able to own it and test it against personal circumstance. Experiential learning invites the head, the heart, and the body to engage with the experience, thus reinforcing the learning. Many a review session has failed because the tutor has overtaught at the expense of enabling students to learn. Some facilitators chew over the designated messages, creating an indigestible pulp of analysis which falls off the flip-chart.

Transference of Learning

A crucial part of the planning of an outdoor programme is the setting of the objectives. These need to be established and understood by the provider so that the outdoor experience can be targeted with optimum orchestration to obtain best results. The outcome could exceed expectations by a wide margin but therein lies a trap. There is little point in sending a group or an individual on an outdoor learning experience unless the likely outcome has been discussed and expectations broadly agreed. The providers of outdoor development have a responsibility to agree, in broad terms, realistic expectations between the provider, the delegate (participant), and the sponsoring organization (client). This agreement is an essential part of the planning process. A manager who returns with a nugget of useful learning which he sees as being relevant to his situation in the workplace, and then finds himself denied the opportunity, authority, and resources to implement his learning, will be disappointed. He will in turn go on to disappoint himself, his superiors, and subsequently his peers and subordinates. The experience will devalue the message as well as the medium and will discredit the management development department within the organization and leave the provider up the creek without a paddle, unable to deliver. It will have been a wasted investment.

Personal Action Plans

It is essential for there to be some structure for participants to enable them to transfer the learning to the workplace. This also provides a tangible next step towards attaining the benefits and can help satisfy cynics and those who manage training budgets aimed at cost-effective short-term pay-offs. Most of the leadership learning on a good outdoor programme will probably be picked up implicitly. Explicit learning once it has been articulated tends to lose its value if it moves from understanding to information. Most leadership should enter the bloodstream, not the handbook. However, explicit action plans have a practical application. Trainers and superiors can offer support and open doors to enable intended actions to be implemented. The delegate himself has a practical plan of implementation. Most action plans fail because (1) they were not really wanted by the sponsors, (2) they were too large (insight gained under a street lamp on the way to Damascus lies in the region of miracles and mirages, and is usually followed by a blinding crash), (3) they were irrelevant or inappropriate to the individual.

Any home work delegates have to do in an action plan is likely to gain their attention if (1) it is chosen by them, (2) it is exciting, interesting, and fun to do, (3) it is clearly attainable and of obvious personal and corporate benefit. Given these criteria, the smaller the content of the action plan the higher the success rate will be. Grander plans which seek to change personality and corporate culture overnight will plummet to the ground.

Action plans which play to strengths should be encouraged. We find the following structure (or something like it) helpful.

1 *Data* Name? Address? Company? Course? Date? etc.
2 *What?* Headline.
3 *Why?* Why are you going to do it? What is the benefit of your intended Action Plan?
4 *Who?* Apart from yourself *who* will benefit?
5 *Who else?* Who else needs to be informed of your intended Action Plan?
6 *How?* Briefly describe the specific physical or mechanical processes you intend to implement to carry your action from your head to its target.
7 *When?* Start time? Finish time?
8 *Authority* Do you have the authority to implement your plan?
9 *Resources* Consider the resources you might need for the proper implementation of your action plan:
   time resources
   material resource
   financial resources
   personal resource.
10 *Hurdles* Anticipate what might become a problem.
11 *Minder* Would you like someone (boss, colleague) to take an interest in your plan?
12 *HWYMYS3MT* How will you measure your success in 3 months' time?
13 *Failure to deliver* What is the cost to the task, the group, and the individual if you fail to deliver?

Conclusion

The well-managed outdoor programme for leadership development is probably the best resource available and has progressed from attempts to develop the whole child (Rousseau) to the whole teenager (Baden-Powell) to the whole officer (Kurt Hahn). Now we need a whole manager who can lead. From listening, talking, and watching the several hundred leaders (male and female) and some of their followers who kindly gave their time to Celmi over the years, I detect some emergent trends and desires which are summarized below and which we are now starting to address in our leadership programmes.

Leaders will become the guardians of our values and will be appointed willy-nilly for their ability to protect those values. The values in question will perhaps become core human values. We will witness a decade or two when individuals become more accountable and take more responsibility for their own destinies. Many individuals will seek personal enrichment to supplement education and career experience and the ability to manage their growing holistic awareness of environmental and human issues.

They will wish to follow firm humanistic leadership in these respects. Some characteristics for leadership will be a shift from solving skills to coping skills as people get fed up as the technological vortex increases and leaves people out of touch with each other and with themselves. The face of perpetual change will increase as the underdeveloped continents develop their markets and productivity. The leader will be caught in a conceptual trilemma (a three-cornered dilemma) between

- ideologies and shifting value systems
- practical and technological advancements and the management of material resources
- the relationships of humankind.

This trilemma itself becomes more dynamic as movement of materials and people speeds up and communication becomes instantaneous. Managing the tolerable equilibrium will become a leadership asset.

Outdoor development for leadership can and should respond effectively to the demand for holistic leadership. The outdoor provider who prescribes stress, threat, and arbitrary challenge and who specializes in exposing individual weakness, abusing the client's vulnerability in the name of management development, is to be viewed with caution. Such attitudes contribute to and endorse malpractice in leadership development.

The early pioneers of education in the outdoors seem to have been primarily concerned with the training and development of 'characters' capable of administering an empire. They saw the natural world as something to be subdued and conquered with benefit to the conquerer. The parallels with outdated management practices are all too obvious. Future leaders will, we hope, wish to stress the notions of empathy and collaboration with human resources and the environment.

2
John Ridgeway's School of Adventure

Manfred F. R. Kets de Vries

Ridgeway offered a new course aimed at jaded businessmen seeking a fresh challenge; this developed into tailor-made courses for multinationals seeking ways of building leadership potential and teamwork among their fast-track executives. As Ridgeway said:

> the people who come here on their own volition are probably the more exciting kind of persons. They are almost certainly going to be put in situations where they are going to be embarrassed physically. To do that in mid-life – as many of them are – takes an unusual type of person. Coming here is like a cleansing experience . . . A number of people come here because of different forms of crisis – not necessarily a family crisis, but a crisis of confidence, business disaster, redundancy or that sort of thing. The person may be exhausted, not working at top efficiency and actually may be getting on everybody's nerves at the office. For such a person it is probably better to have a highly active week and not just sit in a deck chair. The change he gets is as good as a rest. He will be frightened about falling on the rock climbing, worried that he was not going to get to the top of the mountain and be left behind. No one knows who he is. If he is the head man he is not surrounded by people who are always saying yes. It is also a good thing to get away from the family. Holidays spent looking after wife and children are not necessarily very restful. Isn't it true that the worst family rows happen on holidays?

One of the company courses in particular, the so-called 'IBM Course,' was developed to 'discover how individuals behaved while tackling group tasks under stress . . . and is designed to test leadership, participation, planning and organizational abilities to breaking point.' Course participants are put through a series of disorienting and isolating activities while at the same time being given

From 'John Ridgeway's School of Adventure' by Manfred F. R. Kets de Vries, a case prepared to be used as a basis for class discussion at the business school INSEAD, by permission of INSEAD.

punishing outdoor assignments to complete. Sleep and food are in short supply and instructors are deliberately noncommunicative or obstructive, setting unexpected 'surprise' targets. At the end of the course an exercise is conducted which allows course members to award each other points based on trustworthiness and influence on events during the course. According to Ridgeway, 'Someone with a high score on both trust and influence is a born leader . . . The course is not designed simply to reward decency; leadership is seldom a 'popularity contest.'

Such stressful situations brought about unusual reactions. Ridgeway recalls:

> The President of a large organization who participated based on an outline proposal by his second in command. When he arrived he realized that his physical fears were going to be exposed to this team of company people from different backgrounds and countries. He tried to take command so that he could cancel or rearrange assignments he was afraid of but obviously nobody was fooled. It became so bad that the chap who had organized the trip decided to resign. But the course was a success because it got a diverse group of individuals communicating and getting to know each other much more quickly than the usual conference in a comfortable hotel. Inhibitions break down and people talk, real person to real person, rather than the fellow who looks in the shaving mirror in the morning and puts on the face he wants the world to see. There are a lot of anxious people at that level of management.

Despite the early success of the School, Ridgeway's partner, Rod Liddon, decided to leave Ardmore for personal reasons. Ridgeway was thirty-two years old, yet

> with Rod gone I felt I was going through one of the last stages of growing up. Feelings of insecurity and underconfidence, useful spurs in some circumstances, finally had to be confronted. Unfortunately, parting with the Liddons seemed to harden my resolve to stand independent of anyone else but Marie-Christine, and regrettably I began what was to become a fifteen-year separation from my adoptive parents.

With each successive year the School's reputation grew and the popularity of the various courses became established. The facilities at Ardmore were improved – tents were replaced with wooden buildings, the original croft was expanded and an adjacent croft was rebuilt for staff. Eventually electricity was even cabled in and other enterprises such as salmon farming were developed. Now after twenty years, Ridgeway runs team-building courses for new and existing teams at differing levels of management for companies like Plessey, IBM, British Telecom, SEC, Bass, ICL.

Expeditions

Ridgeway's life gradually divided into two complementary parts. In the summer he was fully occupied with the adventure courses, but by October, with the participants departed, he had the opportunity to pursue other activities: 'Each winter I planned to make a journey, either mentally or physically, to broaden my experience of life.'

On one of his expeditions Ridgeway's own leadership abilities were brought into question. In 1978, with his wife and a crew of twelve instructors from his School, he entered the Whitbread Round-the-World Yacht Race in order to celebrate the tenth anniversary of the School's founding. A two-man film crew was also on board to shoot a TV program.

Living in close quarters, with few land sightings, and with the yacht falling behind in the race, the pressure on the crew inevitably grew. As the yacht approached New Zealand, things came to a head. A letter written to Ridgeway by a nineteen-year-old member of the crew summed up the situation:

Dear John,
I feel now that perhaps things on the boat have finally gone too far. When we left Ardmore I felt it was the proudest moment of my life, sailing around the world and with a skipper whom I had complete faith in. Now I feel that I can no longer sail with you unless a lot of changes are made. The crew were at first a close-knit group of friends but have now become divided in attitude towards the venture and I for one find it hard to get on with anyone except a few at the present moment and this is no way to approach the next leg.

I have no wish to persecute you in any way but I feel that you must be held responsible for a lot of the trouble on board. Your continual depression during the last leg was very hard to tolerate after four hard hours on deck. It is very depressing when everyone is doing their best to get the boat moving and then find that nothing seems to satisfy you. The film trouble was I feel unnecessary. [Ridgeway had objected to interviews being filmed without him present.] You yourself said it was to be a true account of what happened but now you seem to be trying to stop people airing their feelings without your consent: Why? You should have nothing to hide. Nobody had said anything up till then.

In a long response to this letter, Ridgeway said:

Yes, that is right, I have been very depressed and the thing is for you to try and help me because I am just an ordinary human being and not the superman you might have once thought I was. Life is not simply black and white and my feet are made of clay just as much as anyone else's. I heard that you had nearly got into a fight in my defence in Cape Town. Well, I don't know what that man said about me – but it is quite likely it was right.

Ridgeway later addressed the crew at a tense meeting in an attempt to 'clear the air.' He said among other things:

Some people haven't had a wash. There are putrid smells coming from various parts of the boat because some lockers and cupboards haven't been cleaned. Certain people are getting set to scuttle off the boat when we arrive at Portsmouth, leaving it in a rather worse condition than they found it. Well, I'm the skipper and the owner of this fine yacht, which has brought you all safely this far round the world. It's my food you have eaten; my drink you have drunk; my clothing you have worn these past six months. Not one of you has contributed a penny towards the voyage. It is in the shadow of my reputation that some of your heads have now grown to the point where you wonder which poor sucker of an owner to freeload off next. A bold cry for people who had hardly been to sea, much less crewed in an ocean race before this voyage.

On his safe return to Ardmore, Ridgeway reflected on the voyage and the tensions on board and commented: 'I thought the sea would be the biggest problem. It was not; it was the people.'

Asked to give his views on leadership, John Ridgeway said:

I have been trained to lead from the age of about twelve, first at Nautical College and then as an officer cadet in the Merchant Navy. Then I spent two years at Sandhurst so really it was the only thing I could do. I think, however, that people with a long military experience are not suited for business leadership. Leadership to me is persuading people that they really want to do this thing which is what I'm doing at the time. Therefore I've got to have enthusiasm. It's largely theatre. I have to psych myself up to be enthusiastic. Enthusiasm is the cornerstone to everything, without it you may as well be dead; finding the enthusiasm or motivation or excitement is the most important thing for me. One thing I've taken as a rule is that you should never make decisions when happy, hungry, angry or tired. Because the decision is likely to be unbalanced in those situations. If you're too happy you're too optimistic, if you're hungry you're going to be pessimistic, if you're angry you'll be unbalanced, and if you're tired you won't even be able to think it out well enough . . .

You've got to get the person committed emotionally to the task. Everyone needs to have a dream. If you have sufficient emotional commitment of the people, they will solve the problem even in the wrong way; they will achieve the results. I like the sort of fellow who always cries in the cinema when he sees a film. That's important, otherwise he's dull and boring. Like a dreary accountant telling you you can earn 4 per cent, who wants to live for that? For leadership you need imagination . . .

But I can't develop leadership potential in a forty-five-year-old manager who comes to Ardmore for a week. If they haven't got it by then, they will never have it. Leadership is really determined by the upbringing and experience of the person. If you look at history and at successful leaders you'll see ambitious mothers. For the younger managers – eighteen to thirty – it's still possible to do something. I think really a lot of people develop leadership after some setback – a physical handicap, a family disaster, bankruptcy, war – and that gives them the determination to succeed. Without that setback you're not the whole person and you must really wonder just how determined you really are . . . In the Army they say there are no bad soldiers only bad officers. I think that's the truth of it. Anybody can do anything if they're properly motivated by whoever's leading. People love direction. We hate not having direction and not knowing what we're doing. Almost anybody can be persuaded to do things otherwise you wouldn't have concentration camps and people putting people in gas chambers. It's a living example. People will do what they're told.

I think the great ideal of continuing to impart secrets of life to ageing business executives after twenty years on the job is somewhat jaded. But the letters I get from people who have come here or have read my books, make you think it is worthwhile doing what you're doing, not just financially worthwhile. In the dark moments – at the end of the day – I would hate lying up there in bed, and saying to someone 'Son, I misjudged the whole thing!'

Chapter 18
Leadership and Team-Building

Introduction

There is nothing simple about building a team. But the reasons why team-building is so difficult are simple: teams are made up of individuals all with their own motivations and idiosyncrasies. Clive Goodworth, in a light-hearted attempt to encapsulate the secrets of moulding a motley group into a cohesive single-minded body, describes a familiar playground scene. 'What happens', wonders Goodworth, 'when people get plonked into the highly artificial work situation'? It is a 'sure-fire certainty' at least that 'while the imposed official hierarchy may hopefully prevail over the natural human pecking order, it will never supplant it.' Some of the sad, lonely, or bullying little bodies identified in the playground should never be allowed anywhere near a team if group dynamics are to work effectively.

Leaders, Goodworth also advises, should not forget that they are as much a part of the team as the most junior member, and avoid such phrases as 'I'd like you to have a go at', instead plumping for the more democratic 'I'd like us to have a go at'. Obvious? Well, perhaps, but the second contribution to this chapter by Robert H. Waterman Jr cites numerous occasions where the we – they split is broken down with impressive results. It was, for example, the starting point for the phenomenal turnaround in the fortunes of General Electric's Appliance Park in Louisville, Kentucky. Roger Schipke, the man who led this particular corporate revolution, resorts to all kinds of ploys: 'I move people from manufacturing to marketing and the other way round . . . I started the Breakfast Club. The top 60 managers in the organization meet once a month at seven-thirty. Otherwise they'd never talk to each other.'

Waterman is also cautious about ambition and competition. Co-operation is much more effective, he theorizes: 'people who are obviously combative, confrontational and prone to win-or-lose situations don't get very far in organizations. They may win a lot of battles one-on-one, but their peers make sure they lose the war.'

From these two articles, there can be no doubt that engendering good teamwork is an essential part of good leadership.

1
Some Thoughts on Creating a Team

Clive Goodworth

You know, it could be said that we managers are nothing if not optimists. We reap ourselves a bunch of subordinates (either through fateful inheritance or by dint of our own splendid efforts at selection) and, provided we're sufficiently with-it, strive like anything to convert this heterogeneous clump of humanity into what the pundits call a cohesive, effective team. And, yes, optimism or not, come hell or high water, it's an extremely important task.

That being so, we must give this boiling priority more than a passing thought.

For starters, I'd like you to take a brief flight of fancy and imagine that you're standing at the side of the playground at your local infant school, just when the wee mites are coming out to play. Observe what happens and note how, quite haphazardly and for no apparent reason, the children tend to coalesce in clusters – and remind yourself, if reminder is necessary, that what you are witnessing is the magical formation of what the textbooks term natural human groups. Keep looking and it shouldn't be long before you notice that, within the groups, there are those little children who, by dint of sheer personality and/or thumping the others, manage to gain the ascendancy and take over control of their respective bands. Yes, you've got it in one – you're privy to a perfect example of the striving emergence of *natural leaders*.

Cast your eyes around the playground. Do you see that hapless little character over yonder, who's going from group to group with the hope of gaining acceptance and, quick as a flash, is being bounced back out of each and every one? That's right, reader, you've spotted a tearful example of what, in jargonese, we term a *reject*. And, hey, what about that little girl who is sitting on the grass at the side of the playground, intent on making a daisy-chain – all

From 'Run a Team, Not a Prison Camp', from *The Secrets of Successful Leadership and People Management* by Clive Goodworth, 1988, by permission of Butterworth-Heinemann Ltd.

alone, but apparently self-content? Yes, the odds are that you've identified an *isolate*, an individual who, for better or worse, deems it best to remain aloof from the common herd.

Okay, now come back down the earth and consider what happens when people get plonked into the highly artificial work situation. Do all the manifestations of natural behaviour (and I've only mentioned a few) go by the board? Once again, the answer is strikingly obvious – no, they don't. None of the organizational and disciplinary ramifications of the workplace will lessen the sure-fire certainty that, while the imposed official hierarchy may hopefully prevail over the natural human pecking order, it will never supplant it. Thus it is that the cohesion of any work group (and that includes *your* lot) can be endangered by the presence within it of:

- a burgeoning natural leader who utilizes the power of a dominant personality to undermine the boss's authority and bend other members of the group to his or her will
- an employee who, for whatever reason, has been 'rejected' by the group and whose enforced presence is therefore heartily disliked
- an isolate-type 'loner', who has no wish to integrate with the group or share in its corporate endeavours.

Having regaled you with that hefty proviso, let's now take a look at the various bricks which, when properly laid, go towards the building of that elusive and intangible thing, team spirit or, as dear old Colonel Blimp would rightly term it, *esprit de corps*.

Common Goals

While all the members of the group must be encouraged to achieve their respective and highly individual objectives, it is no less important that the team as a whole is unified by obtaining an across-the-board recognition and acceptance of common goals. But, once again, beware! The autocratic or simply unwise manager who attempts to impose these overall objectives on his people will very soon find himself on a hiding to nothing. Carefully steered discussion is the only true way to win them round – and, just in case you've a dollop of Machiavellian blood running in your veins, this *doesn't* mean acting the part of a con-man.

Team Identity

There are some executive-type creatures who believe that team identity simply means the organizational name of the group – Sludge Inwards Department, or whatever. But you're not one of them, are you? You and I know that this bit of jargon refers to the awareness of a given band of employees that they haven't just been slung together, willy-nilly, but, rather, that they're valued members of a team – people who, knowing each other and each other's capabilities, *belong* together. Yes, it goes without saying, doesn't it – but, and here's the rub, do we also appreciate that the manager is as much a part of the team as the most junior member?

> Oh, my God, here we go again . . . That's as obvious as the nose on your face. Goodworth – if he's to enjoy any success at all, it stands to reason that the manager's *got* to be part of the team. For heaven's sake, stop teaching me to suck eggs.

All right, smartie-pants – so, tell me, why it is that so many managers address their teams along the following lines?

> Remember the deadline – I want all statements in the post by Friday, at the latest.

instead of

> Hey, remember the deadline – we must have all the statements in the post by Friday, at the latest.

or

> I'd like you to have a go at . . .

instead of

> I'd like us to have a go at . . .

or

> Joe, Sales have just been on the line. They want that Horrocks order completed this week – do you think it can be done?

instead of

> Joe, Sales have just been on the line. They want that Horrocks order completed this week – do you think we can do it?

or

> Okay, that's the set-up – so I'd like you to get cracking.

instead of

> Okay, that's the set-up – so let's get cracking.

The manager who constantly resorts to the first-person pronoun 'I' when addressing his people is the boss who remains aloof from them; the kind of leader who'll never ever be regarded as 'one of us' by the group. Sorry, what was that?

Now you've got me really worried. You're saying that, in order to create a team spirit, a manager should set out to be 'one of the boys' – but I've always understood that that'd be asking for trouble. Surely, a boss has to stay aloof – otherwise, he stands in danger of losing status *and* credibility.

Lest that comment reflects your feeling (which, now that we know each other, would surprise me) it is not only possible but eminently desirable for the truly consultative-cum-participative manager to play the 'one of us' role without losing a shred of status *or* credibility – and play it he should.

Mind you, this business of creating and fostering team identity is not all plain sailing. It's only too easy to overcook things and produce a work group who, because they've come to regard themselves as the bee's knees, compete with other sections and departments in a spirit of destructive rivalry – and, as you'll appreciate, that can be distinctly counter-productive.

Loyalty and Cooperation

The with-it manager who succeeds in inculcating his group with team identity and the need to strive for common goals will, in fact, be thrice blessed – for his people will be well on the way to achieving a corporate bond of loyalty and, just as important, a yen for mutual collaboration. In other words, they'll not only think of themselves as a team, they'll *pull together* as a team – and what could be better?

An Internal Code of Behaviour

Quiz any ex-serviceman on this aspect of 'team dynamics' and the odds are that he'll reminisce at length about the manner in which well-knit groups in the forces develop their own, highly unofficial standards and rules of conduct. Provided the leadership is of the right quality (and here we must call to mind the ineptitude of the democratic leader), exactly the same type of phenomena will occur within any group in business or industry; to wit, an internal code of behaviour which, carefully monitored by the thinking boss, will augment, *not* supplant, his authority and do much to improve the efficiency and well-being of the team, as a whole.

2
The Power of Teamwork

Robert H. Waterman Jr

In today's business environment, more than in any preceding era, the only constant is change. Somehow there are organizations that effectively manage change, continuously adapting their bureaucracies, strategies, systems, products and cultures to survive the shocks and to prosper from the forces that decimate their competition. They move from strength to strength, adjusting to crises that bedevil others in their industry. They are masters of what I call *renewal*.

In the course of extensively researching 45 of these renewing organizations, all of them among the best in their industries or fields, I listened to conflicting opinions about the impact – indeed, even the presence – of politics as a vital force of renewal.

Richard Huber, a former executive with Citicorp, greets the subject with enthusiasm: 'Thank the Lord for corporate politics. How boring life would be without it. I love it. It's wonderful!' He explains that much of his daily job is persuasion – finding ways to persuade other people to do what he thinks is important. 'Is that politics? I don't know, but by my definition it is. It's an essential part of the reality of what we do.'

Others disagree, however. In many discussions at the renewing companies, executives were emphatic: political behaviour simply did not exist in their organizations. A frequent comment was 'What makes this place work is that we have no politics.'

Who's right? Both are. Nothing so clouds the renewal issue or our understanding of management itself as our collective innocence about politics and power in organizations. Few people get ahead who are not good politically. But we have been raised to be so suspicious of power and politics – while

Adapted for *Best of Business International* from *The Renewal Factor: How the Best Get and Keep the Competitive Edge* by Robert H. Waterman Jr. Copyright © Robert H. Waterman Jr, by permission of Bantam Books, a division of Bantham Doubleday Dell Publishers Group Inc.

privately coveting what these forces can bring us – that we deny their very existence.

The importance of the politics issue is explained by P. C. Chatterjee, a former partner in the management consulting firm McKinsey & Company: 'What bars renewal – makes change for the better virtually impossible in most companies I see – is the very high level of politics, low level of teamwork and no general sense of direction.' Chatterjee says that his greatest disappointment, as he moved up in the business world and spent more time inside the inner sanctums of big business, was how difficult it was to do the obvious.

Positive Politics

Well-meaning, honest, energetic managers cannot afford to trust their well-meaning, honest, energetic counterparts. If you get anything done, it is in spite of the organization. If you get too much done, it makes the others look bad; although your colleagues can't agree on much else, they can agree that you are a threat, and they see to it that your next effort is thwarted.

The executives I interviewed recognize the harm that lies in the backbiting behaviour usually associated with politics. They are clearly determined to make politics a positive force by emphasizing teamwork.

From Morgan Bank, Super Valu, Bankers Trust, IBM and Nucor (the minimill steel company) to Olivetti's headquarters in Italy, calm is the pervasive theme. Where is the frenzy? The fervour? The angst? How can these people be so calm yet do so well in today's fast-paced, split-second world?

Teamwork, that's how. Almost without exception, the successful people stress the importance of teamwork. It starts at the top.

Now, you may be thinking, *That's old news. Everyone understands the need for teamwork.*' Not so, according to a study conducted by Robert Lefton, the president of Psychological Associates, an American training company. He found that many executives distrust collaboration because it seems 'soft' and 'unbusinesslike'. They prefer instead the hard-nosed authoritarian approach. The result? 'Less than 40 per cent of the effort expended by top-level corporate teams can accurately be described as teamwork,' Lefton says. 'One-third of the time, the group leader calls the shots to head off opposition.'

Every renewing organization has a chief executive who is clearly in charge. But this individual is seldom the grandstanding, heroic figure – the hard-nosed authoritarian – that the popular press makes such leaders out to be. Leaders are supposed to be charismatic, but that is not how you would necessarily describe the chief executive officers of renewing companies. Their personalities run the spectrum from voluble to taciturn, from extroverted to introverted.

Ralph Waldo Emerson said that an institution is simply the lengthened shadow of a single individual. This may be true of many organizations, especially new or small companies. The Americans' emphasis on individualism and their fixation on heroes encourage them to believe that the one person at the top is more singular than he really is. I had the impression that a dozen or so of the top people in several of the big companies studied had the raw capacity to be chief executive officer at almost any big company. That wealth of talent at the top and the manifest teamwork made for what many described as seamless transitions from one generation of management to the next.

But it truly is a team at the top that makes renewal happen. Yes, there has to be a first among equals. Printing entrepreneur Harry Quadracci has a rule he calls 'president wins' for settling issues when his consensus-driven style doesn't yield a decision (or when it yields one he knows is wrong for the company). But, no, the top person is not as effective when operating as a loner.

At Steelcase Inc., as you might expect of an office-systems company, teamwork at the top is symbolized by office layout and reinforced by computer technology. The two top people, Robert Pew, the chairman of the board, and Frank Merlotti, the president and chief operating officer, have offices that connect via an atriumlike conference room so they can quickly confer. All Steelcase executives, managers, and supervisors are linked by computer terminals that encourage electronic mail; they can call up everyone's schedule at the stroke of a few keys. That almost gimmicky-sounding device makes it so easy for the executive group members to find one another that they end up communicating more often.

At Super Valu, chief executive officer Mike Wright holds forth from a glassed-in office where he is visible to all. He wants others to treat him informally. The nameplate outside his office says MIKE WRIGHT. He tells everyone to call him Mike. 'It's all first names around here; no "mister",' he says. By making his own office physically transparent, and by insisting on informality, he reinforces Super Valu's brand of teamwork.

In companies that aren't well managed, there's an inverse relationship between the small amount of teamwork and the large amount of executive turf-grabbing, each fiefdom jealously duplicating and defending its staff and functions. These companies then wonder why they are so top-heavy with managers. A company that has good teamwork and cooperation at the top enjoys a terrific multiplier effect: that close-knit gang of three or four accomplishes far more than does a throng of managers (and supporting retinues and overhead) three times its size. The teamwork companies enjoy a communication level that seems uncanny to outsiders; important ideas move like quicksilver. Decisions are made in hallways and on telephones. Formal meetings are less frequent and are not all that formal.

Even within the vastness of IBM, with its 400,000 employees, teamwork at the top provides a kind of intimacy. 'We've all grown up together,' says John Akers, the company's president and chief executive officer. 'When we have a meeting of the top 85 or 90 people throughout the company – we call them

Distribution A – I know them all. I've known them all for 20 years! Everybody started out as a clerk or a salesman or a junior engineer or something, and we all kind of moved forward together.'

Smart chief executives like Akers know that they won the top jobs through a combination of ability, luck and perseverance. They accept the fact that if they were suddenly vaporized, a slew of highly talented, qualified men and women in the organization would be available to fill their jobs. To a significant and beneficial degree, the people at the top of a renewing company are interchangeable, although that word is often cast as a pejorative, implying a sea of dull grey look-alikes. To believe that is to miss the point. The members of a senior team represent individual shadings of style and emphasis, but they share the fundamental beliefs, values and skills that drive the company.

A Cushion of Competence

Does the certainty that one can be so easily replaced create fear and anxiety in top executives? It doesn't seem to; if anything, it adds to the calm at the top. An executive knows that he doesn't have to do everything himself, that some superhuman effort on his part not only is unnecessary but would probably be foolish. He knows he is surrounded by smart and capable people who can make the organization run effectively, preferably with him but if necessary without him. It's when you have a brilliant leader surrounded by people who he thinks are incompetent that fear, uncertainty and doubt take hold.

'At one company I visited, they were all terrified of the chairman', says Peter Buchanan, the chief executive at the First Boston Corporation. 'On the company plane he sat off in his cabin, and everyone else sat worrying about what he was thinking. It was worse than what I saw in the military.' At First Boston, though, Buchanan says, 'we look for the guys who will be team players. There's very little hierarchy here.'

'I don't care whether they get along,' says the chief executive officer of a national bank, 'as long as they do a good job.' The position sounds reasonable. But the point is that they *can't* do a good job if they can't work effectively as a team. The top executive team at this company has a huge, politically generated energy leak. The executives spend too much time worrying about, imagining and defending themselves against one another's hidden agendas. At lower levels, if one person works for one group executive and another works in a different group, the two people can rarely collaborate. Either they feel disloyal to their respective supervisors or they've been convinced by their bosses that 'the other side' is up to no good.

Contrast that situation with an experience at one of the renewing companies, where groups from various divisions meet to discuss their common interest in computer-aided design, engineering and manufacturing technology. There is a lot of information-sharing going on. No posturing. Nothing held back. Just an easygoing, cooperative attitude. But it wasn't always this way. 'Several years ago you would have seen just the reverse,' says the president. 'Lots of politics, nobody working together. I finally got so fed up that I picked the two worst offenders among top management. I fired them, and I told everyone why I fired them. We didn't have much trouble with politics after that.'

Corporate Encampments

Outside the executive suite, a formidable barrier to change and renewal is the 'we–they' split that fragments an organization. The we–theys are all around us. The most obvious is the split between labour and management. Then there's the classic line-and-staff split. Marketing versus manufacturing. The new York office versus Chicago. One division versus another (or versus the rest of the company). The German (or French or European) operation versus the domestic operation. The common ingredient in we–they splits is a communication breakdown. Trust disappears – or never gets established. Organizational gridlock is the result.

Sometimes the we–they split is blatantly adversarial. Other times it is subtler, and when it masquerades as consensus, it can be even more destructive. Its symptoms include excessive politeness, excruciatingly correct behaviour and formal 'agreements' that each side promptly goes about trying to undermine in private.

We–they barriers have to be removed, or at least dramatically lowered, in order for renewal to happen. That was the starting point for the phenomenal turnaround in the fortunes of General Electric's Appliance Park in Louisville, Kentucky. The man who led it, senior vice-president Roger Schipke, recalls, 'In the early 1970s we got ourselves in trouble with matrix management. It was the "glamour" style of organization then.' But it had the appliance division broken into so many small segments, with artificial walls between, that it was more confusing than helpful. Schipke remembers, 'By the late 1970s we had 13 corporate vice-presidents in major appliances, and they all had different agendas. We were paralysed. No one could make a decision.'

Schipke sat down and designed an organization that would foster teamwork and strike a balance between short- and long-range thinking. 'I blew up the separate functions and created four major operating units. Two divisions – production, and sales and service – are 'now' organizations. The other two – technology and marketing – are 'future' groups. One problem was that 99.9 per cent of the people here were so focused on making income for the quarter that they had no concern for what would happen two years down the road. I wanted each pair of divisions to get involved with the other – to talk to each other. Linkages between them are crucial.' Schipke comments that swimming against the organizational tide is one of the hardest things he's had to do. 'People seem to want a narrow, functional self-concept. I'm trying to create a one-team business perspective.'

He went to work making sure the people who populated the new organization *would* work as a team, or at least 'a well-coordinated dinosaur', as he refers to the place. 'I said to Jack Welch, "Now, you pick the fellow on the top block [Welch, the chief executive of GE, chose Schipke]; then he can pick his team. Each of them picks theirs, all the way down." In early 1982 we were disjointed; it was a staging year. I worked on team-building and relationships. In 1983 I added a strategic orientation.'

To break down barriers further within Appliance Park, Schipke and his new team made many symbolic moves. One was to take down all the signs from the factories. DISHWASHER, RANGE, LAUNDRY and REFRIGERATION became buildings 1, 2, 3 and 4.

Schipke reports almost immediate results from his efforts to lay waste to the old we–they boundaries.

Shaking up the Status Quo

The main reason he was so effective is the strength of his relationships across organizational boundaries. He and Ken Cassady, the president of the local union, are on good terms. The bond between them, which started with their mutual concern for product quality, was probably forged when Schipke 'sent the message out that we would fire anyone who used anything that was tagged defective'. Others comment on Schipke's singular ability to relate up, down and sideways. Says James Allen, the manager of communication and community affairs at Appliance Park: 'He can stir up the troops, but he also has a big power base from the top.'

Schipke talks about methods he uses to help break down the old walls:

> I move people from manufacturing to marketing and the other way round. Sales trainees spend two weeks in the factories for orientation. I would love to have them spend six months on the factory floor and some time on the retail floor as well.
>
> People are social; they want to be on a team. Plus, they really want to learn more about what's going on around them. So I started the Breakfast Club. The top 60 managers in the organization meet once a month at seven-thirty. Otherwise they'd never talk to each other.
>
> Formerly, central marketing would sign off on all prices. But I turned pricing over to the field. The response was 'That guy is crazy. The whole organization will fall apart tomorrow.' So I started the Price Club, which brings marketing and finance together. They communicate. We haven't fallen apart.'

But as with the other renewing companies, the emphasis on teamwork at Appliance Park doesn't mean that power has disappeared. The last word on

Schipke's political instinct comes from one of his executives: 'Roger picked his own team, and he knows just when to ignore it.'

Many executives I interviewed stressed the importance of talking directly with the people. They pointed out how common it is for some managements to communicate with their workforce only through the unions. The unions may like things that way because it preserves their own power positions. Managers may even think it makes their job easier. But this habit leaves a canyon-size we–they gulf.

Although the gulf that often exists between management and labour is the most obvious we–they barrier in companies, others exist; potential schisms are waiting to open with only the slightest encouragement. There seems to be something about human nature that creates a need for an us-versus-them mentality. Martin Luther King Jr called it 'the drum-major instinct'. By that he meant that each of us has a need to stand out, to be special in some way. But he warned of the good and the bad sides of that instinct. We all like praise; it makes us feel important and lets us know we are being given attention. Good managers energize their people by recognizing that drum-major instinct in us all, by paying attention to us and making each of us feel special.

The destructive side of the drum-major instinct is that it leads us to create and join groups that will make us feel superior because we belong to them ('We're okay; you're so-so'). It's all too easy to slip into the suit of metaphorical clothes that strongly identifies us with those most like us – the union, the factory supervisors, the division, the factory floor, the research-and-development labs, the top executives.

To a certain point, that ability to identify strongly with something small is good. Highly divisionalized companies like Hewlett-Packard, Johnson & Johnson and 3M have been unusually innovative over the years. They renew by being small and big at the same time. But too much identification with the small unit has problems of its own. It creates too strong a sense of 'us'. 'They' become not just outsiders but the enemy. The benefit of being a part of a large organization is lost.

Simple job rotation improves teamwork and dissolves the we–they boundaries before they form. Morgan Guaranty makes a regular practice of job rotation, and senior vice-president Maureen Hendricks explains its effects: 'There's an appreciation at Morgan of the circumstances under which your colleagues are working, because either you've had their jobs or you will someday have them. Since we've been "on the other side", people here tend to be very sympathetic, very willing to cooperate.'

Even with the importance this bank places on teamwork, Morgan's retired president, Robert V. Lindsay, says that recent thinking has shown a clear customer need 'for a close relationship between our securities traders and the people who produce deals for their clients'. Morgan created a single division, he explains, 'which combined trading and capital market activities under one roof, thereby bringing together groups that tended to argue for their spread [their share of the profit margin] against the clients' needs'. The reorganization accomplished two things, according to Lindsay: it eliminated the issue of who gets credit for the spread, and it formed the basis for better chemistry and closer relationships between the two groups.

John F. Ruffle, the vice-chairman, says that the top management team could see strong political camps forming and we–they attitudes hardening between operations (the administrative activities) and the line units. 'We had to decentralize. We eliminated the operations division, and we placed a number of its components in the business units. We also made the operations people feel a part of the business, partly to get more of us orientated toward the client as our master.'

New on the American scene is the shattering of an unobstructive yet influential we–they barrier: the one between a company and its suppliers. Ford plant manager Joseph Bobnar muses that employee teams can accomplish things that management can't. For example, the company wasn't getting the kind of parts or service it needed from an ITT unit. When the problem was bounced up to Bobnar's level, he tried to go through the ITT management to get it fixed. Not much happened. Eventually one of Ford's employee teams met with its counterpart in the ITT organization, and the whole problem was solved with alacrity. Now it is common for the people on the production line at Ford to know their counterparts in supplier organizations. Most things that go wrong can get fixed at that level. Another we–they boundary zapped.

Steven Walleck, a McKinsey & Company partner who specializes in manufacturing, notes not only that we–they barriers between companies and suppliers are coming down but also that suppliers are playing an increasing role in helping their customers renew. 'This is especially evident in manufacturing, where the very existence of many suppliers is dependent on the health of the companies they supply,' he says. 'Some of the important advances in robotics for Ford, General Motors or Chrysler are supplier-driven.'

The conventional wisdom is to set up multiple sources of supply and let them compete for the business. Today the move is toward one, or a very few, trusted sources, trained in your methods and quality standards.

S. J. Morcott, the president of autoparts and industrial-products manufacturer Dana Corporation, and Gerald B. Mitchell, its chairman and chief executive officer, talk about trust all the time. They explain that when you come to work for Dana, you automatically have their trust. They trust you to 'do what's right for Dana'. You trust them to respect you and to build your dignity as an individual.

Morgan Guaranty builds trust into the culture from day one of the training programme. Arthur M. Rogers, an executive vice-president, explains that even a 26-year-old officer at Morgan would have a clear sense of the kind of bank it is, the kind of business the bank wants to do. There isn't the feeling, as there is in many banks, 'that someone is trying to zoom one by you as if you were a hockey goalie. All of us are on the same side of the table. You don't have to question others' motives all the time. Trust. We've all inherited it, and the culture passes it down.'

Walter Gubert, a senior vice-president, feels that trust of a client is an extension of what Morgan practices within the bank. 'When you're working on a transaction,' he says, 'you don't look at the Morgan organization chart. There's no focus on rank – that's just not an issue. When I talk to our Zurich people, I don't care if I talk to the junior person or the senior person, and neither do they. When you are trying to do a transaction, it's better to talk to whoever has the best information at the time. It's important to have an organization where everyone is sharing information with others for results that are good for the firm and good for the client.'

How does Morgan achieve this culture of trust? Top officers explain that the training programme for every new Morgan officer is designed as much to help establish rapport among classmates as it is to build their technical banking skills. With their business dependent on rapid communication, this means everything.

Cooperation is the Key

It's common belief around many organizations that the way to get people to work the hardest is to pit them against one another. Give similar assignments to two or more people, and you don't have to be concerned any further about whether they do their best. It's a safe bet that those involved will scramble to be the first with the most. Sure, some fur will fly – they may even undermine one another in the process – but it's worth the results. If there's going to be a winner, someone's got to lose. Right?

Wrong. Findings from the behavioural sciences suggest that cooperation is much more effective than competition. These studies support what the renewing companies were telling us about the role of trust and teamwork. Alfie Kohn, author of *No Contest*, describes a classic piece of research conducted back in 1954 by Columbia University sociologist Peter Blau, who studied two groups of interviewers in an employment agency. The first group was extremely competitive, personally ambitious and concerned about its own productivity. The second group was naturally cooperative and worked as a team. The second group's results in filling jobs were much better than the first group's.

Two and a half decades later, Robert Helmreich of the University of Texas used questionnaires to relate achievement among a sampling of scientists with various personality traits. He found that the most productive scientists (as measured by how often their work was cited by others) ranked high on traits like work orientation and preference for challenging tasks. But they ranked low on competitiveness.

This intrigued Helmreich and his colleagues, who went on to study other groups. By 1985 they had covered seven categories, including airline pilots, airline reservation agents, college undergraduates (using grade-point average as the measure of success) and businessmen (using salary as the measure of achievement). In each case the result was the same: the Helmreich group found a negative correlation between achievement and competitiveness.

In the literature about competition and cooperation, virtually every experiment spotlighting cooperation yielded much better results than those concentrating on competition. Why? Alfie Kohn provides some clues. 'Success often depends on sharing resources efficiently, and this is nearly impossible when people have to work against each other. Cooperation takes advantage of all the skills represented in a group, as well as the mysterious process by which that group becomes more than the sum of its parts. By contrast, competition makes people suspicious and hostile toward one another and actively discourages this process.' Furthermore, 'competition generally does not promote excellence, because trying to do well and trying to beat others are simply two different things.'

If the research is correct, or even right in direction, we need immediately to reassess our assumptions about 'making it', whether in school in business or in life. It is no wonder that the companies I studied, which are the best at renewal, put such heavy emphasis on teamwork and trust.

Sometimes it's hard to see high achievers as noncompetitive. Perhaps the difference is the degree to which they wear their noncompetitiveness on their sleeves. People who are obviously combative, confrontational and prone to win-or-lose situations don't get very far in organizations. They may win a lot of battles one-on-one, but their peers make sure they lose the war. Moreover, there are situations whose outcomes are too important to be left to one department or project team. Companies deliberately set up two or more teams to develop the same product. Then they have a performance 'shoot-out' to see which one works the best. The difference is that the competition is open, aboveboard and free of the 'win at someone else's expense' mentality. The reason for the competition – the project's urgency – is thoroughly explained.

Bruce Brackenridge, a group executive at Morgan, emphasizes teamwork, even – maybe especially – during a stressful period such as the bank's recent reorganization, which was big enough to be considered equivalent to a revolution. Most organizations are afraid to talk much to their staffs about major reorganization, for fear that the uncertainties generated will be more disruptive than a swift stroke of the structural scalpel. For companies and cultures that are less secure than Morgan, the fear may be justified. But of the recent reorganization, Brackenridge says, 'There was lots of consensus-building. By the time we reorganized, everyone understood that we wanted to get banking and corporate finance together. We talked about it so much that the actual change was ho-hum.'

In his *Essence of Decision*, Graham Allison argues that organization are creatures of habit as well as of rational choice. In that same book, he introduces yet a third model of organization behaviour: a political model. His point, of course, is that the dynamics of all three models are simultaneously at play in any organization. To understand organizations, you can't just look at them one way. They are rational decision-makers. Yet they are 'irrational' products of internal politics and power.

Explaining his political model, Allison says:

> Men share power. Men differ about what must be done. The differences matter. This milieu necessitates that government decisions and actions result from a political process. In this process, sometimes one group committed to a course of action triumphs over other groups fighting for other alternatives.
>
> Equally often, however, different groups pulling in different directions produce a result, or better, a resultant – a mixture of conflicting preferences and unequal power of various individuals – distinct from what any person or group intended. In both cases, what moves the chess pieces is not simply the reasons that support a course of action, or the routines of organizations that enact an alternative, but the power and skill of proponents and opponents of the action in question.

Our collective distaste for politics and power gives us an innocence about them that makes us either bow to those who use force or use it ourselves. We can do better than that. We can start by recognizing that organizations run in part along political lines. Then we can think clearly about the benefits of politics as well as the drawbacks.

The Value of Support

Yet the role of the manager is to get things done. Little change, let alone renewal, happens in this world without a power base. Remember Schipke's experience in Appliance Park. People felt that one of the reasons he was effective was that he had support from all sides – the people in the plant, the union leadership, the chief executive and, of course, the management team that was brought in from other GE operations. He had a power base. He was very effective politically, but nobody would label him 'political'.

The key to being good politically without being political lies in the way historian James MacGregor Burns defines leadership. He calls for recognition of collective purpose between leaders and followers: the followers need something, leadership fills their needs and followers yield power to the leaders. In his classic book *Leadership*, Burns contrasts two styles. The first, which he calls 'transactional leadership', stresses the interaction between leader and follower in 'exchanging gratifications in a political marketplace'.

In contrast, the result of the second style, 'transforming leadership', is to raise the sights and aspirations of the followers to a higher level. Both kinds of leader, says Burns, can contribute to human purpose. Both operate on sets of values, but the transactional leaders' values are those of 'means – honesty, responsibility, fairness, the honouring of commitments'. The transforming leaders elevate the aspirations of the followers through their teaching, mentoring and coaching. They are more concerned with end values – 'liberty, justice, equality'. GE's Schipke; Ford's Philip Caldwell and its chairman and chief executive officer, Donald Petersen; and Chrysler's chairman and chief executive officer, Lee Iacocca, along with many other executives, are playing that transforming role.

It is the transforming leader, not the transactional leader, who renews institutions. And that person need not be a top executive.

Bill McCormick, the chief executive officer of Fireman's Fund Insurance Company, believes that all leaders are political and there's nothing necessarily wrong with that. Many leaders are smart and talented – you don't get to the top without being so – but they are focused mainly on acquiring position. They want to get into the next-bigger chair. Those are the ones who get to the top without having earned it. Others also want to move ahead, but their main concern is 'What can I do to fill the chair when I'm in it?' Their purpose is much bigger than to occupy the position; it's to make a difference in the organization. McCormick, who is clearly in favour of this kind of leader, believes that a big problem in corporate leadership is that too many of the former sort are in positions of power. In his own company, he hopes, he is able to stop people who are interested only in their own advancement or to lead them to change their ways.

The most effective leaders can take on a challenge without getting swallowed up by it. They're willing to walk if they are no longer in a position to lead. Listen for a moment to Jack MacAllister, who accomplished a lot in the Bell System before he left to head US West Inc.: 'I wanted a management challenge, and I guess the Bell System was the biggest one I could find, I decided that never, under any circumstances, was I going to be intimidated by the organization or anyone in it. And, yes, I thought many times about leaving.'

GE's Schipke reinforces MacAllister's point: 'I've always been willing to walk. I say what I think, and I don't get mad at people if they criticize me.' That state of mind gives him a tremendous source of power, although he says he's not a political animal.

Every individual's true source of power over the organization that employs him is his willingness to walk. It's too big a stick to use often, but a lack of willingness to use it always puts people in a subservient role to organizations.

Companies should encourage their members to see this; the last thing organizations need is leaders, managers and subordinates who are overly dependent and submissive. Such people will not speak up on the tough issues. No individual security and toughness – no renewal.

Clarity about your own purpose in the organization – and how far you're willing to go to accomplish that purpose – is crucial. That doesn't mean that you can do everything by yourself or by decree. Effective leaders recognize these limitations and understand the importance of building support networks throughout the organization. That's what led IBM's John Akers to comment, 'You have to be politically capable. You have to be able to sell your ideas and to get people on the team. Those who can't get things done, and who can't get people to work on their problems, don't rise as high as people who can.'

McCormick has made a career of resuscitating troubled businesses. He started in the renewal game with the American Express banking subsidiary; his charge was to 'automate the bank'. He says the biggest problem was that the bank operated in more than 25 countries, and he wanted to design a system that would work in all of them.

He remembers, 'I kept worrying, Is the design right?" But Pano, a member of my team, said, "Bill, you don't understand. The political risk is greater than the technical risk; everybody will want to go their own way." And I said to myself, "The son of a gun is right."'

So they shipped the equipment to the banks in countries that were most critical to the project's success and divided the responsibility for developing the total project: financial accounting went to Italy, client accounts to Germany, foreign exchange to the United Kingdom, fixed-asset accounting to France and so on. McCormick says, 'That step, which was Pano's idea, made it work. And every time we brought another country into the system, we gave them a piece to design. Go anywhere in the world and they say, "That's our system. We built this piece."'

Another source of strength for negotiators and politicians is simply persistence. Like politics itself, this power source is neither good nor bad. It can be used for the wrong ends as easily as for the right ends, so part of being political and positive within this dimension is to keep questioning the merit of causes for which you persevere. But if you have integrity and legitimate purpose, simply hanging in there is another way to get things done without having the power of office.

For years one of the top-performing companies in the American broadcasting industry has been King Broadcasting Company in Seattle. King's owner is Dorothy Bullitt, now in her nineties. As a fairly young woman she inherited a small radio station from her father. She decided to do something with it and, since Seattle is in King County, went after the call letters KING, which at the time were the property of an inactive station. Later she went for and got an affiliation with NBC. Still later she picked up the NBC affiliate in Portland, Oregon, and an ABC affiliate. Quite a success, especially when you consider that she started long before there were many women managers.

Why has she been so effective? 'She's a good negotiator,' one of her colleagues explains. 'She just wears you down. She knows what she wants, and she just leans on you until you say okay.' Obviously she understands the power of persistence.

Politics and renewal are not incompatible. Political power can be used for destructive or beneficial ends. Of course, backstabbing politics has no place in any organization. Yet our culture is so suspicious of both politics and power that we barely have the words to talk about their good side. Some executives told us that the 'good guys' will figure it out anyway. Some *will* figure it out; others will believe management's refrain of 'no politics around here'. The trouble is that the latter group will be 'had' too often by those who have figured it out – and that group will be less effective leaders.

Appendix 1: Steps toward Teamwork

One way to halt negative politicking and move toward the positive is to make your organization one in which teamwork counts. Teams generally get things done in organizations – not Lone Rangers, not yes people and especially not people who are out to serve their own ends. Does your company reward teamwork? Do your employees *like* working with one another?

Teamwork is a tricky business; it requires people to pull together toward a set of shared goals or values. To strengthen the sense of teamwork at your company, take the following steps:

1   *Hire people who both qualify for the job and fit into the culture.* Hire the best people for your own business, not just 'the best people'. There's a danger in having too many like-minded team players, however: big change could catch you unawares. Plenty of employees who may be several standard deviations off the cultural norm nonetheless fit into the cultural envelope.

2   *Destroy at least one we–they barrier a year.* Start with a tiny one for practice. Then, with some we–they combat experience under your belt, knock down some of the big ones. Don't assume that the barriers will stay down. They are deeply rooted in every human being's need to feel special as an individual and as part of a broader whole. Recognize the healthy potential in multiple loyalties. Just as you can be proud of your town, region and country, people can feel a part of multiple groups in an organization without erecting impassable we–they barriers.

3   *Encourage direct talk across the we–they boundaries.* Some companies use consultants to help break down old barriers. But bringing in specialists in group dynamics isn't the only way to open up communication. You can start with your own attitude toward other people's ideas and opinions.

4   *Look outside the company for needless we–they barriers.* No matter how many times it has been said, the barrier that cries out for continuing attention is the one between a company and its customers. Another barrier that's getting increasing attention these days is the one between a business and its suppliers.

5   *Use training programmes to build relationships.* Learning is a lifelong process. When

people are continually being trained and retrained, they are also forging new cross-company bonds.

6 *Build networks.* Much of what happens in the daily life of a company happens through informal channels. You will be effective to the extent that people throughout the organization know you, like you and trust your motives.

7 *Think of the political process as one of conflict resolution.* To a great extent, good politics is the ability to negotiate well. Good deals benefit both parties, and good negotiators don't try to beat the other guy. They solve problems; they look for areas of overlapping interest and expand on them.

8 *Share the facts.* Information is a source of positive power. If you know what is going on when others don't, you are immediately in a position of power. If you try to hold on to that position by not sharing information, you lose trust and, in turn, the power you had.

9 *Win support from the boss.* Although you can accomplish much through sheer negotiating ability, you'll accomplish much more if the boss supports your goals. Remember, however, that misusing your supervisor's support put you in the soup (or it ought to).

10 *Discourage political behaviour that is purely self-serving.* Weed out those who are politicking in the negative sense. The more blatant ones are easy to spot. The difficult ones are those who are especially good at relating upward but not sideways or down in the organization. They're so skilful at getting along with the boss that they mask the fundamental divisiveness of their actions.

11 *Come down hard on political infighting.* Take a cue from an executive who picked the worst offenders, fired them and told everyone why. The action seems unduly harsh, but considering the vigour lost when politics are tolerated, the punishment fits the crime.

12 *Promote transforming leaders at all levels of the organization.* Look for several characteristics: a vision that expresses the thought 'This is what the organization needs, and here is the mark I will make on it'; a record of achievement; the ability to bring out the best in others; and, of course, integrity.

13 *Do not tolerate lack of integrity or of trustworthy behaviour.* An atmosphere that lacks trust breeds bad politics. Don't deal with people you don't trust inside or outside your organization.

14 *If your company runs on mistrust leave.* This is easier said than done, but the alternatives are bleak: become political yourself or watch well-intended programmes being steamrollered.

Appendix 2: A Team by Any Other Name

Corporate teams often fall far short of the goals for which they strive, a fact that explains why teamwork is so often less productive than expected. Most people define any group with a common goal as a team, but Drs. Robert E. Lefton and V.R. Buzzotta of Psychological Associates Inc. in St. Louis, Missouri, have identified four patterns of interaction. Each group probably comprises a mixture of these pure forms, but only one represents true teamwork.

1   *The hierarchical pattern*   Rank and authority are the important factors with this team. Strict procedures are in place for control and for transmission of instructions from the top down.
2   *The formalistic pattern*   Bureaucracy and impersonal organization predominate. The emphasis is on precedent, tradition and routine. Innovation is discouraged.
3   *The circular pattern*   The focus is on camaraderie and congeniality, which are mistaken for collaboration. The leader, equating high morale with high productivity, abides by the motto 'Keep everybody happy'.
4   *The teamwork pattern*   Constructive candour is prized, and collaboration is not an end but a means to results. The leader enlists everyone as needed. Commitment is an obvious consequence.

Chapter 19
Developing Women as Leaders

Introduction

The question of whether women add a unique quality to leadership may be fraught with controversy (see chapter 12), but there is more consensus that the number of female managers who make it to the top is disappointingly low. On both sides of the Atlantic, fewer than 10 per cent of all directors are women. In countries with an exemplary record of equal opportunities, such as Norway and Sweden, the proportion is not much higher.

The cause is certainly not a failure to recruit women into junior management. Look at the graduate intake of Top 500 companies throughout the 1980s and you find that 40 to 50 per cent were female. Similarly, the number of women taking MBA courses increased from an average of just under 5 per cent in most established business schools in 1979 to between 20 and 30 per cent in 1990.

The problem comes higher up in the organization. In the transition from middle to senior management large numbers of women drop out. In many companies women outnumber men by a ratio of two to one in junior management whereas higher up men outnumber women by anything from four to ten to one.

The articles in this chapter offer many explanations, most falling into one of three categories – culture, career management, and children. Clare Bebbington focuses on the third. 'Whichever way you turn to explain why women find it so difficult to make it to the top of companies, she says, 'there is no getting away from the deep-seated assumption that women at some point in their careers will break to have children. This not only detrimentally affects a woman's chances of promotion and access to training opportunities, but it also all too often colours a woman's own expectations of her career.'

Bebbington's article was written in 1988, the year when the full implications of the demographic time bomb were beginning to be discussed in boardrooms and conferences throughout North America and those European countries facing a sharp decline in the number of young people. Child-care support, longer maternity leave, and flexible working were advocated as the key to breaking the glass ceiling which separated women from the board. Career management centred on ways in which 'women returners' could be reintegrated into the mainstream with a minimum of fuss and disruption.

The trouble with the child-care debate is that it detracts attention from the cultural barriers women face in gaining credibility from their male peers. Jaclyn Fierman, in an article written as recently as 1990, argues that many female executives who aspire to the top in the US 'want no special favors . . . These women figure their best shot at success is at gender-blind companies that make no concessions to their needs and require them to work the same hours as men.' As the female vice-president of a computer software company puts it: 'There is no such thing as job sharing or part time at the top.'

Summed up in one sentence, Fierman's article suggests that for the foreseeable future, women will succeed only if they play to male rules. 'Look like a lady, act like a man; work like a dog' is the advice she offers her female readers. Career management should not only reconcile family and professional responsibilities but also ensure that women stay in line management and do not get shunted into dead-end functions like personnel and PR.

Yet she also highlights the appalling cost women pay in the face of male prejudice and the 'no concessions' ethic. Assumptions about boardroom behaviour, for example, force women to tread an uneasy tightrope between abrasive masculinity and wimpish feminity. 'It's as if we're being asked to play a Beethoven sonata in two octaves . . . We need the whole keyboard to show our range', says one interviewee.

Women can have children and succeed, Fierman concludes: but only if they delegate all child-care and household responsibilities to domestic staff and, in effect, put the same distance between them and their children as their husbands. Another female executive interviewed in the article comments: 'I don't cook. I don't do laundry. I don't market. I don't take my children to malls and museums. And I don't have close friends.' To avoid this dilemma, Fierman suggests that women should have children early on in life so that they are free to devote their attention to their work at a time when their children are less dependent.

How does all this affect the training and development women receive in the formative stages of their careers? Should they be treated any differently from men? The final contribution suggests the interventions corporations can make not to 'make things easier' for women in their work *per se* but to ensure they receive the kind of responsibility at an early age which will qualify them for senior positions.

Valerie Hammond from the UK's Ashridge Management College proposes a three-point process which provides women in junior management with mentoring and two-way career appraisal, female middle managers with projects and task force assignments which provide general management perspectives, and senior executives with experience of running major operational units.

Career management is, in Hammond's view, more important than special courses. But she also stresses that the work environment women encounter in senior management needs to be transformed. 'For women . . . to develop their full potential within the corporate framework requires a change in attitude and behaviour of men as well as of women', she argues. 'Outdated assumptions and attitudes are often perpetuated by people who are well-meaning but unintention- ally disabling.'

This does not mean that women need to be let down easy, 'The paternalistic view . . . in some companies . . . can be doubly disabling for women', she says, 'as it protects them from taking risks and meeting challenges which are the most significant growth points.' But she does rebut the view implied in Fierman's article that attitudes in the boardroom are sacrosanct and women should put up with them or get out. Indeed, as she points out, unless companies break the Catch-22 situation facing women in the boardroom, the best female talent will be lost to them as high-ranking women start their own companies as the only means to realize their full potential.

1
Ladies Don't Climb Ladders

Clare Bebbington

Margaret Thatcher and Gro Harlem Brundtland running countries of 57 million and 4 million people respectively? So why does the prospect of a woman at the helm of Philips, Volkswagen or ICI still seem such a long way off? In boardrooms throughout Europe, women are remarkable chiefly for their absence.

In France, just over 2% of top managers are female; 5% of the members of the UK's Institute of Directors are women. Even in the Netherlands the picture is similar. On a recent count there, women represented just under 2% of all supervisory board members. And in Italy, the proportion of women in top managerial positions in the private sector hovers around 2%. That is backed by common experience. Watch passengers getting off any of Europe's short-haul business flights, and there are probably 50 men with briefcases for every woman.

Even in Scandinavia, where many believe opportunities are most equal, women are few and far between in the higher echelons of corporate management. In Norway, less than 9% of all management positions are occupied by women. In Finland, women make up just 11% of managers in the private sector. The statistics vary slightly from country to country, but the general pattern remains the same: all across Europe, women are making slow progress up the corporate ladder.

There is plenty of evidence to suggest that this is not because women are short of management or entrepreneurial skills. Running a large household is very much like running a small business. Moreover, figures from the International Labour Organization indicate that the number of female entrepreneurs is increasing quite rapidly. In Finland, 30% of all entrepreneurs are women, in Sweden 25% in France 21% and in West Germany 20%.

'Ladies Don't Climb Ladders', by Clare Bebbington, from *Eurobusiness*, December 1988, by permission of Eurobusiness Ltd.

Women become entrepreneurs for a variety of reasons. Not all of them are peculiar to women. Anita Roddick of Body Shop (Britain's most profitable company according to a recent survey in *Management Today*) was driven originally by financial necessity and a narrow range of options. However, it is easy to find examples of women who have become disenchanted with the opportunities offered by large organizaitons and have decided to branch out on their own. Ragni Rissanen, owner and managing director of the Finnish hotel chain Rivoli-Yhitot, left the banking industry to set up her first cafe. On her way to creating a company with an annual turnover of Fmk 70 million she is credited with introducing the pizza parlour and nouvelle cuisine to Finland.

First Steps

For many women in northern Europe the battle to gain a first foothold in the labour market has been fought, and is well on the way to being won. Scarce as women may be in the higher strata of corporate life, OECD figures show that over the past two decades female participation in the workforce has increased in every European country. Cultural differences, variations in tax systems, the speed and nature of industrial development, religion, housing costs – the list is endless – account for the very different percentages of women who work.

In some cases, most notably Portugal, the increase has been dramatic, from 25% in 1967 to 57% in 1987. Conversely, in the Netherlands, where the female participation rate is only 40%, progress has been disappointing. Aided by equal-opportunities legislation, economic necessity and changing attitudes, both in the workplace and at home, it will not be long before in one country – Sweden – women will be participating in the workforce at virtually the same rate as men.

But participation rates alone paint an incomplete picture. Women are more likely to be concentrated in the poorly-paid lower grades, and they often work only part-time – 90% of all part-time workers in the UK are female. Susse Meedom of the Dansk Arbejdsgiverforening (Danish Employers Federation) points out that women are also concentrated in relatively few industries. In Denmark, working women are to be found in 30 trades compared with 300 trades for men.

Even in those industries where women are well represented, they still do not progress to senior management. Take the Irish electronics industry. A study undertaken by the Irish Employment Equality Agency, published in 1987, found that whereas 74% of the operatives were female, only 3% of the managers were. Commenting on this, the authors of the study said that:

> In broad outline the Irish situation is similar to that in other countries. In electronics factories all over the world, the best-paid jobs are filled almost entirely be men and the worst-paid jobs almost entirely by women.

Even in areas where women are thought to be well represented (for example, in the media) few make it to the top. A Europe-wide study of television companies found that out of 1,775 managers in the top three grades, only 135 were women.

Is too much being expected too soon? As long as companies make longevity of service a prerequisite of a seat in the boardroom, women will have to resign themselves to a long wait. Cor van der Klugt, Carl Hahn and Helmut Maucher started their careers in Philips, Volkswagen and Nestlé respectively in the 1950s. They reached the top of their companies after 30 years of slow progress. Few women have yet spent similar spells in the corporate foothills.

Marie-Antoinette Hugenin, who was Switzerland's first female bank branch officer, says 'the doors are definitely opening.' There are encouraging signs that the number of women entering certain professions is rising rapidly. Women bankers are on the increase. The number of female members of the UK's Institute of Bankers increased from 20,000 to 31,000 between 1987 and 1988. So too are female accountants and lawyers. But the proportion of women in these profession still falls way below 50%.

The number of women taking MBA courses is also increasing. At Insead, the international management stood near Paris, an average of 12% of the past three intakes has been female. At the London Business School the figure is even higher, at 27%, and at IESE in Barcelona the figure for the current intake is 17%. Ten years ago the figures were under 5%.

But how far have attitudes really changed? Amid much pageantry, *Cosmopolitan* magazine and the Nationwide Anglia Building Society recently ran a competition for high-flying women. The prize was an all-expenses paid MBA course at Insead. Laudable indeed. But why did their press release describe the winner as a 'girl'? Ermine Evans, a gilt-edged saleswoman at stockbrokers Citicorp Scrimgeour Vickers, is 28. It does not need a strident feminist to point out that no man in his late twenties would like to be described as a 'boy'. As time passes, those women already in positions of power will facilitate the progress of others. They will do that either by example, or by creating the corporate environment that encourages more women to progress. Val Hammond, research director at the UK's Ashridge Management College, believes that women executives in Europe are doing more to change their working environment than are their American counterparts, even though their progress up the corporate ladder has been slower.

But for every plus, there is at least one minus. Look at the figures for post-experience executive development programmes (EDP) run by business schools. Only once over the past three years has the proportion of women on Insead's EDP courses for high-flying executives scraped over 4%. At the London Business School, the proportion is marginally higher at a miserable 6%. Neither school expects dramatic changes over the next few years.

Why does this sexual differentiation persist when, as our profiles illustrate, talented women are successfully running businesses all over Europe? Diana

Davies, a participant on the European Women's Management Development Network's study tour to America, says that 'for women to succeed, it was felt that their performance had to be outstanding, whatever difficulties were encountered.'

These difficulties start young. Girls too readily shy away from non-traditional subjects at school. Whereas in Sweden no more than one in ten students studying production engineering at secondary level is a woman, nine out of ten students on nursing courses are female. Family responsibilities still play a far bigger part in a woman's life than in a man's.

As might be expected, Italian husbands were found in 1983 to leave the bulk of housework to their spouses whether they were working or not – encouraged, no doubt, by mothers who do not want to see the next generation of women shed a burden they had to bear. But macho Italian males are not alone in this. A study of women in south-east London found that whereas single women were half as likely to suffer stress as single men, married women were four times more likely to suffer stress than married men.

Whichever way you turn to explain why women find it so difficult to make it to the top of companies, there is no getting away from the deep-seated assumption that women at some point in their careers will break to have children. This not only detrimentally affects a woman's chances of promotion and access to training opportunities, but it also all too often colours a woman's own expectations of her career.

The Need to Move Fast

There are grounds for hoping that slowly such assumptions will hamper women less, although it is unlikely that they will ever disappear entirely. The Employee Benefit Research Institute of America believes that child care will be the fringe benefit of the 1990s. Where America leads, Europe may have to follow. This summer the European Commission was presented with a report from the Childcare Network, set up as part of the Community's second programme on equality. The report noted that:

> In the present situation, not only are women unable to compete on equal terms in the labour market because of the unequal share of family responsibilities that they carry; but variations in policies between member states are an obstacle to the free movement of labour between member states. The current major disparities in child-care services and related policies affecting the employment of many workers with children are not compatible with the concept of a single market.

The recommendations of the report include the issuing of directives on maternity leave; a guide to good practice in child-care services; and a revised draft directive on parental leave to circumvent the current impasse caused by the UK's opposition to its introduction. Many are concerned that such stringent requirements could damage the health of small companies which are the least able to cope with absent staff.

In terms of state child-care provision, maternity leave entitlement, and parental leave, there were wild discrepancies between European countries. In Denmark, 44% of children under the age of two are in publicly funded child-care services, as are 87% of children aged 3–6. In the UK, 2% of children under two are in publicly funded crêches, and 44% of those aged 3–6. So it is no surprise that, in Denmark, 75% of women with children under five work. In Britain, just 28% of such women do. Where public facilities are not extensive, a woman's chances of making it to the top are greatly dependent on the company she works for. In the Netherlands, for example, IBM is a frontrunner in offering maternity benefits.

A demographic time bomb is ticking away which could be of benefit to European working women. Just as the absence of men in the First World War precipitated female emancipation, the decline in school leavers that is inevitable in the mid-1990s must force companies to make better use of female labour and of female skills. The Confederation of British Industry points out that between 1986 and 1994 the number of 16- and 17-year-olds in the UK will fall from 1.7 million to 1.25 million.

The populations of West Germany and Denmark are already declining. These countries are faced with the prospect of a shrinking and ageing workforce. According to the OECD, the projected fall in the youth labour force is likely to be sharpest in Austria and the Netherlands. The proportion of young people in the Dutch labour force could decline from around 20% in 1987 to around 12% by the year 2000. Austria faces a decline from 23.7% in 1985 to 16% in 2000.

As a result, companies are beginning to look for alternative sources of labour to young male school leavers. Not surprisingly, companies in those sectors which rely heavily on school leavers are in the vanguard of firms experimenting with in-house child-care provision, back-to-work schemes, and so on. In the UK, Midland Bank and the Halifax Building Society have just announced that they are to set up in-house child-care facilities. Not, of course, for any altruistic motives. The UK financial sector takes on some 20,000 school leavers each year.

Solving the baby-break problem will not be enough. If European companies want to avoid being short of skills in the demographic squeeze to come, they will have to think much more imaginatively about how to entice and keep female workers. Some have started. The Swedish car-maker Volvo is looking at the question of equal opportunities from an original angle. In its Uddevalle plant, Lena Sperling is heading a project which, by examining the dimensions of the male and female hand, aims to design more egalitarian production-line equipment. The sooner that women climb into the corporate boardroom, the sooner this process will get fully under way.

2
Why Women Still Don't Hit the Top

Jaclyn Fierman

When will women in decent numbers finally make it into the highest ranks of corporate America? The short answer: not in this millennium. By the year 2000 women will make up nearly half of the labor force. But it won't be the top half. The cool reception women once got at the door has followed them up the organizational hierarchy. For all but an exceptional few, the corner office still looks as remote as it did to Rosie the Riveter.

Just wait, was the old excuse. A decade ago even women's staunchest male advocates said time had to pass; women lacked the seasoning and seniority to run the show. Today that explanation rings increasingly hollow. Women have gained access to virtually every line of work and are bulging in the pipeline: The US Department of Labour says they make up 40% of a loosely defined demographic category of managers and administrators that covers everyone from President Bush to the person running the local Dairy Queen. But only a minuscule number of women have top jobs at America's major companies, and not many more are in the zone for promotion to those jobs anytime soon. Says Judy Mello, 46, in the early 1980s CEO of First Women's Bank in New York City: 'My generation came out of graduate school 15 or 20 years ago. The men are now next in line to run major corporations. The women are not. Period.'

Want proof? *Fortune* examined 1990 proxy statements of the 799 public companies on its combined lists of the 1,000 largest US industrial and service companies. The cold-shower findings: of the 4,012 people listed as the highest-paid officers and directors of their companies, we spotted 19 women – less than one-half of 1%. True, there has been progress, but it has been remarkably limited. When *Fortune* undertook a similar project in 1978, out of 6,400 officers

'Why Women Still Don't Hit the Top', by Jaclyn Fierman, from *Fortune*, July 30 1990. Copyright © 1990 The Magazine Company, by permission of the publishers.

and directors on its combined lists, which then included 1,000 industrial and 300 service companies, ten were women.

Further down the ranks the numbers are more heartening. But only slightly. To get an idea of the count – there are no authoritative studies of the number of women in upper management – *Fortune* looked through the names at the back of the annual reports of 255 major corporations. The list often goes as deep in the organization as division head and assistant vice president, and includes positions like corporate secretary that have frequently gone to women. Of the 9,293 names, 5% were women. (Admittedly, some women, especially initial users, may have escaped us, though we did pay special attention to the Leslies, Carols and Gales. And some men may have slipped through our screen, though we did catch Mr Shirley Beavers of First Virginia Bank.)

To once again raise a question *Fortune* posed 17 years ago when it first looked at women in the executive suite, where in blazes *are* they? Many women aren't rising to the top of large corporations because they quit or deliberately leap off the fast track. They miss their children. They miss not have *had* children. A better opportunity comes along. Or they just get tired and want out of the rat race. As comedienne Lily Tomlin quipped, 'If I had known what it would be like to have it all, I might have settled for less.'

For many baby-boom women, the 1980s effectively destroyed the notion that they could have it all: a full-blown career, a happy marriage, well-adjusted children, and cellulite-free thighs. Blessed with first-class educations, middle-class drive, and a sense of unlimited opportunities, these women expected a lot of themselves. They also expected equal treatment in the workplace. And they wanted to give their families – if they ever got around to having them – the same security that June Cleaver gave her children. Well-intentioned but torn asunder, many understandably failed as Supermoms.

But some women were willing to tough it out, stay the course, and make the necessary sacrifices. What they have run up against can only be called discrimination. Discrimination, you scoff, in this enlightened age? Yes, says Ralph Ablon, chairman of Ogden Corp., no. 74 on *Fortune*'s list of the 100 largest diversified service companies. 'Sure there's discrimination. It's stupid to say there's not. Despite our intellectual efforts to deny it, prejudices exist and will exist until a new generation comes along that doesn't have them.' That generation, it bears remembering, was supposed to be the baby boom, many of whose men have already assumed key decision-making roles at large companies.

At age 73, Ablon seems an unlikely harbinger of new thinking. But three years ago he appointed Maria Monet, now 40, as his company's chief financial officer, and he pays her more than $730,000 a year, making her one of the top-earning women in corporate America. Enlightenment, Ablon concedes, has come only with age and a lot of contemplation: 'When I became CEO 29 years ago, I don't believe I could have been as liberal. And I couldn't have gotten away with appointing a woman as CFO. Today I could.'

A recent poll of *Fortune* 1,000 CEOs shows that Ablon isn't alone in finding discrimination at work. Nearly 80% of 241 respondents to a survey conducted by Catalyst, a group that does research on women in the workplace, said there are identifiable barriers that keep women from reaching the top. No, they say, women do not lack the technical skills to make it. After all, they have been going to the same schools as their male counterparts and now represent over half of all college students, 37% of graduate business students, and roughly 40% of law students. The problems, said an astonishing 81% of the CEOs who acknowledged the existence of barriers, are stereotyping and preconceptions.

This is a subtle, tricky, but nonetheless pernicious form of discrimination, more apparent in the result – just look at the numbers – than in anyone's conscious intentions. Ask the typical male executive if he is prejudiced against women, and he will roundly deny it. But when it comes to choosing among several rivals for a top corporate job, he chooses a man. The next time, he does the same thing. And the next. Even Ablon, who recently retired as CEO of Ogden chose not Monet but a man – his 40-year-old son, Richard – to succeed him.

What nonsense, you counter – if women don't get top jobs, they don't deserve them. Undoubtedly so in many cases. Besides, the volume of the uppermost quarter of any pyramid is only 1.6% of the whole, a geometric fact that automatically eliminates most women – *and men* – who aspire to the top. True also that the average CEO is in his mid-50s and most business schools began admitting women in significant numbers only in the early 1970s, which puts them around fortysomething today.

But John Reed had no trouble seeing over his desk six years ago when he was promoted to CEO of Citicorp at age 45. Nor does Cigna CEO Wilson Taylor, who is now 46. Even allowing that many women still aren't old enough or talented enough to be CEO, more should be joining their male contemporaries in the executive dining room. CEO John Mascotte of Continental Corp., a property and casualty company worth $14 billion in assets, was stunned when he started counting. Two-thirds of his 15,000 employees are women, but nine out of ten senior managers are men. Says he: 'It seems idiotic if we're investing in people but making it impossible for them to advance. Are we sending out signals that women need not aspire to the top?'

The signals may be no more than a slight rustling of discomfort, a bit of awkwardness in a man's body language. It may seem surprising in an era sometimes labeled postfeminist, but working closely with the opposite sex continues to make many male executives uncomfortable. Listen to Ellie Raynolds, a partner at the headhunting firm Ward Howell International: 'Corporate males still don't know how to deal with women. They are afraid to yell at them or to give them negative feedback. It's as though they think they are yelling at their mothers or their wives. Men often worry women will run from the room in tears, or worse yet, yell back. They're not really sure the women will come through for them. They just don't trust them as much as the guys with whom they talk football.'

Haven't we heard this before? But after ten years of supposed progress, too many of the old, uncomfortable ways persist. The offense may be as banal as the mere existence of Merrill Lynch's Chowder and Marching Society, a group of men who get together now and then for drinks and dinner. Or it may be tougher to read. 'You'd hear things,' says Deborah Farrington, 39, who went to Merrill Lynch after graduating from Harvard business school in 1976. 'There were innuendoes. If you wore dark blue suits with floppy bow ties, there would be no talk about whether you were being flirtatious. But if you were attractive and dressed stylishly, people took you less seriously.' Farrington, who spent a decade at Merrill, feels she can more easily be herself as head of corporate finance in Hong Kong for Asian Oceanic Group, a small merchant bank.

Try as women have to fit into the male business milieu, men still think they do a lousy job of it. Many believe corporate women are weak in interpersonal skills, a dimension that's largely ineffable but critical to achieving a high corporate position, where competence is assumed and chemistry often becomes key. Sometimes men see women as pushovers. More often they find women overbearing. 'The most common lament of top management men is "She's too shrill. She's too aggressive. She's too hard-edged,"' says Kenneth Brousseau, president of Decision Dynamics Corp., a human resources consulting firm in Santa Monica, California.

Women point to the persistence of precisely this attitude as the most pernicious example of discrimination in the workplace. If they are too feminine, they are viewed as softies; too masculine, and they're abrasive. 'It's as if we're being asked to play a Beethoven sonata in two octaves,' says Arlene Johnson, who directs workforce studies for the Conference Board, a business research organization in New York. 'We need the whole keyboard to show our range.'

The recently decided case of Ann Hopkins, 46, formerly a management consultant at Price Waterhouse, affords a striking example of how such stereotyping works. In May a federal judge ordered the accounting firm to make Hopkins a partner and give her $370,000 in back pay because it had unfairly discriminated against her. The firm, which counts 27 women among its 876 partners, recently filed an appeal.

What happened: In 1982, Hopkins and 87 colleagues, all men, came up for consideration as partners. Though in the previous few years she had played a big part in securing some $40 million in contracts for the firm, an amount she says was more than that of any other candidate for partner in 1982, she was not among the 47 people promoted; Price Waterhouse will neither confirm nor deny Hopkins's claim. 'Any women who can be a success with her clients should qualify as partner,' says Cynthia Turk, 37, who recently resigned as partner from a Price Waterhouse competitor, Deloitte & Touche, to set up her own consulting firm. 'This was a clear case of discrimination.'

The court, in agreeing, found particularly damning a remark made by Hopkins' mentor and chief supporter. 'He told me to walk more femininely, talk more femininely, wear make-up, have my hair styled, and wear jewelry,' says Hopkins, now a senior budget officer at the World Bank. Hopkins, who has two sons, 11 and 12, and a 14-year-old daughter, says the advice was largely useless: 'I already wear jewelry and high heels, and I go to the beauty parlor. But I'm allergic to makeup.' Even if she weren't allergic, Hopkins says applying the makeup would be difficult because she can't see without her trifocals.

Faced with this kind of prejudice, women who set their sights on top jobs and actually get them develop 20-20 vision when it comes to corporate folkways. 'They understand that competence and a bus token will only get them across town,' says psychologist Dee Soder, president of New York's Endymion Co., which counsels women and men who want to scale the corporate Everest. The experiences of the women on *Fortune*'s best-compensated list, plus war stories from Hopkins and other high-achieving women identified by *Fortune*, show just how tricky it is to navigate the ascent.

Go-getters who stand out in the ranks can *stick out* at the top. 'When I first started out, I was extremely rough around the edges,' says Lois Juliber, president of Colgate-Palmolive's Far East/Canada division. 'Bully wouldn't be the right word, but I was the toughest of the tough. I didn't listen well. I had to mellow and learn to trust people.

It may help to regard the experiences of women in business as akin to infiltrating an alien world. Maria Monet of Ogden has been feeling her way and finding it since she emigrated to the US from Portugal when she was 5 years old. 'I grew up trying to fit in with a different culture. I didn't speak English when I went to kindergarten,' she says.

Monet had her share of setbacks on the corporate climb. Twice she hit the proverbial glass ceiling, a barrier that enables women to glimpse but not grasp the corner office. A lawyer by training, she began as an associate at the Wall Street firm of Shearman & Sterling in 1974. But by 1980 it was still largely a white-shoe – no heels – firm, and Monet failed to make partner.

Investment banking, she thought, would be different. After 18 months of round-the-clock dealmaking at Lehman Brothers, she took stock: All the partners were men. So when an Ogden executive whom she met on a deal offered her a job, she leaped again. Monet quickly established herself at Ogden by reducing the time between the start and close of a deal from two years to six months. In three years she rose to chief financial officer.

If women who are puzzling over appropriate boardroom behavior feel as if their heads are spinning, so do male managers. Just what do women want, anyway? The vast majority have lobbied aggressively for special treatment. And they are getting it. Hewitt Associates, a benefits and compensation consulting firm in Chicago, found that 56% of 259 major employers offer some sort of child-care aid, 56% allow flexible scheduling, and 42% grant unpaid parental leave.

But along comes a select group of women who want no special favors – just a top job, thank you. These women figure their best shot at success is at gender-blind companies that make no concessions to their needs and require them to work the same hours as men. 'There is no such thing as job sharing or part time at the top,' says Phyllis Swersky, 39, executive vice president of AICorp Inc., a computer software company outside Boston. Swersky began holding meetings in her living room two days after she came home from the hospital after delivering her third child.

America's most successful businesswomen wave not the feminist banner but the corporate one. 'I've never particularly thought of myself as a woman in business, so I've never let it get in my way,' says Kathryn Braun, 39, senior vice president of Western Digital, a major supplier of personal computer parts in Irvine, California.

These women have interpersonal skills sufficient to finesse them through difficult situations. Edith Martin, 45, who was a Deputy Under Secretary of Defense under President Reagan and is now a vice president at Boeing, recalls the time she went on an executive outing while at Control Data. The luncheon grill was an extension of the men's locker room. Rather than sitting around with a bunch of towel-clad hearties, Martin decided to hit tennis balls while the men ate. 'Yes, there are awkward moments,' she says. 'You can either walk off with a hot head or laugh it off. But after you have a couple of drinks and everyone laughs it off, it brings you closer.' Moral: Greet the wrong gesture with the right attitude.

In breaking through stereotypes, the addage that line jobs are the straightest line to the top still holds. Women should take a lead from men and steer clear of dead ends like personnel and public relations. The most successful have typically sought out risky, thankless projects whose results become immediately apparent on the bottom line. 'You have to prove you're a leader. You have to show you're willing to steal second base. Women don't project that ability well.' says Mary Rudie Barneby, 38, who built from scratch a $3 billion corporate retirement plan business for Merrill Lynch. She now heads a similar division for Dreyfus Corp. in New York City.

Maria Monet stole second while working at Lehman Brothers. Her client, Ogden Corp., wanted to build a waste-to-energy plant in Oregon, but the county thought the financing it would have to provide was too burdensome. Monet calculated that if the county floated variable- rather than fixed-rate bonds to pay for construction, it could save about $5 million. 'I was so new at investment banking, I didn't even realize the problems I had created,' she says. 'Financing a waste-to-energy project whose future revenues were predictable with bonds whose interest rates were not was unheard of.' But Monet persisted, won the bankers' confidence, and caught the eye of Ogden Chairman Ablon. Her creative financing set a new industry standard and, she's convinced, clinched her career.

What Western Digital's Braun calls her acid test entailed resisting Wall Street nay-sayers to buy the assets of Tandon Corp.'s faltering disk drive division in 1988. Braun decided she had no choice: Without disks, she predicted, Western Digital's bread-and-butter business – computer information storage – wouldn't survive. She felt sure that the next generation of storage chips would reside directly in the disks. She guessed right. 'We managed our way through the crisis,' she says.

One of the explanations still cited for why women fail to get to the top is that they don't stick to it; they leave jobs more often than men do. Conclusive evidence on the point is hard to come by. But women do seem more willing than men to act on their desires for something else, perhaps because they are so acutely aware of the personal sacrifices they are making to work. When Opinion Research Corp. of Princeton, New Jersey, asked 26 500 managers in seven large companies whether they intended to quit their jobs in the next year, 17% of women said yes, compared with 11% of men.

If women would just hang in there and be patient, the thinking goes, more might reach their goals. Perhaps, allows Dreyfus Corp.'s Barneby, who in 14 years rose from clerical worker to one of the highest-ranking women at Merrill Lynch. 'If I had waited, I think I would have had a shot at the top rungs', she says. 'But I got tired of pushing. My shoulder started to hurt.'

Don't Blame the Baby is the name Wick & Co., a Delaware consulting firm, gave its recent study of why male and female managers change jobs. The Wick research, a survey of 110 executives, found that most women quit jobs not to rock the cradle but to find greater career satisfaction somewhere else.

Nonetheless, virtually every woman interviewed for this article acknowledged the heavy – and sometimes painful – demands of juggling family or personal life and the fast track. Observes John Rosenblum, dean of the University of Virginia's Darden graduate school of business administration: 'Women are discouraged about their ability to realize a vision of life that has family, career, and happiness all in the same sentence.'

In choosing to make the corporate climb, Monet let some of life's other options go. She has no children and sees her husband, a general partner at Montgomery Securities in San Francisco, once a month. She reports to work every morning at seven at the New York headquarters of Ogden, which operates sports arenas, power plants, and convention centers. She eats lunch at her desk and tops off her 11-hour day with a 1½-hour workout at a nearby health club. 'I used to think I could work, get married, and raise a family,' she says. 'I realize now it's hard enough just to do my job well. It was a rude awakening.'

One very senior woman at a large consumer products company asked not to be quoted by name when she spoke of the price she had paid for success. 'I would never want my mother to know how much it hurts me to be childless,' she says. She is hardly alone. Nearly half the women on *Fortune*'s 1990 list of highly paid women are childless, five are divorced, and one never married. Claudia Goldin, the first tenured economics professor at Harvard, feels she might not have achieved her position had she had a family. 'I'm at the top of my profession now, and it took a tremendous amount of concentration and focus in a brief period of time. If I were married and had kids, I probably wouldn't have had the energy.'

Women who do try to combine traditional and fast-track lifestyles need a rock-solid infrastructure at home. Swersky of AICorp has a live-in nanny to care for her three children, ages 8, 5, and 4. She also has a live-in housekeeper and a supportive husband who runs his own accounting firm. Says Swersky: 'I don't take care of the house. I don't cook. I don't do laundry. I don't market. I don't take my children to malls and museums. And I don't have close friends.'

She typically leaves the house before 8 a.m. and returns around 7 p.m. 'I am often gone longer, not shorter, than this,' she says. 'I am frequently too tired to tell my husband about my day, listen to him tell me about his, or play with the children. It was a major challenge just to figure out a simple hair style and makeup for myself.'

On the question of when to bear the brood, women are often not in sync with their employers. 'From an organizational point of view, the early 20s is the best time to have children,' says Mary Anne Devanna, associate dean of the Columbia University graduate school of business. 'Employers don't care what people do before they enter the work force.' Probably so, but many women don't feel ready at that age. Says Blair Sheppard, 38, director of the human resource management center at Duke University's Fuqua graduate school of business: 'The whole career ladder in the US is predicated on the life cycle of a man. We tell people to prove themselves between 30 and 38. But that's when executive women tend to have babies.'

The lesson: Having it all is easier if you don't insist on having it all at once. Rosetta Bailey, 55, now senior vice president at Citizens Federal Bank in Florida and a member of *Fortune*'s 1990 list, worked as a receptionist and teller in the bank for 15 years while raising two children. 'By the time I got to a management level, it wasn't necessary for me to be with my children all the time,' she says.

Ambitious women would do well to choose employers whose expectations are compatible with their own. Banking has always been fertile ground, perhaps because women have been paying their dues for years and now represent 91% of tellers, for instance. High-tech companies and small startup ventures too bent on survival to be exclusionary are also women-friendly. 'There is no old boy network in my industry, because it's too new,' says Western Digital's Braun. 'So women rise more easily through the ranks.'

In a business where product life cycles are as short as two years, qualified women – and men – tend to be promoted more rapidly than colleagues at mature consumer products or industrial companies. Braun headed for Southern California 17 years ago, a biology and psychology graduate fresh out of Duke University. Her first job was on the assembly line of a minicomputer manufacturer. When she realized that women weren't being promoted into sales, she quit and joined Western Digital in 1978 as a technical support person. Today she heads the company's most profitable division, which so far this year has sold $200 million of intelligent disk drives and other storage products for personal computers.

No business is as receptive as the one whose CEO feels comfortable with women at his side. 'If I were working for my first employer today, I would still be a middle manager,' says Ilene Beal, one of three executive vice presidents at BayBanks, outside Boston. Of her current boss, CEO William Crozier, she says, 'He only cares about getting the job done. Maybe it's because he's married to a Ph.D. who has more degrees than he does.'

Will the glass ceiling ever disappear? Yes, if history is any guide. But it won't crack and fall all at once, or even soon. For most the the first half of this century, married women were almost unemployable; they couldn't even get office jobs. When they entered the work force in large numbers during World War II, it was not so much because men wanted to hire them as because the country needed them.

The next big wave of women – mostly baby-boomers – began working in the 1970s. Men were more receptive to them, but ambivalence abounded; as recently as 1978 there were urinals in the ladies' rooms at Harvard business school. And women managers still make only 64% of what men do.

Harvard's Goldin, for one, argues that conditions for working women will gradually get better. 'While there is still reason to clamor, women have made great strides, especially in the past ten years,' says Goldin, author of a new book called *Understanding the Gender Gap*. She notes that in the Department of Labor's broad management category, the gap between men's and women's wages narrowed 18.5% between 1979 and 1988.

Women who look at the world not as historians but as victims may scoff at Goldin's perspective. They are also the ones least likely to survive in the corporate jungle. 'Our best hope for the future are women who don't see the ceiling but the sky,' says Goldin. Indeed, the best defense in a hostile world is to shed the defensive posture. 'A group wants to feel that you're part of it,' says

Monet. 'If you don't look like them, you already have something to overcome. Most men just haven't had enough experience working with women.'

In the meantime, what can parents do to nudge things along? For starters, they should emphasize self-reliance in their daughters. Superachievers share a gritty, pioneering spirit, says New York psychologist Dee Soder. 'I have yet to meet a truly successful women who didn't have a courage-building experience in her childhood.' Typical is Ilene Beal of BayBanks, whose mother died when she was a child. 'My father brought me up to think I could do anything. If I broke a toy, he taught me to fix it. He brought out the take-charge part of me.'

Another small step: Parents should encourage their daughters to take as much interest in baseball and basketball as in Barbie. Not only would the girls gain fluency in the sports-speak so common in business, but according to a 1986 survey of 2,043 adults by *Sports Illustrated*, one of *Fortune*'s sister publications, sports lovers are more successful in life than nonfans. The poll also found that sports-minded people are wealthier, and perceive themselves as wittier, more popular, smarter, and more competitive than people who don't care about keeping score.

Parents might even inspire their daughters with Dr Seuss's current bestseller, *Oh, the Places You'll Go!* 'Remember that Life's a Great Balancing Act,' says the man who speaks volumes to children. He urges: 'On you will go though the weather be foul. On you will go though your enemies prowl . . . Onward up many a frightening creek, though your arms may get sore and your sneakers may leak . . . And will you succeed? Yes! You will, indeed! (98 and ¾ percent guaranteed.)'

The odds for grownup women, of course, are slimmer, though demographics are on their side. Women and minorities are already the majority in the workplace, and a competitive corporate America will eventually have little choice but to include them in their leadership pool. Until then – for the next few decades, anyway – women may want to heed the following checklist for success, which itself, alas, carries no guarantee: Look like a lady; act like a man: work like a dog.

3
Women Managers: Developing their Full Potential

Valerie Hammond

Today's interest in the development of women managers represents a change of focus from the late 1970s and early 1980s when the concern was how women could enter management. The current focus reflects a growing concern about women's performance as managers, whether they have the same or different qualities as men, how they fare in the promotion stakes, and how they can be retained within the workforce. In short, the need is to benefit from developing the full potential of women as managers.

The expression of this need comes from many different sources: employers who, coming out of the recession, face an urgent need to recruit people with talent; professionals in industry and academics who must arrange appropriate training; students at undergraduate and postgraduate level who wish to research specific aspects; and media people who want sound data on which to base articles and television programmes. This last group represents an important indication of the change that has occurred. It is no longer only the women's or social affairs journalists and programmes that feature these issues, but those concerned with business. It is becoming common to hear men address issues of equal opportunity and women's development and to put this in the context of economic need.

In doing this, journalists and business people are commenting on a cycle of activity that is reinforcing women's role in the workforce. Recent work by Mertha Cassanova, a member of the Naisbitt research and consulting firm that collects data on trends worldwide, notes the interrelationship between the growth in the service economy and in women's participation in the workforce. As services expand, so there is more possibility for women to work outside the home. This in turn gives women access to their own disposable income, which

Original paper written for this publication © Valerie Hammond 1989.

in its turn fuels the growth in services. Cassanova argues that this is a cause-and-effect spiral which will ensure that women remain in the workforce in significant numbers. This being so, it makes sense to look at the distribution of women in the workforce and particularly at those in management.

The entry and progression of women in management varies across the world, reflecting the cultural, social, and legal framework in each country. However, the situation in most Western industrialized nations is similar: women are in mangement but not to the same extent as men. At 35 per cent there is a higher proportion of women managers in the United States than in other countries but in that country, as elsewhere, there is a level above which, it seems, women have great difficulty in being promoted. Only 2 per cent of most American senior executives are women.

Estimates for the UK, based on a new occupational classification sytem used by the Institute of Employment Research, Warwick University, shows that in 1987 women comprised 22 per cent of all corporate managers and administrators and 32 per cent of all managers/proprietors in services and agriculture. (When figures for earlier years are recalculated in the same way, this represents an increase percentage share of jobs amounting to 5 per cent for corporate managers and administrators and 7 per cent for managers/proprietors. It is forecast that women's share of jobs in these groups will increase by 1995 by a further 3 per cent for corporate managers and administrators and 1 per cent for managers/proprietors.)

In the UK women are now represented in management posts in most industries. The few remaining formal barriers to entry are likely soon to fall or fade away. For example, current legislation to allow women to work in coal mines is unlikely to result in many women working at the coal-face but it will influence the number of women managers in the coal industry. This is because a prerequisite for many of the management posts in the coal industry is for some experience of work underground. Women will now have access to this as a right even though the development of mining technology is challenging the relevance of this experience.

This does not, of course, mean that women are equally represented in all industries. According to figures in the British Institute of Management (BIM) Annual Salary Survey for 1988, only in chemicals, metal manufacturing, and mechanical engineering are women not increasing their share of management jobs. By contrast, the survey shows that in textiles, construction, financial, and technical services women have more than doubled their numbers.

Women are more likely to be found in the junior levels of the management spectrum of jobs. However, the BIM Survey found that the women included in their survey tend to be younger than their male colleagues and that their earnings are rising faster, although men still earn more. BIM conclude that these women are on a 'fast track'. It is difficult to determine how representative the BIM survey is of the situation for women managers in UK as a whole but government statistics published annually in the New Earning Survey indicate that women form a small proportion of senior or top managers. This situation is supported by data from studies of the distribution of women's employment within the Institute of Directors where women form approximately 2 per cent of the membership, and by the practical experience of executive search and recruitment professionals.

On the other hand, as indicated above in the figures for proprietors/managers, the number of women who set up and own small businesses is increasing. There are a number of outstanding women entrepreneurs including innovative retailers like Anita Roddick of Body Shop, as well as those creating entirely new businesses in the high tech field such as Steve Shirley who founded the FI Group and Pamela Gray of Sphinx. It is worth noting that these three examples, and there are many more, are all drawn from the burgeoning service sector. Women have not been slow to seize these new opportunties either as business owners or franchisees.

This is an international phenomenon. The percentage of new businesses started by women is especially high in North America and in Canada it is now 86 per cent. In Spain, a country not yet as advanced as others in terms of women's development, none the less embraces entrepreneurial activity. At a 1989 meeting for management women, a young marketing professor quietly demonstrated the strength of her ideas by revealing that she has set up and owns several successful businesses – all in the service sector – which 'I can see from my office window'.

An important issue for the future is therefore not women's capacity for business or whether they can secure management jobs but whether women can survive and thrive within the corporations. The phenomenon of the 'glass ceiling' where women get close but are not appointed to senior posts has been well documented in the USA, specifically in *Breaking the Glass Ceiling* by Morrison et al. (1987). One response to this suggested in *Harvard Business Review* by Felice Schwartz of Catalyst, the US organization that campaigns for women's development, is the creation of an alternative career route: a 'mommy track' which would allow career-breaks as well as the more traditional continuous career track. This is not without its own problems in that women's decisions to have or not have a family tend to change over time and not always for reasons within their control. It is interesting that in the UK where there are a number of career-break schemes they are not described as separated from the regular career route.

Employers are subject to other pressures with regard to human resources. Demographic trends show that the number of school-leavers and graduates entering industry will decline substantially in the 1990s. This places a high premium on young people with talent and means that companies will have to broaden the resource pool of people from whom they recruit and promote. The main ways of achieving this are to make appointments from those in older age-groups, to make more effective use of underdeveloped resources within the company, and to employ more women returners. Women in UK have already increased their participation in the labour force substantially and this is set to increase still further in the 1990s.

This situation is shared with most countries in the developed world, and in some cases the impact will be dramatic. Over the period 1985–2000 for example, countries like West Germany and Italy will face a situation where the numbers of their young people aged 20–4 falls by about half. This compares with a drop of 28–9 per cent for the same age-group in other countries including the UK, Netherlands, and Belgium. Companies will no longer be able to afford to overlook the potential of women employees. As competition for scarce resources increases both within the UK, and increasingly post-1992 throughout Europe, women will choose to join those organizations where they see evidence that women are able to achieve, and do achieve, their potential.

Developing women managers to their full potential therefore calls for attention to three separate aspects of the development process:

- ensuring that women have training and particularly development throughout their careers in management
- giving attention to career and life management for women
- dealing with attitudes, assumptions, and unfair practices in the workplace.

Each of these aspects is discussed below.

Training and Development

Sparking Interest: Pre-entry Awareness of Management Careers

The barriers to women's initial entry to management have diminished, but more work is needed to overcome outdated assumptions in the minds of young people themselves and their teachers as well as of managers in companies. There are initiatives whose effect is to demonstrate to students at school and college that management is a natural and desirable career for women. Examples in the UK include the Young Enterprise programme where young people, girls and boys, form and run real companies for a year and short courses where pupils can 'taste' management. Girls generally perform well in these settings, and this serves to demonstrate to them and to the boys that management is a career that women can choose.

In the UK there is no universally preferred route into management which makes it difficult to track youthful aspirations. Even taking account of current attempts with the Management Charter Initiative to formalize development steps, there will remain diverse routes for many years to come. However, one useful indicator of interest in management is the number of students studying for business degrees. In 1988 this accounts for 5 per cent of all degrees, and women represent 41 per cent of those studying for these degrees.

At the higher level in the UK women comprise only around 20 per cent of people studying for the Master of Business Administration or equivalent qualification. However, the total number of people studying for this qualification in UK and Continental Europe is very small. This is, of course, a very different situation from the USA where an MBA is virtually mandatory for a management career and where women have studied for and gained the MBA in large numbers.

In the UK it is still common for graduates from a wide variety of disciplines to be recruited into management. As part of an initiative to attract some of the ablest young minds, the Foundation for Management Education (FME) have for the past five years offered an introduction to management course for Oxford undergraduates to encourage them to consider careers in management. By 1988 women's participation in the FME course had grown to 50 per cent and discussion showed that they were already forming clear ideas of the companies whom they believed would provide good training and career opportunities. The course includes the opportunity to meet and talk informally with company sponsors, usually people at board or senior management level. The under-graduates, men as well as women, comment on the small number of women who have these positions and can therefore act as role models in a similar way to the men. Very often it is the first time these undergraduates have thought that career success may depend on factors other than ability.

Matching Expectations: The Issue for Management Trainees

If undergraduates generally have been cushioned from this issue, it is clear that women who are successful in obtaining management traineeships soon learn that their male colleagues are more quickly accepted. An in-company study revealed that women's perception was that the men were given more challenging assignments, were moved more quickly, and were given more coaching and counselling by the line managers. Not unnaturally, this caused boredom and frustration among the women who found themselves given routine tasks, sent to unpopular locations or departments, and often left for long periods without feedback on their performance. In these circumstances, it is not surprising that high aspirations dwindled, and in the worst cases the young women left, convinced that they had no career opportunities with the company.

This situation, while it sounds stark, is one which will be familiar to many large organizations. Human resource managers engaged in graduate recruitment may be aware of the abilities of young women applicants but know that their particular organization climate is not yet ready to assimilate more than a very few. Organizations as disparate as the Post Office, Metal Box, Esso, and Oxfam have carried out their own internal studies to see what can be done to improve the work climate for their women. Such organizations are far-sighted in recognizing that they will need women increasingly to play a role in their management team, and that in order to achieve this they need to understand women's experience of the organization and to involve the women in improving the situation for themselves.

Frequently, what is also highlighted through studies such as these is a need to work with the attitudes and practices of existing middle managers, a group usually predominantly male and often with little experience of working with women except in roles such as secretaries, operatives, and sales assistants. This can often colour their assessment of the roles that women can perform.

Therefore while most training for new entrants to management is offered equally to women and to men there is frequently a lack of mentoring or counselling available to the women and they tend to be more restricted in terms of assignments that permit broader development. These differences may have far-reaching effects. The 1987 study by Peppercorn and Skoulding found that 27 per cent of women, as opposed to 16 per cent of men, said that their interest in management was sparked by a mentor, and successful women frequently identify specific individuals who guided their early career steps. Women seem therefore to draw heavily on this type of support and the lack of it may be denying the full development of young women with potential.

A Sense of Self and the Organization for First Line Managers

First management appointments are often those that are narrowly defined within a specialism. Training is typically skills-based and women are generally well represented on formal programmes which cover essential techniques and practices. Training or personal development programmes may be offered specifically for women. The intention is usually for women to grow in awareness of the basis on which 'things are done around here', to gain confidence, and to develop appropriate influencing and other skills. These events range from completely unstructured programmes of self-development to short courses where similar aspects are covered usually in a more formal but highly participative way.

In the unstructured programmes women are supported through a network of colleagues as they identify and meet individual needs. The programme is intended to encourage women to take responsibility for their own development. A report by Boydell et al. in 1986 showed that this type of approach can have a powerful effect in motivating and unblocking women who otherwise feel constrained by the management style and practice in their organization.

A potential difficulty with this approach to self-development is that it places a high premium on confidentiality, and companies may get little or no feedback on the individual's development plans. This can be counter-productive for women's development within the company if it serves to continue to isolate them from the mentoring and counselling which, as indicated above, is often an important part of the informal development process.

This danger has been overcome in those companies, such as National Westminster Bank, where there is clear and, in this case, central responsibility for developing all women on a management career track. This includes providing appropriate training, planning their career steps, having networking meetings and annual interviews.

Overcoming Assumptions: The Challenge for Middle Managers

As people move up through middle management the need is for broader management development. This is typically accomplished by involvement in project work and assignments, membership of task forces, as well as participation in training programmes designed to develop general management perspectives. The issues for women's development here are the role that women play in project work and whether they do have access to off-the-job training.

The role that women play in projects and task forces appears to be under-researched even though these are becoming more prevalent. Typically, women who have achieved career success mention taking responsibility for a major project or study at this stage in their career as being highly significant for their later development. As one senior woman manager from British Telecom explained, 'realizing that I knew more on the subject than the senior people around me increased my confidence enormously.' This was with regard to a fact-finding study which involved travel to many other parts of the world.

We need to know more about the process of selection for project work, whether women perceive its significance and whether they are as likely to be included as men. We need to understand more about the role that women, once part of the project team, typically take, whether it is a lead or a supportive role. These aspects all have significance for the development potential inherent in project work.

This is particularly relevant because research studies such as that carried out by Barham et al. into *Management for the Future* (1988) identified the importance of project work as the means by which companies maintain their flexibility and competitiveness as well as developing their staff. Clearly, women need to participate fully in project and task groups.

In terms of formal training on courses, it is at this stage that women's participation falls away and this may be linked to the fact that this is the level at which women tend to plateau. They may be 'parked' here for some years, usually more than men, and they may leave. This may be to join another firm, to start their own business, for family reasons, or to study for further qualifications. This stage seems to carry with it an element of self-fulfilling prophecy in that if women do not receive clear signals from the company about their career potential, then they are acting perfectly rationally in deciding to leave even though this may then confirm the company's fear that they were a poor risk.

Companies who have a strong equal-opportunity policy are determined to break this cycle by targeting the proportion of women (and minorities) they want to have in each grade and ensuring that training and development is available so that people can prepare themselves and then apply for promotion. In the UK the Littlewoods organization has adopted this approach which might be described as an enabling one rather than a token approach. Results to date suggest that it is effective.

A more ambitious attempt using broadly the same approach is being used by Mobil Oil in the USA with the objective of having a top management team by the year 2000 that reflects the working population. To achieve this will require significant progress to be made by women and by minorities. The process by which it is to be achieved makes use of the company's sophisticated manpower development policy. Under this, three people are identified as potential replacements for each management post, a ready replacement and two others. The company president has instructed that if a woman is not included in the three names, a woman can be added. The significance of the addition is that the woman will then be included in development programmes. The scheme does not guarantee to promote women; it offers development for women to enable them to compete on more equal terms.

It is also during this stage of their career that women have to tackle the issue of overseas assignments. A study of American women managers with assignments in the Pacific Basin by Nancy Adler found that 75 per cent of North American firms believe foreigners are prejudiced against expatriate women managers. The women claimed that the most difficult hurdle in their international career was getting sent overseas in the first place rather than in gaining the respect of the local people. Once the woman had taken up the post, she was promptly regarded as a 'foreigner' rather than as a woman, and therefore not expected to conform to local notions of feminine behaviour. The women in this study describe such difficulties as they do experience as being with expatriate Western managers rather than with the Asian population.

Winning Through: Senior Managers, Directors, and Chief Executives

At senior levels there are inevitably fewer managers and, at this time, very few women. Training and development for senior managers is frequently by postings or responsibility for major operational units. Formal training programmes are offered, but women who attend are part of a very tiny minority.

As with the middle managers, the issue for these women is more likely to be getting the job rather than performing well in it.

The executive women study described in *Breaking the Glass Ceiling* describes just how difficult this is. At this level they use the metaphor of 'hitting a wall of extremely sturdy construction' and conclude that no more than a handful of women will reach senior management level of *Fortune* 100-sized corporations within the next two decades, because 'the barriers that keep women out of senior management today will remain'. If this is the case then there is a catch-22 situation, since if there are no prospects of reward for effort that compares with that attainable by men, it is difficult to see what keeps women within the corporations.

At the highest levels, women's representation is even smaller. In the UK the Institute of Directors estimates that no more than 5 per cent of its members are women. This is in part a reflection of the very small number of women who hold directorships. Women chief executives are even more rare, being confined almost entirely to companies started by women and to some public bodies.

An issue for these women is the double isolation that comes from being a CEO and a woman. To this must be added the media attention that follows their performance as well as handling requests for public appointments and other engagements that reflect their 'experienced woman' and role-model status. These all offer personal development opportunities although visibility means that the price is high.

There is another small group of women who are on the boards of Britain's largest companies but on the whole these are non-executive directors whose experience is not in mainstream management. Over the past three years Ashridge Management Research Group has monitored the appointment of women to the boards of those included in *The Times* Top 100 companies. There has been no change in the total number: only nine women are on the main boards of the UK's top 100 companies. Perhaps even more significantly these appointments appear to reflect a version of the 'old boy network' where people are appointed for family or status connections. Of the present nine directors only three have full-time careers in management. It has to be said, however, that some of the women directors are making an important contribution by their own visibility and by gaining commitment from those at the top of the company to the development of women employees. In this, they may yet prove to be significant agents of change.

Choosing their Own Way: Women Entrepreneurs

Entrepreneurial activity has already been identified as an option which women are increasingly finding an attractive alternative way to develop their full potential. Women in the large corporations are not alone in wishing to start their own business. The study of managers' attitudes to British industry by

Peppercorn & Skoulding shows that this was the ambition of 23 per cent of the managers they surveyed. However, there does appear to be an increase in the number of women who actually take this step, and women now represent 42 per cent of new business start-ups in the UK.

Very young women, as well as those more experienced, are electing for this route to success and in 1989 seven of the ten Livewire awards for the best young business brains in London went to women. These women in their mid-20s had started successful businesses that ranged from a writing, research, and publicity service, and a Filofax-insert production company to hat design. The award, organized by the London Enterprise Agency and sponsored by Shell UK and NatWest Bank, is typical of the initiatives being taken by some major corporations to recognize and promote young entrepreneurial talent and, in so doing, to challenge assumptions about where this talent is to be found. Among the more experienced entrepreneurs the Verve Cliquot award for the Business Woman of the Year which is offered in a number of countries also demonstrates that there is a ready pool of successful entrepreneurial talent among women.

Career/Life Management for Women

Women are making career progress but this requires planning and personal management skills of a high order. It has become the norm for women to work, and in the UK 60 per cent of women aged 16–60 are active in the labour force. This means that many of those working are married and/or have family responsibilities. In the past women were presented with a stark choice: family or career (and then only if they were lucky). Today women are choosing to have a family and career. Among management women this usually means having an exceptionally sensitive and understanding partner, taking the statutory maternity leave, and then organizing full-time or live-in child-care for several years.

Career women have shown themselves willing to pay substantial sums for the peace of mind that comes with reliable home-based child-care. This is frequently the only option in the communter belts around major cities. It is the more remarkable because in the UK this is paid out of taxed income. There are no allowances for child-care such as exist in Germany, for example.

State-provided child-care is almost non-existent in the UK in marked contrast to other European countries including France, Germany, the Netherlands, and the Scandinavian countries. Employer-provided child-care is even more rare, although in a major initiative, Midland Bank who plan to open 300 day-care centres throughout the country, will become the largest provider of child-care in the country. The issue for Midland Bank is to demonstrate a serious commitment to women and to make it possible for them to consider long-term careers. This is part of the bank's response to a tightening labour market in a financial sector where there is keen competition for people of talent.

A number of organizations in the finance sector in the UK now offer career-break schemes where women managers are allowed extended maternity leave for several years providing they attend updating seminars and give an agreed amount of back-up service to their employer each year. For this they are assured of a return to a job in their grade rather than, as used to be the case, going to something at a lower level in the same industry or elsewhere.

This approach, which keeps women in touch and committed to their employer is now being copied by other industries, and in some cases the career-break is shown as an alternative step on a career path, indicating that the experience itself is regarded as a valuable one which can be translated into business terms. This is being used by West Sussex Local Education Authority, for example, in an innovative programme, 'Keeping in touch with teaching', which helps to keep teachers updated, re-skilled, and involved while they are not in full-time employment, with the objective of enabling them to return and ultimately to be eligible for appointment to senior and headship posts in schools and colleges.

An alternative to the career-break is to amend the employment contract to allow the woman manager to change her working hours and/or her work location. For example, around 5 per cent of UK women (and 3 per cent of men) in the corporate manager/administrator classification work part-time. Jobs may be split or shared and the job holders may work from home. Improved telecommunications make this more possible so it is not surprising that there are a number of examples of women working in this way in British Telecom. However, in this corporation as in many others, such possibilities are not widely publicized. Women have to negotiate individual contracts and may have to move to a different part of the business to find a senior manager who is receptive. The process is therefore difficult and acts as a deterrent. A clear, open policy would seem to be advantageous to all.

The trend towards flatter organizational structures is another change which has an effect on women's career choices and therefore on career planning. In some companies the hierarchical management structure has been removed or severely shortened. Frequent re-skilling with new jobs and responsibilities is the norm. This makes conventional approaches to career planning difficult but it does offer new options to people who are flexible and adaptable. It is a trend that is working towards the integration of women into long-term careers since short breaks from the workforce can be assimilated into the overall pattern of change. However, it also requires individuals to be self-motivated and self-directed.

The role of mentors in giving guidance and sponsorship is important in helping individuals to understand the general organizational framework and climate although past experience may be no guide to future success. However, studies to identify the scope and effectiveness of mentoring, such as that carried out by Clutterbuck, find individual mentor relationships but seldom company-initiated schemes. This can be a problem for women since the people most able to perform effectively as mentors are themselves senior people, at this stage mostly men. Clutterbuck identifies worrying problems associated with cross-sex mentoring. This has much to do with the constructions people tend to put on close long-term mixed-sex relationships. Clutterbuck recommends 'a high level of openness and communication with interested observers that leaves no room for rumour' which then allows women to benefit from the advice, guidance, and encouragement of their seniors. Company-initiated schemes could be one way of promoting the necessary level of openness.

More effort is being made to encourage people to take responsibility for their own development. Many companies emphasize the need for self-development and there are numerous examples of initiatives that look at whole-person development rather than just development of skills or narrowly in the job. One of the largest of these is a do-it-yourself development programme for women at the BBC. It is envisaged that several thousand women will complete this programme, which includes three workshops and group work, but mostly depends on individual activities which can be completed in the individual's own time and pace.

An objective behind programmes of this type is to enable women to see and create their own opportunities to develop their full potential. Given a situation where a 'career' may need to span several functions and sectors, to involve frequent retraining, and to embrace both employed and self-employed status, this is essential. However, organizations can do more with regard to the work environment.

The Work Environment

There is a massive change in the work environment. Change, the nature and pace of it, competitiveness, and flexibility are the key words identified in studies such as Management for the Future among many others. It is those companies which are the most adept at identifying and using change to their advantage that will survive. This is forcing companies to identify the management skills and qualities they require. In the UK this search has been fuelled by the Management Charter Initiative, but the quest for management competencies is widespread.

The competencies now being sought place as much emphasis on the 'being factors' – the personal qualities and the perspective of the individual – as much as the 'doing factors' – the action-oriented management skills and techniques. It is sometimes suggested that this will prove favourable to women although it is normally difficult to prove. However, one indication that this might be the case comes from the West German pharmaceutical company, Schering. Following a skill analysis that identified areas of technical competence, managerial skills, and personal qualities, it was noted that it was the last of these three aspects that contained the critical indicators of successful managerial performance. Schering have now designed an assessment centre approach to identify these qualities in individuals, and they report that whereas previously few women were recruited or promoted, now the assessment is showing that women are as suitable as men and more are being recruited and developed.

After first efforts to attract women into management positions and attention to personnel policies and procedures that obviously discriminate against women, many companies have begun to realize that the issue is deep and subtle. For women to have real equality of opportunity and to develop their full potential within the corporate framework requires a change in the attitude and behaviour of men as well as of women. Outdated assumptions and attitudes are often perpetuated by people who are well-meaning but unintentionally disabling. The paternalistic approach that exists as the predominate style in some companies is an example. In the current work climate this disadvantages everyone, as employees must increasingly take responsibility for themselves. It can be doubly disabling for women as it protects them from taking risks and meeting challenges which are often the most significant growth points.

It is to combat unintentional as well as overt discrimination that leading companies offer sexism and racism awareness training, often to all managers and staff. It is no longer a marginal issue but one that is central if all people of talent are to be developed.

Such training can seldom change attitudes overnight. It can raise awareness of reactions to language and behaviour and generate a range of different perceptions that can be shared. It can also help to bring about a new view of what is the norm for organizational behaviour and get everyone engaged in the task of developing real equality of opportunity. To be successful such programmes need a high profile, the active commitment of senior management, and the recognition that change will take sustained work over several years.

It is not only within the corporations that effort is required to encourage the development of women into high level careers. There is still much to be done in terms of tax allowances for working women especially with regard to child-care, but a step is being made in the UK with the introduction of separate taxation. Other issues on the macro stage include parental, as opposed to maternity, leave, the introduction by employers of cafeteria-type benefits so that dual-career couples can build sensible, non-duplicating personal packages, retention of benefits and rights during maternity leave, equitable pension plans as well as locally available child-care for pre-school and older children.

In all these ways women will be helped to reach their management potential and make their full contribution to the competitiveness of their companies and the wider economy.

Summary

There is an increase in the proportion of managers who are women. This is a trend that exists through the developed world although it is most pronounced in the USA. Having gained entry, women are proving able competitors for middle management jobs but few as yet are successful in climbing to the top of corporations. There is a trend for women to set up and run their own small businesses. If companies are to reap the benefit of the full potential of their women managers, they will need to give attention to their needs in order that they may retain them. There is evidence that those employment sectors facing the fiercest competition for human resources are already doing this and that others will have to follow.

References

Adler, N., 1988: Pacific Basin Managers: A gaijin, not a woman, Women in Management Worldwide, Ed. Adler, N., Izraeli, D. N., M. E. Sharpe Inc., 1988.

Barham, K., Fraser, J., and Heath, L. 1988: *Management for the Future*. Ashridge Management College.

Boydell, T., Pedler, M., and Hammond, V. 1986: *A Guide to Self-Development Groups for Women Managers*. Manpower Services Commission.

Clutterbuck, D. 1985: *Everyone Needs a Mentor – How to Foster Talent within the Organisation*. Institute of Personnel Management.

Morrison, A. M., White, R. P., Van Velsor, E., and the Centre for Creative Leadership 1987: *Breaking the Glass Ceiling – Can Women Reach the Top of America's Largest Corporations?* Addison Wesley.

Peppercorn, G., and Skoulding, G. 1987: *Profile of British Industry – The Manager's View*. British Institute of Management.

Schwartz, F., 'Management, Women and the New Facts of Life,' *Harvard Business Review*, Jan.–Feb. 1989, Vol. 67, No. 1.

Chapter 20
Developing International Leaders

Introduction

It has become increasingly vital for competitive corporations to operate globally in order to keep up and survive. Communications, the opening up of Eastern Europe, the EC single market, and demographic changes, in particular static populations in rich developed countries as opposed to a 40 per cent growth predicted in the populations of developing countries over the next twenty years, are all factors contributing to the evolving reality of the Global Village, and the need to compete across national and regional boundaries.

The ability to compete globally depends very largely on the ability of the human resources of a corporation to think and operate globally. This applies especially to those in senior enough positions to have a direct influence on company philosophy and strategy – business leaders in fact.

The two articles in this chapter try to address the double demands required of corporations who not only seek to develop leaders (a difficult enough task in itself), but to develop internationally minded leaders.

In the first article the authors point out that the top management team should set an example in terms of 'internationalism' to more junior corporate teams. Lamentably, this is often not the case, and an effort to foster an international culture further down the company may prove more effective and 'balloon' up through the organization in time. The best way of achieving a global way of thinking is through consistent overseas exposure. Business trips help to give a flavour of foreign business, but there is no alternative to overseas postings, carefully planned and organized. Another outcome, say the authors, 'is a far more forward-looking attitude to manpower planning, based on a close link between human resource management and corporate direction-setting'.

The second article approaches the development of the global leader from an entirely different angle. It suggests that the qualities of leaders and of internationalists are, happily, largely the same, so by aiming to develop one category the other may also be strengthened. As Hogg concludes, 'It would be comforting to think that the knowledge and experience needed to produce the international thinker only serves to strengthen those needed to produce a compelling leader. And vice versa.'

1
Getting the Right Management for 1992

Clare Hogg and Michel Syrett

With human resource management now regarded as a central business issue, the impact of the single European market on the way managers are recruited, trained and developed is likely to be considerable.

British companies, including UK-based multinationals, are particularly affected. A survey last year by the journal *MultiNational Employer* found that other European companies had management teams that were better prepared for post-1992 competition and that UK groups could well lose out in the greater exchange of managerial talent that will result from a freer flow of labour.

Management practice in Europe has already been drawn closer together, well before 1992, by the steady stream of mergers and acquisitions generated by companies diversifying or expanding beyond domestic markets.

A *Financial Times* report last January highlighted no fewer than ten reports of intercountry mergers and acquisitions. According to the European Commission, the number of major mergers involving EC-based companies nearly tripled between 1983 and 1987 and this growth is expected to accelerate.

The result is that many companies are now undergoing a fundamental structural and cultural growth, and the changes involved have prompted a major reassessment of how managers at all levels of the organization are developed.

Initiatives to create top management teams that are adaptable, cosmopolitan and truly international in their outlook and background have, however, been neither consistent nor evenly spread between European countries, though certain companies have combined diversification and expansion with systematic management development.

Daimler-Benz is a good example. Chairman Edzard Reuter, the man responsible for implementing the strategy, says that the key to the success of his

'Getting the Right Management for 1992' by Clare Hogg and Michel Syrett, *Director*, March 1989, by permission of The Director Publications Ltd.

company's expansion was the efforts made to broaden the perspectives and experience of his managers.

Berlin-born Reuter is himself something of an outsider, the company's culture having been dominated by a close-knit group of managers brought up in and around Stuttgart until the latest spate of takeovers brought several new members onto the board.

In Shell, the top management board, known as the Group Managing Directors, shows an impressive richness of experience, all six having spent a good part of their careers overseas.

Forbo, a Swiss firm, has directors from all the countries where it has factories, and by process of foreign acquisition looks like becoming one of the first companies to have a truly global board. Meetings are held in English, French or German.

Most UK-based firms do not compare so favourably. A 1987 survey of 200 top UK companies by the Ambrosetti Consulting Group found that 90 per cent of main board directors are still British. Nearly 80 per cent of the directors surveyed did not speak a second language. In a quarter of the companies surveyed not one of the directors was bilingual.

Most worrying of all, a surprising number of leading UK companies were found to have a totally domestic orientation. Approximately 47 per cent of the directors surveyed had no international experience at all and 8 per cent of the companies had no directors with international experience.

Immediate steps to rectify this situation have often involved recruiting foreign directors onto the board. Storehouse, the retail group founded and run by Sir Terence Conran and now one of the 100 largest companies in Britain, recently appointed Michel Julian, a Frenchman, as chief executive. Colgate has just created an international board to supervise its operations, based at its offices in Brussels.

But European experience has shown that the process of building management teams capable of operating in international markets has to start much lower down in the organization. It encompasses recruitment drives that are international in their scope, general management development schemes that provide international experience, team-building exercises that extend beyond national boundaries and the better use of employee communications and events to foster a truly international corporate culture.

One of the most impressive examples of a truly international recruitment drive is Olivetti's 'No Frontiers' training programme, which aims to fill a demand for more than 1,000 systems support specialists by 1990.

The programme was formulated as an international exercise specifically in response to the increasingly international business of the company's clients. The third intake, for example, included 13 different nationalities in a group of 58. A careful assessment was made of global needs. A worldwide advertising campaign was run entirely in English. Recruiters in the individual subsidiaries were all carefully trained by headquarters instructors to look for the same qualities and to give them the same emphasis. All successful candidates were then flown in to undergo the 'No Frontiers' training programme at the company's headquarters in Ivrea, Italy.

The programme is intensive. Close ties are formed. 'Candidates form a strong personal network,' says Tirad Sorooshian, Olivetti's UK international projects training manager. 'Back at their jobs, they phone each other to talk over problems and help each other.'

Olivetti recruits are all considered potential managerial material, but some companies recruit high-flyer talent at a more senior level. Those in the market for MBA graduates are one example. Top-league business schools such as Warton, London, Cranfield, INSEAD and Barcelona are increasingly operating in an international marketplace for their graduates. Centres based in Europe are increasingly developing closer ties with each other by faculty exchanges, the introduction of European case-study material and joint management programmes.

This in turn helps to create a more identifiable European management style, a fact appreciated by Louis Mallet, UK personnel manager of Eurotunnel. Mallet regularly trawls the top European business schools and reports that competition for the best is strong.

'European MBAs are in the best position to see the European market as a single entity,' he says. 'They keep older, more traditional managers on their toes.'

With the demand for European managerial talent much greater than the supply, many organizations are veering towards a more home-grown approach, however. Shell is a particularly strong proponent of this. Ian Thorely, personnel director of Shell UK, explains: 'We believe strongly that the best training is on-the-job training. We use career development and movement – functionally interfunctionally and internationally – in order to give breadth of experience.'

Thorely laments the dwindling number of overseas assignments, since these provide excellent opportunities for developing managers. 'It means that we are now filling the overseas postings that do arise very carefully,' he says.

Thorley's concern is reflected elsewhere. At merchant bank Kleinwort Benson, expatriate numbers remain stable in overall terms, although traditional postings are on the decline. The effects are being largely offset by increased headquarters and third-country postings, as well as short-term assignments.

Computer giant IBM is doing the same, possibly with a more conscious rationale behind it. Although the company appreciates the value of an overseas posting in terms of the breadth of experience it can give and the entrepreneurial thinking it can inspire, the feeling is that really *international* attitudes are best developed at a major corporate headquarters. The opportunity, for example, of working closely with the chief executive helps to give 'universal' perspective.

Some organizations prefer to give their managers this kind of 'global vision' through more formal training. Fiat's West German managing director recently became concerned at the provincial attitude prevailing within the company. He voiced his concern to Fiat's chief executive Cesare Romiti, who immediately initiated an analysis of the strengths and weaknesses of the attitudes of managers in Fiat in an international context.

An innovative and impressive spectrum of action has resulted. Vittorio Tesio, the executive in charge of the strategy, is at pains to point out that the new training programmes that lie at its heart (some of which are Brussels/Paris based) cover a large proportion of Fiat's managers and are fully integrated into the general corporate management development programme. Less eye-catching but no less important is the increased emphasis on the development of language skills.

Better language training has been a central issue in Britain. Many companies are now investing far more money in language learning. ICI, active in language learning for over 20 years, has a foreign language unit at its Millbank headquarters staffed by in-house linguists. APV Baker and Rowntree Mackintosh have both made videos that illustrate the importance of speaking foreign languages.

Individual examples of companies providing language learning facilities are supplemented by the burgeoning language school market, which increasingly specializes in teaching business people, and the increasing number of business courses offering a modern language option.

Language training is now a strong feature of MBA courses at many of the UK's business schools. Manchester Business School for example, has introduced foreign language tuition as an option on its MBA programme. Howard Ward, who runs the language centre, reports that among the school's UK MBA students the take-up rate of the option has been nearly 100 per cent. The majority are studying French and German, but some classes are being run for beginners in Spanish, Italian and Japanese.

Cranfield has also broken new ground by offering top first-degree linguists a new MA course in European Management. The one-year programme provides linguists with an appreciation of the fundamentals of management and a knowledge of the European business environment. The course covers company organization and operations in France and Germany as well as the economic, political and social aspects of other EC countries.

Course tutor Colin Gordon, one of the co-authors of the influential Handy report on management education, claims a very high success rate in placing students from the MA programme in leading European companies. Cranfield's links with Europe are also helped by the fact that its director, Professor Leo Murray, is a linguist by training.

A final means by which leading European multinationals have inculcated a stronger international feel to management is through the development of a stronger cross-boundary corporate culture.

Organizations have adopted different approaches. For example, some have used training programmes as an opportunity to cross-fertilize managers from local subsidiaries (This was one of the principal benefits of Olivetti's 'No Frontiers' programme.)

Others have encouraged international team-building as a means of drawing together functional counterparts from different countries. NCR recently set up an élite marketing team in London. Half are British but the others (about 15 executives) are drawn from all over Europe. It is a long-term experiment in its fourth year, but so far the project has proved successful, creating a highly motivated group generating many ideas.

A third approach is the better use of employee communications and internal conferencing. The Coats Viyella group recently introduced management conferences to bring together senior people from subsidiaries all over the world. Inchape has recently launched *Inchape World*, a magazine that is specifically intended to foster and sustain a sense of corporate identity across all its divisions. British Airways is extending its suggestions scheme to include foreign subsidiaries.

Whatever the level of preparedness for 1992 among British companies, most are at least now examining their management needs in the light of the single European market and the impact this is likely to have on their training and development programmes.

The result is a far more forward-looking attitude to manpower planning, based on a close link between human resource management and corporate direction-setting. British Steel is a good illustration. Its management succession policy is based on an advanced development programme undertaken by British Steel managers with senior executive potential.

Participants are assessed against a series of key 'competencies' – attributes identified by top general managers at British Steel as being vital to the corporation's future development.

'During the process of identifying these competencies, we were looking well beyond privatization to British Steel's position as an international rather than a UK business,' says the personnel executive in charge of the programme. 'Everyone was tuning what they said in line with this forward view.'

2
World Role for Business Players

Clare Hogg

What makes a good international leader? In a survey carried out by Charles Cox and Cary Cooper and published in their recent book *High Flyers*, they discover that in the early childhood of many successful chief executives there was often an event forcing them on to their own resources.

Other surveys have also shown the value of some time spent overseas in the upbringing of a future internationalist. Sir John Harvey-Jones, the former chairman of ICI, found lessons learnt in his boyhood in India useful in professional later life. However, progress may not merely be a matter of getting into the habit early of understanding other points of view and adapting to different values.

The experience of being 'thrown in at the deep end' in a new school, in a strange country, perhaps speaking another language, may qualify as an event that 'throws the individual on to his own resources', one of the first steps in drawing out leadership potential.

Later on, internationally minded graduates make strenuous attempts to identify a like-minded employer. In their initial training they seek variety, particularly in location, but also in function. This broad experience will also enhance their leadership qualities.

Professor Manfred F. R. Kets de Vries, at Insead, the international business school in France, contrasts successful top executives with those who did not get to the top. The successful graduates have more diverse track records.

An overseas assignment is one of the best ways of introducing variety into an executive career. Those sent abroad, or those involved in setting up new operations, will find themselves dealing with a whole range of activities, from ordering pens to acting as a corporate representative at presidential meetings.

From *The Times*, 11 April 1991 by permission of Times Newspapers Ltd.

According to Professor Kets de Vries, successful executives maintain 'composure under stress'. This ability to deal with pressure is a requirement in the successful overseas assignee.

Research carried out by Dr Richard Caplan has formed the basis of an approach to the selection of expatriates. His hypothesis is that relocating abroad is as stressful an event as marriage, divorce and redundancy. If individuals can cope with one sort of stress, they should be able to cope with others.

Professor Kets de Vries says successful executives have the ability to get along with all kinds of people and to be outspoken without being offensive.

Moran, Stahl & Boyer, the American consultancy, has pioneered a method to help companies to spot employees who might upset overseas clients. The consultancy identifies 'introvert and extrovert' qualities and the consultants warn against anybody who is excessively introspective.

Formal training is being used to reinforce the benefits of the overseas assignment. One successful training programme developed in 1987 is now supported by 31 large companies.

The five-week course aims to 'develop global business leaders who have the mindset, leadership and team-building skills to both lead their institutions and contribute to world economic growth.'

In developing the leadership skills needed in companies with overseas operations, the course explores the participants' assumptions about foreign countries and gives them the opportunity to relate directly with executives from other cultures. The course uses outdoor training and incorporates two weeks spent overseas analysing political, cultural and economic conditions, resulting in a 'business opportunity report'.

Having braved the seas of 'Hurricane Island', and detoured for a day of briefings in Washington, the participants are met at Michigan airport by a battery of media correspondents asking awkward questions about their employers' corporate disasters and scandals. This event is typical, organized specifically to create a sense of what global leaders must face.

The pressure is intended to make them learn quickly. After the event, participants were relatively impressed, although initially some from the West found themselves dumbstruck by a 'subtle' Japanese saying translated for them at 'he who speaks first at meetings is a dumb ass'.

John Danzelsen, the executive director of ICI Paints, says that if he had to arrange an investment in a part of the world about which he knew little he 'would certainly pull a cross-cultural team together to look at the issues'.

Peter Williamson, of London Business School, asks his Master of Business Administration students to 'imagine yourself standing on top of the Empire State Building, trying to direct the New York traffic'. This, he says, helps to give the feeling the business leader must have of being all-powerful, yet powerless.

In the case of an international corporation the dichotomy of this feeling is exacerbated. It would be comforting to think that the knowledge and experience needed to produce the international thinker only serves to strengthen those needed to produce a compelling leader. And vice versa.

Chapter 21
Why Leaders Fail

Introduction

Any study of corporate behaviour indicates that the dividing line between success and failure is often very thin and narrows perceivably as the top of the ladder comes into sight.

No general management development programme or succession planning exercise is fool-proof. Executives with faultless career histories and every prospect of a boardroom appointment fail to live up to their potential, and disappoint their own and their organization's expectations.

The three articles below attempt to pin-point the likely causes. Morgan McCall Jr and Michael Lombardo from the Center for Creative Leadership, North Carolina demonstrate that the characteristics of the executives that 'arrive' at the top and those that 'derail' are in many respects very similar, and that often the strengths that underpin the early careers of successful managers turn into weaknesses as the organizational stakes get higher. As competition increases, deficiencies that may not have mattered lower down, whether connected to gaps in knowledge or a lack of good interpersonal skills, start to count more. Nevertheless, they are able to identify some principal characteristics which distinguish the 'arrivers' from the 'derailers'; and they caution that there is no fool-proof step-by-step formula for success; as Kirkegaard said of truth, it is 'like searching a pitch dark room for a black cat that isn't there'.

Abraham Zaleznik concentrates specifically on the inner conflict and personality changes that can erode a successful executive's standing among colleagues and subordinates and undermine his or her self-respect. He argues that many senior managers fail to come to terms with the consequences of success and recognition in their work and are haunted by a fear of failure. This affects their ability to maintain a firm sense of identity, makes it harder for them to be consistent in the way they respond to colleagues and subordinates, and unselective in the activities and personal relationships they get involved in.

Manfred Kets de Vries focuses on the loneliness of the new leader. 'Leaders should take care of the dependency needs of their employees. Given the universal nature of these needs, however, one must ask who takes care of the *leaders*' dependency needs?' Like Zaleznik, Kets de Vries identifies fear of success as a major cause of derailment. Above all, and most usefully, he makes some suggestions as to how some derailments can be avoided.

All the contributors to this chapter stress that the élitist nature of career advancement and succession planning often causes people to forget that successful executives, like everyone else, are a subtle combination of strengths and weaknesses, and that while there is usually (but not always) an early recognition of the characteristics that denote senior management potential, there is less likely to be an early recognition of the highly successful executive coming off the rails, by either the organization or the individual.

1
The Human Dilemmas of Leadership

Abraham Zaleznik

Not too long ago, the citizens of the United States and of the world became witnesses to a political drama that had all the ingredients of a first-class Greek tragedy. Were it not for the fact that the episode revealed some sense of the nature of power conflicts among influential men, one could safely have stopped reflections on the event at that point where its human interest ended and its deeper significance for leadership began. I am referring, of course, to the Adlai Stevenson episode that exploded on the public scene with an article in the *Saturday Evening Post* by Stewart Alsop and Charles Bartlett.[1]

I do not intend to go into a commentary on this article but, rather, I want to use this episode to launch my reflections on the human dilemmas of leadership as they affect every person who works in a position of authority and responsibility. In the course of the Stevenson affair, we became privy to backstage rivalry among subordinates close to the President. We saw attempts at political homicide and character assassination through the use of 'the leak' of so-called secret positions in the deliberations of high councils of government. We saw the President of the United States drop his guard, if only momentarily, to show us how difficult it is to make or hold friends while in the Presidency. And throughout the revelations, charges, and counterchanges, we learned just what the medium of exchange can be in power conflicts; namely, prestige, personal integrity, friendship and loyalty, jealousy and egotism – all typical human sentiments likely to be found in any human encounter where people care about what they are doing.

In the professional literature on the job of the executive, one seldom finds much reference to or intelligent discussion of the dilemmas posed by the

'The Human Dilemmas of Leadership' by Abraham Zaleznik, *Harvard Business Review*, July–August, 1963. Copyright © 1963 by the President and Fellows of Harvard College, by permission of *Harvard Business Review*.

exercise of power and authority. The dramatists, novelists, biographers, and journalists attempt to portray these struggles in their works, but much is left to the sensitivity and intuition of the audience. And least of all are we ever invited to consider the underlying dynamics of leadership dilemmas and the different forms open to us for their resolution.

I should like to try to lift the veil somewhat on the nature of conflicts in exercising leadership. The two points I want to develop are:

- The main source for the dilemmas leaders face can be found within themselves, in their own inner conflicts.
- Dealing more intelligently with knotty decisions and the inevitable conflicts of interest existing among men in organizations presupposes that executives, at least the successful ones, are able to get their own house in order. It presupposes that the executive is able to resolve or manage his inner conflicts so that his actions are strongly grounded in reality, so that he does not find himself constantly making and then undoing decisions to the service of his own mixed feelings and to the disservice and confusion of his subordinates.

Tendency to Project

Most of us are accustomed by virtue of our training and inclinations to externalize conflicts and dilemmas. If an executive finds himself immobilized in the face of a difficult problem, he is apt to look to the outside for an explanation. He might perhaps say to himself that he is unable to act because he has inadequate authority delegated to him. Or he might hesitate because he feels subordinates are holding out on him by providing too little information, confused positions, and mixed signals. In this case, he is likely to vent his frustrations on their incompetence.

This generalize tendency to place conflicts in the outside world is part and parcel of a well-known mechanism of the mind called *projection*. A person projects when, unknown to himself, he takes an attitude of his own and attributes it to someone else. In the example just cited, the executive who despairs because his subordinates are confused and who charges them with holding back and with indecision may well be reading his own state of mind and attributing it to others.

It is just not within us to be able consistently to separate those issues which arise from our own concern from those issues that reside in the realities of a situation. Let me cite another example:

> The president of a large company became concerned with the possibility that his organization had failed to develop executive talent. This concern of his arose in connection with his own retirement. He organized a committee composed of

assistants to vice presidents to study this problem and to report to him with recommendations.

The president's forthcoming retirement was well known, and there was private speculation as to who among the vice presidents would be named as his successor. This succession obviously implied that several persons among the assistant vice presidents would be promoted. The task force met several times, but its discussions were not too productive or interesting. The group spent most of its time attempting to define what the president wanted the committee to do, instead of dealing with the issues the organization faced in attracting and developing executive talent.

In other words, they projected their own concerns and anxiety onto the president and attributed to him confused motives in undertaking the assessment of the company's needs in executive development. In reality the individuals themselves shared confused motivations. They were in intensive rivalry with one another over who among their immediate superiors would become president and how this change would affect their fate in the organization.

By centering attention on the inner conflicts of the executive, I do not mean to imply that conflicts are not based in the relations among individuals at work. The illustrations presented so far clearly indicate how vicious these relations may become. The point I am suggesting is that external conflicts in the form of power struggles and rivalry become more easily understood and subject to rational control under those conditions where the executive is able to separate the conditions within himself from those existing on the outside.

This process of separation is more easily said than done. Nevertheless it is crucial for the exercise of leadership, and sometimes the separation is the very condition for survival. One wonders, for example, whether the failure to maintain this separation lay at the basis of the breakdown and subsequent suicide of such a brilliant man as James Forrestal. At the very least, by attending to the conditions within himself, the executive can expect to be dealing with those situations most susceptible to his rational control. It is in the long run a lot easier to control and change oneself than it is to control and change the world in which we live.

Forms of Inner Conflict

But before we examine some of the ways in which a man can learn to deal more competently with his inner life, we need to know something more about the nature of inner conflicts. Let us take two types that are quite prevalent among executives in organizations:

- *Status anxiety* This refers to those dilemmas frequently experienced by individuals at or near the top in their organizational world.

- *Competition anxiety*   This refers to the feelings generated while climbing to the top.

These two prevalent types of anxiety, while resembling each other in a number of respects, are worth keeping separate for purposes of furthering understanding.

Status Anxiety

When an individual begins to achieve some success and recognition in his work, he may suddenly realize that a change has occurred within himself and in his relations with associates. From a position of being the bright young man who receives much encouragement and support he, almost overnight, finds himself viewed as a contender by those who formerly acted as mentors. A similar change takes place in his relations with persons who were his peers. They appear cautious with him, somewhat distant, and constrained in their approach, where once he may have enjoyed the easy give-and-take of their friendship. The individual in question is then ripe for status anxiety. He becomes torn between the responsibilities of a newly acquired authority and the strong need to be liked.

There is a well-established maxim in the study of human behavior that describes this situation tersely and even poetically; namely, that 'love flees authority.' Where one individual has the capacity to control and affect the actions of another, either by virtue of differences in their positions, knowledge, or experience, then the feeling governing the relationship tends to be one of distance and (hopefully) respect, but not one ultimately of warmth and friendliness.

I do not believe that this basic dichotomy between respect or esteem and liking is easily changed. The executive who confuses the two is bound to get into trouble. Yet in our culture today we see all too much evidence of people seeking to obscure the difference. Much of the current ethos of success equates popularity and being liked with competence and achievement. In Arthur Miller's *Death of a Salesman*, Willie Loman in effect was speaking for our culture when he measured a person's achievement in the gradations of being liked, well liked, or very well liked.

Reaction and Recognition

In what ways do executives react when they are caught in the conflict between exercising authority and being liked?

Sometimes they seek to play down their authority and play up their likeability by acting out the role of the 'nice guy.' This is sometimes called status stripping, where the individual tries in a variety of ways to discard all the symbols of his status and authority. This ranges from proclaiming the open-door policy, where everyone is free to visit the executive any time he wants, to the more subtle and less ritualistic means such as democratizing work by proclaiming equality of knowledge, experience, and position. And yet these attempts at status stripping fail sooner or later. The executive may discover that his subordinates join in gleefully by stripping his status and authority to the point where he becomes immobilized; is prevented from making decisions; is faced with the prospect of every issue from the most trivial to the most significant being dealt with in the same serious vein. In short, problem solving and work become terrorized in the acting out of status stripping.

The executive soon becomes aware of another aspect of his dilemma. Much to his horror, he finds that attempts to remove social distance in the interests of likeability have not only reduced work effectiveness, but have resulted in an abortion of the intent to which his behavior has been addressed. He discovers that his subordinates gradually come to harbor deep and unspoken feelings of contempt toward him, because he inadvertently has provided them with a negative picture of what rewards await them for achievement – a picture unpleasant to behold. In effect, the process of status stripping helps to destroy the incentives for achievement and in the extreme can produce feelings of helplessness and rage.

There is yet another side to the dilemma of status anxiety which is well worth examining. This side has to do with the hidden desire to 'touch the peak.' Executives frequently want to be near the source of power and to be accepted and understood by their bosses. Such motivations lead to excessive and inappropriate dependency bids, and to feelings of lack of autonomy on the part of the subordinate and of being leaned on too hard on the part of the superior. Under such conditions, communication between superior and subordinate tends to break down.

So far I have discussed the problem of status anxiety as an aspect of seeking friendship, warmth, and approval from subordinates and bosses. Status anxiety is also frequently generated by the fear of aggression and retaliation on the part of persons who hold positions of authority. Executives sometimes report feeling lonely and detached in their position. A closer look at the sense of loneliness reveals a feeling that one is a target for the aggression of others. This feeling occurs because the executive is called upon to take a position on a controversial issue and to support the stand he assumes. He must be able to take aggression with a reasonably detached view, or the anxiety can become intolerable.

If in your experience you have encountered an executive who seemed unable to take a stand on a problem, who seemed to equivocate or talk out of two sides of his mouth at once, then the chances are reasonably good that you have come upon a man in the throes of status anxiety. Sometimes this will appear in the form of hyperactivity – the case of the executive who flits from problem to problem or from work project to work project without really seeing an activity through to completion. In this case, the executive is utilizing the tactic of providing a shifting target so that other persons have difficulty in taking aim at him.

Constructive Approach

Now, in referring to aggression and the avoidance of aggression as aspects of status anxiety, I do not mean to imply hostile aggression. I mean to suggest instead that all work involves the release of aggressive energy. Solving problems and reaching decisions demand a kind of give-and-take where positions are at stake and where it is impossible for everyone concerned to be equally right all the time. But having to give way or to alter a position in the face of compelling argument is no loss. The executive who can develop a position, believe in it, support it to its fullest, and then back down, is a strong person.

It is just this type of person who does not suffer from status anxiety. He may love to provide a target because he knows this may be a very effective catalyst for first-class work accomplishment. He is secure enough to know that he has nothing to lose in reality, but much to gain in the verve and excitement of interesting work. This type of executive is able to take aggression, and in fact encourage it, because he probably has abandoned the magical thinking that seems to equate his position of authority with omnipotence. No one has the power to make everyone else conform to his wishes, so it is no loss to learn that one has been wrong in the face of the arguments aggressively put forth by others. In fact, such ability to retract a stand results in heightened respect from others.

I am suggesting, in other words, that we should not be misled into equating the virtue of humility with executive behavior that appears modest, uncertain of a stand, and acquiescent toward others – behavior which frequently is feigned modesty to avoid becoming a target. True humility, in my opinion, is marked by the person who thinks his way through problems, is willing to be assertive, is realistic enough to encourage assertiveness from others, and is willing to acknowledge the superiority of ideas presented by others.

Competition Anxiety

The second main pattern of inner conflict that badly needs attention is what I have termed competition anxiety, a close kin of status anxiety. It goes without saying that the world of work is essentially a competitive one. Competition exists in the give-and-take of solving problems and making decisions. It also exists in the desire to advance into the more select and fewer positions at the top of a hierarchy. An executive who has difficulty in coming to terms with a competitive environment will be relatively ineffective.

From my observations of executives – and would-be executives – I have found two distinct patterns of competition anxiety: (1) the fear of failure and (2) the fear of success. Let us examine each in turn.

Fear of Failure

You have perhaps seen the fear of failure operate in the activities of the child, where this type of problem generally originates:

> The child may seem to become quite passive and unwilling to undertake work in school or to engage in sports with children his age. No amount of prodding by parents or teachers seems to activate his interests; in fact, prodding seems to aggravate the situation and induce even greater reluctance to become engaged in an activity. When this child progresses in school, he may be found to have considerable native talent, and sooner or later becomes tabbed as an 'underachiever.' He gets as far as he does thanks in large measure to the high quality of his native intelligence, but he does not live up to the promise which others observe in him.
>
> When this child grows up and enters a career, we may see the continuation of underachievement, marked by relative passivity and undistinguished performance. Where he may cast his lot is in the relative obscurity of group activity. Here he can bring his talents to bear in anonymous work. As soon as he becomes differentiated, he feels anxious and may seek to become immersed once again in group activity.

An important aspect of this pattern of response is the ingrained feeling that whatever the person undertakes is bound to fail. He does not feel quite whole and lacks a strong sense of identity. He is short on self-esteem and tends to quit before he starts in order to avoid confrontation with the fear that he might fail. Instead of risking failure he is willing to assume anonymity, hence the sense of resignation and sometimes fatigue which he communicates to those near to him.

A closer study of the dilemma surrounding the fear of failure indicates that the person has not resolved the concerns he has with competing. It may be that he has adopted or 'internalized' unrealistic standards of performance or that he is competing internally with unreachable objects. Therefore he resolves to avoid the game because it is lost before it starts.

If you recall James Thurber's characterization of Walter Mitty, you may get a clearer indication of the problem I am describing. Walter was a meek, shy man who seemed to have difficulty in mobilizing himself for even the simplest tasks. Yet in his inner world of fantasy, as Thurber portrays so humorously and touchingly, Walter Mitty is the grand captain of his destiny and the destiny of those who depend on him. He populates his inner world with images of himself as the pilot of an eight-engine bomber or the cool, skilful, nerveless surgeon who holds the life of his patient in his hands. Who could ever work in the world of mortals under standards that one had best leave to the gods!

You can observe from this description that fear of failure can be resolved only when the person is able to examine his inner competitive world, to judge its basis in reality, and to modify this structure in accordance with sensible standards.

Fear of Success

The fear of failure can be matched with its opposite, the fear of success. This latter pattern might be called the 'Macbeth complex,' since we have a ready illustration available in Shakespeare's *Macbeth*. The play can be viewed symbolically for our purposes:

> Macbeth was an ambitious man. It is interesting to note that the demon ambition is projected out in the form .of the three witches and Macbeth's wife, who, Macbeth would lead us to believe, put the idea into his head to become king. But we do not believe for a minute that the ambition to become number one existed anywhere but within Macbeth himself. You remember that to become king, Macbeth killed Duncan, a nice old man who had nothing but feelings of admiration and gratitude for Macbeth.
>
> As the story unfolds, we find the crown resting uneasily on a tormented head. Macbeth is wracked with feelings of guilt for the misdeed he has committed and then with uneasy suspicion. The guilt is easy enough for us to understand, but the suspicion is a bit more subtle. Macbeth presents himself to us as a character who committed a foul deed to attain an ambition and is then suspicious that others are envious of him and seek to displace him in the number one position. So, there are few lieutenants to trust. And, paradoxically, the strongest subordinates become the ones least trusted and most threatening.

The play portrays in action the morbid cycle of the hostile-aggressive act followed by guilt and retribution. In addition, if we view the play symbolically, we can say that the individual, like Macbeth, may experience in fantasy the idea that one achieves position only through displacing someone else. Success, therefore, brings with it feelings of guilt and the urge to undo or to reverse the behavior that led to the success. If such concerns are strong enough – and they exist in all of us to some degree – then we may see implemented the fear of success.

The form of this implementation will vary. One prominent pattern it takes is in striving hard to achieve a goal, but just when the goal is in sight or within reach, the person sabotages himself. The self-sabotage can be viewed as a process of undoing – to avoid the success that may generate guilt. This process of self-sabotage is sometimes called snatching defeat out of the jaws of victory.

I am not certain just what Theodore H. White had in mind in his book *The Making of the President – 1960*, portraying Nixon's defeat in the 1960 Presidential election, but he certainly conveys the impression that Nixon may have been going through a cycle such as the one described here – the fear of success. There were just too many errors of commission and omission that prevent us from passing off the election simply in terms of external events and forces, as important as these were.

Managing Inner Conflicts

To summarize the discussion thus far, I have called attention to the not easily accepted notion that conflicts of interest can and do exist within individuals and are not restricted to the relations among men in the ordinary conduct of affairs. I have said that the inner conflicts rooted in the emotional development of the individual are at the core of the leadership dilemma. It is misleading, in other words, to seek for causes of conflict exclusively in external forces.

Then, touching on a few of the inner conflicts of executives, I grouped them into two main types: (1) status anxiety and (2) competion anxiety. Both of these forms of inner conflict are rooted in the very process of human development in the strivings of individuals for some measure of autonomy and control over their environment. The forms happen to be especially crucial in the executive's world simply because he acts in the center of a network of authority and influence that at any point in time is subject to alteration. In fact, one can think of decision making and action in organizations as a continuing flow of influence interchanges where the sources of the power to influence are many. But whatever the external source through which any one person achieves power to influence, its final manifestations will reflect the inner emotional condition of the man.

Let us now see what guidelines exist for resolving and managing inner conflicts. There are six ideas I would like to suggest.

The Necessity of Acknowledging and Accepting the Diversity of Motivations

The control of one's own responses and actions presupposes some accurate understanding of one's motivations. Everyone would like to believe that his inner world is populated only by the socially nice drives and wishes. But this is not the case. It is fruitless to attempt to deny awareness of the less nice, but equally human, feelings that we all experience such as rivalry, dislike, rebelliousness, anger, and contempt. I am not urging executives to express these feelings impulsively. I am not of the school of thought that believes the catharsis of feelings in everyday relationships at work and at home is a good thing. But the awareness of how one is reacting in a situation is beneficial and permits more flexibility in thinking and action. Unless an executive establishes a close connection between his realms of thought and feeling, the two can exist in relative isolation from one another to the detriment of his effectiveness as a manager. At the very least, such self-estrangement involves considerable costs in the waste of energy.

The Necessity of Establishing a Firm Sense of Identity

The exercise of leadership requires a strong sense of identity – knowing who one is and who one is not. The myth of the value of being an 'all-around guy' is damaging to the strivings of an individual to locate himself from within and then to place himself in relation to others. This active location and placement of one's self prevents the individual from being defined by others in uncongenial terms. It prevents him also from being buffeted around the sea of opinions he must live within. A sense of autonomy, separateness, or identity permits a freedom of action and thinking so necessary for leadership.

Not the least significant part of achieving a sense of identity is the creative integration of one's past. There is no tailor who can convert a hayseed into a big-city boy – any more than a dude can become a cowboy for all the hours he spends on the range. Coming to terms with being a hayseed or a dude permits the development of a unique person who goes beyond the stereotypes offered to him as models.

The Necessity of Maintaining Constancy and Continuity in Response

Closely related to the need for a sense of identity is a constancy in how one represents and presents himself to others. Constant alterations of oneself are confusing to work associates. These shifts are particularly damaging to subordinates who are entitled to the sense of security that comes from a feeling of reasonable continuity in the responses of their boss. For instance:

> I knew of one group of executives, many of whom had the practice of taking tranquilizers before a meeting with the president of the company. They claimed that they needed the tranquilizers to help them withstand the angry reactions the president demonstrated when people acted as though they had not thought through the ideas they were presenting. I think they were mistaken. They used the tranquilizers because they were very unsure as to just what he would get angry about or when. If they had had some sense of the standards of performance to which he reacted kindly or harshly, they would have been able to spend less time worrying and more time working.

The Necessity of Becoming Selective in Activities and Relationships

Most executives believe that gregariousness and participation in many activities at work and in the community are of great value in their life. In a sense this belief is true. But I would urge that greater attention needs to be paid to selectivity. Without carefully selecting the matters he gets involved in, the executive faces a drain on his emotional energy that can become quite costly. Selectivity implies the capacity to say 'no' without the sense that one has lost esteem. The capacity to say 'no' also implies that one is so constituted that he does not need esteem from diffuse persons and activities to enhance his self-worth.

The Necessity of Learning to Communicate

Conflict resolution, both inner and external, depends on the capacities of men to communicate. Communication is a complex process and one that requires careful thought and attention. Here are two suggestions for improving communication:

1   Try to develop a keen awareness of your own reactions (a point I referred to previously).
2   Try to make your opinions and attitudes known without wasteful delays. (An unexpressed reaction that simmers and then boils within is apt to explode at inappropriate times; this may lead to increased confusion and concern in the minds of listeners, to the detriment of information interchange.)

The Necessity of Living within a Cyclical Life Pattern

The effective utilization of energy seems to involve a rhythmic pattern of alternating between quite different modes or cycles of response. The prototype of alternating modes is probably best found in the comparison of wakefulness and sleep. Wakefulness suggests activity, conscious attention to problems, and the tension of concentration and action. Sleep is the epitome of passivity in the adult as well as in the child; here concerns are withdrawn from the outside world to a state of inner bliss. In this passive state the organism is rejuvenated and made ready for a new cycle of activity.

This prototype can be applied to a wide range of events in the daily life of the executive. Building oneself into a rhythmic pattern, whether it be around work or play, talking or listening, being at work alone or in association with others, may be essential for dealing with the strains of a difficult role.

Summing Up

Training oneself to act and react in the ways just discussed may sound like a formidable task. Formidable it is, but perhaps the basic necessity is to overcome the sense of inertia to which we are all susceptible from time to time. While it sounds puritanical, the most elementary step necessary for achieving a mature orientation as an executive is to assume responsibility for one's own development. Basic to this responsibility is the experiencing of one's self in the active mode. (The sense of inertia referred to before is just the opposite; here life and events appear to occur apart from one's own intentions.) As soon as an executive is able to assume responsibility for his own experience and in the course of doing so overcomes the sense of inertia, he is on the road toward experiencing leadership as an adventure in learning.

Fortunately, increasing recognition by executives of the importance of their continuing development has made it possible for them, in conjunction with universities and institutes, to examine the dilemmas of leadership and to experiment with new approaches for their resolution.

Note

1   'In Time of Crisis,' December 8, 1962, p. 15.

2
Leaders who Self-Destruct: The Causes and Cures

Manfred F. R. Kets de Vries

Why do some people derail when they reach the top? What psychological forces affect executives when they attain a position of power? Why does an executive who seem bright, likeable, and well adjusted suddenly resort to strange behavior when he or she becomes chief executive officer?

There are no simple answers to these questions. In order to address them, we must deepen our understanding of the psychodynamics of leadership and the vicissitudes of power. A number of clinical insights from dynamic psychiatry and psychoanalysis may help in our analysis.

First, however, consider an example that illustrates the kind of irrational behavior described above. Before Robert Clark[1] assumed the presidency of the Solan Corporation, he had always been well liked. His supervisors had been impressed by his capacity for work, his helpful attitude, his dedication, and his imaginative method of solving problems. He eventually crowned his seemingly brilliant career by being selected to succeed Solan's former CEO.

In the period immediately after Clark took over, he received many accolades for his role in taking a number of long overdue steps. Gradually, however, after the initial enthusiasm had cleared up, many of his old colleagues concluded that he had apparently undergone a personality change. He had become less accessible; his once widely acclaimed open-door policy and advocacy of participative management had disappeared. He had become increasingly authoritarian, impatient, and careless of the feelings of others.

The organizational effects of Clark's transformation were quickly forthcoming. In their desire to please him, key executives would jostle for his attention and waste time and energy on power games and intracompany squabbles rather than

'Leaders who Self Destruct: The Causes and Cures' by Manfred F. R. Kets de Vries, SPR89, *Organizational Dynamics*. Copyright © 1989 American Management Association, New York, by permission of the publisher.

on strategic decisions. Company morale sank to an all-time low, and the financial results were predictably dismal.

What happened to Clark – and *why* did it happen? Certain psychological forces – his own and those of his followers – came into play, creating a multitude of problems. Here are three reasons why this occurred:

- Succession to the top leadership position in an organization is necessarily isolating in that it separates leaders from others (who now directly report to them) and leaves them without peers. As a result, their own normal dependency needs for contact, support, and reassurance rise up and overwhelm them.
- Whether consciously or unconsciously, employees expect their organization's leaders to be infallible and even gifted to some degree with 'magical' powers.
- Troubled by guilt feelings about their success and fearful that it may not last, leaders may unconsciously cause themselves to fail.

To some degree, every human being suffers from these reactions and feelings. History has provided us with many examples of leaders whose behavior became pathological in the extreme once they attained power: political leaders such as King Saul, Caligula, Adolf Hitler, and Colonal Qaddafi, or business leaders such as Howard Hughes.

I am not suggesting that each business leader will resort to pathological behavior upon reaching the top of his or her organization. What differentiates those who 'crash' from those who don't is the latter's ability to stay in touch with reality and take these psychological forces in stride. Many leaders are very good at handling the pressures that leadership brings; indeed, some individuals who may previously have been rather colorless turn into great leaders when they attain positions of power. However, some leaders just can't manage; the regressive pulls simply become too strong. Since we are all susceptible to these psychological forces, I will discuss their dynamics.

Isolation from Reality

On June 18, 1982, the body of Roberto Calvi, Chairman of Ambrosiano, Italy's largest private bank, was found hanging under Blackfriars Bridge in London. The exact circumstances of his death may never be known; however, this was certainly an ignominious ending for one of Italy's most prominent bankers. It was also one of the saddest developments in modern Italy's largest financial scandal.

Although the extent of Calvi's involvement may never be known, he certainly carried a heavy responsibility. His secretive, control-oriented management style didn't help, and his remoteness was an added complication. In newspaper accounts of that time, Calvi was described as the most private of financiers, an individual who was very reserved and formal, a man for whom communication was a difficult task. From the various descriptions we have of him, he was apparently a person who would internalize his problems rather than confide in anyone. Here was an individual who had a very detached way of dealing with others.

Why did Calvi get himself into this situation? We cannot really answer this question; however, we do know that, in spite of the sea of executives reporting to Calvi, he apparently ended up very much alone in dealing with his problems. There was apparently no one he could turn to, which seems paradoxical in light of his contacts and his very active life. Unfortunately, this kind of isolation seems all too common among people who head organizations, and it can affect their sense of reality.

The term 'loneliness of command' has been used frequently in the context of leadership. The inability to test one's perceptions, the tendency to lose touch with reality because one occupies a top position, is a danger anyone can fall victim to when in a leadership position.

For example, when Peter Harris became president of the Noro Corporation, he thought that his personal and professional lives would continue more or less as they had before. The appointment had been very routine; as one of the senior vice-presidents of his company, he had been the logical choice for the job.

In reality, however, Harris had to deal with more changes in his lifestyle than he had expected. Soon after he assumed the presidency, he realized that, in spite of his efforts to maintain his previous amicable working style, he was creating more distance between himself and his employees. Although he tried for a while to be one of the boys, he discovered that this was no longer possible. In short, Harris now had difficulty socializing with and having to make tough career decisions about the same person; life seemed much simpler if he retained some distance. He had also discovered that friendliness to an employee was quickly interpreted by others as favoritism; attempts at closeness by an employee were similarly viewed as a lobbying effort.

Although Harris simplified matters by keeping his distance, this had a price. He increasingly felt a sense of isolation, a loss of intimacy. He could talk to his wife, but that didn't seem to be enough. He wanted to confide in someone more familiar with what happened in the business, someone on whom he could test his ideas.

Sometimes he would think nostalgically of the time before he became president. Occasionally, he found himself longing for a way to resurrect the broken network of relationships, searching for a way of sharing, but this had become impossible. A side-effect was that he was becoming increasingly irritated about having gotten himself into this position; it was not what he had expected. He began to wonder if his increasing aloofness was affecting his ability to make decisions.

The examples of Roberto Calvi and Peter Harris show us one of the pitfalls of assuming the position of CEO; for some it becomes a mixed blessing. The organization's leaders are supposed to take care of their organization's existing strategic and structural needs; they are expected to articulate a vision of the future and show others how to achieve it. But there are a number of other aspects to leadership; one of these is that leaders should take care of the dependency needs of their employees. Given the universal nature of these needs, however, one must ask who takes care of the *leaders'* dependency needs? When no such person is available, some leaders may suffer from anxiety associated with loneliness and disconnectedness; some may even lose touch with reality.

When leaders reach the top of their organizations, they may be dismayed to learn that their network of complex mutual dependencies has been changed forever. Some leaders can overcome this and find other forms of gratification; others may even enjoy experiencing a certain degree of detachment. However, many leaders become upset at finding themselves in this situation and may react accordingly. They may feel frustrated and angry and may even experience a seemingly irrational desire to 'get even' with those who have not fulfilled their dependency needs. The resulting scapegoating behavior can create a very politicized organization torn by interdepartmental rivalry.

However, aggression can also be turned inward, which can lead to depression and to alcohol and drug abuse. If these extreme responses continue, they can have dire consequences for the organization.

The Dangers of Transference

Apart from acting as catalysts in the achievement of their organizations' objectives, leaders can also become the embodiment of their employees' ideals, wishes, feelings, and fantasies. By transforming their subjective fantasies into objective reality, employees may imbue their leaders with mystical qualities – a phenomenon that may occur despite their leaders' attempts to resist it. Employees may consciously or unconsciously perceive and respond to their leaders not according to objective reality, but as though the leader were a significant authority figure from their past, such as a parent or teacher. When this occurs, the boundaries between the past and present may disappear.

As with many authority figure, leaders are a prime outlet for such emotional reactions. Given their position, they can easily retrigger in their employees previously unresolved conflicts with significant figures from their past. When this happens, regressive behavior may occur: Employees may endow their leaders with the same omniscience that they attributed in childhood to parents or other significant figures.

This psychological process – the distortion of the whole control of one's relationships – is called *transference* and is present in all meaningful human interactions. Although leaders may find it hard to accept, all interpersonal exchanges involve both realistic *and* transference reactions – and leaders are particularly susceptible to this kind of confusion.

Transference reactions can be acted out in several ways and can affect both leaders and their employees. One common manifestation is for employees to 'idealize' their leaders in an attempt to recreate the sense of security and importance they felt in childhood, when they were cared for by apparently omnipontent and perfect parents. As authority figures leaders fall easily into an employee's subconscious definition of a 'parent' role. Employees may therefore want to endow their leaders with unrealistic powers and attributes, which in turn can inflate their leaders' self-esteem.

During periods of organizational upheaval such as cutbacks or expansions, employees are particularly anxious to cling to their beliefs in their leaders' powers as a way of maintaining their own sense of security and identity. For this reason, employees will do anything to please or charm their leaders – including giving in to their extravagant whims. Thus in times of organizational crisis leaders may conceivably be surrounded by 'yes men.' This lack of critical opinion can obviously have dire consequences for their organizations. If leaders get too much uncritical admiration from their employees, they may begin to believe that they really are as perfect, intelligent, or powerful as others think. Losing one's grasp on reality in this way is a common human failing, but it can be particularly dangerous for leaders since they often have the power to act on their delusions of grandeur. When a CEO stops listening to criticism and embarks on an overambitious expansion or orders the unnecessary construction of a new company headquarters, this process may indeed be at work.

As a result of their grandiose delusions, some leaders will favor highly dependent employees who are in search of an all-knowledgeable, all-powerful leader. However, such leaders can be very callous about these employees' needs; they may exploit them and then drop them when they no longer serve their purposes.

Such employees may legitimately react angrily to this type of behavior. However, another less obvious process may also be at work: Employees may subconsciously blame their leaders for failing to live up to their own exaggerated expectations. Angry about this, and perhaps aggravated by callous, exploitative behavior, these employees may find their attitudes quickly turning from admiration to hostility and rebellion. Like children, such people tend to divide all experiences, perceptions, and feelings into unambiguously 'good' and 'bad' categories. Thus, although new CEOs may initially have been welcomed as messiahs, they may be surprised to find out how suddenly their employees' mood can shift. After one setback, employees may view their leader as being responsible for all the company's problems, even if these problems developed long before his or her arrival.

Faced with this transition in employee attitudes from admiration to rebellion and anger, leaders may become irritated and even develop slight feelings of persecution. But leaders have to realize that this is to a certain extent inevitable and that they must exert a certain amount of self-control.

Some leaders, however, may be tempted to retaliate – possibly by firing their critics. There are some leaders who tend to mentally divide their employees into those who are 'with' them and those who are 'against' them; such an outlook is liable to breed an organizational culture of fear and suspicion. Employees who are 'with' their leaders share their outlooks and support them even if they engage in unrealistic, grandiose schemes or imagine the existence of malicious plots, sabotage, and enemies. Effective leaders, however, know how to contain their excessive emotional reactions and avoid being caught up in groundless fears.

The Case of Ted Howell

To illustrate how these psychological forces can affect a leader, consider the following incident. As a result of the unexpected death of his predecessor. Ted Howell was appointed president of the Larix Corporation, a company in the electronics equipment field. Howell had been found with the help of a headhunter who had highly recommended him. He had previously held a senior staff position in a company in the same line of business; Howell's knowledge of the industry had been a key factor in convincing Larix's board to take him on.

Soon after his arrival, Larix's board members saw signs that Howell was having difficulties dealing with the pressures of the job. A number of rash decisions made in his first week at the office were the first indications of trouble. But in spite of these mistakes, everything initially turned out better than expected. First, one of the company's main competitors went out of business, which freed up an important segment of the market. In addition, one of Howell's employees came up with an excellent marketing idea that he quickly adopted and that proved very successful. Some executives were disturbed because their colleague never received credit for it; nevertheless, these two factors helped to get Larix back into the black.

Unfortunately, this success apparently went to Howell's head. After the turnaround, he embarked on a dramatic expansion program, ignoring cautionary remarks made by his employees, consultants, and bankers. Other steps were taken, including the relocation of the company's headquarters to what Howell thought were more suitable surroundings and the acquisition of an expensive company plane. These two actions put a heavy strain on the company's finances. Those executives who expressed disagreement or concern about the new moves were fired; consultants who suggested that Howell change course suffered the same fate. In the end, only sycophants who were willing to share his grandiose ideas and accept his aggressive outbursts were left.

As expected, the unrealistic plans and high expenditures put the company into the red. However, Howell was unwilling to admit his role in the debacle. When questioned at directors' meetings, he would become defensive and deny any responsibility for the losses; instead, he would blame them on faulty moves made by his predecessor or on vindictive action by executives no longer in his employ. In his opinion, a turnaround was just around the corner. To an increasing number of board members, however, Howell's behavior was becoming unacceptable. Eventually, having become impatient with the continuing losses and with Howell's imperious, paranoid behavior, they managed to remove him.

As in the case of Robert Clark, here was an individual who was apparently well adjusted and who had performed well in his previous job. After his promotion, however, when he was subjected to the pressures of being a leader, this same individual began to behave irrationally.

One contributing factor was apparently the excessively high expectations that Howell's employees had for him. Overwhelmed by all the attention that he was suddenly receiving, he apparently allowed his sense of reality to become distorted. Perhaps because he couldn't withstand these psychological pressures, he may have assumed that some of the qualities ascribed to him were true and behaved accordingly. When his grandiose actions backfired and he couldn't deliver, his employees reacted with anger. Howell began to show signs of paranoid behavior and retaliated by putting the blame on others.

This distortive reaction pattern is another factor that contributes to this strange, irrational behavior we sometimes find in leaders. These reaction patterns are semi-dormant tendencies with which we all have to deal and which arise easily in leadership situations. As I have indicated, some leaders find it very difficult to withstand these pressures.

The Fear of Success

In a success-oriented society, failure is looked upon as a catastrophe, and to some extent we all fear it. But while the fear of failure is quite understandable as a reactivating mechanism for feelings of incompetence, fear of success is more of a mystery. In fact, Sigmund Freud tried to demystify some of the dynamics behind this fear in an article entitled 'Those Wrecked by Success' (1916). He noted that some people become sick when a deeply rooted and longed-for desire comes to fulfilment. He gave as an example a professor who cherished a wish to succeed his teacher. When this wish eventually came true, the professor became plagued by feelings of depression and self-depreciation and found that he was unable to work.

The Case of Ted Nolan

Sometimes we can see how top executives fall victim to this form of anxiety. Reflecting on his career. Ted Nolan recalled being surprised when he was asked to succeed Larry Fulton as president of the Dalton Corporation. Like many of his colleagues, he had thought that the vice-president of marketing was the person most likely to be chosen by the board; however, he certainly didn't protest when asked.

When his appointment came through, however, Nolan noticed that he felt slightly ill at ease, a feeling that didn't go away when he took over. He became increasingly preoccupied with the question of whether he could hack it. He began to have difficulties sleeping at night, tormenting himself by wondering whether his previous day's actions had been correct. He often felt like an impostor, having just been 'lucky' to get the job. To make matters worse, he also developed a full-fledged drinking problem. At work he found it increasingly difficult to concentrate and make decisions. He wondered how many of his problems in handling the top job were noticed by his board members. When were they going to realize that they had made a mistake, and that he was really an incompetent fake?

However, as Nolan said himself, he had been fortunate. His wife had been a great support to him. Because of the changes in his behavior, she had encouraged him to see a psychotherapist. As he explored the underlying causes of his anxiety with the therapist, he began to realize that he had always been anxious whenever he was put in a position of responsibility; previously, however, he had handled it better because there had always been others in a similar situation with whom he could talk. This time, however, he was really on his own.

With the psychotherapist's help, Nolan discovered the relationship between his past and his present feelings. In reviewing his life, he realized how successful he had been, having overcome tremendous handicaps to work himself up to a position far above those held by his parents and siblings. He also recognized that this success had come with feelings of guilt and betrayal of his origins. Having risen so far above his roots apparently contributed to his current anxiety. He had explored these feelings with his psychotherapist and had succeeded in becoming more objective by integrating these feelings with his current situation. Being able to see those connections and working through these insights had brought him greater peace of mind. What's more, he felt he was now doing a fairly good job in his new position.

What Nolan's experience exemplifies is that some people believe, whether consciously or unconsciously, that success can only be attained by displacing someone else. For them, success is perceived as a symbolic victory over the parents or siblings or childhood. This is particularly true for those individuals who have never resolved rivalrous feeling towards the latter. If this is the case, to be successful and to have tangible accomplishments in adulthood can turn into a Pyrrhic victory.

In a case like this, success becomes symbolically equated with betrayal. Success makes these individuals stand out and be noticed; it becomes a provocative, hostile act that not only leads to feelings of guilt but also invites retribution. As in childhood, being in such a position may arouse the envy and resentment of others. Retaliation will be feared from those individuals with whom the person is competing. Thus unresolved competitive feelings from the past become confused with present-day reality. Since success is feared to have negative consequences, these successful individuals may downgrade their accomplishments or even view themselves as impostors. They may have difficulty believing that they have achieved success through their own abilities.

In management situations, these irrational thoughts and behavior patterns may not become evident as long as the executive in question is one out of many. As long as such patterns are not particularly noticeable, the problem may be subdued. But as soon as these people reach a leadership position, they may become anxious, deprecate their accomplishments, and even engage in self-defeating behavior.

Staying on Course

I have described some of the more problematic aspects of leadership, as well as depicted a number of psychological forces that can negatively affect individuals in leadership positions. Many of these forces will often be brought to bear simultaneously; leaders who cannot withstand them will be the ones who cannot manage. Stress reactions may follow, and such individuals may lose touch with reality.

Figure 1 depicts the various forces at work in leadership and the potential dysfunctional outcomes. We see how leadership is part of a complex mosaic of interactive patterns that very much depends on the personality and background of the leader and the nature of the relationship between leader and employee. This all takes place within a specific situational context.

Leaders should be aware of the psychological forces and should be able to identify potential signs of trouble. To prevent stress reactions and irrational behavior from coming to the fore, leaders should engage in a regular process of critical self-evaluation. Those who are interested in the vicissitudes of leadership may want to reflect on the following questions:

- How accessible is the leader?
- How does the leader react to bad news or criticism from an employee?
- Is the leader able to discuss any problems or ideas with colleagues?
- Does the leader think of employees in terms of those who are 'with' and those who are 'against' him or her?

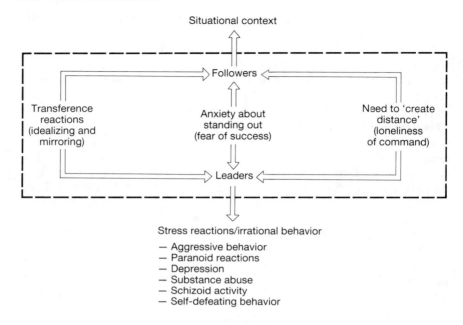

Figure 1 The pressures of leadership

- How realistic is the leader's vision of the company's future? Is there a large discrepancy between his or her own and others' points of view?
- Is the leader willing to accept responsibility if things go wrong, or does he or she blame 'the others'
- Is the leader quick to take offense and feel unfairly treated? Does he or she have a great need to 'blow his or her own horn'?
- Does the leader feel anxious and guilty when he or she is successful and have difficulties believing that his or her professional success is caused by his or her own accomplishments and not by sheer luck?

In considering these questions, we should not forget that the ability to change fantasy into reality, given the power leaders have, can be like the mythological siren's call and may cause an individual to change as soon as he or she attains a leadership position. The potential for losing touch with reality and behaving irrationally is dormant in all of us.

Paradoxically enough, it is sometimes this very irrational quality that is needed to make some leaders effective. Paranoid reactions and visionary experiences may feed very well into certain types of situations, and many political and religious leaders have acted in just this way (consider Joseph Stalin or the Ayatollah Khomeini).

However, in spite of what may have been an initially enthusiastic reception, there is a dark side to this behavior. To evoke regressive tendencies in others and to provoke aggression is to set in motion that which may be impossible to stop.

What Organizations – and their Leaders – Can Do

This cautionary note – on a somewhat lesser scale – is also true in business situations. Here, however, it may be somewhat easier to set up safeguards against the excesses of leadership. Leaders in contemporary society have to deal with the government, unions, banks, or other stakeholders that may take on the role of a countervailing power, helping to keep the leaders in touch with reality. In many large organizations, leaders will inherit an organizational structure with different checks and balances in the form of distribution of key policy decisions over a number of individuals and various agencies that will circumscribe their behavior. Moreover, in large organizations organizational processes find their own momentum and are resistant to dramatic change. Social systems have their own way of providing a 'safety belt' for individuals through their inherent structure.

Apart from the various external checks on leaders' actions that may prevent these irrational manifestations from coming to the fore, leaders themselves can take preventive action. Encouraging frank feedback from outsiders such as external directors, bankers, and consultants is one way of preventing these regressive forces from gaining the upper hand. Individuals from outside the organization usually possess a very different frame of reference, and their vision will be considerably less distorted by the existing organizational dynamics. They can provide more of an overall view and warn about potential sources of trouble. Board members in particular can play a critical role; selecting a strong, independent board that is really willing to enforce its auditing role rather than just acting as a rubber stamp is one of the best ways to keep an organization on course and prevent it from losing touch with reality.

Another useful countervailing force can be participation in top executive training programs. These programs can provide a nonthreatening environment in which leaders can discuss their working experience with colleagues and professionals exposed to similar problems; such situations will enhance reality testing. Mutual comparison of potential problem areas may provide leaders with a revelation, and insight is the first step toward constructive change.

A Shared Responsibility

Leaders and their employees are like partners in a dance: The experience can be very exhilarating, but the dancers can also fall over each others' feet. Both parties carry a heavy responsibility for the interchange to work. To make this possible, they must be willing to listen and have respect for each other's point of view. This requires a certain amount of self-knowledge and a preparedness to reflect on their actions. Empathetic listening becomes a *sine qua non* to a real understanding of the leader–employee dialogue. Thus in spite of all the countervailing forces mentioned, in the end it is the relationship of equity, consistency, and trust that will make for frank interchange between leaders and employees and will constitute the strongest force in preventing regressive behavior in leadership. And given the nature of power in organizations, making this relationship work is the real challenge for all concerned.

Note

1   'Robert Clark', is a pseudonym, and the name 'the Solan Corporation' is fictitious. The following individuals and organizations mentioned in this article are also identified by pseudonyms or fictitious names. Peter Harris and the Noro Corporation; Ted Howell and the Larix Corporation; and Ted Nolan and the Dalton Corporation.

3
Off the Track: Why and How Successful Executives Get Derailed

Morgan W. McCall Jr and Michael M. Lombardo

SENIOR EXECUTIVE. At one time, he was the leading, perhaps the only, candidate for CEO. And then he ran into something he'd never faced before – an unprofitable operation. He seemed to go on a downward spiral after that, becoming more remote each day, unable to work with key subordinates.

INTERVIEWER. Why do you think he derailed?

SENIOR EXECUTIVE. Some of it was luck because the business was going down when he inherited it. Some of it was surrounding himself with specialists who inevitably wear the blinders of their particular field. And some of it was that he never learned to delegate. He had no idea of how to lead by listening.

Few people reach the top of a major corporation without considerable talent and an impressive list of accomplishments. Still, many talented executives rise *near* the top yet are denied the ultimate positions. The quick answers to why this can happen include the ever-popular Peter Principle – rising past one's level of competence – or more darkly, that some managers possess a fatal flaw.

But the grain of truth in these explanations masks the true complexity of the process. As we discovered in a recent study conducted by the Center for Creative Leadership, those who were once quite successful and later derailed differed only slightly from those who reached the top. Some of those who derailed found themselves in a changed situation where strengths that had served them well earlier in their careers became liabilities that threw them off-track. Others found that weaknesses they'd had all along, but which had been outweighed by certain assets, were precisely the things needed as strengths in a

'Off the Track, Why and How Successful Executives Get Derailed' by Morgan W. McCall Jr and Michael M. Lombardo. Technical report no. 21, 1983, by permission of Center for Creative Leadership.

new situation. Yet others became captives of their own success or of events outside their control.

When we began a large-scale study of the key events in the careers of effective, mobile executives, we included a close look at executives who 'derailed' – that is, people who were very successful in their careers (spanning 20–30 years and reaching very high levels) but who, in the eyes of the organization, did not live up to their full potential. What became of these people varied: Some were demoted or transferred, some were fired or opted for early retirement, and some simply stopped advancing. One thing they had in common, however, was that their halted progression was not voluntary. What, we wondered, separated these otherwise successful people from their colleagues who arrived at the very top of the corporations?

To find out, we and our associate, Ann Morrison, worked with several Fortune 500 corporations to identify 'savvy insiders' – people who had seen many top executives come and go and who were intimately familiar with the circumstances surrounding their careers. The executives agreed to participate because of a desire to understand who makes it and how, what pitfalls to avoid, and most important, what they can do systematically to develop future leaders.

In each corporation one of us interviewed several insiders, usually a few of the top ten executives and a few senior 'human resources professionals', people who help make executive succession decisions. We asked them to describe, in detail, first a success story, then a derailment. In all cases, the executive describing the cases knew the people quite well and considered them fairly representative of either success or derailment in that corporation. The interviews yielded about twenty success cases and a comparable number of derailments.

Although the interviews lasted two hours and longer, covering many questions about key events in the careers of forty executives, we have organized the results to answer four questions:

- Why were those who derailed so successful in the first place?
- What events brought their weaknesses to the surface?
- Why did they derail?
- How did they differ from those who remained successful?

Reasons for Success before Derailing

If there is a formula for success, only an alchemist could concoct its magic properties – a great track record, lots of brains and technical acumen, and qualities such as charm, luck, loyalty, ambition, and leadership (see table 1).

Almost to a man (they were all men), derailed executives were identified early as having 'it' and ran up a string of successes in engineering, operations, or

Table 1 Reasons for Success Before Derailment (Based on 50 reasons for success from 20 cases. The average executive had two or three of these characteristics)

1   Outstanding track record – identified early as having high potential and had a string of successes
2   Outgoing, well-liked, charming
3   Technically brilliant
4   Loyal and helpful to management, willing to make sacrifices
5   Ambitious, managed career well
6   Moved up during reorganization or merger
7   Excellent at motivating or directing subordinates

project management assignments. One brought in three huge successes in a row which at one time accounted for half the corporate profits.

About half of the time they were seen as technical geniuses ('This guy is without peer') or brilliant problem-solvers ('He'd do anything to solve a problem – anything'). They were less often well liked or considered charming; their manners were sometimes viewed with suspicion, as if their impeccability concealed a certain hollowness beneath.

Some executives who eventually derailed moved up during mergers or reorganizations, a time when performance is particularly hard to measure. Others were exceptionally hard-working and loyal, managed their careers well, or were excellent at motivating and supporting their subordinates.

Thus far, these men looked much like successes in any field. For one reason or another, they were much better than the competition. There seemed to be little to differentiate them, other than luck, from those who did eventually succeed.

Trail in the Forest

While conducting the interviews, we did not hear many stories about so-called water-walkers, leaders who have no faults. The one 'natural leader' we encountered derailed *because* everyone assumed he could do absolutely anything. At higher levels of management his faults began to show. He became lost in detail, concentrated too much on his subordinates, and apparently lacked the intellectual ability to deal with complex issues. Still, no one helped him. It was assumed that he would succeed regardless. Both the eventual successes and the eventual derailments had plenty of faults to show. What, we wondered, might cause these faults to surface, especially so late in a career?

The events that reveal flaws are seldom cataclysmic. They are more like the broken twigs and crushed leaves in frontier novels that subtly indicate a direction taken, and mark that someone has passed that way. As one executive put it, 'Careers last such a long time. Leave a trail of mistakes behind you, and you eventually find yourself a captive of your past.'

In general, the flaws of the successful and the derailed showed when one or more of five things happened:

- They lost a boss who had covered or compensated for their weaknesses.
- They entered a job for which they were not prepared (another function or a big change in responsibility), usually coupled with having a new boss whose style was quite different.
- They left behind a trail of little problems or bruised people, either because they handled them poorly or moved through so quickly they failed to handle them at all.
- They moved up during an organizational shake-up and weren't scrutinized until during the shake-down period.
- They entered the executive suite, where getting along with others under highly stressful conditions is critically important.

These events, which happened to both types of executives, began to separate the two groups. How an executive dealt with his faults under stress went a long way towards explaining why some arrived and some jumped the track just short of town.

The Faults that Mattered

SENIOR EXECUTIVE.   Successful people don't like to admit they make big mistakes, but they make whoppers nevertheless. I've never known a CEO who didn't make at least one big one and lots of little ones, but it never hurt them.
INTERVIEWER.   Why?
SENIOR EXECUTIVE.   Because they know how to handle adversity.

Part of knowing how to handle adversity lies in knowing what *not* to do when faced with it. A manager does not necessarily have to know the right move, but must avoid making the wrong one. As we were to learn, many patterns of managerial behavior were acceptable to others. The key was in learning which ones were not acceptable.

Just as a successful executive doesn't have all the good qualities, executives who derailed didn't have all the bad ones. In general, ten personal and managerial flaws were cited as reasons for derailment (see table 2); of these, only two applied to the average derailed executive.

Personal Flaws

SENIOR EXECUTIVE.   . . . he wouldn't negotiate, there was no room for countervailing views. He could follow a bull through a china shop and still break the china.'

Table 2 Fatal Flaws: The Reasons for Derailment (based on 65 reasons for derailment from 21 cases. The average derailed executive had two of these characteristics)

1	Specific performance problems with the business
2	Insensitivity to others: an abrasive, intimidating, bullying style
3	Cold, aloof, arrogant
4	Betrayal of trust
5	Overmanaging – failing to delegate, or build a team
6	Overly ambitious – thinking of the next job, playing politics
7	Failing to staff effectively
8	Unable to think strategically
9	Unable to adapt to a boss with a different style
10	Overdependent on an advocate or a mentor

The most frequent cause for derailment was insensitivity to others. Under stress, some of the derailed managers became abrasive and intimidating. One walked into a subordinate's office, interrupting a meeting, and said, 'I need to see you.' When the subordinate tried to explain that he was occupied, his boss snarled, 'I don't give a goddamn. I said I wanted to see you now.'

Others were so brilliant they became arrogant, intimidating others with their knowledge. A typical remark was, 'He made others feel stupid . . . wouldn't listen, had all the answers, wouldn't give you the time of day unless you were brilliant too.'

In an incredibly complex and confusing job, being able to trust others absolutely is a necessity. Some committed what is perhaps management's only unforgivable sin – they betrayed a trust. This rarely had anything to do with honesty (which was a given in almost all the cases), rather it was a one-upping of others or a failure to follow through on promises, which wreaked havoc on organizational efficiency. One executive didn't implement a decision as promised, causing conflicts between marketing and production that reverberated downward through four levels of frustrated subordinates.

Others, like Cassius, were overly ambitious. They always seemed to be thinking of their next job, bruised people in their haste, and spent too much time trying to please upper management. This sometimes led to staying with a single advocate or mentor too long. When the mentor fell from favor, so did they. Even if the mentor remained in power, people questioned the executive's ability to make independent judgements. Could he stand alone, or did he need a mentor for a crutch?

Managerial Flaws

A series of performance problems sometimes emerged where a manager ran into profit problems, got lazy, or demonstrated that he couldn't handle certain kinds of jobs (usually new ventures or jobs requiring lots of persuasion). More important, by failing to admit the problem, covering it up, and trying to blame it on others, the manager showed that he couldn't change. One manager flouted senior management by 'failing' to work with a man specifically sent in to fix a profit problem.

After a certain point, managers cease to do the work themselves, and become executives who see that it is done. Some never made this transition, never learning to delegate or build a team beneath them. Although overmanaging is irritating at any level, at the executive level it can be fatal because of the difference in one's subordinates. When executives meddle, they are meddling with other executives, most of whom know much more about their particular area of expertise than their boss ever will. One external affairs executive who knew little about government regulation tried to direct another with thirty years' experience rather than help him accomplish what needed to be done. The expert balked, and the executive lost a battle that should never have begun.

Others got along with their staff, but simply picked the wrong people – staffing in their own image with technical specialists, or picking people who later failed.

Inability to think strategically was masked by an attention to detail and a miring in technical problems as some executives simply couldn't go from being doers to being planners. Another, related failure to adapt appeared as a conflict of style with a new boss. Although the successful managers had the same problem, they didn't get into wars over it, fought problems with facts, and rarely let the issues get personal. Derailed managers exhibited a host of unproductive responses – they got peevish, tried to shout the boss down, or just generally sulked around.

One manager exhibited both flaws – he couldn't change from a go-goer to a thinker/planner and eventually ran afoul of a slower-paced, more reflective boss.

Every Strength is also a Weakness

The reasons for derailment seemed to be all over the place. Some derailment cases over-controlled, some failed to mind the store. Some were dictators, some were wishy-washy. By going back to why the derailed managers succeeded initially, a pattern emerged that explained how certain combinations of strengths became weaknesses that eventually caused the derailments. In other words, the same attributes that got these men to the top also did them in.

- Executives who were brilliant but not personable derailed because of insensitivity to others or over-managing, or both.
- Executives who were personable but not brilliant derailed because they couldn't think strategically.

- Loyal, hard-working types remained that way and over-managed themselves off the track.
- Ambitious types got skewered for being ambitious. Eventually the trail of bruised bodies became a pile.
- Finally, even those who had it all (brilliant and likeable) sometimes derailed, but the reasons were idiosyncratic. One was too ambitious, one betrayed a trust, another fought with the wrong person.

The Arrivers versus the Derailed

As we stated at the beginning of the report, both groups were amazingly similar in some respects: incredibly bright, identified early, outstanding track records, a few faults, ambitious, and willing to sacrifice. A closer look (summarized in table 3) does reveal some differences and, at the levels of excellence at which executives deal, even a small difference is more than sufficient to create winners and losers.

Table 3   Those Who Arrive Contrasted With Those Who Derail

Similar in many ways:

- incredibly bright
- identified early
- outstanding track records
- have a few flaws
- ambitious
- made many sacrifices.

But those who arrived:

- had more diversity in their track records – had done more *different* kinds of things well
- maintained composure under stress
- handled mistakes with poise and grace
- focused on problems and solved them
- got along with all kinds of people – were outspoken but not offensive.

The Track Records

Derailed executives had a series of successes, but usually in similar situations: They had turned a business around more than once, or they had managed progressively larger jobs, but in the same function. By contrast, the arrivers had more diversity in their successes – they had turned a business around *and* successfully moved from line to staff and back; or they had started a new business from scratch *and* completed a special assignment with distinction. They built plants in the wilderness and the Amazon jungle, salvaged disastrous operations, resolved all-out wars between functions without bloodshed – one even built a town. They showed a breadth of perspective and interest that resulted (over twenty to thirty years) in detailed knowledge of many parts of the business, as well as first-hand experience with *different kinds* of challenges.

Composure

Derailed managers were often described as moody or volatile under pressure. One who could control his temper with top management, whom he sought to impress, was jealous of and often angry at peers he saw as competitors. His too frequent outbursts eroded the co-operation necessary for success as peers began to wonder if he were trying to do them in.

In contrast, the arrivers were calm, confident, and predictable during crises. Quite simply, people knew how they would react and this helped them plan their actions accordingly.

Handling Mistakes

Although neither group made many mistakes, the arrivers overwhelmingly handled them with poise and grace. Almost uniformly, they admitted the mistake, forewarned others so they wouldn't be blindsided by it, then set about analyzing and fixing it. Also important were two things the arrivers didn't do – they didn't blame others, and once they had handled the situation, they didn't dwell on it – they moved on to something else.

Derailed executives tended to react to failure by going on the defensive, trying to keep it under wraps while they fixed it, or, once the problem was visible, blaming it on someone else.

Going after the Problem

Although both groups excelled in this area, arrivers were particularly single-minded. This 'what's the problem?' mentality kept them away from three of the common flaws of the derailed – they were too busy worring about their present job to be eager for their next position, they demanded excellence from their people in problem-solving and in so doing often helped develop them, and they developed many contacts, saving themselves from the sole-mentor syndrome. (In fact, almost no successful manager reported having a single mentor.)

Interpersonal Style

The arrivers, perhaps because of the diversity of their backgrounds, had the ability to get along with all types of people. They either had or developed the skills required to be outspoken without offending people. Rather than being seen as charming but political or direct but tactless, they were described as direct and diplomatic. One arriver disagreed strongly with a business strategy favored by his boss. He presented his objections candidly and gave the reasons for his concerns and for the alternative he preferred. But when the decision went against him, he put his energy behind making the decision work. When his boss turned out to be wrong, the arriver didn't gloat about it – he let the situation speak for itself without further embarrassment to his boss.

Why Executives Derail

Executives derail for four basic reasons, all connected to the fact that situations change as one ascends the organizational hierarchy:

- Their strengths become weaknesses. Loyalty becomes overdependence or narrowness or cronyism. Ambition destroys their support base. Their leadership of subordinates causes them to bog down in operational and technical detail.
- Their deficiencies eventually matter. If talented enough, one can get by with insensitivity at lower levels, but not when one's subordinates and peers are powerful and probably also brilliant. The charming-but-not-brilliant find that the job gets too big and problems too complex to get by on interpersonal skills.
- Success goes to their heads. After being told how good they are for so long, some simply lose their humility and become cold and arrogant. Once someone acts as if there is nothing more to learn, their information sources begin to dry up and people no longer wish to work with them.
- Events conspire too. A few of the derailed apparently did little wrong. They were done in politically, or by economic upheavals. Essentially, they weren't very lucky.

One senior executive, in commenting on this part of the study, said that he thought only two things differentiated the successful from the derailed – total integrity and understanding other people.

Integrity seems to have a special meaning to executives that is vastly different from its Mom-and-apple-pie image. The word does not refer to simple honesty, but embodies a consistency and predictability built over time that says, 'I will do exactly what I say I will do when I say I will do it. If I change my mind, I will tell you well in advance so you will not be harmed by my actions.' Such a statement is partly one of ethics, but more, it may be one of simple practicality. This seems to be the core method of keeping a large, amorphous organization from collapsing in its own confusion.

Likewise, understanding other people's perspectives has the same Mom-and-apple-pie ring to it, but of all the differences between the arrivers and the derailed, this was the most glaring. Only 25 per cent of the derailed were described as having a special ability with people while 75 per cent of the arrivers were spoken of with such warmth. Interestingly, two of the arrivers were cold and asinine when younger, but somehow completely changed their interpersonal style. 'I have no idea how he did it,' sone executive related. 'It was as if he went to bed one night and woke up a different person.' However the feat was accomplished, a certain awareness of self and willingness to change characterized the group. That same flexibility, of course, is also what is needed to get along with all types of people.

A final word, a lesson perhaps, to be drawn from our findings. Over the years, 'experts' have generated long lists of critical skills in an attempt to define the complete manager. In retrospect it seems obvious that no one, the most talented executive included, could possess all those skills. As we came to realize, executives, like the rest of us, are a patchwork of strengths *and* weaknesses. The reasons why some executives ultimately derailed and others made it all the way up the ladder confirm what we all know but have hesitated to admit: There is no one best way to succeed (or even to fail). The fool-proof, step-by-step formula is not just elusive; it is, as Kierkegaard said of truth, like searching a pitch dark room for a black cat that isn't there.

This is a comparison of an executive who arrived with an executive who derailed, in the words of executives who knew them well.

One who Arrived

The man

'He was an intelligent guy with a delightful twinkle in his eye. He could laugh at himself during the toughest of situations.'

Notable strengths

'He was a superb negotiator. He could somehow come out of a labor dispute or a dispute among managers with an agreement everyone could live with. I think he did this by getting all around a problem so it didn't get blown. People knew far in advance if something might go wrong.'

Faults

'He was too easy on subordinates and peers at times. Line people wondered if he was tough enough, and sometimes why he spent so much time worrying about people.'

Career

'He wasn't really developed – rather, he was thrown into special assignments – negotiations, dealing with the press, fix-it projects. He always found a way to move things off dead center.'

And ended up . . .

Senior vice president.

One who Didn't

The man

'He got results, but was awfully insensitive about it. Although he could be charming when we wanted to be, he was mostly knees and elbows.

Notable strengths

'He was a superb engineer who came straight up the operations ladder. He had the rare capability of analyzing problems to death, then reconfiguring the pieces into something new.'

Faults

'When developing something, he gave subordinates more help than they needed; but once a system was set up, he forgot to mind the store. When things went awry, he usually acted like a bully or stonewalled it, once hiring a difficult employee and turning him over to a subordinate. "It's your problem now," he told him.'

Career

'He rocketed upward through engineering/operations jobs. Once he got high enough, his deficiencies caught up with him. He couldn't handle either the scope of his job or the complexity of new ventures.'

And ended up . . .

'Passed over and it's too bad. He was a talented guy and not a bad manager either. I suppose that his over-managing, abrasive style never allowed his colleagues to develop and never allowed him to learn from them.'

Index